NATIVE SOUTH AMERICANS

NATIVE SOUTH AMERICANS

Ethnology of the Least Known Continent

EDITED BY

PATRICIA J. LYON *University of California, Berkeley*

with Tribal Distribution Map by John H. Rowe

WAVELAND PRESS, INC.

Prospect Heights, Illinois

For information about this book, write or call:

Waveland Press, Inc.
P.O. Box 400
Prospect Heights, Illinois 60070
(312) 634-0081

Cover textile design courtesy of the Robert H. Lowie Museum of
Anthropology, University of California, Berkeley.
Photo: P.J. Lyon

PREFACE
AND TRANSLATOR'S NOTE

A book such as this is never the work of a single person, in spite of the fact that only one name appears on the title page. It would be impossible to mention all those colleagues and friends who have contributed to the creation of this text, but there are some who have made especially important contributions. My husband, John H. Rowe, not only provided some of his own material, but also suggested other articles for inclusion, helped check translations and the bibliography, and was a great support throughout the project. Without the initial organization of the paperwork by Rose Marie Jaquith, I might well have become mired in a morass of confusion. Sylvia H. Forman devoted much time and energy to checking the bibliography, as well as helping some with translation. Of the many people who suggested material for inclusion I would especially like to mention Donald W. Lathrap, Waude H. Kracke, Timothy J. O'Leary, Paul L. Doughty, Michael J. Harner, Kenneth M. Kensinger, and Daniel R. Gross. All the publishers and authors of the works included have also been most helpful.

With two major exceptions, and unless otherwise noted, I have translated all foreign-language material in this book. The article by Udo Oberem was initially translated by Alegonda M. Schokkenbroek, whose translation was then edited by Sylvia H. Forman, John H. Rowe, and myself. The article by Gerardo Reichel-Dolmatoff was rewritten in English by the author. All translations were submitted to the authors for approval (with the exception of the articles by Herbert Baldus, Max Schmidt, and José Alvarez, who are dead) and I cannot adequately express my thanks to them for carefully checking the translations.

Following the lead of another translator, Janice H. Hopper, I did not attempt to regularize the spelling of Indian names. I agreed with her conclusion "that the student and the general reader who perused materials on ... Indians ... would encounter a variety of spellings and might therefore profit from exposure to the range of possibilities now" (1967:73). I even went so far as to insert the varied spellings from the original sources in the article by Rodrigues on linguistic groups. Several authors have introduced editorial changes of their own in their articles. I have indicated in the introductions the extent to which each article has been changed from the original.

The bibliographic notations in this book have been made editorially consistent throughout. For in-text citations I decided on a modified version of the form used in the *American Anthropologist,* since it is both economical and one most readers should be familiar with. Insofar as it has been possible, all items included in the bibliography have been checked against the actual publications. When it was impossible to see the actual item, at least two reliable bibliographical sources were consulted to ensure accuracy. It should be noted that in some cases the references cited in an article are anachronistic, that is, an item cited carries a publication date later than that of the article itself. This happens when a work was referred to prior to its publication. In such cases, I have regularly cited the published version.

The cover design is taken from a Piro man's *cushma* collected in 1953 by Esther Matteson on the lower Urubamba River in eastern Peru. The garment is made of cotton cloth with a design that is painted except for a few warp stripes. Such geometric designs are also common among the Panoan-speaking groups of eastern Peru, and may be applied not only to cloth but also to almost any item to be decorated. This Piro specimen is catalogue number 16-7576 in the Robert H. Lowie Museum of Anthropology.

CONTENTS

III   RELATIONSHIPS WITH ONE'S OWN KIND

IV   RELATIONSHIPS WITH THE SUPERNATURAL

V   REACTIONS TO ENCROACHMENT FROM OUTSIDE

INTRODUCTION

This book is primarily intended for use in teaching about the native peoples of South America. Since it is impossible to present either the great variety and richness of South American Indian cultures or the many problems that have drawn the attention of students in this area, I have limited my scope in several ways. I have concentrated on those areas of South America that still contain functioning Indian cultures, and with the exception of one article that was included for comparative purposes, I have excluded material on the Central Andes—highland Bolivia, highland and coastal Peru, highland Ecuador, and highland Colombia. The reason for this particular omission is that the Andean region presents many problems not common to the rest of South America, and it deserves more extensive treatment than could have been given here.

The interpretation of South American prehistory is currently in a state of flux due to the large amount of field research now in progress. It is common knowledge among specialists in this field that by the time an article on South American archaeology appears in print, it is probably already out of date. The most recent major survey of South American archaeology is by Gordon R. Willey (1966–1971:vol. II). Donald W. Lathrap has published a study of the prehistory of the upper Amazon (1970). Betty Meggers presents a viewpoint different from Lathrap's in her survey of prehistoric America (1972).

In spite of growing activity by physical anthropologists in South America, there are as yet few synthetic works on this topic (e.g., Salzano and Freire-Maia 1970: Salzano, ed. 1971). Those readers interested in current work in this field should consult the summaries in the *Handbook of Latin American Studies* and articles in the specialized journals, especially *American Journal of Physical Anthropology, American Journal of Human Genetics,* and *Human Biology.*

The study of social structure in South America is in much the same state of flux, for many of the same reasons. For those interested in the newer material, I suggest the following items: The symposium on recent research in central Brazil organized by Maybury-Lewis (Symposium 1971), Maybury-Lewis' book on Akwe̅-Shavante society (1967), Rivière's book on Trio marriage (1969), Kloos' book on the Maroni River Caribs (1971), Dole's paper on Kuikuru kinship (1969) and Basso's response (1970), Kaplan's material on the Piaroa (1972), Scheffler and Lounsbury's book on Sirionó kinship (1971) and Lave's comment on this work (1973).

The arrangement of articles in this book is intended to prevent the imposition of any particular viewpoint, and an effort has been made to take materials from various theoretical backgrounds. After presenting a section of survey articles, I have chosen to place the remaining articles within four major sections, each encompassing a problem area that must be dealt with by any native culture in South America. The section titles reflect these areas: "Relationships to Natural Resources," "Relationships with One's Own Kind," "Relationships with the Supernatural," and "Reactions to Encroachment from Outside." Within each section certain subjects have been emphasized and illustrated from several points of view, using examples from different cultures.

The section and article introductions are meant to draw the material into a meaningful whole. Even such a loose organization involves certain arbitrary decisions. It may, for example, be unwarranted to separate relationships with outsiders from those among Indians. However, there appears to be a qualitative difference between these two kinds of relationships—a difference marked by many writers' use of the word "inferiority" in expressing the Indians' evaluation of their situation *vis à vis* the whites.

I have endeavored to provide references to additional related items and supplementary materials in the introductions, especially for those articles where such bibliographic information did not appear within the article. These references should suffice to put the reader in a position to continue research on his or her own. It is intended that these selections be used in conjunction with at least two complete ethnographic studies. An extensive listing of monographic studies published in English is available in Michael D. Olien's recent work on Latin America (1973: 384–392), and additional studies in both English and other languages are mentioned throughout the present work.

Twelve of the thirty-nine articles appear for the first time in English. The purpose in presenting these translations is not only to provide stimulating works not easily accessible to most students, but also to emphasize the amount of material not available in English. There is a tendency, particularly in the United States, to assume that any work of real importance will be translated into English. There is no justification for this assumption. To give an idea of the small proportion of material on South American Indians that is available in English, I offer the example of Brazil, which is the area for which we have the best bibliographical inventory. A count of works in English in the first volume of the *Bibliografia crítica da etnologia Brasileira* (Baldus 1954) reveals that only 12.2 percent (218) of the 1,785 articles and books listed are in English. Since this volume includes all published material for the period from 1500 to 1953, the count is probably skewed toward materials in other European languages deriving from the Conquest and Colonial periods. For the period from 1953 to 1960, Baldus' breakdown of 385 publications is as follows: 48 percent Portuguese, 19.7 percent German, 16.3 percent English, with the remainder in Spanish, French, Italian, Russian, Dutch, and Danish (Baldus 1967:209). There is no reason to suppose that the proportions would be changed in any appreciable way in the 664 additional works published between 1960 and 1968 (Baldus 1968), and they probably approximate the proportions for the Spanish-speaking countries of South America, if one puts Spanish in the first place on the list, rather than Portuguese.

Even if we assume that any English-speaking student of South American cultures will read Spanish or Portuguese in addition to English, he or she would still be unable to read one third of all the available material. Much of the foreign-language writing is primary data that are vital to a scholar but do not have sufficient sales volume to make translation economically feasible. Even when translations are available, they are often so untrustworthy that they are useless for research purposes. Nor is the picture likely to change. There is not only a growing number of South American anthropologists who are publishing extensively, but also increasing (and justified) pressure for foreign scholars to publish their findings in the language of the country where the work was done. It cannot be sufficiently emphasized that students who plan to pursue the study of South American anthropology must acquire at least a reading knowledge of several languages in addition to Spanish or Portuguese.

Another point that should be obvious from the references in the selections themselves is the debt we owe to the past. Our current work and knowledge of cultures and culture change depend upon a large and hard-won body of data, much of which refers to groups no longer extant or now completely acculturated. Our understanding of the people of South America is due in large part to those who went before us, without airplanes, helicopters, roads, or motor launches, not to mention freeze-dried foods and modern medicines. Those who read only the most recent work are missing what these people have to say to us, and they have a lot to say.

We have come a long way in the nearly twenty-five years since the *Handbook of South American Indians* was published, but it is hard to evaluate the extent to which we have improved our understanding of the many and intricate problems presented by South American Indian cultures. At the very least there has been a tremendous increase in the amount of data available for study. Nonetheless, it is still difficult to assemble material for any sort of detailed comparative study, since each researcher has emphasized different aspects of the culture he or she was studying. If we are to untangle some of these problems, we need more organized efforts like that directed by Maybury-Lewis and his students among the Northern Gê (cf. Maybury-Lewis 1967:viii–ix; Symposium 1971). Although such projects have been organized by archaeologists for some time, ethnologists have not done the same sort of thing. There have been informal arrangements--many researchers working in the Peruvian Montaña discuss and exchange material on an informal basis—but never before in South America has there been a concerted attack on a given problem such as that represented by the Maybury-Lewis project.

Finally, the subtitle of the book, which may surprise some, is a reflection of simple fact. Not only are the native cultures of South America poorly known, but so are its archaeology, botany, geography, zoology, geology, and so forth. In spite of the increasing amount of material that has been coming out of South America in all fields, our knowledge of the continent is still very poor and in many areas virtually nonexistent. Those who read this book are invited to take up the challenge of the unknown.

INTRODUCTION TO THE WAVELAND EDITION, 1985

Since 1974 our knowledge of Native South Americans has grown; it could hardly do otherwise. We have considerably more information on social organization and religion, but perhaps the most striking advances have been in the area I called Relationships to Natural Resources. It is now clear that, rather than "slash and burn" techniques that simply alternated planting with long fallow periods, native practice involves sophisticated, long-term land and forest management. Unfortunately, encroachment from the outside has increased, often involving the physical destruction of both native peoples and the environment in which they live. In less drastic cases the people are preserved but their culture is endangered. A new response is the formation of native federations to protect their lands and cultures by working through government channels both national and international. With all the new information, the original selection of articles here reissued is still basically sound, forming a framework into which new material can be readily fitted. The invitation and the challenge still stand.

I ATTEMPTS AT CONTINENT-WIDE TREATMENT

Attempts to deal with the continent of South America as a whole have been applied to essentially four kinds of material: (1) archaeological material, with which I will not deal, (2) the classification of cultures, (3) the classification of languages, (4) surveys of specific activities or kinds of man-made objects.

The articles by Steward and Murdock represent classifications of whole cultures, although into rather different sorts of groupings. Murdock uses a straight culture-area approach which is open to all the criticisms that this approach has received wherever applied (e.g., Kroeber 1952: 396–401). Basically the problem is in defining the areas, which almost inevitably tend to blend into one another at the boundaries, but this problem is immediately compounded if the area being classified has any time depth. In South America this problem is still further aggravated by the fact that available descriptions come from many different points in time, so that the culture areas do not represent any situation that ever actually existed.

Steward's classification, upon which the *Handbook of South American Indians* is based, is essentially a broader culture-area classification with an evolutionary ordering of the areas. Steward has, however, had to break up the geographical unity that is considered basic to a culture-area classification, in order to accommodate the evolutionary ordering.

Either of these classifications can be used to make it easier to approach the quantity of material on South American cultures. It must always be kept in mind, however, that both of them have serious faults, and each introduces its own bias into material that should be viewed objectively.

Linguistic classification is aimed at determining genetic relationships between languages. The articles by Rowe and Rodrigues point out that the present linguistic classifications for South America are far from satisfactory, but that there is hope for more successful attempts in the future.

Surveys of specific activities or objects, as exemplified by Schmidt's article, can be made for any number of reasons. Many of them are made in an effort to establish an evolutionary ordering, as was Schmidt's, but such surveys can be very useful for other purposes. For example, a study of lip ornaments such as that published by B. Menzel (1957) could be used by linguists to ascertain the effect, if any, of such ornaments on language.

The tendency today in South American studies is, however, toward the study of more restricted problems, or studies limited to a rather confined geographical area, or both (e.g., Wilbert, ed. 1961; Simposio 1968; Symposium 1971), as well as to structural studies.

The classificatory scheme for South America utilized by Steward is based on a series of evolutionary assumptions which should be obvious to the reader. While deriving the basic scheme from the earlier work of Cooper (1942a, 1942b), Steward was able to utilize a considerably larger data base, the material published in the Handbook of South American Indians. He also had available to him considerably more archaeological data than had been available to Cooper although he did not use it very critically. Archaeological work since the time of Steward's article tends to conflict with his rather simple developmental scheme (cf. Willey 1966–1971). For example, there is ample evidence in Peru for the existence of at least one major state that rose and fell long before the Inca empire appeared (cf. D. Menzel 1964), and recent work in the Andes of western Venezuela indicates that this area was prehistorically tied to the Andean region rather than the Circum-Caribbean (Wagner 1973). Reports from other areas indicate that prehistoric South America presented a constantly changing panorama of areas of contact and cultural interchange, grouping and regrouping, much of which is not at all reflected in any of the modern or historic connections (cf. for example Lathrap 1971).

Further problems in the Steward classification arise from the identification of borrowed elements and lost elements. The author assumes that any element present in, for example, a Marginal culture that does not fit his criteria for Marginal cultures must have been borrowed (usually from the Andean cultures) without any evidence for such borrowing. On the other hand, he seldom recognizes that many of the groups that are today hunters and gatherers were, prior to European pressure, agriculturalists who were either pushed out of areas appropriate for farming, or were forced to adopt a nomadic existence better suited to evading invaders (cf. Hohenthal ms.).

Steward's approach, as exemplified in this article, thus oversimplifies an extremely complex situation, obscuring differences which may be of considerable importance. Moreover, as in any scheme attempting to establish a diachronic picture on the basis of largely synchronic data, the entire structure is likely to crumble at the first touch of real diachronic information.

1   JULIAN H. STEWARD

American Culture History in the Light of South America

In an interpretative summary of the *Handbook of South American Indians,* I have suggested the historical implications of the four cultural types which are described in the first four volumes (Steward 1949). It is my purpose in the present article to show that a comparable typology is applicable to North American and Mexican cultures and to offer a broad, historical framework for native American culture history. I wish to express my indebtedness to the eighty-odd *Handbook* contributors for the mass of factual material on South America, but they cannot be held responsible for interpretations, except as their own classificatory or historical theories are specifically cited.

The four-fold classification of South American cultures used in the *Handbook,* though primarily a convenience for publishing the material, has historical significance. The Marginal tribes were hunting, fishing, and gathering nomads with simple socio-religious patterns. The Tropical Forest tribes differed from the Marginal peoples in possessing farming, dugout canoes, woven baskets, loom weaving, and pole-and-thatch houses. Many Tropical Forest tribes also had a war complex, which featured captive-taking, cannibalism, and display of human trophies. The Circum-Caribbean tribes of Central America, northern Venezuela and Colombia, and the Greater Antilles had all of these Tropical Forest traits, and they also had a class-structured society and a priest-temple-idol cult. The Circum-Caribbean social, religious, and military patterns and the material culture, except such rain-forest traits as dugout canoes and pole-and-thatch houses, occurred also in the early, developmental periods of Central America and the Andes.

Marginal cultures once existed throughout the Americas, but they varied in local configurations, patterns, and culture complexes.[1] In the Andes, farming provided the basis for the development of dense and stable populations. Socio-religious patterns and a material complex similar to those of the Circum-Caribbean culture were established as early as the Chavín and Early Periods. The special configurations and patterns of the Late Periods of the Central Andes represent developments of the earlier potentialities.

The Circum-Caribbean cultures were probably derived from the same source as the early Andean cultures, but they acquired such features as pole-and-thatch houses, hammocks, dugout canoes, and tropical root-crops; that is, they became somewhat adapted to coasts, rivers, and rain-forests. The Circum-Caribbean material culture, but not the social and religious patterns, diffused into the Tropical Forests, where, water-borne, they followed the coasts and rivers, diminishing through loss of

Reprinted by permission of the publisher and Mrs. Julian H. Steward from *Southwestern Journal of Anthropology,* vol. 3 (Summer 1947), pp. 85–107.

All material appearing within square brackets [ ] has been added by the editor of this book.

their characteristic traits at the headwaters of the Orinoco and Amazon, and scarcely penetrating eastern Brazil, the Gran Chaco, Patagonia, or the Chilean archipelago, where the tribes remained Marginal hunters, gatherers, or fishers.

In North America and Mexico, these culture types are roughly paralleled, and they may be recognized despite the variety of local configurations, patterns, and culture elements. Cultures comparable to the Peruvian Early Periods in general type, though not in specific configurations, are found also in Mexico and Yucatán, and they provide the roots of the later civilizations. I shall use the term "Formative Period" to designate the developmental phases of the American civilizations, that is, as an abstraction of the varied local cultures from their earliest agricultural beginnings to the time when they achieved a class-structured society and a priest-temple-idol cult. The concept is not concerned with centers of origin or with local time lags.[2]

Something very like the Circum-Caribbean culture occurred in the southeastern United States, and it gradually diminished through trait loss in the Eastern Woodland area to the north and in the Plains to the west. The remainder of North America, except the Northwest Coast, was Marginal in type. The North and South American Marginal tribes shared a great many culture elements with one another, but all of them had a large variety of configurations and patterns.

It is possible, of course, to overemphasize these North and South American culture parallels, so that American culture history is represented simply as a diminishing spread of the Formative Period culture. Such simplification is not supportable. Nonetheless, the Circum-Caribbean culture is a distinctive type in Central America, Colombia, Venezuela, and the Greater Antilles, and some explanation must be provided for the occurrence of a very similar culture type in the southeastern United States and for the gradual loss of the characteristics of this type northward in North America and southward in South America. An historical explanation is evidently required, but it need not be in terms wholly of diffusion.

The conceptual approach used here is that in each area the exploitation of the local environment by the technological devices culturally available set different limits to the variability of socio-political patterns and other features, so that historical influences were very great, moderate, or ineffective as the social and cultural ecology allowed greater or less latitude in the readaptation of patterns. In many, if not most, of the Marginal areas, the natural environment made aboriginal types of farming impossible. The particular patterns of subsistence activities carried on by the small, nomadic, and unstable groups of Marginal families set narrow limits to the variability of socio-political configurations and to the patterns of religion and warfare. The more adequate subsistence afforded by farming and, locally, by other resources, provided a basis for large, stable communities and thereby allowed greater latitude for variability in the principal configurations and patterns, that is, for the adoption of diffused features as well as for variations arising from local developments.

The concept may be illustrated by a comparison of the Circum-Caribbean peoples with the Araucanians. The former had large settlements, social classes, a strong war complex, and a priest-temple-idol cult, whereas the latter, with equally

Figure 1. *Culture types of the New World.* Solid black: *area of native civilizations in Middle America and Peru.* Heavy hatching: *Circum-Caribbean culture in the Antilles, South America, and Central America; Southeastern culture in the United States.* Light hatching: *diminished Circum-Caribbean–Southeastern culture type (Tropical Forest in South America; Eastern Woodland in North America).* White: *Marginal cultures in North and South America.*

proficient farming and about the same population density, lacked these patterns. The Circum-Caribbean peoples, however, did not simply borrow these features. It is probable that warfare also contributed to the nucleation of the dense population into compact multi-lineage communities of some size—especially in the areas of slash-and-burn farming—and to the differentiation of social status on the basis of war honors. Warfare, coupled with the priest class, which in turn depended upon the temple cult, produced the special Circum-Caribbean class pattern. But it represented a special cultural integration which, though depending on the one hand upon ecological potentialities and on the other upon diffused features, was a distinctive type.

THE MARGINAL CULTURES

The Marginal tribes of North and South America have been the subject of detailed comparisons by Krickeberg (1935), Nordenskiöld (1931), Ploetz [and Métraux] (1930), Métraux (1946:213–214), and Cooper (1942a, 1942b, 1946b). They listed large numbers of elements of split-distribution, that is, elements occurring among the Marginal tribes but not among the agricultural peoples in between, and inferred that these are early American traits that once had pan-American distribution. On the whole, these traits are probably traceable to a single origin, though it would not stretch the imagination to concede the independent invention of such things as wind-breaks, a slightly sunken house floor, leggings, caps, hair nets, hair brushes, animal-skin containers, wedges, clubs, driving game with fire, and the like.

The split-distribution approach to the culture history of the Marginal tribes is not very satisfactory for several reasons. First, these tribes resembled one another more in the absence of traits which occurred among higher tribes than in the presence of any traits among all of them. Second, a large number of the features common to all Marginal peoples did not have a split-distribution but were found also among more advanced American tribes and in other parts of the world. Third, the split-distribution traits did not occur among all Marginals, but tended to cluster in certain groups. Finally, the Marginal tribes had a wide range of socio-political configurations, which were special local traditions and ecological adaptations rather than survivals of an early, pan-American culture.

The absence of several important technologies and material traits distinguished the Marginal tribes from the farming peoples. Marginal peoples were not basket makers, though a few of them made twined baskets and many had adopted coiled baskets, the latter having spread from the western high cultures northward to Alaska and southward to Tierra del Fuego. They had no loom-weaving and made only twined or netted fabrics. They made no pottery or only a crude, unpainted ware. They lacked large, permanent houses and built only simple, domed, conical, or lean-to shaped structures, each accommodating a small, biological family. They had no dugout canoes, and travelled in bark canoes or on foot. They did not practise farming, and they had no domesticated animals, except the dog, which was unknown to many South American Marginal tribes. They lacked metates, mortars, narcotics, stimulants, salt, ear-, nose-, and lip-ornaments, and all musical instruments, except rhythm beaters and perhaps rattles.

This characterization of the principal features of material culture represents the Marginal tribes as if stripped of many traits diffused from special regions. The Northwest Coast had Asiatic features, the Eskimo and some of the Canadian Marginal tribes had certain circum-polar traits, and tribes in the deserts of western North America had many inter-American highland-type traits, such as coiled baskets, metates, and balsa rafts, which spread far beyond agriculture. Some of the eastern Brazilian tribes borrowed farming and other features from their Tropical Forest neighbors, while the culture of the Gran Chaco was strongly influenced by the Andes. It is really in Tierra del Fuego that the Marginal culture survived in its starkest simplicity, and even here archaeology shows important changes, the bola, for example, appearing in the middle periods and the bow being very recent (Bird 1946).

Many of the principal features common to the Marginal tribes occurred widely among other peoples; for example, such material traits as making fire and the use of stone artifacts, spears, harpoons, bows, nets, and containers. Similarly, the Marginals were not unique in their crisis rites: fasting by the mother of a new-born child; isolation of and fasting by pubescent girls; earth-burial, and belief in life after death. Like many other peoples, their shamans usually had a spirit-helper and cured through massage, blowing, and sucking. Also, they believed in nature spirits, omens, and magic. Their uniqueness lay in the manner in which these patterns and culture elements entered into the total configurations, and these configurations varied locally among the Marginals as one or another integrating factor predominated. Ritual elements, such as the drinking-tube, head-scratcher, steam bath, arrow-swallowing, bull-roarer, soul-loss theory of disease, deer-hoof rattle, and the like had quite different roles in each culture.

The scores of items of split-distribution—material culture, games, myth plots and motifs, etc.—did not occur among all Marginal tribes and do not, therefore, reveal the content of an early, pan-American culture. Many of them tended to cluster among certain tribes, and it is possible that more detailed plotting would reveal greater clustering. There is, for example, some evidence of distinctive complexes in the eastern and western parts of South America, attributable perhaps to separate streams of cultural flow from north to south. Differentiation of the Marginal cultures at different periods and in different areas is expectable; for the pre-agricultural period in America lasted some 10,000 to 15,000 years, during which the culture must have become regionally specialized and its history extremely complex.

Some localized elements link particular Marginals of South America and North America. Among the Araucanians, as among some Northwest Coast and Arctic tribes, the shaman was a transvestite and used a tambourine, and among the former, as in California, pubescent girls raced at dawn and carried firewood. The Charrua and their neighbors of the Paraná River, like the Great Plains tribes, practised finger mutilation as evidence of mourning and they fasted for a guardian spirit. Both groups thrust skewers through their flesh—the Charrua during mourning, the Plains tribes during the Sun Dance. The Chaco and western North America shared several traits, some of which also occurred elsewhere: myth motifs, such as the trickster, vagina dentatum, and theft of fire; games, such as ring-and-pin (also Montaña), dice (also Andean), "snow snake" (also eastern Brazil); and gambling (Métraux 1946: 369; Cooper 1949a).

In social and religious features, the Marginal tribes had a wide variety of adaptive patterns. They were similiar to one another only in their simplicity and their lack of a class-structured society, a priest-temple-idol cult, and a war complex that included captive-taking, use of human trophies, and cannibalism. Equipped with poor exploitative techniques and occupying areas of limited resources, the population was sparse and the socio-political group was small and nomadic. It may best be designated a band, and it usually consisted of a lineage or a group of bilateral families. It was loosely structured on the basis of sex, age, and associations; but there was no single configuration which, on the split-distribution hypothesis, can be assumed to have had a former pan-American distribution. To the contrary, there was a great variety of configurations, each of which must be understood in terms of special ecological adaptations.

Among a few tribes, such as the canoe-using and fishing Guató and Mura, and the seed-gathering Nambicuara and western Shoshoni, the bilateral or conjugal family was the only stable social group. It entered into informal and transient association with other families, but the configuration of these larger groupings was very different in each case, being strongly conditioned by the food-gathering regime.

The band of many Marginal tribes consisted of a lineage or extended family. Among the hunting tribes of Tierra del Fuego and southern California, the lineage was patrilineal, exogamous, patrilocal, and land-owning (Steward 1936a). Among the Guayakí and Sirionó, it was matrilineal. Among the northern Algonkian tribes, there was a combination of a system wherein bilateral families owned territories for trapping small mammals but multi-family or bilateral bands owned large areas for hunting migratory game.[3]

Multilineage bands occurred where greater food resources, improved transportation or both enabled larger numbers of people to live and travel together. The Tehuelche, Puelche, Querandí, and Charrua perhaps had single lineage patrilineal bands in native times, but these amalgamated into multilineage bands after the introduction of the horse. The North American tribes of the high Plains evidently developed in a somewhat parallel manner after becoming equestrian. Among certain Chaco tribes, such as the Mbayá, Caduveo, and Abipón, acquisition of the horse so intensifed warfare that warriors acquired special status in an incipient class system.

Among the seed-gathering, foot tribes of the Chaco, and among the Tapirapé and Carajá, society was based on the matrilineal lineage or extended family, but most villages consisted of several lineages. Perhaps at one time, each lineage had been independent, but the lineages later drew together in larger communities when ecological factors made it possible and historical factors gave a reason to do so.

The Ge tribes of eastern Brazil, especially the Northern Ge, had adopted the Tropical Forest type farming. They lived in large, stable communities that were structured on the basis of moieties, age-groups, and societies, most of them for men. These associations proliferated throughout this area. Thus, the Canella were divided into exogamous matrilineal moieties, three sets of nonexogamous moieties, and four men's age classes. The Sherente had exogamous patrilineal moieties with four sibs in each, seven grades in the Bachelor's hut, and four other men's associations. Such developments cannot be attributed to diffusion from more advanced Tropical Forest neighbors, for the latter lacked them. The associations must be interpreted as the crystallization of the sex and age cleavages implicit in all Marginal cultures. The moieties are an eastern Brazilian development, being found among the Tapirapé, Carajá, Bororo, and Caingang. The only other Marginal tribe accredited moieties is the Yaruro of the Orinoco River.

Outside eastern Brazil, formal associations are not characteristic of Marginal tribes, but in North America moieties occurred on the Pacific coast, men's associations in the Great Plains, and sibs among some Algonkians.

In summary, the Marginal tribes all had simple technology, society, and religion, but the wide variety of special configurations, patterns, and culture elements evidences a complex culture history. The pre-agricultural history of the Americas cannot be pictured as if a uniform culture had blanketed the hemisphere for thousands of years, its various traits surviving among some of the Marginal peoples and inexplicably disappearing among others. There were regional differences, which certainly involved the ecological adaptations of social institutions and probably involved the special development of many material, social, and ritual elements. Some local differences may have been established in successive migrations from Asia; others were almost certainly special complexes which diffused within America at widely different periods. Though the complexity of prehistory is well known to archaeologists, it tends to be oversimplified by those ethnologists who rely primarily on distributional methods in dealing with culture elements.

THE FORMATIVE PERIOD AND THE CIRCUM-CARIBBEAN CULTURE

The developmental phases of farming in the high culture areas are still obscure, except for the recent finds in the Virú valley in Peru. The beginnings of the Formative Period must antedate Christ by a long time, for the essential patterns of New World civilizations were established in Mexico and Yucatán at least by the beginning of the Christian era. In the Andes they can be no less old, for maize, a basic crop, probably originated in South America. In Peru, thirty-one domesticated plant species and the domesticated llama and alpaca are known from the Early Periods, and lima beans had already reached the limits of their genetic variability. Prior to this, there must have been a long period of plant breeding.

The early American civilizations, such as the Chavín in Peru, perhaps the San Agustín in Colombia, the Formative Period Maya, and the "Middle Periods" of Mexico, were distinctive in many ways, but a certain general configuration and a good many special elements are found in all.[4] These cultures represent the final phases of the hypothetical Formative Period, and their major features were also found among the Circum-Caribbean tribes at the Spanish Conquest.

The Formative Period and Circum-Caribbean cultures[5] had intensive farming, a fairly dense population, stable settlements (that were usually dispersed around religious centers in the Formative Period but were strongly nucleated in villages in the Circum-Caribbean tribes); a class system in which status was accorded priests; government, as contrasted to informal social controls of the kin group; the beginning of multi-village states, federations, or realms; special privileges accorded a chief, for example extra wives, acts of obeisance by his subjects, use of a special stool, riding in a litter, and burial accompanied by his wives and retainers; a priest-temple-idol cult involving public worship of tribal gods and a ritual calendar; celestial and astral deities; religious mounds, altars, offertories, and shrines; and construction of wattle-and-daub houses, causeways, aqueducts, canals, defensive works, and stone buildings. The Formative Period and Circum-Caribbean cultures also shared many items of material culture: loom weaving of domesticated cotton; cloth garments; armor; painted, negative-painted, incised, and plastic treatment of pottery; and featherwork and feather mosaics. Other elements common to the various Formative Period cultures were sandals, batik and tie-dying, coiled and perhaps woven baskets, and metates.

There is some reason to believe that the Formative Period cultures may have been more widespread than later ones. Archaeological evidence in eastern Bolivia, in the Colombian lowlands, and in portions of Central America, where more primitive cultures are now found, suggests that it was formerly better adapted to rain-forest and lowland areas. Possibly the insecurity of slash-and-burn farming, combined with pressures of a growing population and aggressive warfare, destroyed the older patterns.

There was also an expansion of a similar culture in North America, which, though later than the Formative Period, introduced the Hohokam and Anasazi cultures to the Southwest. The Pueblo may perhaps be seen as the forging of the Formative Period type priest-temple-idol cult and class and status system to conform to the age, sex, associational, and kin groupings of a more primitive type of society. The priesthood merged with clans and societies, the temple cult was combined with the men's club and secret society (kiva) and with ancestor worship (kachinas), and moieties, warrior societies, and curing societies combined with these institutions in endless combinations. Many of the Mexican elements were lost, though even head-hunting apparently reached northern Utah[6] and the Pueblo may once have sacrificed children.

At the time of the Spanish Conquest, the essential features of the Formative Period culture survived in Ecuador and Colombia, in northern Venezuela, in the Greater Antilles, and in Central America. Though perhaps derived from the early Formative Period culture of the northern Andes and Central America, this culture showed considerable influence from the central Andes, especially in Ecuador and Colombia. In Central America, at least in the later, pre-Columbian periods, the cultural flow was predominantly from South America. This is evidenced by such archaeological traits as stone cist graves, deep-shaft graves, stone stools, jaguar-form stools, Manabi type stone slabs, and mace-head clubs, and by such ethnographic traits as the Chibcha language, burial of subjects with a chief, mummification, platform beds, and gold-copper alloys. Most of these traits occurred north to the Maya frontier in Honduras.

Several features, especially rain-forest traits, link the Circum-Caribbean culture with that of the Tropical Forest tribes and distinguish it from both Mexico and the Central Andes: manioc, Muscovy ducks, the babracot, pole-and-thatch house, dugout canoe, palisaded village, hammock, and blowgun. These features do not greatly affect its patterning, in which it resembles the Formative Period culture.

Despite its linkage with both the Andes and the Tropical Forests, the Circum-Caribbean culture was distinctively patterned. Except in Colombia and Ecuador, it was largely coastal and sea-faring; sea resources supplemented farm produce and supported a dense population in large, permanent villages. Society was stratified into (1) nobles or chiefs, who sat on stools, were carried in litters, received obeisance from their retainers, and, at death, were buried with servants, who were slain for the purpose; (2) commoners; and (3) slaves, who were war captives. Warfare was crucial to the class system, for, though some of the higher nobles may have held hereditary status, rank could be achieved through the capture of persons, who either became one's slaves or who were sacrificed and their heads, stuffed skins, or other trophies displayed. There was a temple cult dedicated to tribal gods, which were represented by idols, and often the temples were on mounds. The idols were served by priests, who were sometimes distinct from shamans and whose primary function was to serve as oracles, although some of them conducted tribal rites. Society was predominantly matrilineal.

In diminished form, the Circum-Caribbean patterns and traits occurred among the Antillean Arawak. They also occurred in the Southeast, especially on the lower Mississippi River, and, though these North American tribes differed in some respects from the Circum-Caribbean peoples, a surprising number of traits and patterns were present (Swanton 1946). The Southeast cultivated maize, beans, and sweet potatoes (though not sweet manioc, arrowroot, or peanuts) and used fertilizer, wooden mortars, woven basketry, loom weaving, incised ceramics, dugout canoes, pole-and-thatch and wattle-and-daub houses, platform beds, earthworks, blowguns, cane-slat and hide shields, and monolithic axes. Society was predominantly matrilineal, and there is evidence of a caste system in Florida and of hereditary, caste-like, though exogamous, divisions among the Natchez. Federations were widespread. Chiefs had considerable status, which was evidenced by their use of stools among many tribes, their being carried in a litter among the Apalachi, Chickasaw, and Natchez, and being buried with retainers at death among the Natchez. There was a cult of the dead, involving burial mounds, urn burial, secondary burial, and filling the deceased's skin with sand, the last perhaps related to mummification. In religion, the Natchez and Caddo had a celestial or solar cult. The theocratic aristocracy combined a priesthood with a class system. Temples that contained idols and were placed on mounds were widespread. The war complex resembled that of the South American Circum-Caribbean culture in its prestige-giving objectives, its use of incendiary arrows and sword-like clubs on offense and of palisaded villages on defense, taking of women as captives, torture and killing of men, and use of men's heads or scalps as trophies.

The Southeastern ceremonial mounds were religious centers, but the developed war complex required that the population be nucleated in palisaded villages, which left these ceremonial centers defenseless. Most of them were abandoned before the historic period. This contrasts with the South American Circum-Caribbean peoples, who incorporated their ceremonial center inside the village.

Northward, beyond the Southeast area, the Circum-Caribbean features diminished, as in South America among the Tropical Forest tribes. Farming was less intensive and included fewer crops, the villages were smaller and less permanent, dugout canoes gave way to bark canoes, twined weaving replaced loom weaving, and bark vessels took the place of pottery ones. But, as in South America, various practices not dependent upon large, settled populations were found northward, more or less to the Canadian border. In warfare, for example, there was capture and torture of prisoners, cannibalism, and taking of trophy heads or scalps.

The general patterns of the Southeastern area equally resemble the Circum-Caribbean culture and the Formative Period culture, for all three had a class-structured society and a priest-temple-idol cult. Certain elements of the Southeast were, however, more specifically Circum-Caribbean than Formative Period: thatched houses, dugout canoes, wooden mortars and pestles, blowguns, woven baskets and a war complex.

To explain the Southeastern cultures, one of two general hypotheses seems required. The first is that a Formative Period type culture diffused northward via Mexico and the Gulf Coast. This explanation is difficult in that agriculture and mound-building appeared in the Southeast in the early centuries of the Christian era, but the full complex did not reach the Southeast until after 1000 AD,[7] whereas the Formative Period culture must have existed in Mexico two millennia earlier. The time lag is similar to that in the Southwest, where the Mexican features are manifest in some number during Pueblo II, also dating around 1000 AD. This hypothesis would not account for the differences between the Southwest and Southeast, and it would therefore be necessary to postulate that during this comparatively recent period of diffusion, there was a difference between a highland and lowland Mexican complex. It would have to be assumed that the former carried culture elements, such as stone architecture, metates, coiled baskets, painted pots, balsa rafts, and others to the Southwest, but that the war complex, social strata, and religious hierarchy were reformulated in a democratic society; whereas a lowland complex carried Circum-Caribbean type thatched houses, mortars, blowguns, dugout canoes, incised and plastic pots, a stratified society, the war complex, and the religious patterns into the Southeast. Against this hypothesis is the present lack of archaeological and ethnographic evidence of intermediate links on the north Mexican and the Texan Gulf coasts.

An alternative hypothesis is that the Southeastern patterns, configurations, and elements spread across the Antilles. This hypothesis also encounters distributional gaps in western Cuba and possibly in Florida, but the gaps are perhaps less formidable than those that seem to exist on the western Gulf coast. Moreover, the Circum-Caribbean peoples were excellent navigators as well as farmers, and they might have continued up the Florida coast beyond the mangrove swamps until they found a suitable habitat.

The typological similarity of the Southeastern, Circum-Caribbean and Formative

Period cultures does not, per se, provide an historical explanation, but it is a fact that must be taken into account, whether it is explained by Gulf coast or trans-Antillean diffusion or by independent invention. The choice among these explanations will perhaps depend somewhat upon one's theoretical and methodological approach. In any event, the facts cannot be ignored.

THE RECENT CIRCUM-CARIBBEAN CULTURE

The Circum-Caribbean peoples suffered from the European Conquest perhaps more drastically than any other American Indians. They became ethnographically, if not biologically extinct, in the Antilles, Venezuela, and much of Colombia. Only fragments survive in isolated areas of Colombia and of Central America. Many of the survivors retain a predominantly Indian culture, but it lacks all essential features of the native Circum-Caribbean culture and presents an interesting case of deculturation.

The Spanish Conquest dislodged the tribes from their native habitat, especially on the coasts and the more favored highland areas, and threw them back into submarginal lands where subsistence could not support large population clusters or special classes of artisans, priests, warriors, and nobles. At the same time, the Spanish government seized political controls from the native nobles, and Spanish military power put an end to warfare, thus destroying the class structure. The Catholic Church was substituted for the native priest-temple-idol cult, and human sacrifice was abolished. The distinguishing socio-religious features were thus destroyed, and the more elaborate craft products in weaving, metallurgy, ceramics, building arts, and the like lost meaning, for they had been designed largely for the native upper classes. There remained only a simple folk culture: simple farming people, an unstratified society, shamanism, and unelaborate textiles, ceramics, and other craft products made for home consumption. The surviving tribes retain a native culture which resembles that of the Tropical Forest peoples, who have also simple technologies and a simple socio-religious pattern.

THE TROPICAL FORESTS

The Tropical Forest tribes are linked with the Circum-Caribbean peoples in a considerable number of technological and material traits. They were all farmers, but some of their tropical root crops, especially bitter manioc, arrowroot, and cara (a native yam, *Dioscorea*), may have been locally domesticated. They used pole-and-thatched houses, dugout canoes, domesticated cotton, the loom, and tobacco, and they made woven baskets, ceramics, blowguns, bark cloth, hammocks, rubber balls, and hollow-log drums.

The Tropical Forest tribes differed from the Circum-Caribbean peoples in lacking the class-structured society of the latter. Instead, their society was much like that of the Marginal tribes, being based on the extended family or lineage. It was predominantly patrilineal, however, except in the Guianas, which were in contact with the matrilineal Circum-Caribbean peoples. Typically each lineage occupied a large, comparatively permanent and isolated house, but in some areas several houses comprised a village. The Tropical Forest tribes were quite uniform in social structure, but social integration varied as emphasis fell upon certain factors—for example, the war complex of the Island Carib and the Tupinamba, the ancestor cult of the Tucano, the head-hunting of the Jívaro, the fertility rites of certain Juruá-Purús tribes, or the Grandfather cult of the Tupí. Chiefs of multihouse villages had greater status than lineage heads, but they rarely held a hereditary position. In religion, there were few public rites; instead most religious observances were private. Birth rites were always so; puberty rites were only rarely public, as in the boys' initiations in the Northwest Amazon; and death rites only infrequently involved public ceremonies. The shaman performed witchcraft and curing ceremonies for individual persons. If he worked for public ends, he made war magic, prognosticated, or performed other services through the medium of his spirit helper, rather than by supplicating a tribal god. Warfare was well developed in many Tropical Forest tribes, but it contributed little to individual social status. Instead, it served tribal ends, the captives being either adopted into the tribe or sacrificed in cannibalistic rites and trophies kept.

The Tropical Forest technological and material traits faded out in the headwaters of the Amazon and in other inaccessible and remote areas, just as they disappeared in the northeastern and western United States. Approaching the hinterlands in South America, dugout canoes gave way to bark ones; loom-woven textiles were replaced by finger-woven, twined fabrics; ceramics became crude and monochrome; temporary baskets made of palm fronds occurred in place of woven and twilled baskets; and agriculture took second place to hunting, gathering, and fishing. The Tropical Forest complex finally disappeared in those hinterland areas that form a great, though broken, U around the Amazon basin—the Amazon-Orinoco watershed, parts of the Northwest Amazon, the Ucayali-Juruá-Purús watershed, and the upper Tapajoz, Xingú, and Tocantins Rivers. These areas remained Marginal, and Marginal cultures survived also in the highlands of eastern Brazil, Matto Grosso, the Gran Chaco, the Pampas, Patagonia, and the Chilean archipelago.

The inference from these facts is that the Tropical Forest culture derived its essential technologies and material culture from the Circum-Caribbean peoples, though perhaps producing some of the rain-forest-adapted traits that were common to both. Though horticultural and utilizing certain tropical root crops, it was equally riparian and coastal. It depended upon canoe transportation to exploit river resources and to maintain its settlement patterns. In its diffusion, consequently, it followed waterways, spreading along the coasts and up the main rivers. Probably deriving its essential features from contact with the Circum-Caribbean culture in the Guianas or Venezuela, it diffused down the Guianas and up the Amazon, with perhaps a secondary route via the Orinoco, Casiquierre Canal and Rio Negro. It diminished in the unnavigable headwaters, where the remoter tribes remained Marginal because these traits did not reach them. The Indians of the Ucayali River in eastern Peru, though partially adjoining the Inca, retained Tropical Forest patterns and traits. From the Peruvian highlands they borrowed only particular elements, such as the belt loom, painted cloth, the feather fire fan, the cushma, the platform bed, and perhaps head-taking. There is no evidence whatever that their configurations, patterns, and major elements were derived from the Andes or contributed to the Andes. Even their ceramics are much more like those of the lower Amazon than the Andes. The Arawakan Campa and their neighbors, living immediately below Cuzco in the Montaña, were nearly Marginal in culture. The same is true of the Jívaro and of the Cahuapanan and Záparoan tribes on and north of the lower Marañón River.

South of the Amazon basin, the Tropical Forest culture also followed waterways. Tupian tribes carried it down the Brazilian coast to the Río de la Plata, and across Paraguay to the very foot of the Andes, one of the few cases in which the culture spread is clearly attributable to migration. Another southward thrust was evidently up the Madeira River into eastern Bolivia, where, in a varied environment, it was intermixed with Marginal and Sub-Andean type cultures. In general, its distribution has a remarkably close correlation with that of tropical rain forests.

THE HIGH CIVILIZATIONS

The great New World civilizations have been described so frequently that the concern here is merely to relate them typologically, functionally, and historically to the tentative scheme that is postulated. It is assumed that the Formative Period culture, at least, its final phase, underlay the high civilizations, which achieved distinctive configurations and patterns in the latest periods of Mexico, Yucatán, and the Andes.

The Andes

The Andean Chavín and Early Periods were evidently similar to the Circum-Caribbean cultures in their basic patterns, but certain special trends that increasingly distinguished the Andes from Mexico and Peru were already established.

The Andean subsistence complex became the most efficient in native America, being based upon intensive irrigation, terracing, and fertilization of farm plots. In the low, fertile valleys bisecting the arid coast, tight nucleation of the population became necessary. This settlement pattern, coupled with construction of irrigation canals, roads, and public works, which served many communities, required far-reaching political controls. In the Peruvian Formative Period, there were clearly confederations or states. The late Chimu developed a true empire, while the Inca achieved the largest and best organized empire in the New World.

During the Formative Period, the Andean class structure appears to have been based on theocratic status. Later, as evidenced by ceramic designs, mortuary customs, and other archaeological evidence from the Early Periods, it was also based on war achievements. Probably, as in the Circum-Caribbean culture, war prisoners became slaves if they were not sacrificed. Finally, Peru became so densely settled that there was no room for captive groups, while developed political controls converted warfare into campaigns of territorial conquest, which were designed to extend the empire and to extract tribute from a subject people. Warriors were drawn from a class of commoners who had fixed status. They were regimented in a state army, and they could no longer achieve status by taking captives, for there was no place for slaves in the social scheme; nor was there any need of sacrificial victims, human sacrifice of prisoners having been given up.

The Formative Period religious pattern was probably like that of the Circum-Caribbean culture. Village or tribal gods were publicly consulted or worshipped, and the priest-shaman, whose power came from a personal supernatural helper, directed public ritual. As tribal worship developed, the priest's power increased, but again it was the extension of political controls over large empires that brought the final formulation. When the Inca priest-temple-idol cult was added to the cults of subject peoples, an hierarchy of gods and priests was established. As the hereditary rulers headed the church as well as the state, the priests also acquired hereditary status, and they became distinguished from shamans, who were minor practitioners. The Inca State thus became one of frozen statuses.

Highland patterns disappear east of the Andes as soon as the rain forest is entered, for slash-and-burn farming could not support them. In eastern Bolivia, however, the Manasí and the Arawakan Mojo, Bauré and Paressí, had patterns somewhat similar to those of the Circum-Caribbean peoples, and in this respect are "Sub-Andean." Their subsistence patterns and most of their material culture was Tropical Forest in type, but they had incipient social classes and traces of a temple cult, which was combined with a men's tribal society among the Mojo and with a men's club among the Bauré. The Paressí waged wars of conquest.

In the southern Andes, many culture elements, including farming, weaving, ceramics, llamas, guinea pigs, quipus, slings, blood-sacrifice, and numerous other traits were acquired from the central Andes, but the Araucanians had also such Tropical Forest elements as thatched houses, mortars, dugout canoes, urn burial, and cannibalism of war prisoners. The socio-political and religious patterns of all these tribes, however, were essentially of Tropical Forest types. The Atacameño and Diaguita, having a very sparse population, lived in small settlements consisting only of patrilineal lineages. They had no priest-temple-idol cult, and they lacked social classes, except as Diaguita warriors attained some status through capture and sacrifice of prisoners. The Araucanians, though extremely numerous, were also settled in kin groups. Their ecology would have permitted larger aggregations, but there were no factors that would break down kin separatism. They had loose federations and incipient classes, but no true temple cult or hierarchical priesthood.

Mexico and Yucatán

At the time of the Spanish Conquest the cultures of Mexico and Yucatán resembled each other and differed from the central Andes in the great development of pyramids, temples, hieroglyphic writing, art styles, and other intellectual and esthetic features. Mexico, however, seems to have preserved the basic traditions of the Formative Period culture, whereas Yucatán has unique features, which present interesting problems.

Like Peru, early Mexico from the Formative Periods through the Regional Classical or Teotihuacan Periods seems to have had peaceful, theocratic states. The war complex apparently was introduced in the Chichimec Period.

The Aztec and their neighbors in the Mexican highlands had intensive farming, urban centers that were also ceremonial centers, and socio-political patterns in which warfare was vital. War was waged in order to take victims for ritual sacrifice and for cannibalism, to exact tribute from conquered peoples, and to give status to the warriors. Religion was based on the priest-temple-idol cult, and the sacrifice of war captives was important to it. Social, political, and priestly statuses were strongly developed, but personal attainments, especially in warfare, permitted upward mobility, in contrast to the Andean caste pattern. Similarly, while Mexico brought conquered peoples into a tribute system, it lacked the Andean genius to create politically integrated empires.

In contrast to Mexico, Yucatán was an area of ceremonial centers, not city states. The problem here is not why these "cities" declined and were abandoned, but why they lasted so long. All other New World civilizations developed in highlands or semi-arid areas, and, though traces of high culture are found in rain-forests and other lowland areas, none of these survived. Yucatán is unique in America, and indeed, probably in the world, in that a great civilization was built and survived for 2,000 years or more on the basis of slash-and-burn farming.

In highland Mexico and the central Andes, the dense populations were maintained by permanent farm lands, which were irrigated and fertilized. Slash-and-burn farming, however, rapidly exhausts the soil and requires that new clearings be opened every few years. This sets limits on settlement size, for, when compact urban centers become too big, it is a physical impossibility for human carriers to transport foodstuffs from farm areas to them. To judge by Circum-Caribbean and Tropical Forest communities, a tightly nucleated settlement supported by slash-and-burn farming cannot exceed a few thousand people. The Maya "cities," however, were able to survive by dispersing their populations. Thus, they were not "cities" in any urban sense, but religious centers, around which the population extended many miles in all directions. As the population in these districts became denser, slash-and-burn farming would become more precarious, though it seems likely that an equilibrium might finally be established.

At this point, the crucial factor of warfare must be taken into account. In the slash-and-burn areas of Central and South America, warfare prevented any such large, dispersed settlements as were found in Yucatán, for a dispersed population is too vulnerable. Communities became nucleated, usually in compact, palisaded villages of limited size, and the religious center was generally enclosed within the palisade. It must be postulated, therefore, that the lowland Maya development was possible only because of prolonged periods of peace; for it is difficult to see how populations dispersed around religious centers could have survived serious warfare. Unlike the highland populations, who had hilltop forts to which to retreat, the Maya were defenseless. The abandonment of the older religious centers of southern Yucatán could be explained by warfare emanating from the highlands, where perhaps it had been perpetuated in the old Formative Period pattern. Even a few wars would upset the already delicate balance between man and nature, and even if the people were not driven out, their ill-defended ceremonial centers would easily fall.[8] In northern Yucatán, the distinctive Maya patterns were destroyed when the

Itza brought warfare out of Mexico, converting the religious centers into fortified urban centers and introducing a militaristic ruling group, to whom the priests yielded power, and a serf class (Thompson 1945:13–16).

Seen in these terms, the Maya culture represents an extreme development of the priest-temple cult of the Circum-Caribbean culture and a lack of the war complex, including conquest, tribute, class status for warriors, and taking of captives for slaves and human sacrifice. Peace was evidently achieved through the formation of federations. But it was the priests who were supreme, and they developed the intellectual and esthetic aspects of their cult far beyond the understanding of common people. The downfall of the religious centers was really a removal of the priestly cult. As in the case of the later Mexican-derived cults of northern Yucatán, the religious superstructures were added and removed without very much affecting the folk culture of the common people.

HISTORICAL SUMMARY

During the many thousands of years prior to the development of farming, America was occupied by Marginal type tribes. These tribes were somewhat similar to one another in their simple technology and material culture and in their shamanistic and ritual patterns, but they differed greatly in their socio-political patterns and in many of their culture elements, evidencing a complex history of cultural development, diffusion, and ecological adaptation. At the time of the Spanish Conquest, they survived in vast parts of northern and western North America and southern South America, and in scattered enclaves among the farming peoples. These recent Marginals were distinguished from one another not only by their own special adaptations but by considerable numbers of culture elements that their local groups had borrowed from the farming tribes.

During the developmental phases of American agriculture, the highland areas from Mexico to Bolivia acquired dense populations, large and stable communities, a class-structured society and a priest-temple-idol cult. In the material arts, it produced basketry, ceramics, metallurgy, weaving, stone working, building arts, esthetic expressions in art forms, and water transportation. This is known as the Formative Period culture.

In Mexico, the Formative Period culture preserved its essential features, their development in later periods being marked by intensification rather than change. In Yucatán, the war complex was absent, while the priest-temple-idol complex was developed to a great extreme and served to channel esthetic, intellectual, and constructional efforts. It was the absence of warfare that enabled the Maya to survive on the basis of slash-and-burn farming, for their dispersed populations were vulnerable to attack. Warfare, consequently, was the factor that tipped the balance and destroyed the great religious centers.

The Central Andes became very densely populated and developed the political and practical potentialities of the Formative Period cultures. The war complex was converted into conquests for territory and tribute, society became organized into a structure of fixed statuses, and the religious patterns finally produced a hierarchy of both gods and priests.

Central Andean material and ritual elements spread to the Southern Andes, where the socio-political and religious patterns remained essentially like those of the Tropical Forests.

The Conquest period tribes of the Circum-Caribbean area had a subsistence complex, social, religious, and war patterns, and material culture very similar to those postulated for the Formative Period cultures, but they differed from the latter in rain-forest adaptations, such as thatched houses, dugout canoes, woven baskets, and hammocks. The Eastern Woodland peoples of North America and the Tropical Forest tribes of South America, both adjoining the Circum-Caribbean tribes, borrowed the latter's technologies and rain-forest traits—basketry, pottery, dugouts, thatched houses, root crops, and so forth—but, partly because of less efficient food production and partly because of insufficient contacts with the higher cultures, they did not borrow the class system or the priest-temple-idol cult. Their social and religious patterns resembled the Marginal types.

As the technological and material traits of the Tropical Forest and Eastern Woodland tribes diffused further, one after another was lost in areas which were remote or which were unsuited environmentally for their existence. Thus, in the far north and far south and in unfavorable localities within the farming areas, the tribes preserved the Marginal type of culture.

NOTES

1. "Pattern" and "configuration" have been used interchangeably to denote interrelated modes of behavior of very different magnitudes; for example, the over-all culture, social organization, marriage, or limited segments of kinship behavior. Clyde Kluckhohn (1941) suggests that "pattern" be used to designate overt modes of behavior, "configuration" to designate covert ones, and that orders of magnitude or abstraction be distinguished by "pattern assemblage," "pattern," "sub-pattern," and "pattern part." Useful as this terminology may be for detailed analysis of a single culture, it is difficult to apply to a comparative study of the present kind, where the need is for a fairly crude device by which to distinguish elements or items, interrelated modes of behavior which make up segments of culture (here called "patterns," for example, warfare or religion), and the over-all integration of the patterns (here called "configuration"). This use of "configuration" is perhaps not inconsistent with Kluckhohn's, though the covert factor is not specified in each case.

My choice of terminology springs from the need of distinguishing the totality of culture, which represents a particular historical continuum and is therefore unique in each case, from its component parts, or patterns, which may be abstracted to the extent that similarities may be recognized between their different occurrences.

2. In America, there was a long period following the beginnings of agriculture, during which the population became dense, the communities large, and culture generally rich. By the end of this period, a class-structured society, a priest-temple-idol cult, and many particular culture elements were established in Mexico, Yucatán, Central America, and the Andes. These patterns and elements underlay the later, more specialized cultures.

Terminology for this early period varies. For the Maya area Thompson applied the term Formative Period to the entire sequence from the earliest agricultural beginnings to the final formulation of the basic patterns prior to the Initial Series Period (Thompson 1943, 1945). In Mexico, the sequence seems to begin with more or less full-blown basic patterns, which Vaillant designated Middle Periods, leaving room for the earlier phases, should they be found (Vaillant 1944). In Peru, the Institute of Andean Research found a sequence extending from the pre-ceramic agricultural period, which is called Pre-ceramic, through an early ceramic phase, which is called Early Ceramic, to a long third period in which the basic inventions and technologies and the mounds, social classes, warfare, and religious cult were established. Only the last is designated Formative Period (Willey 1946; Strong 1947).

If interest is centered in the development of the basic social and religious institutions, it would seem advisable to extend Formative to cover the entire period from the beginnings of agriculture to the final formulation of the patterns in question. Thus, Peru and perhaps Yucatán would have the whole period, Mexico the later phases with the earlier ones yet to be identified, and peripheral areas, such as the Southwest and northwest Argentina, the early and perhaps middle phases.

Subsequent to the Formative Period, cultures began to acquire more marked local characteristics. These periods—Salinar and Gallinazo in Peru, Initial Series in Yucatán, and Archaic in Mexico—might be called Regional Developmental. They preceded the final formulation of the Regional Classical or Florescent Periods—Mochica and Nazca B in Peru, Teotihuacan in Mexico, and Classical Maya in Yucatán—when technological and socio-religious developments attained their finest esthetic expressions. The war complex of captive-taking, human sacrifice, and human trophy display appears during this period in Peru and during the following periods in Mexico and Yucatán, the latest periods in all three areas being times of conquest and empire growth with other aspects of culture becoming stilted.

3. I see the Fuegian patrilineal band hunting territory and the Algonkian family trapping territory as very different ecological adaptations, whereas Cooper (1946b) seems to consider them the same thing and to derive them from historical tradition through a split-distribution method. He does not take into account the co-existence of two types of land-tenure among the Algonkians, each related to a special economic activity.

4. For archaeological evidence of inter-American distributions, see Kidder (1940); Lothrop (1942); Uhle (1942); Strong (1943).

5. The concept of the Circum-Caribbean culture was introduced by Paul Kirchhoff, who, utilizing the early Spanish Conquest period chronicles to reconstruct the native cultures of Venezuela, Colombia, and Central America, found abundant evidences of a civilization that compared favorably with that of the Andes though it shared many rain-forest traits with the Tropical Forest peoples. This represents an addition to Cooper's three-fold classification of South American culture types, and it helps resolve the seeming contradiction between the Circum-Caribbean archaeology, which has strong Andean characteristics, and the ethnology of the modern tribes, which is of a Tropical Forest type.

6. Trophy heads are clearly indicated in petroglyphs of the upper Colorado River (Steward 1937: pls. 3 and 5).

7. After agricultural beginnings, the resemblances to the Formative Period and Circum Caribbean cultures evidently began to reach their fulfillment by 1000 AD or later. See, for example, Griffin (1946).

8. Thompson notes that the abandonment of the "cities" probably "was not accompanied by any mass depopulation of the surrounding country" (1945:4).

Extensive comment on this article by Murdock is obviated by the inclusion of Rowe's review which follows. There are, however, a few points that should be kept in mind while reading the following article. Murdock, in attempting to classify all groups recorded for South America in his scheme, runs into the problem of the use of the ethnographic present. He is dealing with data collected over more than 400 years and treating them as if they were contemporaneous. Such a treatment is particularly problematical in establishing areas, since we have many recorded instances of considerable tribal movement, displacement, and even extinction. On the basis of work that has been done in the last twenty years in the Peruvian Montaña, it is obvious that the establishment of the Montaña as a single culture area is indefensible, and his treatment of Brazil contrasts markedly with that of Galvão (1967).

2 GEORGE PETER MURDOCK

South American Culture Areas

The culture area concept, though long since divested of most of the theoretical significance ascribed to it by Wissler, still retains its classificatory importance. It is nearly as useful in ordering the immense range of ethnographic variation as is the Linnaean system in the ordering of biological forms.

For the South American continent, until recently, anthropologists have had only the tentative and impressionistic classification by Wissler (1917). The publication of the monumental *Handbook of South American Indians* (Steward, ed. 1946–1959) makes possible, at last, an approach to a definitive areal formulation.

Despite the immense merit of the *Handbook,* which places the anthropological world in deep debt to the editor, the latter's delineation of culture areas leaves room for improvement. The present writer finds it unsatisfactory on two counts. First, since it utilizes all available cultural data and these are often scanty and of different kinds for different areas, it frequently employs criteria for one area where comparable data cannot be cited to differentiate other areas.

A second and more serious objection is Steward's excessive use of negative criteria. His many "marginal" and "submarginal" areas are based primarily on the absence of traits found in the more complex cultures. The writer, having worked in "marginal" areas like the Plateau, is deeply impressed with the richness of simpler cultures in positive characteristics, and he would define the areas in which they appear primarily in terms of such positive cultural content.

With these objectives in mind it seemed worth while to reassess the data assembled in the *Handbook* and to refer for additional evidence on crucial points to the substantial collections of the Cross-Cultural Survey on the South American Indians. A schedule was drawn up of a selected number of important traits and complexes upon which comparable information is fairly widely available, and the relevant data were abstracted and tabulated for every tribe or group of closely related tribes on the continent. These were then compared, ignoring all other evidence, and a classification into culture areas was made on the basis of the

Reprinted by permission of the author and publisher from *Southwestern Journal of Anthropology,* vol. 7 (Winter 1951), pp. 415–436.

similarities and differences discovered. The major types of information covered by the schedule were as follows:

1. Linguistic affiliation.
2. The incidence and relative importance of the major techniques for securing food.
3. The presence, absence, and relative importance of domesticated animals and the principal cultivated plants.
4. The participation of the sexes in agricultural operations other than land clearance.
5. The incidence of certain selected crafts of varying levels of complexity, notably pottery, loom-weaving, and metallurgy.
6. The prevailing house types and household size.
7. The relative degree of development of trade, social classes, and political institutions.
8. The prevailing form, mode, and rules of marriage.
9. The prevailing types of kin and local groups and kinship terminology.

The twenty-four culture areas emerging from this analysis are listed, named, and characterized below, in an order starting from Central America, descending the Pacific coast, ascending the Atlantic coast, zigzagging through the Amazonian basin, and ending with Venezuela and the West Indies. The accompanying map shows the approximate location of the several areas. It distorts actual distributions only by favoring backward areas interpenetrated by more advanced peoples to the extent of giving the former a slightly falsified continuous distribution.

1. ISTHMIAN AREA

This area connects the Mayan center of Middle American civilization with the Colombian area, the northernmost extension of intensive Andean civilization. The lowland sections of this territory, like Honduras, eastern Nicaragua, and the Pacific coast of Colombia, are occupied by peoples of relatively simple cultures. Interspersed among them, however, are more advanced peoples, especially in Panama, Costa Rica, and western Nicaragua, who possess many of the essential features of the more complex civilizations to the north and south, and who form a bridge across which elements originating in either could have diffused to the other. The dominant linguistic stock of the area is Chibchan, but the Choco in Colombia and the tribes of Honduras and Nicaragua belong to other and usually lesser stocks. Subsistence depends upon a relatively intensive milpa type of agriculture, with hunting and fishing commonly of only subsidiary importance. The staple crops are maize and sweet manioc, the former usually dominating in highland and the latter in lowland regions. Beans and sweet potatoes are also important, but bitter manioc is a post-Conquest importation. Field work tends to be done mainly by men in the highland tribes, by women in the lowlands. Dogs are kept, and the turkey is domesticated in upland Nicaragua. Good ceramics and the loom-weaving of cotton are nearly universal, and work in gold and occasionally in copper occurs sporadical-

Figure 1. Culture areas of South America.

ly through Central America. The prevailing house type is a rectangular thatched structure accommodating a number of families. Large towns are found only in highland Nicaragua, but villages are aggregated into petty states under hereditary paramount chiefs except in a few lowland tribes. Social class distinctions are usually well developed. Though information on social organization is exceedingly meager, matrilocal residence appears to be common, and several Isthmian tribes are reported to possess genuine exogamous matrilineal sibs.

2. COLOMBIAN AREA

The Andean highlands of Colombia and adjacent Ecuador are occupied by a series of peoples nearly all of whom speak languages of the Chibchan stock, the few exceptions speaking Choco, Coche, or unidentified tongues. Their cultures, though closely affiliated with those of the Isthmian and Caribbean areas, show rather more directly the influence of Peruvian civilization. Hunting and fishing are everywhere subordinate to intensive agriculture. Besides maize, sweet manioc, beans, sweet potatoes, and fruit trees, which extend to the Isthmian and Caribbean areas, quinoa, potatoes, and other Peruvian crops assume importance. Women perform most agricultural operations except clearing the land, though in a few tribes the men participate on an equal basis. Domesticated guinea pigs are widely kept. Ceramics and loom-woven cotton fabrics are universal, and most tribes are conversant with metallurgy in gold and copper. Trade is highly developed, and regular markets are widespread. The Chibcha have large palisaded towns, but most of the other tribes live in small villages, hamlets, or communities of scattered homesteads. The dwellings themselves, which usually accommodate only a single nuclear or polygynous family, are often raised on posts. They are circular or occasionally rectangular in shape with thatched roofs and walls most commonly of wattle and daub. Although local autonomy prevails in some regions, communities are more commonly aggregated into districts under paramount chiefs or even, as among the Chibcha, into feudal states with kings. Differentiated social classes are the rule. Polygyny, of either sororal or unspecified form, is reported for most tribes. Marriage, at least in some regions, is effected by payment of a bride-price or by the exchange of sisters, and residence appears to be generally patrilocal. However, matrilineal succession, reported for the Chibcha and several other tribes, suggests matrilineal descent, which is specifically attested for the Pantangoro and Amani.

3. PERUVIAN AREA

The Andean highlands and Pacific coast of Peru and adjacent Ecuador and Bolivia formerly supported the highest civilization of aboriginal South America—similar to but appreciably more complex than the cultures of the Colombian area to the north and the Chilean area to the south. The inhabitants spoke languages of many independent stocks, of which Aymaran, Quechuan, and Yuncan were the most widely distributed. Hunting and gathering contributed relatively little to the food supply, and fishing assumed importance only on the coast and on Lake Titicaca. The economy rested primarily upon an unusually intensive agriculture, often conducted by irrigation and the terracing of fields and supplemented on the coast by the use of guano as fertilizer. More than fifty different species of domesticated plants were cultivated, the staples being potatoes, quinoa, and oca at the highest elevations, maize at lower altitudes, and beans, squash, sweet manioc, peanuts, peppers, fruit trees, and cotton in the deeper valleys and on the coast. Women did the field work in Ecuador, but both sexes participated equally in Peru and highland Bolivia. Domesticated animals included llamas, alpacas, dogs, guinea pigs, and the Muscovy duck. The herding of llamas and alpacas rivaled agriculture in economic importance in the high plateaus. Crafts included superior ceramics, excellent loom-weaving in cotton and wool, and expert metallurgy in gold, silver, copper, and tin. The only boats, however, were rafts. Over most of the area these were crudely made from bundles of reeds, but in a restricted section of the northern coast somewhat better sailing rafts were constructed of balsa wood. Trade was highly·developed, and was facilitated by an admirable system of roads. Architecture reached its climax in magnificent temples, palaces, and fortresses of brick or stone masonry. The common people, however, lived in rectangular single-family huts with thatched gable or hip roofs and walls of stone, sod, adobe, or wattle-and-daub. Among the Aymara, but not elsewhere, these were grouped in extended family compounds surrounded by a wall. Social classes were sharply differentiated, and the entire area, together with parts of the Colombian and Chilean areas, was politically integrated under the massive Inca empire. Marriage was strictly monogamous except in the noble classes, and involved neither bride-price nor bride-service. Local endogamy prevailed, and residence was patrilocal. Though inheritance and succession were patrilineal, descent was bilateral, and kinship terms were of the Hawaiian type. The modern Aymara possess exogamous patri-lineages, but there is no evidence that such groups are aboriginal.

4. CHILEAN AREA

In northern and central Chile and in the adjacent mountainous portion of north-western Argentina reside a group of tribes characterized by a distinctive variant of Andean civilization. Linguistically they fall into a number of isolated stocks—the Araucanian, Atacaman, Comechingonan, Diaguitan, Huarpean, and the unidentified languages of the Omaguaca and Tonocote nations. All these peoples practice intensive agriculture, commonly with the aid of irrigation. Maize is the staple crop, but beans, squash, quinoa, potatoes, and other plants are also cultivated. Manioc and sweet potatoes, however, are absent. Women do nearly all agricultural work, at least among the Araucanians. Fishing and shellfishing are important only on the coast, and gathering only among the inland Araucanians, who make extensive use of piñon nuts. Hunting is everywhere a distinctly subsidiary activity. In all of the aboriginal economies herding holds a position approaching, or in some instances even exceeding, that of agriculture. In addition to smaller animals like dogs and guinea pigs, which are sporadically reported, all tribes raise llamas for their wool, and the Comechingon and Tonocote are even said to have domesticated the rhea or American ostrich. Loom-woven woolen fabrics, made by all tribes, provide a basis for extensive trade with the north. Pottery likewise has a universal distribution, and metallurgy in copper and bronze (sometimes also in silver and gold) is attested for all tribes except the Comechingon and Huarpe. The people live in sedentary villages of rectangular houses, occasionally protected by stockades. The Araucanians have multi-family houses with wooden frames and thatched roofs, but elsewhere the prevailing house type is a smaller structure with dry-masonry walls and a flat roof covered with poles, reeds, and mud. Political integration under paramount chiefs was apparently achieved aboriginally only by the Araucanians and Omaguaca, but most of the tribes of the area were ultimately conquered and absorbed by the Inca empire. Marriage is contracted by payment of a bride-price and is commonly polygynous, especially in the sororal form. Inheritance and succession are patrilineal. Other data on social organization are available only for the Araucanians, who are characterized by patrilocal residence, extended families, exogamous patrilineages, and kinship terminology of the Omaha type.

5. FUEGIAN AREA

The coast and offshore islands of Chile and Tierra del Fuego are occupied by the Chono, Alacaluf, and Yahgan tribes, who speak isolated or unidentified languages. They practice no agriculture, gather few wild vegetal products, and hunt to only a very limited extent. Subsistence depends primarily upon the collecting of mussels and other shellfish, supplemented by fishing, the pursuit of seals and porpoises, and the catching of marine birds. The people make good bark or sometimes plank canoes, but they lack completely such technological arts as pottery, loom-weaving, and metallurgy. They lead a migratory life in small bands and live in single-family dwellings of dome or beehive shape constructed of flexible poles covered with skins or bark. Class distinctions are lacking, though the Chono occasionally hold war captives as slaves. The Alacaluf and Yahgan do not even have local headmen. Marriage is monogamous except for very rare instances of sororal polygyny, and involves no bride-price. Residence is initially matrilocal for a few months, but neolocal or patrilocal thereafter. Descent is bilateral, though patrilocal residence and local exogamy make the band a patri-deme among the Yahgan. This tribe has a kinship system of the Hawaiian type.

6. PAMPEAN AREA

The steppes and pampas of Argentina and Uruguay are the homeland of a group of Chonan, Puelchean, and Guaicuran tribes of fundamentally similar culture. Except for a small enclave on the delta of the Rio de la Plata and the islands of its estuary, occupied by intrusive Tupian and other tribes who subsist by fishing and maize agriculture, the economy of the area is based primarily upon hunting, especially of the guanaco and rhea, supplemented by a certain amount of gathering, particularly of algarroba pods among the northern tribes. Fishing is insignificant and agriculture unknown, except in the afore-mentioned enclave. The dog is the only domesticated animal, but during the eighteenth century all the tribes save those in the extreme south acquired horses and adopted an equestrian mode of life paralleling in many respects that of the Plains Indians of North America. A nomadic life in politically autonomous bands is general throughout the area, and dwellings are either temporary skin windbreaks or insubstantial rectangular or conical structures of poles covered with skins, leaves, or transportable rush mats. Crude pottery is made except by the Ona and Puelche, but metallurgy is absent, and loom-weaving is practiced only by the Tehuelche, who weave fabrics of guanaco wool. Class distinctions, though probably originally lacking, developed among the horse nomads, who usually kept war captives as slaves and recognized social gradations based on wealth or military prowess. Marriage is monogamous, qualified by occasional polygyny, especially of the sororal type. A bride-price is customary except among the Ona. Residence is universally patrilocal or neolocal, though in two or three tribes it is initially matrilocal for a few months. Descent is bilateral and succession patrilineal in all instances, but inheritance rules are lacking because of the practice of destroying a man's personal property at the time of his death. Kinship terms are reported only for the Ona, where they are of Eskimo type.

7. CHACO AREA

In the Gran Chaco reside a series of tribes of the Guaicuran, Matacoan, Mascoian, Vilelan, and Zamucoan linguistic stocks who all practice a certain amount of rather desultory agriculture but subsist primarily by hunting, fishing, and the gathering of algarroba pods and other wild products. The principal crops are maize, sweet manioc, beans, and pumpkins. They are cultivated variously by the men (Mascoi, Pilaga), the women (Choroti, Mataco), and both sexes (Ashluslay, Toba). Most of the tribes have adopted horses, cattle, sheep, and goats from the Spaniards and depend today in some measure upon herding. A semi-nomadic life in politically autonomous bands or temporary villages is the norm. Dwellings are typically circular or elliptical in shape with a frame of poles fixed in the ground and a dome-shaped or conical roof of mats, rushes, palm leaves, or grass thatch. In a temporary settlement they are arranged either in a circle around a central plaza or in a double row on either side of a broad street. Pottery is universal, but loom-weaving and metallurgy are lacking. Except for local headmen, who are usually succeeded by a son, status differences are minimal. Marriage is monogamous with only infrequent exceptions, and the Mataco alone require a bride-price. Extended families are general, their form depending upon the prevailing rule of residence. This is always matrilocal initially and usually permanently, but a shift to patrilocal residence is more or less common among the Pilaga and Mataco. Descent is bilateral. Kinship terms are reported only for the Mataco, where they are of the Hawaiian type. The culture of the Chaco peoples on the whole, when the thin agricultural veneer is stripped off, seems clearly to affiliate fairly closely with that of the Pampean area.

8. PARAGUAYAN AREA

On the upper Paraguay River and in the adjacent flood plains reside a small group of tribes whose cultures are not readily classifiable with any of the larger adjacent areas. They are largely Guaicuran in language, though the Guato belong to an isolated linguistic stock. Interspersed among them, usually in a relationship of dependence to the Mbaya, are a number of small groups of Arawakan speakers known collectively as Guana, of whom the best known are the Terena. The primary dependence of the Guana upon maize and manioc agriculture, their expert loom-weaving of cotton fabrics, and their residence in settled villages of beehive-shaped huts arranged around a central plaza differentiate them strikingly from their neighbors and reflect an old connection with the Bolivian area. The other tribes depend to a much more limited extent, or sometimes not at all, upon the cultivation of maize, sweet and bitter manioc, and sweet potatoes; they do no loom-weaving; and they lead a migratory life, camping only in insubstantial temporary structures or mere windbreaks. Though hunting is important, they spend much of their time in their dugout canoes fishing, gathering wild rice, and engaging in trade and piracy. The fruit of the acuri palm is a staple food, and the Guato are noted for their construction of extensive low mounds to protect the trees from the annual floods. Monogamy is the rule, but polygyny also occurs, usually in the sororal form. Despite the otherwise uncomplicated level of their culture, all the tribes of the area make pottery, slavery and class stratification are found at least among the Guana and Mbaya, and the latter have powerful paramount chiefs who exact tribute from dependent tribes. The family type varies: the Guato have neolocal residence and independent sororal polygynous families; the Guana have matrilocal extended families, while the Terena are organized into bilocal extended families despite a rule of initial matrilocal residence. Descent, however, is universally bilateral, and both the Mbaya and Terena have kinship systems of the Hawaiian type.

9. EASTERN LOWLAND AREA

Southeastern Brazil, portions of adjacent Paraguay and Argentina, and a strip of country extending to the northeast behind the coastal highlands between the Atlantic and Goyaz areas constitute the homeland of a group of Tupian tribes possessing an elaborated version of Tropical Forest culture. A highly successful expansionist people, they were in the process of displacing the backward Atlantic tribes from extensive stretches of the seacoast when the Portuguese first arrived. They fall into three major groups: the Guarani of south Brazil and Paraguay, the Tupi of the Rio São Francisco drainage basin and other interior regions, and the Tupinamba in several scattered sections of the Atlantic coast. Differentiated sharply from all three are the Guayaki, a small Tupian tribe in the forests of eastern Paraguay, who cling to an earlier mode of life without agriculture or permanent settlements, subsisting on hunting, fishing, and especially the gathering of the fruits and pith of the pindo palm. The three dominant groups, whose cultures are strikingly similar, depend primarily upon an intensive agriculture with only supplementary fishing, hunting, and gathering. The men clear the fields, but most of the tillage is done by the women. The staple crops are maize and manioc of both the sweet and bitter varieties, but beans, sweet potatoes, peppers, pineapples, and cotton are also raised. Dogs are lacking, but the Guarani possess domesticated Muscovy ducks. Pottery, loom-woven cotton fabrics (not universal), and bark and dugout canoes are manufactured. Metallurgy is lacking, but the Guarani, when first encountered, had considerable amounts of gold which they had secured by trade with, and raids upon, the outposts of the Inca empire. The major tribes formerly lived in large towns, each consisting of from four to eight huge communal dwellings around a square plaza, the whole surrounded by a double or triple palisade and often also by moats. The houses were rectangular in ground plan with vaulted thatch roofs descending to the ground, and each accommodated an entire extended family numbering as many as 100 or more people. Though local autonomy was the rule, Tupinamba chiefs sometimes extended their authority over several communities. Marriage is effected through matrilocal bride-service, is commonly though not exclusively monogamous, and is contracted by preference with a cross-cousin or a sister's daughter. Though residence is patrilocal for chiefs, other men reside matrilocally in the household of the wife's father, to whom they remain subservient until their eldest daughter has attained marriageable age. Then by marrying her to the wife's brother, her preferred spouse, a man dissolves his bondage to his father-in-law and can remove with his family to his own paternal household. Among the Guarani, patrilocality was apparently more easily achieved than among the Tupi and Tupinamba, and there are suggestions that bilateral descent had given way to an incipient patrilineate. Succession to such offices as household head and village headman is patrilineal in all tribes. Evidence on kinship terminology is abundant but extraordinarily conflicting.

10. ATLANTIC AREA

In the highlands which closely parallel the Atlantic coast of Brazil, and also on the coast itself except where they had been recently displaced by Tupian invaders, the Portuguese found a group of tribes with genuinely marginal cultures. Though speaking languages of several quite isolated stocks, they have been persistently confused with the much more advanced Ge tribes of the Goyaz area. The Atlantic tribes lived for the most part in wandering bands and subsisted by hunting and gathering. They fished very little, and agriculture was absent or minimal except among groups like the Caingang, Camacan, and Mashacali who were most exposed to Tupian influence. Even these tribes cultivated maize and sweet potatoes rather than manioc, which only the Camacan raised to any appreciable extent. The Camacan also stood alone in possessing dogs, building substantial houses, and practicing loom-weaving. Several tribes, e.g., the Aweikoma and Botocudo, even lacked pottery and canoes. Class distinctions were completely absent, and political integration had not advanced beyond the level of autonomous bands or settlements. Dwellings, except for the Camacan with their large communal structures, were constructed of a circle of poles set in the ground, brought together at the top in the shape of a dome or a cone, and covered with leaves or branches. They accommodated only a single family among the Mashacali, Patasho, and Puri, a small extended family among the Aweikoma, Botocudo, and Caingang. Polygyny, especially in the sororal form, was permissible everywhere, but varied in its frequency. Cross-cousin marriage is reported for the Mashacali, and local exogamy for the Botocudo. Residence seems usually to have been optionally either matrilocal or patrilocal, though some tribes tended more toward the one or the other alternative. Unilinear kin groups are reported only for the Caingang, who had exogamous patrilineal moieties. Elsewhere descent appears to have been bilateral, and both the Aweikoma and Botocudo had kinship terms of the Hawaiian type.

11. GOYAZ AREA

The Brazilian state of Goyaz is the geographical center of a nearly solid cluster of tribes who speak languages of the Ge stock. In their midst are located the Tupian Tapirape, who have adopted much of the Ge culture, and the Caraja of the Araguaya River, whose language to date appears independent. The Bororo of Mato Grosso, long classed as linguistically isolated, were shown by Lounsbury in 1950 to belong definitely to the Ge stock, and are included here for cultural as well as linguistic reasons though they affiliate more closely with the Paraguayan area in basic economy. The little-known tribes of the interior of northeast Brazil, speaking Caririan and other isolated languages, are likewise included here on the basis of economic and technological similarities, though their social culture is practically unknown. The characterization of the cultures of this area as "marginal"—an old preconception perpetuated in the *Handbook of South American Indians*—is quite unwarranted, for they clearly constitute a mere variant, albeit a distinctive one, of the widespread Tropical Forest type. Thus, with the sole exceptions of the Bororo and the Teremembe of the Atlantic coast, every group subsists primarily by agriculture, supplemented to varying degrees by fishing, hunting, and gathering. Manioc of both sweet and bitter varieties and maize are staples everywhere, and sweet potatoes, beans, and peanuts are also widely distributed. Except among the Caraja, where the fields are worked exclusively by men, both sexes engage in agricultural operations, though with some variation in relative participation. Domesticated animals and metallurgy are lacking everywhere, and only the Cariri practice loom-weaving. Pottery, however, is universal, being found archaeologically in the few regions where it is absent today. Dugout canoes are also common. All tribes have fixed settlements, though several abandon them seasonally for fishing, hunting, or gathering expeditions. Local autonomy under a headman and council of elders is the rule, but the Tarairu in the northeast have paramount chiefs, and among the Sherente the headmen of a district form a democratic superior council. The typical house form is rectangular or elongated with an arched gable roof of thatch. The dwellings of a settlement are arranged in a circle, semicircle, or oval around a plaza on or beside which stands a men's house. Among the Ge tribes, who have moieties, the houses of the two moieties stand on opposite sides of the plaza, and within each division they are further grouped by sib or extended family affiliation. Age-grades, men's and sometimes women's associations, and special agamous ceremonial moieties are widespread, being present, for example, even among the Tupian Tapirape. Marriage tends strongly toward monogamy, usually strict but sometimes qualified by occasional sororal polygyny. Polygyny, however, is reported for the Tarairu. There are occasional suggestions of unilateral cross-cousin marriage. No bride-price is paid. Residence is matrilocal—permanently so for all tribes except the Sherente, among whom a shift to patrilocal residence is normal. Descent is bilateral only among the Tapirape, who also possess Hawaiian kinship terminology. Matrilineal kin groups—moieties, sibs, or both—are found among the Caraja and most of the Ge tribes. The Apinaye and Caraja show evidences of double descent, and the Sherente have only patrilineal sibs and moieties. The modified Omaha kinship nomenclature of the Sherente contrasts similarly with the Crow terms of the matrilineal Timbira.

12. PARA AREA

Along the south bank of the Amazon River and its southern affluents from the Atlantic Ocean to the Madeira River, mainly in the Brazilian state of Para, resides an almost solid block of Tupian tribes with a characteristic variant of Tropical Forest culture. Except for two small nomadic groups in the east, the Tupian Guaja and the Cariban Arara, all tribes practice an intensive agriculture. Sweet and bitter manioc, the staple crops, are supplemented by maize, beans, sweet potatoes, peanuts, peppers, and cotton. Fishing and the capture of crocodiles and turtles are also very important in the vicinity of the larger streams, and hunting and the gathering of palm fruits and Brazil nuts elsewhere. Though some tribes have dogs, domestic animals are commonly lacking, as is metallurgy. Pottery, however, is universal, and loom-weaving nearly so. The Mundurucu make the finest featherwork in South America. The people live in sedentary villages composed of several rectangular multi-family dwellings with thatched gable or hip roofs. Communities are politically autonomous, but western tribes like the Cawahib, Maue, and Mundurucu reveal an incipient development of paramount chiefs. Preferential marriage with a cross-cousin and/or a sister's daughter is specifically reported for several tribes. Monogamy is the rule. Polygyny, though allowed, is rare, usually sororal, and largely confined to chiefs. Residence is initially matrilocal. For some tribes, e.g., the Tenetehara, it is permanently so, but for the majority it is ultimately patrilocal or neolocal. The eastern tribes are bilateral in descent, and the Tenetehara have a kinship system of the Hawaiian type. In the west, however, the Mundurucu and Cawahib possess exogamous patrilineal sibs and moieties.

13. XINGU AREA

On the headwaters of the Xingu River in the heart of Mato Grosso reside a number of small tribes of homogeneous culture but diverse languages, representing the Arawakan, Cariban, and Tupian as well as the isolated Trumai stock. With them are here included the culturally more backward and linguistically isolated Nambicuara nation, who lie westward of the rest. The food quest differs considerably with the season. The Nambicuara, who carry this divergence farther than the other tribes, lead a sedentary life of agriculture and fishing only during the rainy season, abandoning their villages and splitting into small migratory bands during the dry season to hunt and gather wild fruits, seeds, and roots. The other tribes remain in or near their permanent settlements throughout the year. For them, agriculture is the primary subsistence activity, followed by fishing, although both hunting and gathering are also important. Bitter manioc and maize are the staple crops, supplemented by beans, peanuts, sweet manioc, peppers, and cotton. The Bacairi are noteworthy for transplanting and irrigating wild fruit trees. All tribes except the Nambicuara have bark canoes, but pottery and loom-weaving are confined to some of the Arawakan tribes. Dwellings are elliptical or circular in ground plan with thatched dome-shaped or beehive roofs, and they regularly accommodate a number of families. Except among the Nambicuara, each village has a special guest house, reflecting the importance of intertribal trade. Local autonomy prevails under headmen with little authority, and social classes are lacking. Marriage involves neither bride-price nor bride-service. Monogamy prevails, varied by occasional instances of sororal polygyny. Matrilocal residence is nowhere reported, the Bacairi being neolocal, the Nambicuara bilocal, and the Trumai patrilocal. Descent is everywhere bilateral, though Iroquois kinship terminology is recorded for both the Bacairi and the Nambicuara.

14. BOLIVIAN AREA

Lowland Bolivia (the highlands belong to the Peruvian area) is occupied by a large number of tribes which, despite large gaps in our information, appear to be characterized by a fairly homogeneous variant of Tropical Forest culture with a modest overlay of Andean traits. They belong to a welter of linguistic stocks: both Arawakan and Tupian are well represented, but they are heavily outnumbered by small or isolated stocks—Canichanan, Cayuvavan, Chapacuran, Chiquitoan, Intonaman, Mosetenan, Moviman, Otukean, Panoan, Tacanan, and Yuracarean. Agriculture is unimportant only among the Siriono, and is the mainstay of subsistence in most tribes. The staple crops are maize, sweet manioc, and in some instances peanuts, but sweet potatoes, peppers, pineapples, beans, and cotton are likewise widely cultivated. Potatoes and bitter manioc also occur, but with restricted distributions. Important supplements to the food quest are hunting, fishing, and in some regions the gathering of Brazil nuts and palm fruits. Pottery is universal, and the loom-weaving of cotton nearly so. Metals are not worked, although some tribes have gold ornaments obtained by trade from the highlands. With the sole exception of the migratory Siriono, all tribes live in settled villages, sometimes large and not infrequently surrounded by palisades. They are usually centered around a plaza on which stands a temple, men's house, or chief's residence and ceremonial hall, and they are often laid out in regular streets. The Paressi even construct roads between villages. Communal or multi-family dwellings prevail except in the Chiquitos region; they are usually circular or elliptical in ground plan with thatched roofs. Slavery and social class differentiation are fairly common, but political integration does not go beyond the local community except occasionally among the Chiriguano and Paressi. Monogamy or sororal polygyny is the normal form of marriage. Residence is initially matrilocal and usually permanently so, but ultimate patrilocal residence is reported for the Chiriguano, Macurap, and Mojo. The Siriono are organized into exogamous matri-lineages, and have kinship terminology of the Crow type, but patrilineal kin groups are characteristic of the Chiriguano, Macurap, Tacana, and Yabuti; data are not available for other tribes. Succession to the office of local headman is regularly patrilineal.

15. MONTAÑA AREA

Between the Jurua-Purus area and the civilized peoples of highland Peru stretches a thin band of tribes whose cultures are described with a degree of inadequacy unusual even for South America. Their languages are mainly Arawakan and Panoan; they are organized in politically autonomous villages; and they subsist by the cultivation of sweet manioc, maize, beans, peanuts, and peppers with only subsidiary hunting and fishing. In these and other respects they clearly affiliate with the cultures of the Tropical Forest, and particularly with those of the Jurua-Purus area. They are, however, differentiated from the latter, and affiliated with Peruvian civilization, in several possibly significant respects. In the first place, genuine loom-weaving is general rather than sporadic. Secondly, people live in single-family houses rather than communal dwellings except among the Masco and Yamiaca, and are patrilocal or neolocal rather than matrilocal in residence. Finally, some tribes, e.g., the Campa, possess dogs, cultivate potatoes, and engage extensively in trade—traits unreported for their lowland neighbors. Moreover, not only is the region geographically adjacent to highland Peru, but there are specific historical records of Inca invasions, suggesting the probability of further cultural influences from the west if the ethnographic record were more complete. For these reasons it seems advisable to segregate the Montaña tentatively as a distinct cultural province within the broader Tropical Forest area.

16. JURUA-PURUS AREA

The extreme western portion of the Amazonian basin, centering on the drainage areas of the Jurua and Purus Rivers but also extending eastward and westward respectively into the watersheds of the Madeira and Ucayali Rivers, is occupied by a group of tribes whose cultures appear, on the basis of inadequate ethnographic information, to constitute a special sub-type of general Tropical Forest culture. In language they affiliate mainly with the Panoan and Arawakan stocks, though the isolated Catukinan and Muran stocks are also represented. Agriculture is important everywhere, hunting and gathering taking a subordinate place in the economy except among the Mayoruna. Fishing and the pursuit of turtles and manatees, though also less significant than agriculture in many places, assume a primary position among such river tribes as the Ipurina, Mura, and Paumary. The principal crops are maize and sweet manioc, followed by beans, sweet potatoes, peanuts, and peppers. Bitter manioc is conspicuously absent. Men clear the land, but women perform all other agricultural operations. Domestic animals are lacking. Excellent

bark canoes, or occasionally dugouts, are made. Loom-weaving occurs only sporadically, but pottery is made by all tribes except the Mura. This tribe, which is also
differentiated from its neighbors in possessing only elementary thatched shelters
accommodating but a single family, quite possibly reflects an earlier, pre-agricultural and nomadic cultural phase. The rest of the area is characterized by settled
communities consisting of one, or sometimes two or several, enormous communal
dwellings, usually circular in ground plan with low walls and a conical thatched
roof. These are among the largest houses on the continent and among the stateliest
anywhere on earth. Among the Yamamadi, for example, they attain a height of 70
feet and a diameter of 120 feet. Each village is politically autonomous under a local
headman. Class differentiation is minimal. Monogamy or else limited sororal polygyny prevails, and residence is usually matrilocal with bride-service. The Amahuaca
and Mayoruna, however, are patrilocal, affiliating in this respect with the neighboring Caqueta area. The Chama may possess matrilineal sibs, but otherwise the meager
ethnographic evidence sheds no light on kinship or rules of descent.

17. AMAZON AREA

The islands, shores, and immediate hinterland of the middle and upper Amazon
River are occupied by three groups of tribes with a spectacular elaboration of
Tropical Forest culture: (1) the Cocama and Omagua, Tupian-speaking tribes of the
upper Amazon; (2) the Yurimagua, Soliman, and other linguistically unidentified
tribes of the middle river; and (3) the Juri, Wairacu, Marawa, Manao, and other
Arawakan peoples lying behind the river tribes and in the triangle between the
Amazon and the Rio Negro. The last group, whose cultures are very inadequately
known, may affiliate with the Guiana area, but they are included here because their
largest tribe, the Manao, were famous river traders who brought even gold from the
far west to the mouth of the Amazon in their large dugout canoes and thus gave rise
to the delusive El Dorado legend. All these river peoples, before their reduction or
extinction, practiced agriculture intensively, raising sweet manioc and maize (the
staples), and commonly also bitter manioc, beans, peanuts, pineapples, fruit trees,
cotton, and divers other crops. The tribes on the river banks and islands avoided the
labor of brand-tillage by cultivating the beaches during the season of low water.
Fishing and the pursuit of manatees, turtles, and other aquatic animals were at least
as important a source of subsistence as was agriculture. Metallurgy was not practiced, but excellent pottery and loom-woven cotton fabrics were manufactured.
The people lived in multi-family dwellings—usually circular with conical roofs
among the Arawakans but rectangular with gable roofs among the Tupians. These
were aggregated in large villages. Indeed, so abundant was the food supply and so
dense was the population that the shores of the Amazon were bordered by an
almost continuous line of houses for hundreds of miles. Slaves were held and
traded, and class distinctions were at least incipiently elaborated. Though local
autonomy was the rule, paramount chiefs had emerged in some areas. Polygyny was
permitted and fairly common. Residence, though initially matrilocal with bride-
service, was ultimately patrilocal, and the typical household consisted of a patri-

local extended family. The Tupian tribes accorded a man a preferential right to marry his sister's daughter.

18. LORETO AREA

A group of tribes of the Chapacuran, Jivaran, Tucanoan, Zaparoan, and other small linguistic stocks in the province of Loreto in northeastern Peru exhibit related cultures of Tropical Forest type overlaid with a thin Andean veneer. Though hunting and fishing are important, subsistence depends primarily upon agriculture, which is performed by women. Sweet manioc and maize, the staples, are supplemented by beans, peanuts, and other crops. Bitter manioc is unknown. Ducks, guinea pigs, and even llamas are occasionally found in sections immediately adjacent to the highlands. Manufactures include pottery and loom-woven cotton fabrics, but metals are not worked. Villages, which are politically autonomous, include a number of communal dwellings, each occupied by an extended family. Marriage tends strongly toward monogamy, though this is not absolute. Residence is initially matrilocal with bride-service. In some tribes it is permanently so, but in others ultimate patrilocal residence is the norm. In either case bilateral descent seems to prevail, though the Lama may be patrilineal.

19. CAQUETA AREA

In Caqueta and adjoining territories of southeastern Colombia reside a group of tribes characterized by a distinctive variant of Tropical Forest culture. In addition to the Chibchan Betoi, the Cariban Carijona, and the linguistically independent Tucano, Tucuna, Witoto, and Peba, they include a considerable number of Arawakan tribes—the Achagua, Arekena, Baniwa, Caberre, Caua, Guayupe, Ipeca, Piapoco, Sae, Siusi, etc. All these peoples subsist primarily by agriculture, which is women's work. Fishing and hunting are important; gathering rather less so. The staple crop is bitter manioc, but sweet manioc, maize, sweet potatoes, beans, and peppers are also grown. Simple pottery is made, but loom-weaving, metallurgy, and domesticated animals are lacking. Class distinctions are minimal. The people live in politically autonomous villages which normally consist of a single large communal house, elliptical in shape with thatched roof and walls. By virtue of local exogamy, patrilocal residence, and usually a specific recognition of patrilineal descent, the community constitutes a patri-clan. Marriage tends to be monogamous except for local headmen, and is variably effected by bride-service, payment of a bride-price, or the exchange of sisters. Among the Tucano and Witoto, at least, cross-cousin marriage is common, kinship terms are of the Iroquois type, and succession and inheritance are patrilineal. Exogamous patrilineal moieties are reported for the Tucuna.

20. SAVANNA AREA

In the forest-streaked savanna country of southeastern Colombia, southern Venezuela, and adjacent Brazil reside various nomadic tribes—the Auake, Caliana, Chiricoa,

Guaharibo, Guahibo, Macu, Puinave, Shiriana, etc. Though shown on the accompanying map as occupying a continuous territory, they are actually separated into several isolated groups by intrusive Arawakan peoples of more complex sedentary cultures. The Savanna tribes speak languages of at least seven different stocks, all apparently unrelated to any outside stock as well as to one another. Subsistence is achieved by hunting and gathering, supplemented by fishing. Agriculture is completely unknown except occasionally under Arawakan influence. The people wander in independent migratory bands and live in temporary thatched lean-tos, flimsy pyramidal huts covered with leaves and branches, or portable mat-covered shelters. They make pottery but lack weaving, metallurgy, boats, and apparently even dogs. Their social organization is completely unrecorded.

21. GUIANA AREA

In the Guiana region—Brazilian and Venezuelan as well as British, Dutch, and French—reside numerous tribes who reveal a relatively uniform variant of Tropical Forest culture. The overwhelming majority belong to the Cariban linguistic stock. The only exceptions, except for post-Columbian intruders, are Arawakan peoples, notably the Arawak proper or Locono of the coast, the Wapishana of the interior, the Arua and Palikur at the mouth of the Amazon River, and the Barauna group on the left bank of the Rio Negro. Without exception the Guiana tribes are basically agricultural; cultivating bitter manioc as the staple crop, supplemented by sweet manioc, maize, sweet potatoes, pineapples, and peppers. The men clear the land and either plant the crops or assist the women in doing so, but the latter do the cultivation and harvesting. Fishing is a major supplement to the food quest, hunting and gathering rather less so. The dog is the only domestic animal. Some tribes, e.g., the Taulipang or Arecuna, have only bark canoes, but the great majority possess excellent dugout canoes, sometimes with the gunwales raised with hewn planks. Pottery, excellent basketry, and loom-woven cotton fabrics are manufactured by all tribes, but metal working is unknown. Two major house types are found, not infrequently side by side in the same tribe: (1) rectangular structures with thatched gable roofs and (2) large circular dwellings with conical thatched roofs and walls of wattle, bark, or thatch. Here and there they are elevated on piles. A house is generally occupied by a small number of separate families—most typically by those of a man and his resident sons-in-law—but among the Yecuana one large communal dwelling accommodates an entire settlement. Class distinctions are minimal, although at least the Arawak and Taulipang keep slaves. Communities invariably enjoy political autonomy. Intertribal trade is well developed, based on local specialization in handicrafts. Marriage is normally monogamous, although polygyny, usually of the sororal type, is allowed. Unions with a cross-cousin are preferred, and some Cariban tribes permit marriage with a sister's daughter. Residence is typically matrilocal with bride-service, at least for several years. It is permanently so among the Arawak, Macusi, Rucuyen or Oyana, and Taulipang, but is ultimately neolocal among the Carib proper and Palikur, patrilocal among the Apalai, Wapishana, and Yecuana. All reported kinship systems are of the Iroquois type, but descent is usually bilateral. The Arawak, however, have exogamous matri-sibs, while the Palikur possess exogamous patrilineal sibs and moieties. Local exogamy and patrilocal residence make each Apalai, Wapishana, and Yecuana community a patri-deme. The rule of inheritance and that of succession to the office of local headman appear to be regularly patrilineal.

22. ORINOCO AREA

The delta and lower reaches of the Orinoco River and its tributaries are occupied by a number of tribes who speak isolated languages and subsist primarily by fishing, the collecting of shellfish, and the pursuit of large river animals, notably manatees, crocodiles, and turtles. They also gather eggs, the fruit and pith of palms, and wild roots and seeds, but do very little hunting on land. Agriculture is completely absent among such tribes as the Atature, Guamontey, Guarico, and Taparita, is minimal among the Guamo and Yaruro and distinctly subordinate among the Warrau, and is important only among the Otomac and Saliva, of whom the latter are included in the area only tentatively on the basis of quite inadequate information. That the Otomac represent a local specialization rather than an intrusive element from the outside is revealed by the fact that their staple crop is maize and that this belongs to a peculiar variety found only among them and their neighbors, coupled with the further peculiarity that they utilize the floods of the Orinoco River to fertilize their fields. All the tribes make pottery and excellent dugout canoes, but they lack domesticated animals, metallurgy, and (except for the Otomac and Warrau) loom-weaving. Only the Warrau and possibly the Saliva have substantial dwellings. The other tribes occupy the flimsiest of palm-leaf shelters, especially in the dry season, though the Guamo and Taparita build simple tree dwellings during the wet season. Social classes are lacking, and an extreme form of local political autonomy is universal. Monogamy or sororal polygyny is the normal form of marriage, and residence is matrilocal. The Yaruro have exogamous matri-moieties, matrilineal inheritance and succession, and kinship terms of modified Crow type. For the other tribes there is no comparable information, either supporting or conflicting.

23. CARIBBEAN AREA

Along the Caribbean coast of Colombia and Venezuela and throughout most of the West Indies there extends a diluted version of Andean civilization which sufficiently resembles the culture of the Isthmian area to warrant Steward's union of the two regions to form his Circum-Caribbean area. They do, however, reveal certain regular differences which impress the present writer as barely meriting their separate treatment. The average level of cultural complexity is somewhat higher in the Caribbean than in the Isthmian area, and there are fewer tribes of simpler cultures. These include the Motilon or Mape on the shores of Lake Maracaibo, to whom fishing is particularly important; the Gayon sub-tribe of the Jirajara, who occupy an arid section of the foothills of the Cordillera de los Andes near the present city of Barquisimeto in northwestern Venezuela and who subsist exclusively by hunting and gathering; and the Callinago or Island Carib, who had wrested most of the

Lesser Antilles from their Arawakan predecessors only a few decades before the arrival of Columbus and who largely retained their original, distinctively Guianan type of culture. The following discussion excludes these three tribes. Agriculture is intensive throughout the area, and in several regions is conducted with the aid of irrigation. Bitter manioc and a considerable number of fruit trees are added to the Isthmian roster of important crops—maize, sweet manioc, beans, and sweet potatoes. Both sexes participate in agriculture. Muscovy ducks, turkeys, and bees, as well as dogs, are domesticated by several Venezuelan tribes. Arawakan languages predominate, although Cariban languages also occur, and in a few instances also Chibchan, Chocoan, Jirajaran, and Timotean. Houses are usually circular with conical roofs rather than rectangular, and accommodate only a single family. Loom-weaving and ceramics are general, and all tribes either work gold themselves or obtain ornaments of gold and gold-copper alloy by trade, which flourishes everywhere. Settlements are large and frequently stockaded. Nearly everywhere they are politically aggregated under powerful paramount chiefs or kings, who are frequently regarded as divine, treated with elaborate ceremony, and transported in litters. Social class distinctions are comparably advanced. Evidences of the matrilineate are widespread, although residence is often patrilocal and inheritance and succession patrilineal. Hawaiian kinship terms are reported for the Cagaba, Iroquois terms for the Callinago.

24. FLORIDIAN AREA

The extinct Ciboney of western Cuba and their relatives of southwestern Hispaniola reveal no relationship whatsoever to the peoples possessing cultures of the Caribbean type. Their language, though unidentified, was definitely not Arawakan, and they lacked agriculture, permanent settlements, pottery, metallurgy, and complex social and political structures. They lived a migratory life and subsisted primarily by fishing and shellfishing, supplemented by the catching of turtles and manatees, the gathering of wild vegetal foods, and the hunting of birds, reptiles, and small mammals. In accordance with Rouse's suggestion of their North American origin they are tentatively classed with the Calusa and other non-agricultural tribes of southern Florida in a proposed intercontinental Floridian area.

The various culture areas described above are not, of course, equally differentiated from one another but fall into a smaller number of more general culture types. One such type, the Andean, includes the Isthmian, Caribbean, Colombian, Peruvian, and Chilean areas, and probably also the Mayan and Nahuan areas in North America. A second major type embraces the Tropical Forest areas (numbers 9, 11–19, and 21 above), among which several sub-types are easily distinguishable. The Pampean and Chaco areas clearly constitute a third primary grouping, the Steppe Hunters. The two remaining hunting areas (Atlantic and Savanna) and the four fishing areas (Fuegian, Paraguayan, Orinoco, and Floridian), however, seem impossible to combine into larger constellations by positive criteria at the present state of knowledge.

3   JOHN HOWLAND ROWE

A Review of Outline of South American Cultures

This outline [Murdock 1951a] provides a summary classification of South American Indian cultures into 216 relatively small groups, each group consisting of from one to twelve or more tribes. For convenience of reference, these primary groups are listed in 23 larger units, some corresponding roughly to present countries (e.g., Colombia, Ecuador, Peru) and others to geographical areas (e.g., Patagonia, Amazonia). The chief purpose of the classification is to provide convenient filing categories for data to be incorporated in the Human Relations Area Files.

For each primary group a one paragraph summary of the culture is provided, and the summaries are documented by one or more bibliographical references. Murdock relies extensively but not exclusively on the coverage in the *Handbook of South American Indians*. In general, when a tribe is reasonably well known it rates a primary unit to itself; the tribes grouped together in the classification tend to be ones about which there is little information available.

The primary grouping system is perfectly satisfactory as a filing device but it provides a basis of dubious value for a further simplification in terms of culture areas. The fact that most well known cultures are given separate listing reflects a striking characteristic of South American cultures in general; namely that each one tends to be markedly different from its neighbors. Many of the tribes grouped together will need to be sorted and listed separately in a system of this type when more is known about them, as Murdock himself predicts for the Fulnió group (p. 77).

Murdock still has great faith in the classificatory value of the culture-area concept, however, and near the end of his *Outline* he provides a schematic grouping of the primary cultural units into culture areas (pp. 133–136). The culture areas are discussed in further detail but without additional documentation in an article by Murdock which appeared at about the same time (Murdock 1951b). In this article, Murdock states that his culture areas were set up by comparing the primary cultural units on the basis of "a schedule . . . of a selected number of important traits and complexes upon which comparable information is fairly widely available" (p. 415). The schedule is not reproduced; Murdock simply lists nine major types of information covered by it. From the tabulation "emerged" 24 culture areas somewhat different from Steward's.

This reviewer regards the culture-area concept itself as indefensible on theoretical grounds and as an inevitable source of distortion in presenting specific cultural

Reprinted by permission of the author and the Society for American Archaeology from *American Antiquity*, vol. 18, no. 3 (1953), pp. 279–280.
All material appearing within square brackets [ ] has been added by the editor of this book.

data. Among the various existing culture-area classifications for South America, the only basis for choice is which type of distortion one prefers. Murdock's classification rests on fewer evolutionary assumptions than Steward's, but a sample check on his Caquetá area, run at my suggestion by Dwight T. Wallace, suggests that it is somewhat inferior to Steward's arrangement as a reflection of cultural similarities and differences.

Murdock's areas are far from being comparable units. The Caquetá area involves some real internal comparison, for it includes 4 tribes which have been reasonably well described (Cubeo, Witoto, Yagua and Tucuna); in the Chilean area there is only one tribe (Mapuche Araucanian) on which we have satisfactory data for comparison. The Montaña area is a pious hope; information on all the tribes is grossly inadequate. The Paraguayan area is set up as a catchall for tribes that do not fit well into the neighboring areas; it has no cultural unity at all. Murdock criticizes Steward for depending on negative criteria, but he himself uses them prominently in setting up his Savanna area.

Finally, it may be noted that Murdock gives a list (*Outline*, pp. 137–139) of 60 South American cultures which he regards as a representative sample of the range of cultural variation and the relative incidence of different culture types in the continent; 52 of these are Indian cultures, the rest largely of European or African origin. The idea is an interesting one, but the choice cannot be other than impressionistic in our present state of knowledge and such a sample would not add greatly to the reliability of the results of any statistical study in which it was used. It may have some value in suggesting interesting tribes for treatment in an area survey course.

A seven-page index of tribal names at the end of the *Outline* is one of its most useful features. The maps are highly generalized, but adequate to their purpose.

The next two selections may be considered together. Rowe discusses the major efforts to classify South American Indian languages up to 1954, and Rodrigues discusses the major classification efforts following 1954. Aside from the specific works discussed by these two authors, there are only three others that should be mentioned. The first is a rather lengthy article by Norman McQuown (1955) which is basically no more than an alphabetical listing of the native languages of Latin America keyed into lists by linguistic classification; maps are provided. McQuown himself states that "the classification here put forth represents a synthesis of that presented in Mason's two articles . . . " (1955:511). Since he uses a considerable amount of supplementary bibliography, however, it is impossible to determine, without searching all of his sources, the origin of any given datum that is not taken from Mason. The article does provide a useful alphabeti-

cal key to the Mason classification in the Handbook. *In addition there are some interesting suggestions for future research and cogent remarks on the weak points of previous classifications. On the other hand, given the author's criticism of the classification he is using, it is difficult to see why he thought it necessary to perpetuate it.*

The work of Antonio Tovar (1961) is yet another compilation with little new material. He categorizes his classification as being based on a combination of linguistic and geographical criteria. It is unclear to what extent the author has actually attempted to classify languages himself; but he appears to have relied heavily on the classifications of Rivet, Loukotka and Mason, without having necessarily examined the primary sources. There are 156 pages of extremely useful bibliography, although the entries are of unequal accuracy, and in some cases it is difficult to locate a specific reference. The great importance of Tovar's book is that it provides a major source in Spanish. It is, in fact, the only classification of all the South American Indian languages that has appeared in Spanish with the exception of Brinton's 1891 classification that appeared in translation (Brinton 1946) and two very short publications of Loukotka published in Prague (Loukotka 1935, 1941). The utility of Tovar's work is, however, more as a catalog, which is what the author calls it.

The most recent attempt at classifying all the languages of South America is that of Čestmír Loukotka, apparently completed in 1964, brilliantly and painstakingly edited by Johannes Wilbert, and published in 1968 after the author's death in 1966. Wilbert's preface to the work provides not only a summary of the contents and indications of his own contributions to the final form but also a succinct summary of the history of the classification of South American Indian languages starting with Brinton but mentioning earlier partial classifications from Gilij on (Loukotka 1968:7–23). As in the case of Tovar, it is the bibliography of this work that is its most impressive feature, containing 2,201 references among which are some 346 unpublished manuscripts (Loukotka 1968:16). Thanks to Wilbert's careful work, this bibliography does not suffer from the faults mentioned for Tovar's work and will long be the standard reference for linguists working in South America even though it includes works only through 1964. As far as the classification itself is concerned, it provides no surprises. Loukotka did not change his methods in any significant way, and his conclusions are therefore subject to the same strictures mentioned by Rowe for his earlier works. Again we find a number of languages classified even though there is not a single word of the language preserved. At least these groups are listed with the addition of the word "Nothing" in parentheses following the listing. Loukotka has augmented the sources used from his prior publications, but in at least some cases it appears that he ignored the additional material and based his classification on those data he had used previously. For example, although he lists five sources for Mashco (1968:139), in his vocabulary table

(1968:141) he utilizes only the vocabulary from Farabee (1922:78) which is totally aberrant (cf. Lyon ms.a).

In short, in spite of all the classification efforts that have appeared in the years since the publication of Rowe's article, we have no better general classification of South American Indian languages than we had then. On the other hand, there are many more well-trained linguists working on the problem than there were in 1954. As Rodrigues notes, there are many people collecting primary descriptive data, and there are some who are already publishing carefully controlled classifications of individual linguistic families based on genetic reconstruction. It is on the basis of such work that we can hope to see a reliable classification for these languages.

Rowe's article is excerpted from the original, including only the material directly pertinent to South America. In Rodrigues' article I have inserted the spelling of native languages from the sources to which he refers, as I noted in the Preface.

4   JOHN HOWLAND ROWE

Linguistic Classification Problems in South America

The description and classification of South American Indian languages is one of the biggest pieces of unfinished business in the field of linguistics. Pressing subjects for research can, of course, be found anywhere in the world, and I am not proposing to plead for any special priority for South America. However, it is probably true that we know less about more languages in South America than in any other continental area. We know so little, indeed, that it is difficult to give any figures that can measure our ignorance, but some rather general comments may serve to make the point.

First of all, it has often been pointed out that no other area of comparable size contains so many or such diverse native languages. This is still true, even after four centuries of European violence and cultural pressure have simplified the picture somewhat by extinguishing two or three hundred languages. No general census of the languages still spoken in South America has been made, but I recently collected

Reprinted by permission of the author and The Regents of the University of California from *Papers from the Symposium on American Indian Linguistics,* held at Berkeley July 7, 1951, edited by C. D. Chretien, M. S. Beeler, M. B. Emeneau, and M. R. Haas. University of California Press Publications in Linguistics, vol. 10 (1954), pp. 13–19, 24.

All material appearing within square brackets [ ] has been added by the editor of this book.

some data on the Indian languages still spoken in Colombia, and they will do for a sample. Colombia covers an area a little more than twice the size of France, and in the whole central part of it only Spanish is now spoken. Yet in the rest of the country I counted some eighty mutually unintelligible Indian languages still spoken there, representing between twenty and twenty-five independent families. More than fifty other Indian languages have become extinct since the Spanish conquest. We might hazard a guess that the total number of surviving languages for the continent as a whole is approximately two hundred and fifty; if anything, this figure is too low. It is my present impression that the languages of which we have some record represent nearly one hundred distinct families and isolated languages.

The fact that we are so far from being able to give an accurate figure for the number of languages still spoken is in itself a good indication of the extent of our ignorance. I tried to make a survey for Venezuela like the one I had made for Colombia and had to abandon it when I discovered that the most recent report we have on linguistic conditions in the eastern part of Venezuela is the one made by Alexander von Humboldt about 1804! It seems quite possible that several new languages will be added to the total of those now known in the continent when more field work is undertaken; it is only ten years since Curt Nimuendajú reported to Robert H. Lowie the discovery of five hitherto unknown Indian languages near the mouth of the São Francisco River in northeastern Brazil.[1] Nimuendajú died before he could publish vocabularies of them, but he stated that they did not resemble one another or any Brazilian language known to him. This is a readily accessible part of Brazil which has been under white rule since early in the seventeenth century.

Altogether too often in the South American field, "known" means little more than "known to exist." Many languages, still spoken by several hundred people, are known only from vocabularies of less than forty words. In other cases, the published information is more abundant, but the transcription used is so poor that the material is almost worthless. We do not yet have an adequate published description of a single South American Indian language. Fortunately, a handful of anthropological and missionary linguists are now working in various parts of the continent, and we have grounds for hoping that we will have much better materials soon.

The point I wish to make is that the available materials on South American languages are relatively very much poorer than those available for any other continent. This does not mean, of course, that we have no useful material for South America. For some Indian languages whose phonetic systems are not radically different from those of Spanish and Portuguese, old grammars, dictionaries, and collections of texts give a very fair picture of the sounds and structure, provided that they are used with due allowance for the author's linguistic preconceptions. We also have some extensive vocabularies and grammatical notes made by recent scientific travelers of some phonetic sophistication, like Theodor Koch-Grünberg, Curt Nimuendajú, and Günter Tessmann.

Taking the bad with the good, the bibliography of South American linguistics is at least as abundant as that for North America. The South American literature is harder to use, however, because it is widely scattered in obscure journals and published in eight different languages. It is often a major research problem to find out what has been written about a language or a family in which one is interested.

The quality of the descriptive information available of course sets a ceiling on the quality of any classification that is attempted. However, we can at least expect that an attempt at classification will be based on defensible criteria, consistently applied, and will give us some reliable information that will enable us to distinguish between securely classified languages and those the affiliation of which is dubious. Unfortunately, there is no existing classification that fulfills these expectations.

In the South American field, linguistic classifications have always been compilations of the results of shorter studies concerned with the relationships of a single language or a group of languages. Criticism of the general classification therefore involves two steps: examination of the reliability of the specific studies utilized, and examination of the discrimination with which they are compiled. The first step is made somewhat easier by the fact that the specific studies most extensively used by recent classifiers are the work of only a few men. Curt Nimuendajú, Theodor Koch-Grünberg, Čestmír Loukotka, and Paul Rivet have done the primary classificatory work on the vast majority of South American languages.

The first two, Nimuendajú and Koch-Grünberg, were first-rate ethnographers who assembled large quantities of new and important descriptive information on the languages of the areas where they worked. Their statements on classification refer chiefly to the languages they have studied firsthand and are markedly cautious. Koch-Grünberg published all his descriptive material, and it is easy to check his remarks on classification against the evidence; Nimuendajú left about half of his linguistic data in manuscript, but what he did publish indicates that his classificatory statements are likely to be sound.[2]

Loukotka has done no field work himself and works only with materials collected by other scholars. He is a careful bibliographer and has assembled an important collection of unpublished vocabularies from a variety of sources. His classifications, however, are based on quite different procedures from those of the two scholars just mentioned. He has devised a startlingly simple method for solving classificatory problems, which he describes briefly in the introduction to his 1944 general classification:

> The so-called "mixed languages" have always formed one of the greatest stumbling blocks in South American linguistics; another is uncertainty over the origin of some tribes; it has always been the occasion of many mistakes and much difficulty. On the basis of the special method of a standardized word list, I think I have now put even the mixed languages in the proper order. *This word list consists of forty-five typical words as a sample of each language.* All known South American languages are then evaluated according to the number of foreign speech elements they show. When the total of foreign words is proportionately large, I make use of the term "intrusions"; when it is only trifling, "traces." And, if in some languages the total of established foreign elements passes one fifth of the forty-five typical words, I have called each such language a "mixed

language" and it is dealt with separately in the framework of the language family concerned.[3]

Because Loukotka's list of forty-five "typical" words is not readily available, I reproduce a copy of it as an appendix to this paper. The limitations of his method call for no comment, but I will say something about the consistency with which it is applied in discussing his general classification of South American languages below.

Rivet has done the primary classificatory work on the languages of Bolivia, Peru, Ecuador, Colombia, and western Brazil. His regular procedure, used when fairly extensive vocabularies are available, is to compare the language he wants to classify with whole families. If, for example, he finds a new language, which he thinks may be Arawak, he compares each word of its vocabulary with words of similar meaning in perhaps thirty languages that he has already classified as "Arawak." If he finds any similar form in any of the thirty languages, it is evidence of relationship, and the fact that the total number of similarities to any one "Arawak" language may be very small is lost in the comparative table. Rivet is looking for similarities rather than systematic sound correspondences, and he does no reconstructing. One of the advantages of this method is that the more languages a linguist has put into a family, the easier it is to find cognates for new ones. Rivet has even succeeded in relating Tehuelche to the Australian languages by lumping several probably unrelated families of Australia together for comparative purposes.[4]

Nimuendajú has called attention to some other conspicuous defects of Rivet's methods of comparison:

> Again, what is known of the composition and etymology of the hundreds of words from both sides of his comparisons? He cuts up the words with hyphens, not according to etymological principles but in whatever way is convenient for his comparisons. Another thing that I cannot accept is the way in which he compares words whose meanings are too far apart. He makes comparisons like 'sun' with 'star,' 'stick' with 'smoke,' 'mouth' with 'nose,' etc.[5]

A very small number of resemblances sometimes suffices to convince Rivet of genetic relationship. To quote Nimuendajú again:

> Rivet is in too much of a hurry to establish linguistic relationships, as I found out in a case in which I was personally involved. In a little publication of mine I once compared, out of curiosity, eight words from the Matanawü language with the corresponding terms from the Mura language, of which I then had only very deficient materials. My comparison was enough to make Rivet classify Matanawü with the Mura dialects. Since then, I have collected Mura linguistic material from five different bands and determined that only four of the eight comparisons are valid.[6]

Nimuendajú himself treats Matanawü (Mason's Matanawi) and Mura as isolated languages (Mason 1950:285).

The methods Rivet uses are thus of doubtful reliability even when he is working with relatively abundant materials. When he applies them to languages for which we have no materials at all or at most a very few words, they merit even less confidence. Because of the wholesale destruction of Indian communities by the whites, there are numerous extinct languages in South America on which our material is scanty or nonexistent, and Rivet, like many other classifiers, has not been able to resist the temptation to fit them somehow into his continental scheme.

A typical example of his procedure in such cases is his handling of the languages of the central Magdalena Valley in Colombia, leading to a classification of Yariguí, Carare, Muzo, and Colima as Carib. The only vocabularies from this area are two short ones collected in the 1870's from Indians from the basins of the Opón and Carare rivers; these are plausibly classified as Carib. Rivet assumes, without any discussion, that the Indians encountered on the Opón and Carare in the nineteenth century were descendants of the Yariguí and Carare of the sixteenth century; hence he classifies the Yariguí and Carare languages, of which we have no sixteenth-century records whatever, as Carib. He apparently did not consider the possibility that the nineteenth-century inhabitants might be recent immigrants from the north, where the highland Motilones still speak a Carib language. In the light of the history of the Magdalena Valley, such a migration is a very real possibility. If the nineteenth-century vocabularies do *not* represent sixteenth-century Yariguí and Carare, we have no evidence at all on which to classify the latter languages.

Rivet then turns to the Muzo and Colima, who are known to have spoken a single language. He assigns them to the Carib family also, on two grounds: (1) P. Simón, a seventeenth-century writer, includes the Colima in a list of Carare tribes; (2) one word of the sixteen-word vocabulary preserved by Simón resembles a common Carib word. Since P. Simón's list of Carare tribes need not imply any linguistic connection, and since in any case it is far from certain that the Carare spoke a Carib language in the sixteenth century, the classification of Muzo-Colima as Carib depends essentially on a one-word comparison. The discussion closes with the statement that we can include the Yariguí, Carare, Colima, and Muzo in the Carib family "with complete security" (Rivet 1943:65–69).

In the conclusion to this 1943 article, Rivet suggests, albeit somewhat indirectly, that studies of the distribution of various cultural elements, which he considers characteristically Carib, like ligatures worn on the arms and legs, may enable us to classify additional languages in the Carib family (1943:85).

The above discussion by no means exhausts the pertinent examples in the 1943 article, nor is this the only one in which Rivet undertakes to classify extinct languages on the basis of a word or two or even by nonlinguistic criteria. The article is outstanding chiefly because Rivet has gone to considerable trouble to discuss the evidence that he is using. In some other articles he does not do so, and his procedure is much less clear.

Our analysis of the methods used by the four chief primary classifiers suggests that Loukotka and Rivet use, at least part of the time, methods of very doubtful reliability. Even if we accept most of the conclusions advanced by Koch-Grünberg and Nimuendajú, much checking of primary classifications will have to be made before a reliable general classification can be prepared.

The two most recent general classifications of South American languages that have been published are both based on the primary materials we have been discussing but differ markedly in their results. The first to appear was a classification by Loukotka, published in German in the *Zeitschrift für Ethnologie* in 1944. It has been supplemented by subsequent studies of the Tupí-Guaraní family and of the languages of the Madeira basin, published in French in 1950 (Loukotka 1944, 1950a, 1950b).[7] In 1944, Loukotka recognized one hundred and seven independent families and twenty-seven unclassified languages for the continent. They are arranged in a table with a note on their location and, in most cases, one or more bibliographical references. There is also a seven-page index, which makes the classification very easy to use. Loukotka gives no discussion of the evidence for classification but simply lists his opinion.

Loukotka's classification is unquestionably the best one available at present, but it should be used with due caution. In the first place, as we have seen, Loukotka classifies languages by a very rudimentary method. In the second place, he is not sufficiently critical of his sources. For example, he presents a linguistic family (no. 75) which is based on Jijón y Caamaño's Puruhá-Mochica. This consists of a southern branch, which includes Chimú or Yunga, Eten, and Mochica, and a northern branch, which includes Tumbez, Tallan, Cañari, Puruhá, and Manabí (Jijón y Caamaño 1940–1947). Yunga and Mochica are synonyms and should not be listed separately; Eten is the last surviving dialect of Mochica. In his northern branch, all the languages are extinct, and not more than three or four words are known for any one of them. These languages were clearly not classified by the use of a standard vocabulary, yet for two of them, Cañari and Puruhá, Loukotka notes "traces of Central American languages." If Loukotka were applying consistently the method he describes in his introduction, all five of these northern-group languages would have been listed as unclassified. In this instance, he has abandoned his announced procedure to accept a family set up on other and much less reliable criteria by Jijón y Caamaño. There are numerous other similar cases. Loukotka has classified dozens of languages, and even five whole families, without a single word to go on. This can be done only by using procedures like Rivet's.[8]

The second recent classification is the one by J. Alden Mason, published in 1950 as the sixth volume of the *Handbook of South American Indians*. This classification is in English and in a readily accessible series; hence it is likely to be more widely used in this country than Loukotka's. This is unfortunate, because Mason's work is in many respects less reliable than Loukotka's.

Mason had done little work on South American languages at the time he undertook his classification, and he had no time to go back to the original evidence. The result is that he has turned out a generally uncritical compilation, the unifying principle of which seems to have been a desire to cut down the number of independent families as much as possible. As a result, he proposes a series of superstocks that go far beyond any evidence now available and are more inclusive even than Rivet's.

An outstanding example is his Macro-Tupí-Guaraní superstock, which he has created by adding up the unproven suggestions of some of the least reliable of his predecessors. He includes Miraña, because Rivet considers it related to Tupí-Guaraní, and Witoto on the suggestion of J. P. Harrington (whose chief claim to fame in South American linguistic classification is his belief, which even Mason finds too radical, that Inca is a Hokan language [1943]). He adds Záparo because Jijón y Caamaño considers Miraña, Witoto, and Záparo connected, although he does not join them to Tupí-Guaraní. Here is Mason's diffident presentation of this superstock:

> It is not advanced with any claim to certainty or with any evidence of proof, but as a result of opinions, deductions, and intuitions of the several authorities and of the present writer. . . . As all these families are contiguous a genetic connection is not unreasonable (1950:236).

One wonders whether Mason would have ventured to suggest this classificatory monster at all if he had been aware of the possibility that Miraña, Witoto, and Záparo have been in contact with Tupí-Guaraní only since about 1549, and that before that date they were separated by more than a thousand miles of Amazon jungle. Loukotka and Nimuendajú quite properly treat all four families as independent.

In a number of cases, Mason is just as willing as Loukotka to classify languages without data. For example, he also accepts Jijón y Caamaño's Puruhá-Mochica family. He lists the languages a little differently from Loukotka, but still includes four on which we have no linguistic material. On other occasions Mason becomes unaccountably cautious. He refuses to accept an attribution of the Muniche language to the Cahuapana family on the grounds that we have only a thirty-eight-word vocabulary of it, and "this is hardly enough on which to base any opinion" (1950:262). This caution strikes me as admirable, but it is clearly inconsistent with his willingness to put into the Puruhá-Mochica family four languages for which we have no vocabularies at all.

The classification is deliberately arranged in such a way as to make any count of families difficult, because Mason feels that any enumeration made at the present time would be premature and misleading. He apparently recognizes fifty-two families as probably independent, however, and lists the affiliations of at least a dozen more as doubtful. These figures are far too low.

I do not wish to imply that there are no families well and truly classified in the monographs of Loukotka and Mason. Both classifications, however, are mixtures of reliable and unreliable statements and as such should not be used lightly as sources for answers to common reference questions or as mines of information for general text books. Their proper use is as guides to the source materials on South American linguistics.

· · ·

APPENDIX

Loukotka's Standard Vocabulary[9]

1. head (cabeza)
2. tongue (lengua)
3. tooth (diente)
4. eye (ojo)
5. ear (oreja)
6. hand (mano)

7. foot (pie)
8. water (agua)
9. fire (fuego)
10. sun (sol)
11. moon (luna)
12. star (estrella)
13. earth (tierra)
14. stone (piedra)
15. house (casa)
16. pot (olla)
17. bow, or blowgun (arco, o bodoquera)
18. arrow (flecha)
19. ax (hacha)
20. canoe (canoa)
21. man (hombre)
22. woman (mujer)
23. dog (perro)
24. wildcat (tigre)
25. monkey (mono)
26. tapir (danta)

27. bird (pájaro)
28. parrot (papagayo)
29. snake (serpiente)
30. cayman (caimán)
31. fish (pescado)
32. tree (arbol)
33. maize (maíz)
34. manioc (manioca, cazabe)
35. tobacco (tabaco)
36. white (blanco)
37. black (negro)
38. red (colorado)
39. big (grande)
40. little (pequeño)
41. one (uno)
42. two (dos)
43. three (tres)
44. eat (comer)
45. drink (beber)

NOTES

1. In a letter dated Belém do Pará, December 6, 1941.
2. For references to the linguistic publications of Koch-Grünberg and Nimuendajú, see the bibliographies in Loukotka (1944) and Mason (1950).
3. Loukotka (1944:1); translated by J. H. Rowe; emphasis supplied.
4. The defects of this method have been pointed out before; compare, for example, Nimuendajú and Guérios (1948:233).
5. Nimuendajú and Guérios (1948:233–234); translated by J. H. Rowe.
6. Nimuendajú and Guérios (1948:234); translated by J. H. Rowe. The order of the last two sentences has been transposed for clarity.
7. There is also an English summary of Loukotka's general classification (Salzmann 1951).
8. In fairness to Loukotka, I should explain that he sets up a separate family to take care of each isolated language; of the five families referred to (nos. 51, 52, 53, 61, and 104 of Loukotka's list) each consists of a single language.
9. As used for Ecuadorean languages, reproduced from Castellví (1937:64), with an English translation added by J. H. Rowe. It may be mentioned that items 25 and 27 to 34 (one-fifth of the list) are general terms for which it might be quite difficult to get comparable translations on a quick visit to the tribes of the Ecuadorean Oriente. In languages of that region, there may be separate names for five distinct types of monkey, for example, and no general term at all.

There are five words in this list (canoe, cayman, maize, manioc, tobacco) which are similar enough in English and Spanish so that a historical connection would probably occur to any linguist who saw them for the first time. One wonders whether this fact would give English "intrusions of Spanish" in Loukotka's terminology. If a hypothetical informant had happened to give 'olla,' 'tiger,' 'serpent,' and 'colored' as translations for items 16, 24, 29, and 38, English would have to be considered a "mixed language."

In no case does the standard vocabulary suggest the true proportions of the borrowings from various sources in the total vocabulary of English. Nowhere near one-ninth of the total vocabulary of English consists of Spanish loan words, and on the other hand about half of it consists of loan words from French and Latin, represented in this list only by 'parrot' and perhaps 'pot' and 'monkey,' although the latter came into English through Germanic.

5 ARYON DALL'IGNA RODRIGUES

Linguistic Groups of Amazonia

In discussing the indigenous languages of Amazonia, the first thing to be noted is the radical change presently taking place in the scientific knowledge of those languages. Up to twenty years ago the data available on the languages spoken throughout this immense area were extremely poor in both quantity and quality, reflecting the situation characteristic of the entire South American continent in which a language studied in some depth by any linguist was rare. The great majority of the linguistic data were lexical in nature, vocabularies or short word lists collected by travelers, missionaries not trained in linguistic methods, or non-linguist anthropologists. It is difficult to mention a single specialist in descriptive linguistics who had, up to that time, devoted himself to the analysis and description of any language of the region. The few existing descriptions are due primarily to missionaries and suffer greatly from lack of scientific method.

In contrast to that situation there are now about 150 investigators trained in descriptive linguistics working in the field with about 80 indigenous languages of Amazonia. The great majority of those linguists are members of the Summer Institute of Linguistics (or Instituto Lingüístico de Verano). The work of that institution in the Amazon region began in 1946 in Peruvian Amazonia, being extended, in the last ten years, to the affluents of the Madeira in Bolivia and to Brazilian Amazonia, to the Ecuadorian lowlands and, in the last three years, to the Colombian portion of the area. Also working in Amazonia, principally in Venezuela, Guyana and Brazil, are some missionaries with good training in field linguistics, who do not belong to the Summer Institute of Linguistics but who generally have taken the courses organized by that institute in the United States or in Europe.

The new linguistic documentation resulting from the noteworthy increase in the study of indigenous languages will soon permit us to reexamine the general linguistic panorama of Amazonia on a really solid basis with the necessary scientific rigor; something which up to the present was impractical given the nature of the available data. Those classificatory endeavors that attempted large scale syntheses, in the hope of providing a clearer view of the distribution and interrelationships of the languages and peoples in a region of great linguistic differentiation and multiplicity, have suffered most from the poverty of documentation prevailing until recently. Even the most recent attempts, such as those of Swadesh (1959) and Greenberg (1960) were predominantly based on the precarious documents that have characterized linguistic data in Amazonia and in South America in general. Even a comparative monograph as recent as that of Noble (1965) on the Aruak

Reprinted by permission of the author from *Atas do Simpósio sôbre a Biota Amazônica*, edited by Herman Lent, vol. 2 (1967), pp. 29–39. Translated and edited by Patricia J. Lyon.

All material appearing within square brackets [ ] has been added by the editor of this book.

group is based almost entirely on deficient and fragmentary material requiring real daring from the author in the postulation of many of his results.

At present we find ourselves in the midst of a situation of change in Amazonian linguistic studies. Although it started twenty years ago, the change that is taking place in documentation is only now beginning to yield its first results. It is in the coming years that the impact of these results will be felt on the linguistic knowledge of Amazonia, especially on linguistic classification and related problems such as migration, diffusion and contact. For some groups materials are already adequate to begin detailed comparative studies, and these materials are being utilized by linguists interested in linguistic comparison and reconstruction. In the meantime, any holistic analysis of the linguistic groups of Amazonia can only be attempted on the basis of the state of our knowledge immediately prior to the new phase of linguistic investigation which we are entering.

The present linguistic panorama of Amazonia is characterized by the massive presence of languages of three of the great groups generally recognized as well defined in South America—Aruak, Karib and Tupi. These languages occur side by side or intermixed with various groups of more restricted distribution, in their majority exclusively Amazonian, and with many languages considered isolated or not classified.

Both the Aruak and Karib groups extend outside of the Amazonian area—the former to the south and the north, the latter primarily to the north—but both have the greatest number of their languages within Amazonia, particularly to the north of the Amazon River. At present the Tupi group has a distribution confined completely to the south of the Amazon, the presence of representatives of the group in French Guiana (Oiampi-Emérillon) and the upper Rio Negro (Nheengatú or Língua Geral) being the result of recent displacement. This group also extends outside of Amazonia to the south and the east. The principal groups entirely within Amazonia are the Xiriariá, Tukano, Witoto, Záparo, Kauapana, Pano, Katukina, Arauá and Txapakura. Of the large non-Amazonian groups the Jê penetrate into the eastern part of the area, the Chibcha into the northwest and the Kechua into the west. This broad outline, omitting details of geographic distribution and internal composition of the groups, as well as excluding the languages of either small isolated groups or unclassified groups, although extremely superficial, will serve as a reference point for an examination, also rapid, of the present state of descriptive linguistics in Amazonia.

An examination of the descriptive studies now underway reveals that the group most studied is Aruak, of which ten languages are the object of investigation. To these should be added four more of the Arauá group which is considered probably related to Aruak. Of the subdivisions of Aruak, Pre-Andine is being studied most intensively (five languages). The six languages of the Karib group under investigation are located in the region of the Trombetas and of the Rio Branco except one, Kuikuro, on the headwaters of the Xingu. Of the Tupi group seven languages are being studied, six of the Tupi-Guarani family and only one, Munduruku, that is linguistically distinct from that family. Two less extensive groups that are being intensively worked are Tukano and Pano (especially the languages located in Peru) between the upper Purus, the upper Juruá and the Ucayali. Of Tukano, both the western languages of the Putumayo and the eastern ones of the Uaupés are under investigation, and among the latter, especially those on the Colombian side of the river. Other smaller groups of which more than one language is being investigated are Takana in northeast Bolivia, Kauapana on the Huallaga, Witoto on the Putumayo and Xirianá between the Branco, Negro and Orinoco rivers on both sides of the Brazil-Venezuela border. Of the Záparo group one language is being studied, Arabela. One Amazonian language of the Jê group, Txukahamãe on the upper Xingu, as well as forest Kechua in Peru and Ecuador are likewise objects of linguistic field work. Also Jívaro and three other related languages (Loukotka's Šuara family) are being described in Ecuador and Peru, as well as some twenty more "isolated" languages, especially in Peru and Brazil, but also in Bolivia, Ecuador and Colombia.

This account, although rather superficial, permits us to form an idea of the remarkable and encouraging development that investigations in descriptive linguistics in Amazonia took and have continued to take during the last twenty years. Of the more important groups mentioned earlier only Txapakura has still not been the object of descriptive studies. We must keep in mind, however, the important areas still not covered by the investigations in progress. There are not only a series of "isolated" or unclassified languages but also subdivisions of such extensive and complex groups as Aruak and Tupi. According to the internal classification presently possible Tupi is composed of eight branches or linguistic families (Rodrigues 1964, see also 1958a, 1958b): (1) Tupi-Guarani, (2) Munduruku, (3) Juruna, (4) Arikém, (5) Tupari, (6) Ramarama, (7) Mondé, (8) Puruborá. Of these families, all except the first occur exclusively in Amazonia; Tupi Guarani occurs both in- and outside of this region. The studies now in progress in Amazonia are concerned with languages of only two families, Tupi-Guarani and Munduruku. The other six families, precisely those that were less known to begin with, continue to call for urgent investigation since practically all of them are very close to disappearing completely. In addition, five of these families are located in the same region as the members of the Txapakura group—the zone between the Guaporé and the Ji-Paraná rivers—that is the present Território de Rondônia, the least studied region of Amazonia from the linguistic point of view.

The Aruak group has just been the object of a first intent at internal classification by Noble (1965). This author distinguishes seven branches within Aruak [Arawak]: (1) Arauá [Arauán], (2) Taíno [Taino], (3) Apolista, (4) Chamikuro [Chamicuro], (5) Amuexa [Amuesha], (6) Uru [Uruan], (7) Maipure [Maipuran] (Noble 1965:10). The last of these branches, much more complex than the others, is composed of the languages that, until now, have been accepted without controversy as members of the Aruak group, whereas the first six are formed of languages whose affinity has been extensively disputed. Of these groups only Arauá, Chamikuro, Amuexa and Maipure occur in Amazonia, and among these the first three exclusively, in contrast to Maipure which extends equally to the north and south of this region. Of the exclusively Amazonian groups those presently being described are Arauá (Kulina, Jamamadi, Dani and Paumari) in Peru and Brazil, and Amuexa in

Peru. As for Maipure, extraordinarily extensive and thus greatly differentiated, it is divided into eight sub-groups, six of which are entirely within Amazonia while two of them also have representatives outside of the Amazon area. Of the six Amazonian sub-groups, Pre-Andine is the one being best studied (five languages—Piro, Kampa [Campa], Matxigenga [Machiguenga], Nomatsigenga, Apurinã [Ipurina] — among about ten that are known). Two languages are being investigated in the Bolivian sub-division of the Southern sub-group (Bauré and Ignaciano). In the Eastern sub-group Noble classifies the Aruak languages of the upper Xingu plus Palikur [Palicur] and Marawan, both of the Oiapoque in the Território do Amapá and in French Guiana. Of these languages Palikur is being investigated, but none of the languages of the upper Xingu has yet been described linguistically.[1] Most surprising is that as yet there is no investigation of any of the languages of the largest of the Aruak sub-groups, the northern, that extends along the Rio Negro and between the Rio Negro and the Solimões.

There is a series of isolated or unclassified languages, so considered precisely because our knowledge of them is extremely precarious or practically nil, that are on the point of disappearing within a very short time due to the extermination of the Indians that speak them or to the adoption by them of another language such as Portuguese, Spanish or Kechua. Some of the languages in the Amazonian area that are in this situation are Trumai on the upper Xingu, Arikapu, Jaboti, probably Kanoé and Kapixaná, Uari and Masaká on the Guaporé, Auaké and Máku on the Rio Branco.[2]

In summary, the high priority tasks of linguistic documentation in Amazonia are, at present: investigation in the Território de Rondônia, not yet visited by any linguist, where the languages of the Txapakura family, all of the languages of five families of the Tupi group as well as some of those of the Tupi-Guarani family, and a series of isolated or unclassified languages are menaced with extinction; investigation in the Rio Negro area, especially on the Brazilian Uaupés and the Içana and Japurá; the description of the Aruak languages of the Xingu and the documentation and description of the various obsolescent languages, isolated or not.

Another order of linguistic studies to be considered is comparison. I have already noted that precisely now, while the results accumulate from the descriptive investigations that characterize this moment in linguistic research in Amazonia, the necessary conditions are being created for a resumption of comparative studies on a truly scientific basis.

Two distinct orientations are currently active in comparative linguistics. One, inspired largely by the experience acquired in the study of Indo-European languages, adheres to the rigorous application of the comparative method which leads to the reconstruction of the probable structure of the proto-language from which sprang the languages compared. The other, characteristic of some North American linguists, attempts to discover much more remote relationships than can be found through the strict application of comparative and reconstructive methodology. Whereas linguists devoted to the first orientation use, as a basis to arrive at genetic relationship between two languages, only the occurrence in both of elements that are demonstrably cognate (that is, due to a common origin), linguists of the second orientation postulate hypothetical genetic relationships even where there are formal similarities that cannot be, or cannot yet be, demonstrated to be cognate. This last orientation is that which Charles and Florence Voegelin call "phylum linguistics," since these daring postulations occur only when the establishment of phyla is being considered, that is, groupings of languages of extremely remote relationship (Voegelin and Voegelin 1965:131 ff.).

Representatives of phylum linguistics are Morris Swadesh and Joseph Greenberg both of whom, with some methodological divergence, recently suggested the establishment of linguistic phyla in South America. The classification proposed by Greenberg is the more extreme or, correspondingly, the more comprehensive since it attempts to place all the languages of South America in only three phyla: Macro-Chibchan, Jê-Pano-Karib [Ge-Pano-Carib] and Andean-Equatorial (Greenberg 1960). Greenberg postulates a remote relationship between the Chibcha and Xiriana [Shiriana] groups and the Mura and Warau [Warrau] languages, all included, along with others, in the Macro-Chibchan phylum; among Karib, Witoto, Jê, Pano, Takana [Tacana], Nambikuara [Nambicuara] and others included in the Jê Pano-Karib phylum; and among Aruak [Arawak], Arauá [Araua], Txapakura [Chapacura], Tukano [Tucano], Záparo [Zaparoan], Kauapana [Cahuapana], Kechua [Quechua], Tupi and others placed in the Andean-Equatorial phylum. The postulation of such and so many connections is extremely provocative, as much for the unexpectedness of many of its details as for the apparent simplification of the South American linguistic picture, generally considered to be one of the most complex in the world. For this very reason the Greenberg classification soon achieved a favorable reception from anthropologists and some linguists.[3] There has as yet, however, been no evidence whatsoever published for the connections suggested therein. Greenberg's effort seems especially rash to me, particularly given the nature of the data upon which it must have been based, which could not be other than the old, fragmentary, extremely deficient documentation that preceded the modern research now in progress. This does not mean, of course, that many of Greenberg's propositions will not be confirmed in the light of adequate data; but it is very probable that, at the same time, profound and substantial alterations will have to be made in his classificatory scheme.

Swadesh advanced a much more detailed classification than that of Greenberg, yet the numerous groups proposed are distributed in only nine sections for the entire American continent, of which six occur partially or entirely in South America: W, C, E, SE, S and SW (Swadesh 1959). These sections are what most closely approximate Greenberg's phyla hierarchically, and all of them are represented in Amazonia. The discrepancies between the two classifications are considerable. For example, restricting ourselves to the consideration of the Amazonian groups: whereas Greenberg established one phylum, Jê-Pano-Karib, in which he included, besides the three groups that provide the name, Nambikuara, Witoto and Takana; Swadesh places Jê [Ye] in the SE section, Pano and Takana [Tacana] in Section W, Karib [Caribe] and Witoto [Huitoto] in Section S, and Nambikuara [Nambicuara] in Section E.

In fact, the classifications of Greenberg and Swadesh are not comparable, not so much because they start out from different bases, but above all because neither of the two authors has yet published the evidence which led him to establish them. It is still premature to discuss their validity in more detail precisely because there is no concrete basis upon which to do so. There are, however, some situations that it has been possible to test to a certain extent with results that sometimes favor neither one of the classifications. The following case will serve as an example. Greenberg included the Xirianá group in the Macro-Chibchan phylum and the Txapakura group in the Aruak family of the Equatorial section of the Andean-Equatorial phylum. Swadesh, however, joins Xirianá [Siriana] and Txapakura [Chapacura] in Macro-Xirianá [Macro-Siriana] located in his SE section in which he also includes some members of Greenberg's Andean-Equatorial such as Tupi, but not Aruak [Aruaco] which, for him, belongs to Section C together with Chibcha. Now, I myself have had occasion to test, with negative results, the relationship of Xirianá to Txapakura proposed by Swadesh (Rodrigues 1960). On the other hand, Noble in his recent comparative monograph on Aruak, while stating that his method is based on the same theoretical foundation as Greenberg's, and taking off from Greenberg's classification, specifically excludes the Txapakura [Chapacura] group from his study (Noble 1965:9). One other important group with which I have worked is Tupi. Greenberg places it alongside of Aruak in the Equatorial section of the Andean-Equatorial phylum, whereas Swadesh puts it in his SE section while, as we just saw, Aruak is in his Section C. At the moment I am preparing the evidence for a quite close relationship between Tupi and Karib—which is in Greenberg's Jê-Pano-Karib phylum and Swadesh's Section S—whereas it was impossible for me to find any evidence whatever favorable to a closer affinity between Tupi and Aruak.

These examples give an idea of the aleatory character of those very broad classifications made on the basis of the inspection of inadequate data. The postulated groupings should be considered, more than anything, as suggestions of possibilities with varying degrees of plausibility, not as proven facts. In this moment of transition and important development in our knowledge of the languages of Amazonia and of South America in general, the bold classifications of Swadesh and Greenberg will be of great importance if, as I pointed out on another opportunity regarding Swadesh's scheme (Rodrigues 1963:15), they are taken as a challenge to the investigators who, in collecting and analyzing the data necessary to test the multiple hypotheses implicit in them, will enlarge and deepen our knowledge of indigenous languages. It seems to me that it is precisely the acceptance of this challenge, together with the utilization of the new data offered by the intensive and extensive descriptive activity in progress, that is going to determine the development of comparative linguistics of Amazonia and of the continent in general in the coming years.

In fact, Noble's comparative study of the Aruak group, already mentioned several times, was made at the suggestion of Charles Wagley precisely to attempt to obtain clarification and certainty on a point where there were evident classificatory conflicts. On the other hand, the increasing accumulation of new data for some groups has led to the undertaking of as yet unpublished comparative and reconstructive studies. Irvine Davis, while visiting professor at the Universidade de

Brasília in 1963–64, prepared a work of this nature on the Jê languages (previously the object of a glottochronological study by J. Wilbert based on very precarious material) which is ready for publication in the first number of the new journal "Estudos Lingüísticos" that should appear in São Paulo. The Canadian linguist, Olive Shell, working with the Summer Institute of Linguistics in Peru, undertook a study of the same kind with the languages of the Pano group. In the Museu Nacional do Rio de Janeiro, Míriam Lemle is doing the same sort of work with languages of the Tupi-Guarani family, and I myself am working with the Tupi and Karib groups. It is probable that there are still other comparative studies in progress of which I have no knowledge.

To conclude this exposition and complete this panoramic view of the present state of the investigation of linguistic groups in Amazonia, I will refer briefly to a type of linguistic problem that so far has not been subject to detailed investigation but is also among the most interesting that Amazonia offers to the linguist. I refer to problems of acculturation created by situations of linguistic contact. The first language that attracts our attention in this context is Língua Geral or Nheengatú which, having become a lingua franca and being spread with the occupation of Amazonia since the 17th century, not only is marked in its structure by the contacts, but left its own marks on a great number of other indigenous languages along almost the entire course of the Amazon and its affluents. Although we have a considerable number of documents about this language, we lack modern descriptions of any of its dialects still spoken and, above all, data on the nature of the contact situations in which it is spoken. Aside from the region of the upper Rio Negro and the Içana, where it is still rather widely used although also on the decline, it appears that it is only at occasional points on the right bank of the Amazon that it is still known or remembered, since now it is hardly spoken.

In contrast to Língua Geral that was a lingua franca from the first phase of expansion of Brazilian society into Amazonia with the aspect, therefore, of a "language of civilization" originally foreign to the indigenous populations, there are in this region other languages that, in special situations of tribal contact, have become lingua francas independent of the new European type society. Cases about which we have information but which have not yet been studied are those of Tukano on the Uaupés and Tiquié rivers and of Makurap on the Guaporé. Kechua, used as a lingua franca in Peruvian and Ecuadorian Amazonia, probably combines the two types of situation, being closer, however, to the situation of Língua Geral. In addition, the contact of the languages of the upper Xingu where there is intensive interaction among languages of the Tupi, Aruak, Karib and Jê groups and where it is probable that Kamayurá exercises, to some extent, the function of a lingua franca, should be carefully studied. A no less important object of linguistic investigation is acculturation within each indigenous language that is in more or less intense contact with the "civilized language" in the respective region.

Finally, it should not be forgotten that European languages such as Portuguese and Spanish, in the process of expansion in which they are involved, pass through simple contact situations, frequently assume the role of lingua franca and, finally, become the only language of new populations, offering in all of these phases an infinity of characteristics that must be recorded and analyzed to enlarge our knowledge and our understanding of the processes of linguistic contact and acculturation.[4]

NOTES

1. According to information from the Summer Institute of Linguistics, a study of the Waurá language is being initiated.

2. Ernesto Migliazza just published two studies on Máku (Migliazza 1965, 1966).

3. Even before publication by its author it was adopted by Steward and Faron (1959) and by Sol Tax (1958, 1960). C.F. and F.M. Voegelin also adopted it in their exposition on native American languages (Voegelin and Voegelin 1965).

4. In his recent work on native acculturation Egon Schaden included a chapter on "A aculturação no plano lingüístico" [Acculturation on the linguistic level] in which, emphasizing the lack of studies, he also indicates various aspects of linguistic acculturation that need to be investigated and further points out some cases of probable development of lingua francas in Amazonia (Schaden 1965).

Max Schmidt died in Asunción, Paraguay, on October 26, 1950, after devoting 50 of his 76 years to the study of South American Indians, both ancient and modern. The present article is his last and was published posthumously. Schmidt was not formally trained in anthropology, and his primary interests were in material aspects of culture rather than such areas as social organization or religion. His essays into the field of culture history are all marked by a strong evolutionary bias, as may be seen in the present article. Although Schmidt had published some undistinguished work on Peruvian archaeology (e.g., Schmidt 1929) and, as noted in this article, excavated in various archaeological sites himself, he utilized archaeological data within an evolutionary framework. This tendency can be noted in his comments on the lack of ground stone implements in the sites and the equation of chipped stone with the European Palaeolithic, thus demonstrating his lack of understanding of New World prehistory. His theoretical stance is equally clear in his equation of "simple" with "primitive" and his persistent attempt to arrange the various agricultural techniques into some sort of developmental sequence. Another trap into which the author falls is that of assuming that because there is a native term for a plant the plant must be native. This is the same trap that has led several writers to assume that because there is an Inca word for writing, the Inca must have had some sort of writing, in spite of all evidence to the contrary. Those who have done any extensive fieldwork are quite aware of the extent to which any group may provide perfectly ordinary native words to obviously borrowed items. Thus, the Wachipaeri of eastern Peru have words in their language, that are neither compounds nor borrowings, for dynamite and shotguns. I doubt, however, that these items formed part of their culture prior to their introduction by Europeans. The presence of a native word for an item of culture is a piece of evidence to be used, together with other data, in the formation of hypotheses, but is not in and of itself proof positive of the native origin of anything. Schmidt also overemphasizes the need for large amounts of organized labor to clear fields. He might be correct if one were to think only in terms of large clearings made with stone axes, but there is no reason to assume that all clearings were large. Harner states that each Jivaro household had either one large garden or several small ones. "If a man clears the forest without the aid of neighbors, he tends to make small clearings at different times, while the rarer communal effort results in one large clearing" (1972:47–48). On the other hand, if such an individualistic group as the Jivaro are able to get together for a communal effort, then Schmidt's assumption of the need for complex social organization to effect such work is clearly unnecessary.

There has been considerable recent interest, especially on the part of cultural geographers, in ridged fields (cf. Parsons and Bowen 1966; Parsons and Denevan 1967; Parsons 1969; Denevan 1970b), and such fields have recently been found associated with the lowland Maya (Siemens and Puleston 1972) and in the Chibcha area (Broadbent 1969). This new material should cause one to ponder Schmidt's appellation of "primitive" to this sort of agriculture. Schmidt's rationale for the use of seasonally flooded areas for agriculture is also subject to question. Although it is of some interest to consider the possibility that the lack of tree cover may have made these areas especially desirable to people forced to clear with stone tools, it is also true that periodic flooding annually deposits a layer of rich alluvium on top of the flooded area, thus performing naturally the act that Schmidt describes as being done artificially in the case of the aterrados.

In spite of any theoretical shortcomings, however, Schmidt's article provides a brief overview of plants and agricultural techniques used in South America including material seldom mentioned by other authors. His coverage of plants is rather perfunctory in some respects, and he entirely omits the genus Cucurbita, the third member of the classic trio maize-beans-squash, from his list. Those interested in more detailed or more recent treatment should see Sauer's article on cultivated plants (1950a) and Galvão's survey of Brazilian slash-and-burn horticulture (1963).

In addition to translating this article, I have cut and edited it extensively. Although most of the cutting was to eliminate repetition, the entire first portion was also omitted since it did not pertain to the main topic. I checked all the botanical nomenclature and corrected it where necessary using the following sources: Towle (1961), Mors and Rizzini (1966), and Kelsey and Dayton (1942).

6   MAX SCHMIDT

Comments on Cultivated Plants and Agricultural Methods of South American Indians

[It is patently impossible to encompass all the plants and agricultural methods of South American Indians in an article the length of the present one, hence the title is somewhat misleading. On the other hand, the author has attempted to give a rapid and generalized overview of the major plants cultivated in South America and a brief discussion of some of the major agricultural techniques used among South American Indians, especially in the tropical lowlands. Within this framework he includes some interesting personal observations on little-known techniques. The author provides the following account of the groups, areas and times of his ethnographic and archaeological investigations.]

In 1901 I visited the Bakairí of the Carib linguistic group, who were still living in their traditional manner on the Kulisehu River, one of the headwaters of the Rio Xingu. While there I observed the clearing of a new agricultural field and the Indians allowed me to participate in both the work and the festive ceremony that followed (M. Schmidt 1905:98–104 or 1942a:79–84). In the same year I encountered the large plantations, including fruit trees such as the *piqui (Caryocar brasiliense)*, of the Auetö of the Tupí-Guaraní linguistic group, who lived on the Kulisehu downstream from the Bakairí (M. Schmidt 1905:79 or 1942a:63). In addition to my research among the Bakairí, I was able to study agricultural work during my stay among the Gózarini-Paressí in 1910. These Indians belong to the Aruak linguistic group and, at that time, still lived in a rather primitive state in the region of the headwaters of the Jaurú and Juruena rivers (M. Schmidt 1914b:202–205). In 1914 I was able to observe the cleared fields of the Kainguá (Tupí-Guaraní) living in the vicinity of the village of Ajos in Paraguay and, in 1928, a field and various abandoned houses of the Umotina or Barbados who live on the Alto Paraguay north of Barra dos Bugres (M. Schmidt 1941:22, lám. XVIII, fig. 57). In 1910 I visited the *aterrados* located in the swampy region of the lower course of the Rio S. Lourenço and, especially, along the Furo do Caracará.[1] These aterrados are artificial mounds still used by the Guató Indians for planting . . . (M. Schmidt 1914a:251–267). In 1928 I was able to complete my studies of the aterrados by visiting Aterradinho located on the Alto Paraguay River downstream from Descalvados in Matto Grosso (M. Schmidt 1942b:43–44, 1940:58–60, lám. XXI–XXIII).

Reprinted by permission of the publisher from *Revista do Museu Paulista*, n.s., vol. 5 (1951) pp. 239–252. Translated and edited by Patricia J. Lyon.
    All material appearing within square brackets [ ] has been added by the editor of this book.

CULTIVATED PLANTS OF
THE SOUTH AMERICAN INDIANS

The two most important cultivated plants that were originally domesticated on the American continent are maize and manioc.

Maize (*Zea mays*) is a genus of cereals belonging to the family Gramineae which, through its great variability, possesses greater adaptability to different climates and soil conditions than any other cultivated plant. Although it apparently originated in a hot zone and is frequently cultivated by Indians of the lowland tropical forest of South America, the so-called Cuzco maize grows in a mountainous region up to 3500 m. in altitude with only four months of summer. There is no doubt that maize is a genuine American plant. [Maize has been recovered from very early archaeological contexts in both North and South America and there is still some discussion regarding the precise point or points of domestication.]

Quinoa (*Chenopodium quinoa*) is another cereal that is important as a food source in the highlands from Colombia to Chile and will grow above the range of maize. Among vegetables, the common bean (*Phaseolus* spp.) is noted for its wide distribution. Another plant widely encountered among South American agriculturalists is the chile pepper (*Capsicum* spp.); and the peanut (*Arachis hypogaea*) is also an American domesticate. . . .

Root crops are more numerous in South America than is any other type of cultigen. Among such crops manioc is the most important in native economy. It is known as *mandioca* in Brazil, Argentina and Paraguay, *yuca* in most other South American states and, finally, *cassava* in the Antilles and the United States. Only two varieties of the numerous species of Euphorbiaceae among which this extremely important plant is found have been domesticated. [The two varieties, commonly referred to as bitter and sweet manioc, were long considered to be separate species but recent studies have resulted in their reclassification into a single species (*Manihot esculenta* Crantz).] Probably the cultivation of sweet manioc has extended since the beginning of European contact. At least the Indians of the forested regions of Central Brazil, for whom manioc is the staple crop, knew only bitter manioc until their contact with Europeans. The large roots of bitter manioc may reach some 60 cm. in length and a weight of 4 kg. They contain, like the rest of the plant, a milky juice with a high content of prussic acid, so that consumption of the root without prior preparation would be fatal. Squeezing the grated tubers removes the poisonous substance and the resultant juice may also be transformed into a potable beverage by cooking.

Another tuber, cultivated from the Antilles and Mexico to Paraguay, is the sweet potato (*Ipomoea batatas*) of the family Convolvulaceae. A similar plant was found to have been cultivated by the Polynesians and some authors doubted the exclusively American origin of the sweet potato. More recent investigations, however, indicate that this domesticate originally comes from America having spread to other regions only after the discovery of the New World [cf. O'Brien 1972].

The potato (*Solanum* spp., especially *S. tuberosum*) is a cultivated plant characteristic of the Andes and cultivated from Colombia to Chile in the temperate alpine climate. Among other root crops cultivated in the Andes we should mention *oca* [or *ibia*] (*Oxalis tuberosa*) and *añu, mashua* [or *cubio*] (*Tropaeolum tuberosum*). [Other important root crops are the following: *ullucu, lisa, papalisa* or *chugua* (*Ullucus tuberosus*); *achira* (*Canna edulis* and *C. indica*); *arracacha* (*Arracacia xanthorrhiza*); *uncucha, pituca* (a term sometimes also applied to taro) or *mafafa* (*Xanthosoma* sp.).]

There is still considerable uncertainty regarding the origin of the yam (*Dioscorea*). This plant is widely cultivated in the tropical regions of South America and it was planted and given native names by the Indians of the headwaters of the Rio Xingu who, at the time of their discovery, were still living quite independent of outside influences. Although several species of *Dioscorea* are known to have been introduced to the New World from Africa, there is one American species (*D. trifida*) which may be a true domesticate. The yam would, thus, provide one of the rather rare cases of two plants of the same genus having been cultivated, before the discovery of America, in both the New World and the Old World.

There is further discussion regarding the two subspecies of *Musa paradisiaca*, the plantain and the banana, both of which are extensively cultivated by the Indians of South and Central America and are of major importance in their diet. The evidence is very clear and convincing that the banana was introduced after the European conquest and diffused so quickly that European investigators found it among Indians who, up to that time, had never had direct contact with Europeans. The argument centers around the origin of the plantain which may have been grown in America before the conquest.

I have yet to mention some cultivated plants that do not serve as food. Among these a tree called *urucú*, annatto, *Orléans* [or *achiote*] (*Bixa orellana*) provides a red dye substance. This plant is frequently planted by South American Indians near their houses. *Crescentia cujete* (calabash tree) and *Lagenaria siceraria* (gourd) are also cultivated to provide open and closed containers. Cotton (*Gossypium* spp.) of the family Malvaceae provides yet another example, as does *Lagenaria,* of a genus cultivated in both the Old and New World in pre-Columbian times. Specimens of cultivated *Gossypium* and *Lagenaria* have been found in pre-ceramic archaeological contexts on the Peruvian coast.

Regarding cultivated stimulants, I will mention only tobacco and coca [although there are others]. Tobacco (*Nicotiana* spp.) is cultivated in all the Americas. Of the various species grown by native Americans, the best known is *Nicotiana tabacum.* Coca (*Erythroxylon coca*) has been cultivated in the Andes since ancient times by the inhabitants of Peru and Bolivia.

Aside from domesticated species such as those enumerated above, South American Indians plant and cultivate various plants and, especially, useful trees that also grow in a wild state in the area of their habitations. In most such cases we cannot consider these plants to be true domesticates, since we are often dealing with the simple transplanting of plants from their original site to the environs of the house. It is not yet possible to prove that such transplanting has produced any perceptible variation in the qualities of the respective wild plant.

In the area of the headwaters of the Xingu River, a great quantity of *piqui* trees were planted as well as *mangabeira* (*Hancornia speciosa*), *genipapo* [*jagua, huito*] (*Genipa americana*) whose sap is used to paint the body black, and *ubá* (*Gynerium* sp.), a reed used especially for arrow shafts (cf. Steinen 1894:209).

In the past the Araucanians of Chile cultivated a species of Gramineae, *Bromus mango,* which also grew wild in those regions (Sapper 1936:37). The *acuri* palm was cultivated in great quantity by the Guató Indians, especially on the aterrados, and the *pupunha* palm (*Guilielma gasipaes*) is cultivated in vast regions of Amazonia where it no longer exists in wild form. . . .

AGRICULTURAL METHODS OF
THE SOUTH AMERICAN INDIANS

There are two means of acquiring raw material from the plant kingdom: gathering and agriculture. By gathering I refer to the acquisition of vegetable material by means of seeking and collecting it in those places where it occurs naturally. The concept of agriculture is complex and includes all the manipulations used in the exploitation of cultivated plants through artificial intervention in the natural conditions of their growth in order to promote it.

The gathering of plant materials and agriculture are by no means mutually exclusive but frequently appear side by side. Agricultural groups in South America generally depend on gathering for those plant materials which serve nonfood uses such as wood, vegetable fibers and bark. It is also possible to demonstrate many forms intermediate between the two economic activities so that it is often difficult to specify where one begins and the other ends. Although the Guató gather a great quantity of rice, which grows profusely in Lake Gaíba and surrounding waters, we are not dealing with agriculture even though botanical examination of some seeds that I took to Berlin showed the rice to be the domesticated form, *Oryza sativa,* and not American wild rice. Without doubt this rice originates from that which the Spaniards brought with them to Lake Gaíba in the early days of the conquest in connection with the founding of Puerto de los Reyes. Nevertheless, this is not a case of Guató agriculture because the rice, sowed in the lake by the Spaniards, continues to grow in its new location as a wild plant without the Guató influencing its propagation and growth in any way. . . . Nor does the transplantation of useful species mentioned above constitute true agriculture. It might, however, be considered as transitional between a gathering economy and agriculture. . . .

As the most primitive form of agriculture among South American Indians, we can consider the method employed by the Guazarapo or Guachico, now extinct, who lived on the Alto Paraguay upstream from the Sarigué-Payaguá. Padre Sánchez Labrador refers to their agriculture in his work, *El Paraguay Católico,* as follows:

> They told me (the present chiefs of the Mbaya) that the savages that they called Guachi, Guachies and Guagii, who are the Guachicos of many *parcialidades,* and also the ancient Guató, cultivate the soil and have good fields of maize, sweet potatoes, gourds, beans and much cotton and tobacco. (Sánchez Labrador 1910:v. 2, p. 134; compare Schmidt 1942b: 67)

Comments on Cultivated Plants and Agricultural Methods   63

Elsewhere in the same work Padre Sánchez Labrador, describing the agriculture of the Guachico, says:

> ... they make great plantings of maize, gourds, tobacco and sweet potatoes. They have an abundance of everything because they place their fields in those sites flooded by the river. When the river recedes, the grass and vines dry, and they burn the leaves and plant the seeds. Thus they achieve large harvests. (Sánchez Labrador 1910:v. 2, p. 67)

This primitive method of agriculture, used by the Guazarapo and probably also used previously by the Guató, took advantage of the annually flooded areas which, therefore, lacked a woody vegetation. Corresponding forms are mentioned among the Indians of the middle course of the Amazon River (Solimões) and among the Otomaco in the regions of seasonal flooding of the Orinoco (Sapper 1936:61).

Aside from exceptional cases such as these, that were exploited by the Indians living in appropriate areas, there is an innate obstacle to the practice of agriculture in the tropical regions of South America. Any soil sufficiently rich to grow domesticated plants without the use of artificial enrichment is usually covered by an abundant vegetation, generally virgin forest. Thus, there exist only two possibilities, either exterminate the wild vegetation in order to use the exposed soil for planting, or induce the necessary fertility in sterile soil by the application of artificial means. Since the first type of agriculture, which may be called "clearing agriculture," ["cultivo de rozado"][2] requires enormous labor, one can suppose that it could not arise except in relatively developed stages of culture, thus we must consider the second type of agriculture as the more primitive. Therefore, we will deal with the latter first, distinguishing subdivisions according to the means used to effect the fertilization of the sterile soil.

One of the most primitive methods of creating a fertile soil artificially consists of applying fertile earth to the area destined for cultivation that is, by itself, sterile and, therefore, not covered by thick vegetation. I have elected to use the term "mound cultivation" for this type of agriculture since, by the repeated application of fertile soil, small artificial mounds are created. In the swampy region of the confluence of the S. Lourenço River with the Alto Paraguay and, especially, in sites along the small Furo do Caracará which connects the lower S. Lourenço with the Alto Paraguay, I was able to find and examine such mounds. ... These aterrados are in swampy sites, already somewhat elevated naturally, that have been covered by a layer of half a meter of humus taken from low and swampy places. Since the exhaustion of the soil through cultivation requires the repeated application of new layers of humus, these aterrados, which are quite extensive, have been raised little by little and this fact explains the distribution of the soil in several layers. Even today the Guató live on the aterrados while tapping the sap of the acuri palms planted there, and even today they bury their dead there, which explains the appearance of human skeletons and of cultural remains on these aterrados. The five aterrados that I saw in the region of the Caracará in Matto Grosso were recognizable even from afar by their wooded cover. Of the two of these aterrados that I was able to examine, the larger, more or less elliptical in form, was 140 m. long and 76 m.

wide. The excavations I made in these aterrados revealed that the Indians who made and used them had very simple tools. No tools of ground stone were found but only of chipped stone; thus we are dealing with men whose degree of culture may best be compared with that of European men of the Palaeolithic epoch. My later excavations in the aterrado called "Aterradinho," located where the Talhamar joins the other branch of the Alto Paraguay, yielded similar results, as did the excavations made by Leopoldo A. Benitez in such aterrados located a few kilometers from Pindotí, in Ybytymí (Benitez 1942). Aterrados similar to those described above are also found in various other parts of South America such as Moxos (in northern Bolivia), on the island of Marajó and in the region of the delta of the Rio de la Plata. It thus appears that the form of agriculture that I have called "mound cultivation" has been very widespread for long periods on the American continent. Artificial accumulations of soft soil, arranged in rows 25–30 cm. high and 8–12 feet long, are frequently found in the Antilles but are also scattered in the northern and eastern regions of South America (Sapper 1936:63). . . . I should also mention here that the Uru used, for their fields in Lake Titicaca, a method similar to that used by the inhabitants surrounding Lake Texcoco and Xochimilco in Mexico to make the so-called floating gardens (*chinampas*) (Ramírez 1906:295–296 or 1936: 21).

A certain contrast to "mound cultivation" is formed by a method known only to the ancient Peruvians on the north and south coasts. This technique consists of removing the upper layer of soil, generally consisting of sterile sand, until a fertile and quite moist soil is reached at the bottom in which the planting is done. We can call this agricultural method "sunken cultivation."[3]

The method of applying the necessary nutritive elements to barren or worn-out land by fertilization, is known in South America only for the ancient Peruvians who employed guano collected from the offshore islands and distributed according to rules to the provinces and, within these latter, to individual agriculturalists. These people also used dung from llamas and other species of the genus *Lama* as well as human excrement that was sold in a pulverized state in the markets. Dried fish also served as fertilizer. In the forested regions of South America the Indians never have fertilized their fields since they raise no livestock and thus do not have the necessary fertilizer. . . .[4] These Indians also do not use the hoe and, thus, could not exploit the grassy regions for planting.

The method of creating a soil appropriate for cultivation by artificial regulation of the moisture needed for planting reached its greatest development in Peru in connection with the construction of terraces. Vast otherwise unusable areas were made available through such means. In spite of the great importance of the agricultural methods of the ancient Peruvians, I do not wish to deal with them here more than briefly, since I have no personal experience in the material and I can also refer to the more detailed explanations made in my book *Kunst und Kultur von Peru* (1929:55–61). There is also a detailed description of ancient Peruvian agricultural terraces, with excellent illustrations, written by the botanist of the Yale University expeditions in the Peruvian highlands under the direction of Hiram Bingham (Cook 1916). These investigations indicate that many of the terrace structures that had been held to be fortifications because of the massive character of their walls, were originally destined for planting since the humus artificially placed on the terraces can be clearly shown. The cyclopean walls sustaining the terraces of the celebrated fortress of Ollantaytambo must also be considered to have been gigantic agricultural installations, built as though to last for eternity.

Since the high plains of Peru are generally too high for profitable agriculture, terrace cultivation is restricted to hillsides which are usually quite steep. Terracing is particularly appropriate to the steep, narrow valleys in which the lower parts of the mountain are sustained by walls which, in many cases, reach gigantic dimensions. On the upper parts of the mountain side, however, frequently reaching the snow line, there are simply earth terraces. Those terraces located in the lower river valley differ from the hillside terraces in being much wider.

The ancient Peruvians developed an extensive system of aqueducts. In some places these canals are carried by high walls or are cut through solid rock for considerable distances. Some of these canals are covered and, in various places, are tunneled through mountain spurs. In many cases these systems are connected to artificial reservoirs constructed on the mountain heights and, by installing dams and controlling the passage of water, moisture could be permanently regulated. Drainage ditches were also important in Peruvian agriculture, and were installed in regions of excessive moisture such as the Island of Titicaca in Lake Titicaca. In regions with marked rainy and dry seasons the water control installations functioned for irrigation or drainage depending on the season.

The second principal type of agriculture which I have called "clearing cultivation" is the most common form among native agriculturalists in the tropical forest regions of South America and we must recall that, until their direct or indirect contact with European culture, they had no tools other than the primitive stone ax to use in felling the great forest trees. The numerous tree trunks cut with stone axes that I saw in the abandoned Auetö villages clearly demonstrated the enormous labor the Indians had performed to clear the land of the wild vegetation on the site destined for their fields. Great sections of forest were removed in this way in the vicinity of Indian houses since the soil, prepared in such a wearisome fashion, was exhausted after two or three harvests so that another clearing must be made. Because of the tremendous work involved in clearing such fields with no implement but the stone ax, no other tool has spread as quickly among South American Indians, following European contact, as the steel ax. This spread has been promoted even more by the fact that the stone axes of the Indians, which they gleefully exchanged for the desired steel axes, are objects greatly in demand by ethnographic museums. Thus, even the Bakairí of the Kulisehu, whose methods of making and cultivating fields I will describe below, were already using some steel axes that they had received from previous scientific expeditions that had passed through their territory. Aside from this item, however, their culture and especially the agricultural techniques were not yet transformed by outside influences.

In June, 1901, after returning from my difficult journey to the Auetö, I was able to observe the clearing of a new field in the Bakairí village of Maimaieti. On the night before the day of work itself, two dancers entered the house at intervals of a few minutes, uttering a sharp "kó kohohohóhohó," imitating the song of a bird. They stamped their feet and sang for some minutes and disappeared with the same "kó kohohohóhohó" to continue the song in one of the neighboring houses. On the morning of the next day, the dancers again went from house to house. According to the Indians, the words of the songs contained the exhortation to prepare oneself for the beginning of the coming work. It was primarily the unmarried males, that is young men and boys, who participated and then formed themselves into a closely packed line. Thus they went through the private houses with their bodies bent over and their hands extended, singing a song which refers to the great pretensions of those who order the youth to work, and to the great merits of the youth, as well as asking for the national drink which is made from manioc.

·   ·   ·

The women then carried gourds of the desired beverage to the singers. Then everyone went, singing, to the forest to the work site. In this case, a new field was being made for the foremost medico-priest of the village and, thus, he was director of the affair and of the festivities connected with the work. In this role he danced for a long time on the path leading from the village to the site of the new clearing. The next day, all the men of the village again went, singing, to the forest to the work site and, this time, I followed them to see their work.

A winding path led from the village to the site of the work. Along the way we passed a clearing in which some Indians, mostly heads of households, were making various useful objects from the wood of the trees cut down in the clearing process. One was making a bow, another an ax handle; each one made something for which the available wood seemed appropriate and which he needed. Arriving at the site of the new clearing, I found everyone happy and enjoying himself. The small boys, who had earlier zealously accompanied the singing, cut down the low brush with their little axes and notched the most slender trees, while the young men worked on the larger trees. The Indians did not cut the trees through, but notched their trunks in such a way that they must fall in a predetermined direction, thus knocking down other trees in their fall. Meanwhile, the chief of the village himself was cutting an especially thick tree that was at the beginning of the group of trees that were to be downed. When the remaining trees were all notched this tree was cut through completely. Shortly before this point, all the workers retreated, and with a tremendous noise the entire portion of the forest destined for the new field fell simultaneously. The large tree had dragged with it, in its fall, the nearby trees and these, in turn, dragged down others so that all at once a clearing was formed as if it had been made by a hurricane. The Indians knew how to exploit natural forces as an aid in making a new clearing with their primitive tools. . . .

After about six hours, the work was finished for the day and all the Indians left, singing, to go to the water to bathe. The young men and boys again formed a closed line and thus returned to the village. Sharp cries, "kó kóhohohohóhohó," warned of their arrival from far off. Then they sang a song . . . with the same melody used when they left for work, but with different words. They continued to sing in front of the doors of the houses demanding food [and drink] from the women in recompense for the work that they had done. On this day each family presented each singer with a piece of "beijú" [round flat bread made of manioc flour], a bit of fish and some beans.

.   .   .

On the night of the third day of work we celebrated the fiesta marking the end of work in the forest which consisted of a communal meal. Shortly before the beginning of the fiesta, the same song was sung [from door to door] and food was presented [to the singers]. The young men brought the food to the village plaza where the chief, the other family heads and the boys were gathered around a fire, seated on tree trunks placed on the ground. Each young man then distributed his food among the family heads, offering it piece by piece, usually starting with the chief. The little pieces of fish and a few cooked beans were carefully placed on small pieces of beijú.

When a clearing is prepared in the manner described above, the felled trees are allowed to dry through the dry season and then the cut material is fired so that all the brush and branches are burned, while the more or less charred trunks remain on the ground. Without preparing the soil in any way, planting is done at the beginning of the rainy season. The soil is loosened a bit with a digging stick in those places where seeds or shoots are to be planted.

During my stay in the Bakairí village of Maimaieti, I accompanied a family to their manioc field one day to observe the harvest of this tuber. The man and woman went, together with their children, to that part of the field that belonged to them. On reaching a place where the manioc had suitable roots, the woman, using her fingers and a small digging stick sharpened at both ends, removed the soil from the roots of several plants and then removed these from the ground. The stalks were cut above the tuber and some cuttings, taken from the stems, were planted in the same place from which the plant had been removed.

NOTES

1. ["Furo" is used in Amazonia to mean a natural communication between two rivers or between a river and a lake.]

2. [The word "rozado" (Portuguese "roçado") has no exact equivalent in English. It refers to a clearing, destined for agricultural purposes, made by cutting the tree and brush cover and then drying and burning the cut material. The phrase most frequently used in English to refer to this type of agriculture is "slash-and-burn."]

3. [There is no reason to believe that the sunken gardens used on parts of the Peruvian coast were made to reach more fertile soil. Schmidt's statement that the upper layer of soil in these areas generally consists of sterile sand is incorrect. The purpose of "sunken cultivation" appears to have been to provide a planting surface so close to the level of the water table that the crops would not need additional water (cf. Rowe 1969).]

4. [Here Schmidt is indulging in simplistic "explanation." His statement is logically inconsistent with the data he presented on the Peruvian use of fertilizer. That is, even without domesticated animals to provide dung, it would have been possible for tropical forest agriculturalists to use either human excrement and/or fish as fertilizer as did the Peruvians.]

II RELATIONSHIPS TO NATURAL RESOURCES

South American Indians, like everyone else in the world, live in an intimate relationship with nature, and nature in South America is extremely varied. All available evidence indicates that the vast majority of the indigenous population depended to a greater or lesser extent on agriculture prior to the European conquest (cf. Hohenthal ms.) and it should be obvious from Schmidt's article, as well as the surveys by Steward and Murdock, that not all agriculture is the same. Even excluding the Andean region from consideration, neither the natural potential of the environment nor the techniques of exploiting it are necessarily the same from one group or area to the next. To provide some indication of the variety present, even within slash-and-burn techniques, I have included three selections relating to farming, each written about a different group and from a different point of view.

It is well known that hunting, fishing, and gathering, in addition to being the sole sources of subsistence for some groups, provide considerable if variable contributions to the subsistence of native South Americans as well as providing raw materials for building, clothing, various implements, ornaments, containers, and many other things (see, for example, D. Ribeiro 1955:147–150 and Lévi-Strauss 1950). Detailed ethnographic data on the place of such activities in farming groups are scarce, although increasing interest in ecological studies should soon begin to remedy this situation. Before we can really understand the place of hunting in native economy much more material is needed similar to that exemplified by Carneiro's article on the Amahuaca, Ruddle's on the Maracá (1970), and Holmberg's material on the Sirionó (1969:51–62). Data on fishing or, more generally, the exploitation of riverine resources, are also scarce. There were and are a number of techniques employed in the acquisition of aquatic fauna, but again there are few really detailed studies of the function and extent of such activities for any given group. Gillin's description of fishing among the Barama River Carib is not intended to represent a general picture of riverine exploitation, but rather to indicate the variety of fishing methods used by one group, with a detailed description of fish poisoning, which is widespread in South America and probably unfamiliar to most readers.

Data on gathering (or collecting) activities are probably even less well represented in the literature than are any of the others already mentioned. I would include under collecting activities the acquisition of all material found in its natural state. That is, not just vegetable material, but animals and insects that are not hunted, clay and stone, for example. The acquisition of materials to be used in the manufacture of utensils is especially neglected. Although some groups no longer make pottery because, "there is no good clay nearby" (personal observation), we know very little about where and how Indians select and exploit clay sources, a matter of no small interest to archaeologists, among others. Stone is little used today except in grinding implements, with the widespread adoption of steel tools from the Europeans, but there are still some groups who have made and used stone tools recently enough so that some data could be secured regarding the acquisition and use of this material.

The contribution of gathering to the food supply is still poorly understood. All groups probably consume a considerable quantity of gathered food on an individual basis while engaged in other activities. That is, there is a tendency to gather and eat, on the spot, any edible material that one may come across in the course of the day. It is almost impossible for the ethnographer to gather data on such casual use of collected material. Only when there is a considerable quantity of some item so that it is brought into the settlement will it draw any special attention. The field worker is limited to the observation of the activities of those persons he or she is accompanying at any given time, as noted by Denevan. Questioning informants regarding the amount of food they have eaten while away from the house is not likely to provide very satisfactory results, since this sort of activity is so natural and automatic that informants tend not to remember exactly what they have come across unless it is some especially desirable or scarce commodity or occurred in unusual abundance (in which case it is probably brought back to the house to be shared). I do not wish to imply that it is impossible to study this area of economic activity, but rather to suggest that food gathering is probably more extensive than is suggested by the published literature and must be investigated with some care. Maybury-Lewis (1967) provides an excellent description of Akwẽ-Shavante gathering, to which I might add that, on the basis of his data it would appear that the Shavante regarded manioc flour as another resource to be gathered rather than produced (1967:49). The extent to which the ethnographer should also be included as a natural resource to be exploited is a question that has not received as much attention as it might, and one that could lead to interesting insights into native concepts of exploitation as well as values.

Still less common than detailed descriptions of individual subsistence activities are studies of the relationship of activities to one another and to other aspects of culture. An excellent description of the annual cycle of subsistence activities is provided by Darcy Ribeiro for the Urubu (1955). Although based on data gathered during only eight of the twelve-month cycle, there is a detailed list of materials acquired by the various techniques, the relation of each technique to the others and of these to seasonal variation, as well as the use of the various gathered materials and special restrictions surrounding the acquisition and use of food items. Another excellent work along this line is Bamberger's article on Kayapó ecological adjustment (1971).

Subsistence techniques are being rapidly altered under the impact of European technology (the use of steel axes in clearing is constantly mentioned, but the use of dynamite in fishing, shotguns in hunting, and the introduction of non-native crops are also extremely important). Native groups have been and are still being forced out of areas to which they are accustomed and forced to adapt to niches that they may not know how to exploit as effectively. They are being more or less forceably settled and "introduced" to Western-type agriculture, while often, at the same time, being cut off from the hinterlands they had utilized for hunting, fishing, and gathering by the influx of settlers or livestock as noted by Nimuendajú for the Timbira and Fock for the Mataco (1967) among others. That an understanding of native adaptations to the environment is crucial to our understanding of cultural processes in South America may be easily observed by a quick perusal of some of the recent theoretical discussions (cf. Meggers 1971, 1972; Lathrap 1968, 1970; Wilbert 1972).

The student should not be deceived into thinking that studies such as those noted above can be carried out easily. It is unfortunate but true that most anthropologists know little, if anything, of botany, and few know very much about agriculture. At present, trained ethnobotanists are so rare as to be almost curiosities. Few professional botanists are either willing or able to take time from their own research to accompany an anthropologist in the field, and it is frequently impractical or impossible for the ethnographer to transport specimens to the botanist for study. The wealth of plant species present in South America makes the problem of identification by a nonspecialist (e.g., somewhat knowledgeable anthropologist) excessively difficult and liable to sometimes serious misidentifications. An example of the complexity of such material as well as the kind of data that can be obtained from its study may be found in Bristol's excellent work on Sibundoy agricultural vegetation (1968). In addition, the task of providing botanical identification for even fairly well-known species is further complicated by the fact that the botanical taxonomists are constantly (or so it seems to the outsider) reclassifying plants, as a brief consideration of the material presented in the symposium on the ethnobotany of America will amply demonstrate (Simposio 1968). The situation in zoology is just as bad. It is more difficult to provide specimens for identification to the zoologist. Although some time spent with books on South American mammals (e.g., Cabrera and Yépes 1940) and at a good zoological garden can help considerably in identifying the larger and more common species, the problem becomes acute in dealing with the extremely varied and extensively used avifauna, snakes, fish, and especially insects. The need for team projects is obvious, but the personnel are not always available, and even if they were, field conditions are frequently such that it is not practical for more than one or two people to be present at any given time.

Any student planning to enter the field of South American ethnology should certainly do everything possible to prepare himself to recognize and face some of these problems. He or she should at least learn enough to be able to converse intelligently with specialists. A basic knowledge of the general geography of South America is absolutely essential. Discussions of the geography of South America in general, Amazonia, and the upper Amazon, respectively can be found in the following sources all of which have useful bibliographies (Sauer 1950b; Meggers 1971:6–34; Lathrap 1970:22–44). It should be kept firmly in mind that there is a large and increasing body of material being published by geographers much of which is of immense utility to anthropologists. The works of Gilmore (1950) and Meyer de Schauensee (1970) are indispensable to the student of South American fauna.

This article is already a classic among both South Americanists and those interested in ecology in general. Although Carneiro's theoretical model is based on evolutionary theory, his use of carefully recorded data upon which to construct his developmental scheme lends weight to his argument. There remains, however, the problem of the extreme variability of environmental conditions in South America and the fact that only a minute portion of the continent has been studied in even the most superficial way. Generalizations about agricultural potential depend on such a multitude of variables that each case must be carefully scrutinized with special attention to the comparability of the data used. The need for more, and more intensive, archaeological work is obvious.

Carneiro's emphasis on the fact that slash-and-burn cultivation need not deplete the soil is of special importance. The burden of proof should now rest on those who claim that fields are shifted due to soil exhaustion to demonstrate that such is indeed the case. Although it is well known that there are many reasons other than soil exhaustion that may cause a settlement to be abandoned, e.g., death, warfare, collapse of the house, continued bad luck, etc., the idea that houses are moved because of soil exhaustion has become a commonplace in South American studies. Only now that more critical work, such as Carneiro's and Denevan's studies, is being produced may we begin to get a clear picture of the various factors involved in shifting cultivation.

Further information on the Kuikuru may be found in Carneiro (1959), Carneiro and Dole (1959), Dole (1959, 1964, 1966, 1969), and Dole and Carneiro (1958).

7 ROBERT L. CARNEIRO

Slash-and-Burn Cultivation Among the Kuikuru and its Implications for Cultural Development in the Amazon Basin

I.

The Kuikuru of central Brazil are a more or less typical Tropical Forest society whose mode of subsistence is slash-and-burn agriculture. They occupy a single village near the Kuluene River, a headwater tributary of the Xingú. At the time that

Reprinted by permission of the author and publisher from "The evolution of horticultural systems in native South America; causes and consequences: A symposium," edited by Johannes Wilbert, in *Antropológica,* supplement no. 2 (Caracas 1961), pp. 47–65.

All material appearing with square brackets with an asterisk |*| has been added by the editor of this book.

field work was carried out among them in 1953–54, the Kuikuru village consisted of 9 large, well-built thatched houses, and had a population of 145. The village is situated in an extensive tract of forest within which the Kuikuru make their garden clearings.

The most important crop plant grown is manioc (*Manihot esculenta*), at least 11 varieties of which are cultivated. All of these varieties are poisonous. In the form of a gruel or as beijú cakes manioc makes up approximately 80 or 85 per cent of the Kuikuru diet. Other cultivated plants, including maize, provide only 5 per cent or less of their food, while fishing accounts for most of the remaining 10 or 15 per cent. Hunting is of almost no importance, providing less than 1 per cent of the food supply.

In clearing a garden plot steel axes, machetes, and brushhooks are now used. Before 1900, however, the Kuikuru felled trees and cleared undergrowth with stone axes and piranha mandibles. The system of swidden cultivation employed by the Kuikuru is very similar to that practiced by primitive cultivators in forested regions generally. Shortly after the end of the rainy season the forest vegetation is cut and left to lie where it falls for several months in order to dry out. Just before the next rainy season it is piled up and burned. Planting begins about the time of the first rains. The ground is not fertilized other than by the wood ashes resulting from burning which are washed into the soil by the rains.

Burning does not completely consume the fallen trees, and charred logs and stumps can be seen throughout the fields. The Kuikuru simply plant where they can between these obstructions. Manioc is always planted from cuttings, which are inserted into low mounds made by hoeing up the loose soil. Between 4 and 10 cuttings are planted in each mound. The mounds are located about 4 or 5 feet apart, and in a manioc plot of average size (around 1 ½ acres) there are some 1,500 of them.

Gardens are weeded by hand as well as with hoes. In addition to weeding them, it is also necessary to fence them in order to protect them from the ravages of peccaries. As a preventive measure fencing is not entirely successful, since peccaries often manage to get into the plots anyway by rooting their way under the fences. According to the natives' account, the amount of damage that peccaries do to the manioc crop is considerable.[1]

Virtually all horticultural work is done by men, including clearing, burning, planting, weeding, and fencing the plots. Women only dig up the tubers and carry them back to the village.

Manioc tubers develop to a harvestable size in about 5 or 6 months after the cuttings are planted, but the Kuikuru prefer to wait 18 or 20 months before pulling them out of the ground. This is because at this age the tubers are considerably larger and have attained their highest proportion of starch, about 25 per cent (see Barrett 1928:373). A Kuikuru garden produces about 4 or 5 tons of manioc tubers per acre per year. Of this amount only a part—perhaps not much more than half—is actually consumed by the Kuikuru. The rest is lost to peccaries, and to leaf-cutter ants who in their unobtrusive way carry off rather large amounts of manioc flour from the village.[2]

Gardens are replanted progressively, new cuttings being put into the ground where old plants have been removed after harvesting. This method of replanting has the effect of staggering the times at which the tubers from the second planting reach optimal conditions for harvesting. A third crop may be planted in a garden, staggered in the same way as the second, but after three plantings the plot is abandoned and a new one cleared.

In selecting a new garden site a Kuikuru has a rather wide choice. Within the 4-mile radius which the Kuikuru are willing to walk to cultivate a manioc plot there are some 13,500 acres of usable forest. This area of arable land is so large in relation to (1) the amount of land under cultivation at one time (about 95 acres), (2) the rate at which land is abandoned (about 40 acres a year), and (3) the time required for an abandoned plot to become reusable (about 25 years), that the Kuikuru are not faced with the prospect of ever having to move their village because of depletion of the soil (see Carneiro 1960). Indeed, the Kuikuru have lived in the same locale continuously for the past 90 years. It is true that during this period of time they have occupied four different village sites, but these sites have all been located only a few hundred yards from each other, and the reasons for moving from one to another have always been supernatural, never ecological.

The subsistence economy of the Kuikuru is one of abundance and reliability. There is never a shortage of food, let alone any danger of starvation. When planting, the Kuikuru make allowance for the depredations of peccaries and leaf-cutter ants by planting more than they themselves could consume. So great in fact is the reservoir of manioc in a growing field that even a large and unexpected loss of flour may be no more than an inconvenience. Thus on one occasion when a family lost several hundred pounds of manioc flour (a two-months' supply) in a house fire, the woman of the family simply made good her loss by digging up and processing more tubers; she did not attempt to borrow manioc flour from any other family.

The extra manioc planted by the Kuikuru to defray losses incurred to peccaries, ants, house fires, and the like cannot of course be called a surplus even if it is an amount over and above their own consumption. It is, rather, an *obligatory margin*. The Kuikuru however do produce a *seasonal* surplus of manioc, for during the dry season a number of families move to small garden houses near the plots where women convert thousands of tubers into flour which is later stored in the village. This laying up of stores of manioc flour makes it possible for the women to forego the usual routine of going to the fields to dig up roots every 2 or 3 days during the early months of the ensuing rainy season. Instead, they can spend their time gathering piqui fruits, making hammocks, or in some other activity.

There is no doubt at all that the Kuikuru could produce a surplus of food over the full productive cycle. At the present time a man spends only about 3 ½ hours a day on subsistence—2 hours on horticulture, and 1½ hours on fishing. Of the remaining 10 or 12 waking hours of the day the Kuikuru men spend a great deal of it dancing, wrestling, in some form of informal recreation, and in loafing. A good deal more of this time could easily be devoted to gardening. Even an extra half hour a day spent on agriculture would enable a man to produce a substantial surplus of manioc. However, as conditions stand now there is no reason for the Kuikuru to produce such a surplus, nor is there any indication that they will. The reasons for this failure to produce a surplus of food when, from the standpoint of time and technology it would be perfectly feasible to do so, will be dealt with in a later section of this paper. There we will also consider the implications of this fact for cultural development in general.

II.

The conditions of subsistence which exist among the Kuikuru are, at a number of points, at variance with generally held beliefs about the potentialities and limitations of slash-and-burn agriculture in the Amazon basin. I would like now to examine some of these conventional opinions in light of the evidence provided by the Kuikuru as well as other relevant data from Tropical Forest tribes and elsewhere.

Permanence of Settlement

It is commonly asserted in the literature on swidden agriculture that because shifting cultivators soon exhaust all of the surrounding soil, they find it impossible to maintain their villages in the same location for more than a few years (e.g., Childe 1953:198). We have seen, however, that the Kuikuru have lived virtually on the same spot for 90 years. Furthermore the Waurá, a neighboring society, have likewise maintained their village in the same locale for many decades (Lima 1950:5). A similar degree of village permanence is reported to exist among the tribes of the Rio Uaupés in northwestern Brazil (Brüzzi 1962:171).

We see therefore that the mere fact of practicing shifting cultivation does not necessarily prevent a society from maintaining an essentially sedentary community. If it is true that many Tropical Forest Indians do move their villages at rather frequent intervals, as is indeed reported, then this fact calls for a more refined explanation. To show what form such an explanation would take let us examine the pattern of settlement and movement that prevails among a number of tribes of the Peruvian Montaña.

Except for tribes living along the lower Ucayali, the villages of most Montaña Indian groups are small, with an average population of perhaps 30 persons or even less. Yet despite their small size, these communities are reported to move frequently, the cause usually being given as "soil exhaustion." This fact appears to present something of a paradox. How could villages of such small size exhaust the surrounding forest soil so rapidly when the Kuikuru, five times their size, do not? The explanation suggested below is inferential, but it is the only one which seems to me to resolve the dilemma.

Villages in the Montaña are not only small with regard to number of inhabitants, they also consist of very few houses which are of modest size and of exceedingly simple construction. These houses usually have a rectangular framework of 6 upright posts, a thatched gable roof, and no walls. They are quickly and easily built, which means that they can be just as quickly and easily *rebuilt*. Thus it is probably easier, after a site has been occupied for a few years, to relocate a village at a spot right next to uncleared forest than it would be to walk perhaps even half a mile from the old village to cultivate new garden plots. The successive clearing, planting and abandoning of adjacent areas of forest is therefore a factor in bringing about periodic village relocation, but to say without further qualification that soil exhaustion caused the village to be moved would obviously be a misleading oversimplification.

We can elaborate and generalize this explanation so that it will apply to all shifting cultivators living in areas where, for all practical purposes, the forest is unlimited. In deciding whether or not to move their village, swidden agriculturalists must weigh two inconveniences against each other. One is the inconvenience of walking an increasingly longer distance to cultivate a plot. The other is the inconvenience of rebuilding the village in a different location. If walking the requisite distance to the nearest available garden sites is less bother than moving the village, then the village will remain in the same location. However, if moving the village is less of an inconvenience than walking the additional distance to the fields, then the village will be moved. In a region like the Montaña, where communities are small and dwellings are simple, relocating the village will presumably appear to be the lesser inconvenience before it becomes necessary to walk even a moderate distance to clear a garden. On the other hand, in an area like the Upper Xingú, where communities are larger, and where houses are of good size and carefully built, it is less trouble to walk 3 or 4 miles to the garden plots than it is to rebuild the village closer to them.

The conclusion to which we are led is that village relocation in the Tropical Forest cannot so facilely be attributed to soil exhaustion as it has been the custom to do. Depletion of the soil in the immediate vicinity of a village merely creates conditions under which moving the village becomes, not an ecological necessity, but simply the more convenient of two courses of action.[3]

The preceding argument has considered only some of the factors involved in determining whether or not a village site is to be moved. Other important ones exist. For example in areas where warfare is prevalent the desire for security from attack may lead to successive relocations of the village having nothing to do with the agricultural cycle.[4] Among tribes for whom hunting still constitutes an important part of subsistence, the depletion of game animals in the vicinity of the village may dictate moving long before other conditions would warrant it.

Thus a variety of factors capable of affecting settlement patterns must be known in some detail before we can be sure of why a particular society has moved its village. Lacking this information we are not justified in assuming that the village must have been moved because of soil exhaustion.

Settlement Size

Villages in the Tropical Forest are typically rather small in size. According to the map in the *Handbook of South American Indians* showing community size for aboriginal South America (Steward 1949:676), the median village size for societies in the Amazon basin seems to fall into the class interval 50–150. The reason most commonly advanced to explain why communities in this region should be so small is that slash-and-burn cultivation does not permit large concentrations of population to occur (see, for example, Meggers 1954:807). Meggers has gone so far as to propose the figure of 1,000 as the upper limit for settlement size in the Tropical Forest.

It is not easy to find population figures for Indian villages in Amazonia under aboriginal or near-aboriginal conditions. I have, however, come across at least one instance of a native community in Amazonia exceeding 1,000 in population. This was an Apinayé village on the Tocantins River which in 1824 had 1,400 inhabitants (Nimuendajú 1939:12). There is no reason to suppose that this village was unique in exceeding the figure of 1,000. Elsewhere (Carneiro 1960) I have calculated that under the prevailing system of shifting cultivation, the present-day habitat of the Kuikuru could have supported, on a completely sedentary basis, a village of about 2,000 persons.

It is very unlikely that even a few centuries ago, when the Upper Xingú basin was at its maximum density of population, it supported communities even approaching the figure of 2,000. If Meggers is too conservative in setting 1,000 as the upper limit of settlement size in Amazonia, she is nevertheless correct in stressing the fact that the vast majority of Indian villages in the Tropical Forest had considerably fewer than 1,000 inhabitants. Certain limiting factors did indeed operate to keep community size in the Amazon basin well below 1,000, but slash-and-burn agriculture was by no means the only, or even necessarily the principal one. I would like to argue that a factor of greater importance has been the ease and frequency of village fissioning for reasons not related to subsistence. The Kuikuru themselves, for example, came into existence as a separate village as the result of such a split some 90 years ago. Other instances of village fission are on record (e.g., Crocker 1958).

The facility with which this phenomenon occurs suggests that villages may seldom get a chance to increase in population to the point at which they begin to press hard on the carrying capacity of the land. The centrifugal forces that cause villages to break apart seem to reach a critical point well before this happens. What the forces are that lead to village fission falls outside the present discussion. Suffice it to say that many things may give rise to factional disputes within a society, and that the larger the community the more frequent these disputes are likely to be.[5] By the time a village in the Tropical Forest attains a population of 500 or 600 the stresses and strains within it are probably such that an open schism, leading to the hiving off of a dissident faction, may easily occur.[6] If internal political controls were strong, a large community might succeed in remaining intact despite factionalism. But chieftainship was notoriously weak among most Amazonian villages, so that the political mechanisms for holding a growing community together in the face of increasingly strong divisive forces were all but lacking.[7]

Of perhaps equal importance with weak chieftainship as a factor encouraging fission is the fact that no great ecological deterrents exist to discourage a faction from splitting off from a parent community. Land suitable as a habitat for a dissident group is easily to be found. Thus the combination of weak integrative forces and absence of external deterrents keeps at a fairly low level the threshold of internal dissension that need be reached before a split is precipitated.

Food Productivity

It is sometimes affirmed that the reason why the horticultural Indians of Amazonia did not attain a higher level of culture was the low productivity of their mode of subsistence. For example, in attempting to account for the decline of Marajoara culture Clifford Evans writes that "the tropical forest environment . . . does not permit the intensive agricultural production resulting in high yield per man-hour of output that is essential for the continuing support of an advanced level of cultural development" (1955:90).

The belief that slash-and-burn cultivation with manioc as its principal crop is not especially productive is, however, quite erroneous. As a matter of fact it can be shown that Tropical Forest horticulture, as represented by the Kuikuru, is considerably more productive than horticulture as practiced by the Inca. This is true whether we compare the food productivity of the two societies in terms of food per acre, or food yield per man-hour of labor.

The manioc tubers grown by the Kuikuru produce something over 4,000,000 calories per acre per year. After we subtract from this figure the caloric value of the manioc wasted and that lost to peccaries and ants, we find that the Kuikuru obtain for their own consumption well over 2,000,000 calories per acre per year.

Figures for food productivity in Peru during Inca times are not readily available, but on the basis of estimates of present-day maize production under conditions similar to those of aboriginal times, it appears that an Inca *chacra* (garden) in the highlands yielded at most 25 bushels of maize per acre per year. On the coast, where irrigation and a warmer climate permitted the harvesting of two corn crops a year, the production of maize would have been no more than 50 bushels per acre per year. Translated into calories, the 50-bushel yield is equivalent to about 700,000 calories, or about a third of that of Kuikuru manioc plots.[8]

Let us now compare food production per unit of human labor. We have seen that the Kuikuru gardener spends an average of about 2 hours a day on manioc cultivation. His Inca counterpart, to judge from descriptions of horticultural practices in ancient Peru (Rowe 1946:210) and from observations of similar practices in modern times (Mishkin 1946:415), must have spent considerably more time on agricultural labor.

The reason for these surprising differences in productivity is not far to seek. Manioc is such a high-yielding crop plant that even when indifferently cultivated it yields far more digestible matter than maize or any other grain crop grown under the most intensive cultivation. If conditions of cultivation are held constant, it will also out-yield any other root crop, although not by as wide a margin.

In view of the foregoing evidence it would appear that whatever the factors that enabled the Central Andes to outstrip the Tropical Forest in cultural development (and we shall examine these later), greater food production per unit of land or per unit of labor was not one of them.

The Possibility of Food Surpluses

Another widely-held belief about slash-and-burn agriculture is that it cannot produce a food surplus. Since everyone seems to agree that without the possibility of such a surplus a society cannot develop the craft specialists, centralized political controls, elaborate religious complexes, social classes, and other characteristics of advanced culture, whether this allegation is true or false is a crucial point. Therefore if it can be demonstrated that Amazonian cultures could not, through the limitations of their mode of subsistence, produce a surplus of food, their failure to evolve beyond the Tropical Forest level would be accounted for.

It is true that over the yearly cycle of production Amazonian cultivators almost never actually produce more food than they need for themselves and their families. Nevertheless, taken by itself this piece of evidence is inconclusive. It is of critical importance that we distinguish between the existence of the *technological feasibility* of surplus food production and the *actualization* of such a surplus. It seems to me that what was said above about Kuikuru horticulture clearly indicates that manioc cultivators in the Amazon basin are technically capable of producing food well in excess of what they need for their own consumption. We noted that the Kuikuru do produce a seasonal surplus of manioc, and suggested that with only a very moderate increase in the time and effort devoted to farming they could produce a surplus over the entire year.[9]

Documented cases of true surplus production of manioc by Tropical Forest tribes are on record. For example, during the 1850's the Mundurucú of the Rio Tapajós produced a yearly surplus of between 180,000 and 300,000 pounds of manioc flour which they sold to White traders from the town of Santarem (Bates 1864:273).[10]

The implications of this evidence are clear: production of a true food surplus is not a matter of agricultural technology alone. The presence of certain additional factors—economic incentives or political compulsion—appears to be required before a people's economic system can be made to generate the food surplus which is an inherent potential of almost every agricultural society. Tropical Forest cultivators certainly possessed the technical capability to produce a yearly surplus of food. But with very few exceptions they lacked both the economic and political stimulus necessary to achieve them.

Alleged Absence of Leisure Time

The availability of leisure time is generally held to be a prerequisite for the development of advanced cultures. Leisure is another kind of surplus. It is a surplus of time over and above that required to carry out necessary activities, especially those connected with subsistence. The assumption is sometimes made that since the village tribes of the Amazon basin never attained an advanced level of culture, they must *ipso facto* have lacked leisure time. Once again the facts show otherwise.

We have seen that the Kuikuru, who in this respect are probably not far above average among Tropical Forest tribes, have considerable amounts of leisure time. Thus insofar as a high level of culture depends upon the availability of abundant leisure, one might have expected it to be attained by the Kuikuru. But despite the leisure time available to them the Kuikuru are like the great majority of other Amazonian tribes in showing no tendency to develop features of a higher level of culture. We are forced to conclude, therefore, that the mere presence of leisure time is not enough. It must be organized and directed by certain kinds of special mechanisms before it can be made to yield significant social consequences (cf. White 1959:292–293). If this view is correct, then it is the absence of the conditions which give rise to such mechanisms, rather than a lack of leisure time that has kept the Kuikuru and other tribes of the Tropical Forest from achieving more complex forms of society.

Poverty of the Soil and the Abandonment of Plots

Virtually all slash-and-burn horticulturalists in the Amazon basin, as indeed in most other parts of the world, abandon their garden plots after only 2 or 3 years of cultivation. Most writers, in trying to account for this fact, attribute the early abandonment of fields to the exhaustion of soil fertility. Is this explanation really true? This is an issue of sufficient importance to deserve being considered in some detail here.

It is known that the soils underlying tropical rain forests are poorer in mineral content than the soils of drier and more temperate regions. In addition to having a lower initial fertility, garden plots carved out of tropical rain forest suffer more than those in temperate areas from the leaching of minerals by rainfall and from biochemical decomposition of humus. But even taking all of these facts into account is it actually the case that after only two or three years of cultivation a swidden is so depleted of plant nutrients that it is no longer suitable for planting? The experimental evidence bearing on this problem that I have been able to examine makes such a conclusion appear to be highly questionable. Since this evidence has appeared in sources generally unfamiliar to anthropologists it seems worthwhile to cite some of it here.

Carefully controlled and long-term experiments on the duration of soil fertility under conditions resembling those encountered in slash-and-burn cultivation have been carried out in Rothamsted, England, and at the Missouri Agricultural Experiment Station in the United States. These experiments have shown that even after three decades of continuous cropping, with no fertilizer whatever being added to the soil, fields in temperate areas are able to produce about 70 per cent of the crop yield they produced during the first three years of cultivation (Lawes and Gilbert 1895:168; Miller and Hudelson 1921:32). It does not seem likely that the rate of soil depletion is enough greater in a tropical rain forest environment to force abandoning a field after only 2 or 3 years, when in a temperate rainy climate an unfertilized field can be cultivated at a 70 per cent level of productivity for 30 years. But however suggestive this evidence, it is still based on work undertaken in temperate areas. Now let us review some of the evidence stemming from agronomic research carried out in the tropics.

For more than a decade experiments designed to determine the degree of soil depletion taking place under native agricultural techniques were conducted at the agricultural experiment station at Ibadan in Southern Nigeria. Some of the results of this work were summarized by H. Vine, Senior Agricultural Chemist of Nigeria, as follows (1953:65):

> 1. Yields can be maintained at a good level for considerable periods of continuous cultivation on these soils without the use of fertilizers.

2. Fertility is lost rather slowly if continuous cultivation is prolonged for
more than about 10 years.

Of the three principal plant nutrients, nitrogen, phosphorus, and potash, it is generally believed that nitrogen is the one in most critical supply and the one most easily dissipated in tropical soils. Accordingly, some further observations of Vine's are particularly interesting:

> The experiment started on land newly cleared from young secondary forest, and the results strongly suggest that the gradual decomposition of constituents of the humus accumulated in such conditions can provide a nearly adequate supply of nitrate for 10 years or more in these soils (1953:66).

When the time and resources needed to cultivate an experimental plot over a number of years and to make periodic analyses of the soil are not available, significant information on soil fertility may still be obtained by sampling the soil of contiguous tracts which are at different stages of the cycle of swidden cultivation. Such a study was carried out in Fiji by Cassidy and Pahalad (1953). The investigators selected three sites in the wet southeastern part of the island of Viti Levu where the rainfall is 120 inches a year. At each site there were, adjacent to one another, (1) areas of virgin forest (or at any rate of forest that had been growing undisturbed for at least 30 years), (2) areas currently under slash-and-burn agriculture which were being cultivated without the addition of fertilizers, and (3) fallow areas which had been abandoned earlier after a regime of swidden cultivation and which were reverting back to forest.

Soil samples were taken from various layers of the soil profile from each of the three phases of cultivation in each of the three sites. Analyses were made of the soil to determine the total amount of nitrogen, and the amount of available phosphate and potash. The most significant of Cassidy's and Pahalad's results (1953:83) are given in Table I. [Not shown.]

Cassidy and Pahalad comment on these results as follows: "A statistical examination of the data in Table II [Table I here] shows that the apparent difference in nutrients after cultivation could have been due to chance except in the case of available potash. Here the cultivated plots were significantly higher than both virgin and reverted plots, and it must be concluded that cultivation had brought about a definite release of potash to the soil" (1953:84).

These findings are very striking, particularly in view of the fact that the three cultivated plots had been under continuous cultivation for 4, 5, and 10 years respectively, significantly longer than the 2 or 3 years of successive planting characteristic of the average plot under slash-and-burn cultivation.

For a number of years the Carnegie Corporation of Washington maintained an experimental milpa in Yucatan which was cultivated following the same slash-and-burn techniques employed by the Maya Indians of the surrounding region. Every year an analysis was made of the soil in order to determine the amount of loss of mineral nutrients it had sustained. The results of this experiment are described by Morley as follows:

TABLE I

Condensed Results of Soil Analyses of Three Sites on Viti Levu, Fiji, Involved in a Cycle of Shifting Cultivation.

	Depth of layer	Phase of cycle	Total nitrogen	Available phosphate (p.p.m.)	Available potash (m.e./100 g.)
Site A	(0–12")	Virgin (30+ yrs.)	.221[11]	14[11]	0.27[11]
(Ovea)	(0–12")	Cultivated (4 yrs.)	.193	15	0.55
	(0– 9")	Reverted (8 yrs.)	.135	15	0.35
Site B	(0– 6")	Virgin (50+ yrs.)	.338	28	0.29
(Navuniasi)	(0– 6")	Cultivated (5 yrs.)	.404	22	1.12
	(0– 6")	Reverted (25 yrs.)	.290	20	0.25
Site C	(0– 7")	Virgin (30 yrs.)	.388	7.4	0.50
(Qeledamu)	(0– 8")	Cultivated (10 yrs.)	.244	10.2	0.54
	(0– 4")	Reverted (8 yrs.)	.303	17.4	0.65

After the harvest, each successive year, specimens of soil have been taken from this cornfield; and, over a period of ten years, the annual analyses of these specimens have shown no appreciable decrease in the amount of necessary nitrogenous salts, nor a sufficient amount of deterioration in the chemical composition of the soil to account for the diminishing yearly yield (1947:148).

Morley suggests that the decrease in crop yields observed in the experimental milpa resulted from the increased competition offered the maize plants by weeds and grass. Indeed, there is reason to believe that the invasion of weeds and grass may be the principal reason why shifting cultivators in general abandon their garden plots not long after they begin to till them. At first the crop plants in a garden cleared in the middle of a forest face little competition from other plants, but by the end of three years of cultivation enough seeds of herbaceous plants have been blown in to bring about very heavy competition from weeds and grass. This competition, in which weeds and grass have a distinct advantage, leads to a considerable decline in the yield of the crop plants.

Moreover, to attempt to cope effectively with this invasion by thorough weeding is extremely tedious, and the older the plot, the more difficult it becomes. Thus the amount of time required to weed an old plot may be fully twice as much as that required to weed a new one (Conklin 1957:104). In fact, it often takes more time to *weed* an old garden than to *clear* a new one (Morley 1947:147). In view of these facts it seems quite apparent why shifting cultivators generally should prefer to abandon a 2- or 3-year-old plot and clear another one elsewhere. It would be foolish to do anything else as long as enough wooded land was available.

Thus we see that the abandonment of a plot after a brief period of cultivation can best be understood, not as a necessary consequence of rapid soil depletion in the tropics, but rather as the most economical way of carrying on subsistence farming under the prevailing conditions of technology and environment.

Supposed Lack of Evolutionary Possibilities

A number of writers have maintained that slash-and-burn agriculture, however primitive, is nevertheless the most advanced system of cultivation that can develop in a tropical rain forest environment. Consequently, it is argued, a high level of culture cannot be attained in areas like the Amazon basin. Betty Meggers, one of the most unequivocal advocates of this point of view, has expressed this opinion in the following terms: ". . . the environmental potential of the tropical forest is sufficient to allow the evolution of culture to proceed only to the level represented by the Tropical Forest culture pattern; further indigenous evolution is impossible" (1954:809).

Considerable evidence exists however that while most societies living in regions of tropical rain forest are relatively simple slash-and-burn cultivators, some of them are considerably more advanced. There are a number of instances of complex cultures, a few of them deserving to be called civilizations, which developed and flourished in a tropical rain forest environment. The lowland Maya are probably the best known example,[12] but one can also cite the Anuradhapura culture of Ceylon, the early states of the Malabar coast of India, the Mon Khmer civilization of Cambodia, various states of Java and Sumatra, and the Polynesian cultures of Tahiti and Hawaii.

Of course most of these higher cultures subsisted not by simple swidden agriculture but by more intensive and permanent forms of cultivation. But these more highly evolved farming techniques had undoubtedly been preceded by simpler ones. The fact is, therefore, that swidden agriculture is not a *cul de sac*. Under certain conditions, which it is possible to specify, the agricultural systems of societies inhabiting the rainy tropics do evolve from simple shifting cultivation to more settled and specialized forms of agriculture.

The Evolution of Slash-and-Burn Cultivation as Exemplified in Melanesia

The development of slash-and-burn into something more advanced has received very little attention from anthropologists, probably because its very occurrence lay virtually unrecognized. Recently however a study has appeared, written by the agronomist Jacques Barrau, in which the evolutionary steps undergone by shifting cultivation in various parts of Melanesia have been set forth in a very clear and illuminating manner (Barrau 1958). In this study, which was based on a survey of 17 native groups extending from one end of Melanesia to the other, Barrau convincingly argues that the horticultural systems of many of these tribes represent different stages of a general evolutionary process that has occurred to varying degrees all over Melanesia. Out of a very rudimentary form of slash-and-burn cultivation, which at one time probably covered all of Melanesia, there have developed more intensive, sophisticated, and productive agricultural systems.

In New Caledonia and in certain areas of New Guinea slash-and-burn agriculture in its typical form can no longer be said to exist. Instead it has been superseded by a kind of fallow field system in which plots are cultivated for 2 or 3 years successively, fallowed for 3 to 5 years, and then recultivated. Only after several of these cycles have been completed is the plot taken out of production for an extended time. During the period of fallow tall grass covers the plots, but the time that elapses between abandonment and recultivation is too short for woody vegetation to reestablish itself. Ordinarily, dense grassland turf such as this is avoided by primitive cultivators because it is extremely hard to work. But in New Caledonia it is turned over with long digging sticks by several men working together. The clods of turf pried lose by this technique are broken up with clubs.[13]

To cope with problems of excessive ground water some advanced Melanesian cultivators construct drainage ditches. Others build terraces to combat seasonal droughts. In order to maintain the fertility of the soil at a high level, especially when the land is to be kept under cultivation for a considerable proportion of the time, several Melanesian groups use compost obtained from rotting organic matter, and also employ a rotation of crops. A few societies in New Guinea plant their crops on mounds made more fertile by topsoil piled onto them from surrounding ditches.

Intense, semi-permanent systems of cultivation have been developed in Melanesia as a result, apparently, of increases in population. Some parts of Melanesia have attained surprisingly great concentrations of population. In the Baliem valley of central Dutch New Guinea, for example, the total native population is estimated at 60,000, with a density of more than 100 persons per square mile (Brass 1941:557). One section of the Wahgi valley in Northeast New Guinea has a population density of at least 450 persons per square mile (Brown and Brookfield 1959:25). It is in areas such as these that the most advanced systems of cultivation also occur.

Shifting cultivation in its typical extensive form can be practiced only so long as sizable reserves of forest are available from which new plots can be cleared as old ones are abandoned. However in any region of shifting cultivation where the population increases at a significant rate, a reduction in the available forest reserves necessarily occurs. Ultimately, with continued increase in population, the forest disappears, either virtually or completely. When this happens, no choice is left to the horticulturalists but to till the only form of land available to them, namely, grassland. No longer can fallowed land be allowed to revert to secondary forest as was the custom before. Now necessity dictates that it be cleared and planted after a very few years under grass. Unquestionably, cultivating the grasslands is more tedious and time-consuming than cultivating the forest. But it is not as impossible as primitive swidden farmers, blessed with ample forest reserves, are inclined to believe. It can be done and done successfully, even with no better tools than the digging stick or the hoe.

Expansion of the Theory

The two principal propositions that emerge from the foregoing discussion seem to me to be the following: (1) Soils developed under tropical rain forest can support systems of cultivation more advanced than slash-and-burn, and (2) these more advanced systems arise in response to the increasing pressure of human numbers on the land. These two conclusions suggest a general theory of cultural development which encompasses other spheres of culture in addition to subsistence. I would like now to present the theory in brief form and then apply it to aboriginal South America in an attempt to account for the major features of cultural evolution in that continent.

Our exposition of the theory may begin, or rather, resume, at the point where population pressure has led to an intensification of agriculture. This result has occurred not only in parts of Melanesia, but in a number of other regions of the world as well. But not in all. Those regions where a notable intensification of agriculture followed an increase of population are distinguished by an important characteristic: *They are regions where the area of cultivable land was distinctly circumscribed.* Areas of distinctly circumscribed arable land are, typically, narrow valleys, sharply confined and delimited by mountains or deserts. It is in such areas that most of the early advances in agriculture, and in other aspects of culture, took place.

It is a curious and significant fact that these advances were not made in areas of broad and uninterrupted expanses of arable land, regardless of their degree of fertility. The forested plain of northern Europe, the Russian steppes, the eastern woodlands and the prairies of the United States, today the most important areas of cultivation in the world, initially lagged far behind the narrow river valleys and littorals in their agricultural, and therefore cultural, development. The reason for this relative backwardness becomes evident in the light of our theory: With extensive and unbroken agricultural land at hand, population increase was followed by the dispersion of peoples. With serious pressure on the carrying capacity of the land thus avoided, the ecological impetus required to turn extensive into intensive cultivation would have been absent.

The same squeeze in available arable land that led to the development of more intensive farming in certain areas of the world gave rise to another important cultural phenomenon as well: competition between one tribe and another over land. In areas like the Amazon basin, where cultivable land is abundant and population relatively sparse, competition over land is not well marked. But in areas of the world that begin to experience a shortage of agricultural resources, desire for land emerges as a predominant cause of war. In parts of the Wahgi valley of New Guinea, for example, where land resources are severely limited and population has largely filled up what land there is, warfare over land is beginning to assume important proportions (Brown and Brookfield 1959:41–42).

Warfare, it should be noted, has entirely different consequences in an area of restricted arable land and dense population than it does where land resources are extensive and population is sparse. A village or tribe consistently a loser in war can, in an area of extensive land and moderate population, move somewhere else where, safe from attack, it can continue to subsist about as well as before. However, in a circumscribed, densely settled area a defeated group could not make a strategic withdrawal. There would be no place for it to go; all of the arable land would be occupied. Instead, it would have to remain where it was and suffer the consequences. And the consequences of defeat under these conditions would generally be, first, the payment of tribute, and, at a later stage, outright incorporation into the territory of the victor. Under the necessity of having to pay tribute in kind, the vanquished group would have to work their lands even more intensively than before. While food production had not as a rule previously exceeded domestic consumption, a clear surplus would now have to be wrought from the soil in order to meet the demands of the dominant group.

The ever-increasing need for more arable land would continue to act as a stimulus to war; and warfare, through the process of conquest and amalgamation, would lead to an increase in the size of political units. At the same time it would also give rise to confederacies and alliances, as each tribe or chiefdom sought to strengthen its military position. The culmination of this process locally would be the political unification of an entire valley under the banner of its strongest chiefdom. The ultimate military and political result of the process over part or all of a continental area would be the formation of a large conquest state encompassing and controlling many valleys.

As a society continued to expand through successful competition against its neighbors, corresponding and related changes would take place in its internal structure. Brave warriors and skilled military leaders would rise in status, wealth, and power, and would form the nucleus of a noble class. The military organization that had brought success in warfare would become elaborated and part of it would be redirected to the effective control and utilization of the peoples it had subjugated. War prisoners, at first merely slaughtered or sacrificed, would later come to be exploited economically as slaves. They would be put to work for the benefit of the emerging state, perhaps side by side with "citizens" conscripted by means of the corvée. A large part of this forced or drafted labor would be directed toward meeting the increasing agricultural needs of a rapidly expanding society: the drainage of swamps, the building of terraces, the cutting of irrigation canals, and the like. The incorporation of slaves into the conquering state would complete the stratification of society into four major classes: chiefs (or kings), nobles, commoners, and slaves.

Craft production would be immensely stimulated, not only by the demands made on subject peoples for tribute and taxation, but also by the rise of a class of craft specialists. These artisans would come largely from landless segments of the population throughout the state, and they would gravitate toward the centers of political and religious activity. Their technical achievements in ceramics, weaving, metallurgy, architecture, and the like would enrich the culture of the state and enhance its prestige. The magnificence of the social and religious superstructure thus erected would obscure the origin of the state. It would be difficult to infer from the later history of the state that a shortage of land among simple farming peoples and the ensuing competition between them had given the original impetus to its formation.

Implications for South America

Finally, let us apply the theory just elaborated to the continent of South America in order to see if we can make its ethnographic features and culture history more intelligible. We may begin by looking at the horticultural tribes of the Amazon basin. From the earliest days of cultivation in this region, perhaps 2000 years ago, the technique employed must have been that of slash-and-burn. Since the introduction of shifting cultivation into the Amazon basin, this region has undoubtedly experienced a steady increase in population. However, this increase had been of sufficiently short duration and had taken place within such a vast area, that at the time of earliest white contact it had not resulted in any very dense concentrations of population. If a tendency to overcrowding developed here and there from time to time, it evidently led to the moving away of the "surplus" population, thus relieving the pressure. Indeed, this mechanism has been suggested as the principal means by which Tropical Forest peoples and cultures spread throughout the Amazon valley. With population able to disperse in this manner, no ecological pressure developed which might have led to the intensification of cultivation. With little or no shortage of forest soil, competition over land did not assume significant proportions. Warfare occurred, but its principal causes appear to have been something other than the need for more land. And a village or tribe that met defeat in warfare could easily move to a safer locale which at the same time was suitable for cultivation, thus avoiding subjugation and amalgamation. We see therefore that none of the forms of social development that, according to our theory, are contingent upon competition over land and subsequent conquest could have been expected to develop in the Amazon Basin within the period of time available.

The Circum-Caribbean Area

When we turn to the Circum-Caribbean area we find that the differences from Tropical Forest culture to be noted here appear to go hand in hand with ecological differences. Perhaps the most striking feature of the geographical distribution of Circum-Caribbean cultures is that they are found in habitats which, however else they may differ from one another, have one feature in common, namely, they are regions where the areas of cultivable land are circumscribed. The mountain valleys of Colombia, the coastal strips of Venezuela, and the islands of the Greater Antilles, all centers of Circum-Caribbean culture, share this characteristic.

Ethnologists who try to account for the higher development of cultures in the Circum-Caribbean area than in the Tropical Forest frequently ascribe this differential to the superior soil of the former area. But many areas that supported a Circum-Caribbean level of culture—Puerto Rico, Hispaniola, and the Venezuelan coast, for example—had essentially the same type of soil as the Amazon basin. We must therefore look for other determinants than soil to explain the observable cultural differences.

Technological factors likewise do not offer a solution to the problem. The digging stick was virtually the sole agricultural implement of both Circum-

Caribbean and Tropical Forest peoples. Even such a relatively simple tool as the hoe was absent or virtually so from the entire Circum-Caribbean area, just as it was from the Tropical Forest. It is true that some irrigation and terracing were carried out in the Circum-Caribbean region, but only to a very limited extent. Furthermore, terracing and irrigation are more the product of the organization and direction of labor than they are of mechanical innovation as such.

With soil and technology thus eliminated, we may now consider the explanation proposed earlier: the higher culture level of the Circum-Caribbean area was the result of a series of events which began with competition over land among agricultural societies inhabiting areas of circumscribed arable land. The form of social organization assumed by Circum-Caribbean chiefdoms was an outgrowth and reflection of this competition. The food surpluses known to have been produced by Circum-Caribbean peoples were an actualization of a potentiality present, but never realized, among Tropical Forest cultivators. The process which produced the Circum-Caribbean chiefdoms proceeded at different rates and to different degrees in the various valleys, littorals, and islands of the Circum-Caribbean area. In fact, the cultures encountered here by the Spaniards in the 16th century represented almost every stage and gradation of this process, from just above Tropical Forest to solidly sub-Andean.

The Andean Area

Cultural development in the central Andes was essentially a continuation and elaboration of the evolutionary trends observable in the Circum-Caribbean area. One might say that in the Central Andes these trends merely reached their logical culmination. In matters of subsistence, cultivation in Peru brought agriculture to its highest point of intensification in the entire hemisphere with the establishment of permanent, irrigated, and heavily fertilized fields in the coastal valleys. In the sphere of political organization, the Incas carried the process of conquest and amalgamation to the point of creating a vast empire, in which vanquished tribes and petty states alike were carefully fitted into the administrative structure.

Although the Inca empire went far beyond Circum-Caribbean chiefdoms in almost every phase of culture, it still revealed very clearly the factors which underlay this elaborate development. There is scarcely a better example anywhere in the world of an environment in which cultivable land was restricted in area and circumscribed in boundaries than the already mentioned coastal valleys of Peru. Along the course of the rivers and as far as irrigation canals could extend, these valleys were literally gardens. Beyond, there was nothing but desert. The relevance of this fact for our theory can be seen from the following observation made by Cieza de León (1959:18–19):

> ...although I have described Peru as being three desert and uninhabited mountain ranges, by the grace of God there are valleys and rivers I have mentioned; if it were not for them, it would be impossible for people to live there, which is the reason the natives could be so easily conquered and why they serve without revolting, because if they did so, they would all perish of hunger and cold.

The Inca empire also provides us with a remarkable demonstration of how far culture can advance through the large-scale and efficient organization of labor, without the necessity of a correspondingly extensive development of technology. Donald Collier (1959:282) has pointed this out clearly and succinctly enough to be worth quoting:

> Peruvian technology is notable for its lack of labor saving devices and its failure to exploit sources of power other than human muscle. Instead, production was accomplished by means of the organization of human effort, craft specialization, enormous patience, and an amazing virtuosity in utilizing the simple tools and techniques. During the Expansionist stage a kind of mass production of crafts was achieved not by means of new tools or techniques but simply by a reorientation of ends and more intensive organization of production.[14] [*Translated by R. L. Carneiro.]

Conclusion

A theory of cultural development has been advanced in this paper which explains the broad features of native culture history in South America more fully and coherently than any other single theory previously put forward to account for the same phenomena. The theory would appear to have another scientific advantage in that it shows civilization and the stages of society that led up to it to be, not subtle and unlikely products, to be accounted for by the invocation of "genius" or chance, by the vagaries of diffusion or of "historic accidents," but rather, as strictly determined cultural manifestations, the inevitable outcome, under certain specifiable conditions, of a complex but intelligible process.

NOTES

1. Some writers have the mistaken idea that because of the prussic acid in bitter manioc, "animals do not eat the . . . roots of this plant" (Gourou 1953:28). Actually, as long as it is growing undisturbed the manioc tuber does not contain any prussic acid as such, but only a cyanogenetic glucoside (manihotoxine). It is only after the tubers are pulled out of the ground and exposed to air that an enzyme in the root begins to act on the cyanogenetic glucoside in such a way as to liberate the prussic acid (Watt 1908:767). Thus, since peccaries go after the roots while they are still growing underground, they can eat them with impunity.

2. On one occasion, the famous naturalist Henry Walter Bates almost lost the contents of two bushel baskets of manioc flour to leaf-cutter ants in the course of a single night (Bates 1864:14–15).

3. In the discussion that followed the oral presentation of this paper it was objected that this explanation is anthropocentric. If the argument has been worded anthropocentrically it was done so only to make the explanation appear more immediate and direct. The explanation offered here could easily be translated into a purely culturological one, since this is, in fact, what it actually is. In this instance, as in so many others involving human behavior, individuals may be regarded as objects on which cultural forces act. The overt behavior of individuals thus may be conceived of as the *resultant* of a cultural *parallelogram of forces,* in which cultural forces of different magnitudes pull in different directions and produce an effect which is a summation of them all.

4. Warfare may combine with factors related to cultivation to affect the length of time a village can be maintained in the same location. In some parts of Borneo, for example, head hunting raids were once so common that it was not considered safe to make gardens very far

from the village. Accordingly, the area deemed safe for cultivation was small, and villages had to be relocated about every twelve years (Chapple and Coon 1942:189).

5. "Other factors being constant, the degree of solidarity [of a society] varies inversely with the size: the larger the group the less the solidarity" (White 1959:103).

6. Such a split seemed to have been in the process of occurring among the Chukahamay (Txukarramãe), a Northern Cayapó group of the middle Xingú, in 1954, according to Orlando and Cláudio Villas Boas (personal communication), who on the occasion of establishing the first peaceful white contact with that group, found themselves caught in the middle of an internal dispute which threatened to divide the village into two.

7. Father John M. Cooper is said to have described the power of Tropical Forest chiefs in this way: "One word from the chief and everyone does as he pleases."

8. The difference is less if we compare the productivity of manioc with that of potatoes, which, I am informed by John Murra, were the staple food crop of the highland peasants of Peru in pre-Columbian times. Nevertheless, the comparison still shows Kuikuru horticulture to be more productive, since it is unlikely that the yield of potatoes in the Andean highlands exceeded 80 bushels per acre, equivalent to about 1,500,000 calories.

9. Meggers has argued that even if Tropical Forest cultivators did produce a surplus of manioc, they could not preserve it. Thus, she writes that manioc "cannot be stored in the humid warm climate [of the Amazon basin] without sprouting or rotting" (1957:82–83). While it is true that manioc tubers will begin to rot shortly after exposure to the air (being roots and not stems they will never sprout), it is also true that if manioc is reduced to flour it can be preserved indefinitely in that form, or as beijú cakes baked from it.

10. It may be of interest here to cite an instance of surplus food production from the island of Fiji, where a similar type of cultivation was carried out in a similar environment. During one religious celebration the chiefs of Somosomo, a district of Fiji, made a presentation of 10,000 yams to their gods (Tippett 1958:145). At a military review on another occasion a supply of 40,000 yams and a wall of yaqona roots 7 feet high and 35 feet long were brought forth (Tippett 1958:153).

11. Cassidy and Pahalad give the analysis for the 0–6" and 6–12" levels separately, but for greater comparability I have averaged the two here and made the average apply to the 0–12" level as a whole.

12. Meggers (1954:817), in order to defend her theory against a seeming exception, has contended that while Maya civilization may have *maintained* itself in the Petén, it must have *originated* in some area other than the tropical lowlands of Guatemala. But this opinion has been challenged, for example by Coe (1957, especially p. 331).

13. This is precisely the way in which Inca farmers of the Andean highlands dealt with the grasslands they cultivated, except that their digging stick, the *taclla*, had a footrest and was thus a somewhat more efficient tool.

14. Cieza de León was very much impressed by the same thing: "There is no disputing the fact that when one sees the fine handicrafts they [the Incas] have produced, it arouses the admiration of all who have knowledge of it. The most amazing thing is how few tools and instruments they have for their work, and how easily they produce things of finest quality ... They also make statues and other large things, and in many places it is clear that they have carved them with no other tools than stones and their great wit" (1959:175–76).

The group described by Denevan is quite different from the Kuikuru, both in habitat and culture. The author, a cultural geographer, was in the enviable position of having not only his own work to rely on, but several excellent anthropological and ethnohistorical studies. His data indicate that many of the previously held generalizations about tropical forest adaptations need rethinking.

One point of interest touched on by Denevan is that pets kept by the Campa are sometimes eaten in time of need. Many South American groups keep pets, sometimes a number of them, ranging from birds and monkeys to peccaries and tapirs. Although such pets are frequently mentioned in ethnographies, there is seldom any discussion of their place within the culture and their eventual fate. It is hard to believe that many groups would be able to refrain from the temptation represented by a nice fat tapir or peccary, or even a parrot or macaw (cf. Maybury-Lewis 1967:37; Métraux and Baldus 1946:438). In the light of these cases it is tempting to think of pet keeping as functioning partially as a form of meat storage among groups who do not have domesticated animals.

8 WILLIAM M. DENEVAN

Campa Subsistence in the Gran Pajonal, Eastern Peru

Shifting cultivation, supplemented by hunting, fishing, and gathering, is the common form of subsistence among the indigenous peoples of tropical America. It is characterized by a great variety of methods under an equally great variety of ecological conditions. Numerous studies of shifting cultivation and subsistence systems have been made in Asia and Africa, and enough detail exists for major comparative analyses to have been published (see Spencer 1966; Allan 1965; Miracle 1967). On the other hand, few accounts other than fragments in ethnographical and geographical works are available for tropical South America (see, e.g., Carneiro 1960, 1964c; Leeds 1961). On the basis of these reports several theoretical statements have been put forth on the relationship of subsistence patterns to population density, settlement stability, food productivity, and cultural evolution. To test these theories and to make comparisons possible, ecological fieldwork must be carried out in conjunction with ethnographic and demographic surveys. Such studies should incorporate detailed measurement of inputs and outputs over at least one annual food-getting cycle (Nietschmann 1971; Brookfield

Reprinted with omissions by permission of the author and the American Geographical Society from *The Geographical Review*, vol. 61, no. 4 (1971), pp. 496–518.

All material appearing with square brackets with an asterisk [*] has been added by the editor of this book.

1968). The need is urgent in view of the rapid cultural changes now being experienced by tropical peoples and of the population decline and actual extinction of many tribes. Salvage ecology is needed not just for understanding aboriginal groups but to provide insights into how the settlers replacing the Indians can come to terms with the tropical environment in a productive and nondestructive way.

The present paper, which by no means achieves all the objectives mentioned, briefly describes the subsistence system of the Campa, a representative nonriverine tribe in western Amazonia, and relates the Campa situation to larger issues of population density and of settlement and subsistence stability. Fieldwork was carried out among different groups of the Campa in 1965–1966 and in the summer of 1968, particularly in the Gran Pajonal, but also on the central Ucayali, the lower Ene, the upper Pichis, the lower Tambo, and the Perené-Pangoa rivers. Some groups were visited at several periods of the year, others only once. A major objective was to gain perspective on the variability of subsistence from group to group, rather than to make an in-depth study of a single group. Many of the studies of tropical agriculture are based on one village and are therefore not indicative of the great diversity of practices frequently present within a single culture. Spanish-speaking Campa informants and interpreters were used, and missionaries and others long resident among the Campa were particularly helpful.[1] Relevant details of Campa ethnography and ethnohistory are omitted here, since they have been covered in other recent studies (Varese 1968; Weiss ms.; Lehnertz ms.). Subsistence activities of more acculturated groups of Campa have been studied by Allen and Holshouser (1973) and by Bodley (ms.). The Gran Pajonal has been described by Chrostowski and Denevan (1970) and by the Oficina Nacional de Evaluación de Recursos Naturales of Peru (Oficina de Evaluación 1968).

THE CAMPA

The Campa are an Arawakan-speaking tribe, with several dialects, who live in the eastern foothills of the central Andes. Their territory is roughly bounded by the upper Ucayali, the lower Tambo, the Pichis-Pachitea, and the foothill zones on both sides of the Ene and the lower Apurimac, a total area of about 25,000 square kilometers. I estimate the present Campa population to be between 24,000 and 26,000, making them probably the largest surviving tribe in the Amazon Basin.[2] The population density, then, is about one per square kilometer. A large number still live in the uplands of the Gran Pajonal (Figure 1) and on the western slopes of the Cordillera de Vilcabamba, but there has been a steady movement toward the riverine missions on the Ucayali, the upper Pichis, the Perené, and the lower Apurimac. The population was undoubtedly significantly greater as recently as twenty to thirty years ago, but the later death rate from epidemic diseases has been high. The degree of acculturation is considerable along the rivers and in the west but is relatively slight in many parts of the uplands, and some isolated groups have had no direct contact with whites and are still hostile.

The Gran Pajonal Campa are best described as a seminomadic horticultural tribe with a strong emphasis on hunting, rather than on fishing, as the major source of

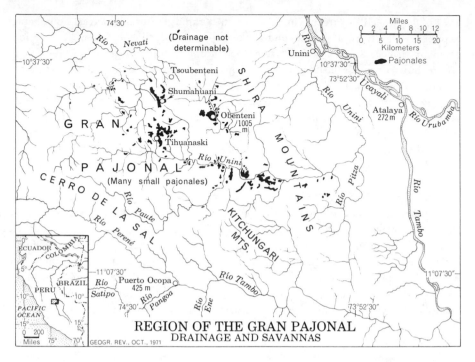

Figure 1.

protein. Socially they are organized into small groups that comprise an individual family or as many as five or six conjugal families, seldom numbering more than thirty-five persons and usually from five to fifteen persons. Settlements consist of from one to five huts (except for the missions, which may have as many as 300 to 400 people). Settlement sites are moved every one to three years for a variety of reasons; hence the designation "seminomadic."

In view of the frequent movement of settlements, it is not surprising that the material culture of the Campa is minimal. Pottery is crude and now absent among most Campa groups, whether or not they have metal pots. Other items include the cushma (tunic), bows and arrows, shoulder bags, *masato* (yuca beer) troughs (Figure 2), looms, and baskets.[3]

Casual observers characterize the Campa as hunters rather than as agriculturists, and most males do spend much of their working time hunting. Nevertheless, most of a family's food, by weight and calories, comes from cultivated plants. Yuca (sweet manioc) is by far the most important crop, but many other plants are cultivated. Still, meat is the main source of protein, and it seems likely that the frequent shifting of fields and settlements is related to the depletion of local game supplies. Ecologically the Campa can be divided into upland and riverine groups.[4] Fishing is of little importance among the upland Campa, the principal focus of this study, but is a major source of food for the riverine Campa, though even in the lowlands many are in the piedmont areas away from the floodplains and are more

Figure 2. Campa woman mashing yuca for the preparation of masato.

hunters than fishermen. The riverine Campa make use of alluvial soils and aquatic resources and tend not to be as nomadic as the upland Campa.

THE GRAN PAJONAL

The traditional heartland of the Campa is the Gran Pajonal, a remote plateau that lies between the Ucayali, Pichis-Pachitea, and Perené-Tambo rivers (Figure 1). The core area, south of 10° S., encompasses about 200,000 hectares of rolling terrain deeply dissected by the gorges of the Río Unini and the Río Nevati and their tributaries. On the more gentle slopes between these rivers are 9000 to 10,000 hectares of *pajonales* (grasslands), which owe their presence, at least in part, to a long history of Campa clearing and burning (Chrostowski and Denevan 1970). The pajonales are in numerous scattered patches along the hill crests (Figure 3); most are less than ten hectares in area, but a few are one hundred hectares or more. The dominant forest vegetation is Bosque Húmedo Subtropical (Subtropical Humid Forest), according to the Holdridge-Tosi classification (Oficina de Evaluación 1968:67–70), and much of it is second growth. The area of pajonales has had the greatest concentration of Campa settlements in the past; recently, however, pressures from settlers, from the Guardia Civil [*Peruvian police], and from a ranch at Shumahuani have forced a movement toward the rugged fringes of the Gran Pajonal and toward the missions.

In the pajonal area elevations mostly range between 1000 and 1500 meters. Temperatures are cool (annual mean 20° to 22° C), but there is no frost; rainfall is

Figure 3. Pajonal *on a ridge near the Franciscan mission village of Obenteni. Such pajonales are probably the result of the concentration of Campa settlements, chacras, trails, and fires on the ridges.*

moderate (2200 mm at Obenteni and 1700 mm at Shumahuani), with a four-month dry season (May through August). Higher mountains rising to 3100 meters surround part of the core area—the Shira Mountains to the east, the Cerro de la Sal and Kitchungari Mountains to the south—and lower, dissected plateau country lies to the west and north. Accessibility is thus difficult, requiring a long hike up from the Pichis or the Ucayali, with the result that until recently the Gran Pajonal has been relatively isolated from outside influences, except for a few missionaries and settlers. Obenteni, with its small airstrip, is the only Peruvian settlement, though from 1953 to 1969 there was a small ranch at Shumahuani, mentioned above, and there are Adventist mission villages at Paute and Tsoubenteni. Today, only a few groups of relatively unacculturated Campa remain in the core area (Bodley 1969). Nevertheless, many of the other Pajonal Campa have retained their traditional economic system.

SHIFTING CULTIVATION

In the Shumahuani area of the Gran Pajonal, three Campa *chacras,* or fields, were each examined in July, 1965, in August, 1966, in November, 1966, and in July, 1968. Some twenty to thirty other chacras in the Gran Pajonal were visited only once. In July, 1968, two weeks were spent living with a Campa family near

Obenteni, and a careful study was made of their six chacras. The chacras were mainly visited during the dry season; nevertheless they were observed during all stages of their annual cycle, since the people in the Gran Pajonal do not adhere to a rigid seasonal pattern of clearing, burning, planting, and harvesting.

The Pajonal Campa, with few exceptions, build their huts on ridge crests and spurs, both forested and in grassland (Figure 4). The reasons are not entirely clear, but among them certainly are a psychological desire, with religious overtones, to be exposed to the sun and probably also a consideration of defense. Chacras are located on the upper slopes close to the huts. Such sites, if steep, usually have relatively poor soils as a result of erosion and of rapid drainage. The intermediate level slopes and the creek bottoms have richer topsoil, since humus is washed down from above, and a higher moisture content. The lower slopes are occasionally planted, especially with crops that demand more nutrients, such as maize, or more moisture, such as plantains and taro.

In spite of poorer soils, the upper slopes are apparently preferred because they offer more sunlight, are easier to burn, and have less of a rodent problem than exists on the more humid lower slopes. Moreover, it is convenient to have the chacra adjacent to the hut for the ready availability of fuel and food. The nights are cold in the Gran Pajonal, and the Campa like to keep fires going at all times both for warmth and for cooking. Star-shaped fires are built with long logs from the chacras, and having large logs close at hand is probably even more important than having the crops nearby.

Figure 4. A newly established Campa settlement and chacra on a ridgetop.

For chacra sites mature forest is chosen over the young second growth, doubtless because of better soil fertility, especially on the upper slopes. Other siting factors being equal, black soils with a high organic content are sought in preference to eroded and highly leached red soils.[5]

The favored time for forest clearing is at the start of the dry season. However, the Campa are known to clear in the middle of the wet season, and I have seen a number of chacras cleared in the middle of, or late in, the dry season. All Campas now use the metal axe and the machete for clearing, but stone axe heads are common on old village sites, attesting to their former importance. Clearing is a concentrated process, and all other activity comes to a near halt, with the possible exception of early morning hunting. Each family is responsible for its own chacra. A man may do the clearing alone or with the help of his sons. Working most of each day, a man can clear an average-size chacra of 0.5 to 1 hectare in one to two weeks. Large trees are cut first, and their falls topple smaller trees and brush; the remaining material is cleared by machete (Figure 5).

Burning does not necessarily take place at the end of the dry season but can occur whenever the cleared debris is dry enough to burn, which may be only two to three weeks after clearing. Such a burn, however, will seldom be a good one, and it is necessary to stack the remaining debris for second and even third burns. I have seen quite green debris burned on cold, misty days, but with ignition on the lower slope and a brisk upslope wind, a partial burn is still possible. Since the Campa use chacra logs for fuel, they probably prefer not to have a complete burn. Also, most chacras are used for only one to two years, and a good ash layer for fertilizer is

Figure 5. A recently cleared Campa chacra.

therefore less important than the removal of the smaller debris to expose ground for planting. Second burns of piled materials provide good ash layers, but these are not particularly sought out for planting.

Planting is done immediately after burning, regardless of the season. I saw fields being planted a month or more before the rainy season began. Occasional light rains, and some heavy ones, fall during the dry season, and although they are not adequate for most crops, yuca does reasonably well.

THE CROPS

Yuca and maize are the first crops planted. These are usually intermixed, but often the maize is concentrated on the lower slopes of fields where the soil is more fertile and more humid. For example, one newly planted chacra had about 60 percent maize plants and 40 percent yuca on the lower slope, 10 percent maize and 90 percent yuca on the middle slope, and 100 percent yuca on the upper slope. Averaging out crop percentages on newly planted chacras, I obtained roughly 25 percent maize, 70 percent yuca, and 5 percent other crops. The maize is harvested at the end of four months and is replaced by yuca and other crops. Other plants are gradually added elsewhere so that by the end of six months the ratio is more like 85 percent yuca and 15 percent other crops. Thus the importance of maize can be overestimated by viewing only a new chacra.

Yuca is planted by digging a shallow hole with a short-handled metal hoe or with a machete. Two or three cuttings, each about a foot long, are inserted in the loose earth piled up at the edge of the hole. The holes are spaced 8 to 12 feet apart where the ground is bare of logs, but there is no attempt to make rows. Maize is planted simultaneously 4 to 5 feet apart between the yuca holes, using a large heavy digging stick to make holes about a foot deep (Figure 6). Three to five maize kernels are inserted in each hole, and loose dirt is scraped into it.

Other crops are included in a chacra wherever there are suitable niches. Taro, yam, dali-dali, and plantain bulbs are planted in clusters just below the surface. A few weeks later when good rains are certain, sweet potatoes are set out in the yuca hillocks or next to the logs. Beans of several varieties are grown but seldom in quantity. Kidney beans are often planted next to stumps of small trees prior to burning, and the area around them is cleared so that few are killed by the fire. Beans are also sown immediately after burning. Most tree and shrub crops are inserted well after initial planting wherever sunlight is good, either in the house clearing, on the fringes of the chacras, or along trails. Some fruit trees germinate naturally from the seed of fruit eaten near the house. Tuber cuttings are clearly selected for desired qualities and are carefully transported to new chacras. Maize and other seeds are stored in gourds for later planting but are seldom stored for food.

In terms of numbers and total weight, the staple crop is clearly yuca, of which there are at least a dozen varieties in the Gran Pajonal. The major secondary crops are maize, taro, impári, sweet potato, and kidney beans. Other important crops include máona, arrowroot, dali-dali, squash, tree bean, groundnut, plantain,

Figure 6. Campa boy planting maize with a digging stick on a recently burned chacra.

pineapple, and papaya. In addition, more than thirty lesser crops are either present or known and planted irregularly. Most of the Pajonal Campa crops are listed in Table I. A few other crops, including rice and cashew, are cultivated by the Campa living along the large lowland rivers, and plantains are much more important there than in the Pajonal.

Several of these crops are Old World in origin and are presumably of post-Columbian introduction (taro, yam, plantain, sugarcane, citrus). Some Campa near Obenteni raise coffee or cacao, often as a cash crop. Two crops not usually associated with tropical forest tribes in South America are the potato and coca. The potato is a small, primitive type identified as the Amico variety.[6] It has also been found in the San Ramón area, which was once Campa dominated, in the Department of San Martín, and at La Libertad on the coast. It grows at Obenteni (1005 m) but is usually found at higher elevations. However, it is uncommon and seems in the process of being lost by the Campa. Coca is grown as single plants, a few in each chacra, and the leaves are mixed with lime and chewed, much as in the highlands. Presumably both crops have been derived from the highland Indians, but the possibility of tropical submontane origins should not be discounted.

Both weeding and harvesting are women's work, though the men help out at times. Weeding is minimal, mainly because it is not a serious problem during the short life of most chacras. It is done mostly by hand rather than by machete, in order to avoid destroying useful plants. Harvesting takes place as crops mature or, in the case of tubers that can remain in the ground for long periods, when needed.

TABLE I

Plants Cultivated by the Gran Pajonal Campa (Incomplete)[a]

Common name	Campa name	Scientific name
Achiote	potsóti	*Bixa orellana*
Achira	antsíriki	*Canna edulis*
Arracacha	tsoría	*Arracacia xanthorrhiza*
Arrowroot (maranta)	tinkótsi	*Maranta arundinacea*
Avocado	atsápa	*Persea americana*
Ayahuasca	kamárampi, hananerótsa	*Banisteriopis* sp.
Banana	avari parénti	*Musa* sp.
Barbasco	kómo	*Lonchocarpus nicou*
Cacao	—	*Theobroma cacao*
Caimito (star apple)	kaimíto	*Chrysophyllum cainito*
Calabash	páho	*Crescentia cujete*
Castor bean	morínaki	*Ricinus communis*
Chili pepper (ají)	tsitíkana	*Capsicum* sp.
Coca	kóka	*Erythroxylon coca*
Cocona	—	*Solanum quitoense* (?)
Coffee	—	*Coffea* sp.
Cotton	ampéhi	*Gossypium barbadense*
Dali-dali	shoneáki, pintshái	*Calathea allouia* (?)
Datura	hayápa	*Datura* sp.
Gourd	shokonáki	*Lagenaria* sp.
Granadilla	shimámpiki	*Passiflora ligularis*
Groundnut	ínki	*Arachis hypogaea*
Guayaba (guava)	tomáshiki	*Psidium guajava*
Hyacinth bean	tsitíoiki	*Dolichos lablab*
Jack bean	matsháki	*Canavalia* sp.
Kidney bean	porótoki, matsháki	*Phaseolus vulgaris*
Lemon	irímaki	*Citrus limon*
Lima bean	tsitíta (?)	*Phaseolus lunatus*
Maize	shínki	*Zea mays*
Mango	mánko	*Mangifera indica*
Orange	naránka	*Citrus* sp.
Pacay	intsípa	*Inga* sp.
Papaya	mapótsha	*Carica papaya*
Pejibaye	kíri	*Guilielma gasipaes*
Pineapple	tivána	*Ananas comosus*
Plantain	parénti	*Musa paradisiaca*
Potato	mosháki	*Solanum tuberosum*
Squash	kémi, tsóri	*Cucurbita maxima*
Sugarcane	shánko	*Saccharum officinarum*
Sweet potato	korítsha	*Ipomoea batatas*
Taro (dasheen)	pitóka	*Colocasia esculenta*
Taro	impári, ónko	*Colocasia antiquorum* (?)
Tobacco	potsháro	*Nicotiana tabacum*
Tree bean (pigeon pea)	tsitíoiki	*Cajanus indicus*
Tuber bean (yam bean)	póe (?)	*Pachyrhizus erosus*
Turmeric	maneónkona	*Curcuma longa*
Watermelon	santí	*Citrullus vulgaris*
Yam (yampee)	máona	*Dioscorea trifida*
Yuca	kaníri	*Manihot esculenta*

[a]Identifications were made from specimens taken to the Instituto Interamericano de Ciencias Agrícolas, Zona Andina (La Molina, Lima), from a list provided by Gerald Weiss (also see Weiss ms.:599–602), and from personal familiarity. Most of the Campa names are derived from the Weiss list, which I used in the field, and are for the river Campa whose pronunciations often vary slightly from those of the Pajonal Campa. Some of the Campa terms used are clearly based on Quechua or Spanish names.

No attempt is made to preserve food. Maize is piled in the roof rafters but is mostly used up within a few weeks.

Productivity was measured only on two first year chacras, totaling 3.4 acres (1.38 hectares), and only in terms of numbers of plants. Where the chacras were intercropped (1.2 acres) there was an average of 7744 maize stalks and 3932 yuca plants per acre. The remaining areas carried about 10,000 yuca plants per acre. A few hundred plants of other crops were planted later, and the harvested maize was replaced with yuca. Crop losses from dry soil, animals, insects, disease, and spoilage were estimated at 20 to 30 percent; the maize loss was higher than that for yuca.

CHACRA USE

Most slope chacras in the Gran Pajonal are planted in only one crop of yuca. The greater part of the crop is harvested after sixteen months, at which time planting and weeding cease and fallowing begins. Nevertheless, perennial tree and shrub crops and some late-planted annuals continue to produce and are collected for food or used for seed and cuttings over the next year or more. Thus a chacra may have a full cropping life of about three years despite only one major crop of yuca. As the first yuca is harvested, often as soon as seven or eight months after planting, the cleared area may be immediately replanted with yuca cuttings from the harvested plants or with other crops (but not maize), thus providing a partial second harvest. In some situations a full second crop of yuca will be planted where the soil is superior or when for some reason a man has not yet cleared a new chacra. I did not see any chacras with more than two full crops of yuca in the Gran Pajonal. The length of the fallow period that follows is at least ten years and usually much longer. In contrast, the riverine Campa frequently clear second growth that is only three to five years old.

Houses usually are not moved with each change in chacra, as long as the new chacra is close at hand. Ideally, each family clears a new chacra each year. The second chacra is adjacent to or at least close to the first. The third year chacra may also be nearby, but usually by the fourth year, if not before, a new chacra site is selected several miles away and cleared. By the time the last full yuca crop from the old site is exhausted, the family will have moved into a house on the new site. For a year or so, though, there may be a fair amount of moving back and forth to work the new chacra and to build the new house and, after moving to the new house, to the old chacras to harvest remaining plants and to obtain seed and cuttings.

The reason for moving is not because land has been exhausted at the initial site, since a great many more chacras could be cropped for longer than one or two years. Perhaps the most critical factor is the depletion of game, a reason that was given several times. Other reasons given for abandoning a house were to escape an enemy or a disliked neighbor, a death in the family, disease, deterioration of the hut, or an influx of pests.

Thus there is an overlapping sequence of chacra making and use. At any given time the basic pattern would comprise tapping residual crops from the chacra cleared two years before, the harvesting of the main crop from the previous year's chacra, and preparation of a new chacra. All three chacras may be at the same place, or one may be at either an old house site or a new house site. The actual pattern may be much more complex, however, since many Campa are not systematic land use planners. A chacra that is still producing may be abandoned prematurely because of a house shift due to a death or lack of game, or a family may move too far away to be able to utilize an old chacra. Relatives may move in and help to deplete a chacra. Because of bad weather, an extended trading or fishing trip, or an injury, a man may not clear a chacra in some years. As a result, some families have plenty of food and their future needs are assured, whereas others are caught short with a chacra depleted before another comes into production. Then they either move in with relatives or live off the land, hunting and gathering, until the new chacra is producing. Such instability of production seems to be common in the Gran Pajonal and helps explain why the Campa frequently clear, burn, and plant out of season. They fully realize that they will not get a good crop, but for one reason or another their cropping-shifting sequence is out of balance, and a poor crop planted at the start of the dry season is better than no crop at all. This does not mean the Campa are poor farmers, however.

Top-soil samples were taken from several chacras over a two or three year period to determine changes in fertility during the cropping cycle. The results were not always comparable, owing to different methods of analysis, but the following examples are believed to be representative. From an upper-slope chacra near Shumahuani, a soil sample was taken in August, 1966, a few weeks after clearing and before burning and planting. A second sample was taken in July, 1968, after the chacra had been abandoned for two to four months and had regrown to 5 to 10 feet high *purma* (second growth) with scattered remnants of yuca, papaya, and plantain. Two years after clearing the pH had risen slightly (4.6 to 5.0), which is not unusual and is probably due to the addition of ash, but there had been a decline in organic matter (7.6 percent to 6.7 percent), in phosphorus (23.0 kilograms per hectare to 11.5), and in potassium (300 kg/ha to 180). On two adjacent chacras on a ridge near Obenteni, one just planted and one cropped for a year, the older chacra's soil was higher in pH (4.6 as compared with 3.7), lower in organic matter (6.6 percent as compared with 6.9 percent) and potassium (240 kg/ha as compared with 300), and was the same in phosphorus (17.2 kg/ha).[7] In general, though nutrient levels declined somewhat, with probable corresponding decreases in crop yields, there is no evidence that this was the main reason for the abandonment of fields after only one or two years. Nor did weeds seem to be a critical factor, as they often are in the riverine chacras.

OTHER SOURCES OF FOOD

Although the Campa obtain the greater part of their food from agriculture (about 90 percent by weight), they are commonly thought of as hunters, and in terms of economic-activity time well over 50 percent is spent on hunting. No meal is considered complete without meat. When a family is out of meat the men and boys go hunting for at least the early part of the day during periods of chacra work and for the whole day at other times. Most hunting trips are no more than a half day's distance from the houses, so the hunters can return at night; however, trips of two or three days or even several weeks are not uncommon. Game is not plentiful in the Gran Pajonal, and a day's results are often pitiful—a few small birds, a bag of snails and grubs, or nothing at all. The Campa will go to great efforts with little return, partly because they enjoy hunting, but probably also because of a need for protein, which is deficient in the vegetable diet with its strong emphasis on starchy tubers.

Many Campa men have shotguns, but shells are not easy to come by, and most hunting is done with the bow and arrow, with which they are quite proficient. A wide variety of arrows are used for different purposes (Craig 1967), with shafts of chonta palm or cane and points of chonta or bone. Blow guns and poisons are not used. Blinds are set up, but I saw no traps.

The main game animals are deer, peccary, paca, armadillo, agouti, coati, lemur, squirrel, and monkeys (capuchin, choro, howler) (Figure 7).[8] Rabbits and sloths are present but are not usually eaten. Tapir is rare. A large variety of birds are hunted for food and for feathers, including partridges, guans, doves, macaws, parrots, toucans, paucars, woodpeckers, curassows, trumpeters, tinamous, trogons, and swallows. The Campa's precise taxonomic classification of birds rivals that of plants. They are knowledgeable about the ecology of each species, and they can identify and duplicate most bird calls.

Most of the large game is seriously depleted in the central Gran Pajonal, even though the Campa population itself has been greatly reduced in recent years. The best hunting areas are near the major rivers below the Pajonal, but these are several

Figure 7.   Campa roasting a choro monkey over a barbecue.

days away and are hunted by other people. Thus the main reliance is on small game—particularly rodents and birds—and on crustaceans, frogs, reptiles, snails, larvae, ants, beetles, and other insects. Children especially spend a lot of time scavaging for insects, and this may reflect their relatively greater need for protein.

The Pajonal Campa "cultivate," or at least protect, an unidentified grub called *poshori* in piles of maize cobs. They also identify five or six species of leaf cutter ants (*Atta* spp.), called *cóqui,* which build mounds in the pajonales. The Campa apparently consciously manage the prized ant resource through the control of encroaching shrubs on active ant hills; the ants are gathered and eaten in October when they swarm (Chrostowski 1973:157–158). A few Campa have a chicken or two, and an occasional muscovy duck is seen. The young of many wild animals and birds are raised as pets, but they usually end up being eaten during times of hunger.

Streams in the Gran Pajonal are generally small and so are the fish. Even the larger Río Unini and Río Nevati are relatively unproductive compared with the lowland rivers. Consequently the Pajonal Campa are at best sometime fishermen. Most Pajonal fishing is with barbasco stupefier or with bow and arrow. They cultivate barbasco, and the local streams are blocked with weirs and poisoned once or twice a year, but the catches are meager. During the dry season many Campa families make a long fishing trip to one of the larger rivers—for example, the Ucayali—and stay for several weeks, often living with relatives. The Campa, including those who live along the large rivers, lack many of the elaborate fishing devices of such true riverine tribes as the Shipibo-Conibo on the central Ucayali. The most common fish caught in the Gran Pajonal, all quite small, are corbina, anchoveta, boca chica, mujalita, carachama, sabalo, pez perro, and several kinds of catfish.

Although the collecting of snails, insects, frogs, crabs, and the like is important and is considered part of hunting in this study, the gathering of wild food plants such as fruits, nuts, and tubers is minimal. Most vegetable foods gathered are actually feral domesticated plants that have grown up near the houses and trails or on old chacra sites, including papaya, pacay, guayaba, pejibaye, and caimito. Palm heart is gathered from several palms, especially chonta (*Euterpe edulis*), and wild fruits are obtained from such trees as *Erythrina esculenta, Bunchosia eliptica, Caryocar glabrum, Rubus urticaefolius,* and species of *Inga, Ficus,* and *Spondias* (Chrostowski 1973:153). A large variety of wild plants are gathered for magical and medicinal purposes, including drugs such as *datura* and *ayahuasca,* which are also planted, and for construction, tools, and fiber. Weiss indicates that of the 385 cultivated and wild plant varieties he found in use by the riverine Campa, 192 have magical or medicinal properties (ms.:599–603, 618).

DIET

The end product of shifting cultivation and other subsistence activities is, of course, the food that is eaten. Diet is culturally determined, within the confines of available foods, and the daily meals reflect cultural and personal preferences, seasonal variability, and the general success of the food quest. The subsistence pattern in turn has a major influence on population density, on village size and stability, and on social organization.

Many Campa meals were observed at different times and places, and the kinds and quantities of food were recorded. For one Campa family of four living about five miles south of Obenteni, everything eaten by each person for one to three days was weighed on a five-pound balance scale. This was clearly not an adequate sample. Ideally, diet should be measured for each member of several families for a period of several days each month over a full year in order to get seasonal variations. The meals recorded were not average in that they contained a higher amount of meat (from a recently killed deer) than did many other meals I observed in the Gran Pajonal. I found that I could record food intakes for only one person at a time and had to stay with him all 24 hours of a day, since he ate frequently between the main meals. The Campa often eat at night when they wake up to tend their fires, and I had them awaken me too.

The family never really understood why I wanted to weigh everything they ate, but they were reasonably agreeable, if not always cooperative. The weighing process did not seem to affect what was eaten or how much. Food was weighed in the ready-to-eat state, and the weights of tubers were extrapolated back to fresh (wet) weight, which is the condition used in most dietary tables. The Institución de Nutrición de Centroamérica y Panamá (INCAP) tables for Latin America and the Collazos tables for Peru (Leung 1961; Collazos and others 1957) were used to determine protein, fat, and caloric content. Although crop varieties differ slightly in nutrient content, the difference is small enough to allow use of standard tables for most purposes. The main objectives were to learn what proportions of the diet came from each subsistence activity and what the quantities and sources of protein and calories were.

The data in Table II show that for the three-day period sampled the diet was more than adequate in both protein and calories. However, on the fourth day, when the venison was exhausted, the same man had only 57 grams of meat (part of a dove), which provided only about 10 grams of protein, and on the fifth day there was no meat. Observations of many Campa meals indicate that the fourth day is the most usual; for on the typical day a family will have a few birds and small animals that provide each adult with about 90 grams of meat containing between 15 and 25 grams of protein. If the vegetable protein averages between 15 and 20 grams daily, the total protein would range from 30 to 45 grams on most days. This is on the minimum side for body needs but apparently suffices.

Data gathered for other family members were inconclusive, but children and mothers seemed to have a more varied diet and obtained relatively more protein than the adult males. Children clearly consume more insects, frogs, and the like than adults do. In general the Campa go to great efforts to obtain seemingly small amounts of meat. Furthermore, all parts of an animal are eaten, including intestines, bone marrow, and the flesh on the skin. This would seem to confirm the indications that the Gran Pajonal Campa have inadequate vegetable protein and are at the lower level of sufficient total protein intake during much of the year.

TABLE II

Average Daily Food Components for One Adult Campa Male[a]

Food	Weight in grams	% of total weight	Protein in grams	Fats in grams	Calories in grams
Yuca[b]	1,049	71.8	10.2	2.6	2,067
Sweet potato[b]	62	4.2	1.4	0.1	84
Maize (roasted)	14	1.0	1.0	0.4	52
Palm heart (fresh)	28	1.9	0.9	0.2	16
Venison (roasted)	307	21.0	90.6	6.8	450
Totals	1,460	99.9	104.1	10.1	2,669
Masato[c]	3,591				

[a]Height 5 ft. 2 in.; weight about 115 lbs. Food intake calculations are based on a three-day sample in the dry season, July, 1968.

[b]The weights given for yuca and sweet potatoes are actual eating (roasted) weights; these were converted to fresh weights, 1,276 grams and 74 grams respectively, for nutrient calculations.

[c]Protein, fat, and calorie content of *masato* (yuca beer) are not given, since the water/yuca ratio was not determined. The masato, however, was thin and little fermented and was used for refreshment on hot working days, in contrast to the heavier, alcoholic beverage. Hence, the nutritional components would be low despite the large quantity consumed.

SOME IMPLICATIONS

The information presented here on the subsistence system of the Pajonal Campa can be related to a number of generalizations and hypotheses concerning cultural ecology of the tropical forest in South America.

1. Most descriptions of shifting cultivation give an impression of cultural consistency in the seasonal pattern of activities, crops grown, and methods. This is not true for the Gran Pajonal Campa, and equally great diversity exists for the riverine Campa. The frequent failure to burn and plant at the optimum time or even to clear a new chacra, resulting in uncertain production, reflects the instability of Campa settlements, the dietary and cultural importance of hunting, the availability of food from relatives, and probably other factors also. I have noticed that even a single family will vary its methods considerably from year to year to accommodate differences in site ecology or for other reasons. Actually, many other shifting cultivation systems also seem to lack seasonal and managerial regularity (Brookfield 1968:421).

2. Seminomadic tribes with a strong emphasis on hunting, such as the Campa, are often thought of as being incipient or primitive agriculturists. However, the large number of crops cultivated and the many varieties of each, plus the utilization of a wide range of microecological conditions, suggest considerable agricultural sophistication, much more than that of the average nonindigenous settler in tropical Peru. The strong emphasis on yuca is misleading. It is a simple, labor-saving way to

provide calories, while a man's greater physical efforts are directed toward hunting for the more basic food element, protein. Although a labor/time study was not made, agricultural productivity seems to be high in terms of time expended, whereas hunting productivity is low for time expended.

3. For the Campa, soil quality does not seem to be the prime determinant of field location, as it generally is elsewhere. More important are the local availability of game and the location of fields adjacent to huts positioned on upper slopes and ridge crests. Within a field, however, crops are sited with respect to variations in soil fertility, soil moisture, and slope exposure.

4. It has been postulated that the greater population densities and more developed cultures have been located along the large Amazonian rivers, in contrast with the nearly empty interfluves, because of the availability of protein-rich aquatic resources which supplement the protein-poor root crops that dominate the diet of Amazonian people (Lathrap 1968; Denevan 1970a). Away from the rivers, game is the main source of protein, but it does not exist in quantities large enough to support large social units, nor is it permanent enough to support long enduring settlements. Hence the aboriginal pattern away from the rivers is one of small seminomadic social groups with a limited material culture.

One of my purposes in studying the Gran Pajonal Campa was to test the above argument, and these Campa clearly fit the nonriverine model. Their total protein intake is low, and they seem to go to great efforts in hunting, with small returns, to stay above the minimum. The result is settlement instability and a low population density. This is not to say that other factors are not important, and a careful sociological study is needed to define these factors, their causes, and their relative significance compared to the dietary argument. In contrast with the Gran Pajonal Campa the riverine Campa are much less nomadic.

Certainly diets can change, and a greater use of protein-rich maize and beans, as in Middle America, would reduce the need for animal protein.[9] The emphasis on protein-poor root crops in Amazonia seems to be culturally determined and, in view of the great productivity and ease of ground storage of root crops, makes sense so long as the population is concentrated along the large rivers where fish and game are found in large numbers. It is interesting to note that the missionaries have been able to establish much larger and more permanent Campa villages along the lowland rivers. On the other hand, the Seventh Day Adventists prohibit meat eating, or at least restrict the varieties of game and fish the Campa in their missions can eat. As a result, severe nutritional problems have arisen in some missions, as on the Perené (Paz Soldán and Kuczynski-Godard 1939:12); elsewhere, the Campa have often ignored the restrictions. More recently, the Adventists have been making major efforts to shift the Campa diet from the traditional yuca toward maize, beans, groundnuts, and other crops with a relatively high protein content and also toward domesticated animals.

5. Betty Meggers (1957) has advanced the controversial thesis that population density, and thus the development of culture, in the Amazon Basin was restricted owing to limitations on agriculture imposed by poor tropical soils. Robert Carneiro (1960) and others, however, have shown that quite substantial settlements and

population densities seemingly can be supported by shifting cultivation. On the other hand, if shifting cultivation does not supply sufficient protein, the availability of unevenly distributed animal protein becomes a limiting factor. Such a limitation, apparently applicable to the Campa, must be viewed as culturally determined insofar as the dietary pattern responsible for it is culturally determined.

6. In another provocative paper on subsistence in the Amazon Basin Carneiro (1970) has taken the protein argument farther by developing a "subsistence quotient," based on the percentages of food obtained from different subsistence activities: $(A + F)/(H + G)$. Here "A is the percentage of subsistence derived from agriculture, and F is the percentage derived from fishing, while H is the percentage derived from hunting, and G the percentage derived from gathering. The higher the numerical value of the quotient, the greater the reliance on those subsistence activities favoring sedentary settlement." Using estimates from his own field research, Carneiro obtained a low subsistence quotient of 1.2 for the seminomadic Amahuaca of Peru, and a relatively high quotient of 19 for the nearly sedentary Kuikuru of Brazil.

However, the application of this index to the Gran Pajonal Campa raises some questions. The Campa obtain at least 90 percent of their food, by weight eaten, from agriculture and at most 6 percent from hunting, 3 percent from gathering, and 1 percent from fishing.[10] This gives a subsistence quotient of $[A(.90) + F(.01)]/[H(.06) + G(.03)]$, which equals 10.1, a figure considerably higher than that for the Amahuaca. The Campa, who move about once every two years, seem to be almost as nomadic as the Amahuaca, who move every eighteen months, but the Campa move shorter average distances (about five miles compared with fifteen).[11] The problem with determining the subsistence quotient is that we have only rough estimates of food-source percentages to work with. The evidence for the Campa, though not precise, does indicate that a tribe consistently thought of as hunting oriented actually may obtain no more than 5 to 10 percent of its total food by weight consumed from hunting. The hunting estimates for other seminomadic Amazonian tribes are probably also disproportionately large.[12]

Possibly a more satisfactory subsistence quotient showing a closer relationship to sedentariness would be simply: F(% of animal protein from fishing)/H(% of animal protein from hunting). It would be applicable, of course, only to cultures whose diet was severely deficient in vegetable protein and did not include much meat from domesticated animals.

The purpose of this paper has been to describe the subsistence system of the Pajonal Campa and relate to it some of the traditional and recent thinking about tropical forest agriculture, diet, demography, and culture. Conclusions are tentative but suggest some new perspectives. What is especially needed before we can proceed with the development of theory on the cultural ecology of tropical-forest people is accurate quantitative data for numerous groups on labor inputs (both time and energy), location factors (distance and site), production factors for individual items, carrying capacity, and actual dietary intakes and their nutritional breakdown.

NOTES

1. Specifically, Burt Watson and Mack Robertson of the South American Indian Mission. In the Gran Pajonal, Moises Cadillo and Teodoro Peña provided considerable assistance and living accommodations.

2. This estimate is based on the unpublished population data for the Campa region for 1970 collected by SNEM (Servicio Nacional de la Erradicación de Malaria). Fast (1962) and the Summer Institute of Linguistics in Lima (unpublished) give a figure of 30,000, but others feel that 20,000 is more realistic. The SNEM data indicate about 500 Campa in the central area of the Gran Pajonal, but their information for this area is incomplete, and a more reasonable estimate would seem to be that of 1500 by John H. Bodley (1969).

3. See Weiss (ms.:591–599) for a detailed list of material culture.

4. Weiss (ms.: 42) makes a sociological distinction between Pajonal and River Campa, based on apparent separate breeding populations.

5. For a detailed description of the soils of the Gran Pajonal, see Chrostowski and Denevan (1970:11–14, 30–36).

6. Dr. Carlos Ochoa, Universidad Agraria, La Molina, Lima (personal communication).

7. Soil analyses were made by the Centro Nacional de Análisis de Suelos, Estación Experimental Agrícola de La Molina, Lima, Peru.

8. For most scientific identifications and full lists of animals (26), birds (80), reptiles and amphibians (11), fish (59), and other biotic resources utilized by the riverine Campa, see Weiss (ms.:605–620). The inventory for the Gran Pajonal Campa includes a few additional items, but the overall diversity is less, especially for fish. Bodley also gives a list of identified game and fish, mainly for the uplands and rivers north of the Gran Pajonal (ms.: chap. 2).

9. However, the Amahuaca of eastern Peru, one of the few tribes in the Amazon Basin for whom maize is the staple rather than tubers, are still seminomadic hunters despite the apparently relatively high protein content of their vegetable diet. See Carneiro (1964c).

10. The hunting figure of 6 percent is based on the estimated average of 90 grams of meat a day per adult and on the measured total of 1460 grams of food obtained in Table II. George P. Murdock (1967:122), in contrast, lists a hunting percentage of from 26 to 35 for the Campa (Murdock's percentages are apparently based on calories rather than on actual food weight, but the results are about the same).

11. Bodley documented four long-distance shifts of Campa homes of from 20 to 80 kilometers; in each case the reason given for moving was depleted game or fish resources (ms.: chap. 2).

12. Carneiro suggests that 40 percent of the total food intake of the Amahuaca is from animal sources (1970); and Murdock (1967:118–122) estimates percentages of 16 to 55 for the relevant tribes that he lists. There have been only a few careful measurements of both meat and crop consumption for tropical tribes in Latin America. For the Miskito of Nicaragua, who obtain relatively large quantities of meat both from the sea and from hunting, only 10 percent (150 grams) of the daily diet comes from meat and fish (Nietschmann ms.:312). For the Bayano Cuna of Panama the daily average of meat was 57 grams and of fish 51 grams for only 5.3 percent of the total diet (Bennett 1962:46). In a more recent study, James Duke obtained a fish and game percentage of 5.5 for the Inland Cuna (1970:346–347). Hence a total of 7 percent meat and fish for the Pajonal Campa is not unreasonably low.

This selection from Curt Nimuendajú's monograph on the Eastern Timbira is almost entirely descriptive but includes detail on ceremonies associated with agriculture and enough data to provide some indication of the effect of the encroachment of surrounding settlers on the native subsistence economy. This description cannot be considered typical of the agricultural practices of the Gê-speaking groups. There seems to be considerable variability among these groups, although all of them appear to practice less intensive agriculture than either the Kuikuru or the Campa. In contrast to the rather extensive list of cultivated plants presented by Nimuendajú, Maybury-Lewis indicates that the Akwê-Shavante planted maize, beans and pumpkins aboriginally, adopting manioc cultivation only recently (1967:47, 29). A more recent work on the Shavante written by the Salesian missionaries who have been working with the group for some time lists, as typical Shavante crops, maize, beans, manioc, squash and sweet potatoes [batatas] (Giaccaria and Heide 1972:70), while Galvão emphasizes the importance of sweet potatoes (1963:134–135). For a description of a very different attitude toward agriculture and plants from that of the Gê, see Goldman (1963:58–65).

It was Nimuendajú's work among the Apinayé, Eastern Timbira, and Sherente that brought these groups to the attention of the anthropological world. The more recent work on these groups, initiated by Maybury-Lewis, is sure to provide anthropology with a body of material of extremely high quality both descriptively and theoretically (cf. Symposium 1971).

9 CURT NIMUENDAJÚ

Farming Among the Eastern Timbira

FARMING

It is erroneous to picture the Gê generically as hunters and gatherers, with at best an occasional group adopting a little cultivation under Tupí influence.[1] Actually, not a single Akwê or Timbira-Kayapó tribe failed to farm; and as to the latter, at least, I am convinced that they learnt nothing from the Tupí about agriculture. Old travelers sometimes decree that such and such a tribe lived "only by hunting" or even "by robbery only." Thus, Saint-Adolphe alleges that the Apinayé had grown accustomed to a vegetable diet only through the plantations made by the military colony of São João de Araguaya (founded in 1797). He overlooked the passage in which Villa Real—four years prior to the establishment of that colony—urged a

Reprinted by permission of The Regents of the University of California from The Eastern Timbira, translated and edited by Robert H. Lowie, University of California Press Publications in American Archaeology and Ethnology, vol. 41 (1946), pp. 57–64.

All material appearing within square brackets with an asterisk [*] has been added by the editor of this book.

treaty of peace with the Apinayé on the ground of their cultivating manioc on a large scale (Viagem 1848:409).

Following Ribeiro and Pohl, Snethlage states that the Timbira when first in contact with civilization already practiced a well-defined system of tillage and rightly surmises that the four species listed by Ribeiro do not exhaust the number of their crops. At present the Rąmkõ´kamekra plant the following species, which shall be divided (according to their own account) into those anciently known and those adopted after intercourse with Neobrazilians.

Aboriginally known:
>Maize, põhị´ (*Zea mays*)
>Sweet potato, yąt (*Batatas edulis*)
>Yam, krẽrõ´ (*Dioscorea* sp.)
>Manioc, kwųr (*Manihot utilissima*)
>Sweet manioc, kwųr-kahą´k (*Manihot aipi*)
>Horse bean, pąnkrịt´ (*Phaseolus* sp.)
>Arrowroot, kurúare (*Maranta* sp.)
>Gourd, kõkónkahą´k (*Cucurbita* sp.)
>Ground nut, kahę´ (*Arachis* sp.)
>[European name lacking], kupá (*Cissus* sp.)
>Cotton, kačą´t (*Gossypium* sp.)
>Bottle gourd, kõkõn (*Lagenaria* sp.)
>Cuyeté, kõ'tõé (*Crescentia* sp.)
>Cuya de rama, ––– (*Cucurbita* sp.)
>Urucú, pų (*Bixa orellana*)

Adopted after intercourse with Neobrazilians:

Rice	Beans	Pineapple
Watermelon	Orange	Tobacco
Banana	Lemon	Tinguy (fish poison)
Sugar-cane	Mango	
Cayenne pepper	Papaya	

The only plant-origin myth relates to maize and coincides with the Apinayé equivalent (Nimuendajú 1939:165–167). It combines two principal motives—the world tree and the star wife. The former occurs among Carib peoples of Guiana, having been recorded by Koch-Grünberg among the Taulipáng, by Brett among the Akawoí, by Im Thurn and Roth for the Carib proper, while Nordenskiöld reports it from the Arawakan Čáne of the northern Chaco. The other motive seems to be derived from the Šerénte, who far more logically connect it not with the origin of maize, but with a visit to the sky.

Nordenskiöld derives Gê yąt (sweet potato) from Tupí yetị´k, which is supposed to point to a transmission of the species from the Tupí. I consider this highly improbable, for the Northwestern Gê would never have lopped off an accented syllable, but would presumably have transmuted the hypothetical loan-word into yetí (cf. below as to the assimilation of Tupí tapití). Further, there is a striking fact: Tupí agriculture stresses maize and manioc, the Northwestern and Central Gê emphasize sweet potatoes and yams, which virtually furnish their daily bread but play a more modest role among the Tupí.

In my description of Apinayé tillage I noted that the Northwestern and Central Gê probably did not acquire manioc from either the Tupí or the Karayá, whose methods of employment and preparation are totally distinct (Nimuendajú 1939:88). Against such borrowing may further be cited the term kwụr, uniformly distributed as it is over the entire Northwestern branch, from the Suyá to the remotest Timbira tribes. From Ribeiro's denial of the Krahō' Indians' familiarity with *the preparation of flour*—"farinha de pau," that is, flour from unfermented manioc (F. Ribeiro 1841:321–322 ¶ 73)—it does not by any means follow, as Snethlage assumes (1931:162), that they lacked manioc altogether. For they may very well have used it as they do today, in the form of pies baked in earth ovens. In recent times the Eastern Timbira have adopted the preparation of flour together with the basketry press, not from the Tupí-Guajajára, but from Neobrazilians. This is indicated by their designating this utensil not by the Guajajára term tipiti, but by its disfigured Neobrazilian form tapití, assimilated to Timbira phonology as tapti. They further give to the roasting pan its Portuguese name, forno.

The species of arrowroot planted by the Rạmkō'kamekra differs from the Neobrazilian form.

Notwithstanding Ribeiro's explicit assertion that the Krahō' of 1816 did not know how to raise or treat cotton, it seems to me to have been native to all Northwestern and Central Gê before the advent of civilization. In the first place, cotton is employed in a variety of ways—in wholly aboriginal forms of industry as well as in ceremonial, notably in the boys' initiation festival. A second argument is the technique of plaiting cotton carrying slings for children, though it must be admitted that according to [*Francisco] Ribeiro (1841:188 ¶ 12) their material was burity bast. Third, there is the form of the spindle, deviating from the neighboring Neobrazilian and Guajajára parallels; finally, all the Northwestern tribes share the same word for cotton.

Ethnographically, however, the kupá is the most important of Timbira cultivated species. This creeper (*Cissus* sp.) has starchy tendrils, which attain the thickness of an inch and are baked in earth ovens. It does not occur wild; is restricted, so far as my information goes, to the Eastern and Western Timbira and the Šerénte, all of them Gê tribes; and is pronouncedly xerophil. Accordingly, it is probably a very old cultivated species peculiar to these tribes, which could not have borrowed it from either Neobrazilians or any of their present Indian neighbors.

As for tobacco, my corresponding comment on it among the Apinayé also holds for the Eastern Timbira. Apparently they were *acquainted* with it before the coming of civilization, but even nowadays they do not plant it, the timid attempts of this or that Rạmkō'kamekra having invariably failed to yield satisfactory results. I did not observe a single case of its magical or ceremonial use among these people. Both sexes, however, are passionate smokers and constantly beg for tobacco. They smoke cigarettes of maize husks or tauary bast; a few also use little clay pipe bowls bent at an angle, with bamboo stems (kačím; Portuguese, caximbo). The chief Kukrāčą́ manufactures very pretty and neatly finished specimens, partly for sale to Neobrazilians, among whom the same form is in vogue.

Urucú and pepper shrubs, as well as sporadic *Crescentia,* mango, lemon or orange trees, are planted beside or behind dwellings, the young plants being guarded against roving pigs and fowls by little fences of vertically set sticks or by circumscribed quadrangles made of former racing logs.

The true plantations are situated in the narrow *galeria* forests by the brooks. Since annually new clearings are necessary, the distance of the plots from the village steadily increases. When the transportation of the crops becomes altogether too cumbersome, the Indians are obliged to move their village near the new plots. Thus, the Ramkṓkamekra migrate with fair regularity about every ten years from the Ribeirāo Santo Estevāo to the Ribeirāo dos Bois. While they are stationed by one of the two creeks for from ten to twenty years, the timber of the other grows again sufficiently to permit the creation of new plots.

Each individual family has its plantation, owned by the woman. No single man owns a plot, but many an unmarried woman claims one and gets her kinsmen to make the requisite clearings, this being an exclusively masculine task. For the last hundred years only iron axes have been in use, different brands being very well distinguished by the natives, who rightly prefer the North American "Collins" blades. No one nowadays is able to haft such stone blades as are still occasionally found. The method of felling timber with iron tools coincides with Neobrazilian practice. Though not every Indian has a good ax suitable for the purpose, he may borrow a relative's.

The several plots belonging to the married woman of an extended family usually, but not always, adjoin one another. At times one individual family may simultaneously own plots in two separate sites. Boundaries between the plantations of different owners are generally marked by rows of maize plants. The size of a plot depends on the tree-feller's industry. One hectare (not quite two and a half acres) is probably the minimum for a single family, many owning double that area, but estimates are difficult because the form is never regular. Pohl sets the diameter of a Pōrekamekra extended family's farm at one hundred fathoms—a somewhat smaller estimate. The yield naturally hinges by no means exclusively on the extent of the clearing and the number of plants, but very largely on the care bestowed on them. In this respect the Eastern Timbira are often incredibly negligent. To be sure, many families violently exert themselves in felling timber and planting their crops, so that they could well harvest far more than the needs of subsistence. But after this initial effort they pay little attention, so that the farm goes to rack and ruin. There is no such personal sentimental bond between cultivated plants and their owner as I discovered among the Apinayé (Nimuendajú 1939:90).

Both sexes jointly plant, weeding is almost wholly a feminine job, harvesting exclusively so. No man will ever haul a carrying-basket with fruits; at most he may carry a few maize cobs or tubers in his hands. At the time of maturation swarms of dwarf parrots attack the plantations, which are mostly guarded by the bigger boys, armed with slings or, more rarely, with pellet bows borrowed from the Neobrazilians.

Except where the plots of the steppe Timbira adjoin impenetrable riparian forests they are protected by coarse, heavy fences made of logs resting on forked supports. These enclosures are to shut out not, as Snethlage supposed, game animals, but rather the cattle of neighboring ranchers, the worst plague that afflicts their fields. But notwithstanding these fences the beasts, particularly if of the zebu breed, often break down the barrier and will within a few hours destroy the whole crop. Fazendeiros have more than once deliberately driven their herds into the Indians' plantations, especially if they were "rightful owners" of Indian lands, in order to compel the natives to abandon the site. Only about ten years ago this was the fate of the Mãkamekra horde of the Krahó' and their plantations at the sources of the Rio Manoel Alves Pequeño. If the Indians then shoot down one of these pests and consume it by way of indemnifying themselves for the loss of their farm, the stockmen wax highly indignant over such "cattle lifting."

Of the wild animals harmful to the crops the dwarf parrots rank as the worst. No sooner has the sun risen than they swarm from their nocturnal resting places in the riparian trees and swiftly pounce upon the crops, screaming aloud. Thus they cause considerable havoc, not so much by what they consume as by the quantities of scattered and spoiled fruit. This applies, above all, to the ripening maize and rice. An Indian who takes no precautions against these birds is sure to lose his entire yield, irrespective of the amount planted. The only antidote is to have a guardian stationed in the plots throughout the daytime during the season so that he may at once repel the intruders. This is achieved by shouts or a variety of missiles—stones, palm nuts, and clay balls hurled with the hand, with slings (hŭkaipē'rča), or with a pellet bow.

Among the Rạmkõ'kamekra and Krahó' I have seen boys setting snares for parrots. To a hoop about 20 cm. in diameter and spanned by a network of cords they attach a dozen nooses of tucum fiber (Rạmkõ'kamekra) or, among the Krahó', of horsehair. After placing some rice ears or similar lures below these snares, they tie the hoop in horizontal position to a wooden fork, which in turn is fastened to the top of as long a bamboo pole as possible. The entire contraption, which is visible from a considerable distance, is erected in the plantation, and as soon as the parrots pounce upon the rice ears their feet are caught in the nooses.

White neighbors are wont to mock at Rạmkõ'kamekra farmers, alleging that they raise nothing or at least nothing worthwhile and that they subsist by theft and begging. Few take the trouble even to look at the Indian plantations. Yet toward the close of 1930 these scoffers were obliged willy-nilly to acknowledge publicly that the Indians had planted considerable crops. At that time part of Maranhão suffered from a famine, for the manioc crop had failed over a wide area so that the generally indispensable flour made from this plant was lacking. In Barra do Corda the scarcity forced the local officials to ration the sale of what little was to be had. At the peak of this plight the Rạmkõ'kamekra suddenly appeared with several horseloads of manioc flour and saved the townsmen since by an odd chance they alone had saved their yield. In the meantime, not only the half-starved Guajajára from beyond the Rio Corda had billeted themselves on the residents of Ponto, but even the Neobrazilians came to offer the Ramkō′kamekra their labor in return for manioc. When I reached Barra do Corda in 1931 and inquired in a shop whether good flour was to be had, the owner answered, "Very good flour, indeed; it's from the aldea Ponto!" Yet in this town many "whites" had declared categorically that they would never eat anything prepared by "these nauseating beasts" (*esses bichos nojentos*). Many Indians are deterred from ampler production of manioc flour for sale only by the lack of means of transport, for hauling a flour sack on one's back over a distance of seventy-eight kilometers is something of a hardship even for a Timbira educated as a log racer.

Ramkō′kamekra economic life was most significantly affected during the last twenty years by the Indians' turning to intensive preparation of manioc flour and to rice cultivation. At present these originally alien articles of food are about to gain ascendancy both in the kitchen and, next to basketwork, in trade. Agriculturally the Ramkō′kamekra have advanced farther since their contact with civilization than the Guajajára, whose aboriginal farming was anciently far more intensive, but whose productivity has since rather diminished than grown.

Even today the Indians in part use their aboriginal planting stick, which is invariably of very hard wood, either pau roxo or pau candeia, 75–100 cm. in length, round and flattened spade-fashion at the butt. Sometimes this flattened section is clearly set off from the round part. The Eastern Timbira term for this implement, pičwapo, means "sharp, flat wood." In probing for tubers, especially for sweet potatoes, these farmers use a special pointed stick some 40 cm. in length, which is often derived from the end of a worn-out bow. These two are the only native agricultural implements that persist in contemporary use in Ponto.

Except for rice and bitter manioc, plants of one species rarely occupy one continuous major strip, the general practice being to dispose them in patches here and there or mixed with other crops.

Among Timbira cultivated plants, maize holds the place of honor, being the only one whose origin is explained by a myth. Though [*Francisco] Ribeiro mentions only two indigenous varieties (1841:187.¶11), the Ramkō′kamekra raise four kinds of small-kerneled maize which they derive from the legendary Star maiden, Kačekwẹ′i, viz. 1, pōhịpéy, true or good maize, with small, white, and very soft kernels; 2, pōhịyaká, white maize, somewhat larger, but otherwise similar; 3, pōhịkreakáre, with small blue kernels; and 4, to′rómre, with black kernels of medium size. The large-kerneled varieties, pōhịti, are additions from the Neobrazilians.

The appearance of the Pleiades (krot) after sunset on the western horizon is a harbinger of the rainy season and indicates the need for starting a clearing in order to plant at the first rainfull. This ushers in the meipimrạk period, roughly coterminous with the rainy season since it ends with the commencement of the maize harvest.

Horticultural rites

A man named Vōkrākẹ′, whose maternal home is on the east side of the village circle, is charged with ceremonially opening the planting as well as the harvesting of maize. On the former occasion there figures a small gourd bowl whose edge is painted with urucú and which is filled with maize kernels. Vōkrākę́ takes this container to the plaza and sets it on the ground, where people dance around it. Then he takes the bowl to his wife's plot and plants the maize, whereupon others are free to follow his example. After this functionary's death his office descends to the matrilineal kinsman to whom he has transferred his name.

When the maize stands about 1 m. high, another ceremony is held in order to induce the Moon, Pųduvrį, to ward off noxious animal parasites from the plants. Clapping together their hands and singing "Pųduvrįre kayē'yē' rivahá vaká mopó tu krére," all the villagers of both sexes then slowly dance in the plaza on a full-moon night, moving from the north southward under the leadership of a precentor wielding his rattle. In the rainy season they fear a lunar eclipse even far more than during the dry period, for they think it would destroy the crops. The relevant ceremonies will be described later.

In case of drought, however, not the Moon, but the Sun, Pųt, is addressed. Three old men then march round the boulevard, singing "kedeti/imąpéy/vayakrį' (Grandfather [= sun],/be good to me and/gladden me [by rain])."

No one—not even the woman owning the plot—is free to eat of the crop until the councilors have tasted of it and declared it mature. The maize harvest is opened by the same man, Vōkrākę́, who inaugurated the planting season. First, a hunting party leaves to secure meat for the village. When they return with game, Vōkrākę́ asks his wife to fetch from the plots a carrying basket full of maize ears, which are husked and cooked into meat pies to be served to the councilors in the plaza. Of the husks Vōkrākę́ makes some twenty shuttlecocks, which his son Rąrą́k takes to the plaza and throws, one by one, into the circle of players. These throw each ball toward one another with the palm of the hand as long as possible without permitting it to drop to the ground. If a player at last allows it to fall, it is not picked up, but Rąrą́k throws a new one into the ring until all the shuttlecocks are forfeited.

After midnight the men of both rainy season moieties assemble by two fires in the plaza, whither a man named Kái brings them a bundle of unfeathered arrows with balls of maize husk covering their points. The players step up in pairs (so as to represent in each case both moieties) and try to hit each other with the arrows, which they throw with their hands.

In 1929, during my first visit, when I had not yet come to understand anything of the ceremonial, I had the following experience. An Indian wishing to show me a special favor had some sweet potatoes brought from the plantation for my delectation before the harvest time had been officially announced. In my innocence I eulogized the generous donor before the elders in the plaza, but at once noted the silent, but significant glances passed among them. The donor was thus placed in an ambiguous position and incurred censure, though in deference to me this was not carried too far. However, the culprit was obliged to hurry to the plaza with a bowlful of baked sweet potatoes for the elders, who consumed them and declared the crop ready for harvesting. Similarly I observed that they received two watermelons when the harvest for these fruits was opened.

Another ceremony, hōčwa (= pointed leaf, i.e., sweet potato), is devoted to the sweet potatoes. It always takes place when these plants produce their vines, immediately preceding the ceremony just described of opening the maize harvest. The performers, numbering some twenty, are organized like the festive organizations, but their activities are confined to this single annual appearance at the hōčwa. As in these other societies, membership is inherited matrilineally with the personal name. The lodge is situated on the north side of the eastern half of the village circle. Like the other societies, this, too, has a leader, the hōčwakédeti (grandfather of the hōčwa). He wears hanging down the nape of his neck from a neck cord a feather from the tail of a red arara. The present incumbent is the chief Hąktokót, but the title hōčwa itself belongs to the bearer of the name Rąrąk, who in this capacity wears falcon down on his body and has a little whistle of Mataco type (Izikowitz 1935:333). The participants also include a precentor and two girl auxiliaries.

The members paint the entire body with white clay, and their faces are marked with two obtuse-angled parallel lines traced with the finger tips with the same pigment. The apex of one of these angles is on the forehead, while its sides extend over the temples; the point of the other angle is on the tip of the nose and its sides are drawn across the cheeks.

The hōčwa actor proper is decorated at sunset. At nightfall a big fire is kindled in the plaza, where the precentor remains waiting. Finally the hōčwa leaves his maternal home and walks to the plaza, where the precentor begins singing to the accompaniment of a rattle, while the hōčwa, with his pinčwę́ipey behind him, sounds his whistle. Thereupon the hōčwakédeti steps out of his maternal house, dances toward the plaza, but immediately returns in order to bring with him the entire membership, who now dance in the plaza with outstretched arms.

Toward midnight all the women and girls come out of their houses and range themselves in groups at the opening of the radial paths leading from their maternal homes to the plaza. The hōčwa march round the plaza from group to group, singing before each of them.

The object of this ceremony is to ensure for each extended family an adequate supply of sweet potatoes, corresponding to the number of its female members.

Sometimes a tamhą́k is made to assume the duty of officially tasting sweet potatoes and gourds prior to the harvest. Thus, the Indians hope to improve their crops at the eleventh hour because the tamhą́k, especially if young and vigorous, are credited with the magical power of improving and increasing the yield. The member chosen is then decorated with the falcon down appropriate to his organization.

Storage
According to [*Francisco] Ribeiro the Eastern Timbira cached their food supplies from year to year in special storehouses (1841:187 ¶ 11). . . . Personally I have never seen anything deserving of the designation . . . storage room—except for the modern, closed attics. Tubers—sweet potatoes, yams, bitter and sweet manioc, as well as arrowroot—are left in the ground, where they keep best. Thence the Indians take just enough to supply several days' need. Gourds and beans are rarely kept for a longer period; ground nuts are stowed away in little baskets and bags of burity

bast. Maize, too, is usually left in the plantation as long as possible and brought home according to demand. Finally, the residue is carried to the house in one lot, the husk-covered ears being hung in bunches below the roof so as to be protected against insects by the smoke. Another way is to fill large burity baskets and stoppered gourd vessels with the kernels, but there they usually soon fall prey to insects. Rice, when ripe, must be harvested forthwith; at first it is gathered in the plantation on a grate of poles covered by a roof, later it is gradually transferred to the village, where it is piled up in the attic in regularly stratified heaps. This process, like rice-growing itself, is derived from the Neobrazilians.

Real care is devoted only to next year's seed-corn, which is stored in firmly corded bags and gourds closed with wax, these containers being packed in baskets usually suspended high up under the roof.

NOTES

1. For a typical expression of this view see W. Schmidt (1913:1023).

This description of field clearing by the Jívaro with stone axes is of some interest in understanding the impact of steel axes on South American farmers. The parallel between this description and that given by Schmidt for the Bakairí is startling. It is apparent from the context from which this selection is drawn, that the author did not actually observe the entire process from start to finish; therefore his statement that the felling of the largest tree took "days and weeks" may be considered as something of an exaggeration. It stands in contrast to the observation of Roquette-Pinto that the felling of a good-sized tree by the Nambikuara with stone axes was accomplished "faster than one would think" (1950:247). Contrary to the general view that the introduction of European tools inevitably increases food production, Harner notes that such is not the case for the Jívaro (1968:379–380).

10 FRITZ W. UP DE GRAFF

Jívaro Field Clearing with Stone Axes

The Antipas . . . are semi-nomadic. The year for them is divided into three parts, not corresponding to the seasons as we know them, but to the capacity of the crops which they plant for keeping them alive; that is to say, they have three distinct homes, some ten or twenty miles apart, each with its own clearing (*chacra* in *Inca*), between which they divide their time. At each homestead they plant fresh crops before leaving for the next, living the while on the produce they find waiting for them on arrival, the result of the last sowing. Each crop takes about eight months to mature, on an average. The exception, of course, is the banana-plant, which bears fruit for many years; the old plant dies each year, after bearing one bunch of fruit, but automatically there spring up round the roots fresh shoots which bear the next year.

Living as they do well to the west of the area which is annually inundated, and consequently being free from dependance on the seasons, they can sow at any time of the year, with the certainty of reaping at the end of the unvarying number of months which are needed in order that the crop may ripen. *Yuca,* for instance, is ready in six months; Indian corn in three months; yams (a potato which grows there to four feet in length and fifty pounds in weight) in a year; sweet potatoes, peanuts, and tobacco are also cultivated in large quantities.

If you saw the one-handed stone axes which are the only tools these people have with which to fell the enormous trees, many of them three to five feet in diameter, to make their clearings (often five acres in extent), you would wonder how it were possible to accomplish this feat. It is a feat of patience rather than of skill. The wood is not cut, but reduced to pulp, six or eight men working round one tree at the same time.

The first step in making a *chacra* is to remove the undergrowth; the soft stems are cut with hard-wood machetes, what can be torn up by the roots is torn up, and the small saplings are snapped off by main force. Then the attention of the workers is turned to the larger trees. A ring is cut round the trunks of all the trees within a radius of, say, a hundred feet of some picked giant, enough to weaken them, and prepare them for the final strain which breaks them off. Finally the giant itself is attacked by a party with axes which works for days and weeks, until at last there comes a day when the great trunk has been eaten away sufficiently for it to crack and fall. But it does not fall alone, for it drags with it all the smaller trees in its vicinity which are bound to it and to one another by an unbreakable network of creepers among the upper branches. With a rending crash, a hole in the roof of the forest is made, and the sunlight pours in. At the same time the Indians pour out,

Reprinted by permission of Dodd, Mead & Co., from *Head Hunters of the Amazon,* by F. W. Up de Graff (Duffield and Company, 1923), pp. 202–204.

leaping for their lives not only from the falling trees, but from the myriads of ants, bees, wasps, hornets, scorpions and centipedes which have been aroused. . . .

After leaving the trees to lie for several months during the dry season, the Antipas fire them, a process which eliminates all the smaller limbs and bush, leaving only the trunks, to deal with which they have no tools. I have examined the stumps of these fallen trees many a time; they resemble in every respect those of a clearing made by beavers.

The Amahuaca differ from the preceding groups in both culture and environment. However, all of these groups, except the Jívaro, use or used the bow and arrow for hunting, as do many South American Indians. Carneiro provides us with a glimpse of the knowledge of his environment that is necessary to the successful hunter in the tropical forest, his attitudes toward the game he hunts and toward the chase itself, as well as his beliefs.

Although, as usual, this description cannot be taken as typical for any group other than the one discussed, it does introduce a number of points of interest. One of these is the general picture of animals in South America. Unlike many other parts of the world, most animals in South America are solitary or only gather in small groups. Exceptions to this rule among the larger land mammals are white-lipped peccaries (Tayassu pecari), guanacos (Lama glama guanicoe) and the rhea (Rhea americana and Pterocnemia pennata), large flightless birds which, together with the guanaco, were especially important in the economy of the southern part of the continent. The scarcity of herd animals is probably basic to the fact that most South American tropical forest Indians hunt in a solitary or semisolitary fashion. One frequently notes the comment that group hunting only takes place within a given tribe when a herd of white-lipped peccaries is located. It should be pointed out, however, that the hunting pattern is different in those areas where there is open country, as opposed to forest. In such areas, fire is frequently used in hunting drives, or was until European invaders introduced cattle to the open areas and made such hunting impossible or dangerous. For excellent first-hand descriptions of hunting in such open country see Maybury-Lewis' account of his fieldwork with the Shavante (1965) as well as the sections on hunting in other works on the Gê. Harner provides a fine description of the use of blowguns in hunting (1972:55–60). Many South American natives also use a variety of traps, snares, and deadfalls to procure animals, and Cooper has provided a survey of such use (1949b:265–273), as has Rydén (1950).

If there is considerable variation in hunting practices in South America, there is probably still more variation in beliefs associated with hunting. In spite of the fact that hunting provides, in general, only a small proportion of the food supply for any given group, it tends to have an importance in the minds of the people completely out of proportion to its nutritive contribution, or even to the amount of time spent in the activity (see, for example, Maybury-Lewis 1967:35–36). Hunting also often confers considerable prestige and is of general interest to the group, frequently being associated with much magico-religious belief.

Parallel to the belief that agricultural plots are shifted because of soil exhaustion, is the belief that native groups frequently clean out the game in a given area and thus must move. Personal observation among the Wachipaeri in eastern Peru as well as conversations with a number of colleagues have led me to believe that the game exhaustion factor may be overemphasized. Denevan quotes the Campa as citing depletion of game as a reason for moving. On the other hand, while Harner notes a marked difference between areas that had been hunted and those that had not, he does not mention severe depletion of game, but rather states: "virtually all of the Jívaro territory has been hunted efficiently for a long period of time, with the result that game is not as abundant as in regions unoccupied by the Indians" (1972:56). As is true of soil conditions, faunal abundance doubtless varies considerably from one area to another. Data on such variation are almost nonexistent. Certainly there are still many groups who are doing very well by hunting.

For further information on the Amahuaca, in addition to that cited in this article, see the selection by Dole on endocannibalism.

11   ROBERT L. CARNEIRO

Hunting and Hunting Magic Among the Amahuaca of the Peruvian Montaña[1]

The Amahuaca Indians inhabit the heavily forested region between the Ucayali and upper Juruá and Purús rivers in Eastern Peru. At its greatest extent their territory encompassed perhaps 20,000 square miles (see map in Carneiro 1962:29), but today it has diminished to about a quarter of that size. The

Reprinted by permission of the author and publisher from *Ethnology*, vol. 9, no. 4 (1970), pp. 331–341.

population of the Amahuaca, estimated at 6,000 to 9,000 around 1900 (Hassel 1905:31), is today no more than about 500. Population density, formerly something like one person per two or three square miles, had diminished at the time of field work in 1960–61 to roughly one person for every eight or ten square miles.

Amahuaca settlements are small. About fifteen persons, occupying three or four houses, form the average community. Settlements are located on or near small streams, usually several hours' walking distance apart. Each community is completely autonomous economically as well as politically. Indeed, the same might almost be said of each nuclear or extended family within a community. There are no headmen or shamans, no kin groups larger than the extended family, and very little ceremonialism. All told, Amahuaca social organization is exceedingly simple.

Feuding among Amahuaca communities is very common, and sometimes they fight with their traditional enemies, the Yaminahua. The result is that an Amahuaca settlement is often on the alert against the possibility of attack.

Subsistence is divided almost equally between hunting and horticulture. To be more precise, I would say that about 50 per cent of the food consumed by the Amahuaca is derived from horticulture and 40 per cent from hunting, with the rest coming from fishing and gathering. Although hunting is thus not quite half of subsistence, it nevertheless plays a very important role in determining the small size of Amahuaca local groups, their location, and the frequency with which they are moved, which is about once every year or two.

The habitat of the Amahuaca is an unbroken expanse of tropical rainforest. There are no grasslands anywhere, and even abandoned garden plots revert directly to secondary forest without passing through an intermediate grass stage. The terrain consists of a series of rugged hills and ridges, often rising 200 or 300 feet above the adjacent streams. The heart of the Amahuaca territory is the height of land between the Ucayali and Juruá and Purús river systems. Here the headwater tributaries are born, and as they flow out of this area, are still narrow and shallow. The fish in these streams are small enough in size and few enough in number to make fishing an almost negligible part of subsistence. The primary source of animal protein is hunting, and the forests of the region are well stocked with game.

Meat is an important part of the Amahuaca diet, and no meal is considered really complete without it. A man who is a good provider sees to it that his household never lacks for meat.

Every man is a hunter, and every good hunter enjoys the chase. Such a man may go hunting even when there is still meat at home. Those not so skilled go less often, but because meat is commonly shared among all families in a community no one is without it for long.

The game found in the surrounding forests is abundant and varied. No single species predominates. Being generalized hunters, the Amahuaca seek out and kill most species of mammals in the area. These include monkeys of several kinds, deer, tapir, peccaries (both collared and white-lipped), agoutis, pacas, capybaras, anteaters, armadillos, sloths, porcupines, coatis, and squirrels. Most species of large game birds are hunted, including curassows and partridges. Caimans, lizards, and turtles are also taken.

The only class of animals not eaten by the Amahuaca are carnivores, including jaguars, pumas, ocelots, jaguarundis, tayras, otters, and various types of wolves or wild dogs. A few noncarnivorous animals are also avoided as food, principally giant armadillos, silky anteaters, raccoons, rabbits, opossums, bats, and mice. Other animals not eaten include snakes, vultures and eagles, and a number of smaller birds.

According to Robert L. Russell of the Summer Institute of Linguistics, who has lived in close contact with the Amahuaca for a number of years, the order of importance of game animals in terms of the weight of meat derived from them is as follows: (1) tapir, (2) howler monkey, (3) spider monkey, (4) deer, (5) collared peccary, (6) paca, (7) cebus monkey, (8) paujil (wattled curassow), (9) guan, (10) pucacunga (bare-faced curassow), and (11) agouti. As far as taste is concerned, the two kinds of game most favored by the Amahuaca are tapir and spider monkey. Despite such dietary preferences, however, it is difficult to predict what a day's hunt will bring. For example, on one occasion two brothers living in adjacent houses shot two tapirs in three days but went several weeks before killing another one.

The hunting technology of the Amahuaca is very simple. The bow and arrow constitutes their principal weapon, and almost their only one. Spears and blowguns are lacking, as are snares, nooses, pitfalls, deadfalls, and any kind of hunting traps or nets. Except on rare occasions when a number of men may co-operate in attacking a passing herd of white-lipped peccaries, there is no collective hunting.

The bow and arrow is the inseparable companion of every Amahuaca man. Not only is it the means of obtaining much of his food, but it is also his principal weapon of attack or defense in a frequently hostile environment. Rarely does a man so much as leave his house without taking his bow and arrows with him. And in the hands of an Amahuaca, trained from childhood in its use, the bow and arrow becomes a very effective weapon.

The stave of an Amahuaca bow is made from the wood of the *pihuayo* or peach palm (*Guilielma speciosa*). This is the strongest and most resilient of the palms in the region, and probably equal or superior to any bow wood available in Amazonia.[2] The average length of Amahuaca bows is between 6 and 6½ feet, but occasionally they are up to a foot longer.

The bowstring is made from the inner bark fibers of the *setico* tree (*Cecropia leucocoma*), twined by the hunter on his thigh.[3] In total length a bowstring may be 15 feet or more, the extra length being wrapped around the upper limb of the bow to use as a spare in case the bowstring should break. The Amahuaca always keep their bows strung, ready to use. The resiliency of *pihuayo* wood is such that it loses little of its "cast" even when kept under continuous tension for a long time.

Some men wrap a thin strip of smooth, flattish bark from a vine around the bowstave in order to protect the bow hand from the fine slivers which, with repeated flexing, sometimes separate from the bow.

Arrows are somewhat over 5 feet in length. The shaft of the arrow is made from the long straight flower stem of the cane *Gynerium saggitatum*.[4] Into the soft pithy center of this cane is driven a foreshaft of hard wood, usually *pihuayo*. The most common type of point attached to this foreshaft is made from bamboo. It is lanceolate in shape and some 12 to 15 inches long. As these arrow points are dulled or broken in use, they are resharpened, and an old point may have been trimmed down until it is no longer than 5 or 6 inches. While designed especially for use against large game, such as tapir, deer, and peccaries, bamboo points are commonly used against game of any size.

Bamboo, which has a thin siliceous layer on the outside, takes a fine cutting edge and a very sharp point. Thus an arrow with such a point has great penetrating power.[5] Sometimes, however, the sides of a bamboo point are not left smooth, but are notched to make it more difficult for an animal to shake itself free of the arrow.

A less common type of arrow point consists of a somewhat longer *pihuayo* wood foreshaft, self-barbed, and sharpened to a point. A sliver of monkey bone, sharpened at each end, may sometimes be attached at an angle to the tip of the foreshaft. Arrows of these two types are designed for use against smaller game—monkeys, birds, rodents, etc. Blunt-headed wooden arrow points are occasionally made for shooting birds. Their advantage is that they do less damage to the bird's plumage, and are not so likely to stick in the trees.

The Amahuaca do not poison their arrows. They do, however, apply a thin layer of an orange-colored resin—apparently a form of copal—to their bamboo points. Although the Amahuaca believe that this resin will cause a wounded animal to die faster, it seems in fact to be more of an irritant than an actual poison.

Arrow feathers are attached only at their ends,[6] and are applied with a slight spiral so that the arrow rotates in flight, thus increasing its stability.

A hunter draws his bow to a point well behind his ear, and at full draw the average bow pulls 60 to 75 pounds. This relatively heavy bow weight, combined with a sharp, tapering bamboo blade, can send an arrow entirely through an animal.

Hunting is a year-round activity. During the dry season, when a man spends a good deal of time clearing and planting his garden plot, he hunts less frequently, but during the rainy season, when no such chores occupy his time, he goes hunting about every second or third day. Some men prefer to hunt alone, but two men, especially brothers or a father and son, may often hunt together. Generally, though, no more than three men comprise a hunting party, since more than this are said to frighten the game. Rarely, a man may go into the forest with his wife, spending the day hunting while she collects fruits, nuts, or other forest products.

Hunters leave early in the morning, often before six o'clock, to take full advantage of the daylight hours. If he sees little game, a man may spend the entire day looking, returning home around dusk. Even if successful, a hunter may stay out a good part of the day, killing as much game as he can before returning. Some men go hunting without breakfast and take no food with them, feeling that the added incentive of hunger will help them make an early kill. Others, however, take a little food with them in a small carrying basket, or perhaps wrapped in a leaf.

Sometimes a man may set out to hunt a particular kind of game, especially tapir or spider monkey, because these are the animals whose flesh is most prized. Tapirs may also be hunted for their fat, which is mixed with achiote (*Bixa orellana*) for body painting during feasts. Similarly, a man may hunt agoutis or pacas expressly for their chisel-like incisors. In such instances, the hunter heads toward an area of the forest where he has reason to think these animals are most likely to be found. When hoping to kill a tapir, for example, an Amahuaca often heads for the Curiuja River, an area where there is less hunting and therefore more game of every sort. On a relatively long trip like this a hunter may spend the night in the forest and return home the next day. He does not encumber himself by taking along his hammock, but, when night overtakes him, makes himself a sleeping mat out of palm leaves and erects a simple shelter.

The Amahuaca do not have defined territories, and a man may hunt in any area of the forest, even if it is close to another settlement, without asking permission and without being considered guilty of trespass. Because Amahuaca communities are so small, so widely scattered, and so frequently moved, there is little reason for them to demarcate a territory precisely, or to try to keep others from hunting in it.

When a hunter sets out, he usually avoids an area recently hunted by someone else, since the game there may have been shot or driven away. A network of hunting trails fans out from each settlement, and hunters follow these trails, at least at first. Often the hunter makes a circuit, leaving by one trail and returning by another, thus seeing more of the forest and increasing his chances of finding game.

After following a trail or a stream bed for awhile, a hunter may then cut across to another trail or stream. He is always on the alert, listening for animals, watching for movements of the undergrowth or of branches which may reveal their presence. If he hears the cry or the movement of an animal, he hurries toward it, yet moving carefully and taking advantage of the natural cover in order to conceal his presence. Whenever possible, he stays downwind of the animal.

Disguises are never worn in hunting, but a man may occasionally make some attempt at camouflage by sprinkling or smearing himself with the juice of the huito fruit (*Genipa americana*). When exposed to the air for an hour or two, the juice of this fruit turns black, and the mottled pattern formed on his body renders him less conspicuous. To cover up his scent a hunter often rubs aromatic leaves, such as vanilla, over his body, or places these leaves under his belt.

Although an Amahuaca is a good marksman with bow and arrow, what makes him an outstanding hunter is not so much his archery as his skill in tracking game and in working in close enough for a good shot. Every significant detail of the life habits of game animals is part of an Amahuaca hunter's knowledge. He knows the sound of their cries, what food they eat, and what their excrement looks like. He can detect the presence of peccaries or howler monkeys by their sharp scent, and can identify spider monkeys by the characteristic noise they make while eating fruit in the trees. From the tooth marks on a fruit he can tell what animal has been feeding on it, and approximately when it left.

If a hunter comes upon the trail of an animal, and it is fresh enough, he will follow it. The freshness of a set of tracks is gauged not only by how wet it is but also by the amount of dust and debris that has accumulated on it. On soft ground a man can tell not only what animal's tracks he is seeing, but also how large it was, how fast it was moving, and how long ago it went by.

The tracks of virtually every game animal are readily distinguished. During one hunting trip on which I accompanied two hunters I had pointed out to me the tracks of an armadillo, a raccoon, a deer, an agouti, a collared peccary, a paca, a giant armadillo, an otter, a tapir, a caiman, and an oriole.

If animal tracks are old, or if the ground is hard and the tracks are not readily visible, a hunter may still be able to detect the recent presence of game. He scans the forest floor for bits of fruit or fresh excrement, and studies the displacement of leaves and twigs. From the amount of exudation on a broken twig, for example, a hunter can judge how long ago an animal passed by.

When a hunter hears an animal, he attempts to fix its location more precisely by imitating its cry and trying to get it to respond.[7] Monkeys may reply by chattering, and a tapir by giving its shrill whistle. A deer may paw the ground. In any case, the animal's response enables the hunter to ascertain its position more exactly and thus to approach closer. The hunter may even succeed in drawing a curious animal close to him. For example, should a hunter chance upon some young, such as a fawn or a baby peccary, he will seize it, knowing that its plaintive cry is likely to bring the mother within arrow range.

The whole purpose of tracking and mimicry is to allow the hunter to approach as near as possible before shooting. Long distance shots are avoided, not only because marksmanship decreases with distance, but also because the intervening foliage can easily deflect an arrow. Generally, a hunter tries to close to within 40 feet or less before shooting. When he finally looses an arrow, he aims for a vital spot if he can, often just behind the rib cage. A bamboo point has such a long cutting edge that it may sever many blood vessels and cause considerable bleeding. If wounded by a well-placed arrow, an animal may be unable to travel far before collapsing. Barbed arrows do less cutting, but, lodging in the animal more securely, they help slow it down by rubbing or catching against the brush as it attempts to flee.

If two or three men are hunting together, they generally separate when they hear an animal and attempt to close in on it from opposite sides. The first one to shoot an arrow at the animal may be allowed to finish it off. But if it appears likely that the animal is about to escape, his companions shoot too.

As mentioned earlier, the only occasion when a number of men co-operate in hunting is when a herd of white-lipped peccaries is detected near the settlement. Unlike collared peccaries, which travel singly or in pairs, white-lipped peccaries travel in herds of up to 100. A group of hunters may be able to kill as many as ten peccaries before the rest take flight. A lone hunter coming upon a herd of feeding peccaries from the downwind side, approaches them stealthily and attempts to kill one or two before the others discover his presence. Once alerted, the peccaries either flee or charge. Because of their sharp tusks and their compact ranks, their charge is dangerous, and a hunter caught in their path can save himself only by climbing a tree.

The Amahuaca have dogs, and these are an important asset in hunting.[8] By catching the scent of animals and following their spoor, dogs enable the hunter to locate more game than he could by himself. Dogs are also very helpful in locating animals living in burrows or hollow tree trunks. Besides finding game, dogs also help in killing it by bringing it to bay, or by so annoying an animal that it stops to bite or snarl at his pursuers, thus allowing the hunter to catch up with it.

The Amahuaca erect hunting blinds at places where animals come to drink, or where the ripe fruit of a tree are falling, or some other place which game is likely to frequent. Blinds are sometimes also built near garden plots if agoutis or deer or other predators have been eating the crops. They are made by inserting the butt ends of four or more palm leaves into the ground, and drawing together and tying the upper ends. Here and there the leaflets are separated to provide peepholes. A blind is about 5 feet in diameter and tall enough to allow a man to stand inside.

Sometimes a man builds a blind in the trees to hunt monkeys, such as red howlers, which frequent the higher branches and are not easily seen from the ground. Or a hunter may simply climb a tree to a vantage point above a passing troop of monkeys and shoot down on them. In this way he may manage to shoot two or three monkeys before the rest realize what is happening. Tree climbing is usually done by means of a climbing ring made by coiling a length of thin vine. The ring thus formed is placed around the insteps, and permits the climber to brace his feet against opposite sides of a small tree, as he reaches up to take a firm handhold. Once he has his new hold, he then pulls his feet up behind him.

A few other hunting techniques used by the Amahuaca may be mentioned. In hunting tapirs, use is sometimes made of a palm-wood sword up to four feet long with sharp edges tapering to a fine point. A cornered tapir is stabbed with such a sword.

Clubbing is the usual way to kill an armadillo, since its carapace is hard enough to ward off an arrow. Clubs may also be used against white-lipped peccaries, caimans, and agoutis.

Burrowing animals like armadillos or agoutis may be lured out of their holes with cries, or smoked out with dry palm leaves which have been ignited. If this fails, one end of the burrow may be stopped up and the animal dug out.

To bring back the game he has killed a hunter accommodates it in a palm-leaf basket which he braids on the spot and carries on his back by means of a tumpline. Smaller game, like monkeys, is brought back whole, but larger game may be cut up for easier carrying. The two feet on each side of a deer may be tied together, the hunter's arms inserted through the loops thus formed, and the animal carried home like a knapsack.

Tapirs, which may weigh as much as 500 or 600 pounds, are naturally too large to bring back in one trip. A hunter will cut up a tapir, remove the viscera and other internal organs, and carry these and as much of the meat as he can back to the house. The parts of the animal left behind to be retrieved the next day must be carefully protected from scavengers. Leaves are usually placed over them, weighted down with sticks, and then covered with dirt. This prevents jaguars and other carnivores from catching the scent.[9]

That evening, when he is back at the settlement, or early next morning, the hunter hoots in a conventional way to inform the rest of the men that he has shot a tapir and is going to retrieve it. This is an invitation to others to come along, and those who accompany him are allowed to keep the portions of the carcass they bring back. When the men go out to retrieve a tapir, their womenfolk spend a good part of the day gathering firewood and making a babracot on which to roast the meat.

A lone hunter, returning from the forest, may appear at his house sad-eyed and empty-handed, as if he had had no luck. But this is often a deception, and a carrying basket full of meat may at that moment be sitting by the trail just outside ...e clearing. When the hunter finally tells his wife about it, she goes to fetch it. It is considered impolite to ask a hunter who has just returned from the forest what success he has had, for if he has caught nothing, he is embarrassed, and the Amahuaca never embarrass one another.

Large game, even if brought back by the hunter unaided, is often shared with other families. Smaller game, however, is consumed by the hunter's family alone. A tapir may provide meat enough for a week, even if shared. To preserve it that long the meat is roasted over a slow fire until thoroughly dry.

There are no rules for the distribution of game. No specific portion of the animal is reserved for the hunter or for particular kinsmen.

HUNTING MAGIC

It has often been observed that supernaturalism tends to surround those activities which are either uncertain or hazardous or both, while, conversely, little or no supernaturalism accompanies those spheres of life where security and predictability prevail.[10] The Amahuaca certainly bear out this generalization. Almost no supernaturalism is connected with horticulture, which yields very abundantly and reliably. On the other hand, hunting, whose outcome is never certain, and often involves an element of personal danger, is attended by considerable supernaturalism.

Not all aspects of Amahuaca hunting are, however, permeated with magical practices. For example, propitiation of the spirits of game animals, so prominent a feature in hunting among North American Indians, does not occur among the Amahuaca. Only a few game animals are thought to have spirits, and these are never propitiated, either before or after the animals are killed.[11] Nor is any attempt made to secure the assistance of animal spirits in hunting.

The Amahuaca do not have totem animals, and do not prohibit the killing of any animal, whether it is eaten or not. It is true that certain animals—especially carnivorous ones—are not eaten, but the failure to eat such animals appears to derive from a general repugnance to their eating habits rather than from an explicit religious prohibition.[12] Vultures, for example, are considered unfit to eat "because they eat rotten things."

Also absent from Amahuaca hunting magic are rituals designed to make animals increase in numbers. The depletion of game in an area is recognized as being the result of overhunting, and the only remedy sought is the purely rational one of moving the settlement to another part of the forest.

Amahuaca supernaturalism, as it relates to hunting, can best be summarized by saying that it is positive rather than negative. There is little or nothing that a hunter must not do to have success in hunting, but there are many things he can and does do. Positive kinds of hunting magic vary considerably. Some of it acts on the hunter himself, or on his weapons, helping him to find game sooner, to see more of it, or to make his arrow fly truer. Other hunting magic acts on the game, making animals "tamer" so they can be seen and shot more readily. Some of these practices may now be examined.

Smearing blood from an animal on the bowstring or bowstave is thought to make the bow more effective against other animals of that species. This is done especially with a new bow, or with blood from the first animal of that species killed with the bow. Arrows as well as bows may be magically treated. A man may run the further end of his arrow through the body of an animal several times, smearing it with blood and thus making it shoot straighter.[13] Some hunters say that the blood of certain animals—a small lizard, for example—is particularly effective in this respect.

The blood of an animal may also be applied to the hunter's own body. It is common for a boy who is beginning to hunt to have the blood of a tapir rubbed over his body so he will turn out to be a successful hunter. Some informants reported that the blood of the tapir, peccary, agouti and spider monkey was occasionally drunk for better luck in hunting these animals.[14]

Plants of various sorts also figure in hunting magic. Certain kinds of leaves are often wrapped around the bowstave or tucked under a hunter's belt for luck. Herbal infusions are also employed. Most common among these is *kumbra ra'o* (called *chiricsanago* in Peruvian jungle Spanish), which appears to come from a species of *Rauwolfia*. The roots of the plant are scraped into water, which is then heated almost to boiling. After drinking this potion a man becomes dizzy and his body feels cold, "as if it had rained on you," one informant said. After taking it, one's aim improves and game animals become "tame," allowing themselves to be easily killed. Various kinds of *kumba ra'o* are specific for particular species of animal.

Another class of plants used in hunting magic are called *sako* in Amahuaca and *piripiri* in jungle Spanish. Most of these appear to be sedges of the genus *Cyperus*. The leaves are crushed in water and smeared on the arms and wrists. Or the infusion may be boiled and applied to the body. As with *kumba ra'o*, there are *piripiri* plants specific to various game animals. *Piripiri* is said to enable a man to see a lot of game.

Still another type of hunting magic involves drinking the excrement of the boa constrictor. Picking at certain scales on the tail markings of the boa is also thought to be magically effective. In addition, an infusion made by boiling hawk's talons may be smeared on the hands and wrists of a boy or young man to make him a better hunter. The talons themselves may be scraped along the back of the hands until blood is drawn, "so that no spider monkey will escape."

Strips of inner bark from a tree with a very caustic sap are occasionally tied around a boy's wrists or forearms, burning a ring around the arm which remains as a permanent scar. This is done so that, again, "no animal will escape." During one hunting trip I observed a man crush the leaves of a certain plant in his upraised hands and allow the caustic juice to trickle down the inside of his arms to the biceps. This, he said, would bring him luck in hunting spider monkeys.

Stronger forms of magic are sometimes resorted to, especially if a hunter has had several unsuccessful hunting trips in succession. He may cut a wasps' nest from a tree and stand holding it, allowing himself to be stung by the wasps. If the pain becomes unbearable, he runs through the forest, still carrying the nest, so that fewer wasps will sting him. For the next two or three days he may be very ill and badly swollen from the effect of the stings, but he is sure to emerge from the ordeal a better hunter.[15]

But the strongest hunting magic of all is for a man to inoculate himself with the very toxic secretion of a small frog which the Amahuaca call *kambó*.[16] This secretion is scraped off the back of the frog with a stick. Then, taking a live brand, a man burns himself in several places on the arms or chest, and rubs this secretion into the burns. Within a short time he becomes violently ill, suffering uncontrollable vomiting and diarrhea. For the next three days, while under the influence of the toxin, he has vivid hallucinations which are regarded as supernatural experiences.[17] When he finally recovers, he is convinced that his hunting is bound to improve.

Even dogs are treated magically. To enable a dog to find land turtles, an infusion from a certain *piripiri* plant may be given to it to drink or put into its nose or eyes. The owner of a dog which is no longer hunting well attempts to sharpen its scent by putting tapir dung, pepper juice, or a paste of ants' nest up the dog's nostrils. A poor hunting dog may even have its tail docked, to see if this will help.

SUMMARY

Although the Amahuaca have practiced horticulture for centuries, they continue to rely heavily on hunting in their subsistence. The dense forest in which they live provides game in variety and abundance. Highly skilled in the use of the bow and arrow and in tracking and stalking animals, the Amahuaca are very proficient hunters. But not content with their physical skill alone, they attempt to improve their hunting by magical means. The effect of this magic, as the hunter sees it, is, on the one hand, to enhance his own ability and, on the other, to increase the susceptibility of the game.

NOTES

1. Some of the data incorporated into this paper were very kindly provided by Mr. Robert L. Russell of the Summer Institute of Linguistics, who has worked among the Amahuaca for a number of years. However, Mr. Russell is in no way responsible for any errors of fact that may appear here.

2. In the ethnographic literature for the Montaña one often finds the statement that bows are made of "chonta" palm. This term is a rather indefinite one. It is sometimes applied to *Guilielma speciosa,* but also to palms of the genus *Bactris,* and, by popular writers, to almost any palm.

3. *Cecropia* bast fiber, which is very strong, appears to be the favorite material for the manufacture of bowstrings among Amazonian tribes generally.

4. This type of cane grows wild in the low marshy areas bordering the Urubamba River, but not in the hilly regions where the Amahuaca live. However, the Amahuaca plant *Gynerium* in their gardens, or in special plots, especially for the arrow cane. When the cane flowers, the long straight flower stems are removed and stored in barkcloth cylinders suspended from the roof of the house until needed.

5. Even when propelled by only the force of gravity an arrow can penetrate deeply. One Amahuaca was said to have been killed when his own arrow, falling out of a tree as he attempted to retrieve it, pierced his neck and entered his chest cavity. Two other men whom I knew each bore a couple of scars on their bodies where they had been wounded by their own arrows in the same manner.

6. This is the so-called "bridge feathering," typical of the tribes of the Ucayali basin. Some Amahuaca had arrows showing "Peruvian cemented feathering," in which the feathers are secured in place by being wrapped along their entire length with cotton thread, and then cemented with beeswax. The Amahuaca appear to have learned this type of feathering from the Yaminahua to the east.

7. Once, when I asked a man to demonstrate the art of imitating animal cries, he proceeded to imitate no fewer than 35 different animals, one after another.

8. The dog may well be post-Columbian among the Amahuaca, as it seems to be among most Amazonian tribes. There is little direct evidence for this, but the Amahuaca do call the dog *indo,* the same term they use for jaguar.

9. If an animal is killed early in the hunt its carcass may be placed in a stream to retard spoilage until the hunter is ready to return and retrieve it.

10. " . . . supernaturalism varies inversely with the extent and effectiveness of naturalistic control. In activities where man has little actual control, or where chance and circumstances play a prominent part . . . recourse to supernaturalism is great. In activities where man's control is extensive and effective . . . resort to supernaturalism will tend to be meager and perhaps only perfunctory" (White 1959:272). See also Linton (1936:429–431), Malinowski (1954:30–31), and Oberg (ms:151).

11. For an account of Amahuaca spirit beliefs see Carneiro (1964a).

12. A number of Amazonian tribes do not eat deer because they believe it to be the ultimate repository of human souls. The Amahuaca have no such belief.

13. One Amahuaca, on the island of Chumichinía in the Ucayali River, told me that if a man had sexual relations before going hunting his arrow would miss its mark. This belief, however, seems to have been derived from the neighboring Conibo or Campa, and is absent among the Amahuaca on the upper Inuya. There, a man may have sexual relations with his wife even while he is out hunting with her in the forest. Moreover, the behavior of women who remain at home while their husbands are out hunting is in no way restricted.

14. The Amahuaca sometimes drink human blood, too, but not as part of hunting magic. It is usually done by the close female relative of a man who has been wounded by an animal or an arrow. The blood may be drunk directly from the wound, or collected in a small bowl and drunk from this. The practice is considered therapeutic for the injured man.

15. I have also seen a hunter allow himself to be stung by ants he encountered on the trail in the forest, for the same purpose.

16. I was not able to identify this frog, but it may be related to the *kokoi* frog, *Phyllobates bicolor* (or *Dendrobates tinctorius*) of Colombia, whose secretion is used by the Chocó Indians to poison their blowgun darts (Wassén 1935:99–100; 1957:78–81). *Kokoi* poison has recently been discovered to be the most toxic natural substance known (Anonymous 1965:112).

17. The Amahuaca also drink *ayahuasca* (*Banisteriopsis caapi*) to induce spirit visions, but do not do so to assist them in hunting.

The rivers of South America provide a wealth of potential food. This food occurs not only in the form of fish, but also turtles and turtle eggs, caimans, and aquatic mammals such as the dolphin and manatee, although the former is seldom eaten. Many groups settled along productive rivers derive almost all their meat protein from fishing and do little hunting (cf. Goldman 1963:53–56). As is true with all subsistence pursuits, the rivers are more productive at certain times than at others. The European invasion of South America has been especially destructive of riverine resources. Major sources of food were river turtles and their eggs that were gathered in tremendous quantities (see Gilmore 1950:400–405). Both turtles and eggs could be stored, many groups keeping the turtles penned up for considerable periods of time, eating one whenever they felt like it. The European conquest brought with it intensive exploitation of turtle eggs for the oil they contained. Almost any account of travel through the Amazon at the proper season until late in the nineteenth century contains a description of crews of men shoveling up thousands of turtle eggs and processing them for the oil at any sand bar where they were to be found. Such wholesale destruction must eventually destroy even the most prolific species, and the species of turtle that have been exploited are now in danger of extinction. Such depletion of a major food source cannot but have had drastic effects on the native inhabitants who were accustomed to relying on this resource. In the same way the manatee has been hounded almost to extinction, also for oil. The caiman, described at one time as virtually lining the river banks, has also been sorely reduced in numbers, largely for its hide. Thus, of the major riverine resources available to the natives prior to the advent of the Europeans, only fish remain in any quantity, and of course, these too are being overexploited. The use of fish poison by those whose interest is a big haul now, not plenty of fish for one's entire lifetime, the use of dynamite in fishing, and pollution are slowly but surely reducing the fish population. Of the riverine resources just mentioned, fish are the only ones that are available in greater or lesser supply in all the rivers of the continent (with the possible exception of some of the very high Andean rivers).

This selection has been excerpted from a monograph-length study of the Barama River Carib. Reading of the entire study will provide the framework necessary to understand the importance of fishing in this culture. For more recent studies on other Carib groups in the Guianas see Hurault on the Wayana (1968), Fock (1963) and Yde (1965) on the Waiwai and Kloos (1971) on the Maroni River Caribs.

12 JOHN GILLIN

Barama River Carib Fishing

European fish hooks are obtained in trade. If these are unavailable, hooks are made from common pins or from a certain thorny bush of the jungle. Fish rods of yarriyarri (*Anaxagorea* sp.) are the most common; the line is made of kraua fibre. Rod fishing is most commonly done from korials, although frequently little boys amuse themselves by fishing with a rod from the bank. Each night a man, if his settlement is near the river, puts out a set line, to which are attached several hooks. These set lines are stretched across the river, fastened at either end to a stake of yarriyarri set in the water near the shore. Usually each hook has to be visited in a korial, although some more ingenious members of the tribe, perhaps through outside suggestion, have rigged up pulley arrangements at the opposite shore so that the line can be set and pulled in by a man standing on the bank.

Fish are also shot with arrows . . . especially made for the purpose. This seems to be a method very rarely used at the present time, and during my sojourn in the Carib country I saw it employed only twice. The men say that fish shooting is difficult because of the vegetable stain in the water which reduces visibility, and is only effective near rocks where the marksman can gain a steady perch high enough above the water to see the game.

The most productive fishing method is poisoning. The haiari root (? *Lonchocarpus* sp.) is the most generally used poison on the Barama. Two varieties are recognized, the "black haiari" (? *L. densiflorus*) and the "white haiari" (? *L. rufescens*). The former is the most commonly found and oftenest used for fish poisoning. The two other fish poisons generally used in the Barama country are konami (? *Clibadium* sp.) and wa'u (Creole, mora balli). Other poisons used in the Guianas are mentioned by Roth, but I have failed to find evidence of their use in this area.

The river itself, as well as practically all of its tributary creeks, is regularly poisoned, although I understand that this practice is forbidden by colonial law because of the devastating effect which it is supposed to have on the fish supply. As one proceeds up the Barama one is impressed by the fact that across the mouth of almost every creek stands a wickerwork fence of nibi (a bush plant which is also used in making basketry), a sure sign that the creek has been poisoned, because the fence has been placed there to catch the dead or stupefied fish as they float downstream under the influence of the poison. When it is decided to poison a creek or river, the whole settlement usually turns out and the affair is made a sort of picnic or field day. The women bring supplies of cassava bread and peppers, and build fires near the site of the poisoning for the purpose of cooking the fish, part of

Reprinted by permission of the author and the Peabody Museum from "The Barama River Caribs of British Guiana," in *Papers of the Peabody Museum of American Archaeology and Ethnology,* vol. 14, no. 2 (Harvard University, 1936), pp. 10–14.

the catch being eaten as part of the picnic lunch. Usually the men have preceded the women to the spot early in the morning, built a fence across the water downstream and collected a supply of haiari root from which they have removed the bark and which they have split into shreds. Each man has also cut a club or beater of yarriyarri wood two and one-half to three feet long, with a smooth handle fitted to the hand and a head of larger diameter. They bring the shredded haiari and the clubs to a point in the stream where semi-submerged logs or rocks arise from the water, which, below this point, must be relatively quiet and sluggish so that the poison is not too quickly borne away. Each man takes an armful of haiari and his club and chooses a suitable rock or log on which to pound the haiari, while he stands in the water alongside. In the meantime the women and children have deployed downstream, armed with cutlasses and knives with which to kill the stupefied fish. Each man then takes a small bundle of his haiari root and begins systematically to pound it on the rock or log which he has chosen, dipping it frequently into the water to free the juice until the haiari is exhausted of its poison. The juice when first freed has a whitish milky appearance which clouds the water. It seems to be heavier than the water itself and turns a rusty red with age. In the shallows of the stream which has recently been poisoned one sees the reddish viscid remnant of the haiari which has collected on the bottom. There seems to be some mystery concerning the effects of the poison on the fish and the opinion among the Caribs is divided as to whether the haiari would actually kill fish or merely stun them. They become sluggish and tend to float belly upward on the surface, but I have noticed that a fish "poisoned" by haiari, even when apparently dead, quickly revives when put into fresh unpoisoned water. On the other hand, the Indians also use the juice of the haiari to poison the ground around the roots of the tobacco plants, in the belief that it poisons the root grubs which kill the plants.[1]

The women and children, along the banks or in the water, kill the apparently stupefied fish by slashing them with their cutlasses and knives. The fish are then put in carrying baskets and carried to the picnic spot. For the picnic lunch the smallest specimens only are eaten, usually being roasted over the fire on the ends of fresh green sticks, in the same way in which we roast picnic frankfurters. The small fish, from which the heads and scales have not been removed, are then put with a small pepper into a sort of sandwich of cassava bread and eaten with much relish and gay talk, punctuated by the necessity of inserting the fingers in the mouth to remove those bones which cannot be chewed and swallowed. The larger fish are deprived of their scales with the help of a piece of wood which has been sharpened to a chisel edge. Then they are disembowelled, decapitated, and split sagittally along the back without removing the vertebrae or other bones. They are placed in carrying baskets with moist leaves and carried back to the settlement. If the people have a supply of trade salt, a number of slits are made parallel to the ribs and the meat is rubbed thoroughly with salt and placed out in the sun to dry. If there is no salt the meat is slit in the same way and dried over a babracot.

The wa'u poison is hacked into small chips and these are thrown into the water. Only the heart of the tree is used. The chips are thrown into the water in the evening, several hours being required for the poison to take effect. The next morning the dead fish may be collected. The wa'u is apparently less successful than haiari and is only used in the absence of the latter.

The poison made from konami is called sokoi. The konami leaf is pounded into a mash which is mixed with grated, unsqueezed, bitter cassava, and baked into small balls which are dropped into the water where they are swallowed by the fish. A fish which has been gullible enough to swallow this fraud soon loses control and floats to the surface where it is captured by the fisherman.

I did not observe nor hear of the use of fish traps or of nets, although these appliances are reported from other parts of the colony.

The fish most commonly used for food are the haimara (*Hoplias macrophthalmus*), huri (*Hoplias malabaricus*), yarrau (*Hypostoma* sp.), low-low (*Silurus* sp.), pirai (*Pygocentrus*), cartabak (*?Tetragonopterus*). The moracot, so well known for its fighting tendencies and flavor in other parts of the colony, is found only in the tidewater portions of the Barama. Hook baits include spiders, calabash pap, cassava bread, and various worms.

Among other food products obtained from the streams are sting-ray (caught on hooks and tasting somewhat like tripe when cooked), small periwinkles or "snails" of two sizes called respectively mari (small) and kue (large), frog eggs.

NOTES

1. See Roark (1933): "Rotenone, $C_{23} H_{22} O_6$, a colorless, odorless, crystalline constituent of certain tropical fish-poison plants, is thirty times as toxic as lead arsenate as a stomach poison to silkworm, fifteen times as toxic as nicotine as a contact insecticide upon bean aphids, and twenty-five times as toxic as potassium cyanide to goldfish, and yet is harmless to birds and mammals eating it. . . . Rotenone is a constituent of the following plants, comprising seven genera of the bean family (Fabaceae or Leguminosae): *Cracca cinerea, C. virginiana, Derris Chinensis, D. elliptica, D. malaccensis, D. polyantha, D. uliginosa, Lonchocarpus nicou* (cube), *Lonchocarpus* sp. (haiari), *L. chrysophylus* (?) (Nekoe), *Millettia, Mundules suberosa, Ormacarpum, Spatholobus roxburghii.* . . . Rotenone is now known to be harmless to mammals when taken by mouth, but many early writers on derris spoke of its dangerous poisonous qualities. . . . Buckingham in 1930 made numerous tests on dogs, cats, pigs, sheep, cows, chickens with rotenone and with the ether extract of derris. He concluded that, when administered by mouth, pure rotenone produced no visible effects in dogs, pigs, or sheep in doses (for dogs) up to one grain per pound of body weight and expressed the opinion that even larger doses would be harmless." Roark summarizes other experiments showing the non-toxic effects of rotenone on mammals, concluded that rotenone, the poisonous principle of haiari, is a stomach poison, although the physiological effects are not described. On this subject see also Killip and Smith (1930, 1931) and Roark (1931).

III RELATIONSHIPS WITH ONE'S OWN KIND

The papers in this section relate to interaction in several different spheres of culture. Although both Sorensen and Roth deal with extensive extra-tribal contacts, these are presented from quite different viewpoints. Sorensen discusses the effects of extensive trading and linguistic exogamy on language and the formation of multilingualism, as well as the effect of multilingualism on culture. Roth deals simply with trading, but over a considerably wider area than that discussed by Sorensen. The implications of Roth's study to considerations of culture contact, culture change and craft specialization are obvious. Although Ribeiro's article includes material on intertribal contact, it is from the point of view of the Kadiwéu, who either dominated or assimilated other groups.

Crocker and Murphy deal with a rarely discussed aspect of culture, but one that is universal—sex. Both writers illustrate the way in which sexual practices relate to other elements of culture, including social control. Yet another form of social control is presented by Titiev in his discussion of singing among the Mapuche as a means of smoothing interpersonal relationships. Conflict resolution is the topic of Fock's brief article on the Mataco, ranging from interpersonal disputes to those that may involve several villages. It is Anthony Leeds, however, who embraces the broadest theme in seeking to elucidate the connection between human relationships and supernatural relationships.

Even as Rodrigues was writing his article on Amazonian linguistics, Arthur Sorensen was investigating some of the points that Rodrigues indicated as needing research. Something like the situation described by Sorensen almost certainly exists in many other parts of South America. It is difficult to imagine how the kind of trade described by Roth and Oberem could have taken place without some multilingualism on the part of the traders. There is considerable evidence that a situation of multilingualism existed along the upper reaches of the Madre de Dios River, at least at the turn of the century (Lyon ms.a). Anyone reading the accounts of the Spanish conquistadores soon notes frequent references to interpreters, many of whom appear to have been multilingual. Widespread occurrence of multilingualism might account for some of the "mixed" languages in Loukotka's lists.

It is easy to imagine how an individual trying to collect a vocabulary during a brief stay with a group, or upon a chance encounter with a family of Indians, might end up with a mixed lot of words if the individuals providing the material were multilingual. The chances for such a mixup are even worse if the vocabulary is collected, not from a single person, but from men, women and children as they come to hand. Rarely when such vocabularies are presented is there any specific indication of how many or what sort of informants were used, and never, to my knowledge, which words came from whom.

13   ARTHUR P. SORENSEN, JR.

Multilingualism in the Northwest Amazon [1]

THE CULTURAL, SOCIAL, AND LINGUISTIC UNITS

Setting and Culture Area

In the central part of the Northwest Amazon, there is a large multilingual area encompassing many tribes, each possessing its own language, where almost every individual is polylingual—he knows three, four, or more languages well. The area of multilingualism coincides largely with the area in which the Tukano tribal language is a lingua franca. This area can be roughly defined as the Vaupés River and its

Reprinted by permission of the author and the American Anthropological Association from the *American Anthropologist*, vol. 69 (1967), pp. 670–684.

tributaries. (The Vaupés flows into the Rio Negro, which in turn flows into the Amazon.) The region is the size of New England, or slightly larger. About half of it lies in Colombia and half in Brazil. The population is sparse, about 10,000.

The area is in tropical rainforest, its terrain transitional between rolling plain and hilly upland. Geologically it is the most westerly extension of the Guiana highlands. Although some of the rivers are large—the Vaupés is over 1,000 feet wide—navigation, because of the many rapids, is restricted to dugouts and to small boats that can be hauled. This has made for a relative inaccessibility that has helped protect the Indian culture, especially during rubber boom times. The area, however, has not been isolated: there has been continuous contact with civilization since the rubber booms began around 1875.

Most tribes occupy a delimited, continuous stretch of a river; a few have a discontinuous settlement pattern. Altogether they form one large, homogeneous cultural group in the center of what is identified in the literature as the Northwest Amazon culture area. (For culture area descriptions, see Steward, ed., 1946–1959, Goldman 1948, Murdock 1958, Steward and Faron 1959, and Galvão 1960.) There is historical as well as traditional evidence that some of these tribes may have originated outside of the Vaupés area, subsequently acculturating to the general central Northwest Amazon culture. Other tribes seem to have originated locally, from proliferation by fission. Koch-Grünberg (1909–1910), for instance, considers the Wanano newcomers (among others). Although it has not been especially noted in the literature, some tribes present social organizations that are atypical for the area. The Piratapuyo, for instance, retain moieties, which until recently functioned as exogamous intermarrying units in an otherwise tribally exogamous and moiety-lacking culture area. Goldman (1963), who noted multilingualism, also reports on the diverse origin of various sibs among the Kubeo. On the other hand, field notes on the Tuyuka-Yurutí (or Dochkapüra-Uaiana [the *Uaikana* are the Piratapuyo]) set of tribes and languages suggest their derivation from a common source.

A couple of the larger tribes do not live in one continuous area, but in several areas. The numerous Tukano tribe occupies several continuous stretches of the Vaupés River and its principal tributaries, the Tikié and the Papurí, and also sites at the mouths of tributaries to these rivers. Historically, they have exerted a dominant influence in the area. The Tukano tribal language serves as the lingua franca of the entire area. (Its use as a lingua franca antedates the appearance of other linguae francae in the region.)

The various tribes making up this large, homogeneous cultural group contain about 90 percent of the people in the area. The remainder consists of two ethnic groups. One is the Makú Indians, who live away from the rivers and are more or less nomadic. They do not intermarry with the riverine Indians. The other consists of the non-Indians, who call themselves *blancos* (in Spanish) or *brancos* (in Portuguese), and who number perhaps 1,500. Most of them live in the two or three air-strip towns. Their economy is centered around rubber gathering, and they include about 150 missionaries, who maintain some dozen missionary posts. The non-Indians have a strong monolingual tradition, speaking only either Spanish or Portuguese. They have shown little inclination to learn the Indian languages or to participate in Indian culture.[2] There is little intermarriage between Indians and *blancos* (who mostly consist of *mestizo-criollos*).

Here, then, is a large, culturally homogeneous area where multilingualism—and polylingualism in the individual—is the cultural norm. Anthropologically, this is a culture trait, and it is an outstanding culture trait of the area.

Social Units

Social units of primary importance to the analysis of multilingualism in the central Northwest Amazon culture area are the nuclear family, lineage, sib, tribe, phratry; the longhouse group; the linguistic group; and the exogamy group. Secondarily important, as they represent aggregations from among the above, are the mission village, the rubber-working group (an incipient *patrón-peón* group), and the nationality group. In the structural interrelations of all these groups, the sib occupies a focal position.

Several nuclear families may be found in a lineage, and several lineages in a sib (or patrilineal clan), which is the named and localized unit of social organization. A tribe is a named political and ceremonial unit, consisting of several sibs; it has a separate history and is identifiable by a distinct language. Barring the few exceptions where some of its sibs belong to a different phratry from that of the majority, each tribe is aligned with one of five phratries. Each phratry is a named, exogamous group of sibs that marries into the other phratries in the area. A phratry is not a political or ceremonial unit per se.

The basic political and ceremonial unit of the Northwest Amazon is the longhouse group, which is also the basic unit of economic redistribution. (The nuclear family is the basic economic unit *before* redistribution.) A new longhouse unit is often created by several classificatory brothers, not necessarily from the same parent longhouse. The one among them who is felt to have the best leadership qualifications becomes chief of the new longhouse group. Sometimes, also, a growing lineage group establishes a new longhouse, with its patriarch as chief. (Each nuclear family has its own area in the longhouse, and each married woman has her own hearth in this area; her husband smokes his fish and game on a rack lowered from the rafters above her hearth. All men and boys are served at one time at the center front of the longhouse by the women, who bring what they have individually prepared at their hearths, including some of their husbands' fish and game, and lay it out for all the men to share. After the men have eaten, the women and girls eat. Then each woman reclaims her own prepared food and what is left of her husband's catch.) A well-established longhouse group becomes, over a period of time, a cluster of lineages. A tribe is represented by a series of longhouses, located several hours' paddling distance apart from each other along a river and often situated at rapids for good fishing.

The tribe is co-extensive with the linguistic group, which is composed of those individuals who are expected to have used the language as their principal language when they were children in their nuclear family of orientation. The language that identifies the linguistic group is, then, at once the father tongue, the longhouse language, and the tribal language of each member; it is *not* the language that identifies the mother's linguistic group.

The exogamic group is the phratry. Cultural emphasis is more on nonendogamy within the phratry than on prescribed exogamic alliances among the phratries (although suggestions of such may be found among some of the tribes). Informants, however, claim that the unit of exogamy is the tribe. The few exceptional cases of tribes whose sibs belong to more than one phratry are well known and are taken for granted as minor exceptions to the stated rule. This rule is expressed in a formula that one does not marry inside of one's own tribe-and-language group because one would then be marrying a brother or a sister. Although informants do not explicitly refer to it, they recognize exogamy at the phratry level, and all marriages conform to a rule of phratry exogamy as well as of tribal exogamy. Recognition of the multitribal composition of the phratry is expressed as: "A Tukano will not marry a Baré because the Baré are brothers and sisters with the Tukanos."

The exogamic phratry system is extended fictitiously to all tribes peripheral to and beyond the central Northwest Amazon area, even though members of these tribes may not themselves be aware that they fit into such a system. Despite this fiction, it is safe to assume that any marriage with a member of one of these tribes will be phratry-exogamous. The nonriverine, marginal Makú of the interior lands back from the Papurí River, with whom the riverine Indians described in this paper do not intermarry, are considered to belong to the phratries to which the Tukano belong (the "Tukano-Makú") and to which the Desano belong (the "Desano-Makú"), and are said to intermarry among themselves accordingly.[3]

A larger mission village is a unit that has been created by missionaries from two or more longhouse groups representing two or more tribes (hence linguistic groups) that have been required to tear down their longhouses, move together, and build separate adobe huts for each nuclear family. A larger mission village also contains a contingent of non-Indian missionaries and a boarding house of school children from nearby settlements. A smaller mission village is a single longhouse group that has been persuaded to tear down its longhouse and substitute a series of adobe huts, one for each nuclear family.

The rubber-working group, for the Indian, is a unit of eight to ten months' duration per year, to which he belongs over a period of several years, usually in his youth. There are a great many such groups in the Upper Vaupés-Apaporis rubber-gathering area, each operating out of a camp, to which the Indians of the Middle Vaupés region are recruited. Properly speaking, the group includes one or more non-Indians, who are the patrón and his foremen, but they tend to keep themselves apart socially and linguistically from their Indian workers. The rubber-working group forms economically a patrón-peón system, or, more precisely for the Vaupés area, a patrón-padre-peón system. A benevolent role of missionaries in the Vaupés has been to minimize the depredations and excessive abuses of the rubber-working barons by requiring them to acquire their Indian workers through the missionaries as middle men.

A clear distinction is made between tribal group and nationality; a word glossing as "landsmen" is the term used in Tukano for nationality group. There are two nationality groups among the multilingual Indians described in this paper—the Colombian Indians and the Brazilian Indians (the periphery of the multilingual area may include some Venezuelan Indians)—and even the members of the longhouses in the zone most unacculturated to "civilization" know whether they are Colombians or Brazilians. Also, Indians and non-Indians both agree that there are two clear-cut categories of people in the Vaupés: in Spanish these are called the *indígenas,* or Indians, and the *blancos,* or non-Indians (including Negros). However, the Indians feel uncertain and confused about ethnic and presumably "tribal" groups among the non-Indians. A favorite topic of conversation with me was inquiry about ethnic descent groups among such known nationality groups as Colombians, Brazilians, Venezuelans, and "Americans" (of the U.S.A.). Apparently the Indians are trying to set up a folk taxonomy for non-Indians within the Indian frame of reference. They have long been familiar with members of Dutch, German, English, Spanish, and Portuguese ethnic groups; they are confused about the nationality as against the ethnic status of some of these, especially of the latter two. Many Colombian and Brazilian nationals whom the Indians frankly regard as mestizos or creoles claim not only to be blancos but also "Spaniards" or "Portuguese"; yet they do not resemble the Dutch, German, or English blancos. (In Tukano the word for "blanco," best glossed from Spanish as "non-Indians," is derived from a form also used in the derivations of "fire, shotgun, fireplace"; the occasional blanco-sponsored request for a new form in Tukano that would gloss as "white" is consistently rejected.)

Although the Indians reckon, for reference, in terms of ethnic groups, their attitude toward non-Indians is roughly the same as that of Americans in the United States toward European immigrants, who are looked upon as potentially becoming more and more American. I observed that Indians behold the visitor as potentially becoming more and more Indian-like unless he actively rejects Indian food, customs, and so forth. Most non-Indians are unaware of this attitude, and many would be contemptuous of it if they did know of it.

With respect to the Dutch, Germans, etc., an identifying criterion important to the Indian is that each of these ethnic groups is a separate language-bearing group. I was surprised that Indians do not naïvely assume that the English-speaking "American" necessarily belongs to the English ethnic group; the occasional North American traveler who insists (in Spanish) that he is "American" by *tribe* as well as by nationality is simply not believed. The North American who can be more explicit about his ethnic background is appreciated, especially if the background includes languages other than English and more than one ethnic group (thus simulating in form the exogamic language-bearing groups among the Colombian or Brazilian Indians). The Indians have also noted the widespread and, to them, notorious endogamy of the non-Indians and figure that there must be some sort of sib exogamy. The Indians ask a great deal about non-Indian marriage customs—partly because missionaries at times have suggested that the Indians' exogamy system is cumbersome and un-civilized, and that it promotes close cousin marriage, whereas the Indians feel that it is the non-Indian, with his lack of a clearly definable exogamy system, who is indiscriminate.

As for nationality-and-language, the Indians know that Spanish is the language of non-Indians on the Colombian side of the border and that Portuguese is the corresponding language on the Brazilian side of the border. They also know that Spanish is the language of Venezuela and that English is the language of "America." Nationality has no bearing on exogamy.

The Tribal Unit

In the central Northwest Amazon the term "tribe" has been used both for individual language-bearing units and for composites of these units sharing the same culture. In general practice, the designation of "tribe" implies a distinct culture-bearing entity. But the use of "tribe" for social units in the central Northwest Amazon has been ambiguous because of the use sometimes of linguistic and sometimes of cultural criteria. The problem of identifying tribal units has been recognized on a more general level in South American ethnology by Steward and Faron (1959:17, 21), and the concept of "tribe" in the world-wide anthropological literature has most recently been challenged by Fried (1966), who indicates that assumptions regarding the diachronic and politico-evolutionary status of so-called tribes need re-examination.

The Tukano, Tuyuka, Barasana, and other Eastern Tukanoan-speaking Indians of the central Northwest Amazon have no simple term for "tribe" in their languages, nor for "lineage," "sib," "phratry." In discussion these units are designated by proper names (e.g., "the Tukanos") or, if the context is clear, by demonstratives suffixed with one of the various classifiers glossing as "group," "class," "persons," any one of which may pertain to any of these social units. When Spanish is used, however, *tribu* is applied by Indians to the language-bearing unit only, whereas *familia* and *grupo* are applied to various units, including the tribe. When an informant is asked to explain the meaning of "tribu" in Tukano (or in another Eastern Tukanoan language), he invariably gives the proper name of the language-bearing unit, and follows up further questioning about other social units by giving the proper names of those that he knows, especially of those in his own lineage-sib-tribe hierarchy, and he concludes with a statement such as, "They're all my relatives." If recourse is made to Spanish to explain a hierarchical arrangement, an informant will say something like "*Este grupo tiene tres grupos.*" In Tukano he would say, "This-group is three-groups: the 'Anteater' people are three-groups: the A are at X rapids, the B are at Y stretch of the Papurí River, and the C are at Z mission village." Linguistically, the name for the language is the name for the tribe in the plural possessive form, nominalized; the plural infinitive of the word for "to speak" is the form glossing as "language," and if this form also appears along with the tribal name, then the plural possessive form of the tribal name also appears but it is not nominalized.

As travelers, missionaries, and rubber-gatherers became familiar with the area, they noted that certain bonds of preferential hospitality and recognition existed among the longhouse groups representing sibs of the same (father-) language group, and that this unit occupied a given, continuous territory. The missionaries and rubber-gatherers, as representatives of the colonial situation, tended to deal with each language-bearing unit separately, designating each one as a "tribe."

Nevertheless, some writers, such as Reichel-Dolmatoff (1963), have referred to the composite of all the Indian tribes (except the Makú) that share the same homogeneous culture and that participate in the system of exogamous phratries as the "Tukano tribe." In this definition, the social aggregate circumscribed by the phratry system is the tribe. Martius (1867) and Markham (1910) likewise spoke of the "Uaupês" Indians. Another argument for regarding this larger social unit as the one that could appropriately be designated as the "tribe" has been its tendency at times to be organized, partially at least, as a confederacy (Markham 1910). Continuing acculturation throughout the area at the present time may indeed lead to the loss of internal lines of social differentiation, resulting in the emergence of a single, regional society (Galvão 1959) in much the same way that the diverse Mapuche groups have emerged as a single tribe (Faron 1961). I believe that such a society here, unless interfered with, will retain a marriage system marked by exogamous, father-language groups of sibs.

At present, however, Indians recognize the set of longhouses speaking the same father-language as the maximal unit, and this is the "tribe" that is exogamous; that is, it is of these units that the exogamous phratry consists. As mentioned earlier, many of these units appear to have separate histories. The Indian identification of this exogamous, language-bearing unit as the maximal one is crucial in the analysis of multilingualism in the central Northwest Amazon. I shall use the term "tribe" in accord with this identification.[4]

Languages: Degree and Nature of Relationships

The criterion used in this paper to differentiate languages is mutual unintelligibility. The Indians' identification of tribe with language was initially relied on to prepare a tentative list of languages, as the listing of "tribes" was ostensibly also a listing of "languages." For the many informants asked, the criterion of tribal distinctiveness includes, by their own cultural definition, mutual unintelligibility between languages. It seemed premature to construct formal tests to explore degrees of mutual intelligibility between languages that were obviously genetically related (Voegelin and Harris 1951), but when asked directly, informants confirmed their mutual unintelligibility. The field procedure that I preferred and used was to watch for occasions when an Indian would comment that he had not understood someone else in a discussion where more than one language was spoken, at which time I would inquire what were the languages concerned. I depended on an Indian commenting in Tukano to identify non-understanding situations, but I was also able to pick up cues of "I don't understand" that I recognized in a number of the other languages. Thus I learned that such apparently closely related languages as Desano and Siriano, and even Tuyuka and Yurutí (see next two paragraphs), are mutually unintelligible. These and similar languages that are very closely related genetically make the central Northwest Amazon area an excellent one for close examination of the problem of language versus dialect (see Haugen 1966a).

Several language families are represented in this multilingual area: Eastern Tukanoan, Arawakan, Indo-European, Tupí-Guaranían, and others that remain undetermined (cf. Mason 1950, Noble 1965). Of these, the family most widely represented and with the largest number of languages is the Eastern Tukanoan, a family that seems to be contained entirely within the Northwest Amazon. The following discussion of my impressions is limited to this family.

I have made a preliminary attempt to reconstruct the Eastern Tukanoan family, using the comparative method on 13 of its languages on which I have field materials. The resulting subgroupings (see list in the appendix) definitely do not correlate with *phratric* groupings. Apparently the language most closely related to Tukano is Tuyuka, which is not intelligible to Tukano-speakers, not even "with difficulty." In phonology, morphology, and lexicon, one is considerably more distant from the other than Jutish is from Standard Danish (cf. Haugen 1955). However, in the field and on paper a person can not help but note the close similarity between others of these languages, e.g., between Tuyuka and Yurutí, or between Desano and Siriano. Discussions with informants of the Desano linguistic group, some of whom knew Siriano and some of whom did not, and with informants of the Siriano linguistic group, reveal that Siriano is not immediately intelligible to Desano-speakers but becomes largely intelligible after continuous exposure for at least several days. It so happens, however, that all members of the Siriano linguistic group know Desano, at least to understand it, because of polylingualism. Desano informants who know both Spanish and Portuguese recognize the relationship between Desano and Siriano as being on a par with that between Spanish and Portuguese (which are definitely recognized among Indians as being quite similar).

The degree of relationship among these Eastern Tukanoan languages can not be rigorously stated yet, but it is my impression that the languages separated by commas in the list in the appendix are a little farther apart than are the languages in the Romance group or in the Scandinavian group. One can look at the Romance languages as a dialect chain, but in the Eastern Tukanoan language family the *intermediate* "dialects" are missing, except perhaps for those languages in the appendix connected by "and." Central Algonquian languages (Bloomfield 1946, Hockett 1948) are more closely related than the Eastern Tukanoan languages seem to be. Approaching the problem from the opposite perspective, that is, from the point of view of reasonably demonstrated *dialects* within a language, the correspondences among the Eastern Tukanoan languages do not present the tightness or neatness that is so evident among those of the Karen dialects as drawn by Jones (1961).

Structural interrelationships are generally close among Eastern Tukanoan languages, but in the finer details of their similarities the languages do not coincide. In *broad* phonetic transcription, most of the Eastern Tukanoan languages share most of the same grid of phones, but the patterning of phonemes and the distribution of allophones vary from language to language. (Eastern Tukanoan languages, incidentally, have phonemic tone and phonemic stress.) To the unaccustomed ear, the Eastern Tukanoan languages all sound fairly similar and, indeed, can be recognized as Tukanoan by contrast with Indian languages of other families. After a person becomes familiar with one of them, the other Eastern Tukanoan languages begin to sound different to him; but the "Tukano ear," while helpful in recording Eastern Tukanoan languages, turns out not to be helpful in recording phonetic detail from languages outside of the Eastern Tukanoan family. The speaker-hearer of an Eastern Tukanoan language is culturally very sensitive to the fine phonetic detail, which he perceives in the form of an "accent." Such detail varies considerably from language to language and, even within some languages, from region to region.

Phonologically, differences in accent reflect a number of things: allophonic fronting of vowels, or lowering of vowels; more opening or less opening of the mouth during production of the vowels; incomplete (versus complete) closure of obstruents in syllables that are not marked by strong stress; more or less contouring of canonically level tones in given environments. These differences are mostly very subtle in quality, and usually speaker-hearers are unable to describe the specific phonological details involved in what they hear as an "accent."

The morphologies of these languages are generally similar, but they vary considerably on specific points. There can even be said to be an Eastern Tukanoan type, but each language still has its own distinctive differences. For instance, most Eastern Tukanoan languages have only two general forms for person in the verbal paradigm, but not all: Piratapuyo has three. The participial system seems to be more developed in some languages than in others. In lexicon, there is again general similarity, but not coincidence, between languages. In the exceptional area of kinship terminology, for example, more relatives may be distinguished in one language than in another, and what appear to be cognate terms in two languages may not refer to the same relative.

I have observed that when an Indian knows how to speak two closely related languages (of the sort connected by "and" in the appendix), he carefully and even consciously keeps them apart. It has occurred to me that the exogamic and other cultural institutions to be discussed below may be exerting a force that makes a speaker want to render closely related languages farther apart, even to an artificial extent, but so far I have detected no linguistic innovations to this end. Here, however, I run the risk of overstating the dialect problem. As Weinreich has pointed out (1968: section 1.3), the learning of a new dialect presents the same situation as the learning of a new language.

The Eastern Tukanoan languages clearly share the same syntax. By this I mean that they share the same types of multiword constructions. For example, they share a preference for a series of clauses in parataxis with a strong avoidance of hypotaxis; the same preferred (and not rigidly fixed) word order prevails (subject-object-verb); the same kinds of multiword constructions are used as techniques for apposition, statements of purpose, and "afterthought" statements of consequences or conditions; the same procedure is followed for developing a discourse topic, the sentence being prolonged by clauses in parataxis so as to provide more and more specificity to an original proposition stated in a main, and usually first, clause; listeners show the same pattern of response, attentively, politely, or disinterestedly repeating the last verb of the speaker's sentence. (I do not have enough material from languages of the other Indian language families to be able to comment on their syntaxes.) It is important for this discussion that Indian speakers do not ascribe the Tukanoan type of syntax to Spanish. Neither is the full syntactic range of Spanish as used by Colombian non-Indian Spanish-speakers found in the Indians' Spanish. As a result of much Spanish-to-Tukano and Tukano-to-Spanish work with informants, I can say that the Indians' Spanish is spoken in shorter and more numerous sentences than is the normal case in either Spanish or Tukano; dependent clauses are mostly lacking, with sentences supplied instead in an approximation of the paratactic subordinate clause of Tukano.

Further evidence comes from the response of Indians to metalinguistic questions. Monolingual Spanish-speakers, when quizzing Indians for forms in their language, typically ask for the forms one word at a time, following the order of the Spanish sentence (which may be phrased quite elegantly to ensure getting elegant Tukano). The translation process breaks down almost immediately; new Tukano forms for former Tukano forms are given as the Spanish sentence progresses, and the Spanish-speaker decides the Indian must be very indeterminate in whatever he says. The actual manner in which an Indian normally translates from Spanish to Tukano is so regular that it can be stated almost as a rule: the Indian remains silent until the full statement has been made in Spanish, he waits then for a few seconds until apparently the way he would say it in Tukano comes to him, and then he restates it in a normal Tukano sentence that generally has a syntactic structure very different from that of the Spanish sentence. This suggests that most Indians may be "coordinate" in their knowledge of Spanish and Tukano rather than "merged" (Weinreich 1953). Or, the cultural pattern may favor coordinate rather than merged control. This procedure can be enervating, culturally, to the monolingual Spanish-speaker, who expects to be replied to almost without audible pause between the end of his statement and the beginning of his responder's statement in rapid-fire repartee.

Anything said in Spanish is customarily repeated aloud in translation, even when all the Indians present already know Spanish. For the Indian, repeating a part of what a speaker says is a formal conversational device indicating understanding, assent (dissent if repeated with a negative suffix), and respect. In a formal gathering, as in the men's circle in the evening when the day's tasks are over, the amount of respect accorded to the older men who begin the session is indicated by how much the listeners repeat them. In the same setting, the remarks of a visitor speaking in another language are repeated in their entirety if someone present does not understand the language; as the conversation acquires more informal character and smaller conversation groups form, the repeating is dropped except for the respectful, assenting repeating of the last verbs of clauses and sentences; the visitor, indeed, may change to the language of the longhouse, if he knows it.

Repeating in translation something said in Spanish or Portuguese takes place in an interesting culture-contact situation. The encounter is rarely in a formal context for the Indian. It may be on a river bank, or on a trail, or on boats with the paddlers holding on to each others' boats and holding on to vines, or it may be on the street in a mission town. It almost never takes place in a formal gathering of Indians, as many situations calling for formal gatherings are discouraged by non-Indians. Nevertheless, many, or all, Indians of the settlement may be present. The repeating is first of all a respectful recognition of the Spanish-speaking non-Indians, but there also seems at times to be an additional quality of defensiveness connected with the practice. The repeating seems to serve as a stalling device so that the Indians can evaluate something of the intentions of the non-Indians, as indicated by their demands, their mood, and their degree of tolerance of Indian habits (for example, whether they permit beer, or admonish women—and men—for going without upper garments). Most non-Indians issue orders and interrogate loudly, according to the Latin American stereotype of the way to speak to Indians, rather than "converse" with them. The Indians, for various reasons, want to be sure that they have heard every question and order correctly. Consequently, repeating serves as a double-checking device, for corrections in translation are supplied unhesitatingly and immediately by other listeners following the translator. In sum, then, repeating is a formal conversational device indicating respect that also has an adaptive defensive function.

Inasmuch as the Eastern Tukanoan languages share the same general syntax, the Indians' ability to recognize and cope with the different syntactic system of Spanish suggests that other Indian languages and language families in the Northwest Amazon may have different syntactic structures, too.

Certain formulaic communication styles—regardless of Indian language family—are probably the same throughout the area, particularly greetings on entering a new longhouse in traveling. I have witnessed and participated in many such situations where the longhouse language was unknown either to me or to some of my Indian traveling companions, and always the content of the initial sequence of bilingual statements was clear to all (namely, the assertion that one has arrived; from which direction—upriver or downriver—one has come, and from what named spot; how many days one has been traveling; and who one's father and mother and brothers and sisters are, and how they are faring). There are other occasional formulaic conventions, especially those involving repeating, that can help a novice gain familiarity with a language. Many languages also seem to share interjections. (In these respects the central Northwest Amazon area may constitute what J. Neustupny has termed a *Sprechbunde* [speech area].) "Semicommunication" (Haugen 1966b) based on a partial knowledge of a language that is closely related to one already known may also occur.

MULTILINGUALISM

Because descent is patrilineal in the Northwest Amazon and residence is normatively and predominantly patrilocal, an individual belongs to his (or her) father's tribe, and to his father's linguistic group, which is also his own. Because of exogamy, his mother always represents a different tribe—tribal membership does not change for her upon marriage—and a different linguistic group. A woman invariably uses the language of the longhouse—her husband's language—when talking directly with her children. But she is usually not the only woman from her tribe in a longhouse. In a longhouse of any size there are usually several women of her tribe, as well as groups of other women from other tribes; and during the course of a day, these several groups of women usually find occasion to converse with each other in their own original languages.

In addition to these multilingual contacts in the longhouse, others occur as a result of considerable traveling. Youths travel to investigate and evaluate available brides. A prospective bridegroom, if he does not know it already, learns his prospective wife's language from his prospective mother-in-law. Families also travel to visit relatives and affines. And there is travel for the sheer sake of travel.

A man's *mother's* language may be quite important because of the preferential marriage system. There is a preference, though not an obligation, to marry his cross-cousin, particularly his mother's brother's daughter, real or classificatory. (The kinship system is of Iroquoian type [Fulop 1955].) She will, of course, be of his *mother's* tribe and speak his *mother's* language. Therefore there is an added cultural incentive for a man to know his mother's language. If he has little opportunity to learn it—if she, for instance, is the only one of her tribe in the longhouse, and her tribe lives at a distance—his mother, nevertheless, will teach him lists of words in her language and how to say various things in it. Children are usually bilingual in both their father's and their mother's languages, but commonly use the former.

A child is frequently exposed to the other languages spoken in the longhouse by the married women, who are ordinarily from more than one outside tribe, and by visitors. Visitors, especially, expose him to the lingua franca (which may also be the father's language or the mother's language for some individuals). Most children remain bilingual or trilingual in speech (with the lingua franca Tukano as the third language) until adolescence.

In the course of time, an individual is exposed to at least two or three languages that are neither his father's nor his mother's language. He comes to understand them and, perhaps, to speak them. I observed that as an individual goes through adolescence, he actively and almost suddenly learns to speak these additional languages to which he has been exposed, and his linguistic repertoire is elaborated. In adulthood he may acquire more languages; as he approaches old age, field observation indicates, he will go on to perfect his knowledge of all the languages at his disposal.

Each individual, then, has a personal repertoire of languages. Each longhouse, too, has its own characteristic language repertoire. Thus, the second longhouse up the Inambú River is a Tuyuka tribe longhouse that speaks Tuyuka; one third of the married women there are from the Barasana tribe, another third from the Desano tribe, and another third from the Tukano tribe. Careful field checking definitely corroborates that all individuals of this longhouse actually control at least these particular four languages within their individual repertoires. Most individuals know other languages besides these, but all share the basic longhouse inventory. The longhouse language, Tuyuka, is used to men and among men; women use the longhouse language with each other, but women who are classificatory sisters and hence from the same tribe have the option of using their own language when women from another tribe are not actually in the active conversation group, although other women (and men) within hearing understand it. All children use the longhouse language (i.e., their father's) to both their father and mother. As one continues up the river to the next longhouse, the proportion of Barasana women increases as the proportion of Desano women decreases, although the same four languages remain in a common longhouse repertoire shared by the individuals of that longhouse. Eventually a point will be reached where one of these languages will drop out of the longhouse repertoire, and perhaps another language (e.g., Tatuyo or Paneroa) will enter.

I must emphasize again that it is not just scattered individuals who know the various languages used in a given longhouse; but *all* the longhouse residents know them. In the mission villages, where what formerly were two, three, or more longhouses are now gathered together in one village of adobe huts, the linguistic picture resembles that of the single longhouse, but usually more than one father-language is present, for most missionary villages contain men from more than one tribe. There seemed to be an incipient age-grading pattern between two father-tongues at one of the missions, but not at the others.

Periodically the missions have tried to prohibit the use of Indian languages, but these efforts were subsequently dropped. In aboriginal settings, in the mission compounds away from face-to-face contact with the missionaries themselves, and in any gathering of Indians, whether traveling, visiting, working rubber, no Spanish or Portuguese is used (except occasionally when Indians drink alcoholic beverages!). The field worker must rely upon a knowledge of at least one of the Indian languages in order to keep track of what languages are actually being spoken.

The Indians are quite unself-conscious about their multilingualism. They take it for granted. There is no development of cross-linguistic puns. There is no stylistic device of switching from one language to another or of interspersing one's conversation with quotes from another language. Conversations in two or more languages indeed occur on occasion, as in visiting, but no one takes special note of it. Each individual initially speaks in his own father-language during such a conversation in order to assert his tribal affiliation and identification, but after a while the junior persons change, without comment, to the longhouse language, to Tukano as the lingua franca, or to another language, whatever one is most convenient for the others. A person usually cannot enumerate how many languages he knows, and is perplexed at being asked to do so. The interviewer has to go over with him one by one the whole list of languages spoken in the area. But when approached, in this way, each individual definitely knows his own repertoire and can state what languages he speaks well, what ones he only understands but does not speak, etc.[5]

I observed no tendency for people to claim knowledge of a language not actually known. I also observed that the Indians' terms for rating fluency, when translated into English, are *under*estimates. Thus when an Indian says he speaks such-and-such a language "some," we would be more prone in English-speaking culture to say he speaks it "quite well." The unequally weighted rating scale used by informants in Tukano is perhaps best rendered by these English glosses and paraphrases: (1) "none"; (2) "hardly any" or "just a few words"; (3) "some, but not *well*" ("well" referring to pronunciation), or "half-way"; (4) "*almost* all" or "just a little lacks"; (5) "all." To an unqualified question, an informant usually gives his *speaking* fluency rating. He must be questioned separately for ratings on languages he understands but does not speak or "hardly speaks." All these observations make it appear that the Indians are indifferent or, perhaps, blasé about their multilingualism.

Their orientation to multilingualism is instrumental and practical, but not devious. The languages used in a given situation are not chosen with motives of concealment from others. Politeness leads visitors to use their hosts' language, if they know it. Reliance on one language as against another is not considered impolite, however, and only on rare occasions, when such a reliance is exaggerated insistently and provocatively, can it signal the expression of anything resembling a militant tribal rivalry. This may, but need not, occur during beer-drinking bouts, as at a formally arranged product-exchanging and friendship-renewing ceremony between two longhouses representing two tribes; but here it should be viewed as a means for expressing and releasing accumulated, and usually minor, tensions rather than as a product of the drunken brawl pictured by most non-Indians. The stereotypes of unsympathetic non-Indians may have prejudiced accounts of some of the unsuccessful ceremonies that have received notoriety. Overt rivalry in most of these ceremonies seldom needs to go beyond the all-night competitive dancing of the separate rival troupes; and by the second day, the older men's chanting may end up entirely in the host-longhouse's language, while the younger men form one cooperative, consolidated dancing body. During the course of the ceremony, the women group according to their own tribal affiliations and sing as choruses in their own father-tongues. Married women alternate between singing in their original father-language, in their husband's language, and in the longhouse language of the hosts.

If neither one's father nor mother is Tukano, one nevertheless will speak Tukano as a lingua franca. Indirect evidence suggests that Tukano existed aboriginally, or at least early in the historic period, as a lingua franca, although its epicenter may have formerly been in the Lower Vaupés. The Tukano tribe may even have been the dominant group in a confederation or nation of sorts (Markham 1910). At any rate, the Tukano are widely and strategically located and appear to have exerted a dominant influence in the whole area. The Tukano claim a mild prestige as the senior sibs of the area and regard all the other tribes as young-brother sibs in a particular rank order (see Fulop 1955); this ranking is accepted by the other tribes.

Because the Tukano tribe is so widespread, almost every longhouse has at least one Tukano woman in it. Therefore, persons who do not have a Tukano for father or mother still have someone in their longhouse from whom they can absorb the correct pronunciation of Tukano.

Now, the Tukano language contains at least six dialects. As a lingua franca it is not pidginized but is learned in one or another of its tribal dialect forms, whatever one the learner is exposed to. Speakers for whom Tukano is not their father- or mother-language can still be identified as to regional dialect. Tukano, incidentally, is not an easy language to learn. It has a great many phonemes and an intricate tonal system; and apart from the tonal system, it has an intricate system of stress. This suggests the hypothesis that sheer intricacy may foster an all-or-none attitude toward learning to speak a phonologically elaborate language. Maintenance of Tukano as a lingua franca has probably been reinforced by there being some 25 or more language groups that it serves.

The Indians do not practice speaking a language that they do not know well yet. Instead, they passively learn lists of words, forms, and phrases in it and familiarize themselves with the sound of its pronunciation. The diverse and discrete phonologies of these languages and their dialects loom very prominently in the Indians' regard. They may make an occasional preliminary attempt to speak a new language in an appropriate situation, but if it does not come easily, they will not try to force it. One of the preconditions of language-learning in the area is a passive familiarity with lists of words (including inflected and derived forms) in languages likely to be learned. Much language-learning (especially of linguae francae) takes place within the peer group. Among closely related languages, a stage of "semicommunication" (Haugen 1966b) may be important in learning. Informants estimate that it takes them from at least one to two years to learn a new language fluently, regardless of language family. Most of them also estimate that it takes longer to learn Spanish than to learn Tukano or another Eastern Tukanoan language.

An Indian, then, does not want to try to speak a language until he knows it quite well. He is conscious of his pronunciation in it and deliberately tries to sound like an authentic speaker. Each language has its own phonetic niceties, nuances of voice placement, and other details of accent not unlike the sort that distinguish some regional dialects of American English. Some languages (e.g., Tukano, Desano, Kubeo) exhibit more than one accent because they have regional dialects. There is such a phenomenon, then, as speaking Tukano with a Tuyuka accent, and vice versa, although many Tuyukas speak Tukano without a Tuyuka accent. A mild Siriano accent is acceptable to speakers of the Upper Papurí River dialect of Tukano, where the Siriano tribe is located. A Tukano child of this area with a Siriano mother who has a Siriano accent in her Tukano will himself speak Tukano without a Siriano accent.

The early non-Indians who started coming into the area brought with them another language as lingua franca: Nheengatú (Inekatú), also called Tupí, and also commonly referred to as *lingoa geral* (which means "lingua franca" in Portuguese) or just "Geral." This is a Tupí-Guaraní language, and it is still spoken, even monolingually, along many portions of the Rio Negro by the detribalized Indian and White-Indian population, collectively known as *caboclos*. Nheengatú spread as the lingua franca of the early rubber boom days, 1875–1920. When the rubber boom declined with the development of rubber plantations in Malaysia, the use of Nheengatú declined also. Now only some older people in the multilingual area described in this report know Nheengatú. Some younger people can repeat lists of words and forms in it, but they do not speak it. According to informants, it can be heard conversationally in the lower portions of the Vaupés, but I have not heard it used conversationally in the Middle Vaupés region. It was originally brought up the Amazon and to the Rio Negro by the Jesuits as the language of instruction; and it was well established there by the 18th century, when a contest with Portuguese began (Martius 1867). Its grammar, originally adapted from a Latin model, was artificially built on a Tupí-Guaraní base similar to that of present-day Guaraní.

After Nheengatú, Portuguese came in as another lingua franca. It is now the language of the non-Indians on the Brazilian side of the border and the language taught in the mission schools there.

On the Colombian side, Spanish is the official lingua franca. There was much learning of Spanish in the rubber-gathering area during the rubber boom, and Spanish superseded Nheengatú as the dominant lingua franca there. The increasing importance of Spanish at the expense of Portuguese and the already fading Nheengatú coincided with a change in the rubber industry: to extract the *siringa* type of rubber, found in abundance in the Upper Vaupés River and Upper Apaporis River region of interior Colombia, instead of the less valuable but more widespread *balata* type found in both Colombia and Brazil. The stability of Tukano during this period of change probably enhanced its position as a lingua franca. The Upper Vaupés–Upper Apaporis region is just outside of the culture area being described in this paper, and it includes Indian workers who have come in from still other culture areas. While the knowledge of Spanish is spreading, via this rubber-gathering area, into the adjacent culture areas, the knowledge of Tukano is also spreading.

For about 20 years there has been a concerted attempt to teach Colombian Indians Spanish in the schools. Perhaps one-third to one-half of the Indians already know Spanish as a second lingua franca. Many learned it when, as youths, they worked a few years in the rubber-gathering area. Theirs is good, understandable, and effective Spanish, although it may lack the subjunctive and certain other details of normative grammar. It cannot be called a "broken Spanish." At the missions, the insistence on using only Spanish has at times had an effect the reverse of the one desired and has invigorated Tukano and the other Indian languages. Along with measures to civilize the Indian linguistically and get him out of the longhouse and into civilized villages, there have been attempts to detribalize the Indians by de-emphasizing exogamy. All these efforts, however, have only served to reinforce the persistence of the native languages.

Because this area is politically divided by the boundary between Colombia and Brazil, an Indian from Brazil who knows Portuguese finds that when he goes any distance into Colombia, Portuguese is not understood. Conversely, Colombian Indians find they cannot use their Spanish in the interior of the Brazilian section. They then resort to their principal lingua franca, Tukano, which is understood on both sides of the border. And this situation obviously helps also in continuing Tukano as the main lingua franca.

IMPLICATIONS FOR SOME CURRENT ISSUES

The One Language/One Culture Image

As I have shown, the multilingualism in the homogeneous culture of the central Northwest Amazon area serves to demarcate distinct, exogamous social units. Homogeneity of culture in this area does not mean homogeneity of language. And to speak of one language is not to speak of one entire culture. Indeed, with minor regional variations, the larger Northwest Amazon cultural area extends far beyond the bounds of the central, multilingual area described in this paper. Moreover, the cultural area includes some societies acculturated to lesser or greater degree to civilization but whose populations still prefer to speak aboriginal languages and to coin new terms in their own languages rather than borrow alien words. Data from the central Northwest Amazon bear directly, therefore, on the prevalent one language/one culture assumption, which, as Hymes (1964) and Gumperz (1961) point out, needs critical review.

The homogeneous culture area of the central Northwest Amazon has been circumscribed, perhaps somewhat artifically, as the area characterized by multilingualism as a culture trait. Within it there is no one language that is father-language to all, nor is there any one language that is mother-language to everyone. What is father-language to some is mother-language to others and an unknown language to still others, all people who bear the same culture. The distribution of Tukano, as the lingua franca, does largely coincide with the extent of this culture area. But this is partly because a lingua franca accompanies multilingualism, and it is this trait of multilingualism that sets off the cultural area. The widespread distribution of Tukano and its near coincidence with the central Northwest Amazon culture area does not lend any special monolithic quality to Tukano such as is revealed in the promulgation of Spanish and Portuguese. Despite much situational reinforcement, Tukano continues to exist as a lingua franca at all only because it has tenuously and flexibly become amalgamated into the cultural picture. Indeed, the linguistic area of Tukano merges into the area of Nheengatú and thence into the area of Portuguese; the cultural areas of tribal Indians and of detribalized caboclos have perimeters that differ from those of the linguistic areas.[6]

Implications for Transformational Linguistic Theory

A number of details in the preceding description of the multilingual society in the central Northwest Amazon force some reconsideration of certain basic premises of transformational linguistic theory. Chomsky (1965:3–9) states that linguistic theory is concerned with the tacit knowledge of an ideally fluent speaker-hearer in a homogeneous speech community. An ideally fluent speaker-hearer in the central Northwest Amazon has to be someone who is *not* monolingual. This poses the question of whether the ideally fluent speaker is to carry one model of Language or several models, one for each of his languages, in his head. Even very closely related languages appear to be kept fastidiously apart by speakers, and the very differences among these closely related languages often are of the same kind of subtlety, especially of surface structure rules and near-surface structure rules, whose exposure has been a major contribution of transformational linguistics. This leads to the further question of how any one language, which forms only part of a normal polylinguistic individual's repertoire (which in turn varies from individual to individual), is to be accounted for. There is also the question of what is to be considered a homogeneous speech community. I have suggested that the best candidates in this community are the longhouse group and the mission village group, whose members share common poly- and multilingual patterns. This necessitates our recognizing hundreds of distinct homogeneous speech communities in the one culture area.

To treat the description of any *one* of these languages as representing the tacit knowledge of a speaker of the language of a speech community is clearly unrealistic. The one language represents only part of the individual's competence in Language, and only part of the speech community's configuration of languages. Description of only one language necessarily can account for only part of the grammatical sentences an individual within a speech community may utter—unless the description of a "single language" can incorporate several, or alternative languages. A linguistic theory limited to one language/one group situations is inadequate to explain the actual linguistic competence of the people of the central Northwest Amazon.

APPENDIX: INVENTORY OF TRIBES AND LANGUAGES

The following tribes and languages have been noted and checked directly in the field.

1. Tribes and languages directly involved in multilingualism:
    A. Eastern Tukanoan language family, arranged in subgroupings suggested by a preliminary attempt at reconstruction by the comparative method (there are probably a few more languages to be documented in this group in subsequent field trips): Tukano, Tuyuka and Yurutí, Paneroa and Eduria, Karapana and Tatuyo, Barasana; Piratapuyo, Wanano; Desano and Siriano; Kubeo.
    B. Arawakan language family: Tariano; Baré. Most Tarianos now use Tukano as their household or father-language, and they marry Tukanos; many younger Tarianos do not know Tariano, although they are polylingual in other languages. The Baré along the Middle and Lower Vaupés use either Tukano or Nheengatú as their household or father-language, and very few speakers of the original Baré are left; the Baré are largely detribalized and cabocloized.
    C. Several tribes-and-languages of various families of the Pirá-Paraná (Moser 1963) await direct checking in the field: Tabaino, Erulia (distinct from Eduria), Makuna, Yekuana, Datuana, and others. The status of some of

these as dialects or languages also remains to be determined. For example, Tatuyo informants have mentioned an Owa language spoken by some Tatuyos, but there has not been an opportunity to check this out. The few Mirititapuyo of the Middle Tikié appear to use either Tukano or Desano as their household or father-language.

    D. Tupí-Guaranían language family: Nheengatú.

2. Tribes and languages bordering the multilingual area (many members of these tribes may be bilingual or even polylingual, but multilingualism is not widespread in a given tribe; many Indians of the multilingual area may include one or more of these languages in their repertoires):

    A. Arawakan language family: Kuripaka and Baniva. These are reported by some informants to be almost mutually intelligible.

    B. Undetermined language families: Karihona, Guayavero. I also have names, in Tukano only, of some dozen other languages spoken around the periphery of the area and along the Rio Negro.

3. Languages spoken in the multilingual area, but by speakers who do not possess multilingualism as a culture trait:

    A. Undetermined language family: Makú (Makú may be more than one language). A few Makú know Tukano or Desano or some other language, including Spanish or Portuguese, but most Makú do not; a few Tukanos, Desanos, Piratapuyos, and Tuyukas know some Makú.

    B. Indo-European language family: Spanish, Portuguese, Italian. Two Colombian dialects of Spanish are found: Antioqueño, spoken by most missionaries, and Llanero, spoken by most rubber-gatherers. "Vaupense" Spanish is basically Llanero Colombian Spanish with the addition of many Nheengatú and some Portuguese terms for things pertaining to the tropical rainforest.[7]

    C. A special case is provided by languages neither spoken in the area nor represented there by groups of speakers. Small lists of words in Dutch can be obtained from older Indians on the Papurí, even though the former Dutch Montfortiano Fathers did not attempt to use Dutch with the Indians. Some Indians, moreover, have learned a considerable amount of Latin.

Spellings

Most names for languages and tribes in the literature are Nheengatú names, carried over into Spanish, Portuguese, German, English, etc. There is great variation in the spellings. The spellings in this paper tend to follow those of Koch-Grünberg, who still remains the general authority for the area as a whole. His spellings are close to those used for Nheengatú. They generally conform with those used for world-wide ethnographic spellings; in addition, they seem to have been the spellings more commonly used in English, German, Portuguese, and Spanish ethnographies on South America.

Population Estimate

Population figures are hard to estimate. The following are very impressionistic. Tribes with 1,000–2,000 members: Tukano, Kubeo, Baré; Spanish-only speakers. Tribes with 500–1,000 members: Piratapuyo, Wanano, Desano. Tribes with 150–

500 members: Tuyuka, Yurutí, Paneroa, Eduria, Karapana, Tatuyo, Barasana, Siriano, Tariano, Tabaino, Makuna, Tekuana, Datuana; Portuguese-only speakers. Of the latter tribes, Yurutí, Yekuana, and Datuana may number fewer than 150 members. A few Salesian missionaries, in Brazil, are Italians.

There are probably a few hundred Makú in occasional contact with the multilingual Indians in this area.

Non-Indians probably number about 1,500 and are concentrated in the few air-strip towns.

For a very round figure, a population of 10,000 has been estimated for the multilingual area in which Tukano is the chief lingua franca. Of these 10,000, only the non-Indians, the Makú, and some of the Kubeo are not multilingual, so that over 80 percent of the population is multilingual. As the non-Indians are concentrated in the few air-strip towns and a dozen missionary posts, the effective distribution of multilingualism is much higher; close to 100 percent of the communities encountered in the area are multilingual. Of the multilingual Indians, well over 90 percent know Tukano at least as a lingua franca, with young children accounting for the majority of the few who do not.

NOTES

1. This report is an expanded version of a paper presented to the Tenth Annual National Conference on Linguistics in New York on March 13, 1965. Field work was done in the summers of 1959, 1960, and 1962 and from June to December 1963. It was supported during much of this time by USPHS Research Grant MH-17,258. I wish to acknowledge the hospitality and cooperation extended to me by the Xaveriano missionary order in Colombia and the Salesian missionaries of the Brazilian Vaupés region. Various drafts of this paper were read by Drs. Charles Wagley, Harvey Pitkin, Robert F. Murphy, and Dell Hymes. I am indebted to them for their criticisms and encouragement.

2. Notable exceptions have been Father Kök of the Montfortiano Order, who was in the Colombian Vaupés until the late 1940's and wrote a grammar (1922), and Father Giacone of the Salesian Order, in Brazil, who has just published a grammar (1965, not yet seen by this writer; also 1939). Many missionaries can understand an Indian language to some extent and listen to confessions in it.

3. According to informants from the still-Indian Middle and Upper Vaupés area, the area of this paper, it seems likely that the *caboclo* population of the Lower Vaupés River and adjacent areas along the Rio Negro continues to observe some sort of exogamy. Caboclos are detribalized (deculturated) Indians who, through the processes of loss, acquisition, and intermingling of Indian and European (Portuguese) culture traits, have acculturated to a relatively stable but impoverished type of "backwoods," riverine culture. Caboclo culture depends on the extraction of natural products, such as rubber, accompanied by some subsistence farming, fishing, and hunting. The caboclo population functions as a marginal, and usually indebted, rural peasantry in the national economy (Wagley 1953, 1964; Oberg 1965). Much of the population living along the Amazon and its tributaries consists of caboclos. The caboclo population is mostly of the Indian physical type, but it may include some non-Indian admixture. The term *"caboclo"* is Portuguese; in Vaupense Spanish it is *"cabuco,"* and in Tukano it is a form glossing as "mixed one." Some downriver segments of such Indian groups as the Tukano and the Desano, and particularly the Baré, are now considered by the other Indians as well as by the non-Indians to be caboclos.

4. The identification of "tribe" with patrilocal language groups and, consequently, with a "linguistically and culturally hybrid social unit," suggests a possibility for widening the research problem recently described by Owen (1965). See Naroll (1964), also, on types of cultural units.

5. These statements are based on 167 formally recorded interviews taken along the course of the Papurí and some of its tributaries, such as the Inambú and the Paca, and on the upper- to

middle-Tikié. However, the representation by tribe, river, age group, mission, etc., is not comprehensive enough for a statistically controlled comparison. Many informants' statements were checked and double-checked, and some were cross-checked through other informants or at other times; they were found to be constant. Most interviewing was done in Tukano. Informants consistently tended to underestimate their linguistic repertoire, and these underestimates, as given, have been retained in the field notebook. I observed that, perhaps owing to the census-like nature of this activity, informants registered some uneasiness, although they did not cease to maintain rapport with the field worker, so the program was dropped and only occasional interviews thereafter were recorded. (In the following year a governmental census was indeed taken.) At one mission, I secured accurate data *about* each informant's linguistic repertoire, but the informants gave spurious names (each other's names in many cases) as a maneuver not aimed against the researcher but intended as a kind of practice session in preparation for coping with a locally rumored politico-religious threat based on missionary rivalry.

6. There still exist abrupt cultural and linguistic lines of demarcation between Tukano and Spanish, which are separated from each other either by a geographical no-man's-land or by figuratively walled towns; but there is now a tendency to adapt to a caboclo type of culture on a semipermanent basis by some Indian nuclear families in the rubber-gathering Upper Vaupés-Upper Apaporis area. They represent a stage of acculturation similar to the one described by Murphy and Steward (1956) for the Mundurucú. Indeed, there are a number of parallels with the Mundurucú (Murphy 1960).

7. See Rivera's powerful, authentic novel *La Vorágine* (1948) for Vaupense Spanish terms. The setting for much of this novel is the Colombian Vaupés region and the adjacent Casanare region (not dealt with, except indirectly, in this report). Rivera projected his morally and passionately torn protagonist, Arturo Cova, in ever-increasingly involved relief against the convoluted setting of the exploits of the notorious rubber barons. His Indians show up only as shadowy figures in the background—no doubt the way the rubber-gatherers, caught up in their own problems, saw them as they paused in dimly lit longhouses for their night's rest.

Roth's material presents a situation that was probably relatively common in aboriginal South America. The material gathered by Oberem tends to support this view, as does an article by Wassén dealing with pre-Columbian trade in Colombia (1955). These descriptions stand in marked contrast to the opinion expressed by Lieutenant Lardner Gibbon regarding the Indians of Mojos in Bolivia:

> *The Mojos Indian never would have known there was such a plant in the world, if the sugar-cane had not been carried to him. He does not travel abroad himself, but remains in his own district, as the wild animals do, living upon whatever may from time to time be passed over into his plate. . . .*
>
> *The old Indian seems perfectly comfortable now that he has milk and sugar. If he was wise enough to know anything about the advantages of commerce, it is doubtful how far he would exert himself. He is rather an indolent fellow. The Indians want nothing particularly; clothing they get from the bark of the tree, or the produce of the cotton plant. Yuca is their bread; there are fish in the stream, and beeves on the pampa; coffee, chocolate, and sugar. (Herndon and Gibbon 1854: Pt. II, p. 224)*

This opinion sounds suspiciously like an inference from the European stereotype of the indolent native.

It should be noted that Roth's work, rather than being an analysis of trade, is a compilation of existing data drawn from his own fieldwork and that of others. In many cases data from other writers are used with the barest rewording or are essentially direct quotes although not so indicated. Nonetheless, the impressive assemblage of data provides a picture of extensive and intensive trade not only among Indian groups, but also between these groups and the so-called "Bush Negroes" and Europeans. The thoroughly ethnocentric observations that occur from time to time simply serve to point up the vast differences in values between the observers and the people with whom they were dealing.

14 WALTER EDMUND ROTH

Trade and Barter Among the Guiana Indians [1]

In his description of the Arawak on the Berbice, Pinckard states what is equally applicable to the Guiana Indians in general: They have no interest in the accumulation of property, and therefore do not labor to obtain wealth. They live under the most perfect equality, and hence are not impelled to industry by that spirit of emulation which, in society, leads to great and unwearied exertion. Content with their simple means, they evince no desire to emulate the habits or the occupations of the colonists; but, on the contrary, seem to regard their toils and customs with a sense of pity or contempt (Pinckard 1816:v. 1, p. 519). But this perfect equality does not necessarily imply a state of socialism; far from it. They have not a community of goods, individual property being distinctly marked between them. But this property is so simple and so easily acquired that they are perpetually borrowing and lending without the least care about payment (Hilhouse 1832:231).

In trade and barter the value of an article to an Indian depends upon his temporary want of it and not upon its intrinsic worth (M. Schomburgk 1847–1848:v. 2, p. 393). Thus, the Santo Domingo natives bartered their gold . . .

A compilation reprinted by permission of the Smithsonian Institution Press from "An introductory study of the arts, crafts, and customs of the Guiana Indians," in the *Thirty-eighth Annual Report of the Bureau of American Ethnology, 1916–1917* (1924), pp. 632–637; and from "Additional studies of the arts, crafts, and customs of the Guiana Indians," in *Bureau of American Ethnology, Bulletin 91* (1929), pp. 101–103.

for tags, nails, broken pieces of darning needles, beads, pins, laces, and broken saucers and dishes (Chanca 1907:452). An Indian at one time shall require an ax, in exchange for that for which at another he will demand only a fishhook, without regarding any disproportion between their value (Bancroft 1769:335). For what one Indian [Warrau] would want a gun or an ax, another, for the same thing, would want a couple of fishhooks, some beads, or a comb (M. Schomburgk 1847–1848:v. 1, p. 175). One Makusi woman offered me a cow for two "flash" finger rings, of a value under 16 cents, whereas at Samarang, on the Brazilian side of the border, I had to part with my trousers for two hind quarters of fresh beef. Similar experiences have been recorded in plenty; e.g., among the Oyana and the Trio (Herderschee 1905b:939). In the former case we notice, says Herderschee, during the trading, how peculiar the taste of the Indian is, and from what an entirely different standpoint he regards the worth of an article to what we do. A beautiful feather article, e.g., for which we offered a few penknives and a scissors, was not handed over, but they were willing to exchange it for a little mouth harmonica that was worth much less (Herderschee 1905b:901–902).

Crévaux was the first to draw attention to the ignorance of the aborigines with regard to the custom of presents: "When I give a knife," he says, "they always ask me 'What do you want?' " (Crévaux 1883:262, 404). The converse is equally true; e.g., if the Uaupes Indians show one hospitality in the way of cassava, smoked fish, etc., they expect something in exchange, and often show themselves very exacting in this respect (H. Coudreau 1886–1887:v. 2, p. 171). At the Patamona village of Karikaparu the chief's brother upon seeing me walk in lame and weak on arrival gave me a long hardwood stick to help me support myself. I accepted it and asked him how much, but he refused to take anything, saying it was a present for me. About a week later, when opening my "trade," he saw some knickknack that took his fancy; he asked me for this, reminding me of his previous present to me of the stick. It seems probable that in the olden days trade was not run on the lines [present for present], article for article. Perhaps they learned such a thing from the bush Negroes. They have, however, made that method quite their own, and I saw bartering take place between an Oyana and a Trio in exactly the same way [i.e., article for article]. Besides that, the least greedy likewise practice the old style; a present whether all or nothing is asked for it. The other party must, in his turn, occasionally give something, but he is not bound to time and a fixed rate (Herderschee 1905b:958).

In the absence of a medium of exchange an Indian has nothing to sell unless the buyer happens to be in possession of what he wants. Thus among the Uaupes River Indians when we first arrived, writes Wallace, almost the whole body of the inhabitants came to visit us requesting to see what we had brought to sell. Accordingly we spread out our whole stock of fishhooks, knives, etc. . . . which they handled and admired in unintelligible languages for about two hours. It is necessary to make this exposition in every village, as they will bring nothing to sell unless they first know that you have what they want in exchange (Wallace 1889:207).

But cases often arise where the article of traffic is of such a nature as not to lend itself to exchange, or, rather, where the article required in exchange is not immediately forthcoming, and under such circumstances no inconsiderable amount of trust and confidence is necessarily imposed upon both parties to the transaction. In the purchase of corials and canoes, their [Arawak] most expensive articles, the buyer is frequently credited to what we should call a ridiculous extent, especially as the means seldom exists of enforcing payment (Hilhouse 1832:231). The Boni [bush Negroes] who come and do business in the Roucouyenne country are obliged to pay for hammocks which will not be handed over to them until the following summer (Crévaux 1883:262).

When buyer and seller are not in immediate touch the intermediary may be direct or indirect. The Atorai obtain their graters from the Taruma not only for their own use but to sell again to the Indians of the Takutu (H. Coudreau 1886–1887:v. 2, p. 308). The Arawak sometimes undertake long voyages to the remote Warrau villages to buy the canoes which they in turn will sell to the settlers (Brett 1868:165). In Surinam many bush Negroes have among the Indians their "matti" (= mate, friend). Such a matti acts principally the part of a trade agent and commercial traveler. When a bush Negro comes to an Indian settlement it is the matti's chief business to see that he is well treated and looked after. The middleman, however, will often take measures to prevent direct trade between buyer and seller. Thus from Surinam come some very interesting records showing the means adopted to obtain such an end, followed by bush Negroes and Trio. The Indians in the interior obtain what they want in the way of products of European industry in large measure through the intervention of the bush Negroes. As the latter do very well in that trade it is of great importance to them to take care that the Indians never come into direct touch with the whites. At the beginning the Joeka (bush Negroes) told them that they had a village somewhere near the sea where they themselves made axes, beads, cotton, etc. They further once upon a time took Indians with them to Poeloegoedoe and then told them it was still a formidably long distance from there to the sea. Besides that, the tempestuous water would perhaps capsize boats and the whites stood on shore ready to murder every Indian whom they saw. . . . When the expedition went up the Tapanahoni Captain Arabi [bush Negro] sent on a message that all the Indians must make their escape as quick as possible, as the whites were coming with a large force to plunder the villages and kill the populace. The Trios then abandoned their village and kept themselves hidden in the forest until news came from Arabi that there was nothing to fear. . . . The Joeka likewise tried to work on the whites. They several times reported on the coast that such dangerous Indians were still living up yonder. . . . It was the same bush Negroes again who in 1878 made the Trio fly before Crévaux by circulating the story that he was bringing a serious disease with him, and that he had some evil-minded Negroes in his following. The Oyana who accompanied Crévaux in order to prevent their own trade being harmed considered it profitable to leave the Trio in that erroneous opinion (Herderschee 1905b:944–945). So again Herderschee was himself tricked by having withheld from him by the Trio and Oyana the existence of a second trail leading from the Arakoepina to the Wana or Wanama (presumably the Wanamu of Schomburgk). The reason of this secrecy was also not far to seek: they prefer the white man not to bring his wares direct to their fellow-tribesmen. The billet of middleman yields a profit not to be despised (Herderschee 1905b:966).

The Indian knights of the road do not hesitate to puff and advertise their wares to the best advantage on lines similar to those employed by their more civilized brethren. Thus, in the well-established trade and barter carried on between the Saluma [Taruma] and Trio, the former tell the latter that the glass beads which they are selling them grow on bushes which they themselves plant (Goeje 1910:26). In the same way, Koch-Grünberg tells a story—a satire on the Indians who, after temporarily working in British Guiana, return home and report all possible exaggerations—where guns, shot, powder, etc., grow on trees which have only to be shaken for the ripe guns, etc., to drop (Koch-Grünberg 1917–1928:v. 2, p. 150). In Surinam, de Goeje states that when making a purchase the buyer will put some turalla, a vegetable talisman, between his lips to prevent the seller overreaching him. I have elsewhere (Roth 1915:sec. 233) discussed the subject of such charms. It is possible that procedures somewhat on these lines have led up to the trade ceremonials, etc., traces of which are still extant. Thus, Hilhouse writes as follows of the Warrau: "I bought several of these [bisee tree] craft in the Iterite, where a depot of them had been collected. . . . But the bargaining, except as an instance of national manners, was sufficiently tedious. First came a multiplicity of questions, then a jorum of beer made of the fermented fruit of the ite—acid, astringent, and a red oil floating on top—this being returned by a glass of rum, the trading treaty was concluded . . . one of which [craft] I bought for four axes. This, however, I found was only the basis of the bargain—a cutlass, a knife, paper of hooks, scissors, needles, pins, a razor, beads, and five yards of salempores being understood as all included in the term four axes. This was a mere feeler. As soon as the old chief or captain saw the complexion of my wares, and that I bled freely, five or six other craft gradually made their appearance, which I bought reasonably enough, and then was proclaimed a general dance (Hilhouse 1834:328).

The length of journey and time spent on the trading expeditions often proved to be formidable enough, occupying, as it did, from months sometimes to a year or more. From their settlement on the Cunucunuma, a tributary of the upper Orinoco, the Maiongkong followed the Orinoco to the Cassaquiare, then the Rio Negro, then up through the mouth of the Rio Branco to Fort San Joachim, and so through the Takutu and Mahu to Pirara, about 1,000 miles in three months, partly by land and partly by water (M. Schomburgk 1847–1848:v. 1, p. 402). The migratory movements of the Akawai were all conducted with profound forethought and according to a regular system. . . . There are certain friendly villages where these roving traders are sure of getting cassava bread on their long journeys. Their expeditions sometimes occupy months, sometimes years (Brett n.d.:198). They have been called, from their roving propensities, the peddlers and news carriers of the northeast coast, and are in constant communication with the inhabitants of Venezuela and the Brazils as well as with the colonists of Demerara, Surinam, and Cayenne (Brett 1868:143). Of course, it is somewhat difficult now to estimate how far these lengthy expeditions were limited by the huckstering or by the fighting which usually accompanied them. Certain it is in some cases that the organized system of traffic has opened up new trade routes in the strict sense of the word. Thus, near Waru, at the head of the Quitaro River, there is a path which leads to the Taruma Indian country on the upper Essequibo which was made by those Indians who used to come from these parts to barter with the Wapishana.

In Surinam the lines of communication of the Joeka bush Negroes, the Oyana (who with the Oepoeroei total some 1,000) and Trio (about 800) have all been recorded. The Oyana are in direct communication with the Joeka and Boni Negroes, the Oyampi [on the Oyapok], Emerillon, Aparai, and Trio. The Trio are in direct intercourse with Joeka, Oyana, Okomajana, the Eastern Trio also with the Aparai. The Western Trio keep up a lively trade with the Saloema and on that account are called Saloema matti, i.e., Saloema friends [=?Zurumatta]. They are furthermore in connection with the Sikijana, Toenajana, and probably other tribes living more to the westward (Goeje 1908:1119). The trade of the Pianocoto is carried on exclusively with the Roucouyenne of the Paru. The Roucouyenne receive their merchandise from the Mécoras (Boni Negroes) of the Maroni. Either the Boni come to the Oyana of the Yary or the Oyana go to Cottua on the Maroni. The Oyana of the Yary sell to the Roucouyenne of the Paru, the Roucouyenne to the Pianocoto, and the Pianocoto to the Indians of the Poanna. One can imagine what the cost of an ax or a cutlass must be when, already tariffed at 100 per cent profit by the Boni, these articles reach the hands of the Pianocoto of the Poanna (O. Coudreau 1901:165).

Each tribe had its own home products, whether manufactured or in the rough— in the later case anything from dogs to timbers—and, in a sense, each had a reputation for the articles it was especially accustomed to barter. For example: The Otomac women were noted for their clay pots (Gumilla 1791:v. 1, p. 170); the Arekuna for their cotton and blowpipe; the Makusi for their curare poison; the Maiongkong (M. Schomburgk 1847–1848:v. 1, p. 402) and Taruma (Brown 1877:248) for both cassava graters and hunting dogs; the Warrau for their corials; the Waiwai for their fiber (H. Coudreau 1886–1887:v. 2, p. 379) of tucum and kuraua; the Guinau for their hammocks, cassava graters, aprons, girdles of human hair, and feather decorations (R. Schomburgk 1841:453); the Oyapock River natives for their "spleene and mateate" stones (Leigh 1906:313). Nothing came amiss, a market being always forthcoming sooner or later for everything—even for dried turtle with its preserved eggs and extracted oil (Pons 1806:53); slaves, dried fish, hammocks, and green stones (Barrère 1743:75), smoked and salted fish (Hilhouse 1832:239), sandstone for sharpening knives (M. Schomburgk 1847–1848:v. 1, p. 210), even bark shirts (M. Schombrugk 1847–1848:v. 1, p. 402). In spite of the statement made (Im Thurn 1883:271) of the Akawai alone having no special products interchangeable, there is evidence of their bartering the kishee-kishee bird (Brett 1868:181), which seems to have commanded a high price, a sort of arrow-root (Brown 1877:19), and the roots of the hai-ari (*Lonchocarpus*) for fish poisoning (Bancroft 1769:106), articles which do not appear in the commercial stock lists recorded of the other nations. As a matter of fact, the hai-ari root continued to be bartered by them to the coast tribes for quite a century later (Brett 1868:143).

Curare constituted a very important article of trade throughout the western Guianas. Gumilla mentions how the Caberre, the only nation on the Orinoco who, he says, manufactured it, derived a rich income from all the others who bought it from them either directly or through a third party (Gumilla 1791:v. 1, p. 125). Indians of various nations on the lower Orinoco proceeded to the annual market (*feria*) for curare and returned with the little clay pots more carefully guarded than the most precious balsams, etc. (Gumilla 1791:v. 2, p. 133). Now, although the Orinoco and Rio Negro Indians prepared the article, caravans nevertheless were wont to come from both of these places all the way to the Canuku Mountains to trade with the Makusi for the superior article made by them (M. Schomburgk 1847–1848:v. 1, pp. 445–447). The Arekuna secured their supplies from the Makusi in exchange for finished blowpipes or even for the pure reeds of the *Arundinaria schomburgkii,* which they in turn got from the Maiongkong (M. Schomburgk 1847–1848:v. 2, p. 239). On the upper Amazon the curare was obtained only from the Indians who lived beyond the cataracts of the rivers flowing from the north, especially the Rio Negro and Yapura (Bates 1892:296). In the more eastern Guianas curare is traded to the Waiwai, Parikutu, etc., who use it for shooting howler and other monkey. It probably comes from the Trio who manufacture it (Herderschee 1905b:943).

The stone-chip cassava graters of the Uaupes River Indians were also articles of trade in all the upper Amazon, as they were cheaper than the copper graters used in other parts of Brazil (Wallace 1889:336). Those of the Rupununi River Makusi were brought into Surinam by Carib in the way of barter (Kappler 1854:281). I had learned from the Wapishana, who obtain their graters from the Taruma, that the Makusi received theirs in trade from the Arekuna. The Makusi confirmed this statement, adding that the usual price was at least a flask of gunpowder, but generally very much more. I was, consequently, a good deal surprised to learn from the Arekuna (or rather the Taulipang branch of them) that they do not make these articles themselves, but trade them from the Maiongkong. It is this same tribe who are carrying on a brisk trade in graters from the Orinoco to the upper Rio Branco (Ule 1913:291).

The trade in good hunting dogs was likewise a well-established one. The Waika [Akawai] often make long journeys in order to trade and barter with the Colombian and Brazilian tribes for their breeding dogs (M. Schomburgk 1847–1848:v. 1, p. 198). Similar practices are reported from the eastern Guianas, where the Boni (bush Negroes of the Maroni River) annually travel more than 250 miles (*cent lieues*) to obtain good dogs from the Carib of the Ytany and Yary Rivers (Crévaux 1883:49). Barrère also speaks of hunting dogs constituting an article of trade between the Indians and French of Cayenne (Barrère 1743:154). Hunting dogs constitute the most important trade product of the Trio. They breed these animals with great care and supply them not only to their nearest neighbors, the Joeka, but also via the Parou and Yari to the Boni bush Negroes (Herderschee 1905b:942).

The pottery trade appears also to have been all-important—traces of it are still to be found between the Arawak and Carib—but few, if any, reliable particulars have been handed down to us with regard to the routes followed and the commodities exchanged; e.g., Otomac women manufactured clay pots for their own purposes as well as for trade use (Gumilla 1791:v. 1, p. 170).

In the early days the following particulars of the articles usually bartered to the Dutch by the Akawai have been noted: Balsam capivi [*Copaifera officinalis*], a balsam called Arrecocerra [*Protium aracouchili*], hai-ari roots, oil of Caraba [*Carapa guianensis*] ... different kinds of curious woods, letter wood [*Brosimum*], ducolla-bolla [?Dukalli-balli], ebony, likewise vanilla, annatto [*Bixa orellana*], *Cassia fistularis, Canella alba,* wild nutmeg, wild cinnamon, monkeys, parrots, parroquets, etc. In return, the Dutch gave them India salempores with which they cover their nudity, hatchets, knives, fishhooks, combs, and small looking-glasses, together with beads of red coral on which they put an immoderate value, and glass beads of different colors (Bancroft 1769:263, 269). Attention had already been drawn to the letter wood by Harcourt, who wrote: "There is also a red speckled wood in that Countrie called Pira timinere, which is worth thirtie or fortie pounds a Tun. It is excellent for Joyner's work" (Harcourt 1906:385). Silk grass (*Bromelia*), the pero of the old Spaniards and flax of the English (Wilson 1906:349–350), seems likewise to have been an important article of commerce in the early days, if only to judge by what Leigh says of it: "At my arrivall here I found a Dutch shippe, and sithence here have arrived another; they buye up all the Flaxe they can get, and pay so deere that I can get none; yet they have not gotten so little I thinke as ten tunnes of Flaxe within these two months" (Leigh 1906:320). In more modern times the bladder of the gilbagre (*Practocephalus*) has been and is still a not insignificant article of British Guiana and Surinam trade (Appun 1871:v. 2, p. 126). Among present-day articles of trade from the Dutch particularly favored by the Trio are: White buttons on cards, purple beads (*silirman*, Goeje 1908:1036), and especially balsam of Peru (Goeje 1908: 1048). The Oyana seemed very keen on salt (Herderschee 1905a:141), as also I found the Waiwai and Taruma were.

NOTES

1. This article represents a collation of the pertinent sections of Roth 1929 with the 1924 work of the same author.

The Kadiwéu are the only remaining group of the Mbayá, who, at the height of their expansion, dominated an area extending from Asunción, Paraguay, to Cuiabá in Mato Grosso and from the Chiriguaná settlements in the west to the banks of the Paraná. They did not actually control this area, but raided through it, capturing resident natives as well as Spaniards and Portuguese for slaves. They considered themselves to have a divine right to make war upon, enslave and demand tribute from all other peoples. Nonagriculturalists themselves, they demanded tribute from surrounding agricultural groups. Only recently have they been forced to perform some farming which supplements the hunting and gathering pattern attributed to them since the earliest reports. The Mbayá had slaves at the time of first contact. There is no reason to assume that the highly stratified nature of their society was due to the adoption of the horse, although their warlike activities were greatly aided by the introduction of this animal. There is as yet no proper ethnohistorical study of this fascinating group, but considerable background material on their history may be found in D. Ribeiro (1950), Oberg (1949) and Métraux (1946). Ribeiro's work on the religion and mythology of this group (1950) is basic to any further study.

The present article includes a description of the mechanism by which slaves were incorporated into Kadiwéu society. Such incorporation was necessary to maintain the population. It is obvious that, in spite of the sad straits in which this group now exists, they still retain much of the spirit that characterized them when they were truly the lords of all they surveyed.

Although Darcy Ribeiro is probably best known to American anthropologists for his works on Indian policy and problems of contact between Indians and the outside world, he has a record of excellent and penetrating publications in "pure" anthropology. It is only on the basis of such scientific and disinterested observation and study that one may build a proper basis for deciding matters of application and policy. Darcy Ribeiro's stature in these latter areas is firmly grounded in his profound knowledge of the people for whom he speaks.

15 DARCY RIBEIRO

Kadiwéu Kinship[1]

The Kadiwéu constitute one of the few remnants of the Guaikurú speaking groups who dominated great extensions of the Chaco until the end of the eighteenth century, forming a major obstacle to the expansion of European civilization and constantly menacing the Spanish establishments in Paraguay and access routes of the boat expeditions [monções] from São Paulo to Cuiabá. They now live in the south of Mato Grosso on a reservation that extends from the Serra da Bodoquena to the Paraguay River between the Aquidavão, Neutaka and Nabileque rivers, forming a triangle of about 100 square leagues of grassland and forest. This reservation was granted by the state government in 1903 and has been administered intermittently by the Indian Protection Service [Serviço de Proteção aos Índios].

The Kadiwéu began to settle permanently on the left bank of the Rio Paraguay at the beginning of the nineteenth century when they initiated peaceful relationships with the whites, relations that were only stabilized a century later with the total cessation of warlike activities and the adaptation, still in process, to those means of gaining a living that are approved by the dominant whites. Today, although they dress like their neo-Brazilian neighbors and raise cattle, hunt and cure hides by the same methods, they still preserve many of the characteristics of the lordly people, the celebrated Indian Cavaliers, who dominated almost all the tribes of the Chaco, enslaving many of them.

At the time of our visit the population consisted of 235 people: 94 near Posto Indigena Presidente Alves de Barros at the foot of the Serra Bodoquena, 60 km. from Coronel Juvêncio, station of the Northwestern Brazil Railway; 66 people in the vicinity of the Posto de Criação Pitoco, 24 km. from the previous one; 11 people in Limoeiro, the isolated residence of the most prestigious religious leader, 20 km. from Pitoco and 31 people in Tomásia, the most isolated community, 54 km. from Pitoco. Twenty-six Kadiwéu are still outside the reservation working on the Fazenda Francesa and at the Carandazal station of the Northwestern Brazil Railway. In addition to the Kadiwéu groups, five Tereno families comprising 28 people live on the reservation.

In the present article we will attempt to describe the Kadiwéu family system just as we saw it functioning. We are deliberately avoiding a diachronic treatment, indispensable for explaining the present day cultural reality of the Kadiwéu, both because the brevity of our stay among them did not permit the collection of sufficient data on many aspects of the kinship system, and because the various early sources on Guaikurú groups, written by missionaries, military men and travelers,[2] although very rich in data on other matters, are lamentably poor regarding kinship.

Reprinted by permission of the author and publisher from *Revista do Museu Paulista*, n.s., vol. 2 (1948), pp. 175–192. Translated and edited by Patricia J. Lyon with the approval of the author.

All material appearing within square brackets [ ] has been added by the editor of this book.

We will, therefore, limit ourselves to a simple description of the kinship system and its principal connections with current social organization and cultural configuration.

RESIDENCE GROUPS

The most important functional unit in Kadiwéu society is the residence group, that is, a nucleus of biologically or socially related individuals who live in the same house. The residence group functions as a cooperative unit with a high degree of internal solidarity, and is the center of economic activity. The women work together, helping each other in domestic activities, the gathering of wild and cultivated foods and the manufacture of artifacts. The men, although without a strict division of labor, prefer collecting and hunting, cattle herding or agriculture. Each one works according to his likes and aptitudes, dividing the products of his activities with the others.

According to the results of the census we took, of the 27 residence groups on the reservation, 23 are located near others in three villages and four are isolated, each forming an independent unit. Analyzing these groups from the point of view of relationships among the members of each one, we find the following types of family association: a) conjugal families consisting of a married couple with their children and, sometimes, a close relative of one of the spouses; b) consanguineal families composed of a group of biologically related individuals, usually sisters, their spouses and children; c) groups of married couples socially related by ties of servitude between one member of a couple and other individuals in the group, or by intermarriages that led to the settling of the families of the two spouses in the same residence. Table I shows the distribution of these types of family association in the residential groupings, and the number of married couples and individuals within each type, and in the three principal communities and in the four isolated ones.

The data demonstrate the predominance in both number of people involved and frequency of occurrence, of residence groups composed of consanguineal families. Next in importance are the socially determined groups. Of these, those related by intermarriage are less stable, since all such cases are seen as provisional arrangements in the face of temporary difficulties, the component families being expected to dissociate later. Those groups related through servitude were much more important until a few years ago, many of them having disintegrated through the separation of the slave components who established themselves as conjugal families near the posts. In the table, the conjugal groups appear of greater consequence than they really are. It was determined, by studying the composition of each of them, that two of the five indicated at Presidente Alves were recently established there after splitting off from groups in which they had the status of slaves. The group at Pitoco was formed in an unusual manner; the husband bought his wife, who was a slave, and settled down with her. The families listed at Tomásia and in the isolated groups, although living in their own houses, are separated, in each case, by only a few meters from the house of the wife's family with whom their members function as an economic unit.

TABLE I

Residence Groups[a]

	Residences						
Type of family association	*P. Alves*	*Pitoco*	*Tomásia*	*Isolated groups*[b]	*Total*	*Married couples*	*Individuals*
Conjugal	5	1	1	2	9	9	39
Consanguineal	5	3	1	3	12	23	104
Intermarried	2	–	1	–	3	9	43
Servitude	2	–	1	–	3	5	22
Totals	14	4	4	5	27	46	208

[a]Three families that were off the reservation and one man who lives alone are not included.

[b]Including the groups of Jatobá (2 married couples, 7 individuals), Curicaca (3 married couples, 10 individuals), Morrinho (3 married couples, 11 individuals), and Limoeiro (3 married couples, 11 individuals).

We should also note disturbance of the social organization, affecting the Kadiwéu family system as well, that is caused by the presence of an official administration foreign to the group. The relatively great concentrations around the posts are largely due to the possibilities for work and assistance that the posts insure, making them more or less independent of the exigencies of an economy based on hunting, gathering and herding, which demands large areas for each family and a number of members larger than that usual in a conjugal family. Such a relationship is indicated by the fact that the majority of the conjugal groups are near the posts.

MARRIAGE AND SEPARATION

According to data obtained from various Kadiwéu, both men and women, girls can marry immediately after the initiation ceremony celebrated following first menstruation, and boys "when they find a woman." Our observations confirm these data. The youngest wife that we know is 16 years old and was married two years ago, and the youngest husband is 18, his case being exceptional as we will see. The data from the census we took in December 1947 indicate that the common age for first marriage is 20 for men and less than 16 for women. Of the 18 men between 16 and 20 years of age, 14 had not been married. Of women over 15 years old, only one had not been married and all individuals over 25 years of age had been married at least once. These data also show that women first marry men at least five years older than they are. The disproportion between the number of men and women under forty years of age who are either unmarried or separated—24 men to 9 women—is probably one of the factors causing men to marry later than women, since it increases the competition in acquiring a wife.

Marriage may occur earlier when it is contracted by the parents. In this case two persons can be considered to be married at any age by an agreement and exchange of presents between the parents. The boy will visit the girl's house periodically, bearing gifts and receiving others, going to live with her immediately after the initiation ceremony. The Kadiwéu[3] speak of this kind of marriage as one of the ordinary possibilities, but one occurring rarely, and mention some people that were married in this way. The usual marriage, however, occurs at the ages noted, formally on the man's initiative, it being common for the girl to insist on the boy's approaching her parents.

The Kadiwéu always emphasize that girls should be virgins when they marry, although they recount the love life of each woman, which generally includes premarital sexual relations. According to these sources, a woman's first sexual experiences occur shortly before initiation and generally with boys of the group from which will come her future husband, so that then they can settle on marriage partners, considering the girl's preferences. Not uncommonly a man has sexual relations with his future bride even before proposing. We heard from some young men of the relationships they are maintaining with their young girlfriends. According to these stories such encounters take place during mixed bathing and, more frequently, on nights when there are festivals or in the girl's house when her parents are absent. Concerning the pattern of virginity, the following commentary of a Kadiwéu[4] is revealing. It refers to the chief of a Tereno family who did not let his daughters participate in the festivals: "It's stupid to hang on, girl is like fish [piaba], the tighter people hold on the more she slips away. You grab her but she slips up the creek, Caracará[5] comes and yanks her under water and goes and breaks her winkle wide open."

Marriage between persons who call each other "sibling" is prohibited, except for socially determined "siblings," when marriage is permitted with some disapproval. Recently, the parents of a girl gave her in marriage to her mother's slaves' grandson who they found sleeping with her. They said, at the time, that it was better to have them married in the sight of all, but when there was a disagreement between the girl's parents and the son-in-law, they threw him out, although a daughter had already been born, stating that marriage between "siblings" was not permitted.[6]

According to João Apolinário, an extremely prestigious religious leader, on the occasion of her first marriage, a girl's father and mother should be asked for her hand, although if they have separated, then after the marriage of the daughter in question. For following marriages it is enough to ask the mother. If a girl has no parents, her hand should be asked of her closest relatives, those with whom she is living, or her elder brother. The request may be made by the interested party himself, but the custom is for the prospective groom to transfer this duty to his "best friend," if not to do the asking, at least to sound out the situation and prepare the ground.

A first marriage is considered ideal when it occurs between young people who have never been married; in that case the parents of the girl and of the boy give parties. Only the first marriage is celebrated in this way. The parties consist of Kadiwéu dances to the music of flutes and drums and Brazilian dances to the music of guitar and accordion, plenty of unsugared mate [Paraguay tea] and plenty of cane alcohol served ceremonially, sometimes a horse race and hand to hand fights and, when the parents' wealth permits, the butchering of one or more steers for the guests. The parents of the newlyweds participate in these parties as they do in those held for initiations, which are the largest, only to serve the guests.

The groom must give a present to his bride and others to her parents; he also receives presents from the bride and his parents-in-law. In the case of subsequent marriages, the consent of the mother and the exchange of presents, which can take place later, is followed by the groom's moving into the bride's house.

The Kadiwéu are strictly monogamous. Marriages generally last only a short time, especially among young people, but no man has more than one woman as a wife and no woman has more than one husband at a time. Residence of the couple after marriage is matrilocal. At least during the first years, a husband lives in his wife's house and can never leave the village with her to attend any festivities unless accompanied by other residents of the house. Likewise, when a husband goes to work on the neighboring plantations he cannot take his wife with him. With the passing of the years, generally after the death of the wife's mother, the married couple, if it is still together—which is very rare—acquires greater independence and can establish their own residence.[7] The husband, after marriage, not only moves in with his wife's relatives, but also becomes a part of their economic unit, separating himself from his previous one. He takes with him to the new residence all his cattle, which are henceforth at the service of the woman's group. We noted, however, that the belongings of the woman are never mixed up with those of her husband. Cattle, as well as all other possessions, are always distinctly separated, and the man never loses contact with his own family group; he frequently visits his sisters and also maintains close relations with his brothers.

The average length of conjugal unions is very short, as we said, seldom more than two years among young people. Separation can be effected on the initiative of either of the partners or the girl's parents. When it is on the initiative of the man, he generally alleges infidelity on the part of his wife. A Kadiwéu man about 30 years old, Antonio Mendes (É-txuá-uô), who had been married six times between 1940 and 1947, told us: "I've no luck with women, they go around doing bad things, run around with other men; you can't quarrel with the men, can't beat the women, just have to get out."

According to the accounts we collected about the motives behind the most recent separations, when a woman takes the initiative she makes accusations identical to those of the husband and, also, that he does not work or that she does not like him. The parents, or those responsible for the woman, take the initiative when they feel themselves exploited by the son-in-law, who is not contributing to the subsistence of the group to the degree they had expected, when he mistreats his wife or is disrespectful to them. The birth of a child is sometimes a motive for separation among young married people because a pregnant woman must sleep in a separate bed, abstaining from relations with her husband, for a period of approximately two months before, and one year after, the birth of the child. This practice, today little respected by newly married couples, is probably one of the factors that make abortion and infanticide so frequent among the Kadiwéu. In the case of infanticide, the period of abstention from sexual relations after birth is one or two months; in the case of abortion it is even less. Sometimes men separate from their wives while expecting a child, marry another woman, and return to live with the first a year later. We knew one couple in this situation; the man had left his wife pregnant and married another and everyone said that, after the period of abstinence, they would go back to living together.[8]

Marital infidelity is considered good justification for separation but married couples do not always separate on this account, and there does not appear to be any resentment toward the person with whom the husband or wife had relations, at least not to the point of causing conflicts. There is no great secret made of one's own amorous adventures, nor of those of other people. A husband will be told of his wife's adventures and vice-versa without the least reserve. The expectation among young married people seems to be that, given the opportunity, they will be unfaithful. This expectation is manifest in the continual vigilance that they maintain towards each other.

It is common to see men and women who get married and separate almost yearly. We already noted one man who got married six times from 1940 to 1947. In the same period another[9] also was married six times and one woman[10] had seven husbands.

KINSHIP SYSTEM

The Kadiwéu have a classificatory type of kinship system, that is, they include under a single term groups of relatives of the same generation who are somehow equivalent in social relations (Radcliffe-Brown 1930–1931). The system is also bilineal, involving both paternal and maternal lines without emphasizing either of them. The Kadiwéu have no institution based on unilineal exogamous divisions. Kinship terminology reflects not only the family relationships of the Kadiwéu but also other aspects of social organization and the current cultural configuration. Some terms are employed to designate, in addition to relationships of consanguinity and affinity, certain kinds of socially determined kinship, such as those established between slaves and masters, godparents and godchildren. Also reflected in the kinship terminology are the modifications that occur in family relationships upon the death of a relative.

Kadiwéu kinship is very similar to the Tupí system (Wagley and Galvão 1946), the most notable differences being due to a greater elaboration of the former, which distinguishes a greater number of kin relationships, and to the correlations between the two systems and their respective social organizations.

I. Consanguineal Kinship

Table II presents a diagram and the terminology of consanguineal kinship, clearly indicating the tendency to designate groups of relatives of the same generation by a single term.

1. All the individuals of the grandparents' generation are classified as "grandmother" or "grandfather," according to sex.

TABLE II

Consanguineal Kinship

Terminology from the point of view of a man (upper number) and a woman (lower number). A circle signifies female; a triangle, male; parallel lines indicate marriage. All the terms are given in the possessive, "my father" not "father." The terms are transcribed following Portuguese pronunciation except the *h* which is pronounced as in English; the *gu* has the same value as in Portuguese *guia* [or English guide]; dashes indicate a glottal stop.

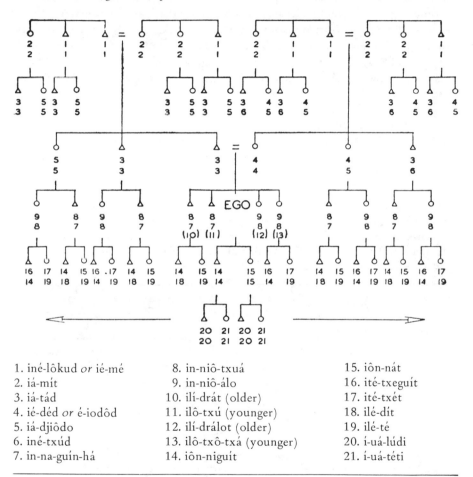

1. iné-lôkud *or* ié-mé
2. iá-mít
3. iá-tád
4. ié-déd *or* é-iodôd
5. iá-djiôdo
6. iné-txúd
7. in-na-guín-há

8. in-niô-txuá
9. in-niô-álo
10. ilí-drát (older)
11. ilô-txú (younger)
12. ilí-drálot (older)
13. ilô-txô-txá (younger)
14. iôn-niguít

15. iôn-nát
16. ité-txeguít
17. ité-txét
18. ilé-dít
19. ilé-té
20. í-uá-lúdi
21. í-uá-téti

2. In the parents' generation there are different terms for "father," "mother," "father's sister" and "mother's brother" (woman speaking). A man classifies as "father" his father's brother and mother's brother, and as "mother" his mother's sister, using another term for father's sister, which is the same one used by a woman for mother's sister and father's sister. A woman classifies her father's brother as

"father" and designates her mother's brother by another term. The same terms applied to brothers and sisters of the father or mother are also applied to the children of the grandparent's generation.

3. Ego classifies as "sibling" all relatives of his own generation, not distinguishing between cross- and parallel-cousins. Siblings of the same sex as the speaker are designated by a single term, and two other terms are used for siblings of the opposite sex. There are special terms for older and younger siblings.

4. Correspondingly, in the children's generation, when a man speaks, he classifies as "son" or "daughter" the sons and daughters of all the relatives that he calls "brother" (same sex) and designates by other terms the sons and daughters of those he calls "sister" (opposite sex). When a woman speaks, she classifies as "son" the sons . . . of the relatives she calls "sister" (same sex) and uses other terms for the daughters of "sisters" and of "brothers," and the sons of "brothers."

5. All relatives of the second descending generation are classified as "grandsons" or "granddaughters" according to sex.

II. Affinal Kinship

Table III presents a diagram and the terminology of affinal kinship.

1. The father and mother of the husband or wife are designated by the same

TABLE III
Affinal Kinship

Affinal kinship terminology from the point of view of a man (smaller numbers) and a woman (larger numbers). The divided circle and triangle indicate married persons who are separated.

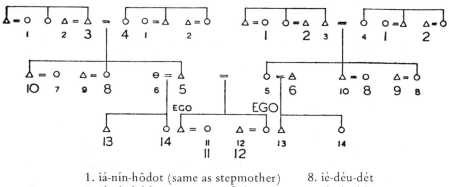

1. iá-nín-hôdot (same as stepmother)
2. iá-nín-húdi (same as stepfather)
3. iô-txí-hádit
4. iô-txí-hát
5. iô-dauát (childless)
   iô-txá-háua (with children)
6. in-nála-túdi (separated)
7. i-lát
8. ié-déu-dét
9. iá-níu-údit
10. ié-déu-dít
11. ihá-tét
12. ihá-dít
13. é-inigui
14. é-iná

terms, "father-in-law" or "mother-in-law," depending on sex. A father's or mother's brother's wife or sister's husband is designated by the same term as a father's wife (stepmother) or mother's husband (stepfather).

2. The married couple call each other by a single term that varies depending on whether they have children or not; there is a special term to designate a married person who is separated. A husband's sister, a wife's sister and a brother's wife (woman speaking) are designated by the same terms. The husband or wife's brother is also designated by a single term, the same being true for a sister's husband (man or woman speaking) and there is a special term for a brother's wife (man speaking).

3. Two terms are used to designate a son's wife and a daughter's husband, these terms being applied to the spouses of all those individuals designated in the system as sons or daughters. There are separate terms for son and daughter of one's spouse by a previous marriage (stepson and stepdaughter).

III. Death and Kinship Terms

As is the case among various indigenous groups, among the Kadiwéu the death of an individual occasions many modifications in the relationships among his relatives. Thus, the tribal names of the dead are never pronounced by any person who may have been biologically or socially related to him, and all such persons change their own tribal names after the death of a relative. Such influence extends even further among the Kadiwéu, however, since death is also reflected in consanguineal kinship terminology. Table IV shows the modifications that occur in the designations of parents, parents' siblings and sibling's children, when a father, mother, brother or

TABLE IV

Effect of Death on Kinship Terminology

Modifications that occur in kinship terminology on the death of a relative. A cross indicates the dead relative.

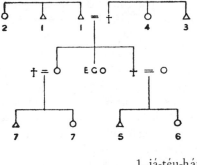 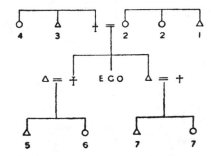

1. iá-téu-hát
2. iá-té
3. iú-ihát
4. ida-gát
5. iá-tín-niguít
6. iá-titxút
7. ilá-bát

sister dies. These changes are made always maintaining the principles of the classificatory system of kinship.

1. The designations for widowed father and mother are also applied to the brother or sister of the father after the death of the mother, and to the brother or sister of the mother after the death of the father. There are two other terms for brother and sister of a defunct father, also applied to the brother or sister of a dead mother. Here, the distinctions between father's siblings and mother's siblings that we see in ordinary terminology disappear.

2. Ego designates the children of a dead brother by the same terms as those of a dead sister. Another term is employed to designate the children of a widowed brother or sister. Brothers and sisters, for this purpose, are all the relatives so designated in the system.

IV. Relationships of Servitude

Kadiwéu social structure is based on an ethnic division into two strata: masters and slaves, the slave stratum consisting of individuals captured or bought from other tribes and of their descendants in the first and second generations. Investigating the ethnic origin of the inhabitants of the reservation more than 16 years old that represented themselves as Kadiwéu, we found that only 10 men and 9 women, of a total of 144, are "pure" Kadiwéu, that is, descendants of parents and grandparents all of whom were Kadiwéu. We also determined that 11 men and 13 women came from other groups, 14 of them having entered the reservation while still children and been raised as Kadiwéu with the status of slave, or "captive" as they say. The remaining 101 are descendants of "captives," 63 in the first generation (one or both of their parents slaves) and 38 in the second generation (one or more grandparents slaves). Aside from the 10 individuals that settled among the Kadiwéu as adults, the rest identify themselves as Kadiwéu and speak only the Guaikurú dialect of this group in addition to the Portuguese known by the majority.

Relationships between masters and slaves are asymmetrical, the latter submitting to the former, and the common form of address between them is "my master" and "my captive." Masters expect slaves to maintain a respectful attitude and, in many cases, to render services without expecting recompense and to give over part of the products of their work. This pattern is clearly manifested in the following state-ment that we heard from a female "captive,"[11] "One respects the master more than other men, and when he comes to the house one has to give him the best to eat," and especially in the conflicts we observed in Pres. Alves originating in differences in expectation between masters and slaves. In all cases the masters demanded gifts or services, coming in conflict with the slaves who refused to provide them. The community, in these cases, always sided with the slaves, berating the "master" because "Now there are no longer captives, we are all brothers."

We know some slaves who live in their masters' house where they are treated as lower status members of the family, provide service as slaves and are very attached, emotionally, to their "masters." The behavior of slaves and masters, when a relative of either one of them dies, is the same as that among consanguineal relatives and slaves are buried in the family plot of their masters.

The following are the kinship terms used to designate relationships between slave and master:

1. The adult "captive" designates his captor as "my owner" (iá-dji-miguít) or "my master" (iniô-tágod), or even as "my grandfather" (ié-mé); if he was taken as a child, as "my father" (iá-tád); the captor's wife is "my mistress" (in-niô-tágod) or "my grandmother" (iá-mít), or even "my stepmother" (iá-nín-hôdot); he is called "my captive" (iô-taguít) or "my grandson" (í-uá-lúdi).

2. A captive's son designates the captor of his father or mother as "my grandfather" (ié-mé) and his sons as "my father" (iá-tád), and both as "my master" (iniô-tágod); he is called by the first "my grandson" (í-uá-lúdi) and by the second "my son" (iôn-nát) or "my captive" (iô-taguít).

3. A captive's son designates the grandson of his father's captor as "my brother" (in-niô-txuá) and is called the same in return.

The modalities that kinship terms take at the death of certain relatives [see Table IV] are also applied to the descendants of captives after the death of their slave parents.

Thus, the reciprocal address of the sons of the captor and the sons of the captive, iá-tád/iôn-nát, on the death of the captive's father change to iá-téu-hát/iá-titxút, on the death of the captive's mother the terms change to iú-ihát/ilá-bát.[12]

As can be seen, the kinship terminology clearly reflects the process of integration of the slave into Kadiwéu society, the descendants of captor and captive progressively approaching one another in social level, generation after generation, at a certain point coming to classify each other as brothers. The relationship between these brothers is not symmetrical as are those between consanguineal brothers, since the descendant of slaves may, at any time, hear a malicious allusion to the origin of the kinship that links him to the descendant of the captor. But as the designations "my master" and "my captive" disappear, so do the obligations that they imply.

V. Adopted Children and Godchildren

We found in the households some individuals called "son" or "daughter" besides those so classified in consanguineal kin terms and the slaves. These are persons adopted due to the death or incapacity of their parents and brought up as sons or daughters. They have the same status as the children of the family and are designated by the same terms.

Another focal point of socially determined kinship relations is the institution of "baptism" (dji-leguí-nal). The ceremony that originates this relationship consists of a party, during which the name of an infant and the identity of his "godparents" (inibedón-nuhúd) are communicated. The party is organized by the parents of the child with the help of the friends chosen as godfather and godmother; if means are lacking they do without the party, bearing the baptized child from house to house to communicate the name it received. In either of the two forms, they try to emphasize the relationship established between the parents of the baptized child and the godparents. They have no words in their language to designate these relationships, using the Portuguese terms *compadre* and *comadre* which they repeat innumerable times during the party. This event terminates only when alcohol is served, the co-godparents then committing themselves to maintain close friendship and to live as brothers.

Children are "baptized" before reaching five years of age, this being the only ceremony for boys, whereas the girls later have an initiation ceremony. Although they use the same terms to designate the Catholic institution of baptism and their own, they consider them to be different. Parents, given the opportunity, "baptize" their children in both forms, seeing nothing incompatible between the two. The same child may be baptized three or four times and each new baptism establishes a new series of relationships, defining a rather precise status for the godchild, the godparents, the co-godparents and the respective families.

Relationships between godchildren (inibedón-niguít) and godparents are perfectly defined. They must help each other, and the godchild, at any time, may go to live in the house of his godfather. Marriage between a godchild and the children of his godparents—classified as siblings—is disapproved although it may not be impossible. Co-godparents and godchildren must be invited to all parties given by a godparent, and they must go or be represented by a close relative, receiving privileged treatment. Relations between co-godparents should conform to the relations between consanguineal siblings. We found in some family groups individuals whose relationships with other members were explained to us as being of this type, and the principal cooperative relationships that we observed were between co-godparents, such relationships being surpassed only by those between children of the same parents.

RELATIONSHIPS WITHIN THE FAMILY

The interrelationship of biologically or socially related individuals are of familiarity or courtesy depending on the nature and degree of kinship. Relations between consanguineal and affinal relatives of different generations are respectful, members of the older generation (parents and grandparents) being allowed to have a joking kind of familiarity toward those of the following generations (children and grandchildren). Relationships are familiar among relatives of the same generation, and they joke with each other. Sex is one of the common themes of verbal jokes, but sexual relations per se are prohibited between related persons. Respect between individuals of the same social level, e.g., consanguineal grandfather and grandson, is different from the respect that a slave owes his master. This latter type admits of sexual relationships, although with some disapproval.

A man, in the matrilocal residential groups, always being able to go to neighboring groups for parties and hunting, relates more than does a woman to all the paternal relatives of his own generation, his parents' generation and that of his children. A woman's relationships remain more or less confined to those relatives of her mother who dwell in and frequent her own house, thus being less broadly integrated in the kinship system than is a man who relates to a larger circle, a fact that is reflected in the kinship terminology.

The degree of solidarity among biologically or socially related individuals varies, depending on the familiarity they maintain with one another. Close relatives are clearly differentiated from distant ones, although they may be classified by a single term. The strongest bonds are those uniting parents and children, and siblings of the same parents, equally in the conjugal and the consanguineal groups; next strongest are those among members of the same residential group and, gradually weaker, those among relatives of the same generation and among those of different generations.

Living with the Kadiwéu in their own houses, we were able to observe some of the typical relationships among relatives but for the following description we are using data from various Indians and from Sr. Anaudelino, agent at P.C. Pitoco, who has lived among the Kadiwéu since 1941 and speaks their language quite well.

I. Relationships Between Parents and Children

Women have children only after age 20, and the majority of them later still, not allowing those conceived earlier to "mature." Few Kadiwéu women have more than three children, it being more common to have one or two, and the great majority of them only allow a new child to be born after the previous one is more than three years old.

Abortion and infanticide are widely practiced, as we said. Abortion is accomplished by means of a decoction of bitter roots, principally *fedegoso* (axalá-krí),[13] or by mechanical means, pounding the fetus in the mother's belly until it is killed. If the mother cannot manage alone, she asks the help of a specialist who, for abortions, is always a man. They kill the fetus mechanically, without the mother, who lies on the ground for this purpose, feeling any pain. Infanticide, to which they resort when attempts at abortion were not successful and, primarily, when a child is born who is not of the desired sex—boys are generally preferred—is performed by the mother or by a "killer." In such a case, they break the child's neck or asphyxiate it and bury it inside the house underneath the platform bed on which the parents sleep. The father cannot see a child that is not to be allowed to "mature." Men cannot practice infanticide, it being a function exclusive to women. There is presently a great battle within the group against abortion and infanticide, but both continue to be practiced on a grand scale, as evidenced by the composition of the Kadiwéu population.[14]   Recently, a woman obliged her niece, who lives with her and is married to a son of a Xamakoko, to abort, saying that she did not want a Xamakoko grandson; she herself, however, is a descendant of that tribe.[15] Among the justifications that I heard for practicing abortion and infanticide, those that occur most frequently are that there is no clothing for a new child and that the last one is still very small. Probably abstinence from sexual relations between the parents before and after the birth of the child is still one of the factors.

Kadiwéu mothers care for their children with the greatest vigilance, leaving them only when they are asleep, accompanying them all day long, watching their slightest move. A woman generally stops cooking for her husband, he himself preparing the meals if they live alone, and only at night will she go to bathe and wash clothes. We heard from Julia (In-nium-nalôe) of Pitoco the following commentary about the work that children cause: "You have to keep watching all day long, a kid is an animal, it doesn't know anything, if you leave it it might even eat chicken shit, any filth off the ground." Children are nursed for two years and sometimes considerably longer. There are no secrets for children, everything can be heard, the adults converse in front of them with no constraint whatsoever. Their questions are always patiently satisfied with all the details that they want about anything. The father and the mother feel equally responsible for the orientation and teaching of the children, which is never done formally. For this purpose boys are more attached to their father and girls to their mother by virtue of the division of labor by sex, but the entire maternal group collaborates in the education of children. The authority of parents over their daughters is greater than that of husbands over their wives. This pattern is seen in the conflicts that occur between father-in-law and son-in-law in which, generally, the son-in-law is separated from his wife. Sons and daughters inherit equally when their parents die and the property rights of each member of the family are perfectly defined.

II. Relationships Among Siblings

Siblings, in general, are socially equivalent, reciprocal dealings differing according to the nature of the kinship, degree of familiarity and age. They are very united and are always visiting each other, especially brothers visiting sisters. The first house to which a man moves after separating from his wife is the house of a sister, which he considers as his own. Within the group of siblings defined by the system, solidarity is greatest, first among sisters, second between brothers and sisters, third among brothers. Parallel- and cross-cousins, although classified as siblings, are linked by a much lesser degree of solidarity, it being more intense among those living in the same house. Relations between siblings whose kinship is determined by servitude are asymmetrical, although a joking familiarity is permitted. Relations between older and younger brothers, especially after the former marry and move to their wives' houses, are also asymmetrical. The older brother is, for the younger, a kindly authority who helps to solve problems and brings presents when he visits.

III. Relationships Between Husband and Wife

The social position of the husband, as well as that of the wife, varies with the type of family. In conjugal groups he is the uncontested chief, having marked dominance over her. This type of family is that which best fulfills the obvious aspirations of Kadiwéu men to dominate their wives, aspirations which are manifest in the fact that the men querulously attribute the conjugal infidelity of the women to matrilocal residence. Commenting on the amorous adventures of a young married woman, one Kadiwéu said to us:[16] "If it were me, I'd drag her out of her father's house, even by force, and then I'd like to see her mess around with other men." Within the extended family a man's social position is markedly inferior to that of a woman. Husbands under 40 years of age are almost always treated as outsiders in these residence groups, being integrated into the group and improving their status only after that age when they finally settle down with one woman, then becoming one of the most prestigious elements of the group.

The social position of the woman varies correspondingly, greater submission in conjugal groups and greater independence when she lives with her own family. Since the number of unmarried and separated adult women (17) is much smaller than that of men in the same condition (29) competition for women becomes extremely intense, increasing their worth and thus helping to improve their social position. All the women under 40 who are separated had been "divorced" shortly before and are, with the exception of two who are under treatment for illness, being contended for by the men. Also influential in the present status of the woman is the role she plays in the group economy, especially her connection with the economy of the neighboring neo-Brazilians. One of the few means the Indians of the reservation have for acquiring money is the sale of plaited work. By virtue of the rigid division of labor in this field, women manufacture the greater part of these items and precisely the more profitable ones. Men plait only hats.

Even in consanguineal families, the married couple and their children are not completely absorbed into the family unit; they always maintain some liberty, functioning as small sub-groups with a higher degree of internal solidarity for the provision of food and the education of the children.

Young married couples are generally very affectionate and spend almost all the time the husband is at home together, telling stories and laughing, while the man plaits hats or tends to his riding gear and arms and the woman cares for the children, cooks, and makes plaited work or pottery. The man's obligations are caring for his own cattle, which are generally few but always give occasion to spend part of the day outside far from his father-in-law's farm, and hunting, which still represents a substantial source of food. Women, older men and children take care of gathering fruit, palm hearts and honey and, with few exceptions, only the older men in extended families and chiefs of the conjugal groups have cultivated fields. Before marrying, boys help their fathers a little, but principally they dance, make music and hunt. After marriage they continue the same way of life for several years, depending on their father-in-law's field or those of the older men of their wife's group.

Relations between separated married people are strictly regulated. They must maintain a respectful attitude toward one another and become good friends as soon as the resentment has passed. An ex-husband is, as are brothers, one of the people to whom a woman can appeal in case of troubles, especially if they have children. He is also the cause of friction between the woman and her new husband.

When a person dies, the Kadiwéu burn the house in which he lived and take his objects of personal use to the cemetery, the rest being distributed among the relatives. There are, however, still no universally accepted patterns regarding inheritance of the property of the dead and one of the uncertainties is whether the last wife has a right to inherit if she had no children by the dead man.

IV. Relations Between Son-in-Law and Daughter-in-Law — Father-in-Law and Mother-in-Law

A son-in-law never speaks directly to either his father-in-law or his mother-in-law. This pattern is considered to be a symbol of the respect that they must maintain toward one another. "If a father-in-law or mother-in-law speaks to his daughter's husband, it is because he does not like the son-in-law any more, and he can pick up and go right now," a Kadiwéu told us.[17] We observed that parents-in-law do not, even indirectly, take part in the conversations of groups in which the son-in-law may be present. When they want to speak to him they direct themselves to their daughter as though the son-in-law were not present. They also avoid looking at one another. According to information from chief Lauriano, confirmed by a story from the agent of P. C. Pitoco, if on a trip or hunt the wife's father or mother find themselves alone and need to say something to the son-in-law, they speak without looking at each other, the parents-in-law addressing themselves to their daughter and the son-in-law to his wife, as if she were present. This pattern is strictly observed by all Kadiwéu. Sons-in-law and parents-in-law, whether they live together or not, never speak to each other.

The daughter-in-law converses freely with her father-in-law and mother-in-law. These relationships are, according to a comparison made by one Kadiwéu,[18] similar to those that should be established as a rule between distant relatives of different generations.

NOTES

1. This article is based on data collected during research carried out by the author in the last two months of 1947, among the Kadiwéu, as part of the program of the Research Section of the Indian Protection Service.

2. The principal sources of information on the early Guaikurú are the following: Dobrizhoffer (1784) [1750–1762], Sánchez Labrador (1910, 1917) [1760–1767], Prado (1839) [1795], Serra (1845–1850) [1803], Azara (1809) [1781–1801], Boggiani (1945) [1892 and 1897].

3. Ilidio and Luz Preto (Acía-toho and Habí-uá) of Tomásia.

4. Antonio Rufino (Omá-txé) of Pres. Alves.

5. Trickster hero of Kadiwéu mythology. [The caracará is a bird of the family Falconidae]

6. Berenicia (Ná-ué-ná) and Joaquim Mariano (Nôo-ták) of Pres. Alves.

7. Data provided by Luiz Pinto (Habí-uá) of Tomásia.

8. Nií-la of Pitoco and Rafael (Náo-umiligue) of Morrinho.

9. Eucrídio Pinto (Dibí-té-ho) of Pitoco.

10. Amélia Marcolina (Abú-gô) of Morrinho.

11. Idalina (Liguí) of Campina.

12. All these kinship terms are from a man's viewpoint. For the opposite case, woman speaking, see Tables II and IV.

13. Leguminous member of the Caesalpiniodiae, genus *Cassia*, probably *Cassia occidentalis*.

14. Leading this fight are "father" João Apolinário and chief Lauriano, the former in the name of sacred values and the latter "so as not to finish off the nation." From these men we obtained the data recorded on abortion and infanticide.

15. Maria (Anoã) of Pres. Alves.

16. Barbosa (Â-gô-lá) of Pitoco.

17. Mariano Rostes (Nôo-ták) of Pres. Alves.

18. Mariano Rostes (Nôo-ták) of Pres. Alves.

The lack of information on aboriginal sexual practices to be found in the anthropological literature on South America is conspicuous. The basic reason for this lack is probably largely reluctance on the part of European anthropologists to inquire into what, to us, is (or was until very recently) an essentially taboo subject. Many anthropologists live in a separate house from the group they are studying, so that direct observation of sexual activity would be difficult; and no one would be so insensitive as to follow a fond couple into the fields or the woods. There also exists the possibility that many anthropologists are in possession of data on the sex life of the people with whom they have worked but have simply not published it. Until recently it has been more than a little difficult to get such data published unless written in Latin, a language no longer known by many anthropologists. (Compare Holmberg 1950:63–65 with Holmberg 1969: 159–170). In addition, anthropologists, knowing the attitude of most Christians towards any kind of "non-standard" sexual practices may have suppressed data in the belief that they were doing so in the best interests of their informants. Such an explanation might be especially true of an anthropologist publishing in the language of the people in a position to influence the future and well-being of the group in question. Certainly such practices as those described by Crocker, if known to the surrounding population, would lead the outsider men to feel that any Canela girl was fair game and could thus cause considerable difficulties. Even without such knowledge, the attitude of the average backwoodsman toward Indian girls tends to be one of sexual dominance, as may be noted in the article by Frikel.

Crocker's discussion of attitudes toward extramarital sex raises some interesting questions. One point that is immediately obvious from Crocker's study is the degree to which extramarital sexual activity is related to other aspects of the culture. Extramarital sex is probably no more extensive among the Canela than among the Kuikuru (Carneiro 1959), but we do not have comparable material on child socialization for the latter group, so that a full comparison is not possible at present. The attitude toward a husband's knowledge of his wife's sexual activities is markedly similar to that described by Laraia for the Surui. It would be interesting to know whether such sexual jealousy might not be more influenced by neo-Brazilian standards than the author suggests. There is no reason to believe that proprietary attitudes toward one's wife's sexual favors is a human universal, and the very structure of Canela society would tend to militate against such attitudes.

Those interested in reading further about the Canela should see, in addition to the items in the Bibliography cited in this article, Crocker (1964, 1965, 1967, 1971a, 1971b). At Crocker's request, the orthography of Canela words has been changed.

Extramarital Sexual Practices of the Ramkokamekra-Canela Indians: An Analysis of Socio-Cultural Factors

Extramarital sexual intercourse is practiced extensively among the nearly 400 Jê-speaking Ramkokamekra-Canela Indians of the northern edge of the Central Brazilian Plateau. Comparing this practice cross-culturally, the Canela variety in sexual partners and also their frequency of extramarital intercourse seem unusual.

Most students of Brazilian ethnography are familiar with the extensive works of Curt Nimuendajú, the German-born, self-trained Brazilian ethnographer. In fact, they usually study his largest monograph, *The Eastern Timbira,* in which there is a detailed account of how these same Ramkokamekra-Canela lived about 30 years ago. In his writings, most sectors of Canela life are described with relative accuracy, but the information presented on the extramarital sexual activities is incomplete and some aspects need to be restated.

Nimuendajú's time with the Canela totaled 14 months in his many visits. The writer of this paper has spent 24 months during 1957 through 1960 living in the two Ramkokamekra-Canela villages and was adopted into a family in both of their communities. The advantages of having the information of the first monograph to utilize as a basis for the second study were very significant, and it seems appropriate at this time to express a strong appreciation for Nimuendajú's difficult and extensive research work among the Canela.

The main objective of this article is to present an analysis of some of the factors contributing to the operation and maintenance of this extramarital sexual inter-course sub-system of the over-all Canela socio-cultural system. First, the day-to-day, informal extramarital practices will be described. Then we will examine some aspects of the questions: how are Canela individuals socialized into performing these practices, and how are these practices sanctioned and supported as customs? Next, in order to understand better how this sub-system operates we will examine a factor which contributes conspicuously to disrupting this sub-system and then we will analyze some of the ways in which this disruptive factor is controlled. Finally, some social ramifications and acculturative aspects of this sub-system will be discussed.

This ethnological reconstruction will be presented as it is believed to have been operating around 1910, before the current social disintegration had progressed to any great extent. Most of the behavorial patterns handled, however, were known to be occurring at the time of this investigator's visits.

Reprinted by permission of the author and publisher from "Beiträge zur Volkerkunde Süd-amerikas," *Völkerkundliche Abhandlungen,* vol. 1 (1964), pp. 27–35.

THE INFORMAL EXTRAMARITAL PRACTICES

The matrilineal and matrilocal Canela are strongly monogamous, and divorce is rare after the birth of a child cements the marriage. Both the husband and the wife, however, are likely to be having extramarital relationships of a brief and sometimes of a lengthy nature during the entire course of their sexually active lives. If a man or a woman has a strong desire for an appropriate member of the opposite sex, these feelings are communicated directly to the desired person or a message is sent indirectly through known channels with the result that a rendezvous is usually arranged. Regardless of who takes the initiative, the man eventually finds himself obliged to provide the woman with gifts as part of the arrangement. These extramarital encounters go on all the time and it is only the spouse who is not supposed to know about them. There is good evidence that this always was the accepted pattern and that the trend is toward a reduction rather than an increase in these practices. The Canela have attempted to hide these facts from outsiders for fear of embarrassing them and of receiving disapproval. Adherence to the practice of marital fidelity is a Christian ideal which has been affecting Canela behavior since the beginning of their more extensive contacts with local Brazilians in the 19th century. Extramarital relations, nevertheless, were never grounds for divorce according to any of this researcher's informants including two men over seventy years of age. (Cf. Nimuendajú 1946:128.)

In addition to these more informal ways for individuals to fulfill sexual desires, there are a number of patterns for extramarital contacts in which the partners come together for social reasons rather than as a result of personal choice and preference. For instance, several women or girls without children are invited by male groups, or designated in the morning council by the elders, to be present during the resting period before the almost daily afternoon sportive log races. Any of the numerous male racers who wish to can take turns in having brief sexual relationships with these women who receive any non-relatives in rapid succession. The group gives the girls some sort of token payment to please them, and though these activities are seen to some extent as a duty, they are also very much enjoyed. Another example is that any expeditions such as work parties recruited for road building, group farm work, or the gathering of needed natural materials, are likely to be accompanied by at least two girls who will gather firewood, carry water, and provide sexual outlets for the men. A third example is that a man who has performed some service for the head of another family will often be paid by being given access to an appropriate girl of that family.

ASPECTS OF SOCIALIZATION

In investigating the socialization procedures of the Canela in order to throw some light on how they develop into adults who maintain the extramarital practices described above, two aspects, among others, of the child training patterns seem to be outstanding. These are (1) the social atmosphere in which sex is learned and (2) the permissiveness which is characteristic of most of the child training.

Concerning this social atmosphere, the Canela child is raised in an environment in which, in his presence, sex is talked and joked about with great delight between certain consanguineal relatives. This large category of fun and joke-oriented kin consists of all the consanguineal relatives not classed as parents, siblings, and children. As boys and girls grow older, they enter little by little into sex joking-relationships with any of these joking relatives, at first mimicking the words and tones of an older sibling and later making up provocative statements and sex-loaded jokes on their own. In this way, children are first hearing and then using sexual expressions before they can understand what is meant, and they are always learning about sex in a context of fun. On certain very festive occasions, children will see women standing, singing, and moving their hips in imitation of the movements of intercourse. They may also see men of the Clown Society repeatedly making thrusting motions with their penises while dancing around and shouting. In both these cases, these movements are performed to express great joy—*amyi-k^hin*—or in Portuguese, *alegria*. It is hypothesized herein that, brought up in such an atmosphere, the child learns to enjoy and to place a high value on sexual activities.

Turning to the development of personality traits that are important to the operation of this extramarital sub-system, it is clear that in several of the more conspicuous training procedures the baby learns to expect relatively often to obtain what will give it pleasure and to surrender relatively easily to others what will give them pleasure. The breast feeding practices, for instance, are among the many patterned experiences through which babies learn these emotional orientations. When they want the breast, they are given it; the mother, or a mother surrogate, is always around. They seldom let a baby cry for long, for this in itself is considered evil. Because of these practices, and for other reasons, babies experience relatively little frustration in this area of socialization.

The patterns are similar in weaning and in toilet training. The mother frustrates the child to a minimal extent, waiting months, and finally rewarding the child with affection for doing what she wants it to do. The child learns to expect to do what it wants to do relatively often and its tolerance of frustration remains relatively low, but it also learns to enjoy doing what the mother wants. The two outstanding exceptions to this permissive sort of socialization pertain to fighting and incest. Such offenses against society are considered intolerable and are punished quickly and severely.

These patterns are typical of the socialization process until puberty, so it is hypothesized that they are contributing factors in the development of much of the characteristic adult behavior. An example of the adult patterns is that when a legitimate sexual object is strongly desired, the man or woman expects, with great self-assurance, to attain the objective and cannot withstand frustration for long. Another example is that adults very conspicuously enjoy pleasing and gratifying other people. The act of giving themselves sexually to members of the opposite sex who express strong desires is consistent with this pattern. The person who refuses is felt to be stingy, and may become the objective of retaliatory witchcraft. One of the most common forms of black magic is a sickness "thrown into" a woman by her rejected lover. Deaths of this origin have caused tribal schisms and inter-tribal hostilities.

A boy, at the age of puberty, often has his first sexual experience with his naming uncle's wife, upon her initiative. When his other mother's brothers hear of this, they order him to have sexual relations just occasionally and only with middle-aged women so that he will grow strong and big. By the end of his adolescent initiation cycle, when he is about twenty, he can break these restrictions and marry. This course of behavior is held to be the ideal pattern, but occasional exceptions clandestinely practiced are understood by everybody to be the rule. By 1910, marriages were beginning to occur individually and at a much younger age as a result of the breakdown in the practice of a group rite in which all the members of an age class were ceremonially married on a day following the termination of their initiation cycle. Some of these youths were in their late teens, but most were in their twenties.

A girl may be contracted for marriage before or around puberty. She often has her first sexual experience with the contracted youth, but just as often her virginity is "stolen" in an encounter with a lover. When the men of the community know that she has had sexual intercourse, they consider her available for casual sexual relationships. This is especially the case after she has received her ceremonial belt (i?pre). If she refuses these attentions for several months, a number of men, when they can catch her alone away from the village, will force her to give, each taking his turn. Her family is so ashamed that her stinginess provoked such a course of action among the men that even if she had been injured in resisting such an encounter, her maternal uncles would not make a claim to be given a compensatory payment from the assailants, as would be the custom under other circumstances. Eventually, when used to the experience, she learns to like to give herself in these group situations which take place in a spirit of gaiety, and in which the men are flattering and attentive.

From her introduction into sex until the birth of her first child, a girl experiences great freedom and has a lot of "fun," as they say. She is married during most of this time, but is receiving attentions frequently from most of the non-related men in the tribe. Especially after she has won her belt, she will be expected to answer the frequent summons to go off as an attendant on the daily log races and other semi-public events. Later, however, as a mother, she is obliged to stay with her babies most of the time, though she still can arrange private meetings.

SOME FESTIVAL ACTIVITIES

The Canela festivals consist of a number of dramatic acts comprising pageants which last for several days. Since the performances in these pageants are traditionally prescribed and considered "right" and "good," they carry the weight of tribal law for the informal interpersonal relationships in the non-festival periods. An account of a number of these performances, or rites, will now be presented.

Prepubertal girls are likely to have their first close personal contact with the festival extramarital practices during the carrying out of their roles as girl associates of a men's society. These girls are assigned in pairs, usually one virgin and one non-virgin, to the many societies for men which average about 25 in membership. At certain times, the non-virgin has to give herself to some or to most of the male members, one right after the other. The virgin is not touched, but since she remains in the vicinity, she is aware of what is going on and may wish she were part of the fun.

During a certain festival occasion, the Wild Boar Log Race Day, which occurs about every other year, the commandant of the troop of adolescent novices procures three or four middle-aged women and orders all the boys of the troop beyond puberty to have sex in turn with one of them (Nimuendajú 1946:169, 197). Being in the vicinity, the pre-pubescent boys also are fully aware of what is going on and may be anticipating the day when they can join their seniors. These formal events contribute toward the socialization of the boys and tend to sanction the pattern for the informal utilization of one woman by a number of men in succession.

On the same Wild Boar Log Race Day, the men of each moiety as a group go with the wives of the men of the other moiety into different areas. With their spouses far away, couples arrange to meet discreetly in the bushes for brief periods. This formal occasion sets the pattern for the informal rendezvous of men and women of any age and with any number of children. The conditions of this particular festival situation make it easy to leave children and babies with relatives.

On the annual *Aylεn* Day (Nimuendajú 1946:168–169), young-married women, with few or no babies, secretly indicate as part of a rite their choice of a hunter to procure wild game for them. Publicly designated, the hunter awaits a secret message so that he will know where to take his kill in the late afternoon in exchange for sexual relations. This rite supports the informal patterns of the secret rendezvous. It also sets a precedent for the man giving the woman a gift even though she had taken the initiative in choosing *him* as a partner.

During the midday period of any festival, and this amounts to from seven to ten times a year, each moiety will conduct a conga line-like dance with the wives of the men of the other age class moiety interspersed in a long, sideways-facing file. After performing this very energetic *Mεaykʰē* procession for an hour, each moiety dancing in opposite directions around the village circle, the performers of each group and their female partners disappear into different areas for sexual relations. One group may stay in the village using their communal *Wëʔtë* house, while the other group may use the forests by the stream. The younger age classes of both moieties, however, were excluded from such activities by the members of the older age classes, in their thirties, forties, and higher. This practice may be seen as a traditional sanctioning pattern for denying the youths access to the young girls and for the reservation of the latter for the older men, at least in the more public occasions.

DISRUPTIVE FACTORS AND THEIR CONTROL

The kind of behavior which most frequently disrupts this system of extramarital practices is jealousy on the part of the left out spouse. Though the importance of being generous with a spouse is portrayed in myths, traditions, and festivals, still jealousy and hostility are expressed when a person is confronted with the evidence of extramarital relations, though this could *never* justify divorce. The joking relatives lecture the angry person energetically, and at great length, saying that jealousy and fighting are hideous and bad, and that generosity is the great Canela virtue. In more extreme cases, a person's ceremonial and informal friends, as well as the ceremonial and political chiefs of the tribe, will call upon him to forget his grievances and wounded pride.

In such a society where sex is so evident and available, it is not surprising that incest lines are strongly maintained from childhood on by severe punishments. Intercourse with distant relatives occurs, but it is believed that such behavior will shorten a person's life considerably. Intercourse with a biological sibling, they say, results in madness and death, a point which they believe they can prove by referring to examples of such occurrences. They can show the interested observer a pigpen-like structure in an old village site which was used to confine a Canela who became violent in 1938–1939 after he had purportedly broken this tabu.

A person will feel the need to display anger especially when he or she catches the spouse in the sexual act with another person, and he will feel this need even more strongly when the act is taking place on the marital platform bed. Then the infraction is taken as a deliberate insult and lack of respect for the offended spouse, because if the offender cared more, he or she would not have taken such a chance at being discovered. Even when the spouse is caught in the act, however, neither fighting nor divorce is considered a justified course of action though there may be a fight and there is most likely to be a temporary separation and a demand for payments to erase the shame "passed onto the face" of the injured spouse.

There are many cultural devices which serve to prevent a person from being confronted with the information and evidence about extramarital activity on the part of a spouse. In the festival situations, for instance, spouses are invariably separated by their having to go with opposite moieties so that there can be no actual confrontations. In such cases, a person knows his or her spouse may have had relations with others but can neither be sure about it nor can the partners be identified. This tends to alleviate any feelings of jealousy.

Another striking cultural device for preventing disruptions can be found in the use of the ceremonial linguistic form of the second person singular, *ye,* instead of the informal morpheme, *ka.* In relationships concerning a person addressed as *ye,* the speaker should always express respect and honor and never discourtesy. Causing a *ye*-addressed person embarrassment is ugly behavior. For instance, a good Canela woman should not even tell her son about his wife's extramarital affairs because she should feel honor-bound to protect this daughter-in-law whom she addresses as *ye.* Most of the affinal relationships fall into this pattern so that such news is prevented from reaching a spouse through most of his or her close consanguineal relatives. In contrast to this kind of behavior of a mother with respect to her daughter-in-law, a wife's sister does not address the husband as *ye.* In fact, she can have sexual intercourse with him though the wife does not want to know about the relationship. Therefore, the wife's sister is also jealous of the husband's exploits with other women and may run to tell the wife about them.

Joking relatives do not tell a person about his or her spouse's affairs. They want to avoid the possibility that the person might get jealous and take some form of action. Their interest is centered around enjoying the person's own extramarital affairs which they discuss among themselves in his or her presence deriving a great deal of amusement from this source. Joking-related people take a special pride and pleasure in each other's sexual adventures often arranging them for each other. From the point of view of the social control of extramarital practices, it seems important that there exists such a group of relatives with whom a person must share the superficial aspects of extramarital sexual life. This sharing of information allows certain social pressures, such as support and disapproval, to be applied in these situations. Being kept within certain limits in this manner, the informal love affairs and the one-time encounters are less likely to endanger a marriage, to break incest lines, or to disrupt other social aspects.

SOME SOCIAL RAMIFICATIONS

Considering the social ramifications of the extramarital sub-system from the point of view of their relationship to the whole socio-cultural system, a number of observations can be made. For instance, with respect to social solidarity, loyalty between *ye*-related affinals is enhanced by the necessity to keep amorous trysts a secret, as already described, and the mutual arranging and sharing of information about sexual activities is a factor in building up the social cohesion among the consanguineal joking-related groups. Besides these ties, a man has a connection with any family to whom he is not related affinally or consanguineally because all non-related women of his generation are sexually accessible to him. Because of this, the man will call these women "my wife" (*iiprō*) whether or not he has had sexual relationships with them. Moreover, he will speak to the consanguineal relatives of these classificatory wives utilizing the appropriate affinal terms of address. He will even refer to their children as "my children," and he must behave towards them with the seriousness required in carrying out the paternal role. A result of this sexual accessibility to all non-related women of the same generation is that a secondary affinal system of relationships is maintained so that almost every non-consanguineally related person in the entire society becomes a relative in either the primary (*-mpey*) or the secondary (*-kahɔk*) affinal systems. The secondary affinal relationships are clearly less serious and can be broken with relative ease. They form a social network, nevertheless, that is an important factor in the maintenance of the Canela high degree of social solidarity.

A great deal of gaiety and fun accompanies any potential or realized extramarital relationship so that at least certain members of almost every non-related family can be approached and associated with in this spirit, an aspect which may partially account for the pervasion of this attitude as a morale-building factor throughout the entire society. Both the high morale and group solidarity can be shown to be important factors in the Canela survival as a tribal unit into present times and in the maintenance of their conservatism with respect to their traditions.

High social cohesion often has a price which has to be paid psychologically by the individuals of a society. In a social unit in which almost any forms of intra-group aggression, hostility, and fighting must be suppressed in order to enhance group solidarity, alternative outlets often exist so that such frustrations can be reduced indirectly. The Canela have a number of such culturally approved emotional outlets. If a person is angry or unhappy, his associates usually try to get him to redirect his concerns into singing in the street or into making overtures to some sexually accessible women. It is expected that after being involved in such activities, he will soon be feeling happy again. Pleasures are quickly substituted for pains. It is hypothesized herein that the easy availability of frequent and varied sexual outlets is one of the factors contributing to the reduction of individual hostility and frustration, and consequently, to the maintenance of group morale and solidarity. The Canela suppression of almost any manifestations of intra-group hostilities is so striking that there must be extensive traditional outlets for the individual frustrations that are necessarily built up in the maintenance of such a high degree of apparent group cooperation and the perpetual display of amiable attitudes on the part of the individual.

It might be thought that the position of women would be very low in a society where it is the custom for women to give themselves, even willingly, to groups of men. This is not the case with the Canela. Although women are not directly involved in the political administration and governing of the tribe, nevertheless, they exert a strong influence on the men of their families, a pressure which is translated into policies maintained in the council meetings. Women are not seen as being inferior but rather as being very different creatures though equally deserving and valued. Their relative lack of dependence upon their husbands is ensured by the matrilocal arrangements for living. Moreover, a woman receives a considerable amount of support socially and economically from her classificatory husbands from whom she can expect and demand gifts and services at any time. Ceremonial sanctioning for this sort of obligatory behavior can be observed in the Pεbye Festival, for instance, wherein a novice's sister requires a lover to carry the novice on his shoulders (Nimuendajú 1946:189). The unmarried non-virginal women of the so-called "wanton" category (Nimuendajú 1946:130–131) can even support themselves and their children largely through their influence over their often numerous lovers so that they can be relatively independent of their matrilineal relatives economically.

Before the strong authority of the older generations over the younger ones broke down in the 1940's and especially in the 19th century before marriages began to take place at an earlier age, young men in their teens were not supposed to have sexual relations with the girls of the same age, even though this was the great flowering period of beauty and attractiveness for Canela women. These young men, undergoing post-puberty restrictions and disciplines of a variety of types were supposed to have sex only with vigorous and firm-charactered women in their forties and fifties so that they too would grow strong. Similarly, the lovely young girls were reserved for the men in their late thirties, forties, and fifties. Young people would grow up weak and soft-natured if they indulged themselves in sex with their luxuriant contemporaries, it was thought. Such practices are patterned after certain festival acts and especially after the Mεaykʰε̄ dance which is performed frequently during the summer ceremonial season. Besides serving to maintain the authority of the older generations, such practices must have furnished gratifications to people at a period in their lives when sexual powers were waning and when such psycho-cultural supports were welcomed. In any case, this practice can certainly be considered a factor which contributes toward building up group morale and social solidarity.

A Canela man's loyalties and interests were widely spread among a number of institutions. Correspondingly, his emotional attachment to his spouse was relatively weak since it was diluted by his responsibilities to his consanguineal relatives, his age class associates, his informal and formal friends, the ceremonial and political chiefs, the council of elders, and his lovers and their children and families. His control over his wife, as over his few material possessions, was very much conditioned by the influences from these various categories of social agents. A Canela lived to a relatively large extent for these agents and their activities and to a relatively lesser extent for himself and his wife. In such a society, people cannot be very individualistic; exclusiveness is seen as stinginess so that even spouses have to be shared. This practice, however, is clearly consistent with the general notions about ownership and sharing, and it is in this light that the extensive sharing of sexual attributes must be viewed in order to be understood.

ACCULTURATIVE ASPECTS

The extensive Canela extramarital practices are important contributing factors in enhancing high morale and group solidarity but are, on the other hand, deterrents to the development of individualism and notions of private ownership and industry. The little that is known about these sexual practices by the neighboring hinterland Brazilians and the Indian Protection Service representatives runs more strongly counter to their feelings and moral senses than any other Canela set of behaviors except, most certainly, for cattle stealing. It is not surprising, therefore, that significant pressures have been brought to bear upon these Indians to change or at least to conceal these practices (Crocker 1958:2).

With the arrival of the Indian Protection Service personnel in the early 1940's, unmarried women found they could no longer spend nights in the plaza without running the risk of being embarrassed by outsiders. From that period on, all group-sponsored extramarital practices had to be confined to the stream gallery forests, the savannas, and the farm plot shacks, though the Wë?të houses could be utilized if certain precautions were taken. The Canela became well aware during this period of their existence that they would be made to feel very ashamed of these activities by almost any hinterlander who became aware of them.

Especially since the mid-fifties, therefore, with their giving up of their negative attitudes toward the local Brazilian way of life, feelings that extramarital practices may actually be uncivilized and wicked have been changing many aspects of the Canela traditions. It has become increasingly difficult to oblige girls to take part in the group activities involving sexual relations and even to obtain their families' permission for them to be installed in the formerly honored roles as girl associates of the festival societies. The private rendezvous affairs are considerably less affected by these new ideas than the traditional behaviors with greater social visibility. It is these more conspicuous practices, both of the daily and the festival varieties, which are being viewed by many younger women, and some men in their roles as fathers and young husbands, as being increasingly undesirable. Sexual jealousy is not suppressed as effectively as it used to be so that angry young husbands with new ideas about marital rights, unfaithful wives, and prostitutes can cause a considerable amount of inter-family trouble and serious intra-tribal bad feeling by demanding large compensatory payments and through involving the entire tribal judiciary system in the resolving of their untraditional problems (Crocker 1961:81).

Observing these trends, the ethnologist wonders how a reduction in the availability of girl associates and extramarital sexual outlets will affect the festival system. Will just the rites involving these practices be omitted or will the festivals themselves be abandoned or drastically transformed? And, with the decrease in the daily availability of extramarital opportunities and the consequent loss of these outlets for the reduction of personal frustrations and generalized hostility, how will group morale and social solidarity be affected? Moreover, what will be the effects on ownership of private property and the nature of the marital bond?

After assembling for the assessment and resolution of these questions data, which cannot be discussed here, from several other sub-systems of the Canela socio-cultural system, I think it is most likely that as a result of the changes in the attitude toward extramarital sexual practices, the nuclear husband-wife family unit will be increasingly emphasized at the expense of the activities of the joking relative group and the secondary affinal family relationships; that the many hours spent in singing, dancing, log racing and in festival performances will be reduced, along with the loss of their sexual components, so that more time will be spent in the farm plots and in a broader number of economic pursuits learned in relation to the needs of the hinterland Brazilians; and that the tribal authority over the individual, which operates through his many diffused social responsibilities, will be weakened so that greater independence in living arrangements and in property ownership will become feasible. Living away from the tribe and marriage outside the group to hinterlanders and Guajajara Indians will then become possible though not frequent.

All of these predicted trends are in the direction of hinterland culture and Brazilian national life. It is not to be expected that the Canela will develop culturally in a direction that is to the side of and parallel to Brazilian society, as has been largely true of the Canela acculturative situation in the past. The Canela at this time are too completely dominated from the outside, too few in number, and too much in awe of the major culture surrounding them to develop independently in the future. Besides, they are already pretty well convinced, especially the youths, that the Brazilian way of life is "superior" to their own. Nevertheless, the outcome may be very different from anything that can be anticipated herein. Already, largely because of the provocations of a Ramkokamekra-Canela religious revitalistic movement of considerable proportions, they have been driven out of their ancestral savanna lands. This occurred in July of 1963 when 190 hinterland gunmen were summoned and hired by the local ranch owners to do the job by force of arms. It is surprising that only five Canela men were killed and twelve wounded. Following this culturally and psychologically traumatic experience, adaptation to forest life and to the immediate presence of Guajajara Indians have become the major challenges which the Ramkokamekra-Canela are currently facing. To survive the inroads of their new acculturative situation as an on-going and independent social unit, they will be required to utilize their characteristic flexibility, imagination, and sense of group cooperation to the fullest extent.

It is obvious that drastic changes are taking place in the Canela extramarital socio-cultural sub-system as well as in their whole ecological setting. It is also clear that because of the extensiveness of the ramifications of these extramarital practices throughout the social system, and because of their basic importance as factors in the maintenance of group morale and social solidarity, their reduction will be an important factor in bringing about very serious acculturative and personality adjustment problems in the next five to ten years.

SUMMARY AND FINAL COMMENTS

In order to present this material on extramarital practices in the form of an analysis of a sub-system of the over-all Canela socio-cultural system, first the informal day-to-day extramarital practices were described and considered as the patterns being maintained by the operation of the sub-system. The most important of these patterns consist of frequent sexual contacts of a brief or lengthy duration begun on the initiative of either the man or the woman and carried out when desired during most of the sexual life span. These patterns include the frequent utilization of one woman by a group of men.

Following this account of the practices, the next part of the article was devoted to examining some of the factors operating to maintain the sub-system. Starting with socialization, it was hypothesized that two of the more significant factors (and most certainly there are many others) which may be related to enculturating individuals into the performing of these extramarital practices are the constant association of sex with joking and gaiety, and the general permissiveness and timing of rewards in the child training procedures. Then, a number of traditional rites were described which sanction the informal day-to-day extramarital activities. Sexual jealousy was next taken up as the strongest factor contributing to the disruption of the sub-system, and some of the factors contributing to the control of this disruptive element were portrayed—such as prohibitions against fighting, the use of an honorific form as an affinal term of address to aid in inhibiting the passage of provocative information, and the existence of a group of consanguineal relatives who cooperate to keep the extramarital activities within safe limits.

In the final portion, a number of ramifications of this sub-system were discussed including the relationship to tribal morale and group solidarity, the position of women and the diffused nature of the marital bond, and some acculturative aspects and predictions.

Such a sub-system of the over-all Canela socio-cultural system as extramarital practices is too extensive and intricate to be completely analyzed and described at this time. The more important factors, however, in the operation of this system have been presented and some related aspects have been discussed.

The following two articles by Murphy, although written a year apart, form a unit. The Mundurucú obviously have quite different attitudes toward sex from the Canela, but it nonetheless pervades many aspects of their culture. Although each of the following two articles deals with social control and sex, in one sex is the social control, whereas in the second sex is the cause of the social control. In the case of Warú, we see how the Mundurucú can express group sentiment through extremely personal individual activity. In the case of Borai, however, at least half the society acted as a unit in establishing virtual ostracism.

From these two articles, the preceding one by Crocker and the later one by Laraia, one can imagine the avenues of investigation that might be opened to us if we had more such studies. Sex is, after all, a basic and omnipresent human activity.

Murphy has made some minor editorial changes that do not change the sense of the original.

17 ROBERT F. MURPHY

Deviance and Social Control I: What Makes Warú Run?

Warú,[1] the young chief of the Mundurucú[2] village of Uari, visited the village of Uakuparí with great frequency. So frequently in fact that he once made the ten hour round trip in one day. Inquiry revealed that Warú was on the horns of a dilemma. Though he was chief of Uari, he kept a young and pretty wife in the house of his father, the chief of Uakuparí. Whenever he visited his wife, his "followers" in Uari busied themselves in plotting against him. Hearing of these threats to his authority, he would immediately dash back to reassert his position of leadership. But as soon as he was out of sight of Uakuparí, the men of that community sought to tarnish the virtue of his wife; this was not a difficult task, and half the men of the village ultimately enjoyed her favors. Their exploits were well publicized, and Warú, hearing of his cuckoldry, would hurriedly retrace his steps. During most of the time we lived in Uakuparí, Warú gravitated between the two communities—to the great amusement and deep satisfaction of his fellow Mundurucú.

On the lowest level of explanation, I have already stated what makes Warú run.

Reprinted by permission of the author and the Kroeber Anthropological Society from the *Kroeber Anthropological Society Papers*, no. 24 (Spring 1961), pp. 55–61.

But the key questions of why the men of Uari plotted against him and why those of Uakuparí pursued his wife can only be answered through an analysis of Mundurucú society and culture and of Warú's position within it. For Warú was a marginal man trying to play traditional social roles to which he had not been socialized, and he failed to define correctly the nature of the role expectations or the values that pertained to specific social situations. His cumulative blunders finally threatened the stability of this small society, and certain processes were set in motion to reestablish the normal flow of social interaction. Anthropologically, this is a study in deviance and social control. Humanistically, it is a tragedy, but like many tragedies, one that has overtones of comedy.

II

Warú's personality was most deviant, and I shall spell this out in terms of his manifest behavior, as it compared with the normal behavior of Mundurucú men and their chiefs. I know nothing of the socialization of Warú, only that at an early age he went to live in the household of a local Brazilian who traded in the village headed by Warú's father. He came back to live among his people, but he was no longer a Mundurucú, any more than he was a Brazilian. When I first met Warú, he addressed me in backwoods Portuguese and in a swaggering manner introduced himself as "Warú, son of José [the chief of Uakuparí] and chief of Uari." This contrasted markedly to the diffident and self-effacing way in which most Mundurucú addressed me, and each other. Though I was an outsider, I had at the time been several months with the group and this departure from what I expected of a tribesman upset me considerably. Warú turned out to be a great problem in other ways. He cited his own importance as a justification for the demands that he made on me for gifts. And he bragged continually of his ability to deal with whites, to lead his followers, to hunt, or to do almost anything in either the realm of traditional Mundurucú activity or in their relationships with the outside world. He strove desperately and openly towards the acquisition of prestige and of material goods, which he had accepted as indicators of prestige. For this reason our mosquito boots were admired greatly, as this would surely differentiate him from his barefoot Indian fellows—shortly after one of his visits my wife discovered that her boots were missing. And we met no other Mundurucú so brash. They felt free to enter our house at all times, but only Warú would demand a cup of coffee and then lie in our hammocks; he was quite offended when we pointed out to him that his body paint was staining them. Warú had other unusual characteristics. He spoke freely and critically of other men to us and did this even in the presence of third parties. Nor did he bother to conceal his hostility and contempt when someone inimical to him was near. But underneath this facade, Warú was a frightened and anxious man. He would often confide to me darkly that "people are talking about me." Lest this be interpreted as paranoia in the clinical sense, I should stress that people were indeed talking about him, and Warú had every reason to be anxious. Not only his ego but his very life was in danger.

III

Warú's behavior grated against almost every single point of Mundurucú expectations regarding how a chief should act and how men, in general, should behave. Mundurucú society is intensely egalitarian and based upon the principle of maintenance of solidarity among a group of males who are conceived to be peers. It has a peculiar structure in that it is divided into patrilineal moieties, which in turn are differentiated into a number of patrilineal clans. But the normal mode of residence is matrilocal, and men generally move to the villages of their wives. This disperses the clans throughout all the villages, for a young man, when he marries, leaves the father from whom he obtains clan membership. It also produces a dualism of loyalties in which the man maintains a clan identity and, with it, defined role obligations and also acquires membership and roles in the village of his wife. This produces a classic form of organic solidarity, for the society is bound together by cross-cutting segments. But it is a very simple form of organic solidarity and an extremely brittle one. Social cohesion must be vigorously maintained and individual strivings muted, for alliances in cases of conflict cannot range along simple segmental lines. To support a fellow-clansman in a crisis may pit a person against his village mates and vice versa. In a society with a population of only 1,200, living in communities of 60 to 100 persons, such stresses are serious threats to social stability in any event; in one of the Mundurucú type they may be totally disruptive. The social system not only produces solidarity but also requires it for maintenance.[3] Given the structure of Mundurucú society, the effective social actor was one who was cooperative, unaggressive, serene, quiet, and willing to place the will of the collectivity before his own. It may be immediately perceived that Warú presented a threat to propriety and to the social system. He was belligerent, loud, self-centered, and acquisitive—all the things that a Mundurucú should not be.

Like all people, the Mundurucú are, to an extent, prestige-seekers, but there are cultural differences in the coinage of status. The traditional culture placed no value upon material acquisitions, and, although this was slowly changing, Warú's tastes were inordinate and clearly derived from his experience among the Brazilians. He thus violated a value standard and at the same time offended the entire community by self-consciously and openly trying to raise himself above his fellows.

Warú not only misconstrued the ends of Mundurucú prestige but he also misunderstood the means for their attainment. The primary rule, and the one he most flagrantly violated, was that one should not *seek* prestige but let it come to him naturally. For example, bravery in war was highly valued but the posture of bravado was ridiculed. A coward was relegated to the lowest end of the status scale, but one who boasted of the damage he intended to inflict upon the enemy in the coming battle was placed in the vanguard of the attack. To attain prestige a man should be modest and unassuming, while observing all the traditional expectations of what constitutes valued behavior. But primarily, he should act always as if he had only the collective well-being and goals in mind. Warú's braggadocio, individualism, and competitiveness had violated every rule of the game, and he won dislike and contempt, rather than the esteem and power he wanted so badly.

Disturbing though all this was to the delicate adjustment of Mundurucú social structure and contrary though his behavior was to the values that bound this adjustment, Warú had committed *the* cardinal error. He had allowed his grievances against certain individuals and groups to come out into the open and alignments emerged for and against him that cut across both village and clan-linked role commitments. Hostilities and latent factions are part of the tribal life of the Mundurucú, but they are carefully repressed—a requisite for the functioning of Mundurucú society. The average Mundurucú is well trained in disguising aggression and in presenting the bland face of neutrality, but Warú's own socialization was in part derived from Brazilians and was not adjusted to the functional needs of the Indian society. Like any cuckold, he had some cause to feel aggrieved. His error was in openly objecting to the offense against him, a normal course for a Brazilian cuckold, but not for a Mundurucú victim.

IV

Warú's alienation from Mundurucú society induced severe anxiety and intensified his quest for a favorable identity. He sought this through his role of chief of the village of Uari. The contemporary Mundurucú chieftaincy must be understood as a boundary role. The dependency of the Indians on manufactured goods, obtained through the sale of wild rubber, has given the Brazilian traders a position of great influence among them, which they exercise through the chief. When the trader wants increased production he tells the chief, who then is supposed to exhort his followers to greater effort. Correspondingly, the chief acts as bargaining agent for the village in trade negotiations, and the people interpret his role to be in large part that of their representative to the outer world. If the trader is sufficiently well established with a village, he can do much to influence the choice of a chief. But since he cannot completely counter the patrilineal rule of inheritance of the chieftaincy, it is common practice to select one or two possible heirs and rear them in his household; this is what happened to Warú. This is agreeable to the chief, for he gains the favor of the trader and, with it, preferential treatment in sales and purchases. It is clearly beneficial to the trader, as he hopes thereby to install a chief who will be responsive to his wishes, even at the expense of the Mundurucú villagers.[4]

The contemporary Mundurucú chief is in a dilemma. If we look upon a boundary role as one in which both ends have to be played against the middle, we see the chief caught between the interests of the trader and those of his followers; these interests rarely coincide. It is a difficult position, but one that can be maintained by maximal adherence to the traditional behavior expected of chiefs and minimal acquiescence to the demands of the traders. Warú's father, José, played a comparatively successful role. If the trader told him that the villagers were heavily in debt to him, José would communicate this fact and suggest that it would be well to collect more rubber; he never attempted even verbal coercion. He also sincerely sought to obtain the maximum return for his people.

José embodied many characteristics of the traditional chief. An older man, he carried himself with a modest and unassuming dignity. He guided, persuaded and cajoled, but he carefully refrained from ordering people, and all decisions of communal significance were made in consultation with the mature men of the village. Beyond this, José knew Mundurucú traditional knowledge and lore and attempted to perpetuate it.

Warú's position was very different from that of his father, for he was the prototype of the Indian boy who had been "educated" by a trader and later installed as a chief. He had no legitimate claim to the position, and it was necessary for the trader to insist that he would recognize only Warú in dealings with Uari. The residents grudgingly assented, but they regarded him as chief only in trade relations. The most influential man of the village was, in reality, a renowned shaman who was the son of the last chief and was considered the legitimate heir to the office.

Warú's precarious situation was made worse by the fact that he was under thirty years old and the junior of many men in the village. To complicate matters, he had no supporting group of kinsmen in Uari. Matrilocality, I have said, is the normal mode of residence among the Mundurucú, but the sons of chiefs generally remain with their fathers after marriage. From the point of view of conscious motivation, the sons of chiefs remain patrilocal because their fathers are influential enough to persuade men to relinquish their daughters to them as a means of solidifying relations with them. By the same line of reasoning, a young man who marries the daughter of a chief is willing to join a prestigeful father-in-law. But from the point of view of social structure, the function of the patrilocality of the chief's family is twofold. By keeping the sons, the chief is able to transmit authority to them without the discontinuity that would result if they were resident in the villages of their wives. Moreover, the chief is surrounded by a group of patrilineally related kin, a small and solidary patrilineage. His position is further enhanced by the fact that he has sons-in-law within the village. Much as this may reenforce his prestige, it does not enable him to exercise unilateral authority, for the rest of the village men are ever-watchful and jealous of the chiefly family and would be quick to resist, however passively, what they considered to be high-handedness. Warú, however, did not have the surrounding group of relatives that might have given even minimal support to his claim to leadership. Rather, he depended upon the trader and his father and relatives in Uakuparí to buttress his position.

Given his delicate status, Warú proceeded to worsen it through a misinterpretation of the chieftaincy. He had listened to his father's nostalgic tales of the role of the chief in times past, and one might say that he had some knowledge, in a purely cognitive sense, of the traditional culture. It is highly dubious however, that Warú had internalized sufficient culture to make him an effective actor within the system of social relationships. Warú knew that "in the old days, chiefs were powerful men who directed their people and bought goods for them." This view of the past may or may not have been true, but it surely did not apply to the present. Warú, nonetheless, announced at large that he was eminently qualified to be chief, as only he knew how to deal with the trader and only he had the force to tell the people how, when, and where to work. I was a special recipient of this information, for Warú found it most important to gain stature in the eyes of a prestigeful outsider. But Warú also told all the others of his importance, and the people of Uari stated that he indeed relayed the demands of the trader in forceful terms. His "followers" saw him solely as an agent of the trader in their village, and they were certain that his only function was to promote their exploitation and defraudment. Their analysis was correct, but I doubt that Warú thought his role to be at all antisocial. There is no evidence to substantiate this, for only he could tell me whether he was aware of the machinations of the trader, and he did not. But I believe that Warú saw the trader as a paternal figure, many of whose values he had internalized and subscribed to as legitimate. And he also saw himself to be in the position of a strong and traditional leader.

Warú had learned something else about the chiefs of times past, and this was the fact that many were polygynous. Polygyny was possible only for chiefs, for the matrilocality that applied to most of the population made it most difficult to have plural wives unless they were sisters. Even for a chief, however, polygyny was a difficult and stormy relationship, and it was evidently never of very great frequency.

Warú did not have the implicit and unconscious ability to understand the fine points of Mundurucú social structure that a man raised in a village would have, and he made some of his most serious blunders in marriage. Soon after assuming the chieftaincy of Uari, he married a woman of the village, a widow several years older than himself who, through the situational variability of post-marital residence, had a strong nucleus of kin in the village. Though I have no data upon which to make a firmer statement, it is quite probable that he married the woman—frankly a crone—in order to enlist the sympathies of her relatives. But Warú was a young, handsome and virile man, and he subsequently sought a wife more to his liking. He located a pretty girl of about sixteen years in the village of Kapikpík and brought her home to Uari. This enraged the first wife, who berated Warú, assaulted the girl and complained to her brothers. The latter expressed their disapproval of the polynynous union to Warú, and the rest of the village supported them. Warú's general behavior and his exercise of his "chieftaincy" had already outraged them, and this offense against his first wife, a native daughter of the village, was beyond their endurance. Warú refused to divorce the new wife, to whom he was greatly attached, but took her to Uakuparí where he left her in the care of his father. He validated his polygyny by pointing to the tradition that this was a prerogative of chiefs.

V

This brings us through most of the key features of Mundurucú culture and social structure and to the point at which this paper began. And since this is in essence a tragic tale, we will see in this final section how the ring must inevitably close on

Warú. He had offended all the Mundurucú canons of taste and ethics and had become a source of strain in this small and tightly knit society. Now the forces of social control became operative and he felt the heavy pressure of his fellow men.

Having left his pretty bride in the "safe" confines of his father's house, Warú returned to Uari to set matters right and quiet the discontent. But he continued in his arrogant and demanding ways and the sentiments of the villagers became further inflamed, with no small assistance from his first wife and her family. There grew among them a firm determination to kill him, and the intention might have been immediately carried out were it not for his ties in Uakupari. This was an important collective decision by the residents of Uari, for his execution would set off a train of repercussions that would seriously disrupt their relations with Uakupari and with the trader. Moreover, Warú did not have shamanistic power and the usual post-hoc explanation for the killing of a deviant—that he was a perpetrator of black magic—could not be used in his case. But his continued presence was even more disruptive, and Warú's life was placed in serious jeopardy.

In the meantime, the person of the young wife was not as secure as Warú thought it would be. Her husband was away and she was a rather wayward girl; whatever rectitude she possessed was certainly no match for the insistent attempts of the men of Uakupari. Soon, all of the men of the village except those prohibited by incest regulations—and there were some exceptions even to this—were enjoying the favors of Warú's young wife in the underbrush surrounding the village, at the stream, in the forest, in the gardens, or wherever they might find her alone. The enthusiasm of the men was understandable from her physical attractiveness, but there was another component to their attentions. Whenever they related their exploits to me, the men would express great satisfaction *at what they were doing to Warú,* for the Uakupari men, too, disliked Warú with some intensity. Even in his father's village, his presence threatened the smooth tenor of social relations, and he was considered unbearable. But physical sanctions against Warú would have been impossible in the village in which his father was a chief, and the men of Uakupari attacked his manhood instead. There could be no doubt about the aggressive character of their seductions, nor of its success in dealing a mortal blow to Warú's prestige by reducing him to a helpless butt of laughter.

Warú soon heard of the events in Uakupari from members of his family and immediately returned. He made frontal accusations against many of the men and even mentioned my Brazilian assistant as being among those who had cuckolded him. The village reacted to his charges ambivalently. They were highly amused at his discomfiture and humiliation, but they were seriously concerned about the open accusations and threats of violent reprisal. Not only was this a breach of fundamental rules of deportment, but if violence were to break out the social system would be seriously threatened. The village soon became ranged on two sides. Warú's family supported him, but the majority of the population were ranked solidly against him. Thus, the threat of conflict had spread from Uari to Uakupari. And Warú ran back and forth between Uari, where they plotted against his life, and Uakupari, where they took more covert measures against him through his wife.

The balance of power and of moral correctness lay with Warú's opponents, and the task of his supporters was made most difficult by virtue of the fact that Warú had almost ceased to be a social person—the rules no longer applied to him. We left the field before the curtain fell on our little drama, but one could already predict the conclusion. This was seen most clearly when, shortly before our departure, José fell from a palm tree and lay seriously injured for several days. Knowing that the people of Uarí would kill him as soon as they were assured of his father's death, Warú came immediately to Uakuparí and remained there until the old man's recovery was certain. During this period, Warú approached me and said, "You know, if my father dies, I will leave this land and go to live on the banks of the Tapajós River." I asked him why, and in fine Warú style, he answered, "Because it is so beautiful there." Warú knew that his life as a Mundurucú was finished.

NOTES

1. All proper names are fictitious.
2. The Mundurucú Indians are a Tupian-speaking people of the upper Tapajós River in the state of Pará, Brazil. My wife and I carried out a one year fieldwork program there in 1952—53 with the support of the William Bayard Cutting Traveling Fellowship granted by Columbia University, and a Research Training Fellowship of the Social Science Research Council.
3. A more complete description and analysis of the relation between Mundurucú social structure and the positive evaluation of male solidarity has already been published . . . (Murphy 1957).
4. I have discussed the general structure of authority and its relation to Brazilian society in detail in my book, *Headhunter's Heritage* (Murphy 1960).

18   ROBERT F. MURPHY[1]

Deviance and Social Control II: Borai

This is the second of two articles . . . presenting case histories and analyses of tragedies in social life. In both, individuals through no essential fault of their own deviated from the moral order of Mundurucú society and by so doing became alienated from their fellows. In neither of these cases was effective control actually exercised over the individuals, but the control process and the means by which the body politic healed its wounds are manifest in both instances. In the first case, a young chief named Warú attempted to exercise authorities and prerogatives that were not his by right of office, and we saw the exquisite and inexorable means by

Reprinted by permission of the author and the Kroeber Anthropological Society from the *Kroeber Anthropological Society Papers*, no. 27 (Fall 1962), pp. 49—54.

which he was destroyed as a social person. The present article gives another case of radical deviation from role, but the principal actor is a woman; her sin was that she loved too many, too much, and too often. It is on the surface a prosaic and unimportant story, and I will relate it as it unfolded before us in just this way. But it is exactly in the vagrant episodes of social life that we see structure, and the conclusion of this contribution will present an analysis of the significance of the events described to an understanding of Mundurucú society and, perhaps, to societies everywhere.

We first met Borai[2] at the house of a trader who maintained a wattle and daub establishment on the banks of the upper Tapajós River. My wife and I were about to embark on the second half of our study of the Mundurucú Indians in central Brazil, and the trader was to supply us with transportation to the Indian villages of the interior. He was a small, wiry Portuguese who had spent most of his life on the Tapajós River trading pots, pans, cloth, tools and tobacco to the Brazilian *caboclos* and the Indians in return for wild rubber. The houses of all these traders harbor a number of dependents, some of whom are related and others of whom simply become attached to the *patron*. And in this area, the trader's family always includes a few Indians who live there for varying lengths of time, working for him and receiving food and whatever they can cajole. It was no surprise then to find two Indian girls helping in his kitchen.

The Indians are always curious and somewhat bemused at the sight of urbanites traveling in the wilds, but they try not to show it. One of the trader's Mundurucú girls maintained the usual pose of embarrassed reserve in our presence, but the other made no effort at all to hide her delight with the obviously out of place New Yorkers. This was Borai. Her free and out-going manner aroused our curiosity, but our inquiries only drew from the trader the muttered reply that she was "shameless." It became apparent that he would like to get her off his hands, and it soon developed that he had promised her a free ride to Uakuparí in our boat. The canoe was large, and there was ample room for Borai and her eight-year-old daughter. We agreed to take her. Actually, we had little choice in the matter.

The purpose of Borai's trip to Uakuparí was to visit "relatives," as she phrased it. This could hardly be taken as a narrowly descriptive statement as all 1,200 Mundurucú believe themselves to share a common kinship. In a more specific vein she had told us that she wanted especially to visit her "father," which, in the moiety system, cut the field of relatives down to half the men of the tribe in her father's generation. Whatever the distance of the relationship of this particular father, she evidently did not intend to live in his house. As we unpacked our things, Borai busied herself hanging her hammock and her daughter Cristina's in the far corner of the uncompartmented house. This provoked a hurried conversation between our interpreter, Chico, my wife and me. Chico thought it quite clear that Borai had adopted us and had every intention to remain part of our household. We were equally convinced that this would rob us of our last shred of privacy and would prove a heavy drain on the family economy. She had to leave, but it was decided to wait a while before telling her.

While this conversation was going on, Borai disappeared from the house. She and Cristina soon reappeared with gourds full of water from a nearby stream and proceeded to make coffee. The house was a shambles. The originally hard-packed clay floor had crumbled and become dusty, making a wonderful home for fleas, and litter was scattered all about. Without any suggestion on our part, Borai improvised a broom from branches and swept the floor as well as possible and then sprinkled it with water to settle the dust. After this was done, she went to the house next door and borrowed an axe, with which she chopped a two-day supply of firewood. All three of us began to look at her thoughtfully by this time, and when she appeared with a haunch of deer for dinner, we decided that another conference was in order. Chico was strongly in favor of keeping Borai, for he was thus relieved of all the household chores. Since Chico did his best work as an interpreter and his worst as cook and general factotum, this seemed an ideal resolution of our field problems. It was agreed that we should say nothing to Borai about leaving and gave her a dress and a handful of beads to insure the opposite result.

After a few days had passed, it became increasingly evident that Borai was not a very typical Mundurucú woman. Her physical appearance was much like that of the other women in the mid-twenties age bracket. Several pregnancies and hard work gave her a stocky body. She was strong, but her abdomen was distended and her breasts hung low. And like all Mundurucú, her front upper teeth were missing. It was rather in the realm of expression and demeanor that Borai was different. Old Mundurucú women are shown great deference and have considerable freedom to express themselves and to make demands on others, but a young woman like Borai is supposed to comport herself submissively and with reticence before men. She should not look directly at a man and she should never catch his eye. And when she smiles or laughs, the proper young lady turns her head to one side and covers her mouth with her hand. Borai did none of these things. When she itched, she scratched, and she usually itched and scratched in places considered private by most Mundurucú women. She eyed all the men with an alert, sparkling gaze, and she expressed amusement by throwing her head back and laughing deeply and libidinously. Borai was wonderfully good-natured, and she had a keen sense of humor. Chico and I made a sport out of catching her reaction to earthy comments or to leading questions about her love life.

My wife immediately recorded her life history, a routine chore in most instances, but in this case a lively one. Borai was first married at the age of twelve or thirteen, but soon left her husband for another man. She bore him three children, of whom one died, another was adopted by a man who had no children, and the other was Cristina. She deliberately aborted herself during a fourth pregnancy in retaliation against her husband, who beat her regularly. The husband died, a victim of witchcraft, and Borai wandered through Mundurucú country living with relatives or lovers. She then left and lived with Brazilian rubber tappers on the Tapajós River and in the houses of traders, but she was homesick when we met her.

Although her traveling days were at least temporarily ended in Uakuparí, Borai's inclinations still wandered. The men recognized her symptoms long before we did—in fact Borai had already achieved some fame throughout Mundurucú country.

She occasionally went to fetch water or firewood by herself and thus announced her availability, for any lone woman is considered fair game. And though the men all slept in the men's house, this did not prevent them from visiting Borai after they thought we were asleep. We soon found out, for it is very difficult to conceal a love affair that takes place in a hammock tied to the beams of a house of bark and thatch placed over a light framework.

After a series of romances, Borai rested her sights on a young man whose Portuguese name was Pedro. He was a strong and handsome person, a few years younger than she, and his attentions grew quite serious. Borai dropped her other lovers, and we had high hopes that a marriage was in the offing. My wife and I made every effort to encourage a more permanent liaison as, once embarked on the accumulation of an extended family, we could see its advantages. Among the Mundurucú, residence is preferentially, and in fact most commonly, matrilocal, and although the bridegroom lives in the men's house and not actually in the wife's house, he owes obligations to it. Since I was the head of Borai's household, I would therefore be able to exert a certain amount of influence over Pedro and perhaps extract some work from him. Our immediate aims were simple: we wanted game, and the roof needed repair.

The situation was complex, however, and our plans failed. One of the girls in the village had already borne Pedro one child and was pregnant again by him. She claimed that Pedro was her husband, but he just as vigorously denied the marriage. The dispute was rather academic, as marriage is legitimized only by public recognition of the state and symbolized by the fact that the husband presents the product of the chase to his wife. Pedro had stopped bringing his take of game to her, but he apparently had not put sufficient distance between himself and his former spouse. Neither of the women wanted to share the connubial state, and Borai was quite frankly afraid of the first wife. The affair ended when Pedro decided that Borai's notoriety would reduce him to an object of humor, and his nocturnal visits stopped.

The unhappy termination of her love affair convinced Borai of the necessity of changing her way of life. Not only had her promiscuity ultimately cost her Pedro, but also the other women of the village had become hostile. "They are talking about me," said Borai—and this is one of the worst things that can befall a Mundurucú. Determined to rid herself of her compulsion, she went to one of the village shamans. Such problems as Borai's are quite sensibly viewed as medical in nature, rather than moral, and the shaman proceeded to make his diagnosis. He made a huge cigarette with a bark wrapper, lit it and blew its smoke over Borai's body. He then stared at her in deep concentration for some time and finally announced that she was a *yapö*, or the victim of a love charm. If a shaman desires a woman, he makes a concoction out of the powered ashes of the *uirapurú* bird and magically sends it into the body of his intended paramour. The uirapurú, incidentally, is used as an ingredient of love potions throughout the Amazon because of its beautiful song and its supposed ability to attract all the birds of the forest. Among the Mundurucú, the bewitched woman develops an insatiable desire for any and all men, not just her bewitcher, and she becomes a yapö until cured.

The cure would take a few days, so Borai left our house and stayed with the shaman. He blew more smoke on her body, massaged her and sucked out the malignant charm. To complete the cure, he directed her to spread on her face and body a mixture of tree sap and the earth upon which a jaguar had rolled. She would thus partake of the repulsive qualities of the jaguar and men would no longer be attracted to her. After the cure she returned to our house.

The change was dramatic. Borai no longer laughed at our jokes, but turned her head or pretended to go to the stream to fetch water. She sought the company of the other women and the security from the men that this implied. When she felt impelled to smile, which she did quite demurely, she covered her mouth with her hand. And she no longer scratched herself in public. We were quite impressed with the transformation and took care to treat her with the deference and respect that befitted her new role. A couple of weeks elapsed—rather dull and quiet weeks in our house—and then one day we noted that Borai laughed rather openly at a story that was not even intended for her ears. As the days passed by, the other familiar traits reappeared. She began to scratch her crotch again, and she stared at the men with renewed boldness. Instead of shunning our company, she welcomed the teasing.

Some days later I asked the shaman, "Have you watched Borai recently?"

"Yes," he answered heavily.

"But I thought that you cured her of her troubles."

The shaman paused and then shrugged, "Sometimes the treatment works. Sometimes it doesn't."

I have deliberately presented Borai's story in the simple way that it appeared to two amused outsiders. The reader may well wonder why it was described at the outset as a tragedy, but I would ask, who was the greater comic bumbler: Shakespeare's Hamlet or Charlie Chaplin's Tramp? To the true humanist, comedy and tragedy are inseparable. It was only after we had known Borai for many months and had understood Mundurucú society better that we realized that she was desperately lonely and in deep danger. Borai had by her promiscuity transgressed the female role and had invaded the domain of the men. Moreover, by playing fast and loose with her procreative powers, she had removed this function from the control of the men and had jeopardized the legal status of her potential offspring in this patrilineal society. The Mundurucú are not puritanical, and her crime was not a delict against good taste and propriety; rather, it was an infringement of the public order. This was not a problem that could be handled by ignoring it—a common technique of social control among the Mundurucú, and elsewhere—for Borai had continually made public her state by dropping the distance-maintaining mechanisms associated with the social use of the eyes and mouth. The totality of her behavior was in violation of Mundurucú standards and elicited countervalence as part of normal social processes.

In another publication, I outlined the structure of sex groupings in Mundurucú society and outlined the corrective steps usually taken against deviant women (Murphy 1959). Of these, the most theatrical was gang rape, and one could ask why this had not happened to Borai. The reason for this is quite simple; she was under my protection, and as long as I vouched for her status she was safe. This bespeaks a fundamental fact about Mundurucú society that I have not previously enunciated— a woman's legal status, as long as she is in her child-bearing years, is contingent upon the integrity of her relationship with a male. That I was a prestigeful outsider no doubt contributed to this protection, but most cases of gang rape in Mundurucú are with the tacit consent of the husband or kinsmen of the woman. Our protection could not be relied upon indefinitely, however, and it is significant that she sought a cure for her condition only after her effort to secure a husband, and respectability, had failed and only in view of the inevitability of our own departure. Borai was well aware of what happens to the unprotected yapö.

The ideology of male control over the women and over their reproduction appears also in the beliefs surrounding the making of a yapö, for it is significant that she is not, herself, responsible for her condition. That she is the victim of a form of bewitchment and that the spell can be cast only by a man stresses the fact that women are incapable, themselves, of assuming an aggressive posture in sex relations. Granted that once bewitched she is partially out of the control of the men, it is a man in the first instance who controls her sexuality. It is not, therefore, paradoxical that she is punished for something for which she is not responsible. Her problem is treated as are other forms of illness, and she has recourse to a cure before any further steps are taken. It is exactly those women who do not choose to be cured or are recidivists who court the danger of public sanctions; I believe that we can find ample analogues of this in ailments defined as social in our own society. Borai would have been fully restored to society if the treatment had been efficacious. That she at least underwent the treatment served partially to restore her.

The pressures upon Borai arose from the women as well as from the men and were more intense from that source and of a different quality. Whereas watchfulness, combined with zest, characterized the male attitude, the women of the village were indignant and resentful of Borai. They were also extremely uneasy about her fate, for nothing disturbs them collectively more than a gang rape, which they quite correctly interpret as an assault upon all women. The women were embattled and sought protection in propriety. Borai had alienated herself from the company of the women not only because she had dallied with the husbands of some but because she had made them vulnerable to the men through a breach in the ranks. As Simmel (1955:96) noted of the treatment of radical deviation among women: "In respect to a particular woman, women as a rule know only complete inclusion or else complete exclusion from the realm of custom." Nobody falls from grace more spectacularly than a woman and nobody judges her more harshly than her fellow-woman.

As in the case of Warú, I cannot tell you of the denouement of our tale, for we left before it. In fact, we may well infer that there could have been no climax as long as she remained in our house. Personally, our antipathy for Warú was matched only by our fondness for Borai, but both shared the element of humanity and lostness that is man's fate, for both were thrust into a struggle against society that they neither understood nor invited. This is not a distinctively Mundurucú saga, for who of us has not known a Warú or a Borai, and who of us is not in some small way a Warú or a Borai?

NOTES

1. I wish to express my deep appreciation to my wife, Yolanda, not only because of her continuing encouragement and support, but because she collected *all* the data upon which this article is based.
2. All proper names are fictitious.

Social control and sex again enter into this article, which also deals with another neglected aspect of South American Indian culture—singing. Many of the songs presented by Titiev deal with sex in one form or another, e.g., a spouse complaining of his or her mate's coldness or ardor, or courting songs. Mapuche singing may be considered to operate on several levels. The songs sometimes function directly as a conflict resolving mechanism, as in cases where an individual replies immediately to an accusation by promising to reform. In other cases the songs serve to involve segments of the community of varying size, ranging from immediate family to all the old men, in active intervention, or to alert the community to the possibility of future conflict. Singing appears to be a widespread mechanism for social control in South America, especially in connection with drinking parties, but precise data are scarce (cf. Lyon ms.b, Wistrand 1969). It is interesting that the Araucanians, noted for their oratory, should use a poetic and verbal form to settle internal conflicts.

19   MISCHA TITIEV

Social Singing Among the Mapuche [1]

This article is based on material that was gathered in the course of a field trip to Chile from mid-February to mid-August, 1948. The trip was made possible by the combination of a sabbatical leave from the University of Michigan and a

Reprinted by permission of the author and publisher from *Anthropological Papers*, no. 2 (Museum of Anthropology, University of Michigan; 1949), pp. 1–17.

generous grant from the Board of Governors of the Horace H. Rackham School of Graduate Studies, to whom grateful acknowledgment is made.

INTRODUCTION

Over the years since 1629, when the "happy captive," Francisco Núñez de Pineda y Bascuñan, first noted that his captors were much given to song, numerous examples of Mapuche singing have been reported and published.[2] Since the contents of the songs are usually packed with meaning, they are properly classed together with such other aspects of oral literature as proverbs, riddles, folk tales, genealogical accounts, and historical recitals. Skill in oratory and associated arts was once a fundamental prerequisite for chieftainship, and even today verbal ability is much esteemed.

To achieve success in this regard is no simple matter, for the Mapuche employ a highly figurative style, full of nuances and subtle turns of expression. Then, too, as Guevara has pointed out, they like to use phrases that are markedly elliptical and laconic, with very few words serving to suggest complete thoughts (Guevara Silva 1911:9–10). Moreover, most of the references that are sprinkled throughout the oral literature derive so much of their significance from close familiarity with Mapuche culture, that outsiders are apt to find them meaningless or enigmatic.

The term for a song is *ül,* and the verb "to sing" is *ülkantun.* As a rule, the songs have neither fixed numbers of syllables nor regularly determined verse lengths. Instead, they get their effects from a combination of clever wording and rhythmic phrasing in conformity with the patterns of Araucanian speech. If a particular passage is well received, it may be repeated at the option of the singer.

Mapuche songs cover a wide range of topics, including prayers and supplications for supernatural aid, love and courtship, lonesomeness, sorrow, grief resulting from bereavement, enforced separation, poverty, or failure to have offspring. Some classes of songs are rendered by special personages such as chiefs or medicine women,[3] and others are sung in conjunction with the performance of particular activities.[4] Both of these types may be rendered in traditionally fixed forms and are generally accompanied by musical instruments.[5]

A great number of unaccompanied songs are improvised at public gatherings by men or women who take advantage of these occasions to "blow off steam," or to call general attention to some matter of personal concern to the singer. Songs of this kind are called "assembly songs," and their moods may vary from naïve and joyful to slanderous, bitter, or ironic.

Not many "assembly songs" have been published, and scarcely any have been analyzed in terms of their social and cultural meanings. It is the purpose of this paper to call attention to this interesting but little known aspect of Araucanian culture, by providing examples of representative texts, translations, and interpretations.

SOCIOCULTURAL BACKGROUND

During recent decades the Mapuche have been living in a large number of districts or reservations, known in Spanish as *reducciones.* Each of these communities comprises a varying number of households whose male occupants are, as a rule, patrilineally related. Postmarital residence is patrilocal, and most marriages are exogamic with respect to the husband's *reducción*. Unilocal residence formerly prevailed, since married sons continued to live under their father's roof;[6] but the modern tendency, at least in the region north of the Cautin River, has been for sons at marriage to build independent houses (*rucas*) on their natal reservations.

Araucanian communities are characterized by an absence of physical cohesion. There are no streets, no central plaza, no stores or public buildings, in short, nothing that suggests the spatial arrangement of a village or town.[7] Correspondingly, it is not surprising that there should be a minimum of community enterprises. Weather permitting, a fair amount of visiting takes place among friends and relatives who live on the same reserve, but inter-*reducción* contacts are comparatively few. This is particularly true during the cold and rainy months of winter, when roads wash out and travel becomes all but impossible. For several months of each year, therefore, every community tends to be cut off from its neighbors.

The virtual isolation that prevails in winter is relieved in the spring and fall when intergroup gatherings known as *kawin* or *trawin* are held. Members of a given reservation act as hosts, and guests are invited from other districts. Various motives may serve to bring about these meetings. They may be held for the purpose of reaching policy decisions that affect all the participants, to announce important events or news items, to honor a person returning from Argentina or some other distant place, to celebrate a holiday, to hold a thanksgiving ritual or a housewarming fiesta, or simply for the sake of friendship and sociability.[8] Whatever their particular aims may be, all such assemblies are welcome events that provide opportunities for friendly conversation, courtship, gossip, and the exchange of news. Regardless of special functions, too, these events always include in the schedule of activities, feasting, drinking, oratory, and singing.

It is on such occasions that some of the celebrants, generally under the stimulus of drink, may give vent to their inner feelings by improvising songs (cf. Guevara Silva 1911:9). The effects of these improvisations are not necessarily slight or temporary. They may lead to the correction of abuses, or they may serve a totally different purpose, for auditors sometimes memorize the songs that strike their fancy and later repeat them from time to time at home. Children are thus given an opportunity to become acquainted with various compositions, which their elders encourage them to learn to sing. The Mapuche recognize that this is an educational technique, and informants point out that it enables youngsters to acquire skill in singing at the same time that it gives them an awareness of the subtleties of their native tongue and an insight into the customs and traditions of their tribe.

ASSEMBLY SONGS: TEXTS, FREE TRANSLATIONS, AND INTERPRETATIONS

The material contained in this section was obtained in Santiago late in May, 1948, from Mr. J. M. Collío Huaiquilaf,[9] and was rechecked with him about two months later. He wrote out the texts in his own hand, using a system of transcription that consists essentially of the values given to the Spanish alphabet, with the sole addition of a Germanic *ü*. Because of the metaphorical quality of the language, it was impossible to translate the texts literally, but the free translations given here were gone over word by word with Mr. Collío. The interpretations are, in all instances, based on data furnished by him, but I have supplied some additional material.

Mr. Collío unhesitatingly affirmed that the custom of singing at assemblies is still practiced throughout the Araucanian region. As a tribal leader he travels widely in central Chile, and he claims to have attended a great number of public gatherings at some of which he heard renditions of the songs given below. In Collío's home reservation, however, where I spent approximately six weeks, informants were not familiar with the texts of these songs. Apparently none of them has more than a local distribution in the vicinity in which it was composed.

Woman's Song No. 1[10]

kanin peuman
petu ñi ilchalen
ñi femguechi
niyer keael meu.

Free translation. I dreamed of a vulture when I was a young virgin, little realizing that I was destined to submit to such a man.

Interpretation. The singer complains that her husband is rapacious and inconsiderate. According to Collío, she is also implying that her spouse does not satisfy her sexual desires.

Man's Reply[11]

felelai papai
eimi palelai
inche ta eimi
deuman piuke
fente ini ayufiel
kimwe laimi piyael
fei-ula doi ayueyu
felen meu feipien
eimi ta sakin domo.

Free translation. It is not so, my dear *papai* (literally, "mother," but used as a courteous or affectionate term of direct address by any man speaking to a mature woman). No matter what you say, I'll never hurt your feelings. My heart beats (*deuman,* literally, "is self-made" or "manufactured") only for you. You don't know what you are saying, because I love you very much. You are my dearest woman.

Woman's Song No. 2

tregul peuman
kuifi meu kai
welu fele pulai
alka pülelen.

Free translation. I dreamed of a lapwing[12] a long time ago, and now I am like a hen under the wing of a rooster.

Interpretation. In explaining this song my informant said that it is of the type sung by a young wife to call attention to the fact that her husband is sexually overactive. On hearing such a complaint, her relatives and friends try to advise her spouse to moderate his marital behavior. Sometimes a group of elderly men will arrange to meet the husband in private, without the wife's knowledge, in order to give him the benefit of their experience. Among other things they may tell the husband not to seek sexual satisfaction daily and to abstain from intercourse for at least twelve hours after a meal.

Man's Reply

ñuke anai ñuke
ñochi müten kimei
mute dungulmi
ñillatu piuke nguea fun
piukeye niye eli
fele kayu müten
tayu poyen külen
inchiu meu ta
dungu kilpe che
inchiu müten kisu.

Free translation. Wife, dear wife,[13] it would be better if you went more slowly and did not talk so much, or else there may be someone else asking for my favor (literally, *piuke,* "heart"). If you feel the same love for me that I do for you, just be quiet. Don't set people to talking about us; this is our own affair.

Woman's Counterreply

koñi anai koñi
müna küme küllüi
tami feipi fiel
ruf künu lan tatei.

Free translation. Husband, dear husband,[14] what you have said shows that you just jumped at conclusions. I wasn't speaking seriously.

Interpretation. It seems evident from the readings of the free translations in this group of three songs that a young wife sought to take advantage of Mapuche custom to draw attention to her husband's faults. When he called her to task in his reply, she tried to pass the matter off as a kind of joke.

Woman's Song No. 3

ngüru peuman
ni wesayauan meu
chum nguea afui
femguei feleael.

Free translation. I dreamed of a fox. It was bad for me, but there is no help for it now, since that is the way it turned out to be.

Interpretation. After having been married for two years or so, a wife has come to realize that her husband is like a fox, in the sense that he is given to thieving and wrongdoing.[15] Interested auditors, acting on this hint, make it a point to advise the husband to mend his ways. They also remind him that he has now been married long enough to realize that he ought to settle down and accept the responsibilities of a married man.

Man's Reply

müna wesa pimi
nai piche ñuke
femkefuli ofpe
fachi antü kimgue
eimi meu müten
puai ñi lelilen
wesa dungu afai.

Free translation. Things are not as bad as you have said, my little cousin (wife). If I have done anything wrong, it's all over now. Only on you do my eyes gaze. Let everything bad be ended.

Interpretation. The husband expresses remorse for his errors and promises to mend his ways at once and henceforth to keep his mind only on his wife.

Woman's Counterreply

feula anai koñi
tami un meu
kimael ayüpen
fei-ula nay ñi piuke
femül mi kimei
rume ayüeyu ula.

Free translation. Just now, dear cousin (husband), I have heard what I wanted to hear from your own lips. Now my heart is restored to its proper place. If you do what is right, I shall love you more than ever.

Woman's Song No. 4

cod-cod peuma
küme peuman
fei neu felen
ñi rumue küme füta.

Free translation. I dreamed of a deer. It was a good omen, and that is why I find myself with my lovely husband.

Interpretation. To dream of a deer is particularly auspicious. The deer is regarded as a gentle and good animal that never hurts anyone and never spoils or destroys anything. When a wife sings in this fashion, all the auditors congratulate the happy couple, who are in need neither of advice nor guidance.

Woman's Song No. 5[16]

rumel re ko peuman
famguechi ñi konpayam
ko engu pod fotra kei
fei neu dungu ka lei.

Free translation. I always dreamed only of clear water. That is how I thought things were going to be, but water and dirt make mud, and that is far from good.

Interpretation. A wife sings in this vein to make it known that she is maltreated by her husband's family, with whom she has to live according to the custom of patrilocal unilocal residence. On hearing such a complaint people speak to the singer's parents-in-law, urging them to be more considerate of their daughter-in-law.

Woman's Song No. 6

weda lerkei puñmo
dungu allkutun
fotum müten mülei
domo nguerke lai.

Free translation. Things are very bad with me. My father-in-law pays attention only to his son, while I am dismissed as if I were dead.

Interpretation. Once again the strain put on a woman by the custom of patrilocal unilocal residence is brought out. A wife is a newcomer to her husband's household and is very much subject to her father-in-law throughout his lifetime.[17]

Woman's Song No. 7

weda peuman
trafia müten
ñi fillka duam
me peuman müten.

Free translation. I had a bad dream just last night. On account of my brother-in-law (*fillka*) I dreamed of nothing but dung.

Interpretation. This song expresses unhappiness because a woman's brother-in-law is about to marry. Through the workings of the custom of unilocal patrilocal residence his marriage means that another woman will come to live in the singer's household and will share in the conduct of its affairs. Women who are married to brothers often are so hostile that they call each other *medomo* ("feces woman") (Félix José de Augusta 1916:v. 1, p. 133).

When people hear a song of this kind, which is sung in the presence of the brother-in-law concerned, they keep it in mind but can take no action, since the marriage has not yet occurred. They note the hint of impending trouble, however, and prepare to serve as mediators and conciliators at the first sign of strife. Toward this end a secret committee of friendly and related women may be formed in order to establish amicable relations between the singer and her prospective sister-in-law.

Woman's Song No. 8

re kochü dungu
piyeninga welu
afkerkelu kochütun
fei ula fre letui
tami dungun
ellaka feipi feli.

Free translation. At first you used to say only sweet things to me, but now the sweetness is gone and your speech is bitter. Please speak to me as you used to do in the beginning.

Interpretation. Acting on the complaint expressed here, a group of responsible men may take it upon themselves to find out what has gone wrong and to take steps to bring about a reconciliation. Since Mapuche men talk more freely than do women about their private affairs, the group usually has some prior awareness of the husband's side of the case; but the wife's point of view may be entirely unknown up to this moment. As a matter of fact, Collío expressed the opinion that a woman would not sing in this way unless she had been long married and had acquired a feeling of security as the dominant female in her household.

Woman's Song No. 9

maicoño kuntrul
inaful inche meu
pün-pün külei
inche püle müten
tenguechi peuman
tañi ñadu nguen meu.

Free translation. A flock of turtledoves[18] flutters constantly by my side, wherever I may happen to be. In this way did I dream because of my *nadu* ("husband's sister").

Interpretation. Although this type of song is called *wenañkun* ("sadness") it really expresses the opposite emotion. It reveals the good news that a woman's sister-in-law is about to be married. By the rule of patrilocal residence it follows that the singer is about to lose the companionship of her husband's sister, who was always fluttering about her. Deep down, the singer is pleased at the prospect of being left alone in her house with her husband and children.[19] Indeed, everyone may be said to be pleased: the prospective bride, her brother, her sister-in-law, and those of the bystanders who entertain hopes of taking part in the wedding celebration. Thus, this song "hurts no one," as Collío put it, and people hasten to wish joy to the girl whose betrothal the singer has announced. Just the same, Collío added, no woman would sing publicly in this manner, unless she were herself long-married and confident of her own security.

Man's Song No. 1[20]

kiñe ngue meu
ella lelien feichi
elu ad laen
rume kutrantun
tami fem fiel
re kura piuke
ütruf niyen.

Free translation. Only with one eye do you glance at me at present. When you hide your face, I might as well be dead. Why must you ever show me nothing but a heart of stone?

Interpretation. A boy sings in this fashion to his sweetheart, either during a family visit to her home or at an assembly where members of both families are present. It reveals the fact that he has failed to win the girl of his choice, and it also serves to test her reaction. In accordance with Mapuche conventions it is not proper for a young woman to accept a proposal too quickly or too directly. Hence, she answers in the manner of the reply given below. If the affair reaches a stalemate the suitor's father, confident of the singer's sincerity, may take steps leading to a formal betrothal.

Woman's Reply

müna koila wentru
piuke meu feipilai
re mellfu-un meu
müten feipi kei
angue ta pengue
küle kei müten
piuke ellka lei.

Free translation. Men are all liars, they speak only with the lips, not with the heart. They show their faces uncovered, but not their hearts.

Interpretation. By singing in such a vein, a girl who is being courted makes it clear that she is not to be taken lightly. The implication is that she may consider a serious offer of marriage but that she is unwilling to take part in a mere flirtation.

Man's Song No. 2

chumül anchi
inche kiman
tami piuke
ni inchü ngueael
feipi keeli
feichi dungu
allkutu anai
küme pichi ñuke.

Free translation. When will the time come when I shall know what is in your heart? Why don't you say the word that will allow us to be united? Please listen to me, my little cousin.

Interpretation. A lover will sing in this way if a sweetheart continues to show reluctance even after some of the preliminaries to marriage have been carried out. The intent is to persuade the girl to set a wedding date.

Woman's Reply

prolei ñi piuke
feipi keeli arol
piuke ta pekan
fam tuku keel
troki kifilngue
rulpa fingue
amulechi antu
fei ula kimaimin.

Free translation. At this moment my heart is tied in a knot, so I cannot reply. The heart is not a toy to be lightly given away. Please do not hurry me. Let the ever-moving sun go on, then you will learn what is best.

Interpretation. In these words a girl expresses her unwillingness to set a definite wedding date. Her song implies that she may yet be willing to marry her suitor, but is not interested in a casual love affair.

Man's Song No. 3[21]

inaltu mahuida
amulerpu fun
welu pela eyu ñuke
cheu anta mülei
tami piuke am
inche kutran piuke
eimi ayene-en
papai anai papai
chumül chefel
inche ta eimi chachai.

Free translation. Along the edge of the forest I happened to go, but I failed to see you, cousin. Why are you so heartless?[22] While I am sick at heart, you are laughing at me. Mother, dear mother,[23] when will you say, "I am yours, daddy."[24]

Interpretation. Here a lover complains that his sweetheart is not responsive to his advances. No serious offer of marriage is proposed, however.

Woman's Reply

koñi anai koñi
müfüchi ñuke
rume piyaimi

welu rüpü kilñe
kiso lelmi rume
feipi afeyu
trig mapu meu
wefpalen inche
pu che meu ta tripan.

Free translation. Cousin, dear cousin, no matter how often you may call me *ñuke* ("cousin" or "wife"),[25] you are on the wrong road. Let me remind you that I did not spring from a hole in the ground, but was born from a human body.

Interpretation. In this song a young woman expresses her refusal to engage in an irregular love affair with her father's sister's son. Because this type of cross-cousin marriage was the Mapuche pattern, young men were apt to regard all of their *ñuke* (mother's brother's daughters) as potential mistresses, if not wives. Parents were, of course, fully cognizant of this attitude and took pains, accordingly, to warn their eligible daughters not to yield too readily to their importunate cousins.

CONCLUSION

The songs contained in the preceding section represent only a part of the repertoire of a single, well-versed informant. No doubt vast stores of similar material await systematic collection. Unquestionably, too, they will yield many insights into the workings of Mapuche culture and its effects on the temperaments of the people.

For women, especially, the device of assembly singing seems to afford an important emotional outlet. Traditionally, Araucanian social organization has a strong masculine emphasis, and women have only minor and subordinate status.[26] This is particularly apparent in the marriage customs, for women have scarcely any voice in the selection of mates, they have nothing to say about where they are going to live, and they have little expectation of being sole mistresses of their own households. That these matters trouble them is clearly evident from the way in which wives take advantage of a socially approved safety valve that gives them an opportunity to "blow off steam" regarding their marital problems, without fear of criticism or reprisals.

It is the postmarital residence pattern that appears to put the greatest strain on a newlywed woman. While a groom continues to live on his natal *reducción*, sometimes in the very house in which he was born, a bride must go to live among strangers in a strange place. Not only must she work out an adjustment to her husband but also to such of his relatives as happen to live under the same roof. Some of the personality clashes that are likely to grow out of this situation are revealed in "Woman's Song" Nos. 5, 6, 7, and 9.

Another aspect of Mapuche social organization that finds recurrent expression in the songs is the emphasis on cross-cousin marriage. So close is the bond between a man and his mother's brother's daughter (*koñi-ñuke*) that one may use the term *ñuke* for a wife or sweetheart who is not a daughter of one's maternal uncle.

The assembly songs also serve to call attention to several items of Mapuche religion. Belief in dreams as omens is frequently reiterated, and there is one interesting example of the widely held notion that heart, soul, shade, and reflection form a single complex. Furthermore, there are some references to bird and animal lore, with mention being made specifically of the deer, fox, vulture, lapwing, turtledove, hen, and rooster.

In conclusion, it may be said that these songs give proof of the high poetic quality of Mapuche oral literature. At the same time they throw light on numerous aspects of social organization and provide important clues to an understanding of the interplay between Mapuche culture and personality development.

NOTES

1. For practical purposes the terms Mapuche and Araucanian are interchangeable. They may be applied either to the aboriginal language that was widespread in central Chile before the conquest, or to the natives who speak that tongue. At present the main body of Araucanian speakers resides between the Bio Bio River and Chiloe Island. In their own language Mapuche means "people of the land."

2. Convenient bibliographic references to these works are given in Brand (1941:29 *et passim*).

3. Best known in this category are *machi ül,* sung by female shamans or *machis,* in conjunction with curing rites or public ceremonies.

4. For example, songs designed to bring victory in hockey games are known as *paliwe ül* ("hockey game song") and are sung before a match begins.

5. The most commonly used instruments are listed and described in Cooper (1946a:738).

6. For a discussion of the significance of unilocal residence, see Titiev (1943).

7. The limits of each *reducción* are defined by legal title to a given piece of land. These titles were originally allotted to recognized chiefs, who assigned particular portions to their descendants and followers. The collapse of the old system of chieftainship has resulted in much confusion with respect to land holdings.

8. Public assemblies may be called *kawin* or *trawin.* These words are variously spelled by Spanish writers, and some authors try to distinguish between them on the basis of function. All assemblies, however, share so many features that it seems permissible to treat them together. On this point compare Robles Rodriguez (1912:359 and footnotes 1 and 2, same page).

9. Mr. J. Martín Collío Huaiquilaf is not entirely unknown to North American anthropologists. He was in the United States after the close of the first World War, and he occasionally served as an informant to Dr. Speck and Dr. Hallowell at the University of Pennsylvania. He also conferred with Dr. Brand in Santiago in March, 1941, and Brand has published a trilingual text furnished by Collío (Brand 1941:24; Collío Huaiquilaf 1941; see also Hallowell 1943).

Mr. Collío formerly lived on the *reducción* called Carrarriñe, near Cholchol, but for some years past he has been a resident of Santiago. He speaks Araucanian and Spanish fluently and has some knowledge of English. I found him to be a helpful and reliable informant, and I am deeply grateful for all the assistance he gave me.

10. Women's songs are generally but not invariably shorter than are men's. The numbers attached to the successive texts are purely arbitrary and are used only for convenience in making references.

11. There seems to be a tendency for singing to develop into a sort of contest, for many songs make accusations which are answered by the person concerned.

12. Fray Félix José de Augusta (1916:v.2, p. 213) identifies the tregle bird as *Vanellus chilensis,* the Chilean lapwing. As Collío described it, however, it was somewhat reminiscent of the European cuckoo, in that he claimed it was noisy, frequented muddy places, and had no nest of its own, but laid eggs anywhere.

13. Traditionally, and to some extent at present, a Mapuche man was expected to marry the daughter of his mother's brother. The term for this cross-cousin is *ñuke* and may be used either in the literal sense of "wife" or else somewhat loosely to connote "sweetheart."

14. A woman calls her husband *koñi*, the term for father's sister's son, because in former times she was expected to marry such a cross-cousin. Compare footnote 13.

15. It is a Mapuche convention that a man whose faults are publicized in an assembly song must neither show anger nor seek to punish his wife. Nevertheless, an ominous tone runs through the husband's reply to Woman's Song No. 2; and the wife's counterreply is distinctly conciliatory.

16. This song and the next two were termed *piñmal kaun* ("ironic" or "sarcastic") by Collío. According to him, songs of this type comprise an important form of social control among the Mapuche. Sometimes, it is the only way in which conduct can be regulated. For example, a man who beats his wife may be induced to stop if people are sarcastic to him.

17. There is reason to believe that in former times a mature man maintained strong control over the inmates of his household. Normally, these consisted of his wives and unmarried offspring and his married sons and their wives and unwed children.

18. Félix José de Augusta (1916: v. 1, p. 128) identified *maikoño* as *la tortola*, the turtledove (*Zenaida aurita*).

19. Contrast a wife's bitterness, in "Woman's Song No. 7," at the prospect of having a new sister-in-law move into her household.

20. "Man's Songs" No. 1 and No. 2 were called *dakeltun ül* ("pact-making song") by Collío. As he used the term it had the connotation of a love pact.

21. Strictly speaking this song is not rendered in public. It deals with a request for a private love affair and is addressed only to the girl concerned. Nevertheless, the lover may make his plea during the course of a large assembly.

22. *Tami piuke am* means literally, "your heart soul." However, *am* also means "shade" or "reflection." Thus, the lover wants to know where is the soul, shade, or reflection of his cousin's heart. This connotes that she appears heartless to him.

23. For the use of *papai* see the free translation of "Man's Reply" to "Woman's Song No. 1."

24. *Chachai* is a familiar term for father. It may also be used as a friendly greeting by a young woman addressing an older man.

25. Compare footnote 13.

26. The fact that most of the religious leaders (*machis*) are women makes an important exception to the general rule.

Like the three preceding articles, this one deals with social control, the punishment of deviance and resolution of conflict. In this case, however, we are dealing with situations of a somewhat more serious nature than those handled by Mapuche singing.

Fock shows us the range of variation in control from strictly interpersonal action to involvement of the several sibs and villages. All these articles indicate a close relation between social organization and the form taken by the conflict itself and conflict regulation.

For further information on Mataco conflict resolution, see Fock (1972), an article also containing material on the Waiwai and the Quechua. Fock has introduced minor editorial changes in this article that in no way change the sense of the original.

20 NIELS FOCK

Mataco Law

The Mataco Indians inhabit the western areas of the Argentine Chaco between the Río Pilcomayo and the Río Bermejo. They have for centuries been in contact with civilisation, but as a frontier tribe they seem to have built up a special traditionalism as a protective bulwark. Particularly the northeastern Mataco at the central Pilcomayo have preserved their ancient traditions to this day, and the occupational system is still stamped by the collecting by women and the fishing of the men.

The Mataco possess a legal system whether one applies a strictly formal or a more elastic criterion of justice. Adamson Hoebel's formal definition lays down that "A social norm is legal if its neglect or infraction is regularly met, in threat or in fact, by the application of physical force by an individual or group possessing the socially recognized privilege of so acting" (1964:28). Thus limited, there exists among the Mataco at all events what Radcliffe-Brown calls a law of private delicts centred around homicide, adultery and theft (1965:212). If regarded from a functional angle, as, for example, by Bohannan, law however is merely the manner in which people handle disputes and cases of trouble in order to settle breaches of standard destructive to the community (1967:46). Thus defined the Mataco also possess a law of public delicts, particularly in connection with the excessive sorcery of the medicine man and the representative behaviour of the chief. However, I shall attempt to confine myself to the so-called private delicts in order through the violating acts to bring to light the social values that are considered so basic that infringement of them is punishable.

Although the sharing of products is carried to great lengths in a Mataco village, theft is by no means rare. The theft of field crops is the most common, and tobacco particularly constitutes a temptation. As a rule the thief discloses his identity by the footprints he leaves behind him; every Mataco claims to recognize the footprints of his fellow villagers. When, therefore, the owner of a field suspects a definite person, he lies in wait to catch the culprit in the act. This can develop into a struggle, but normally the owner is content to issue a warning, which ends by telling the thief to take home the stolen property. "I shall come home to you and work out what I consider you owe me," he may well say. In one illustrative case it was a matter of a youthful thief, and the owner involved therefore applied to the offender's father, who compensated for the stolen property by handing over two goats which in value far exceeded the goods stolen. The father reproached his thieving son, saying that he must not harm the owner as the latter might become angry and cause them still further loss. "When you need anything you must not take it, but ask for it from someone who possesses it. When he harvests he is not

Reprinted by permission of the author from *Actas y Memorias, XXXII Congreso Internacional de Americanistas, España, 1964*, vol. 3 (Seville, 1966), pp. 349–353.

only harvesting for himself, but for all." In other cases where the identity of the thief is disclosed without his being caught in the act, it may happen that whilst the delinquent is out hunting the aggrieved person sends some of his family over to select a goat or a sheep from the thief's flock. Whilst this animal was brought home and slaughtered, a number of people assembled—as is always the case with such incidents—perhaps also members of the culprit's family, and the aggrieved person took the opportunity to justify his action by remarking: "I do not normally make a practice of slaughtering another man's beast, but do so now with a clear conscience. When we have something it is not only for ourselves, but for us all. We have acted thus because we have no desire to hurt any family; no human lives have been lost, there has been no strife." Later in the day when the thief returned and the meat had been cooked, the victim of the theft sent over a piece of meat to the house of the thief, who was unaware that it was a matter of his own animal. This was a peculiarly subtle form of correction. Not until later did his family tell him about it, and his father exhorted him not to be angry, but to learn instead to cultivate himself the crops he needed. As a rule practical instruction of this kind causes a young man to cease being a thief.

The treatment of hardened offenders is less lenient. The owner of a field who had discovered that a person of this kind was ravaging his field, found the place where the thief climbed over the fence, and placed below it a dangerous poisonous snake he had caught for this purpose. Placing a cord round its neck he tethered it to a pole and placed some twigs over it. When the thief arrived and started rummaging about near the fence, the snake became irritated, and when the man jumped down he was bitten. The owner of the field did nothing more about the matter, but the thief was also punished indirectly, for he had to seek assistance from the medicine man and pay for his cure. In similar cases owners can also use cactus thorns hidden in loose soil in a small pitfall where the thief usually enters. In this way his identity is discovered. The owner is never held responsible for his act of vengeance, but nor does he obtain compensation for his lost products. Others do not concern themselves with the matter, but discuss it and agree that the owner has acted correctly.

Three principles seem to dominate these anti-theft sanctions: a compensatory principle when merely going to the thief's father and demanding indemnification, a retaliatory principle when the family is sent out to bring back some of the thief's property, and, finally, a retributive principle where the thief can suffer bodily harm. Whether theft among the Mataco can be termed private delict seems very doubtful. It is not the rights of private ownership that are infringed, for it is seen that some of the same benefits that were subject to theft could have been requested—and obtained. In reality it is laziness that is punished, for given sufficient industry, a person can himself produce and obtain by barter what he needs. Here it is therefore more a matter of taking the law into one's own hands for the sake of private gain, an act directed against the community economy, and consequently more a case of public delict.

With the Mataco two other offences can, like theft, be punished by corresponding economic sanctions. These are rape and homicide. In the event of rape the man, if married, also comes under the sanctions valid for infidelity, but in addition the raped woman and her family are allowed to capture and slaughter, say, a goat and a sheep from the flock of the delinquent. If he or his family angrily ask what it is all about, the woman's family at first says nothing, but gradually explain. The whole matter is then regarded as settled.

Among the Mataco monogamy is strictly enforced, and no form of extramarital sexual relations is socially allowed. In case of infidelity within a marriage, distinction is made between the unfaithfulness of a man and a woman, the latter's being considered the more serious offence. In that case the wife—when she realizes what is going on—with some of her female relatives, attacks the girl. For this reason, in earlier days particularly, girls never cut their nails in order that they could draw blood from any rival. It is noteworthy that whereas the wife obtains the help of her female relations, the same is not so in the case of the intervening girl. Her family maintains "that is not worth fighting about," but in view of the absolute solidarity that is customary within families, it must mean that her conduct is regarded as positively wrong by her own kin, that is to say, socially.

In the event that a man should have fled with the intervener, the wife and her female relatives pursue them and attempt by force to drag back the man. As a rule they are successful in this, because the other men will not concern themselves about it, considering it a purely feminine affair. When a man is unfaithful and is regarded as the active party, he also risks being beaten to his senses by his wife and her female relatives. No one in the village wishes to intervene. A man who persists in infidelity will be reproached, even by his own relations, and his wife has the right to leave him without incurring censure.

As a rule a woman's unfaithfulness will have more far-reaching results than that of a man. In the first place the husband does not trouble to consider whether the wife is the seducer or the seduced, but always gives her the blame. Her fate depends upon the temperament of her husband. If he discovers her, he can beat her in order that her behaviour shall be improved, and in that event he seldom does anything to his rival. As a rule, however, he will at once divorce her and chase her away. Her family will make no protest, and will at most vilify her for having behaved badly. It is said that the reason why a man wants to be divorced at once is because he thinks that she will be unfaithful to him again and again, so that at last he will lose his head and attempt to kill her and her lover. There are numerous examples of this.

Unfaithfulness is one of the chief reasons for divorce, which is a quite frequent occurrence with the Mataco. If on account of infidelity a man is divorced from his wife, he himself leaves the house taking with him only his personal effects such as fishing net, tinder, bow and arrow, etc. He moves first to his parent's house, and later to the family of his new wife. Under these circumstances he cannot take his children with him unless they are so big that they themselves desire it. If the woman's unfaithfulness is the cause of the divorce, she will be evicted from the house, and not until later will her family come and fetch her personal property such as clay vessels, yicas, harvest of forest fruit, plus any goats and sheep. The children then stay with the father and can be brought up by his mother or some other female relative. It is always a general rule that at divorces the injured party retains house and children, and only the personal property is divided.

Whatever the reason for a Mataco divorce, it is always a heavy blow, both morally and economically, for the spouse that is left. The economic loss can only be made good by re-marriage, and this nearly always takes place. A person who feels himself rejected or a victim of unhappy love sometimes commits suicide, which with the Mataco appears to occur particularly in this connection. In cases of suicide the spouse of the dead person will always be pointed to as the one responsible. In consequence, the family of the dead person will in many cases start a campaign against that of the spouse to obtain blood vengeance or, more probably, to secure economic compensation.

According to Mataco unwritten law infidelity is severely punished by the loss of home and children. This should occasion no surprise, for adultery, on account of band exogamy, is the main reason for blood feuds and inter-band warfare. The marriage system thus obtains a far-reaching political influence.

We have seen how infidelity normally entails the imposition of sanctions by the injured party, in that the offender must leave home and children. However, when infidelity leads to homicide as a result of jealousy this is regarded as too stern a sanction, and is immediately countered by another: a blood-feud or some other form of compensation. In case of homicide resulting from jealousy, the lesser offence is completely expunged by the greater, and the adulterer's family become justified avengers.

The sanctions imposed against a killer—and one who has caused the suicide of another is also regarded as such—are of three kinds: The most simple—but today rather rare—are the retributive killings, where one or more of the deceased's sibs arm themselves, and with loyal kinsmen, engage on a feud with the killer's sibs and those who support him. However, the only result of this is to spread the conflict and make it a general one between several local groups. It is far more usual for the sibs of the murdered man to put on full war paint and visit the killer in his village in order to demand "blood-money." The villagers are aware that a force of this kind comes to demand its rights, and accordingly receive it well, though with extreme caution. Some of the close kinsmen of the deceased go forward to the killer, gripping him by the chest whilst threatening him with their spears. Meanwhile the remainder approach ominously, the one man after the other cursing the killer, and striking him at the same time. During such a tense situation the women often take to the woods with their belongings, but when they discover that the contending parties have begun to haggle about a reasonable compensation for the crime, they often return with some of the goats and sheep to the village. The killer might, for example, offer 10 goats, 5 of which are with kid, and the punitive expedition agrees to be satisfied with this. As soon as payment has been made to the leader of the deceased's family, they stop all abuse, saying, for example: "Very well, my friend, every thing is as before. Should anyone tell us anything bad about you, we shall not believe them. All is forgotten." When the warriors leave the village they wave greetings, and everybody is relieved that the matter has been settled amicably. On the way home the goats could be distributed to the various sibs who had helped to enforce the law. The family of the murdered man might, for example, retain 3 goats themselves, but these animals were not eaten, but incorporated in the family flock, their issue being gradually divided among the families which received nothing in the first instance.

Finally, an interesting third procedure was formerly resorted to if, say, an intoxicated person slew another man. The killer could then go on the war path and bring back a scalp from a hostile neighbouring tribe. Although the family of the murdered man did not completely forgive the crime, the general acceptance by the village of this settlement would normally cause the deceased man's sibs to refrain from further sanctions.

The three methods of easing the situation after a homicide: compensation in the form of "blood-money," a blood feud between the parties involved with its tendency to spread to other sibs, and the collection of a scalp from a hostile tribe, evince various stages of the conflict's polarization, as the sib, more sibs or villages and, finally the whole tribe are respectively involved. Whilst the conflict extends the personal risk of the killer is reduced. The fact that the acquisition of a foreign scalp is regarded as an adequate sanction for a homicide appears to suggest—as was the case with theft—that the homicide is regarded as a public delict: the life taken from the public mass is replaced by the death of an enemy; balance has been restored.

What is punished with the Mataco, and which therefore falls under the legal system, appears always to be offences committed against the community, its property by theft, its basic principle by adultery, and its life by homicide.

Leeds' article can be viewed as an "ethnotheology" of the Yaruro. The author demonstrates convincingly that "the cosmos, society, and man are a single system in Yaruro thought," and, by an analysis of Yaruro ideology, provides important insights into the world view and self-conceptualization of these people. His description of Yaruro cosmology also provides interesting contrasts and parallels with those described in the next section for the southern Quechua, the Campa, Kogi, and Jívaro.

Leeds has revised the orthography used in the original and provided a key to the pronunciation of Yaruro words (see footnote 2, page 234).

21 ANTHONY LEEDS

The Ideology of the Yaruro Indians in Relation to Socio-economic Organization

It is the purpose of this paper to show the correspondence between the principles of socio-economic organization of the Yaruro Indians and their ideology and to isolate some dimensions of ideology which may be used for comparative purposes. It is hoped that by further isolation of such categories it will eventually become possible to compare the structure and content of widely different ideologies, as we today are able to compare kinship systems, so that we may be able to recognize synchronic regularities of a functional order and diachronic regularities of an evolutionary sort. Yaruro religious and philosophical beliefs are reduced to a series of postulates or axioms about the nature of the universe and man in an analysis somewhat like Kluckhohn's study of Navaho philosophy (1949) and Opler's of Apache themes (1945). No Yaruro would be able to express the axioms nor see them in the logical series as presented here, yet each would recognize them, when couched in the phrasings of his own language, as referring to his particular *Weltanschauung*. The postulates are derived from direct statements by informants about the cosmos or about human living, from other verbal materials such as discussions of disease and social organization, and, more occasionally, from observed behavior. The generalized titles introducing each of the summarized postulates appearing at the end of the paper comprise the dimensions, here inductively arrived at, which may serve for cross-cultural analysis.

The Yaruro Indians have been living in the savannas or llanos of Southern Venezuela for an unknown number of centuries. They have developed a socio-economic life well-articulated to the geographical conditions of life.

The gross geographical characteristics of the alternately desert-like and flood-covered llanos cause all the best economic resources to be concentrated along the west-to-east flowing rivers in ribbons some kilometers wide. Most significant fauna and flora of economic use occur in these ribbons. This ecological distribution of resources governs subsistence activities whether they be mainly hunting, fishing, collecting, or horticulture.

Yaruro subsistence comprises all these activities.[1] Horticulture in the rainy season appears considerably to outweigh all other sources of food together, but in the dry season, hunting, fishing, and collecting perhaps equal or outstrip horticulture. In any case, slash and burn gardening of manioc, corn, plantains, and a number of lesser crops is by far the single most important economic activity. The technology is exceedingly simple in all aspects of production, the main tools being the machete and digging stick. The most elaborate technology occurs in the

Reprinted by permission of the author and the Sociedad de Ciencias Naturales La Salle from *Antropológica*, no. 9 (Caracas, 1960), pp. 1–10.

conversion of food into edibles and in the manufacture of hammocks, pottery, objects of wood such as canoes, and woven containers of all types.

The economic organization displays a sharp division of labor between men's and women's work. Men do all hunting and fishing, make all objects of wood, haul lumber and householding materials, make hammocks, and carry out the heavy labor of gardening. Women do most of the collecting of roots, seeds, and fruits. Since collecting contributes a substantial portion of the food supply in summer, women's contribution, here, is of considerable communal importance. Women's work, a continuous activity from dawn to dusk, is, first, the conversion of raw foodstuffs into edibles. Second, women make all pottery, mats and baskets, the manioc squeezers, and much of the cord used to make hammocks. Another important contribution of women is their help in harvesting in the gardens. Men sometimes help the women with the cookery.

Men may work alone, in groups of 2 or 3, or in larger groups on rare occasions. No occasion exists for all men to work at a single task since there is no technological need for it. Women's work groups for collecting or householding are of similar size. Work group alignments are often based on choice or accident but in other instances coresidence and kinship are determinants. The household, however, constitutes the only really necessary cooperative group for production. The man is a funnel for produce which the woman converts to make it usable. The need to eat makes woman's work more or less continuous, while the nature of production does not make man's work continuous. As long as there is food in the village, the man may rest, help his wife, or engage in non-food production such as canoe-making, as he chooses.

Objects used by men are men's property and are inherited by the men; objects used by women are women's property and are inherited in the women's line. Immovable property such as gardens and houses are said to be inherited by the decedent's children of both sexes. Male animals, such as boars and dogs, are owned by men, the females by women. Thus the division of property is as sharp as the division of labor, a fact reflected throughout the ideology.

No two producers produce the same quantity or inventory of goods, especially as each has great freedom to concentrate in the productive activities he prefers to the exclusion of others. Yet each producer contributes to household and community in what is felt to be equivalent value since most foods are considered good and of equal worth. Each household producing unit distributes supplies of raw or cooked foods to other households along the lines of coresidence and kinship. In this way, all villagers, as consumers, receive the same total amount of food and no one goes without. Thus all persons and households in the community are equivalent as producers, distributers, and consumers. All are tied together in a loosely formalized network of coordinate reciprocal exchanges and obligations in which scales of value are not necessary, since each person contributes approximately equally of all values. In this situation, accumulation of wealth by individuals is out of the question and management of production or of wealth distribution is unnecessary. Consequently, there are no economic status differentiations and no effective leadership among the Yaruro.

Similarly, no purely social differentiations based on status ranking occur in Yaruro society, except by casual deference to those of age and experience like shamans and village spokesmen, called *"capitanes."* The status of women is coordinate with that of men. The complementary and coordinate units, a man and a woman, combine into a series of coordinate but semi-autonomous units, the households. A group of these constitute the Yaruro social unit, the neither endogamous nor exogamous (Murdock's "agamous") village. All these units are tied together by links of bilaterally traced kinship, with coordinate relations on both sides, the ultimate tie being the reciprocal marriage of cross-cousins. Marriage is ideally matrilocal, and occurs most frequently within the village. As a consequence, the most immediate kinship ties in the village are matrilateral, whereas kinship among the men is more diffuse. The villages themselves are tied together by kinship ties, real or imputed, as well as by marriage and visiting, but by no other ties of an all-tribal nature. People who are known to any particular village—to "us"—are considered part of our village's family, since their kinship ties to our members can be discovered or invented freely. Persons recognized as being of our linguistic and cultural stock will be included under the general term *pume*[1][2] but may not be considered "of our family" unless the kinship ties are recognized. Thus there is a Yaruro people, but no Yaruro tribal unit. Even the persons included in "our family" do not constitute a unit, since there are no cross village unifying institutions other than real or imputed bilateral kinship ties. Even these vary from village to village, since each village constitutes a separate and independent center of relationships with neighboring villages and consequently has its own unique assortment of outside relationships, based partly on choice. This situation, like so many other aspects of the socio-economic organization, is reflected in the cosmology.

According to the Yaruro, the cosmos originally lacked not only humans, but even gods. There existed only three concentric, rigid, blue, celestial domes; below them, a flat, undifferentiated, vast savanna all of sand; and a cold, dark, flat underworld. Beyond these there was, and is, nothing. Thunder, already then, was to be found between the upper celestial domes, while Sun, his wife, Moon, and their children, the stars, were already revolving between the lower two.

Into this cosmos were spontaneously born the primordial gods. The goddess Kumā[1], the grandmother of us all, who lives in a land to the west, out of the savanna created the discrete lands of her fellow gods and of the Yaruro. She created the non-Yaruro peoples, the *nive*[1], first, and the Yaruro, the *pume*[1], last, which is why there are so few—there were few left to create. She ordered Kibero[1], the female toad who lives in the dark underworld to give fire, which she belched from her belly. Kumā[1] created the foods which are collected and the modes of preparing them. She instructed the men and the women in their crafts. She ordained the social order. Her husband, Poanā[1], the snake god, who lives in a land to the south, created the characteristic savanna features: the rivers, the woods, the grasses for the animals to eat.

He taught men the technology of horticulture and gave them the seeds of the garden crops. He, with his fellow god, Ici'ai''[1], who lives in a land to the north and was born a boy given to troublemaking though he later matured, then taught the arts of hunting and fishing. Poanā' son, Hacha'wa, who lives in a land to the east, created only the ceremonial cigarettes. The four godly other-worlds lie beyond the Great Water which surrounds, but is not quite contiguous to, the Yaruro hither-world. This geographical break in the cosmos is negligible, however, since the hither-world and the other-worlds become continuous in the thought and action of the Yaruro. The Great Water continues in an endless expanse beyond the four other-worlds, according to one interpretation, while in another, it is said to be enclosed by limitless, unpeopled and empty savannas. The four Yaruro other-worlds are also inhabited by a younger generation of gods all possessing Spanish names. Some interpreters identify these with the primordial gods. Others do not. According to some informants, they live in the same lands as the older gods. Others say they live in different lands. Such variations of religious interpretation occur frequently despite general agreement in all essentials. Individual freedom of choice and interpretation, already noted in connection with economic choice and social inter-relationships, is also found in relation to ideology.

The godly other-worlds are generally described as idealized versions of the Yaruro habitat. This is true also of a fifth other-world, one which is discontinuous geographically, conceptually, and behaviorally with the rest of the Yaruro worlds, though similar in form. This is the land of Dios, the God of Christian Venezuelans, which lies between the two lower celestial domes and existed prior to Kumā'.

It is to be noted that Kumā' was not responsible for creating her fellow primordial gods. She is not an omnipotent creator but is fundamentally limited to creating other-world and hither-world things familiar to the Yaruro. She exists in an independent but loosely coordinate status with other celestial beings or phenomena like Thunder, Sun, Moon, the stars, the rainbow, and possibly Dios—the prototype for personal status among the Yaruro. Furthermore, despite wide variation in creation myths, the fact stands out, too, that she must almost equal honors with Poanā' in the creation of all that is vital to the Yaruro in the hither world in a creational division of labor closely paralleling the division of labor found in the actual economy. Further, Kumā' and Poanā' by the link of marriage, provide a prototype for the essential productive and distributional unit, the household. Hacha'wa, their son according to some informants, and Ici'ai'', Poanā' sister's son, both boys at the time of the creation, contribute little and are as much nuisance as help until they have matured, an apt reflection of the position of children in Yaruro economy. Today Poanā' and Kumā' seem preeminent in status among the gods, but at the same time are definitely merely *primi inter pares,* occupying the position of more experienced elders within the community of the gods, each of whom acts autonomously according to his own dictates.

The community of the gods is again prototypic for Yaruro hither-world life. Each god and his land constitutes a sort of village community populated by the god or gods, by dead *pume',* by dead animals, and by the regular other-worldly animal population, especially jaguars in human form and dress. The human-like inhabitants of the other-world eat, drink, dance, have sex relations, and visit from god's land to god's land. They enter into the web of kinship which ties the gods to each other, to the dead Yaruro, and to the live *pume'* of the hither-world in complex, if varying, genealogical connections. Even the great jaguar god, Tio' whose bailiwick is the first celestial dome and whose main task, under the general direction of Kumā', is to cure, is considered distantly related and of the family of Poanā'. A number of animal species are similarly distantly related, but like those Yaruro who cannot be fitted into the kinship system, are merely connected to us nominally. The gods, the dead, and the live *pume*' equally observe kinship obligations. Thus kinship and visits among the autonomous lands of the gods are the chief ties holding the four other-worlds together, a prototype for Yaruro village and social structure.[3]

However, in relationship to the living, Kumā' is "our chief." More than any other god, she is turned to for advice, for ethical reaffirmations, and for fulfilment of needs. It is first to Kumā' bright and golden land that the *pume*' go at death, during unconsciousness, in dreams, and during the religious ceremonies, the *tɔŋhe*'. The other lands are visited later and are less important in the other-worldly journeys made by the living. The dead of Kumā' land are the first to be called upon by the shaman when, during the *tɔŋhe*', he arrives in the other-worlds. He asks them, as well as Kumā' and the other gods, to return to earth and guide the community. In this manner, Kumā' is a center of gravity of the Yaruro ideological life. She is the center of a communications network which ties the Yaruro of the hither-world, those of the other-worlds, and the gods all in one continuous system of personal and social relations. This is somewhat the position of the spokesman or "*capitan*" in the community life of the Yaruro, though he has proportionally much less influence in his village than Kumā' has in her universe.

In sum, the gods and the dead are conceptualized as continuous with those of us on earth. Conceptually they appear to constitute the two highest steps in the age levels: infant, child, young adult, elder, the dead, and the gods. The last four classes are increasingly instrumental in teaching the ethics of living in tranquility, of respect and deference to one's spouse and to all members of one's people, and in teaching the values of the community. They exhort but never compel the community to follow these ideals. These precepts are followed not only among the egalitarian gods in their autonomous other-world communities, but in the personal and social relations between the gods and the hither-world *pume*'. The relations between men and gods, the communication between the hither- and other-worlds, the cosmography itself, all show quite clearly that there is no separation of "natural" and "supernatural" as discrete classes of events. The cosmos, society, and man are a single system in Yaruro thought.

The nexus through which the flow of life in the other-world and the ongoing rhythm of daily life in the hither-world are meshed into a single system is the religious ceremony, the *tɔŋhe*'. Some description of the *tɔŋhe*' will afford us further insight into Yaruro ideology.

During the night-long *tɔŋhe*', the entire community sits behind the shaman, ranged roughly by age levels. The women sit to his right, the men to his left. At dusk he begins to sing as he starts his journey to the land of Kumā' through the dark, cold land of Kibero', the toad who gave man fire. In hundreds of improvised verses and melodies, he describes his journey, and then, after his arrival about midnight, his adventures in the lands of Kumā' and subsequently of the other gods.

In each verse, the shaman sings an intonation which the entire community repeats in an identical antiphon. Thus the full experience of the shaman is transmitted to and shared by every member of the community. All is public; there is no secret knowledge. The shaman urges his people to sing with him and the other-worldly beings, to share in the responsibilities and joys of the community in supporting their individual members whether the shaman in his journey or the sick person for whom the tɔŋhe¹ may be being held. At the same time, in Kumā¹land, he urges the other-worldly beings to come to advise his people and teach them. Later, the verses are no longer sung by the shaman, but rather by the dead and the gods who arrive in the husk of the shaman which he has left behind as a channel of communications for the other-worldly beings while his divisible self travels abroad. As these beings arrive in the shaman's husk, all members of the community may greet them by putting their arms around them or giving them cigarettes or drink. This is done separately by women, sometimes in groups, and by men. Throughout the ceremony the chief link between the sexually divided community is the shaman or the gods in the shaman's husk upon whom both sexes are focusing their attention. The shaman's position as link is emphasized by the fact that his wife invariably sits next to him during the tɔŋhe¹ to minister to him and to supply him with cigarettes and drink. Thus, the socio-economic link of the household is also the unique link between the sexes in ceremonial life.

The various forms of socio-economic and ceremonial division of the sexes is even more remarkably underscored by the existence of female shamanism. As one might expect, shamanesses behave differently from shamans. Shamanesses sing only in the day-time. They, like Kumā¹, sing from hammocks whereas men sing sitting on the ground or dancing. Furthermore, messages transmitted to them from Kumā¹ are sent only to them, though the men hear and understand them. The men listen to these messages with care and respect and with the air that there are things to be learned from them which they would otherwise not hear. The shamanesses cannot receive male gods or their messages. Female shamanism seems to be an affirmation of the kin-bonds of the matri-centered local group as well as a means of asserting the values and rights pertaining to the women's world. The women's experience, ideologically, as well as socially and biologically, is recognized as being systematically distinct from men's experience in life.

Behavior in the tɔŋhe¹ is very relaxed. Villagers laugh, joke, sleep, play, get up, walk about. Sometimes persons may even fail to attend if they have chosen to go to work the next day. The only thing explicitly forbidden, because Kumā¹would consider it most indelicate, is sexual intercourse. Otherwise, the lack of formalism and freedom of individual behavior so often noted before is again found here.

The importance of the tɔŋhe¹ as the foremost way of reinforcing social relations and communal values as well as for curing is seen in several ways. First, when there has been no tɔŋhe¹ for several days, one begins to feel and hear a bruiting for another tɔŋhe¹. It is felt that much time has elapsed since the last tɔŋhe¹. Someone asks what's wrong that we haven't had a tɔŋhe¹ in so long. Another says we need a tɔŋhe¹. Rumors of tɔŋhe¹ begin to be heard. By the fifth or sixth day another tɔŋhe¹ is held and community bonds are again reasserted. Again, the sexual division of labor and social life observed in the other- and hither-worlds is systematically carried through into religious observances. We have mentioned the seating of men separate from women and the separate greetings given to the gods. This theme is carried still further in the exclusive women's shamanism and the equally exclusive capacity of men to do curing, either as shamans or as purely private individuals.

The *tɔŋhe'* illuminates much about Yaruro ideology. First, shamans both male and female are not considered authorities possessed of special gifts and prerogatives who interpret lore for the entire community. Rather they are considered merely the community religious spokesmen for the public expression of community values and for curing, who, by their own choice, enjoy and are willing to undertake the long, arduous work of training and practice. They reaffirm community bonds by repeating in endless verses the precepts and knowledge contained in the Yaruro ideology. All knowledge and all experience is, at least potentially, open to all members of the community and even the private or personal experience of each is made known to all. Any member of the community may do the shaman's work if he chooses, just as any can travel to the other-world or commune with the gods, although, because of age, temperament, or individual taste, not everyone does so. There were, in fact, two shamans among the nine men of the writer's village, as well as a number of men who cured and who occasionally sang verse intonations in the *tɔŋhe'* although they were not shamans. The shamans are no more than respected community members outside the ceremony. Here again we observe the egalitarianism and individual self-determinism which is so much a pattern of this culture.

The *tɔŋhe'* also clearly shows the relationships which prevail between men and gods. The shamans and the other adults of the village converse with the gods in great mutual respect. They do not manipulate them nor minister to them, nor implore them. Before the gods, they are in a position corresponding to active and adept junior members of the village before their elders and especially their lineal ascendants. Furthermore, in a very real sense, no individual person, *qua* person, deals with the gods. The community, with its religious catalyst, the shaman, is the unit of action. The only individual relations with the gods occur in dreams, unconsciousness, and death. Dreams about gods are made public by singing aloud in sleep, the experience of unconsciousness is recounted publicly, and death, too, becomes public because the dead man is accessible through the *tɔŋhe'*.

The directness of contact between man and gods again emphasizes the unity of cosmos, society, and man. Within this unity, the sharp division of a male sphere from a female sphere is found. These quite coordinate spheres, in the other-worlds as in the hither-world, in religion as in socio-economic life, are linked through the household.

In conclusion, I would like briefly to review the major dimensions of Yaruro ideology. We may state these as a set of propositions, each presenting a major dimension of the ideology.

1. Cosmic structure. *The cosmos is static, limited, concrete, and internally continuous in that no barriers separate man and his society in the physical world from the nonphysical world.* The parts of the universe together form a rather rigid,

symmetrical, architectonic structure, although each individual Yaruro may vary the description of the whole to suit his particular taste. All parts are of roughly coordinate importance. The major motions of nature, such as thunder and lightning, the revolutions of sun and moon, are often embodied, personalized, and independently operating entities, moved by semi-human motivations.

2. The good. *Goodness inheres generally in the cosmos as a system. The goodness manifests itself in understood causes and concretely and describably known parts of the cosmos which, whether places, persons, or things, are given exact locations.* Conversely all known and localizable objects, persons, or places and understood causes are generally good.

3. The not-good. *Evil, which is not polar to good, finds its locus in specific persons, things, or events inside or outside the cosmos, and is manifest in specific results. The underlying causes of evil, however, are inaccessible to the senses or to understanding.* For example, all cosmic or extra-cosmic personnel whose locations are variable, vague, or unknown, are capable of doing evil. Being neither known nor localizable, they are not part of the unified kin and cosmic structure in which gods, the dead, and men and their respective lands are tied together. They exist outside society, hence only loosely attached to, or even outside of, the cosmos. Thus disease and death are both caused by sorcerers (*brujos*, Sp; *yarəkə'*, Y.). These are described as wandering about freely in the savannas where they attack persons. Not only can the Yaruro advert to them only in the most indefinite way with regard to form, but they also specifically deny that human beings are or can be sorcerers or that human beings practice witchcraft. Thus, to the Yaruro, the major evils of disease and of wicked hearts (*corazones malos*) of individual Yaruros are caused by unknowable spirits. Even the chief and father of the *yarəkə'*, Abaka'ri, is as indefinite in form as his sons, and the Yaruro either do not locate him at all, or are very much disagreed as to his locus. No proper Yaruro self has any personal contact with him. Though the *yarəkə'* are kin-related among themselves, they are not "of our family" (*de la familia de nosotros*), hence outside of our society.

4. The good society. *In the good cosmos, the good society consists of kin-related gods, the dead, communities and individuals of largely coordinate and reciprocal statuses living in tranquility and sharing all things.* Gods, community, and individuals are all actors knowing the general principles of the cosmic society. Such principles include kinship, equivalent rights and privileges for all.

5. The determinants of action. *In the good society, action is guided by precept, suggestion, and by sensibility to the wants of others and of self, but compulsion and hostility are not permissible.*

6. Nature of precepts and principles of action. *In the good society, precepts and principles are general rather than specific and prescriptive.* The result is that patterns of behavior and thought in Yaruro society are quite unformalized, unritualized, and unspecified. All classes of behavior show a great range of variability and flexibility. The individual can choose to fulfil his obligations to the community, and the community to the cosmos, in various ways.

7. Freedom or restriction of will. *The individual not only has a broad range of choice of actions but is not compelled by the nature of the cosmos nor by the*

personnel in it to follow any particular path. He has free will with regard to the ordained order of things.[4] Each man is, in theory, as in fact, to a remarkable degree self-determining in actions and thought. Except in extreme divergences, he need not account to anyone.

Several dimensions which appear as dualistic distinctions in western thought are conceptually single in Yaruro ideology. The self, as the experiences in shamanism, dreams, unconsciousness, and immediately after death show, is conceived as being undifferentiated and unitary, though divisible into like, but unequally active parts. No mind-body distinction is made. Again in a static and limited universe within which, however, all parts, visible and invisible, sensible or not directly sensible, are in a flux of interaction, all things have some degree of reality. The distinction "real-unreal" as it is understood in the West is lacking among the Yaruro. Further, in this same universe, those parts which we might designate "immaterial" are, to the Yaruro, quite as concrete and sensed as the so-called "material" objects and events. The western distinction between "material" and "immaterial" is not a meaningful one to the Yaruro. Finally, the unity and continuity of what westerners would call "natural" and "supernatural" has been discussed above. Such a distinction is not made by the Yaruro.

NOTES

1. The present description applies to the Cinaruco River Yaruro where the major part of the writer's field work, supported by a grant from the Social Science Research Council, was done. The Capanaparo River Yaruro were reported by Petrullo (1939) and Le Besnerais (1948) as being hunters and gatherers, although Le Besnerais observed small horticultural patches which he claimed were diffusions from Venezuelan farmers which had occurred recently. Le Besnerais in 1954 states directly that they were horticulturalists, omitting any mention of possible diffusions from Venezuelans. The passing mention of horticulture by Fiasson (1947) confirms the present writer in his opinion that, although horticulture may be more restricted on the Capanaparo than on the Cinaruco and Cunaviche-Arauca (where the writer also spent several weeks) which are not discussed at all by Petrullo or Le Besnerais, nevertheless, the absence of horticulture is probably not aboriginal with the Yaruro as has been suggested by Kirchhoff (1948a:456). Rather the restricted gardening is a result of ecological conditions on the Capanaparo which are less favorable to horticulture than on the neighboring rivers, combined with extremely violent acculturation, including large-scale massacres of natives. The only other possibility, in my opinion, is that horticulture was introduced by the missionaries in the early part of the eighteenth century, which is certainly the period when the Yaruro first became acquainted with iron tools (cf. Baltazar de Lodares 1922).

2. In the orthography of Yaruro words, vowels and consonants, in general, have values approximately like those of Venezuelan Spanish. /c/ represents /ts/; /ə/ a high, central, unrounded vowel. The tilde represents nasalization—there is a complete set of nasalized and unnasalized equivalent vowels in Yaruro. Stress is marked by /'/ or where there are two stresses, by /''/ as the main one.

3. Eliade (1954) emphasizes this prototypic quality of "primitive" ideologies throughout the book.

4. Petrullo (1939:299) first noted this aspect.

IV RELATIONSHIPS WITH THE SUPERNATURAL

There are probably more data on the religion and folklore of South American Indians than on any other aspect of their cultures. Although much of this material consists of isolated accounts of myths and tales or descriptions of a single ceremony with no cultural context, frequently collected by a passing traveler, there also exist some surprisingly good accounts of religious beliefs from periods as early as the first years of contact. The official basis for conquest was to bring the benighted savages of the New World to the True Faith, and many missionaries sent to perform this task realized that, in order to accomplish it, they must first understand the native belief system. For a discussion of Spanish attitudes toward the Indians at the time of the Conquest and later, see Hanke (1959).

After the Jesuits were expelled from Portuguese territory in 1759 and Spanish domains in 1767, many of them devoted themselves to writing down the observations made during the period they had spent among the savages; and some of these accounts provide priceless data for that period, e.g., Sánchez Labrador (1910, 1917), Dobrizhoffer (1784), Eder (1791), Gilij (1780–1784) and Veigl (1785). In some cases these are the only record we have for groups who have either been wiped out or totally acculturated (e.g., Eder's material on the Mojo).

The nineteenth century was the century of travelers and naturalists. At the end of that century, work by professional anthropologists, or at least work directed primarily at collecting anthropological information began, often as part of large expeditions. Reports from such sources frequently present some isolated data on belief in the supernatural, generally consisting of a collection of "myths" or rather superficial statements about native religious beliefs.

It is only in the twentieth century that we begin to get important and relatively sophisticated treatment of native South American relationships to the supernatural world. An early and important contribution to this area of knowledge is represented by Nimuendajú's impressive study of Apapocúva Guaraní religion (1914), followed by Koch-Grünberg's work on the myths and legends of the Taulipáng and Arekuna (1917–1928: Vol. II), Goeje's comparative work (1943) and Métraux's many contributions including his summary article on religion in the *Handbook* (1949a) which is an excellent source for bibliography on the earlier work, to mention only a few.

Since World War II, a number of additional works have appeared, many by German authors such as Zerries (1954), Hissink and Hahn (1961), Bödiger (1965) and Münzel (1971). The most important influence on such studies today, however, is unquestionably that of Claude Lévi-Strauss resulting largely from the publication of *Mythologiques* (Lévi-Strauss 1964, 1966, 1968, 1971). The influence of the Lévi-Straussian approach is clearly visible in the articles by Melatti, Reichel-Dolmatoff and Clastres that follow, as well as the work of Laraia (1968) and Ortíz (n.d.) and Reichel-Dolmatoff's recent study of Desana symbolism (1968), published in English as "Amazonian Cosmos" (1971).

The earliest descriptions of Inca religion are almost entirely devoted to the state religion, the major ceremonies and celebrations associated with the ruling class and the capital city, Cuzco. Every effort was made by the Spanish invaders to wipe out this religion, including razing monuments, constructing Catholic churches on the site of native temples, and destroying cult objects. Something, however, persisted, and when the Catholic church sent out investigators to ascertain the success of the indoctrination procedures they discovered that, in spite of the fact that the state religion was no longer practiced, there were extensive "idolatrous" practices among the conquered population. There followed an intensive and well-documented effort to extirpate these idolatries. A recent study by the French historian Pierre Duviols analyzes the situation from 1532 to 1660 (1971), and Juan Ossio has edited a volume (1973) on messianism in the Andes.

Many of the idolatries mentioned at that time are still being practiced and are among the practices mentioned in Núñez del Prado's article. In conversation with the author, I discovered that we had independently arrived at the conclusion that the practices noted by him and other fieldworkers are occupying today the same position they occupied at the time of the Conquest. That is, local and individual religious manifestations do, and did, coexist with the state religion, previously Inca, now Christian.

An important point made by Núñez del Prado is the division between the deities and their habitats. That is, the Quechua do not worship mountains, but rather the spirits that inhabit them. A study by Henri Favre (1968) provides interesting comparative material from the area near Huancavelica in the central Andes. Although there are some parallels, there are many contrasts to the system described here, and it is of some interest that the form of human sacrifice described by Favre is more similar to that known for the Inca than is that described by Núñez del Prado.

It is not obvious that the Quechua here discussed see the cosmos, society, and man in quite as unified a system as do the Yaruro; nonetheless, it is worthy of note that in both systems the Christian deities, although integrated into the whole structure, are placed at a greater distance from man than are the native deities.

The work from which this selection is extracted includes descriptions of both the aboriginal and western elements of the supernatural world of the Quechua, in addition to descriptions of many minor spirits. In accordance with the wishes of the author, this version is a rewriting in English rather than a translation.

22 JUAN VÍCTOR NÚÑEZ DEL PRADO B.

The Supernatural World of the Quechua of Southern Peru as Seen from the Community of Qotobamba

The present work is an attempt to delineate the structure of the supernatural world of the Quechua according to the concepts of informants in the community of Qotobamba. It also suggests some tentative generalizations about an extensive area of southern Peru on the basis of this material combined with my own small-scale surveys in a number of other communities and information recorded by other investigators.

To provide the reader with an idea of the kind of material utilized in the synthesis and the amount of variation between areas, I include the texts of two myths. These texts, from Q'ero and Qotobamba respectively, reflect the differential acculturation of the two communities. Q'ero, which is geographically isolated, has preserved its mythology relatively free from outside influence, whereas in Qotobamba there is considerable religious syncretism due to the more intimate contact with the Westernized culture of the country.

It is possible that this initial study may suffer from mistakes or omissions since the information needed to carry it out is very difficult to acquire, particularly in the case of a mestizo investigator, due to the fact that the Indians are conscious of the disdain and contempt with which their beliefs are held by individuals of the dominant mestizo stratum. For this reason informants consistently tend to present their beliefs in the closest possible approximation to those that they suppose to be the most acceptable to the mestizos, whose support they do not wish to lose. That is, they try to bring their beliefs as far as possible into line with the concepts imparted by priests and catechists.

·   ·   ·

CONCEPT OF THE UNIVERSE

The universe is conceived as being divided into three great estates:

Hanaqpacha (Upper World). Estate of promise and abundance in which are found God, Christ, the Virgin Mary, the saints and the spirits of the dead who led

Excerpted by permission of the author from "El mundo sobrenatural de los Quechuas del sur del Perú a través de la comunidad de Qotobamba," thesis presented in the Department of Anthropology, University of Cuzco, 1970, pp. 3–4, 21–45, 85–89. Translated and edited by Patricia J. Lyon with the approval of the author.

Portions of this thesis have been published in Spanish in the following journals: *Allpanchis Phuturinqa, Orakesajj Achukaniwa,* vol. 3 (Cuzco, 1971), pp. 57–119; *Revista del Museo Nacional,* vol. 26 (Lima, 1970), pp. 143–163.

All material appearing within square brackets [ ] has been added by the editor of this book.

exemplary lives during their stay on earth; men can reach it only after death. Around it is *Limpu* (Limbo), to which the spirits of unbaptized children go, and Animal Towns to which the spirits of animals go after death.

Kaypacha (This World). In this estate are located the earth, *Roal,* the entire gamut of spirits of the mountains, evil spirits, man, animals, plants and inanimate objects. Although I have not been able to establish it definitely, I believe that the sun, the moon and other celestial bodies also form part of this estate.

Ukhupacha (Inner World). Estate of which very little is known except that it is inhabited by some small and delicate little people and their diminutive animals that can be harmed by earthquakes and electrical storms (lightning) caused by the careless discarding of, respectively, coca quids and *llipt'a* (ash of the quinoa stalk kneaded into a mass to chew with coca). Nor are the activities of these beings known in detail except it is said that, in general, they are similar to those of men. In some cases Ukhupacha is also identified as the Hell of Catholicism and it is designated as the abode of the *Supay* (Occidental Devil).[1]

The earth is similar to a top floating in space (this concept may possibly be derived from what children are taught in public schools). We are on its upper part and on the lower cone are the *ukhupacha runa* (little people of Ukhupacha). The sun stands still in the universe and the world is constantly turning, producing the phenomena of day and night. When it is dawning for us, night is falling in the world of the ukhupacha runa. To quote one of our informants, "We do not fall off of the world for the same reason that an ant does not fall off a rock when we pick up the rock with the ant on it."

MYTHOLOGICAL ERAS

Within Quechua mythology three mythological eras can be distinguished, as will be shown in the texts:

The Era of the Spirits. In this era there was first Roal, then the stars, the earth, the spirits of the mountains and *Pachamama.*

The Era of the Ñawpa. These beings were created by Roal in an unknown manner. Their form was similar to that of present day man but they were more powerful than he is. This era ends, in some cases, with the rebellion and punishment of the ñawpa by Roal, and in others by the crucifixion and death of Christ, who belongs to the lineage of the ñawpa, followed by the punishment of the ñawpa by God.

The Era of Man. This final era begins with the creation of man by either Roal or Christ and is the one in which we are presently living.

MYTHOLOGICAL TEXTS

Version from Q'ero [Department of Cuzco, Province of Paucartambo].

> There was a time in which the sun did not exist and on the earth dwelt men whose power was capable of making rocks move at their will or

turning the mountains into plains with a single shot from their slings. The moon shone in the dimness, poorly illuminating the activities of those beings, known by the name of "ñaupa-machu."

One day Roal, or the creator spirit and chief of the Apus, asked these beings if they would like him to invest them with his power. Full of arrogance, they responded that they had their own and needed no other. Annoyed by this response, he created the sun and ordered it to rise. Terrified and almost blinded by the coruscation of the star, the ñaupa sought refuge in small houses, the majority of which had their doors oriented toward the place where the sun would rise daily; its heat gradually dried them up, turning their muscles into flesh that was desiccated and adhered to their bones. Nevertheless they did not die, and are now the soq'a who come out of their refuges some evenings when the sun sets or at the time of the new moon.

The earth became inactive and the Apus decided to form new beings; they created Inkarí and Qollari, a man and a woman full of wisdom. They gave to the former a golden crowbar and to the latter a spindle, as symbols of power and industriousness.

Inkarí had received orders to found a great city in the place where, when it was thrown, the bar would remain upright. He tried the first time and it fell badly. The second time it stuck in between a cluster of black mountains and the banks of a river. It fell at an angle and nevertheless he decided to build a town, which was Q'ero. The conditions were not very propitious and in the same region he thought he should build his capital, working industriously on the construction of what today are the ruins of Tampu.

Tired by his labors, dirty and sweating, he wanted to bathe but the cold was intense. He then decided to cause the hot springs of Upis to spring forth, constructing some baths that still exist.

Inkarí raised his city in contravention of the mandate of his Apus. To make him understand his error, they allowed the ñaupa who, full of envy and rancor, were observing Inkarí, to come to life again. Their first desire was to exterminate the son of the spirits of the mountains. The ñaupa took gigantic blocks of stone and rolled them down the slopes toward the place where he was working. Appalled, Inkarí fled in terror to the region of Titicaca, a place whose tranquility allowed him to meditate. He again returned toward the Vilcanota and stopping on the peaks of La Raya threw the bar for the third time. It fell to stand vertically in the center of a fertile valley. Here he founded Cuzco, living there for a long time.

Q'ero could not remain forgotten, and the firstborn of his sons was sent there to populate it. The rest of his descendants were scattered in various places, originating the lineage of the Incas. His labor completed, he decided to go out again accompanied by Qollari to teach the people his knowledge and, again passing through Q'ero, he went into the jungle, not without first leaving testimony of his passage in the footprints that are seen in "Muju-rumi" and "Inkaq Yupin" ... (O. Núñez del Prado 1957:4–5).

Version from Qotobamba [Department of Cuzco, Province of Calca, District of P'isaq], collected by the author. There are several versions of the example presented here, and we have selected the one that includes the greatest number of events.

In the beginning there existed only Roal (sometimes God) and other spirits similar to him but of lesser power and rank. Roal decided to create the moon, the earth, then the animals and plants and, finally, some beings who inhabited the earth before men known by the name of ñawpa machu (ancient old ones) who were morphologically similar to men although they were much more powerful and learned than he is.

Since the sun had not yet been created, the moon stood in its stead. It happened that the ñawpa sinned and made themselves enemies of God who decided to cause his son, Christ, to come to the world. Christ was born a very long time ago when the sun did not yet exist. He grew, reached adulthood and began to pursue the ñawpa, enemies of God. Commanding his hosts that consisted of saints (the saints also belong to the same lineage as the ñawpa) he attacked the ñawpa, pursued them and destroyed them until many of them united to defeat him (Herod, Pilate, Caiaphas), succeeding in overcoming him, taking him prisoner and killing him. Christ came back to life and ascended to Hanaqpacha, next to his father. Then God decided to call the ñawpa (Jews) to account and said to one of them: "Come, you and your brothers, I want to talk to you." The ñawpa so addressed ignored the word of God, without even bothering to communicate the message to his fellows. God notified two more, with similar results. Since they paid no attention to his summons, he called a bird, the hak'achu (Colaptis rupicola puna [Andean flicker]) and ordered it to communicate his command to the ñawpa; it carried out the divine order and, on hearing the message, the ñawpa replied that they had no reason to see God and if he wanted to talk to them he could come and look for them. The flicker went and delivered the reply to God, but he did not place much confidence in its words since the flicker had the reputation of being a liar. To verify the information he called the urpi (dove), sending it with the same message. It went to their village and told them that they should go to see God to give an accounting of themselves. The ñawpa gave the dove the same answer that they had given to the flicker and it returned to God, crying, and told him that they had refused to pay it any attention. Annoyed, he called the q'enti (hummingbird) and said to it, "Go and tell the ñawpa that if they persist in disobedience, I will cause fire to rain on them that will annihilate them." The ñawpa, instead of obeying, decided to build stone houses on the slopes of the mountains to protect them from the rain of fire. They began the task very enthusiastically but each time that they were about to complete it the walls fell down; they began again more vigorously and, when they were on the point of finishing, the same thing happened. In this situation the rain of fire began and, terrified, they ran to take refuge in their half-finished houses where they were trapped in attitudes of terror, some doubled up clutching their knees, others covering their faces with their hands and many crouched on their haunches (all positions in which mummies in pre-Columbian tombs are ordinarily encountered). Many ran to springs thinking that the water would protect them but were nonetheless reduced to a state of helplessness. The spirits of these beings refused to give an accounting of themselves to God and therefore have remained confined to the earth, sometimes being able to harm people. They are the *soq'a machu,* the *soq'a paya* and the *soq'a pukyu* (evil old man, evil old woman, and evil spring, respectively).

After the rain of fire, the earth was unpopulated and God, or Roal (depending on the case), thought to repopulate it. First he created the sun to light the new inhabitants of the earth and at the same time to keep the ñawpa from reviving. He then created Arran (possibly Adam [Adán in Spanish]) and placed him in some very beautiful and fertile gardens. One day the man saw a pair of flickers making love and said, "How I would like to have my mate, too!" God, who heard him, caused Arran to sleep and, meanwhile, created Iwa (possibly Eve [Eva in Spanish]). On awakening, the man saw her next to him and felt very happy.

In the gardens where the man lived there was one apple tree from which God had forbidden them to eat. One day, while Arran was working his fields, a serpent said to Iwa that that apple had a very special flavor, much more agreeable than the others, and that God selfishly wanted it for himself alone and therefore had forbidden them to eat it. Iwa believed the serpent and when Arran returned she urged him also to eat of it. Arran put up some resistance but finally listened to his wife. Then came the wrath of God that cast the couple from those fertile lands where man had assured harvests, making him adapt to those that we now occupy, subject to drought and disaster. Had it not been for the error of our progenitors, we would still be in that place and man would suffer neither hunger nor poverty.

In the preceding tale some identification between God and Roal is noticeable, and sometimes they are merged. We can also see that, in an effort to understand the imported system, European mythology has been tied into the native tradition in such a way that it agrees with the existing ideas.

THE SUPERNATURAL IN GENERAL

The religious system of the Quechua of southern Peru is very different from the Catholic system. Although it is manifestations of the latter that are ordinarily expressed in public, in the final analysis they do not constitute the essence or the basic structure of the functioning system. This system is based on a series of native deities who very actively influence the life of the people.

The fact that the cult of the deities themselves is not expressed publicly is easily explained if we keep in mind the fact that the society under investigation has been subjected to more than 400 years of domination by another society with a European or Europeanized culture which, at least initially, pursued and punished all worship not directed to its own gods. This activity was followed by the inevitable presence of Catholic parish priests protected by the Peruvian state which, although its constitution guarantees freedom of religion, proclaims Catholicism the state religion, protecting it and giving it every opportunity for diffusion, including it in the curricula of both primary and secondary public schools.

Indian society, in the face of this constant religious pressure, has defended its own beliefs by converting them into expressions of covert culture. In spite of this measure and the strength of the native system there have been a series of influences from the religious system of the invading culture, which has in turn been influenced, as we shall see.

In the present study I refer to acts and concepts that could be associated with religion or with magic without separating them. In the Quechua religious world these two spheres are so closely related that were I to separate them it would have to be on the basis of personal and ethnocentric criteria. Likewise I am not dealing with practices and liturgy in the detail that might be expected, because I consider them to be incidental to the system rather than essential to it. The intention of this work is to analyze the substratum of Indian religion, its deities and their nature and the way it operates and influences men's lives.

The indigenous religious system has often been conceived of as naturalistic, [animatistic] and even pantheistic. I perceive it, on the contrary, as essentially spiritualistic and animistic with something of naturalism. It has generally been considered, for example, that the Indians worship the mountains and the earth. In my judgment, worship is directed to the spirits that inhabit the mountains and the earth whose existence is independent of their material habitats, as may be noted in the following list of concepts:

urqo (peak or notable hill) and apu (spirit of the mountain)
moqo (knoll or rounded hill) and awki (spirit that inhabits it)
allpa (earth) and Pachamama (spirit of the earth)
qaqa (cliff) and tira (evil spirit)
wiñaq rumi (emerging stone) and ñust'a (spirit that inhabits it).

The system in general is structured around the two great deities, Roal and Pachamama. The former is the creator spirit who occupies the top of the hierarchy, while the latter permeates the system from top to bottom, being linked with femininity and fertility.

In contrast to the Christian religious system in which the relationships between men and God are quite distant and sometimes diffuse, in the system to which I refer the gods are regularly involved in the daily life of individuals; they are intimately related to common activities and intervene directly in determining the success or failure of such activities in accord with the conduct of the individual and the quality of his relationship to the gods. Furthermore, in the complex of Occidental beliefs, the reward for an exemplary life or the punishment for a dissipated and sinful existence is very remote and contingent on the individual's abandonment of this world. In the world of indigenous belief, however, man is subjected to a series of supernatural punishments in this life, as a consequence of his evil actions, in addition to the punishments and rewards reserved for the afterlife; consequently, beliefs in the supernatural have a much stronger normative function in Indian culture than in Westernized culture. Furthermore, Catholic religion also provides a means of attaining absolute forgiveness in the eyes of God by means of confession which, at any given moment, can erase the entire black record of an individual, no matter how evil he may have been or how many rules he may have transgressed. Catholic confession has entered the Indian culture and is practiced, not in the Occidental sense, but rather as a means of initiating relations with or drawing closer to Christ, the god specializing in justice.

In some cases, such as adultery, these beliefs are an efficient means of uniting the members of a community to apply social sanctions to the transgressor, since, according to the beliefs, such misconduct leads not only to the obligatory punishment of the guilty party, but also to calamities of great magnitude to the community that shelters this individual and even to neighboring communities. For example, in July, 1968 there occurred a heavy snowfall, quite unusual in the area, at the same time that a case of adultery had occurred in the neighboring community of Kuyo Chico. All the residents of Qotobamba and various nearby communities agreed in blaming the catastrophe on the guilty pair and exerted so much pressure on the adulterous party, in this case the woman, that she finally had to leave her community.

The Indians also maintain a close relationship with their gods, who can be consulted at any time through an *altomisayoq* (the most important religious specialist with power to conjure up the highest ranking deities). In such sessions the voices of the gods can be heard answering the questions that are formulated about personal problems.

THE DEITIES

Roal

He is the creator spirit (*Kamaq*) primal, unique and ubiquitous. He has no known form and is invisible, although when he communicates with men he speaks as a male and consumes such food and drink as have been prepared for his enjoyment. He has existed since the dawn of time and before anything else. It was he who originated the universe and the other spirits of lesser rank such as the Apus and the Aukis. He created all the animals and plants that we know and also the lineage of the ñawpa and, in those myths that we consider purest, such as that from Q'ero, he originated the lineage of the humans in the persons of Inkarí and Qollari. A similar concept was held in ancient Peru, but concerned Wiraqocha: "The greatest god was the Creator, a being without beginning or end, who created all the other supernatural beings, animals, and men . . ." (Rowe 1946:293).

He governs the forces of nature and maintains their equilibrium. The powers of the lesser spirits, or Apus, to whom he delegates or assigns the supervision of specialized activities, come fundamentally from his person. The mountains he inhabits serve him as lookouts from which he can oversee all the activity taking place around him. The various and simultaneous residences of Roal are in a number of high mountains distributed through the area of southern Peru. In the Cuzco region he inhabits the snow-capped peak Ausangate or Powerful Ausangate. Rowe tells us, "The powerful peaks of Ausangate (visible from Cuzco), Vilcanota, Coropuna, and Pariacaca were widely worshiped." (Rowe 1946:296) For a vast region of the Department of Apurimac and part of the Department of Cuzco, Roal resides in the snow-capped peak Salqantay; for a certain area of Arequipa, he resides in the volcano Pichu-Pichu. For the area of Carabaya in Puno, Roal inhabits Allinqhapaq and for the area of Abancay and surrounding towns he is located in the snow-capped peak of Ampay. Nevertheless, one should not visualize a multiplicity of supreme spirits; rather we are dealing with the same deity who resides in the highest mountain of each zone and takes, for the purpose of liturgy, the name of the peak that he inhabits in each case.

There is a close correlation between the elevation of the mountains and the hierarchy of the spirits that inhabit them (Rowe 1946:296), so that the highest in each area is reserved for Roal, those that are next highest for the highest ranking Apus, and so on down the scale.

Roal is a being generous and accessible to humans, who can achieve direct communication with him by means of an altomisayoq. People consult him regarding their problems and receive from him instructions for solving them and, sometimes, reprimands for improper attitudes or actions along with advice for bettering their behavior and situation. There are communities in which the word Roal has been confused with that of Apu and both are used interchangeably as a generic term for the spirits of the mountains; such is the case in the community of Wanqara in Urcos (Bonino Nieves ms.) and in Kuyo Grande (Casaverde 1970), but the concept of a spirit of the mountains superior to the others exists. In contrast, the clearest distinction and the purest concepts, to our way of thinking, are found in Q'ero (O. Núñez del Prado 1957, ms.). Between these extremes occur a series of variants such as that of Qotobamba in which, although the distinction between the terms Apu and Roal is clear, the concept of the latter is syncretized with the Occidental Eternal Father as can be seen in the account presented at the beginning of this study. Nevertheless, Roal is more deeply involved in the process of the daily life of the people and God in matters relating to the ultramundane life of man, post-mortem judgment and the imposition of the corresponding rewards and punishments in the afterlife.

Pachamama

The origin of this deity is pre-Columbian and about her Rowe says: "Of equal importance with the sky gods were the female supernaturals, Earth (Paca-mama, 'earth mother') . . ." (Rowe 1946:295). I typified Pachamama as a feminine deity specialized in agriculture and occupying a position immediately below Roal, alongside the great specialized Apus. Nevertheless, I am now doubtful of this attribution, and it seems to me that she could, in some circumstances, have a position similar to Roal, since her powers are not subject to him nor have they been delegated by him as is the case with the great Apus. She may well be, rather, a being of pan-earthly powers who intervenes as the feminine factor in the origin of things. Holding sway in agriculture, she is also related to females in the origin of animals and is linked to the warmichakuy (traditional marriage) ceremonies, in which she is directly related to the woman and feminine occupations, since ordinarily a woman, on invoking Pachamama, says: "Pachamama: awaq-masiy, pushkaq-masiy, wayk'oq-masiy.

Pachamama: companion in weaving, companion in spinning, companion in cooking."

Pachamama resides in the bowels of the earth and her powers have no territorial limits with the exception of lakes and the sea, sites in which she is not encountered.

She is generous and tolerant and is propitiated by sprinkling chicha [corn beer] on all occasions in which it is drunk. She also likes to share the food of men, and is invited to do so with small portions cast upon the ground at the beginning of daily meals. Since her field of greatest power is agriculture, the importance of this deity among people wholly devoted to farming, such as those we are discussing, and their constant preoccupation with maintaining good relations with her, is understandable. She is sensitive and is angered by one who forgets her. Nevertheless, at the same time she is generous and, at most, will cause partial loss of the crops of those who may not have propitiated her duly.

The most formal and important propitiations to this deity are made in the months of August and September, coinciding with the beginning of planting. On these occasions a "pago" is made;[2] this consists of offering her, through the mediation of a *paqo* (generic term for native religious officiants, excluding the *layqa* [evil sorcerer]), portions of food and chicha together with a "despacho."[3] In return for this offering she receives the seeds that are cast on her bosom with goodwill and affection and makes them abundantly fruitful.

Pachamama sometimes receives the name of Juana Puyka or Mama-Puyka, sometimes (Totorani, Q'ero area) being identified as the wife of Roal. Other times she is identified or confused with the Virgin Mary (Sonqo and Qotobamba).

In some cases wiñaq rumi (emerging stones) are considered to be manifestations of Pachamama. These are rock outcrops shaped like a shaft that are believed to issue from the center of the earth. The female spirit who inhabits these rocks is called *ñust'a*. In Qotobamba they remember one occasion when they tried to remove one of these stones in order to enlarge some fields and an extremely severe thunderstorm occurred only over the place where the rock was. Those that were trying to remove it suspended their work, and at that instant the phenomenon ceased.

·   ·   ·

Pachaqaqa or Pachatira

There is another being close to Pachamama known as Pachatira, Pachaqaqa or simply Pacha, this last name being most frequently used to identify it. In contrast to Pachamama, he is masculine and of a perverse nature; he inhabits precipices, cliffs and gullies, and it is he who originates a series of catastrophes such as earthquakes; the great landslides that destroy agricultural fields; the fall of stones down hillsides; the collapse of houses, irrigation ditches, bridges and other constructions; people and animals falling from cliffs, and other accidents without number. He also eats the hearts of people that fall asleep on the road, thus producing in them the sickness called *pachaq hap'isqan* (caught by Pacha), from which people die spitting blood. It is he, also, who traps and holds the *ánimu* (a person's psyche), an act which can also cause death. He is very jealous of the integrity of the earth and, therefore, in those cases when it is necessary to disturb it, be it for the excavation of a house foundation or the construction of an irrigation ditch, it is first necessary to placate his ire offering him "pagos." The presents may consist of *k'intu* of coca (clusters of specially chosen leaves), "despachos," small animals such as guinea pigs and lambs and, if the work about to be initiated is of great magnitude, even men, preferably madmen who are buried alive in the base of the construction. If such actions are not taken it will be impossible to complete the work; if it is concluded, it will not last.

If Pacha is not placated he does not wait to be offered the appropriate tribute but rather takes it by his own hand. Thus, if he feels the desire to drink, he causes the receptacles of chicha or other drinks to turn over; if he is hungry, he will cause the food or coca to be scattered. He acts in the same fashion in cases when it is necessary to offer him animal or human tributes. The following case will serve as an example: The Indians of Kuyo Chico . . . began excavation work on a long irrigation canal without having taken the precaution of offering the proper tribute to Pacha. Shortly after the initiation of the work, however, there were two successive accidents that cost the lives of two people. It was Pacha who was collecting, with interest, the tribute that was owed to him for disturbing the earth (J. Núñez del Prado ms.). A demonstration of the extent of the ideas referring to the need to make even human offerings is found in a case taken from the archives of the Program of Applied Anthropology in Kuyo Chico. A woman from the community of T'oqra (Paucartambo) arrived at the offices of the Program, inquiring if anyone might know about the death of her mad son who had disappeared. She had been told that, "it was possible that, since her son was 'simple,' they might have buried him under the piers of the new bridge that, at that time, was being built over the Vilcanota River at P'isaq."

We have discussed Pachatira before the great specialized Apus, not because he has a rank similar to Pachamama since, although maleficent, he is not as powerful as she, but because Pacha is always close by Pachamama and there are cases in which the concepts have been confused or syncretized, combining the two beings into a single ambivalent deity.

The Great Apus

Within the territory controlled by Ausangate, this category is composed of three great Apus: Apu Wanakawri, Apu Qañaqway and Apu Qolqepunku, who derive their powers from Roal and play a specialized role with regard to certain types of activities. Within this category we also consider Christ who, in spite of being an Occidental god and not dependent on Roal, has been fitted into the general system by a process of syncretism and shares some characteristics with these deities. Similar groupings are established in each of the areas influenced by the mountains specified as residences of Roal. Thus, for example, within the jurisdiction of Salqantay this category would be occupied by Apu Wayna-Qorqor, Apu Runtu-qayán and Apu San Cristóbal (San Cristóbal is the name of a mountain) (personal communication from Dr. Demetrio Roca W.).

Apu Wanakawri. He resides in the peak of the same name located to the southeast of the city of Cuzco and his worship dates from the time of the Inca empire. Rowe tells us: "The most important huaca outside of the temples of the sky gods was Huanacauri (*Wanakawri*) . . ." (1946:296). He specializes in watching over the good behavior of men. It is he who oversees the behavior of individuals, watchful that they perform their activities within the norms established by society and attain total well-being. It is said that he is the Apu of *allin kausay,* an expression whose meaning implies a combination of material well-being and tranquility proceeding from good relations with all other people. One resorts to him for advice about the rules to be adopted in difficult circumstances and the means of correcting the behavior of third persons who may adopt deviant conduct.

Apu Qañaqway. He inhabits the mountain of the same name located in the eastern cordillera to the east of the province of Paucartambo. He is a god specialized in rain and livestock raising, protector of this type of activity. . . . On the flanks of the mountain that he inhabits this Apu has great herds of stock in the care of several herdsmen. The livestock is of a special type called *salqa enqaychu,* consisting of a kind of supernatural breeding stock that favors those individuals who are on good terms with the Apu, impregnating the females of their flocks and generating exceptional offspring. . . . This Apu is consulted about problems related to livestock raising, such as instructions for curing animal diseases and the whereabouts of lost or stolen animals. One who is not on good terms with this Apu will suffer gradual but certain decrease in his stock until it is entirely gone, unless the relationship is improved before that point, it then being very difficult to reestablish the stock.

He is propitiated by means of "despachos," *t'inka* (sprinklings of chicha or cane alcohol) and k'intu of coca.

Apu Qolqepunku. He inhabits the mountain of the same name situated at the foot of the valley of Qollpak'unku (Q'ero area) (Escobar Moscoso 1958). His specialized occupation is guarding man's health; he watches over it and is profoundly knowledgeable about the etiology of illnesses. He is appealed to in petitions concerning health. He is especially important in the process of curing and in diagnosis practiced by the paqo by means of *qollpasqa.* In this process the specialist boils *qollpa* (potassium carbonate) with the patient's urine and diagnoses the illness by observing the manner in which bubbles form in the resultant foam. This Apu is also propitiated by means of "despachos," k'intu of coca and t'inka of alcohol and chicha.

It is possible to establish direct relations with the three great Apus through the mediation of an altomisayoq, and forgetfulness or carelessness in propitiating them can cause grave harm to men in spite of the fact that they are tutelary deities. The protective concept is very well expressed by the Indians who, when the occasion calls for referring to the Apus generically, do so with the phrase *runa micheq* (shepherd of men). What really appears to happen is that, if one neglects his relations with the Apus, their protective action is removed, permitting a series of evil spirits, who are the real cause of catastrophes, to act.

Christ. In this section we deal with him as the Son of God who was pursued by his enemies in ancient times and with his character as a deity specialized in justice, the aspect in which he appears acting with the greatest vigor. His residence is established in Hanaqpacha and, in contrast to the native gods, he is more distant. Individuals cannot establish direct relations with him nor such direct communication as with the others. Nevertheless, it is possible to achieve a certain relationship through the Catholic priests, and he is propitiated by practicing the Catholic sacraments and by attending masses and having them said. It should be noted that, aside from this aspect, Christ is presented in several others. . . .

One applies to him for the mitigation of one's sorrows and sufferings caused by others and to enter complaints about injustices suffered. It is paradoxical that, besides introducing many injustices and an implacable tyranny, the invaders were also the bearers of a deity to whom the specialty of dispensing justice has been assigned.

[In the original there follow sections on: local Apus, other beings, celestial bodies and forces of nature, the coexistent system (Catholicism), religious specialists, the supernatural life of man.]

CONCLUSIONS

The structure of the supernatural world that I have described is susceptible to generalization over an extensive area of southern Peru. I base this opinion on the fact that great mountains exist throughout the southern area of the country that are inhabited by a spirit with a rank superior to all the other deities and that, around such mountains, are distributed others also inhabited by spirits but of a lower rank (the Apus and Aukis). Likewise the worship of Pachamama occurs generally. There also exists an almost uniform concept of the afterworld. This interpretation is reinforced by the considerable amount of supporting material found in both published and unpublished sources cited throughout this study. It must be emphasized that the generalization applies to the structure and organization of the religious system and not to the local variations in form to which it is subject, just as a cultural complex may cover an extensive area, presenting some variability in its components and characteristics according to the subareas.

The phenomena of religious syncretism that have been observed appear to arise from two major factors. The first of these is the parallelism existing between the two coexistent structures. Such parallelism is the basis for the identification of God with Roal and vice versa or the substitution of one of these beings for the other in myths, as well as the corresponding identification of Pachamama and the Virgin Mary. The second source of syncretism seems to be the complementation of one of the systems by a deity or idea from the other; an example would be the case of the consideration of Christ as a deity specialized in justice. The degree of obvious syncretism varies notably from one subarea to another as can be clearly seen by comparing the mythological versions from Q'ero and Qotobamba.

We also find, in general terms, that the transferred elements have been strongly influenced by the structure receiving them. Thus, for example, crosses have received a series of characteristics of the spirits of the mountains; the cross itself is considered as only the habitat of a spirit whose power is in direct relationship to the size of its habitat.

In spite of the amount of blending, however, we find that there is a clear dividing line between the native structure and the coexistent one, since the native specialists cannot establish contact with nor propitiate the Occidental deities and, equally, the priest who propitiates the latter cannot communicate with the native supernatural beings. Therefore I have treated each system separately in the discussion.

Within the native structure, black magic is confined to the manipulation of lesser deities; the manipulation of the great gods to the end of causing harm is in no way possible. On the other hand, within the coexistent structure, even God may be manipulated to cause death (e.g., by performing a funeral mass for the living and by lighting candles turned upside down).

Agriculture as the focus of the Indian culture is projected even into the afterlife, since, for example, Hanaqpacha is a place of agricultural activity in which even children work and its paradisiacal condition lies in the fact that lands are abundant and fertile and harvests are not subject to losses or calamities. This concept contrasts with the Occidental concept of paradise which is presented as a place of eternal leisure.

The Indian supernatural world has immediate power in governing human conduct, since an individual's errors or sins receive immediate and tangible sanctions. A clear example is seen in the case of adultery. On the other hand, in the Catholic world punishments or rewards are remote, being subsequent to the death of the individual who, meanwhile, always has the opportunity of obtaining a complete pardon by means of repentance and confession, no matter how evil he may have been. It is perhaps this factor that has produced a slackening of standards in the *cholo* [upwardly mobile Indian], since he, in the process of acculturation, gradually loses many of his Indian ideas of the supernatural world which restrained and regulated his conduct.

We find that the supernatural world has characteristics very similar to those that it had during the Inca empire, although the worship of some deities has died out and the veneration of others appeared. The surprising thing is not, however, that the supernatural world has changed, but rather that it has not disappeared entirely, considering that the culture under investigation has coexisted for 400 years with another that has constantly tried to eliminate native beliefs and replace them with its own. We can attribute the phenomenon of persistence to the fact that the pressure, discrimination and segregation applied to the Indians, first by the invaders and then by the dominant mestizo group, have generated a protective barrier behind which the native tradition and rituals have been able to maintain themselves thanks to their clandestine practice.

NOTES

1. A similar description of the estates is given by Casaverde (1970).
2. [The term "pago" (literally "payment") refers to the entire offering including the nonmaterial (e.g., prayers) as well as the material (e.g., food, drink, "despacho") components.]
3. [A "despacho" is an indispensable element in all major offerings. It is composed of a number of different elements (e.g., animal fetuses, fat, shells, coca, incense, various minerals, special paper, etc.) the number and selection of which vary depending on the use to which the despacho is to be put. Despachos may be purchased in markets. For detailed information on kinds and contents of despachos see Casaverde (1970:225–236).]

The cosmology of the riverine Campa described in this article provides interesting similarities and contrasts with that of other cultures, especially that of the Quechua, since these two cultures have a long history of contact, and one would expect to encounter some similarities or evidences of communication. In fact there are not very many such similarities, and some of these occur more widely, such as a universe consisting of layers, and the important place of birds in mythology. In contrast to the importance of mountains in Quechua religion, Campa belief merely locates good spirits along mountain ridges. Specific similarities may be seen in coitus with evil spirits resulting in death, and evil spirits with an extremely enlarged penis, both elements having a much wider distribution. The motif of transformation of people into rocks is widespread throughout the Andean region. Perhaps the greatest contrast between the Campa view of the supernatural and that of the Quechua is the way man relates to supernatural beings. The Quechua believe in the direct intervention of good spirits in the life of man, but this intervention is dependent upon man establishing the proper relationship by means of offerings and orations. The Campa, on the other hand, consider good spirits to be basically indifferent to man and, rather than positively seeking aid, the Campa must avoid doing evil things in order to avoid punishment, an attitude somewhat similar to that of the Aymara (cf. Carter 1968).

In addition to the material cited in this article, further data on Campa religion may be found in Weiss (1973) and Garcia (1935), the latter being the first article in the series entitled "Mitologia Machiguenga" although it bears a different title from the remainder of the series. Weiss has made some minor editorial changes that do not appreciably alter the sense of the original.

23 GERALD WEISS

Campa Cosmology[1]

The Campa of eastern Peru, who number perhaps 30,000 (Fast 1962), occupy a large territory that includes the watersheds of the Ene, Perené, and Tambo rivers, plus the Gran Pajonal (see Map 1). These four geographic terms—Ene, Perené, Tambo, and Gran Pajonal—correspond to four cultural regions differing to a certain degree in dialect and other cultural details, the Gran Pajonal region being

Reprinted by permission of the author and publisher from *Ethnology*, vol. 11 (April 1972), pp. 157–172.

the most divergent. Between the Campa of the Ene, Perené, and Tambo rivers and those of the Gran Pajonal there is long-standing enmity, little contact, and very little intermarriage. This situation suggests that there may be not one but two Campa tribes, which might be called the River Campa and the Pajonal Campa respectively, with two different cultural systems. The information on cosmology set forth in this paper was drawn from the River Campa cultural system, though undoubtedly the Pajonal Campa hold many similar beliefs.

A further qualification should be made explicit. No single Campa has in mind all the ideas and details that will here be set forth as River Campa cosmology. Each idea, each detail, has its own distribution, its own frequency of occurrence, within the River Campa population. Some surely are universal in that population, others nearly so, but many are more limited in their occurrence. Nevertheless, certain general understandings are shared by all members of the tribe in terms of which their more specific cosmographic and cosmogonic ideas make sense. The result, it seems, is that these ideas are by and large compatible with each other even when they are not held by the same individuals. When the cosmological ideas elicited from different informants are pieced together, the result is not a collection of heterogeneous elements but rather a single completed picture of which each individual Campa has come to possess some fragment, however large or small. In addition to these distributional differences there are variational differences, e.g., different versions of the same myth, but again the differences are not as important as what is common to the several versions.

THE CAMPA UNIVERSE

The Campa identify themselves as *ashaninka*, "our fellows."[2] They understand themselves to occupy a definite region on a flat earth extending out in all directions to unknown limits. They recognize that they are surrounded by neighboring tribes and peoples, each occupying its own territory: the Amuesha (*amáisha*), the Cashibo (*kashivo*), the Conibo (*konivo*), the Shipibo (*shipívo*), the Piro (*shimiríntsi*), the Machiguenga (*machikénka*), and the Highland Indians (*chóri*). Finally, there are the invading Caucasians (*virakócha*), believed to have been fished up initially out of a lake in Campa territory, a lake within which they originally resided, but whose present homeland is far downriver in the vicinity of the river's end.

The land beyond the circle of neighboring tribes is largely *terra incognita,* until the limits of the conceptualized or "known" world are reached. Good spirits reside there, and it is there that two important geographical features are located: River's Beginning and River's End. The main river that courses through River Campa territory—the Apurímac-Ene-Tambo-Ucayali—has its source at River's Beginning (Intatóni) at the southernmost point on the rim of the known world, and its termination at River's End (Otsitiríko) at the easternmost point, where the main river falls through a hole into the underworld, to proceed no one knows where. Many Campa believe that a gigantic crab (*antári oshéro*) lives in this hole, and that its movements regulate the river's level. Both at Intatóni and at Otsitiríko there are important settlements of good spirits.

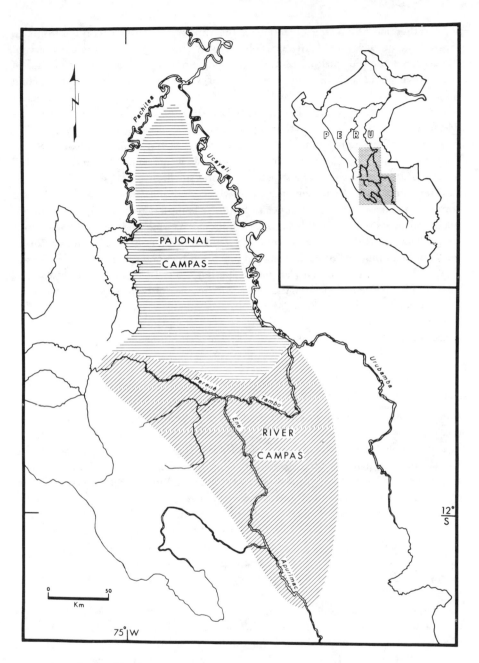

Map 1: Campa Territory

Another important spirit center on the rim of the known world is Irimáka, located in the west, and quite possibly derived from reports of the existence of Lima (if not the old spiritual center of Rimac). Some Campa extend the radius of the known world a little farther, speaking of settlements of good spirits beyond those mentioned, such as Otiriáni, the place of the thunder spirits, situated just beyond Otsitiríko. What lies beyond these frontiers of the conceptualized world—whether there is land or anything—is completely unknown. The earth, as thus described, is commonly and quite simply referred to as kipátsi, "land"; those Campa who give it a specific name refer to it as Kamavéni, "the land of death," because it is on the earth that all mortal creatures, including man, dwell.

The Campa view Kamavéni—the earth which they inhabit—as one of a series of strata arranged one above the other to form the complete universe. Each stratum is inhabited by its own class of beings, for whom it is as solid underfoot as the earth is to us. The sky, Inkíte—also referred to by the term henóki, "up"—consists of an indeterminate number of such strata, all inhabited by good spirits. Through the sky flows an invisible river called Hananeríte (perhaps derived from the Milky Way but not at present identified with it). Between the sky and the earth lies the intermediate stratum of the clouds (Menkóri), also inhabited by good spirits. Beneath the earth, some Campa recognize the existence of a stratum called Kivínti, again a residence of good spirits. The lowest stratum of the universe is Sharinkavéni, the stronghold of demons.

THE GOOD SPIRITS AND GODS

For the Campa the universe is inhabited not only by the living forms that they can observe, but also by hosts of beings normally invisible to human eyes. These are the spirits—immortal, powerful, capable of rapid flight and of instantaneous transformation. Through such transformation a spirit takes on one or another visible form or reverts to its true form—human or humanoid but invisible. Two main hosts of spirits are recognized: good spirits and evil spirits.

The good spirits are frequently called asháninka, "our fellows," which reflects the close friendship and even kinship ties that the Campa feel to exist between themselves and the good spirits, for many of the latter were once Campa here on earth. A more specific term applied to the good spirits is amatsénka, which might be translated as "our spirit fellows." Good spirits are also known as maninkari, the "hidden ones."

The good spirits reside in settlements located (1) on the mountain ridges in Campa territory (these are the otishisáti or "mountain ridge dwellers"), (2) along the rim of the known world (these include the intatonisáti, the otsitirikosáti, and the irimakasáti), and (3) on other strata in the universe—the celestial strata, the stratum of the clouds, and the first subterranean stratum inhabited respectively by the henokisáti, the menkorisáti, and the kivintisáti. In these abodes the good spirits live in their true or human form, much as the Campa live except that they have all good things and know nothing of sickness, misery, or death. They periodically rejuvenate themselves by bathing in Hananeríte, the celestial River of Eternal Youth.

Some of the *henokisáti* or "sky dwellers" are visible as stars (*impókero*) in the night sky. The Pleiades are Mashíkinti with his family; as a Campa here on earth, Mashíkinti was the first to use *kamárampi* (the hallucinogen ayahuasca, *Banisteriopsis* sp.) and to instruct the Campa in its use. Mashíkinti and his family reached a state of perfection by taking ayahuasca with suitable continence over a period of time, and flew to the sky and immortality on a raft. The belt and scabbard of Orion is Porínkari. In one version, Porínkari was Mashíkinti's brother-in-law, whom Mashíkinti so loved that he let down a rope from the sky for Porínkari and his family to clamber up. In another version, Porínkari was a Campa pursued by a warrior wasp (still in human form at that time); Porínkari escaped by climbing a rope connecting earth and sky and then cutting it, but not before receiving an arrow in his leg. Another *henokisáti* is Kirákiri, the red star Antares in Scorpio; a nearby dark streak in the Milky Way is *itsakaménto Kirákiri*, "Kirákiri's digging stick." Kirákiri taught the Campa how to cultivate their gardens; when Kirákiri is overhead at nightfall, it is time to plant maize (*shínki*). Other features of the night sky are recognized. For example, the Campa have names for the planets, and they identify the Larger Magellenic Cloud as a sloth (*soróni*) and the Coal Sack in the Southern Cross as a bees' nest (*aéri*). But the Campa do not presume that all the stars are *henokisáti,* or even to know what they are.

As with mortals, there are both male and female spirits, and they have offspring. The good spirits, however, are equipped with diminutive genitalia, lack the passion of lust, and reproduce by means other than sexual union. Furthermore, they are spared the burden of infant and child care; their offspring are born standing, and reach adulthood in a single lunation or so.

In their true form, the good spirits are human in shape but invisible to the normal human eye. Only shamans have the ability, because of their special powers, to see spirits in their true form, both when good spirits come to visit and when the shaman himself (or rather his soul) goes to visit them at their places of residence. The good spirits, however, do take on visible forms when they visit or pass through Campa territory. Lightning flashes mark the passage through the air of good spirits or of the souls of shamans traveling to or from distant places.

Good spirits can also assume the guise of certain species of birds and animals. The sacred birds of the Campa—those which are good spirits in visible form—include *ashívanti* (the swallow-tailed kite, *Elanoides forficatus*), *tsonkíri* (hummingbirds, fam. Trochilidae), *neorónke* (a particularly small species of hummingbird), *kamévira* (a particularly large species of hummingbird), *tsiróti* (the yellow-rumped cacique, *Cacicus cela*), *mankóri* (the scarlet-rumped cacique, *Cacicus uropygialis*), *pichoti* (the paradise tanager, *Calospiza chilensis*), *pitóroro* (the barbet, *Eubucco* sp.), *yoríni* (the cock-of-the-rock, *Rupicola peruviana*), *áávo* (the white-necked heron, *Ardea cocoi*), *katári* (the anhinga, *Anhinga anhinga*), and *shankénti* (the timelo, *Parra jasana?*). These are the most commonly recognized sacred birds; there are others whose recognition is less common. The highest-ranking sacred bird is *ashívanti*. In each case, the visible bird is understood to be the "clothing" of the good spirit appearing in its form.

Significantly, the Campa have chosen as the material manifestations of their good spirits living forms possessing a power denied to themselves—that of flight—

and especially the forms most beautiful in plumage or most stately in flight. Their sacred animals are the otters, both the small and the large species (*parári* and *charavapána*). Generally speaking, these sacred birds and animals are referred to as *itómi Pává*, "sons of the Sun." The Campa also believe that good spirits, when they so will, can materialize in visible human form to lead and instruct a group of Campa for a time; an interesting case is reported by Padre Sala (in Izaguirre 1922–1929:v. 10, pp. 532–533, 546).

Certain game birds are understood to be raised and thus provided by the good spirits who reside on the mountain ridges. The Campa call these birds *ivíra itómi Pává* or *ivíra otishisáti*, "creatures raised by the children of the Sun, or the mountain ridge dwellers." They include the toucan *chári* (*Ramphastos ambiguus*), the razor-billed curassow *tsamiri* (*Mitu mitu*), and the guans *kanári, sankáti,* and *tsióni* (*Pipile cumanensis,* etc.). The mountain ridge dwellers also raise the game animal *kapéshi* (the coati, *Nasua nasua*) as their equivalent of the dog (*irotsítite otishisáti*). The peccary (*shintóri*), an important game animal, is *ivíra Pává.*

In addition to the sacred beings mentioned, there are a few creatures with an ambivalent status; they are good spirits rather than demons, yet they do only harm of some sort. One is the *yaanáite,* described as a kind of arboreal beast living in the mysterious, uninhabited mountain reaches of Campa territory. These *yaanáite* kill and eat any Campa intrepid enough to enter their habitat, yet they are not demons for they are identified as *itómi Pává.* It is impossible to determine from its description whether the *yaanáite* is an entirely imaginary creature, an actual species of animal that lives at higher elevations, or a composite of several animals.

Two species of birds may be noted in this connection: *amémpore* and *etsóni.* From its description, *amémpore* would appear to be the condor. In Campa thought, Amémpore—i.e., the "father" of the *amémpore* birds—resides between earth and sky. The danger is that the soul of a Campa may encounter Amémpore, take him to be the "true God," which he is not, and remain with him. *Etsóni* is another species of bird, with dark plumage and a white throat. What seems to have caught the imagination of the Campa is the sight of flocks of these birds wheeling in circles in the air. The shamans say that when *etsóni* fly in circles, they are playing panpipes and dancing (as if they were human). The souls of recently deceased Campa rising to join the good spirits in the sky are intercepted by Etsóni, i.e., the "father" of the *etsóni* birds, and flung back down if they are not sufficiently good. Souls which fall thus from the sky are seen as meteors. Amémpore and Etsóni, the "fathers" of the *amémpore* and *etsóni* birds, are recognizable as "species masters," each being a spirit which personifies and controls an entire species.

Sacred plants include the tobacco plant and the hallucinogenic ayahuasca vine (*Banisteriopsis* sp.), used by shamans to perfect their powers. Associated with each species of sacred plant is a specific group of good spirits. From among their number a shaman takes one or more spirit "wives," with whom relations are purely spiritual. Shamans use a special word, *nomankiáro,* to signify "my spirit wife, my narcotic drink."

At the pinnacle of the hierarchy of good spirits stands a small number of beings, the most powerful in the universe, whom we may identify as gods. The Campa term for them is *tasórentsi,* the substantive form of the verb "to blow." The Campa believe that these beings have the power to transform one thing into another, that the typical way they effect such a transformation is with a simple puff of breath, and that the universe as it exists today is partly the result of many such transformations. Another term used by the Campa to refer to their gods is *pinkátsori,* "ruler," literally "he who is feared." The most important of the *tasórentsi* are Avíreri, Pachákama, Inkanítari, Kashíri, Pává, and Inka.

Avíreri is the great mythological transformer of the Campa. According to the mythology, Avíreri was originally a Campa; he lived with his grandson, whom he carried on his back wherever he went, and habitually visited his sisters to drink manioc beer and to socialize. In the course of time, as related in a lengthy myth cycle, Avíreri transformed many of his nephews into rocks, monkeys, and nests of insects, thereby bringing these things into existence; he created the alternation of day and night, of the dry and wet seasons; and he attempted to dam the main river at Kentipánko on the Tambo, only to abandon his project (the dam-like mountain of Kentipánko is the remains of this earthwork).

A number of natural features along the Tambo River are understood to be human beings or objects transformed by Avíreri into imperishable rock. On the face of a cliff overlooking the little salt spring of Tivíha on the right bank of the Upper Tambo is a natural rock formation roughly human in outline. This was once the "owner" of the spring, a malevolent person whom Avíreri, passing by, transformed into rock. A large stone of unusual shape, on the left bank of the Tambo below Tonkáma, is regarded as the petrified remains of a woman caught in her bath by Avíreri and transformed. The huge rock called Manihiróni (the Peña de Wertheman), located on the right side of the Tambo just below the mouth of Onkonéni, was formerly a launch manned by Caucasians heading upriver to molest the Campa, transformed to stone by Avíreri.

Avíreri's life among the Campa ultimately came to an end. A sister became so angry at him for transforming her sons that she plotted with her husband to get rid of him. The brother-in-law excavated a hole under the dancing area of the settlement, leaving it covered with a thin roof of earth. Avíreri, invited for a visit, was induced by his sister to dance, whereupon he fell through into the hole. When he was not given any assistance, he transformed his sister into the tree *shimáshiri* and his brother-in-law (who had wrapped himself in his sleeping mat out of fear) into the armadillo *etíni.* He then used his power to extend the hole to Otsitiríko, River's End. Here he emerged and was greeted by Pachákama who, not wanting him to return and wreak more havoc, requested his assistance in holding up the earth. A strangler vine wrapped itself around Avíreri, and there he remains to the present day. The hole into which he fell (*imóro Avíreri*) is still to be seen just above the tributary Yorináki on the left side of the Upper Perené River.

Avíreri's grandson, Kíri, who had been left behind, was heartsick for his grandfather and set out for Otsitiríko. However, he was pursued and overtaken by a number of the other relatives. They tried to kill him for his complicity in Avíreri's activities, but were unable to do so. Finally, on Kíri's instructions, they drove a wooden stake into his head, down through his body, and into the ground, whereupon he was transformed into the *kíri* or pihuayo palm (*Guilielma speciosa*), whose fruit is used today by the Campa to make a wholesome fermented drink. In another version of the same myth, the figures of Avíreri and Kíri are not distinguished, and it was Avíreri who became the *kíri* palm.

Pachákama is the god who holds up the earth at Otsitiríko. He seems to have certain tree-like properties. The distinction made by the River Campa between Avíreri and Pachákama does not appear to be made by the closely related Machiguenga, who use the two names interchangeably in referring to the equivalent of Avíreri in their mythology (see García 1935–1937:v. 18, p. 11). This suggests either that the Campa have divided one deity into two, or that the Machiguenga have merged two into one. In either case, the name Pachákama is surely derived from that of Pachacamac, the deity worshiped on the coast of Peru in pre-Conquest times. While Avíreri is widely known among the River Campa, the recognition of Pachákama appears to be limited for the most part to the Perené region.

Inkanítari is the god of rain (from *inkáni,* "rain"). He resides at the level of the clouds and is the ruler of the good spirits of that realm. He does not play a part in Campa mythology.

Kashíri is the moon. He is male (as are all the Campa gods) and is the father of the sun. At first, the Campa knew nothing of cultivation and subsisted on a diet of earth, specifically the nests of the termite *katsíkori* (from which the Campa themselves had originally been fashioned). At that time Kashíri appeared to a young girl in her menarche hut, introduced her and her people to manioc and its cultivation, and took her to wife. She became pregnant and gave birth to the sun, but was burned to death in doing so. Kashíri's stay on earth ended in the following manner. He began taking his nephews (the sons of his sister) on hunting trips into the forest, where he slaughtered and ate them. Finally, when his brother-in-law found out and threatened to kill him, he escaped by rising into the sky, where he now resides. His cannibalistic tendencies still continue; the waxing of the moon is understood as the filling of Kashíri's belly with the souls of the dead that he has succeeded in capturing.

Sometimes the Campa use the term Tasórentsi to mean not "god" but "God." When they do so, it is usually possible to determine that they are in fact referring to the sun, commonly called Katsirinkáiteri, "he who is hot," but spoken of in a theological context as Pává, "our Father." It is true that the paramount god of the Campa is Pává, the sun. From Pává flow all good things—warmth, light, the useful products of the earth, the good order of the universe. The Campa are forever grateful to him and at their festivals dance with panpipes in his honor.

According to Campa mythology, Pává was born on earth as a Campa, but he gave off so much heat that he burned his mother to death. The young Pává matured rapidly, and his body heat also increased until it became clear that he would incinerate the earth if he were not raised to the sky. The manner in which this was accomplished varies in different Campa accounts. According to one version, Pává's mother's father carried him in tongs to the western end of the earth and set him in his trajectory. Another version states that a number of different flying creatures attempted to carry Pává to the sky, until at last one species of bird, *kentiparo,* after wrapping him in layer after layer of new cushmas[3] to protect themselves from the heat, succeeded in the difficult task. Yet another version describes how Pává ascended to the sky with members of his terrestrial entourage by means of a vine connecting the earth with the sky, after the tiny hummingbird *neorónke* had carried one end of the vine to the sky and attached it there. In any event, Pává is today a celestial being, rising at Otsitiríko in the east and setting at Irimáka in the west. How Pává—or, for that matter, any of the celestial beings—returns from west to east is a matter concerning which the Campa readily admit that they have no knowledge.

One other deity should be mentioned. The Campa believe in a technological genius named Inka. Originally an important man among the Campa, Inka was swept on a raft in a flood downstream to *virakócha* territory, where he was taken captive by the Caucasians. It is he who has given his captors their superior material culture. His attempts to return to Campa territory have failed thus far, because the Caucasians do not want the technological imbalance between themselves and the Campa reversed, but time may be on the side of the Campa since Inka is immortal.

Generally speaking, the quality of the good spirits lies in their being good, not in their doing good. They are paragons of virtue, of chastity, of beauty, of excellence, and so are admired and revered by the Campa. Though they personify Campa ideals, however, they are not expected to be beneficent toward human-kind. They come and go, appear and disappear as they will. They are contemptuous of human frailty, and no Campa expects any good spirit to come to his aid no matter how desperate his circumstances.

THE DEMONS OR EVIL SPIRITS

Demons, who are legion, are called *kamári,* a term applied in a broader sense to refer to anyone or anything repugnant, malevolent, or reprehensible. If the good spirits keep themselves aloof from mere mortals, the demons consider human beings (i.e., Campa) their legitimate prey. Indeed, it would appear that the hordes of evil spirits in the universe are driven by an insatiable urge, automatically triggered, to attack and inflict maximum damage upon any human being they encounter. The breeze stirred by a passing demon (*atántsi kamári*) causes sickness; the attack of a demon, or even the mere sight of one, causes either immediate death or a form of a madness in which the victim does himself physical injury until he is finally killed by his own people out of fear.

Sharinkavéni, the nethermost stratum of the universe, is the abode of vast numbers of demons and is ruled over by the Lord of Demons, Korioshipíri. Belief in the existence of Sharinkavéni is probably indigenous among the Campa since it was reported more than two centuries ago (Adam 1890). But demons also abound on the stratum of Kamavéni, the earth. Here they inhabit, not the ends of the earth as do the good spirits, but actual Campa territory itself, lurking in its forests and teeming in its waters, and thus constitute an ever-present danger.

Among the different kinds of terrestrial demons distinguished by the Campa, the élite are the *mankóite,* who reside within the great cliffs of Campa territory.

They are described as human in form, but with mane-like hair, dressed in old cushmas, with a red parasitic plant (*anánta*) instead of proper red macaw feathers stuck in their wicker crowns. The *mankóite* are mighty demons, with powers approaching those of the gods. A Campa who sees a *mankóite* can expect instantaneous death. Usually, however, the damage they do is to cause sickness by their *atántsi* (the breeze of their passing). Living as they do in the cliffs overlooking the rivers, their specialty is capturing the souls of children voyaging on the rivers with their elders.

The *katsivoréri* are demons that live in caves in the hills and go abroad at night. They are small, black creatures with wings, and each carries a smaller companion on its back. From such a demon there emanates a light, which can be seen flying through the air as the demon makes its nocturnal forays. The demon will attack any human being it encounters, holding him with its powerful grip and driving its gigantic penis into his body, thereby killing the victim or transforming him into another *katsivoréri*.

Sashínti, another type of demon, is distinguished by its extreme thinness, a quality which the Campa disparage, probably because they associate it with the emaciation due to sickness. When a *sashínti* appears to someone, it "breaks" his body into pieces, then reassembles and blows on them to revive him. The victim, remembering fully what has happened to him, returns home to sicken and shortly die.

The *irampavánto* are demons who raise *opémpe* toucans (*Ramphastos cuvieri*) as domesticated fowl. An *irampavánto* may appear to a man alone in the forest in the form of an attractive woman, with an *opémpe* on her shoulder, and excite him to coitus. Or it may appear in the form of a man to a woman with the same results. Afterwards, it informs its victim of the truth, thereby frightening him into helplessness, and beats him "to death." The victim later revives, returns home with full remembrance of what has happened, sickens, and dies. Alternatively, the victim becomes insane.

A *mironi* is a demon that takes the shape of a large tapir or mule with huge eyes and a gigantic penis, or alternatively, of a little old man dressed in an old cushma, carrying a walking stick, and possessing the same genital abnormality. In either form it is a powerful demon. It will attack a solitary man in the forest, driving its member into his body. The victim dies and is transformed into a female *mironi*.

A *kasónkati* likewise appears either as a large tapir or mule, or in human form. This demon has a hole in one or both knees, into which it blows to produce a fearful noise. It likes to kill people by crushing their bones.

The *korínto* are man-devouring monsters as big as houses. They are no longer to be found in Campa territory; shamans long ago trapped them all in a cave near the headwaters of the brook Tsikiréni, a tributary of the Ene River.

The *imposhitóniro* and *shonkatiníro* are water demons who live in the whirlpools and bad passes of the river, where they wait to drown and eat voyagers passing by. The father of the *shonkatiníro* is Tsomiriníro, who collects the souls of drowned Campa in his stomach and then transforms them into *virakócha* to be the husbands of his daughters. The *keátsi* are spirits in human form who live in the rivers and lakes. They are not actually demons, for some are good and some are bad. When a drowned person's soul does not return to make noises, it is presumed that the person still lives but has joined the *keátsi*.

In the foul places of the rivers and streams reside demons in the form of zungaros marked with longitudinal stripes. They collect food wastes thrown into the water and practice witchcraft with them, bringing sickness to those who ate the food. A rainbow is the smoke from the campfire of one of these demons, or else, some Campa believe, is the demon's cushma. Both the demons and rainbows are called *oyéchari* or, alternatively, *tsaviréntsi*.[4]

Another kind of partially visible demon is the small whirlwinds or dust devils that kick up dust and leaves and swirl around the clearings of the Campa settlements from time to time. They are variously called *kaviónkari, tiviónkari,* and *shinkíreri* and are believed to cause *atántsi* sickness.

A number of insects are demons. The morpho butterfly (*Morpho* sp.), called *sánta* or *ankáro,* is one example. Another is the owl butterfly (*Caligo* sp.), called *maatsarántsi* or "old clothes" because it has the drab color of old cushmas and is supposed to be what becomes of the old clothing of a bad person when he dies. The adult ant lion or *shiénti* (fam. *Murmeleonidae*), with its thin body, is also a demon. All these insects cause sickness. In addition, the scorpion (*kitóniro*) is a demon, and all verminous insects are believed to be of demonic provenience.

A number of birds are demons, including all owls (*mamáro*), the vulture (*tisóni*), and the *aróni,* an unidentified large black bird of rapine with a white breast. The drab-colored hummingbird *tsiísanti* is unique among the hummingbirds in being regarded as a demon. Several other species of birds are also believed to be demons, as well as a number of animals including jaguars (*maníti*), bats (*pihíri*), and rabbits (*kíma*).

The Campa have also adopted the widespread *pishitáko* belief of the Peruvian Highlands, according to the Campa form of which there are diabolical Caucasians in the towns who kill Campa to extract the grease from their bodies for use in automobiles and airplanes. The Campa, indeed, cast a suspicious eye on all Caucasians; there is something demonic about them, for they are powerful yet not benevolent, wealthy yet not generous. Are they human, are they mortal? There appears to be a tendency for the Campa to consider the *virakócha* as *mankóite*.

Witchcraft constitutes a special category of demonic activity. The Campa term for witch is *mátsi,* and the Campa believe in the existence of both human and nonhuman witches. Nonhuman witches are the various species of ants and bees. They take food refuse and exuviae to their nests to practice witchcraft upon them, producing sickness in the individual from whom the materials came. The symptoms vary with the species of ant or bee involved. When someone falls ill, and the shaman's diagnosis is that a particular species of ant or bee is causing the sickness by witchcraft, the members of the community go out to search for the nests of these insects in the vicinity, to destroy them and with this hopefully the materials being used for witchcraft.

Human witches are almost always children, usually girls, who bury such materials as pieces of mat, bones, and manioc cores around the house; these materials then enter someone's body and make him seriously ill. Children are seduced into witchcraft by any of a number of species of demonic insects and birds. The katydids *shiínti* and *tsináro* (fam. Tettigoniidae) and the cricket *tsivivínti* (fam. Gryllidae) are demons that teach witchcraft to children. There is also supposed to be an insect which only witches can see, called *tsempokiríriti,* that does the same. The birds *tsiváni* (the squirrel cuckoo, *Piaya cayana*) and *eentiopéti* (unidentified) are likewise demons that teach witchcraft to children. When they appear to children for this purpose, they do so in human form. A child approached in this way is innocent but defenseless, and once it becomes a witch it is a social menace. When a shaman diagnoses an illness as being due to human witchcraft, he designates some child in the community, perhaps even in the victim's family, as the witch. This child is treated brutally and forced to dig up the materials it has buried. If the victim recovers, the accused child may be let off with a warning to desist from further witchcraft; if the victim dies, however, the child is killed or traded to the Caucasians.

The demons of the Campa universe are both real and imaginary beings that embody some combination of repulsiveness and harmfulness. The qualities which the Campa consider demonic can be identified with particular clarity in the demons that are not wholly imaginary. Whatever can do serious physical harm to human beings is a demon; thus jaguars and blood-sucking bats are demons. Whatever is excessively thin, thereby recalling the emaciation due to severe illness, is a demon; therefore the extremely thin *shiénti* (adult ant lion) is a demon. Whatever has the drab color of decay—the color that the Campa call *kamára* or *kamárari*—is a demon; therefore the drab-colored hummingbird *tsiísanti* and the butterfly *maatsarántsi* are demons.[5] Whatever appears to be other than it is—whatever presents a false appearance—is a demon; therefore the katydids *shiínti* and *tsináro,* insects that look like leaves, are demons. Whatever would serve as a bad example for human imitation is a demon; therefore the *tsiváni,* a bird that is not only ugly in Campa eyes but also a slovenly nest-builder, is a demon. The same qualities, in various combinations, are attributed to the imaginary demons as well. It is the imaginary demons who do the greatest harm in inducing sickness, madness, and death; if they wear clothes, it is old clothes (*maatsarántsi*) with their characteristic *kamára* color; and one important category of demons—*sashínti*—is distinguished precisely by its extreme thinness.

Certain other characteristics which are repulsive or even frightening to the Campa are attributed to some of their imaginary demons. Among these characteristics are old age, with its decay and presentiment of death, and excessive sexuality; thus some demons are seen as little old men, and some are visualized as possessing enormous genitalia. The Campa themselves, of course, do not make such interpretations as these; they are content to recognize the several categories of demons with their distinguishing characteristics. But Campa demonology does appear to lend itself to this kind of interpretation.

THE NATURE AND DESTINY OF THE HUMAN SOUL

Every Campa is mortal—he will die. But within him is his soul (*ishíre*), which can leave his body in dreams while he is alive, and will survive his death to join one or another of the hosts of immortal spirits. An individual's soul looks like him, though it is normally invisible. The soul is centered in the heart; indeed, the same term is used for both: *noshíre*, "my soul, my heart."[6] The soul is what animates the body; if it remains away from the body for any considerable length of time, as when it is captured by demons, the body will waste away and die. For short periods the soul can leave the body without ill effects, as when one's soul goes abroad in one's sleep, or when a shaman sends his soul on a flight to distant places. One point of interest should be noted: an individual says that he has gone here or there in his sleep, and a shaman that he has flown to distant places, thereby apparently expressing a belief that an individual's soul is that individual. Indeed, the Campa say the body is only the "clothing" or "skin" of the soul. In general, Campa thought seems to vacillate between a view of the soul as something that "I" have (e.g., "my" soul) and a view of the soul as the essential "I."

When a Campa dies, he (i.e., his soul) may join the good spirits as a *manínkari* if he was sufficiently good in his lifetime. However, with their strong sense of human frailty, the Campa consider it far more likely that a deceased individual's soul (*ishíre*) will become a malevolent ghost (*shirétsi*, "unpossessed soul"), revisiting the settlement where it had lived and attacking the living there. For this reason, the Campa commonly abandon a settlement where someone has died, moving some distance away to establish a new residence. *Shirétsi* can wander the forests in their human, though normally invisible, shape at least for a time; they can join one or another category of demons, becoming one of their number; or, alternatively, they can become *peári*. A *peári* is the soul of a dead person, or any demon, that takes the form of a game animal or game bird; it looks like that animal or bird but is in fact a demon. When a hunter bags an animal or bird and discovers that it has no body fat, is infested with worms, or has pustules, tumors, patchy fur, or unhealthy looking organs, he knows that it is a *peári* and is consequently unfit for human consumption. The suffix *-niro*, meaning "looks like," denotes particular *peári;* thus a *peári* in the form of a peccary (*shintóri*) is a *shintoriniro,* and a *peári* in the form of a deer (*maníro*) is a *manironiro.*

The soul of a Campa attacked by a demon will, after death, become a demon of the same type. When a witch is executed, its soul joins the particular class of demons that taught it witchcraft and becomes one of them. To prevent this from occurring, the corpse of a witch or madman is sometimes cremated in the expectation that the potentially dangerous soul will be destroyed by the flames along with the body. The souls of those who, in their lifetimes, committed such heinous offenses as incestuous fornication, are punished by torture in Sharinkavéni by Korioshipíri and his demon cohorts. In the end, the tortured soul is eaten by the demons, or becomes one of their number, or else is purified and joins the *manínkari.*

THE CAMPA COSMOS

In Campa thought, the universe in its present form came into existence through a series of transformations and, at some time in the future will be destroyed by the will of Pává. For the Campa there is no such occurrence as the creation of something out of nothing, but only the transformation of something out of something else. Consequently, in their thinking, the original condition of the universe was not nothingness but somethingness. The general structure of the universe existed to begin with, as the stage on which all the dramas of Campa mythology were to be acted out. When the curtain goes up, the actors are already on stage: the primal Campa, human beings living here on earth but immortal, many with powers exceeding those possessed by mankind today. There were some special features, later to be changed; thus the sky was much closer to the earth, and the earth spoke. Whatever else existed in the universe at that time is indicated only sketchily in the mythology, but it was an impoverished universe lacking many features that would come into existence through transformation only with the passage of time. Campa mythology is largely the history of how, one by one, the primal Campa became irreversibly transformed into the first representatives of various species of animals and plants, as well as astronomical bodies and features of the terrain. In each case the mechanism of change was either the action of a transformer deity or auto-transformation.

The development of the universe, then, has been primarily a process of diversification, with mankind as the primal substance out of which many if not all of the categories of beings and things in the universe arose, the Campa of today being the descendants of those ancestral Campa who escaped being transformed. Mortality came also to be added as a feature of human life and, with the increasing frequency of death, the earth gradually ceased to speak. The widening gap between mortal life and that of the good spirits was punctuated by the moving apart of the sky and the earth. When the present universe is destroyed, the Campa will be destroyed with it and a new world will take its place, with immortal inhabitants. The sky will again be close to the earth, and the earth will speak once more.

And what is the nature of the universe in which the Campa find themselves? It is a world of semblances; for example, what to us is the solid earth is airy sky to the beings inhabiting the strata below us, and what to us is airy sky is solid ground to those who inhabit the strata above. It is a world of relative semblances, where different kinds of beings see the same things differently; thus human eyes can normally see good spirits only in the form of lightning flashes or birds whereas they see themselves in their true human form, and similarly in the eyes of jaguars human beings look like peccaries to be hunted. It is a world in which there exist beings with powers out of all proportion to their appearance; thus, for example, the gods, though visualized as human in size and form, can bring about sensational transformations by simply expressing their will or with a puff of breath, and have the physical strength to throw up mountains. It is a world operating according to mechanical principles of the sort we would call magical; thus, as a form of homeopathic magic, both prospective parents during pregnancy refrain from eating turtle meat, for fear that this would make their child slow-moving and slow-witted, and, as a form of contagious magic, a witch supposedly utilizes someone's food refuse or exuviae to strike him with sickness—these are examples of "action at a distance," the distinguishing characteristic of magic. It is, again, a world of transformations, of beings and things passing in and out of visibility, in and out of tangibility. It is, finally, a world which, for the Campa, is one of death, of debility, of sickness, of tragedy, because as "mere mortals" they are the weakest of beings and are in constant danger of being crushed by the greater forces of the universe. Yet, despite their understanding of their predicament, the Campa laugh, act vigorously, cling to life, and survive.

It would be easy to dismiss the cosmological thinking of the Campa as false in its assertions of fact, as absurd in its premises, and as childish in its simplicity. But to do so may be an error. We must recognize that the Campa, like every other human group, have attempted to make sense out of existence, have had to do so on the basis of limited information, and have succeeded adequately for their purposes. They may personify forces that we would view as impersonal, but this permits them to think concretely instead of vaguely about matters that affect them intensely. What would be the point of telling the Campa that a diseased game animal is not really a demon, when its flesh is actually dangerous for human consumption and the central meaning of *kamári* is "deadly"?

With a clarity that can best be obtained from simplicity, the Campa have incorporated into their cosmology a number of fundamental moral concepts of the utmost relevance to the human predicament. They distinguish between good and evil, dividing the beings of the universe into two great hosts on this basis, and they revere the good while despising the evil. They recognize the difference between good and bad actions, wishing that their actions could be only good but knowing that bad actions are all too easy, and their mythology is full of cautionary tales about Campa who were transformed into lesser creatures as punishment for objectionable behavior. They have intuited the contrast between chastity and lust, cosmologically expressing their admiration for the former and their contempt for the latter by the way in which they describe both the anatomy and the actions of the good spirits and the demons of their universe. And they have grasped the essential ingredient of human dignity, that of acting properly and with pride in self, rather than corruptly and ignominiously. The Campa recognize their own imperfections and limitations, and consequently in the ideal cosmos of their imagination they place themselves in an intermediate position between the cosmic forces of good and evil, and far less powerful than either. In contemplating data such as these, we may well ponder with special irony the earlier view of, as Darwin (1936: 489) expressed it, "the low morality of savages, as judged by our standard."

NOTES

1. The author's field work among the Campa was conducted between 1960 and 1964, funded in part by the American Museum of Natural History, National Science Foundation, and Social Science Research Council. The present paper is a summary of a much more extensive report on the subject (Weiss ms.).

2. The River and Pajonal Campa are more likely to call each other by the less friendly term of *ayómpari*, "our trading associates." The Pajonal Campa are referred to as the *keshisáti*, "grassland dwellers," by the River Campa.

3. "Cushma" is the local Spanish term for the cotton robes worn by the Campa and neighboring tribes. The Campa name for the garment is *kitsárentsi*. When new, it is clean and white, with woven stripes, and is worn only on special occasions. Once soiled, it is dyed brown and used for everyday wear, becoming increasingly dark, dirty, and tattered.

4. Zungaros are the giant catfish of these rivers. They do not have longitudinal stripes. The stripes ascribed to the demons of this category are therefore imaginary, and probably relate to the stripes of the rainbow on the one hand and, on the other, to the vertical stripes on the cushmas worn by Campa men.

5. *Kamára* is a color category that includes the various shades of cream, khaki, tan, brown, olive drab, and lead. The term is translated as "drab" in this paper as a simplification.

6. An alternative term is *nasánkane*, with the same double meaning.

Rather than describing the entire belief system of the Krahó, a Timbira group, Melatti discusses Krahó shamanism in the light of how one becomes a shaman, and how this process is related to a certain myth. The process contrasts in most respects with that of the Cashinahua described by Kensinger, and in many respects with Harner's description for the Jívaro, especially in the lack of the use of any drug in association with the experiences described by the shamans. A rather startling parallel may be noticed in the technique of transmission of a magical substance from a shaman to his apprentice which is described by Melatti from Nimuendajú (1939:150) and by Harner in the following article. Melatti's study, as well as those of Kensinger and Harner that follow, points up how little detailed descriptive material we have on the formation and/or training of shamans, in spite of such excellent works as Wagley's on Tapirapé shamanism (1943) and Kloos' on the Maroni River Carib (1968).

The author has provided a note which is appended to the translation of his original article indicating where the original interpretation requires modification in the light of later research. He has also changed the orthography of Krahó terms to a somewhat simplified version of the phonetic transcription of Pike. Since the publication of this article, Melatti has published considerable additional material on this group (cf. Melatti 1967, 1971, 1972) and is currently preparing a book on Krahó rites. Roberto da Matta has also published important material on Timbira myths (cf. Matta 1971).

In the original Melatti referred to the Portuguese version of Nimuendajú's monograph on the Apinayé (1956). With the author's approval I have changed all such references to the corresponding pages of the English version of that work (Nimuendajú 1939).

24 JULIO CEZAR MELATTI

Myth and Shaman

The object of the present study is to point out the relationship between certain myths of the Krahó Indians and the stories of experiences that some members of this native group claim to have had on being transformed into shamans.[1] The same relationship may occur in the other Timbira groups since they share the same mythology, use similar shamanistic practices, possess a social organization based on the same fundamental principles and, according to their traditions, perhaps have a common origin. The ethnographic data of Curt Nimuendajú, as we shall see, seem to us also to confirm this idea.

CHARACTERIZATION OF THE SHAMAN

The Krahó shaman is generally male. One informant affirmed the existence of female shamans, who, however, are satisfied with simply seeing spirits (*ka'rõ*). The shaman occupies two distinct roles: that of "curer" (*vaya'ka*), when he uses his powers to benefit society, that of "sorcerer" (*kai*), when he uses them to cause harm and death (see paragraph 4, page 274). Naturally, no one admits to being a sorcerer in view of the threat of death that hovers over anyone doing so. Generally, an individual only brings accusations of sorcery against those shamans who are not considered to be related to him. It might, therefore, be legitimate to include the cases of assassination of sorcerers, which are very frequent among the Krahó and other Timbira societies, as an aspect of the rivalry between kin groups. This topic, however, is beyond the scope of the present work.

The knowledge of plants whose leaves, roots or fruits, when rubbed on the body, drunk mixed with water or put on incisions made in the skin, bring success in hunting certain animals, cure determined diseases or improve the efficiency of the individual in log races, is not exclusive to the shaman. In a general way, all adult members of the group, in accord with the interests of each sex, know how to use some of these resources. The shaman, however, besides knowing a reasonable number of magico-medicinal plants, can see the spirits of the dead, enter in contact with them and consult them. He can talk with certain animals from whom he learns new remedies. He possesses magical substances within his own body, knows how to remove or cast pathogenic objects, and can cause the reentry into a person's body of the spirit that has left it. These are the powers that distinguish him from the other members of Krahó society.

In Krahó society nothing is given away; nothing is done for another person

Reprinted by permission of the author and publisher from *Revista do Museu Paulista*, n.s., vol. 14 (1963), pp. 60–70. Translated and edited by Patricia J. Lyon with the approval of the author.

All material appearing within square brackets [ ] has been added by the editor of this book.

without something being received in exchange. The shaman does not escape the rule. Each time he successfully exercises his powers to help someone, that person pays him with money or some other commodity. In rendering certain services to the entire community such as making the rain stop so that some task may be performed or attracting fish so that they may be poisoned, he also has the right to payment. Likewise, in the relations of the shaman with the supernatural, the same principle applies; he generally avoids killing and eating animals of the species he credits with having transmitted shamanistic powers to him.

THE "INDIVIDUAL MYTH"

Since we proposed to indicate the existence of a relationship, it is necessary to identify the elements to be related. Let us begin with one of them: the manner in which certain individuals are said to have been transformed into shamans. We will summarize four personal statements that we have selected and then point out the uniformities among them.

First, we have the story of the curer, Zezinho (Ha'poro Wa'khe), of Aldeia do Posto. He told us that once, when he still lived in Aldeia de Canto Grande, he fell ill. No one went out hunting for him. He decided to go out by himself to find some animal to kill. In spite of the advice of his wife, he went out to the plateau. He felt worse and worse and, therefore lay down with his body all feverish. A hawk appeared to him and he informed it of his misery. The hawk departed, and returned shortly with a *juriti* [a kind of pigeon or dove] that Zezinho had to eat raw, as it was. The hawk then ordered him to vomit; he obeyed and a small ball of blood came out. It then caused Zezinho to see the village, and then advised him to care, henceforth, for all those who were sick.

The second statement is that of the Indian Clóvis (Pōhï' tɔro Ya'txu Tu'mãi), brother of Zezinho's wife, and living in the same house. He says he began his career as a shaman in the vicinity of the Aldeia do Posto itself. One time he was sick. Even so he decided to go fishing in spite of the opposition of his sister. He went to the Ribeirão dos Cavalos. He did not manage to catch anything, but the fish and the caimans drew closer and closer around him. He was frightened and almost ran. Behind him, meanwhile, there appeared a fish transformed into an Indian. Clóvis was frightened, but the fish calmed him. Perhaps it was God [Deus][2] who had sent it, according to the informant, since he was sick. . . . The fish asked him to make a cigarette for it and then blew smoke on him for some time until pork fat, the cause of all his illness, came out of his body. The fish then indicated a desire to turn him into a curer. First, however, it wanted to sate his hunger and, therefore, producing from its own body a table, tablecloth, spoon, plate, rice, beef, chicken and even coffee, it served him a copious meal. While he ate, Clóvis noticed the fish's wife and desired her, but he could do nothing. Having satisfied himself, he saw the table and all that it contained disappear. The fish then indicated to him a series of foods to be avoided until the next moon. It then introduced into Clóvis body a number of things including a radio, a knife, a bowl, rice, the meat of various animals, etc.[3] Clóvis began to see, from right there, the Canela village, the Apinayé village,

Conceição do Araguaia, Carolina, in short, all places. The fish then ordered that, before leaving, he try out the powers received from it. Clóvis took a little cotton and threw it into the trees; they immediately caught fire and a thunderclap sounded. He then returned home. He lost all his powers through breaking the food taboos that were imposed on him. Before losing them, however, he once went to the heavens. He went up one night. There, on high, he saw the same things that are here below: he noted the presence of Indians, civilized people and animals. Everything was clean, however, and there were no fallen leaves on the ground. He descended after making his observations.

The third story recounts the experience of young Itu"ëp of Aldeia do Posto. He told us that it was a *xupé*, a kind of bee, that gave him shamanistic powers. He was still a boy and was living in Aldeia de Canto Grande. One day he went deer hunting. He was facing a gallery forest when there appeared to him a xupé who, on being informed of the reason for his presence in that area, advised him to seek game elsewhere. Itu"ëp returned to the village and fell ill; his body felt too hot. During the night the xupé came to his house. It transformed itself into a black man with lank hair, cast a substance into his head, his heart and his arms, curing him. This substance also made it possible for Itu"ëp to cure the sickness of others. He never cured, however, nor did he ever harm anyone. He no longer wanted to be a curer, and the xupé returned to his house to recover the magical substance.

Finally we have the story of the shaman Aniceto (Mam'pok Rom'rɔ Ĩtxo'tuk Ka'mõk) of Aldeia de Pedra Branca. Once, in that village, he was sick. He sent his wife to her brother's house and remained all alone, crying. . . . A *seriema* [large bird of the Fam. Cariamidae] approached the house, arrived at the door and greeted Aniceto. Learning of his sickness, it gave him "things" and arranged to meet with him two days later. Aniceto went to look for the bird in the agreed upon locale and, with its aid, was cured. To try out Aniceto's powers, the seriema cast a pathogenic object into its own nestling and asked him to remove it. The Indian removed the egg of a *calango* [small lizard] from the little bird and it was well.

Studying the four narratives presented above we see that they possess something in common; they recount similar events arranged in the same diachronic order. We can, therefore, analyze each of these stories into a series of propositions, each of which will consist of the application of a predicate to a subject.[4] If we write out each account in a line, so that one is placed beneath the other, then similar propositions will be grouped into vertical columns. We conclude from this fact that the four stories possess the same structure. If we then present the content of each column in a single proposition, we have a scheme that could be considered a model of the stories and would approximate the following (see paragraph 1, page 274):

1) A man is sick;
2) the man is alone;
3) an animal appears to the man;
4) the animal cures the man's sickness;
5) the animal feeds the man;
6) the animal gives magical powers to the man;

7) the man tries out the acquired powers;

8) the man goes up to the heavens (see paragraph 2, page 274);

9) the man loses the acquired powers (see paragraph 3, page 274).

One or another of these elements is lacking in some of the stories, but the majority is present in all of them. Some clarification is needed with respect to the last two items. Item number 8 appears in only one of the depositions. Clóvis, the Indian who claims to have ascended to the heavens, says he did so some time after having received the shamanistic powers although, in the original account, the fish promises several times to send him to the heavens at the moment in which it bestows the powers on him. The position of this item in the sequence, therefore, does not necessarily have to be that in which we have placed it. Moreover, numbers 4 and 5 can also appear with their positions reversed. As far as item 9 is concerned, it can only appear, naturally, in the depositions of those who, temporarily or permanently, ceased being shamans.

THE "COLLECTIVE MYTH"

In our presentation of the relationship between two elements we have now described the first, the "individual myths," a term by which we are designating the stories experienced by shamans on receiving their supernatural powers. Let us move on to the account of the second element, a story preserved in tribal tradition and one in which all members of Krahó society believe. We have decided to call this story the "collective myth" to distinguish it from the four already presented. It deals with the adventures of a man who went to the heavens. We will attempt to summarize the version we obtained from the Indian Messias (Ha'wët KrΛk Pïrï'pok).

Once upon a time there was an Indian named Tïr'krē. One day he went to his field, collected some manioc, grated it and, finishing the task, fell asleep. However, an ant entered his ear, which began to swell continuously. At this time his village was moving to another site. His wife, who was deceiving him, having sexual relations with her husband's brother, asked him to wait there until the house was completed in the new village. Tïr'krē, however, was forgotten and abandoned. A flock of vultures [urubus] found him and resolved to take care of the sick man. They called in various little birds until one of them succeeded in removing the ant from his ear. Then the vultures bore him up to the heavens after first arguing with the King Vultures [Sarcoramphus papa] who said they had more strength to carry the man, a statement denied by the vultures. Having arrived in the heavens, a hawk, a very good curer, went hunting and brought back a jaó [bird of the Fam. Tinamidae] which Tïr'krē had to eat raw (see paragraph 6, page 275). Then the hawk caught a young rhea, which he also ate raw. Then a vulture went down to earth and gathered human excrement but the Indian refused to eat it. Tïr'krē got well. At that time the festival of Pembka'hΛk was celebrated in the heavens. The Indians of that time did not know how to do it. Tïr'krē was the one who taught it to them when he returned from the sky. Later, the hawk took him to visit the lightning (A?khrā'ti) (see paragraph 5, page 274). Lightning took dry buriti palm, set fire to it and threw it into a river, causing a thunderclap. It was then decided to try out Tïr'krē's powers (see paragraph 6, page 275). A bird, Tεp'khriti, went down and caught two fish and put them on top of a log. Tïr'krē transformed himself into an otter and ate them. He then transformed himself into a *tututi* [bird of the Fam. Columbidae]. The hawk doubted that the Indian wanted to return home. It ordered the vultures to take his belongings down to earth, and Tïr'krē himself descended transformed into a sambaíba leaf. He stayed in his mother's house. Perceiving now that his wife was deceiving him with his brother, the good curer surprised them together one day and, transforming himself into a large ant, bit each of them on the genitals. Later, when they, all unknowing, came to him complaining of the animal that had wounded them, Tïr'krē cured them. Since his wife was pregnant, but persisted in denying it, he caused the child to leave her belly. Another curer, called Khïok, challenged Tïr'krē to show his powers (see paragraph 6, page 275). He proceeded to transform himself into various birds while the challenger could do nothing.

We have another version of the myth in which the last episode, the contest between shamans, is omitted and Tïr'krē is asked to repeat the action of Aʔkhrā'ti, also throwing burning buriti into the river and causing a thunderclap. Various isolated data add that, in the heavens, the hawk taught Tïr'krē to be a curer.

RELATIONSHIPS BETWEEN THE "COLLECTIVE MYTH" AND THE "INDIVIDUAL MYTH"

If we take the myth presented above and divide it into small units of the same nature as those proposed for the four previous accounts, we will be reducing it into what Lévi-Strauss called "mythemes" (Lévi-Strauss, 1958:233,236). Arranging the mythemes in the order in which they occur in the myth, we will find almost total conformity with the model of the shamans' accounts already presented. There are, however, some differences that we will point out. In the first place, Tïr'krē comes in contact with more than one being, not with just a single animal as the shamans who were interviewed claim to have done. These several beings, however, perform the same actions which, in the curers' depositions, are done by a single one: curing, feeding, bestowing magical powers and making the recipient try them out. In the second place, the myth of Tïr'krē presents two elements not found in the model we constructed: a) the failure of the curer's wife to observe her conjugal duties, and b) the contest between shamans. Now, the first element could only occur among married shamans; but there are single curers. In addition, the wife's irresponsibility presents two aspects. At the beginning of the myth it serves to explain the state of abandonment, of isolation, in which Tïr'krē is found, and this satisfies our model. At the end of the myth it becomes a pretext for the shaman to use his resources as a sorcerer, that is, to cause harm, an eventuality to which every Krahó curer is subject although he would never admit it. As far as the contest of shamans is concerned, it certainly refers to the confirmation of the magical powers by the community. Those shamans who flagrantly failed in the use of their powers would be ostracized. This fact may, perhaps, be related to the loss or giving back of powers that we saw in two of the summarized statements. It would be an explanation for failure with temporary or permanent effect on prestige in the community.

It should be added that these two items are also lacking in another Krahó myth that, otherwise, follows the model that we are presenting. This myth deals with the story of a pot-bellied, geophageous little boy who was carried off by a caiman under the waters of a river. The caiman cured him and fed him for some time, during which it taught him to sing and to cure. After the instruction, the boy returned to the village where he transmitted the art of singing to the other Indians.

We believe we can conclude, therefore, that the "individual myths" lived by the shamans, and certain myths traditionally known and accepted by all of Krahó society, such as that of Tïr'krē, are adapted to the same model; thus, they possess isomorphic structures. The relationship that we desired to indicate was, then, a relationship of identity. Some individuals, if not all, on becoming shamans, relived the myth of Tïr'krē.

THE PROBLEM OF THE APPRENTICESHIP

We do not have sufficient information to state with certainty that all shamans have relived this myth. We do not know if there could be another means of achieving the status of curer. By any means, the individual would necessarily have to learn shamanistic techniques in some way. To state the problem in other words: we know the only way—or one of the ways—by which someone believes he became a shaman, but we do not know the manner in which he really learned to act as such, that is, how he was trained.

Our data indicate that candidates for shaman learn from more experienced curers (that would be formal apprenticeship) and that there is also, among those individuals familiar with the magical sphere, a certain mutual observation (that would be informal apprenticeship). We do not, however, have details of such apprenticeship.

According to Curt Nimuendajú, among the Ramkokamekra an apprentice shaman must abstain from "meat pies" and any other form of meat for a month, must avoid sexual relations and rub his body with pieces of a certain yellow root in order to be visited by the spirits who finally appear to him in dreams. After announcing this result in the plaza, he will be considered a shaman (Nimuendajú 1946:239). However, the Indians themselves, when sick, could seek instruction from the spirits of their ancestors without the aid of a curer. For this purpose seclusion is necessary: one must surround his bed with mats, use a scratching stick and avoid conversation with anyone. Thus, he can hope to see the person he is seeking in his dreams (Nimuendajú 1946:237). The Apinayé Indians, as we can infer from Nimuendajú's data, attain the status of shaman with the help of a supernatural vision, or even without it. As an example of the first case, we have the story of Katam who dreamed of his dead brother who advised him to take care of the well-being of the village and promised to teach him to cure illness. Some time later, Katam tried to cure his chief, Matuk, and being successful, came to be considered a shaman by everyone (Nimuendajú 1939:143). In the second case, a shaman chose a little boy after examining the palms of his hands and his eyes. He taught him the use of tobacco, fasting, sexual abstinence and rubbed his hands and chest with magical substances. Finally, the teacher drew his own powers out of his hands and chest, passing them to his apprentice. However, referring to this last case, Nimuendajú states that he never saw one of these disciples (1939:150).

We can hypothesize that apprenticeship among the Krahó, whether formal or informal, instead of being an independent process leading to the office of shaman, is combined with the reliving of the myth. We imagine the following on the basis of Nimuendajú's data, especially that on the Ramkokamekra, which we have cited: abstinence from certain foods and other conduct to be followed by the shaman's disciple would act to put him into a condition of physical weakness and a psychological state that would culminate in the supposed contact with the spirits. Nimuendajú does not describe for us in detail the dream of any of these apprentices, but it would not be impossible that it have the same structure as the Krahó myth of Tïr'krē. Besides, the Ramkokamekra have at least two myths that fit the same model set out in the course of this study, the myth of Yawę and that of Hąhąk (Nimuendajú 1946:246–247), and the Apinayé have one, "The visit to the sky" (Nimuendajú 1939:184–186). All three of these may, however, be other versions of the myth of Tïr'krē.

This reference to Nimuendajú's data was aimed at demonstrating that, a) among the other Timbira nothing appears to prevent the shaman's apprentice from reliving the myth of Tïr'krē and b) if the Krahó possess a similar formal apprenticeship it could not only be combined with the reliving of the myth, but also favor the appearance of such a psychological phenomenon.

CONCLUSIONS

If we accept the existence of the relationship that we just indicated between the advent of a new shaman and a determined myth, we can arrive at three conclusions:

a. Along with objective apprenticeship, Krahó society offers candidates to the office of shaman a structured, subjective access route, the knowledge of which they acquire by means of a myth.

b. Since all members of the society believe in this myth, the shaman, having relived it, acquires a precedent considered to be real which permits him to believe sincerely in his own powers, legitimating his actions.[5]

c. Each of the shaman's successes contributes to the increasing vigor of the belief of the members of the society in the myth that the shaman relived.

This study was inspired by the article by Lévi-Strauss, "The structure of myths" (1958:227–255), in which the author seeks a formula for the interpretation of myths. Here, however, it was not our intention to explain, but rather to identify some versions of a single myth. Anyone proposing to interpret it, on consulting all of the published Timbira mythology, would perhaps be able to include as versions of it many variants that, at first sight, seem to be related to entirely different motifs.

Such may be the case of the myths of "Aukê," "The tapir that impregnated the woman" and "The woman and the snake," collected by Harald Schultz from the Krahó (Schultz 1950:86–92, 153–154, 156–158). The collection and interpretation of all the versions of this myth would obviously contribute to a better comprehension of the function of the shaman within Krahó society.

AUTHOR'S NOTE

This article was written almost ten years ago. In its general lines it is still acceptable but certain details should be modified.

1. It is not only animals that transmit magical powers to human beings. Plants such as manioc or *abacaxi* [a variety of pineapple], mythical heroes such as Sun and Moon and other elements such as rum [*cachaça*] can cause an individual to be transformed into a shaman in a manner similar to the cases recounted in the article. For example, one informant told me that a woman once went to the garden, ate an abacaxi and also gathered some to take back to the village. On arriving, her stomach ached from the juice of the abacaxi and she began to see the abacaxi itself that wanted to talk to her and make her a curer. Since another person approached her, however, the abacaxi went away and the woman lost the opportunity to become a shaman. The woman was sick and alone, but the breaking of her isolation prevented her receiving the magical powers. Therefore, the model that we constructed on the basis of the four statements examined in the article—1) a man is sick; 2) the man is alone; 3) an animal appears . . . , etc.—should be revised in the light of these other data and may be expressed as follows: 1) an individual (either male or female) is sick; 2) the individual is alone; 3) a non-human being appears . . . , etc.

2. Item 8 of the model can be eliminated. Of the several accounts that we collected, only one shaman admitted to having visited the heavens and this event did not occur at the moment in which he received his magical powers. The ascent to the heavens of the mythical hero Tïr'krẽ simply accentuates his separation from other human beings at the moment in which he receives his magical powers; it reiterates the need for isolation. Therefore, the isolation of the future shaman, even here on earth, is sufficiently equivalent to the period Tïr'krẽ spent in the heavens.

3. Item 9 can also be eliminated. In the myth, Tïr'krẽ does not lose his magical powers, and it appears that the shamans do not lose theirs either. We observed that those who told us of having ceased to be shamans continued to exercise their magical activities in a normal fashion. They had probably lied to us to avoid a possible request for the demonstration of their powers or questions about accusations of witchcraft.

4. It seems that the terms *kai* and *vaya'ka* are not translated by "sorcerer" and "curer" respectively, since both of them may be used in the second sense. We do not have sufficient information to distinguish between the two terms.

5. The being called *A ʔkhrā'ti*, whom we identified as the lightning, is actually identified with meteors as may be seen in Nimuendajú (1946:233) and an article by Vilma Chiara (1962:374–375) which also presents a version of the myth of Tïr'krẽ (1962:339–350).

6. Finally, since this article was written as briefly as possible to be read at the VI Reunião Brasileira de Antropologia held in São Paulo in 1963, we had to summarize the myth of Tïr'krē considerably, omitting, due to our inexperience, details that we now consider important. Thus, we failed to say that Tïr'krē, on eating the raw flesh of *jaó*, vomited the blood of this bird. As far as the testing of Tïr'krē's powers is concerned, the initiative appears to have come from the bird Tɛp'khriti (of the genus *Ceryle*), but our field notes are not clear on this point. With regard to the dispute between Tïr'krē and Khïok, it is the former who challenged the latter, although provoked by the doubts of Khïok.

NOTES

1. We were in the Krahó Indian villages nearly four months, from September, 1962, to January, 1963, carrying out our first period of investigation of the social organization of these Indians, an integral part of the project of Prof. Roberto Cardoso de Oliveira, "A comparative study of indigenous Brazilian societies."

2. "*Deus*" is the translation that the Krahó generally give to the term *Pït*, that is, the Sun. They also customarily identify Pïdli'rɛ (Moon) with St. Peter.

3. The Krahó have been in permanent contact with the Brazilians for more than a century. Thus, it should not cause surprise that their supernatural experiences include the presence of plates, bowls, knives, radio receivers, etc.

4. We are attempting here to use a technique recommended by Lévi-Strauss: "each myth is analyzed independently, seeking to translate the succession of events by means of the shortest possible sentences. Each sentence is written on an index card which bears a number corresponding to its place in the story. It will then be noted that each card consists of the assignment of a predicate to a subject. In other words, each gross constituent unit has the nature of a *relation*" (Lévi-Strauss 1958:233) [emphasis in the original].

5. Since we showed our surprise when the curer Zezinho told us that a hawk taught him to cure, he queried: "And was it not the hawk who taught Tïr'krē?" as if to say: If Tïr'krē, in whose existence, and the truthfulness of whose story, we all believe, received instruction from a hawk, why cannot the same happen to me?

A new emphasis in the study of South American Indian religion has grown out of the increasing realization of the extent to which hallucinogens are used in religious contexts (cf. Furst 1972). This realization, coupled with current interest in drug use throughout the world, has resulted in a spate of potboilers purporting to be scholarly or at least first-hand studies of such activity in South America. Harner's is most definitely not such a work. Although the article presented here was written for a nonspecialized audience, it is the result of years of research not only among the Jívaro but also in the area of hallucinogens and their use in culture. In addition to other articles (cf. Harner 1962, 1968), Harner has published a book on the Jívaro (1972) and edited a collection of articles on hallucinogens and shamanism (1973).

One respect in which the Jívaro curing shaman differs from either the Cashinahua or Krahó shaman is in the object of his attentions. That is, he cures solely on an individual basis and is not called upon to perform any sort of activity in behalf of the collectivity.

25 MICHAEL J. HARNER

The Sound of Rushing Water

He had drunk, and now he softly sang. Gradually, faint lines and forms began to appear in the darkness, and the shrill music of the tsentsak, *the spirit helpers, arose around him. The power of the drink fed them. He called, and they came. First,* pangi, *the anaconda, coiled about his head, transmuted into a crown of gold. Then* wampang, *the giant butterfly, hovered above his shoulder and sang to him with its wings. Snakes, spiders, birds, and bats danced in the air above him. On his arms appeared a thousand eyes as his demon helpers emerged to search the night for enemies.*

The sound of rushing water filled his ears, and listening to its roar, he knew he possessed the power of tsungi, *the first shaman. Now he could see. Now he could find the truth. He stared at the stomach of the sick man. Slowly, it became transparent like a shallow mountain stream, and he saw within it, coiling and uncoiling,* makanchi, *the poisonous serpent, who had been sent by the enemy shaman. The real cause of the illness had been found.*

The Jívaro Indians of the Ecuadorian Amazon believe that witchcraft is the cause of the vast majority of illnesses and non-violent deaths. The normal waking life, for the Jívaro, is simply "a lie," or illusion, while the true forces that determine daily events are supernatural and can only be seen and manipulated with the aid of hallucinogenic drugs. A reality view of this kind creates a particularly strong demand for specialists who can cross over into the supernatural world at will to deal with the forces that influence and even determine the events of the waking life.

These specialists, called "shamans" by anthropologists, are recognized by the Jívaro as being of two types: bewitching shamans or curing shamans. Both kinds take a hallucinogenic drink, whose Jívaro name is *natema,* in order to enter the supernatural world. This brew, commonly called *yagé,* or *yajé,* in Colombia, *ayahuasca* (Inca "vine of the dead") in Ecuador and Peru, and *caapi* in Brazil, is prepared from segments of a species of the vine *Banisteriopsis,* a genus belonging to the Malpighiaceae. The Jívaro boil it with the leaves of a similar vine, which probably is also a species of *Banisteriopsis,* to produce a tea that contains the powerful hallucinogenic alkaloids harmaline, harmine, d-tetrahydroharmine, and quite possibly dimethyltryptamine (DMT). These compounds have chemical structures and effects similar, but not identical, to LSD, mescaline of the peyote cactus, and psilocybin of the psychotropic Mexican mushroom.

When I first undertook research among the Jívaro in 1956–57, I did not fully appreciate the psychological impact of the *Banisteriopsis* drink upon the native view of reality, but in 1961 I had occasion to drink the hallucinogen in the course of field work with another Upper Amazon Basin tribe. For several hours after drinking the brew, I found myself, although awake, in a world literally beyond my wildest dreams. I met bird-headed people, as well as dragon-like creatures who explained that they were the true gods of this world. I enlisted the services of other spirit helpers in attempting to fly through the far reaches of the Galaxy. Transported into a trance where the supernatural seemed natural, I realized that anthropologists, including myself, had profoundly underestimated the importance of the drug in affecting native ideology. Therefore, in 1964 I returned to the Jívaro to give particular attention to the drug's use by the Jívaro shaman.

The use of the hallucinogenic *natema* drink among the Jívaro makes it possible for almost anyone to achieve the trance state essential for the practice of shamanism. Given the presence of the drug and the felt need to contact the "real," or supernatural, world, it is not surprising that approximately one out of every four Jívaro men is a shaman. Any adult, male or female, who desires to become such a practitioner, simply presents a gift to an already practicing shaman, who administers the *Banisteriopsis* drink and gives some of his own supernatural power—in the form of spirit helpers, or *tsentsak*—to the apprentice. These spirit helpers, or "darts," are the main supernatural forces believed to cause illness and death in daily life. To the non-shaman they are normally invisible, and even shamans can perceive them only under the influence of *natema.*

Shamans send these spirit helpers into the victims' bodies to make them ill or to kill them. At other times, they may suck spirits sent by enemy shamans from the bodies of tribesmen suffering from witchcraft-induced illness. The spirit helpers also form shields that protect their shaman masters from attacks. The following account presents the ideology of Jívaro witchcraft from the point of view of the Indians themselves.

To give the novice some *tsentsak,* the practicing shaman regurgitates what appears to be—to those who have taken *natema*—a brilliant substance in which the spirit helpers are contained. He cuts part of it off with a machete and gives it to the novice to swallow. The recipient experiences pain upon taking it into his stomach and stays on his bed for ten days, repeatedly drinking *natema.* The Jívaro believe they can keep magical darts in their stomachs indefinitely and regurgitate them at will. The shaman donating the *tsentsak* periodically blows and rubs all over the body of the novice, apparently to increase the power of the transfer.

The novice must remain inactive and not engage in sexual intercourse for at least three months. If he fails in self-discipline, as some do, he will not become a successful shaman. At the end of the first month, a *tsentsak* emerges from his mouth. With this magical dart at his disposal, the new shaman experiences a tremendous desire to bewitch. If he casts his *tsentsak* to fulfill this desire, he will become a bewitching shaman. If, on the other hand, the novice can control his impulse and reswallow this first *tsentsak,* he will become a curing shaman.

If the shaman who gave the *tsentsak* to the new man was primarily a bewitcher, rather than a curer, the novice likewise will tend to become a bewitcher. This is because a bewitcher's magical darts have such a desire to kill that their new owner will be strongly inclined to adopt their attitude. One informant said that the urge to kill felt by bewitching shamans came to them with a strength and frequency similar to that of hunger.

Only if the novice shaman is able to abstain from sexual intercourse for five months, will he have the power to kill a man (if he is a bewitcher) or cure a victim (if he is a curer). A full year's abstinence is considered necessary to become a really effective bewitcher or curer.

During the period of sexual abstinence, the new shaman collects all kinds of insects, plants, and other objects, which he now has the power to convert into *tsentsak.* Almost any object, including living insects and worms, can become a *tsentsak* if it is small enough to be swallowed by a shaman. Different types of *tsentsak* are used to cause different kinds and degrees of illness. The greater the variety of these objects that a shaman has in his body, the greater is his ability.

According to Jívaro concepts, each *tsentsak* has a natural and supernatural aspect. The magical dart's natural aspect is that of an ordinary material object as seen without drinking the drug *natema.* But the supernatural and "true" aspect of the *tsentsak* is revealed to the shaman by taking *natema.* When he does this, the magical darts appear in new forms as demons and with new names. In their supernatural aspects, the *tsentsak* are not simply objects but spirit helpers in various forms, such as giant butterflies, jaguars, or monkeys, who actively assist the shaman in his tasks.

Bewitching is carried out against a specific, known individual and thus is almost always done to neighbors or, at the most, fellow tribesmen. Normally, as is the case with intratribal assassination, bewitching is done to avenge a particular offense committed against one's family or friends. Both bewitching and individual assassination contrast with the large-scale headhunting raids for which the Jívaro have become famous, and which were conducted against entire neighborhoods of enemy tribes.

To bewitch, the shaman takes *natema* and secretly approaches the house of his victim. Just out of sight in the forest, he drinks green tobacco juice, enabling him to regurgitate a *tsentsak,* which he throws at his victim as he comes out of his house. If the *tsentsak* is strong enough and is thrown with sufficient force, it will pass all the way through the victim's body causing death within a period of a few days to several weeks. More often, however, the magical dart simply lodges in the victim's body. If the shaman, in his hiding place, fails to see the intended victim, he may instead bewitch any member of the intended victim's family who appears, usually a wife or child. When the shaman's mission is accomplished, he returns secretly to his own home.

One of the distinguishing characteristics of the bewitching process among the Jívaro is that, as far as I could learn, the victim is given no specific indication that someone is bewitching him. The bewitcher does not want his victim to be aware that he is being supernaturally attacked, lest he take protective measures by immediately procuring the services of a curing shaman. Nonetheless, shamans and laymen alike with whom I talked noted that illness invariably follows the bewitchment, although the degree of the illness can vary considerably.

A special kind of spirit helper, called a *pasuk,* can aid the bewitching shaman by remaining near the victim in the guise of an insect or animal of the forest after the bewitcher has left. This spirit helper has his own objects to shoot into the victim should a curing shaman succeed in sucking out the *tsentsak* sent earlier by the bewitcher who is the owner of the *pasuk.*

In addition, the bewitcher can enlist the aid of a *wakani* ("soul," or "spirit") bird. Shamans have the power to call these birds and use them as spirit helpers in bewitching victims. The shaman blows on the *wakani* birds and then sends them to the house of the victim to fly around and around the man, frightening him. This is believed to cause fever and insanity, with death resulting shortly thereafter.

After he returns home from bewitching, the shaman may send a *wakani* bird to perch near the house of the victim. Then if a curing shaman sucks out the intruding object, the bewitching shaman sends the *wakani* bird more *tsentsak* to throw from its beak into the victim. By continually resupplying the *wakani* bird with new *tsentsak,* the sorcerer makes it impossible for the curer to rid his patient permanently of the magical darts.

While the *wakani* birds are supernatural servants available to anyone who wishes to use them, the *pasuk,* chief among the spirit helpers, serves only a single shaman. Likewise a shaman possesses only one *pasuk.* The *pasuk,* being specialized for the service of bewitching, has a protective shield to guard it from counterattack by the curing shaman. The curing shaman, under the influence of *natema,* sees the *pasuk* of the bewitcher in human form and size, but "covered with iron except for its eyes." The curing shaman can kill this *pasuk* only by shooting a *tsentsak* into its eyes, the sole vulnerable area in the *pasuk*'s armor. To the person who has not taken the hallucinogenic drink, the *pasuk* usually appears to be simply a tarantula.

Shamans also may kill or injure a person by using magical darts, *anamuk,* to create supernatural animals that attack a victim. If a shaman has a small, pointed armadillo bone *tsentsak,* he can shoot this into a river while the victim is crossing it on a balsa raft or in a canoe. Under the water, this bone manifests itself in its supernatural aspect as an anaconda, which rises up and overturns the craft, causing the victim to drown. The shaman can similarly use a tooth from a killed snake as a *tsentsak,* creating a poisonous serpent to bite his victim. In more or less the same manner, shamans can create jaguars and pumas to kill their victims.

About five years after receiving his *tsentsak,* a bewitching shaman undergoes a test to see if he still retains enough *tsentsak* power to continue to kill successfully. This test involves bewitching a tree. The shaman, under the influence of *natema,* attempts to throw a *tsentsak* through the tree at the point where its two main branches join. If his strength and aim are adequate, the tree appears to split the moment the *tsentsak* is sent into it. The splitting, however, is invisible to an observer who is not under the influence of the hallucinogen. If the shaman fails, he knows that he is incapable of killing a human victim. This means that, as soon as possible, he must go to a strong shaman and purchase a new supply of *tsentsak*. Until he has the goods with which to pay for this new supply, he is in constant danger, in his proved weakened condition, of being seriously bewitched by other shamans. Therefore, each day, he drinks large quantities of *natema*, tobacco juice, and the extract of yet another drug, *piripiri*. He also rests on his bed at home to conserve his strength, but tries to conceal his weakened condition from his enemies. When he purchases a new supply of *tsentsak,* he can safely cut down on his consumption of these other substances.

The degree of illness produced in a witchcraft victim is a function of both the force with which the *tsentsak* is shot into the body, and also of the character of the magical dart itself. If a *tsentsak* is shot all the way through the body of a victim, then "there is nothing for a curing shaman to suck out," and the patient dies. If the magical dart lodges within the body, however, it is theoretically possible to cure the victim by sucking. But in actual practice, the sucking is not always considered successful.

The work of the curing shaman is complementary to that of a bewitcher. When a curing shaman is called in to treat a patient, his first task is to see if the illness is due to witchcraft. The usual diagnosis and treatment begin with the curing shaman drinking *natema*, tobacco juice, and *piripiri* in the late afternoon and early evening. These drugs permit him to see into the body of the patient as though it were glass. If the illness is due to sorcery, the curing shaman will see the intruding object within the patient's body clearly enough to determine whether or not he can cure the sickness.

A shaman sucks magical darts from a patient's body only at night, and in a dark area of the house, for it is only in the dark that he can perceive the drug-induced visions that are the supernatural reality. With the setting of the sun, he alerts his *tsentsak* by whistling the tune of the curing song; after about a quarter of an hour, he starts singing. When he is ready to suck, the shaman regurgitates two *tsentsak* into the sides of his throat and mouth. These must be identical to the one he has seen in the patient's body. He holds one of these in the front of the mouth and the other in the rear. They are expected to catch the supernatural aspect of the magical dart that the shaman sucks out of the patient's body. The *tsentsak* nearest the shaman's lips is supposed to incorporate the sucked-out *tsentsak* essence within itself. If, however, this supernatural essence should get past it, the second magical dart in the mouth blocks the throat so that the intruder cannot enter the interior of the shaman's body. If the curer's two *tsentsak* were to fail to catch the supernatural essence of the *tsentsak*, it would pass down into the shaman's stomach and kill him. Trapped thus within the mouth, this essence is shortly caught by, and incorporated into, the material substance of one of the curing shaman's *tsentsak*. He then "vomits" out this object and displays it to the patient and his family saying, "Now I have sucked it out. Here it is."

The non-shamans think that the material object itself is what has been sucked out, and the shaman does not disillusion them. At the same time, he is not lying, because he knows that the only important thing about a *tsentsak* is its supernatural aspect, or essence, which he sincerely believes he has removed from the patient's body. To explain to the layman that he already had these objects in his mouth would serve no fruitful purpose and would prevent him from displaying such an object as proof that he had effected the cure. Without incontrovertible evidence, he would not be able to convince the patient and his family that he had effected the cure and must be paid.

The ability of the shaman to suck depends largely upon the quantity and strength of his own *tsentsak*, of which he may have hundreds. His magical darts assume their supernatural aspect as spirit helpers when he is under the influence of *natema*, and he sees them as a variety of zoomorphic forms hovering over him, perching on his shoulders, and sticking out of his skin. He sees them helping to suck the patient's body. He must drink tobacco juice every few hours to "keep them fed" so that they will not leave him.

The curing shaman must also deal with any *pasuk* that may be in the patient's vicinity for the purpose of casting more darts. He drinks additional amounts of *natema* in order to see them and engages in *tsentsak* duels with them if they are present. While the *pasuk* is enclosed in iron armor, the shaman himself has his own armor composed of his many *tsentsak*. As long as he is under the influence of *natema*, these magical darts cover his body as a protective shield, and are on the lookout for any enemy *tsentsak* headed toward their master. When these *tsentsak* see such a missile coming, they immediately close up together at the point where the enemy dart is attempting to penetrate, and thereby repel it.

If the curer finds *tsentsak* entering the body of his patient after he has killed *pasuk*, he suspects the presence of a *wakani* bird. The shaman drinks *maikua* (*Datura* sp.), an hallucinogen even more powerful than *natema*, as well as tobacco juice, and silently sneaks into the forest to hunt and kill the bird with *tsentsak*. When he succeeds, the curer returns to the patient's home, blows all over the house to get rid of the "atmosphere" created by the numerous *tsentsak* sent by the bird, and completes his sucking of the patient. Even after all the *tsentsak* are extracted, the shaman may remain another night at the house to suck out any "dirtiness" (*pahuri*) still inside. In the cures which I have witnessed, this sucking is a most noisy process, accompanied by deep, but dry, vomiting.

After sucking out a *tsentsak*, the shaman puts it into a little container. He does not swallow it because it is not his own magical dart and would therefore kill him. Later, he throws the *tsentsak* into the air, and it flies back to the shaman who sent it originally into the patient. *Tsentsak* also fly back to a shaman at the death of a former apprentice who had originally received them from him. Besides receiving "old" magical darts unexpectedly in this manner, the shaman may have *tsentsak* thrown at him by a bewitcher. Accordingly, shamans constantly drink tobacco juice at all hours of the day and night. Although the tobacco juice is not truly hallucinogenic, it produces a narcotized state, which is believed necessary to keep one's *tsentsak* ready to repel any other magical darts. A shaman does not even dare go for a walk without taking along the green tobacco leaves with which he prepares the juice that keeps his spirit helpers alert. Less frequently, but regularly, he must drink *natema* for the same purpose and to keep in touch with the supernatural reality.

While curing under the influence of *natema,* the curing shaman "sees" the shaman who bewitched his patient. Generally, he can recognize the person, unless it is a shaman who lives far away or in another tribe. The patient's family knows this, and demands to be told the identity of the bewitcher, particularly if the sick person dies. At one curing session I attended, the shaman could not identify the person he had seen in his vision. The brother of the dead man then accused the shaman himself of being responsible. Under such pressure, there is a strong tendency for the curing shaman to attribute each case to a particular bewitcher.

Shamans gradually become weak and must purchase *tsentsak* again and again. Curers tend to become weak in power, especially after curing a patient bewitched by a shaman who has recently received a new supply of magical darts. Thus, the most powerful shamans are those who can repeatedly purchase new supplies of *tsentsak* from other shamans.

Shamans can take back *tsentsak* from others to whom they have previously given them. To accomplish this, the shaman drinks *natema,* and, using his *tsentsak,* creates a "bridge" in the form of a rainbow between himself and the other shaman. Then he shoots a *tsentsak* along this rainbow. This strikes the ground beside the other shaman with an explosion and flash likened to a lightning bolt. The purpose of this is to surprise the other shaman so that he temporarily forgets to maintain his guard over his magical darts, thus permitting the other shaman to suck them back along the rainbow. A shaman who has had his *tsentsak* taken away in this manner will discover that "nothing happens" when he drinks *natema.* The sudden loss of his *tsentsak* will tend to make him ill, but ordinarily the illness is not fatal unless a bewitcher shoots a magical dart into him while he is in this weakened condition. If he has not become disillusioned by his experience, he can again purchase *tsentsak* from some other shaman and resume his calling. Fortunately for anthropology some of these men have chosen to give up shamanism and therefore can be persuaded to reveal their knowledge, no longer having a vested interest in the profession. This divulgence, however, does not serve as a significant threat to practitioners, for words alone can never adequately convey the realities of shamanism. These can only be approached with the aid of *natema,* the chemical door to the invisible world of the Jívaro shaman.

Although the author has centered his article on medicine, it is clear that the "medicine men" are functionally similar to the shamans described by Melatti and Harner. That is, they cure and can also cause sickness, and they maintain a relationship with supernaturals. With this third account of how one becomes a shaman, it would appear that there is a tendency, at least, for shamanism to be arrived at by a combination of apprenticeship and supernatural experience. Among the Cashinahua, however, the functions of the shaman are more specialized, so that there is an herbalist who does not require any supernatural aid in practicing his profession. He cures but cannot cause illness. On the other hand, there is the shaman who also cures, but is solely involved with the supernatural realm.

The Cashinahua medicine men are specialized in more than function and method; they are also more specialized in the source of knowledge than are either the Jívaro or the Krahó, assuming Melatti is correct in assuming some sort of apprenticeship in this latter group. The Cashinahua herbalist learns his skills entirely from mundane sources without supernatural intervention, whereas the shaman learns his techniques entirely from extramundane sources—the spirits. Dealing with the realm of medicine, Kensinger refers to a point also mentioned by both Harner and Melatti, but frequently neglected by ethnographers, namely the area of popular medicine shared by all or most members of a group, in contrast to the specialist's knowledge that must be acquired by special training or experience.

26 KENNETH M. KENSINGER

Cashinahua Medicine and Medicine Men

Medicine, *dau*, is an important domain in both the thought and behavior of the Cashinahua. This paper summarizes my data on this domain, focusing primarily on the medical specialists.[1]

The Cashinahua are a Panoan-speaking tribe living along the Curanja and Purus rivers of southeastern Peru. Approximately 400 people are distributed among seven villages ranging in size from 22 to 98 persons. Each village is politically, socially, and economically autonomous. Although contact between villages is sporadic, the Cashinahua consider themselves to be a single society, bound together by a common ethnic identity, *huni kuin* "real men," by a common language, *hancha kuin* "real words," by patrilineal moieties, and by extension of kinship terminology to include all persons who are *huni kuin*. The patrimoieties regulate marriage, naming, and ceremonial activities. Each village ideally is composed of two patrilines bound in a symmetrical marriage alliance. In reality, they consist of two matrilocally extended families, bound by affinity and consanguinity, plus assorted hangers-on. Kinship terminology is of the Dravidian type. Hunting and slash-and-burn

This article was written especially for this book.

horticulture are the basis of subsistence. Fishing and gathering provide variety to the diet.

The Cashinahua distinguish two major categories of medicine, *dau bata* "sweet medicine," and *dau muka* "bitter medicine." Each type is distinguished from the other by the manner in which a practitioner becomes a full-fledged specialist, his methods and materials, as well as the social values attached to his role.

Dau bata is associated with the role *huni dauya*, literally "man medicine-with," often also called *huni bata dauya* "the man with sweet medicine." It consists of herbal remedies which either grow wild in the jungle or, less frequently, are grown in the gardens. Glands and glandular excretions of some animals are also classed as *dau bata*. Most faunal medicines are used as charms, and all such medicines are connected to rituals. Also included in this category are the ornaments worn for rituals and festive occasions. Although this subclass of medicine is known and made by all post-initiate members of the society, the *huni dauya* is the recognized authority on this medicine.

Muka dau "bitter medicine" is an ill-defined spiritual quality possessed by the *huni mukaya*, literally "man bitter with," which is obtained from the spirits during the process of becoming a specialist. Some informants claim that there are different varieties of *muka* depending on the spirits from which it is obtained, and that each variety is used for a different kind of treatment. Most informants argue that *muka* is *muka*, but when pressed about it, quickly said that they did not know much, if anything, about the subject.

THE *HUNI DAUYA*

The *huni dauya* is essentially an herbalist. He is qualified to treat two types of disease: (1) those which the patient "has" *haya*, including fungi, swellings, sores, dysentery, boils, etc.; and (2) those which the patient "feels" *tenei*, or "is," such as pain, nausea, laziness, sleeplessness, failure in hunting, anger, selfishness, and feelings of personal inadequacy. In general both types of disease are thought to be of natural origin (very few informants ever told me that these diseases were due to supernatural causes even though speculation about supernatural causes is very frequent when illness occurs.)

Each symptom is thought to be a separate illness and is given a separate name which describes either the appearance of the ailment, the physical sensation it produces, its location, or the natural causative agent. What Western medicine considers a single disease exhibiting various symptoms is thought by the Cashinahua to be not a single disease but several diseases occurring simultaneously. For example, the fever, chills, dizziness, and nausea which accompany malaria are four different diseases each of which must be treated separately because each may occur in combination with other symptoms at other times. Thus, nausea, whenever it occurs, requires the use of the same medicines no matter what other symptoms are present.

For each disease (symptom) there is a single medicine or class of medicines used as treatment. Each is named, the name reflecting the nature of the disease for which it is a cure, or some particular physical or therapeutic characteristic of the herb itself. Some herbs are disease specific, but most are used for more general treatment.

All Cashinahua adults know (or, as they say, have) some medicine much as most Americans know simple first aid. This does not make them herbalists who are recognized as particularly knowledgeable specialists who are consulted in cases where "first aid" fails to produce a cure.

In general any man or woman may become an herbalist,[2] if he demonstrates sufficient interest, ability, and willingness to work for a long period of time under an older specialist, and manifests a sincere desire to be helpful to the society in general. Medical knowledge is generally passed on from father to son or father-in-law to son-in-law, mother to daughter or mother-in-law to daughter-in-law. The herbalist-to-be apprentices himself to an older herbalist who takes him into the forest and teaches him the skills while gathering the herbs needed for treatment of a disease. He first learns the names, appearance, and location of all medicinal materials and the diseases against which they are effective. Secondly, he is taught how to diagnose diseases. He then begins to practice his skills under the watchful eye of his mentor.

The herbalist rarely treats the patient personally. When his services are requested, he goes to the jungle, gathers the appropriate herbs and upon returning to the village, presents them to the person making the request with instructions for their use. The person requesting the medicine or the patient then gives/takes the treatment in the prescribed fashion.

According to the Cashinahua medicine always works. But where cures do not follow the treatment, the following excuses are given: the medicine was improperly given or taken, the diagnosis was incorrect, or the disease has a supernatural cause and will not respond to normal treatment. The herbalist is not held responsible for the failure to produce a cure or for deaths which may follow treatment. However, if his patients consistently die or fail to improve, his reputation as a curer is weakened or destroyed and he will be consulted with less frequency.

Herbalists are highly valued by the Cashinahua, each community desiring to have a successful, well-trained one residing in the village. At present only two men, who reside in different villages, are recognized as first class herbalists. Members of the other five villages consult these men when their own less skilled herbalists are unable to produce cures. To my knowledge neither of these two men has apprentices at the present time.

THE *HUNI MUKAYA*

The *huni mukaya,* the man with bitter medicine, functions as shaman, diviner, sorcerer and prophet. In the capacity of shaman and diviner he is consulted openly, particularly with reference to sicknesses which fail to respond to the treatment of an herbalist or which exhibit unusual symptoms not generally treated by an herbalist. Such illnesses are thought to be of supernatural origin. Upon request he takes snuff made from locally grown tobacco and goes into a trancelike state. He then runs his hands over the body of the patient who is lying before him in a hammock or on the floor. When aware of the cause of the problem, he either recommends treatment or, if a foreign object is present in the body due to sorcery, he removes it by sucking on the part of the body nearest to its location. Treatment prescribed by the shaman frequently includes herbs which must be obtained through the herbalist and taken along with the obligatory fasting which always follows (and may precede) any treatment by the *huni mukaya.*

In his capacity as sorcerer the *huni mukaya* may be requested by a member of his local community to practice witchcraft against a personal enemy who generally is a person residing in another village or a member of a neighboring tribe. (If the person who is the object of sorcery is a local resident, he will not be a member of the social core of the local group, i.e., he will not be a member of the *huni mukaya's* extended family or the extended family to which it is linked in a marriage alliance.) Such requests are made in utmost secrecy.

In his capacity as prophet, the *huni mukaya,* at the request of the headman of the village, attempts to learn from his spirit familiars either what is happening in other places or will happen at a later date which will affect the members of the village. Such a request is frequently made in order to obtain additional information following an *ayahuasca* session. (Any adult male may take *ayahuasca,* a hallucinogen, which is taken in order to learn about events removed in time and/or space) (Der Marderosian, et al. 1970; Kensinger 1973). The information gained from these sessions is often incomplete and since the *huni mukaya* is able to communicate with the spirit world without the use of *ayahuasca,* he is requested to get additional details.

Informants are unclear about the manner in which *muka* is used. Most informants however are agreed that a person who has *muka* has power to influence the supernaturals to do his bidding. Unlike the herbalist who learns his trade from a successful and accomplished practitioner, the shaman learns his art from the spirit beings who give him *muka.*

Any person, male or female, with a propensity for dreaming may become a shaman. The Cashinahua believes that dreams occur when a person's *nama yuxin* "dream spirit," one of his five personal spirits, leaves his body during sleep. The dream is thought to be the actual activity of his dream spirit while absent from the body. A person desiring to become a shaman "pursues dreams," that is, he takes whatever steps are necessary to maximize the number of dreams he will have in any night. My informants were very indefinite about how such steps were taken, emphasizing rather, the results of excessive dreaming. The person in pursuit of spirits and of *muka* becomes listless, somewhat withdrawn from the other members of his society, loses his appetite, expresses his disinterest in sexual matters, both verbally and physically, and becomes unsuccessful at hunting. This last, according to the informants, is due to the fact that when the person goes hunting, the animals try to talk to him and treat him as a friend, therefore, he is unable to shoot them. He wanders about the village and into the jungle as if in a daze, and after an indefinite period of time he is "seized" by the spirits and falls to the ground unconscious or in a trancelike state. This is the point at which he receives *muka* from the spirits. After regaining consciousness or recovering from the trancelike state, he requests from the herbalist spirit medicine with which he bathes his body in order to avoid further seizures. Some shamans become unconscious or go into an involuntary trancelike state after the initial experience and are said to obtain additional *muka* with each new occurrence. The shaman does not lose any of his *muka* either through using it for a client or through failure to practice his art. He may lose some or all of his *muka*, however, while dreaming, when spirits with whom he is not familiar or spirits working at the behest of another shaman steal it from him.

Persons who dream a lot but do not wish to become shamans request medicines from the herbalist to calm their dream-spirit and to prevent it from becoming friendly with other spirits.

The degree of success and thus power of the shaman is directly related to the number and variety of spirit beings with whom he is familiar. Lack of success by the shaman is credited to either his not having sufficient *muka* or to the overpowering strength of spirit forces hostile to the shaman.

The Cashinahua are very ambivalent about shamans and shamanism. A *huni mukaya* who practices his art for the benefit of his community is highly valued. However, his presence in the community constitutes a continual threat to the other members of the group, in that wherever and whenever a shaman is present, the number of spirits, both friendly and hostile, is considerably increased. In addition, deaths which are diagnosed as being caused by sorcery may be avenged by the kinsmen of the deceased who may kill either the shaman or any of his close kinsmen.

At present I know of no powerful shamans practicing among the Cashinahua. Several informants claimed that one man had a little *muka*, but when I asked him about it, he hesitatingly admitted that at one time he had some; but claimed that he has lost it. At least, he does not at present seem to be practicing the art. The last powerful male shaman died about 1950 or 1951, and a woman known as "a little shaman" died in 1964. During the summer of 1966, none of the Cashinahua were actively trying to become a shaman, rather, two men were taking medicine to avoid becoming one. Both insisted that the process was dangerous and inconvenient; it interfered with or negatively affected their skill as hunters.

CONCLUSION

Although both systems of medicine have been affected by the increased contact with outsiders during the last three decades, the *huni dauya* has been more fortunate than the *huni mukaya*. Although neither system proved adequate in the face of the influx of new diseases resulting from contact, the medicine of the *huni dauya* continues to produce cures for many diseases. In addition, his pharmacopoeia has been expanded by the addition of Western medicines obtained from traders and missionaries. On the other hand, given the general ambivalence of the Cashinahua toward *muka dau* and the absolute failure of the last powerful *huni mukaya* to deal with disease brought into the village by traders (he died in an epidemic he failed to halt), there has been a serious decline of interest in the role. All informants agreed, however, that the absence of any *huni mukaya* seriously jeopardizes the health of the tribe, since only a *huni mukaya* has the power to deal with the spirits with relative safety.

NOTES

1. Most of these data were obtained between May and August 1966 when I was working as an apprentice to Inkamatsi, the principal herbalist in the village of Xumuya. Additional data were gathered during 82 months of field work in 1955–63. The 1966 study was supported by a grant from the Joint Committee for Latin American Studies of the Social Science Research Council and the American Council of Learned Societies. An earlier version of this paper was read at the 1969 Northeastern Anthropological Association meeting in Providence, Rhode Island. I have greatly benefited from the criticisms and comments of Luis S. Kemnitzer, Bette Landman, Elmer S. Miller, Patricia J. Lyon, Paula Wineberg Sabloff and John Szwed, none of whom is responsible for any deficiencies.

2. Since I was unable to obtain data about female specialists, the present descriptions refer only to males, although my informants told me that the same rules apply for females.

With the Kogi, we turn to another type of religious practitioner, the priest, who is the holder and interpreter of the group cosmology. We also turn to another aspect of relationship with the supernatural, the treatment of the dead. William Carter in his fine article on Aymara death ritual discusses the difficulty of studying death rituals (1968:238–239). It is obvious that if the ethnographer is to describe such a ritual someone must die during the period of study. Not only must there be a death but the investigator must be in a proper position to be allowed to observe all the attendant activities. The failure of these two factors to coincide with great frequency may well explain much of our lack of knowledge of the details and meaning of funeral practices. For example, Clastres, whose article follows, was unfortunate enough to be temporarily absent from the Guayaki settlement when the last cannibal meal was carried out. It would be unusual, except in the case of some sort of calamity, for more than one or two deaths to occur in a small group during the more or less standard one year period that the ethnographer spends on a study. Thus, large bodies of comparative material are simply not available from any one group. It is, nonetheless, quite possible to use a single occurrence of a rite to very good advantage as Carter did and as is demonstrated in the present article.

It is unfortunate that the work of Gerardo Reichel-Dolmatoff on South American religion had to await the publication of his latest work to achieve general recognition (cf. Reichel-Dolmatoff 1968 or 1971). Perhaps due to the limited number of copies published (500), the second volume of his work on the Kogi which deals essentially with the belief system of the Kogi (1951b), was largely overlooked. It is, however, unfortunately true that works published in South America and in Spanish or Portuguese frequently fail to have the impact on the anthropological world that they should. In fact, in the English-speaking world (of anthropology), any work not published in English is likely to find itself doomed to obscurity until, if ever, it is translated into English.

The present article is a summary of Kogi cosmological thought, and anyone wishing to probe further into this fascinating and complex belief system should make an effort to secure a copy of the more extensive work referred to above. This earlier work becomes even more significant in view of the striking parallels between Kogi and Desana cosmology.

The author's final comments on potential changes in Kogi philosophy are of considerable interest. It would appear, from the timing of such incipient changes, that they were triggered by problems of acculturation brought on by increasing outside pressure within the traditional Kogi domain. We can observe similar philosophical adjustments on the part of other groups. For example, the Kadiwéu origin myth shows slight but significant alteration to accommodate to the change from being the dominant group in the area to being a despised minority confined to a reservation (D. Ribeiro 1950:21–33). Weiss mentions the Campa explanation of their technological inferiority to Caucasians, and we have seen how the southern Quechua have accommodated their view of the universe to include the Christian deities, as have the Yaruro to a lesser extent. Many examples of such accommodation are to be found in the South American Indian literature.

As noted, we have little good data on the intellectual basis for burial customs. Most ethnographies describe burial, but few explain why what is done is done. The following two articles also deal with the disposal of the dead, though from different points of view.

27 GERARDO REICHEL-DOLMATOFF

Funerary Customs and Religious Symbolism Among the Kogi

Near the Caribbean seaboard in the northern lowlands of Colombia rises an isolated mountain massif, the Sierra Nevada de Santa Marta. At the time of the Spanish Conquest, in the early sixteenth century, the foothills and lower valleys of

This English version published by permission of the author. The original Spanish version appeared in Razon y Fabula, no. 1 (Bogota, Universidad de los Andes; 1967), pp. 55–72. Copyright © by Gerardo Reichel-Dolmatoff. This article was translated and revised by the author.

these mountains were occupied by the Tairona Indians, a native tribe which had reached a level of cultural complexity equal, if not superior, to the Muisca culture of the Andean highlands of the interior. At the present time there still remain several thousand Indians who are descendants of the Tairona and who continue to live in relative isolation in the cool uplands of the Sierra Nevada. There are three tribes, all of them speaking dialects of the ancient Chibcha language: the *Kogi,* the *Ika,* and the *Sanhá,* numbering about 6,000 individuals in all. The Kogi are still very little acculturated and occupy mainly the northern slopes of the Sierra Nevada, but some groups live on the western and eastern slopes, in close vicinity to the Ika and the Sanhá whose tribal territories cover rather the southern and southeastern slopes.[1]

Although these three tribes present marked physical and linguistic differences, they all share many cultural traits which form part of a common tradition, and the Sierra Nevada thus represents a single cultural area. The Ika and Sanhá are considerably more acculturated than the Kogi, especially in their economic activities, and they look with contempt upon the Kogi whose fields, houses, and general subsistence level they consider to be very deficient. However, in everything concerning the religious sphere, the Ika and Sanhá recognize quite openly the superiority of the Kogi. As a matter of fact, the religious system of the Ika and Sanhá is, in essence, a less elaborate variant of Kogi religion and to the former the Kogi are, and always have been, the possessors of a body of esoteric knowledge which is extremely important to *all* tribes of the Sierra Nevada. This dependence manifests itself in the fact that the other two tribes will approach the Kogi to consult them on religious matters or to ask them to officiate on a variety of ceremonial occasions.

The Kogi, on the other hand, certain of possessing the secrets of the "true" religion, assume in front of their neighbors the attitude of benevolent "elder brothers" of mankind and are, therefore, obligated to propagate the true faith and to teach their "younger brothers," the Ika and Sanhá. It therefore quite frequently happens that the Kogi visit the villages of the neighboring tribes in order to take a leading part in their religious activities.

In all three tribes the men who are specialists in the interpretation, transmission, and execution of religious principles, are designated by the term *máma* and generally they are old men who have spent many years of apprenticeship at the side of a specialist of high reputation. These men are not shamans or curers, but constitute a class of tribal priests who are highly respected. The *mámas* of the Kogi enjoy very high prestige all over the Sierra Nevada because they are said to have a very profound knowledge of the tribal traditions and, in particular, of the rituals which are necessary to guarantee the order of the universe. Thanks to the *mámas* of the Kogi the sun follows his daily round; the seasons change in an orderly fashion, and the great principle of fertility, central to all religious thought, continues to manifest itself in nature as well as in all living creatures. The *mámas* celebrate the various rituals of the individual's life cycle, and also officiate at the collective ceremonials, the dances, offerings, and other occasions.

In the present paper I shall refer to one of these ritual occasions, specifically to a burial rite, which I was able to attend during recent fieldwork in the Sierra Nevada. The ritual took place in the village of *Seráncua,* a small Ika settlement on the headwaters of the Cataca River. Seráncua is only a few hours from *Mamaróngo,* a major ceremonial center of the Kogi, and the Ika living in the surroundings are therefore strongly influenced by their neighbors.

The Ika of Seráncua had invited a Kogi priest from Mamaróngo to officiate in some minor rituals such as the purification of several houses and the preparation of collective offerings. On the first day of the priest's arrival there occurred an incident which was very characteristic of Ika-Kogi relationships. As soon as the *máma* arrived the Ika hurriedly took several sick people to the house where he was staying and asked him to cure them. There was a man who had a spell of fever, a woman who suffered from hemorrhages, and another man who had broken an arm. The *máma* looked stoically at the sick. After a while he said slowly: "I do not know how to cure the fever; I do not know how to stop bleeding. Neither do I know how to set broken bones. All I know is to talk to god." He said these words in a quite superior and ironic manner as, obviously, he felt somewhat offended by the fact that the Ika were taking him for a simple curer, he being a high-ranking priest. Having thus made clear his status, he was treated from then on with great respect. At nightfall he joined the men who had gathered in the ceremonial house, where he spoke to them in a low voice, advising them on how to prepare their offerings and inquiring discreetly into village affairs, always with great patience and with a faint smile of tolerant ennui.

During these days a young unmarried Ika woman had died. When news of her death became known in the village, the *máma* gave orders to prepare more offerings and gave notice to the family of the dead girl that, in the afternoon, he would officiate at the burial.

The cemetery was located on a hill slope, about 200 meters to the south of the village. The ground was covered with high grass and there were several irregular stones, half buried in the soil, marking the individual graves. At a short distance there was underbrush and then the forest began, but on the burial ground itself no trees were growing. On the day of the burial the following people gathered at the cemetery: the Kogi priest, the local Ika priest, the parents and the maternal grandmother of the dead woman and three maternal cousins of the woman's father. After discussing for a while in low voices the best location for the burial pit, the Ika priest walked away from the group toward the east and then sat facing toward the west. He now concentrated in order to divine the precise spot for the burial. Chewing coca leaves and watching the clouds on the western horizon he sat in silence for about half an hour. Meanwhile the Kogi priest sat down next to me and said: "The Ika are our younger brothers. They don't quite know yet how to bury their dead," and then, looking around at the others, he added: "I have to teach our younger brothers; such is the law."

Now the ritual was beginning. The Kogi priest stood facing toward the east and, with a mute gesture, delimited before him a small stretch of ground, perhaps one meter square; he ordered the men to clear the ground and, with their bush-knives, they now cut the grass and scraped the soil, cleaning it of roots and pebbles. Then the men stepped back and the priest took several dry coca leaves from his bag and, holding some leaves in each hand close to his chest, stepped into the middle of the space which had been cleared. He then turned toward the south and slowly moved his hands, always close to the chest, as if weighing the leaves, sometimes lifting the right hand, sometimes the left. After a minute or so he turned to face the north and repeated the movements of the hands, again starting with the left hand in a slightly lower position, lifting it up higher until the right hand was lower. Then he turned toward the east and, standing at the western edge of the space, pulverized the dry leaves between his fingers and let the dust fall to the ground, first from the left hand and then from the right. While doing this he said: "This is the village of Death; this is the ceremonial house of Death; this is the house of Death; this is the uterus. I am going to open the house. The house is closed and I shall open it." He now took from his bag a small wooden spade and with it picked up some earth from the eastern side; turning to the left he deposited the soil on the western side. There he picked up soil and, turning again, put it on the eastern side. Then he picked up soil from the south and placed it on the north where, again, he picked up soil and deposited it in the south. He now said: "The house is open," and ordered the men to start digging. At this moment the Ika priest changed his position; walking toward the west he passed by the group of people and sat down again, this time turning his back to us. The men worked in silence, digging a round hole. When they had reached a depth of about 50 cm. the priest ordered the dead woman's father and another man to bring the corpse which was lying in front of the ceremonial house in the village. While the other men continued to dig, the two descended to the village and soon returned with the corpse which was wrapped in a large carrying net. They deposited their burden at the southern edge of the pit and now the dead woman's parents began to prepare the body under the supervision of the priest. The deceased had been dressed in a white cotton garment of the kind unmarried girls wear and had been tied with ropes into a flexed position, with the knees drawn up to the chest and the hands touching the chin. After having taken the corpse out of the carrying net, the father pressed down the eyelids of the dead girl, to make sure they were closed. He then placed the body on a large piece of white cotton cloth and began to wrap it beginning at the feet. The girl's mother had brought with her two skeins of whitish sisal fibers and the father took one of them and twisted a long string. With a bone needle the mother had brought, he now sewed up the corpse, beginning at the feet and forming, eventually, a compact bundle. When he came to the head he took the remaining skein of fibers and twisted from them a stout rope of more than one meter length, one end of which he tied firmly to the hair on top of the head of the corpse. He then continued to sew the cloth until he covered the head also. Then, with the help of the other men, the father placed the body into the carrying net again, tying it firmly into a bundle and fixing to it a loop of rope to serve as a handle.

While the men were thus busy with the corpse, the mother and the grandmother who were sitting nearby began to intone a slow dirge, a long-drawn wailing song without words. From their carrying bags they took some small bundles of dry maize leaves which they opened and from which they extracted a few small marine shells, some of them of conical gastropods. Holding the shells in their hands they addressed them in low voices saying that they were "food for the dead." They then gave the shells to the men who placed them into the folds of the carrying net which held the corpse.

The *máma* stood now at the northern edge of the burial pit and, with deliberately slow movements, took off his cap, then his two carrying bags, and lastly the small bag of coca leaves he had been wearing. Taking once more some dry leaves in both hands he repeated the gestures of "weighing" the content of each hand, lifting or lowering one hand or the other. He then scattered the dry leaves over the bottom of the pit which, by now, was about one meter deep. Taking from one of the bags several small bundles of leaves, he stepped into the pit and slowly untied the little packages of dry maize leaves. Extracting from them some pulverized stones, seeds, and cotton fibers he deposited these in the center of the bottom. Stepping out of the pit again the *máma* now approached the corpse. There was a moment of great tension; everybody looked at him watching anxiously every gesture, every expression on his face. Standing with his feet well apart, planted firmly on the ground, as if preparing himself to lift up a heavy weight the *máma* bent over and grasped the rope handle with both hands, trying to lift the corpse. By his bodily position as well as by his facial expression he made it understood that he was making a great effort and that the corpse was very heavy. As a matter of fact, it seemed that he could hardly lift it from the ground; he lowered the corpse again and looked around at the others with a gesture of impotence, of doubt. After a short while he stooped again and tried to lift the carrying net but soon he straightened again, giving the impression that his strength had failed him. There followed long minutes of anxious silence. At the third attempt the *máma* pretended that the corpse was somewhat less heavy then before. He smiled and, looking at the others as if to encourage them, he bent down again to lift the corpse. Nine times this act was repeated and each time the *máma* made it understood that the corpse was becoming lighter and lighter. At the ninth time, smiling, he picked up the corpse as if it was almost weightless, as if it were something small and light. People looked at each other with relief. The *máma* placed the corpse carefully on the ground and walked to the other side of the pit. After throwing a few coca leaves into it he directed the father to place the corpse in the pit, lying on its left side and with the head toward the east. The father now went to the underbrush and soon returned with an armload of green fern leaves which he spread carefully over the corpse. The *máma* now ordered the men to fill the pit with earth, but when it was half full he interrupted them in their work and took from his bag five small bundles the contents of which he placed in the pit at the four cardinal points. There were some very small stones, some seeds, and some white cotton. The contents of the fifth bundle he placed in the middle of the pit, directly on top of the corpse.

During the entire process of filling in the grave care had been taken not to bury the rope which was tied to the dead woman's hair, and the *máma* often reminded the men not to lose sight of it and to keep it taut. When finally the pit was completely filled in the *máma* asked one of the men to bring a thin rod, about 80 cm. long. The father now tied the free end of the rope to this stick which he pushed vertically into the soft soil while twisting the remaining rope loosely around it. In the meantime the other men had brought a heavy stone which they placed over the pit, next to the rod. Then the men stepped back while the *máma* placed the contents of another leaf bundle at the foot of the rod. He then again took his little spade and now "closed" the grave, this time in the inverse order, by carrying earth from south to north, north to south, west to east and east to west.

The *máma* now called the parents of the dead woman and asked them to stand in front of him, at the western side of the grave. He said to them: "Turn around completely to the left." The two did as told. "Now turn around completely to the right," he continued. The two turned rapidly and the *máma* said: "Now go away while turning left." The couple began to descend the slope, turning and turning until, after a while, they continued to walk toward the village. Then the others passed before the *máma*, turning first to the left, then to the right. "Get going, get going!" the *máma* said. When all had left he walked back to the grave and stood facing toward the east. Very slowly he turned to the right and then, three times, to the left. With the last turn he started to walk downhill, always turning, until the burial ground was far behind. While all those who had touched the corpse now went to a nearby creek to wash their hands and arms and to clean their bush-knives, the *máma* went directly to his house.

Nine days later, ·the *máma*, followed by the dead woman's parents, returned to the burial ground. The *máma* grasped the end of the rope which was tied to the rod and pulled at it, lightly first, then more strongly. The fibers were already rotten and when suddenly the rope broke, they all smiled and nodded and returned to the village.

The burial rite I have described so far lasted approximately two hours and was carried out in almost complete silence. Except for the women's dirge only the *máma* had spoken a few times, but there had been no prayers, nor chants; only a few short indications given to the men who were digging the grave, and to the parents as they prepared the corpse. However, it was a ritual in which every phase, every step, had been carried out with great precision.

A casual observer could easily think that this was a very simple rite and he might deduce, from what he had seen, that the burial rites of these Indians were limited to a few quite elementary practices. Worse still would be the conclusions of an archaeologist who, at some future time, in digging up this grave would find nothing more than a simple pit, with a flexed skeleton facing east. But perhaps both—our casual observer and the imaginary archaeologist of the future—would be very much mistaken. As a matter of fact, behind this apparently very simple ritual I have described there exist complex ideas and there lie religious and philosophic concepts of unusual interest.

I shall try now to isolate the different components of the ritual, to identify and analyze them, in order to appreciate their function within the wider context of Kogi culture.

In the first place, I shall list the symbolic elements which were observed during the burial. This list is the following:

1. Verbalization of the cemetery as the "village of Death" and as the "ceremonial house of Death"; verbalization of the burial pit as a "house" and as a "uterus."

2. Flexed position of the corpse, placed in a carrying net, with a rope tied to the hair.

3. Corpse resting on the left side and with the head oriented toward the east.

4. Marked emphasis on right and left: position of hands; position of the corpse; left turns and right turns.

5. Placing of offerings at the sides, the center and the top of the burial pit.

6. Verbalization of the offerings as "food for the dead."

7. Attitude of "opening" and "closing the house."

8. Purification by turning.

Let us see now to what extent these diverse symbolic acts are related to the cosmogonic and socio-religious concepts of Kogi culture.

Underlying many forms of thought and action among the Indians of the Sierra Nevada is a concept of dualism which expresses itself on many different levels. On the level of the individual as a biological being, it is the human body which provides the model formed by the concept of opposed but complementary principles. It is the apparent bilateral symmetry of the body and the sexual differences, which provide the norm. On another level, that of the social group, we find another dualistic division, this time between "people from above" and "people from below," terms which do not refer to altitudinal differences in the habitat of certain groups living on the mountain slopes, but which express the existence of groups of opposed but complementary segments of society. The villages themselves are divided into two parts and the dividing line, invisible but known to all, separates the village into two sectors. The ceremonial houses, too, are imagined as being divided into two halves, each with its own central post—male and female—and with a dividing line running diametrically between the two doors and separating the circle of the ground plan into a "right side" and a "left side." On a cosmic level, the same division separates the universe into two sides, determined by the sun, which, going from east to west, divides the world into a right and a left half. The dualistic elaborations of this type are innumerable: male/female, man/woman, right hand/left hand, heat/cold, light/dark, etc., and they are furthermore associated with certain categories of animals, plants, and minerals; with colors, winds, diseases and, of course, with concepts of Good and Evil. These ideas manifest themselves in all religious practices. Of course, many of the dualistic manifestations have the character of symbolic antagonists which, in the final analysis, share a common essence. Just as the tribal deities which, in one single divine being, unite benefic and malevolent aspects, thus man carries within himself this vital polarity of Good and Evil.

The Kogi believe in the existence of a principle of Good (right), the presence and benefic function of which is determined by the simultaneous existence of a principle of Evil (left). In order to guarantee the existence of Good it is necessary to foment Evil because if the latter should disappear—finding no justification for its existence—the principle of Good would disappear as well. It is deemed necessary then that a person should occasionally commit sins which bear witness to the active existence of Evil. It is here where, according to the Kogi, lies the main problem of human existence: in finding a balance between these two opposed but complementary forces and in establishing a harmonic relationship between them. The basic concept is called *yuluka*, a term which might be translated as "to agree," "to be equal." This idea of "agreement," of knowing how to balance the creative and destructive energies on the path of life leading from east to west, is a fundamental principle of human conduct. It is for this reason that the *máma*, by "weighing" in his hands the coca leaves or other ritual objects, first tries to establish this balance, until, at least, the right hand, i.e., the principle of Good, "weighs more."

Beginning with a dualistic concept of complementary opposites, the dimensions broaden now and lead to a structure consisting of four points of reference. This is still a static concept, a bidimensional one, in which, on the horizontal plane, the world is divided into four segments. The paradigmatic model is the four cardinal points: North/South/East/West. Associated with them we find a long series of other concepts, mythical beings, animals, plants, colors and attitudes. In the first place, the mythical ancestors of the first four clans, together with their wives, occupy the four cardinal points: in the North the opossum and his spouse the armadillo; in the South the mountain lion and his spouse the deer; in the East the jaguar with his spouse the peccary, and in the West the eagle and his spouse the snake. As we are dealing here with a system of patri- and matrilines in which descent is reckoned from father to son and from mother to daughter, the relationship of complementary opposites is expressed by the idea that each "male" animal (opossum, mountain lion, jaguar, eagle) feeds on the "female" animal (armadillo, deer, peccary, snake), all ancestral couples forming antagonistic pairs. Then follow certain color associations: North-blue, South-red, East-white, and West-black. On the other hand, the color red (South) is classified as a "light" color and forms, together with the color white (East) a "good side," in opposition to an "evil side" formed by the North and the West which have "dark" colors. There are countless other associations with each cardinal point because each clan is, at the same time, the spiritual "master" of certain animals, plants, minerals, atmospheric phenomena, manufactured objects, dances, songs, and other elements.

The four points of the cosmic structure are also found in many microcosmic versions. The world is sustained by four mythical giants; the Sierra Nevada is divided into four sectors; the villages are traditionally constructed with four entrances and, surrounding them, there are four sacred sites where offerings are deposited. The ceremonial houses have a cosmic structure and in their interior there are four hearths around which gather the members of the four principal clans. Besides, in the ceremonial house the line which divides the circle into two segments also divides the men into two antagonistic groups: those of the "right side" (red) where sit the men who "know less" while those of the "left side" (blue) "know more," the latter being closer to the negative forces which dominate the universe.

But a scheme of four points necessarily leads to a fifth—the central point, the point in the middle. The symbolism of the central point is of great importance to the Kogi; it is the center of the universe, it is the Sierra Nevada, it is the central point of the circle of the ceremonial house where the sacred offerings are buried and where the *máma* sits when he wishes to "speak with god." In divinatory practices, the person places on the ground four ritual objects, or groups of objects: stones, seeds, or shells, orienting them toward the cardinal points. But in the center he will place a tiny stool, a little bench carved of stone or of wood. This is his "seat," sitting upon which the essence of his being—a diminutive and invisible replica of his person—receives the answers to the questions the diviner formulates.

The next step in this scheme is a tridimensional system with seven points of reference: North/South/East/West/Zenith/Nadir/ and the Center. The cosmic axis formed by the last three points also has its associations in the form of "masters," animals, and colors. Again, it is a static system of fixed points circumscribing the universe which, according to the Kogi, has the shape of an enormous egg. But now there appears a new concept, this time a dynamic one, formulated in terms of developmental phases: the concept of the nine stages.

The great Mother Goddess was the creator of the universe and of mankind. She had nine daughters and each daughter represents a different kind of agricultural soil: black soil, brown soil, red soil, sandy soil, and others. These soils form a series of horizontal layers within the cosmic egg and symbolize a scale of values. Mankind lives on the fifth layer, the layer of black soil, the "middle layer," while above and below there follow four different layers of soil, four different worlds.

The great cone-shaped mountains of the Sierra Nevada are imagined as "worlds," as houses, with exactly the same structure; and also the ceremonial houses are microcosmic models containing four layers of circular shelves in the interior of their conical roofs. In a negative sense, it is imagined that the structure of these houses continues underground, so that a ceremonial house is a replica of the cosmos, and its center is the "center of the world."

But the associations continue. The universe, the cosmic egg, is interpreted by the Kogi as a uterus, the uterus of the Mother Goddess, within which mankind continues to live. But also our earth is a uterus, the Sierra Nevada is a uterus; every mountain, every ceremonial house, every dwelling and, finally, every tomb is a uterus. Caves and crevices are openings which lead into the body of the Mother Goddess. The huge round roof apices constructed in the shape of funnels, which crown the ceremonial houses, are her sexual organs where offerings are deposited representing a concept of fertilization. These apices are the "doors" which open and connect with the cosmic levels of "above." From the highest point of the interior of the conical roof of the house there hangs a rope which represents the umbilical cord and it is thought that through this cord the *máma*, sitting in the center, establishes contact with the supernatural powers.

We can now understand the symbolism of the burial rite. The dead person returns to the uterus, in a flexed foetal position; wrapped in a carrying net which represents the placenta, and connected with this world by an umbilical cord which is cut after nine days, after which follows rebirth into another world. When the *máma* lifts the corpse nine times, he symbolizes by this action the return to the uterus because he makes the corpse return to an embryonic state by leading it through the nine months of intrauterine gestation. At the same time, the tomb is the cosmos, the world. Offerings are deposited in the seven points of the sacred space: North/South/East/West/Zenith/Nadir/Center, and the head of the corpse is oriented toward the east, the direction where the sun, the light, life itself are reborn every day. The burial rite then was an act of "cosmification."

We must discuss now in more detail the concept of offerings. In their material aspect the offerings consist generally of small stones, seeds, small marine shells, pieces of thread or cotton, or fingernails and hair. All these objects have to be collected in certain spots and under certain circumstances because each supernatural power demands offerings of specific materials, forms or colors. The material is then wrapped into small thin leaves taken from the interior of a dry corncob which are then tied into a tiny bundle with a short piece of fiber or string. In preparing these offerings several symbolic acts have to be performed. In the first place, it is necessary that each offering be identified with the person who performs it. In order to do this, the small bundle is taken into the uplifted left hand and a circular movement is made with it around the head, in order to "extract the evil"; then the same movement is repeated with the right hand to "introduce good." In the second place, in tying or untying the bundle of leaves, a certain order has to be observed. The piece of dry leaf on which the material of the offering is placed has an oblong shape and the two protruding ends represent the North and the South respectively. These two ends are now folded upwards and downwards in such a manner that the southern end comes to lie on top of the northern end. The fibers or threads are now tied from east to west, and when the bundle is being opened in order to deposit its contents on a sacred site, the reverse order has to be followed.

All offerings are meant to be "food" and are verbalized as "food for the dead," it being understood that the category of "the dead" comprises not only the spirits of specific ancestors, but also those of mythical beings, of the "masters" of animals and plants and, of course, of the total concept of "Death." For the Kogi there exists a close relationship between eating and sexual intercourse. In myths, dreams and, as we have seen, in the rules of exogamy, the act of eating symbolizes the sexual act. The contents of the offerings have thus a double significance: they are "food," but at the same time they are a fertilizing matter, they are male semen which impregnates the supernatural personification which, being the anthropomorphic counterpart of a plant or animal, thus maintains its creative and multiplying quality. If, for example, a Kogi makes an offering to the Mother of Maize, she is not only nourished by his offering but is inseminated and will procreate more maize. A third interpretation compares an offering with a uterus, that is, the wrappings represent the placenta, the thread represents the umbilical cord, and the contents of the bundle have an embryonic character. As a matter of fact, on certain occasions the Kogi weave diminutive bags, one or two centimeters in length, which contain offerings and which are directly designated as "little wombs." We can now understand the symbolism of "opening" and "closing" of the homologous series: burial pit/uterus/offering.

I have mentioned that while the women were singing they handled several small sea shells which were deposited with the corpse. In many ritual practices the Kogi employ small marine shells, as offerings or as personal amulets. Bivalves represent the female principle while gastropods represent the male one, and both are offered to the Mother Goddess in order to increase fertility. The little shells, however, which were buried with the corpse represented the surviving members of the girl's family. The largest shell was a gastropod which symbolized a husband for the girl because, if this object were not put into her grave, once in the Beyond she might ask for a husband and thus might cause the death of a young man of the tribe.

I also mentioned the act of turning left and right, when the participants in the ritual left the burial ground. There are several interrelated concepts connected with this act. On the one hand, many religious contacts between the individual and the supernatural powers are conceived of in terms of a union which is established by a connecting thread. Also all diseases are "like a thread" which entwines the sick person, and a strong cotton thread tied around the wrists or the ankles hinders the entrance of diseases to the body. On the other hand, many sacred songs are thought of in terms of "threads" which connect the singer with the deity to which he addresses his song. One must untie these threads in order to avoid evil influences, or one must tie oneself firmly to those forces which are benevolent. When turning around next to the burial pit, the person unties the thread of Death and, at the same time, forms a cosmic axis. It is also thought that when turning rapidly several times one becomes invisible to Death. Turning rapidly "one does not see" and, therefore, "one cannot be seen." When walking away from the cemetery, turning and turning on their axis, people free themselves from the invisible threads of contagion and, besides, become invisible and invulnerable.

I also mentioned that nine days after the burial the *máma* demonstrated that the rope which was tied to the hair of the corpse was broken. The nine days represent again the nine months of gestation and the rupture of the rope symbolizes the cutting of the umbilical cord at birth. According to the Kogi, the soul of the dead wanders for nine days and nine nights on the dangerous trail which leads to the Beyond where, upon its arrival, the dead are reborn. But not all connections with the world of the living are severed; through the offerings the dead continue to participate in the nutritional and sexual spheres of the living, punishing with diseases should they not fulfill their duties or rewarding them with the fertility of their crops and families.

In the foregoing analysis of the symbolic elements observed during the burial rite, we have seen that the Kogi conceive the world in terms of a series of points of reference with which they connect categories that are of importance to the individual, to society, to nature, and to the supernatural forces. Starting with a basic principle of dualism, of antagonistic but complementary pairs, the scheme continues to develop into a four-fold structure, bidimensional, and fixed in space. A third dimension is then introduced, formulated in terms of "above" and "below," now containing a central point and being penetrated by an axis. Across this static structure of fixed points there now move the nine developmental stages. This macrocosmic structure is then repeated and reproduced in a series which diminishes in extension and leads to the microcosmic vision, repeating in its different forms the same patterns which control the cosmos. These are binary chains of associations which form a harmonic whole within whose dimensions all phenomena fall into recognizable, manageable categories, and any person who knows the barest outline of cosmogony can readily identify the religious and moral codes he has to obey.

It is surprising then that this great design, so complex but, at the same time, so harmonic and predictable, does not satisfy some of the *mámas* who see in it an oversimplification of human destiny and of the place Man occupies in the Universe.

One might say that the structural concepts, from dualism to the construction of sacred space, are based essentially on the empirical observation of nature. In the first place, it is the human body and the sun which establish the basis of this dichotomy of the division of space and of the successive phases of developmental cycles. But this observation of nature at times lacks precision because occasionally there appear phenomena which are quite unforeseen in the established scheme and which seem to throw doubt on the absolute validity of the cosmic vision and of its human projections.

While the great mass of the people accept the premises and postulates of their traditional religion, the *mámas* are preoccupied by certain facts which seem to point to other possibilities, to other dimensions of being and becoming, and which still escape the established norms. These exceptions are, for example, the left-handedness of some people, a phenomenon which leads to the inversion of "right side" and "left side." Which, then, is the "good side,"—the positive, the vital one? Some cases of hermaphroditism have been observed, of bisexual individuals whose very condition contradicts the clear distinction between a male and a female principle. A child born seven months after conception seems to invalidate the theory of the nine developmental stages of intra-uterine life, and an eclipse of the sun or the moon shows that not even the heavenly bodies always follow the same predictable path. Of course, not all the Indians of the Sierra Nevada have realized the importance these phenomena have for the philosophical basis of their culture, but some of the priests recognize that there do exist problems which do not have an easy explanation.

However, it is not so much the question of *what causes* these phenomena which occupies the priests, but the problem of *how to integrate them* into the established cosmogonic scheme. What is certain is that there exist *other* dimensions, *other* categories which are still unknown, but—who are their "masters"? What are their associations? In which direction do they lead? What ritual or moral attitudes do they imply for the individual and for society?

There is still much doubt and uncertainty, but among some of the tribal priests new ideas are arising. The most disquieting question is the one referring to the directions in which men go toward their final destiny. In the course of his life man follows the path of the sun, from east to west, from birth to death. But after death man must follow other directions, other trails which are determined by his moral conduct on this earth. Those who have been virtuous used to go toward the east or the south while those who had done evil went toward the west or the north. But nowadays, the *mámas* say, the principle of Evil is increasing. The ancient traditions are being forgotten; the old customs are disappearing; theft, lies, and aggressiveness are the rule. In what directions do these sinners go? What will be their destiny? What powers lead them on and make them commit so many sins? Under these circumstances—how can the balance of the Universe be maintained?

The old division of the circle into a cross formed by four cardinal points is now being subdivided and the *mámas* speak of the "in-between ways": northeast, southeast, northwest and southwest. But each one of these segments is now being subdivided into eight "ways of the soul." It is not clear yet where these ways are leading, and who will have to travel on them and why. The priests are trying to divine it and to revise their traditional theories. And—if the horizontal plane contains that many intermediate points and directions, that many new categories and clusters of concepts—how many new points of reference might not be contained in the tridimensional structure of the cosmic egg?

In these preoccupations we can observe the dynamics of a culture in which the apparently rigid premises of a philosophical-religious system are being transformed by the thinking of a few priests who do not conform to the basis established by tradition, but who glimpse new horizons and new dimensions in which human destiny might fulfill itself.

NOTES

1. For more detailed treatment of this area and its inhabitants see Reichel-Dolmatoff 1950, 1951a, 1951b, and 1953.

Perhaps because of our own practices of interment or cremation, we may sometimes forget that there are other ways to dispose of the dead. The following two articles deal with one of the more exotic methods, as well as with one of the most obscure and debated aspects of South American Indian culture—cannibalism, more specifically, endocannibalism. Dole had the opportunity to observe the more common form of endocannibalism, the drinking of the burned and ground up bones of the dead, while Clastres had the only opportunity given to a modern anthropologist to work with a group practicing a much less common form of endocannibalism, consumption of the flesh of the dead. Dole had no opportunity to see Clastres' material, since his fieldwork was done after her article was written. Obviously Clastres never saw her material, or he might have had to modify some of his conclusions. Each author attacks the problem with a different question in mind, but the data are complementary. Although it is possible that some of the data cited by Dole for the existence of flesh endocannibalism may be subject to question, certainly the quantity and quality of the material on the Mayoruna, at least, are sufficient to make it highly unlikely that it was all invented. Osculati's account of the old man's desire to be eaten by his relatives is especially suggestive in the light of Clastres' material. The data assembled by Dole tend to make the dichot-

omy between exo- and endocannibalism suggested by Clastres much less apparent. It is obvious that a thoroughgoing study of all the literature on cannibalism in South America is in order. The probability of acquiring much more first-hand data on flesh cannibalism is very slight, so the concentration must be on published data and more investigation of the philosophical basis for the drinking of the ground bones of the dead.

Dole's effort to establish an evolutionary sequence in the data is interesting but impossible to verify. There is already one article devoted to reversing her order of precedence written by Hans Becher on the basis of his work among the Surára and Pakidái (cf. Becher 1968). A more promising line of inquiry is the function of cannibalism within the culture on both the utilitarian and supernatural levels. It is interesting that, according to Padden's data, the Araucanians, who had never been cannibals, adopted the custom of eating the Spanish and upon occasion not only ate the flesh but also burned and ground up the bones and drank them in wine.

The data presented by Dole and Clastres, as well as other material available in the literature, suggest that cannibalism is not a simple matter at all. It cannot be treated as a contrast between eating the flesh and drinking the ground bones, since there are also cases where only a small portion of a dead person is eaten, as opposed to the entire body. Perhaps too much attention has been centered on the simple fact that it is human beings that are being consumed in one way or another, and not enough on the real purpose and meaning of such practices.

28 GERTRUDE E. DOLE

Endocannibilism Among the Amahuaca Indians

The eating of human flesh by human beings has been extremely widespread. It has apparently been practiced all over the world by peoples on all levels of cultural development.[1]

The purpose and meaning of the practice may differ radically according to the social relation that exists between the body consumed and the person who eats it, that is, according to whether the subject eaten belongs to the in-group or the

Reprinted by permission of the author and publisher from *Transactions of the New York Academy of Sciences*, vol. 24, series 2 (1962), pp. 567–573. © 1962 The New York Academy of Sciences.

All material appearing within square brackets [ ] has been added by the editor of this book.

out-group. Hence, this dichotomy serves as a useful device for classifying the numerous instances of cannibalism. If an enemy or other person outside the local or kin group is eaten, the custom is referred to as "exocannibalism"; the term "endocannibalism" refers to the practice of consuming members of one's own group (Steinmetz 1896:1). Another rare type of cannibalism that has been reported is the eating of one's own flesh. The Iroquoian Indians of New York and Canada are said to have forced prisoners to swallow pieces of their own flesh (Hrdlička 1911:201). This type might be termed "autocannibalism."

For the purpose of the present study both exocannibalism and endocannibalism will be further divided into two types according to whether their functions are biological or supernatural. These two types are (1) gastronomic, in which the subject is eaten for its food value, and (2) ritual or magical, in which the spirit is absorbed.

Gastronomic endocannibalism has occurred in civilized and primitive societies alike, arising out of dire need for food. Scarcity of food has not infrequently forced arctic peoples, for example, to eat members of their own groups. And from the pioneer days of the United States, we recall the Donner Party for the fact that its members resorted to endocannibalism because of hunger.

In contrast to hunger endocannibalism, the ritual type is usually restricted to uncivilized peoples. At the time the great voyages of discovery took place, Europeans had very little acquaintance with cannibalism. When Spanish and French explorers in the Antilles discovered that the Carib (or Caniba) Indians ate their slain enemies and captives, they were horrified and adopted the name of these natives to refer to the practice (Humboldt 1852–1853:v. 3, p. 214; Barcia 1881–1883). The conquistadors and the missionaries who followed them were determined to stamp out this "bestiality" wherever they came across it, and as a result of their tireless efforts the custom has been abandoned by most of those who formerly practiced it. One group in South America that has had very little contact with Whites and has maintained the custom to this day is the Amahuaca of eastern Peru.

The Amahuaca are a very small population of Panoan-speaking Indians who live in very small settlements along the border of southeastern Peru and western Brazil. They depend about equally on hunting and horticulture for their livelihood. Their staple crop is maize, but some sweet manioc and other crops typical of the tropical forest are raised. Amahuaca material culture is exceedingly simple. Steel tools were introduced by pioneers of the rubber and lumbering industries some 70 years ago, but until that time only stone axes and wooden clubs or tortoise-shell hatchets were used to clear the land for gardening.

During recent field work among the Amahuaca a death occurred in a polygynous extended family, and the following is a description of the funerary rites that took place on that occasion.

THE AMAHUACA FUNERARY CEREMONY

An infant died in the night. When this fact was discovered at dawn, the little corpse was flexed and wrapped in its mother's skirt and a blanket. The bundle was firmly bound with bast. The mother of the infant, Yamba Wachi, took the bundle and wailed over it as she sat on the floor of her house. Tears flowed, and her eyes swelled. Occasionally she wiped mucus from her nose.

A grave was prepared immediately in the middle of Yamba Wachi's house floor. It was dug by a young man, Hawachiwa Yamba, who was Yamba Wachi's prospective son-in-law. Except for two young boys, all of the people of the community attended the burial. All the adults sat or stood quietly near Yamba Wachi, while the children roamed in and out of the house at will. When the grave had been dug as deep as Hawachiwa Yamba could reach with his arm, he gently took the bundle from the mother, placed it in one of her cooking pots, and adjusted another pot over it in the grave. He tucked some of Yamba Wachi's palm-leaf mats tightly around the pots in such a way as to prevent dirt from falling into the lower one and pushed loose dirt into the grave to cover the pots.

Then Yamba Wachi searched out and burned a few rags, corncobs, and an old hammock that had been in contact with the baby before its death. Still wailing, she sat down again and with a smooth pebble pounded the surface of the grave lightly with slow even strokes until it was quite even and firm. When this was finished, she swept the dirt floor and threw out the refuse. She then returned to her place beside the grave and continued to wail intermittently throughout the rest of that day and for about ten days thereafter.

One week after the date of burial, the corpse was cremated. Early in the morning Hawachiwa Yamba and four other young men cut a large quantity of very hard dry firewood. They also split Yamba Wachi's grinding trough into long sticks. These sticks and the rest of the firewood were piled up carefully, leaving a depression in the middle for the burial vessels. Hawachiwa Yamba lighted the funeral pyre. He and one of his helpers opened the grave with machetes and removed the two burial pots, taking care not to open them. Nevertheless the odor of decaying flesh escaped as Yamba Wachi took the vessels fondly in her arms and wailed over them, caressing the lower one.

At this point Yamba Wachi's husband, Maxopo, approached her beside the grave, put one hand on the vessels, and began to wail with her. Although he had previously shown no grief, he now generated tears, and mucus dripped from his nose. After a short time Hawachiwa Yamba took the burial pots from Yamba Wachi. He quickly dumped the decaying remains into a third pot in which he had broken a small hole in the base, covered this pot with another, and placed them on the flaming pyre. When they had finished doing this, Maxopo suddenly dashed toward the fire with hands outstretched as if to retrieve the corpse. His gesture was apparently a part of the ritual and was anticipated by the helpers, who joined in restraining him. They all crouched in a huddle near the fire and chanted and wailed loudly as the fire blazed.

When the fire had burned for about an hour, Hawachiwa Yamba lifted the charred remains with a long pole and shook them. Rib bones, calcined and white, were seen separated from one another. However, charred flesh still clung to the rest of the skeleton. The remains were stirred, and wood was placed in the pot to finish burning the flesh. After about an hour and a half longer, the flesh was entirely consumed. The pot was removed from the fire and soon Yamba Wachi, still wailing and weeping, began to slowly and laboriously pick out of the cremation pot the tiny bits of whitened bones that remained with the hot coals and ash.

Maxopo ceased to wail. He brought out a bowl of cornmeal and chatted and joked with Hawachiwa Yamba as they sat together and ate cornmeal. Yamba Wachi, on the other hand, continued to wail and search for bits of bones for about four hours. Finally she arose and put the cremation pots, together with the ashes, into the open grave and covered them with the loose dirt from the grave. She scooped up the charcoal from the funeral fire bed and put it into a carrying basket, which she lifted onto her back with a tumpline. She carried the basket down the hill to the river and put the charcoal into the water. This ended the day's ceremony, which had lasted nine hours.

Yamba Wachi continued to wail intermittently a few more days, holding the bowl of bones on her lap. During this time her adult son cut a new grinding trough for her. When the trough was finished she ground some corn and made gruel. Into this she mixed the bone powder and drank the mixture.

In the Amahuaca funerary ceremony, the primary concern of the participants is to appease the spirit of the deceased while it is at hand by expressing affect to it. When the body has been disposed of, the spirit is thought to disappear also. But until this is accomplished, there is some anxiety lest the spirit of the deceased cause trouble, as it "hangs around wanting to kill someone." The prescribed way for the closest relatives to express concern to the spirit is by weeping. As one observer commented with reference to the Cashinahua, who are closely related to the Amahuaca, "The more one moans and sobs, the better the deceased's shade is appeased. The depth of one's sorrow can be measured by the length of the mucus hanging from one's nose" (Tastevin 1925:34). The mother continued to mourn until she had consumed the last vestiges of the infant, whereupon her attitude changed radically, as had her husband's earlier. She became voluble and happy, with no suggestion of her bereavement.

DISCUSSION

Amahuaca endocannibalism is not an isolated phenomenon in South America. It was reported among most of the Panoan peoples in the Ucayali valley. Among three of these groups the funerary rites are restricted to consuming pulverized bones or ashes as among the Amahuaca (Carvalho 1931:230, 254; Izaguirre 1922–1929:v. 2, pp. 246–247; Villanueva 1902:67). But ten other Panoan groups consumed the flesh of their dead, five of these going so far as to kill the sick and aged for this purpose (Maroni 1889–1892:v. 27, pp. 84–85; v. 30, p. 133; Figueroa 1904:118; Izaguirre 1922–1929:v. 1, p. 227; v. 9, pp. 41, 104; v. 12, pp. 445–446; Oppenheim 1936:148; Tastevin 1925:34).

Endocannibalism occurred somewhat less frequently among peoples outside the area occupied by the Panoans. Nevertheless many instances have been reported throughout the continent among peoples of Marginal, Tropical Forest, and Circum-Caribbean culture types.[2] It does not appear likely therefore that its occurrence in

South America can be related to the influence of any restricted group of people or correlated with culture level. Nor does the pattern of its distribution lend itself to an interpretation through the concept of age area. Hence we must look for other factors to explain its occurrence and distribution here.

The meanings of customs as expressed by those who practice them, although frequently mere rationalizations, sometimes yield clues to the function and development of those customs. Let us consider, then, the meaning of endocannibalism expressed by the Amahuaca and other Panoan peoples.

As we have already seen, among the Amahuaca consuming of the pulverized bones of the deceased is apparently an attempt to banish the spirit. The Conibo cremated the corpse in order to prevent the spirit from reoccupying the body and drank the ashes in order to forget the dead (Maroni 1889–1892:v. 30, p. 133). The reason given by the Remo and Cashinahua for consuming the remains was to put the dead to rest (Carvalho 1931:254, 227). Another report on the Cashinahua indicates that the deceased was mourned to appease the spirit and that when the body had been eaten, the spirit would fly away to the west (Tastevin 1925:34). For these people, eating the flesh was clearly a duty and a disagreeable one. The shaman is said to have forced everyone in the group to eat a piece of the roasted corpse, and everyone went to a secluded corner to eat his piece "with much weeping for the dead man and the sad lot of humanity" (Tastevin 1925:34). The Capanahua's reason was "piety," or a desire to honor the dead (Izaguirre 1922–1929:v. 9. p. 41).

But in spite of the obvious supernatural element in Panoan funerary endocannibalism, some of the data indicate that there is also a gastronomic aspect to the practice. The Capanahua, for example, roasted the body "like game," and it is said that they found this food agreeable, drinking the blood as we drink wine (Izaguirre 1922–1929:v. 9, p. 41). The Cashibo ate their old people with delight (Bastian 1878–1889:v. 2, p. 761). They and the Mayoruna killed the old and sick, the Mayoruna doing so before they could grow thin (Izaguirre 1922–1929:v. 12, p. 4; Martius 1867:v. 1, p. 430). Figueroa's description of their endocannibalism suggests a thorough confusion of the supernatural and gastronomic elements.

> When a parent, son, or other relative dies, they weep, and then, between floods of tears, they cut him into pieces: they boil the flesh or roast it and eat it as fresh meat; the rest they smoke to be eaten on other days. They usually place the entire corpse on a fire, where they remove small pieces of meat from it as it is roasting, and eat between wails and weeping, which they mix with the mouthfuls, until the deceased is entirely eaten. . . . They save the heads until they are full of worms in the orifices and brains, and they eat these, for they like them very well mixed with chili pepper (Figueroa 1904:118) [Translated by G. Dole].

A Mayoruna man on the point of death made explicit the gastronomic value of the practice. He had fallen gravely ill while away from home. Expecting to die shortly, he was loudly bemoaning not his illness but the thought that he would be interred and would thus be eaten by worms; he would have preferred, according to ancient custom, to serve as food for his relatives instead (Osculati 1850:210–211).

Other peoples have expressed the same reasons as those voiced by Panoans, and demonstrate a similar confusion of practical and supernatural objectives. (See, e.g., Roth 1915:158; Sumner 1906:331–333; Sumner and Keller 1927:v. 2, pp. 1237–1239). In eastern Amazonia, among the Botocudo, the flesh of a dead child was eaten "with tenderness" by its mother (Waitz 1859:v. 3, p. 446). Other Tapuya peoples believed that the soul would live again in the eater (Anonymous 1874:297), and that the deceased could not be preserved in any better way than inside their relatives (Pompeu Sobrinho 1934:25). A Camacan mother ate her dead infant because it had come from her body and should return to it, being a prize too precious to leave to the worms (Castelnau 1850–1851:v. 4, p. 382).

A frequent reason given for consuming human remains is that the good qualities of the deceased will thereby be transmitted to the eater. In the northwest Amazon area the Cubeo expressed this belief succinctly by saying that in this way they incorporated all the energy of their forebears (H. Coudreau 1886–1887:v. 2, p. 173). An instance of flesh endocannibalism reported in Colombia is suggestive. It is said that funeral feasts were "the only time the Sae ever tasted meat" (Kirchhoff 1948b:390).

Another consideration that may be of significance in the development of endocannibalism is warfare. Among many peoples, including Panoans, the eating of flesh of one's own people was associated with warfare. The Comobo and Ruanahua, for example, were said to kill and eat people who were old and unable to serve for war (Izaguirre 1922–1929:v. 1, p. 277). Endocannibalism was associated with warriors also among the Indians of Bonda on the north coast of Colombia in the 16th century. Here the liquids derived from drying a corpse over a slow fire were drunk by the most valiant warriors (Reichel-Dolmatoff 1951a:92). Even among some groups that practiced only the bone-ash type of cannibalism there is a suggestion that it had been associated with warfare. For example, the Island Caribs were said to have practiced it for the purpose of absorbing the spirit and valor of the dead (Koch [-Grünberg] 1899:84), and later abandoned the practice because they had no more warriors (Borde 1886:253).

The possibility of a functional relation between endocannibalism and warfare is strengthened by a high correlation of these two phenomena. The Panoans were at war with one another at the time of the first White contact and, elsewhere in South America, warfare was most intense in those areas where flesh endocannibalism occurred. Moreover, many groups practiced both revenge and funerary cannibalism, and the forms of the former custom resembled those of the latter.

The available data suggest that the eating of flesh is an early phase of ritual endocannibalism, and that the drinking of ground bones is a ritual survival of the simpler form. If this is so, consuming the flesh of one's relatives becomes more understandable as a custom adapted from revenge cannibalism.

I have noted the gastronomic aspect of flesh endocannibalism. It may be that a need for meat is another significant factor in the development of endocannibalism. (Of course, warfare and hunger do not necessarily operate independently; rather it might be expected that they reinforce each other.) In spite of repeated denials of the relevance of hunger to ritual endocannibalism, this question has never been adequately investigated. The reports of ritual endocannibalism record an established custom that has been perpetuated through predilection for human flesh or supernatural beliefs or both. Neither its inception nor the conditions which gave rise to it are described. Valuable data on this question may soon be supplied by a group of Indians (Pacaás Novos) in western Brazil, recently publicized by the magazine *O Cruzeiro* (March 3, 1962). These Indians are described as starving and at war with their Indian neighbors and with Whites. They eat the flesh of both enemies and relatives because of hunger and lack of other food.

NOTES

1. Surveys of the distribution of cannibalism may be found in Andrée (1887), Koch [-Grünberg] (1899), Linné (1929), Loeb (1930), Métraux (1947, 1949b), Schaafhausen (1870), Sumner (1906), Sumner and Keller (1927), Steinmetz (1896), and Thomas (1910).
2. Space here does not permit mention of all the forms and instances of endocannibalism in South America. I intend to publish a survey of this material elsewhere.

The Guayakí are a group now living by hunting and gathering in Paraguay who have been the subject of considerable interest to anthropologists but have remained elusive as a subject of study. The following article is based on a period of eight months' fieldwork, from February to September of 1963, among recently "pacified" Guayakí (P. Clastres 1968b:101; Sebag 1964:2181). In July of that year, the author and his coworker, the late Lucien Sebag, read a paper at an anthropological meeting in São Paulo on the topic of cannibalism and death among the Guayakí which was later published (P. Clastres and Sebag 1963). A comparison of that work with the present article is of considerable interest in understanding how interpretations can change in the light of further data.

The reader will note that the reason for Guayakí cannibalism is still not entirely clear. The nutritive aspect is logical to anyone who has lived for long periods of time on game animals with no auxiliary source of fat, since game animals are generally quite lean. The question of protecting the living from the souls of the dead is not, however, entirely resolved, since at least some close kin of the dead may not eat the body and must be subject to attack. If the soul will not depart while there is someone who is subject to attack, then it would appear that there are still aspects of the entire practice that need further clarification.

The article from which the present selection is excerpted is one of a series (see also P. Clastres 1966, 1968a), and the author has also written a book on the Guayakí (1972). Hélène Clastres published a work on Gua-

yaki funerary customs (1970), and Lucien Sebag published a study of the dreams of a Guayaki woman (1964).

Portions of the original chapter on cannibalism have been omitted and some additional bibliography has been inserted with Clastres' permission.

29 PIERRE CLASTRES

Guayaki Cannibalism

Permanent confrontation between the living and the dead, and the constant necessity of the former to defend themselves from the latter, may assume brutal forms and lead to the banishment of the souls by consumption of the bodies: for the Guayaki are cannibals. Anthropophagy is a practice so profoundly foreign to Western civilization that this civilization, in the face of cannibalism, has continually oscillated between fascination and disgust, ready to see it as a dimension of and proof of barbarism, the better to be horrified immediately. On the other hand, accusing the Savages of committing the sin of eating their fellows provided the Europeans with an excellent justification for their enterprise of conquest. Any scruples were superfluous, even sinful, in the face of such wickedness and one had the right and duty to make war on the Cannibals for the purpose of terminating practices so dangerous to the well-being of their souls. Thus, one could, throughout the 16th century, reduce to slavery and decimate entire tribes with the most perfectly clear conscience. If, however, some societies such as the Tupinambá really did practice anthropophagy, it was quite simply invented for others, since the Spanish and the Portuguese used this pretext to devote themselves to slave raiding and to legitimate it in the eyes of the governments in Madrid and Lisbon, so that, among the numerous Indian tribes accused of cannibalism in the 16th and 17th centuries, doubtless many of them did no such thing. Thus it is with good reason that, as a consequence, Americanist ethnology, lacking more reliable data, has rejected some testimonies too suspect of being self-interested. This attitude of critical skepticism was surely necessary; it was necessary to separate the serious reports from the immense jumble of fanciful statements among which they were lost. But the "mania" of the soldiers, missionaries, explorers and adventurers of past centuries to see a cannibal in every Indian, was answered by a reverse exaggeration on the part of some scholars that drove them consistently to doubt all

Excerpted by permission of the author and publisher from *Journal de la Société des Américanistes*, vol. 57 (1968), pp. 30–47. Translated and edited by Patricia J. Lyon with the approval of the author.

All material appearing within square brackets [ ] has been added by the editor of this book.

statements of anthropophagy and thus to reject some reports, extremely valuable due to the personal character of their authors, but tainted as were the others by suspicion and immediately discredited. Such is almost exactly the "ethnological history" of Guayaki cannibalism. Mayntzhusen . . . was the first to achieve peaceful contact with these Indians. He gathered several dozen [plusieurs dizaines] around him, lived a number of years among them and thus could gather a rich, as yet [largely] unpublished, documentation on this mysterious South American tribe [cf. Mayntzhusen 1913, 1926]. Now the statements of the German scholar are clear: the Guayaki practiced anthropophagy and, more precisely, an endocannibalism presenting some traits doubtless unique on the continent. Mayntzhusen's seriousness, his knowledge of the language and his intimate acquaintance with the Guayaki, confer on his writing very great scientific value, and the information that he provides about cannibalism merited being taken into consideration for the same reason as the other data. Furthermore, that is what Prof. H. Baldus did in an article devoted to the formation of power in various Indian societies among which figured the Guayaki (Baldus 1939), as well as in "Sinopse da cultura guayaki" [Synopsis of Guayaki culture] published later, wherein he wrote: "Mayntzhusen received from numerous Guayaki such minute descriptions of the tribal endocannibalism of certain extraordinarily despotic and brutal chiefs that it is difficult to doubt these reports" (Baldus 1943:152). This being the case, it is surprising to see that the chapter of the *Handbook* devoted to the Guayaki and written by A. Métraux and H. Baldus, principally on the basis of materials gathered by Mayntzhusen, is quite reserved regarding his statements on the problem of anthropophagy; as a result Prof. Baldus in 1946 writes nearly the opposite of what he had written in the 1943 article: "Certain chiefs are reported to be inveterate cannibals, who prey on the members of their own (!), as well as of neighboring, bands. Most sources agree that the *Guayaki* are cannibals, but the evidence is not always convincing. The endocannibalism described by Mayntzhusen is open to strong doubt and requires careful checking" (Métraux and Baldus 1946:441). Doubtless these fluctuations are a mark of the difficulty that Americanists have in addressing the question of cannibalism, even when it really exists. For Mayntzhusen is by no means mistaken; the information that he has furnished is absolutely accurate and our own residence among the Guayaki permits us to confirm and state precisely what in fact has been known for 50 years about the anthropophagy practiced by this tribe.

· · ·

From a review of cannibalism in South America [cf. Métraux 1949b; Fernandes 1952; Zerries 1960] we can extract the following characteristics:

1. Exocannibalism consists of eating the roast flesh, and not the bones, of the enemy.

2. Endocannibalism amounts to absorbing, in liquid form, the bones of relatives, and not their flesh.

3. Exo- and endocannibalism appear to be exclusive of one another.

It is in the light of these general traits that one should examine Guayaki cannibalism, which we are now going to describe.

THE CIRCUMSTANCES OF THE DISCOVERY

Let us point out immediately that, of the two groups studied, the Yñarö group, or Aché Gatu, practices cannibalism. The other tribe, or Yvytyrusu group is totally ignorant of this ritual and submits its dead to a treatment quite different from that inflicted by the Aché Gatu on their dead relatives. In fact Guayaki anthropophagy is essentially endocannibalism. On our arrival in the field we were absolutely unaware that the Guayaki might be cannibals, and it is perhaps not without interest to recount the circumstances of this discovery. L. Cadogan had begun his research on these Indians by questioning some adult Guayaki captured by the Paraguayans several years previously who, while maintaining their own language, had more or less learned Guaraní. Some of these informants belonged precisely to the Aché Gatu group, and from their accounts it resulted that there were Guayaki cannibals named, by them, Aché Vwa. Therefore, L. Cadogan translated this expression as "eaters of Guayaki" (Cadogan 1961). When later the Aché Gatu had joined the camp of Arroyo Moroti, the Paraguayan scholar went there but could not get confirmation of the accounts previously obtained about the Aché Vwa. He then supposed that his first translation was erroneous in favor of accepting that *vwa* mean "incorporated," and that Aché Vwa designated those alien Guayaki incorporated into the group of the informants, and not Guayaki cannibals. Such was our understanding at the moment when the inquiry began. And in fact, questioned about the burial ritual observed by the group, the Indians were unanimous in affirming that the dead were carefully buried (*juta*), lying on their backs in a long horizontal grave (*wykwa*). It was exactly Occidental burial! This identity was disturbing but could also be nothing more than a simple coincidence. In any case, the Guayaki spoke well of the Aché Vwa, but as if referring to an alien Aché group, and nothing in their conversation indicated that they might be acquainted with cannibal practices. It seemed then that L. Cadogan had rightly modified his first hypotheses and that there was no trace of anthropophagy among the Guayaki. Now, about two months after the beginning of our research, while we were in the course of questioning an old woman, the oldest of the group, about the burial of one of her relatives killed long ago by the Paraguayans, she answered us firmly, even with irritation, that this Guayaki had never been buried, rather he had been roasted and all the group had eaten him. Questioned immediately about what had happened to other ancestors, she gave us the same response in each case: the body was roasted and eaten by the band to which it belonged. Provided now with these extraordinary reports, we immediately called for an explanation from the Indians who had obligingly described to us the supposed funeral ritual of inhumation. Not in the least troubled, they confirmed on all points what the old woman Jygi had innocently confided to us. They admitted that their grandparents were cannibals, Aché Vwa, and were hilariously amused that they had lied to us from the first. Asked the reason for the double falsehood (positive in that they had described something that did not exist among them, burial; by omission in that they had avoided saying that their immediate ancestors were cannibals), they explained to us that it was for fear of our reaction: "so that you would not hit us!" We learned thus that the Paraguayan peasant who "led" them and who was aware of their ancient practices had explicitly forbidden them to speak of it to anyone. But from the time that we were aware of it, there was no longer any difficulty in investigating this theme. On the contrary, a conspiracy could even be formed between ethnologists and savages in the face of the "civilized person." By common accord these questions were never raised in the presence of the Paraguayan, and as soon as he was absent the Guayakí spoke to us with delight of their free life in the forest with no restriction. . . .

Although, in fact, the Guayakí admitted voluntarily that their grandparents ate their dead, on the other hand they denied grimly that they themselves had ever eaten the least little bit of human flesh; they buried their dead, they maintained, they never ate them. . . . Their attitude was, however, too calculated, too different from the truth and from what they really thought and believed not to be rapidly abandoned; and it was quite soon known that, with the exception of children less than 10 years old, *all the members of the tribe had eaten human flesh*. For anthropophagy was by no means stopped after the disappearance of the Aché Vwa, that is, the direct ancestors of the Aché Gatu. The Aché Gatu themselves had maintained the funerary ritual applied to the dead, and it was possible for us to establish that the last cannibal repast, in the course of which a woman was eaten, took place about 5 years before the "surrender" of the tribe, that is, about 1954. The participants in the feast had, however, no difficulty in telling us about it and it was thus possible to obtain an extremely detailed description not only of the progress of the anthropophagic feast, but also, later, of the way in which the Guayakí think of their own cannibalism. Be that as it may, we could observe to what extent the Aché Gatu *are* cannibals, how great is their greedy relish of human flesh and with what nostalgia they evoked the banquets still so recent and which one could even qualify as sinister, so fresh is the "cannibalistic" spontaneity of the table-companions, and authentic as well as disquieting their healthy appetite: *"uré rö Aché Vwa, Aché kyravwa,"* they proclaimed with pride, "We are eaters of men, eaters of human fat." They really were, and 4 years of living in contact with civilization had in no way changed this very profound tendency of their culture. In the month of July, 1963, unfortunately in our absence, an anthropophagic repast took place, doubtless the last one celebrated by the Aché Gatu. In the course of an epidemic of influenza and measles that killed 16 Indians, above all old people and the majority members of the noncannibal group of the Yvytyrusu, a child, a little boy about 20 months old, died of the sickness. It appears that, demoralized by the sickness, disheartened by this new life to which they had not succeeded in adapting, the Aché Gatu, at least those present at the camp, wanted to reimmerse themselves momentarily in the atmosphere of days gone by. They chose to carry out that which for them constituted the exclusive singularity of Guayakí life, the absolute difference of their culture, the cannibal feast; thus little Brikugi was cooked and devoured. He was the only child in the group born into the civilized world of the Whites, and he was also the last Guayakí to die according to the custom of their ancestors. We have questioned all the participants in the repast; none refused to tell about it, but it was particularly the father, the mother and the sister of the child who gave us the most exact information. It should also be mentioned that not only Aché Gatu attended and took part in this repast but also several children of the noncannibal group. They were, moreover, the first to announce to us on our return to the camp that, "the child of the woman Baipugi had been eaten." This experience had amused them greatly. Our inquiry into cannibalism thus unfolded throughout our stay among the Guayakí. The sudden and unexpected resurgence, in the month of July, of the anthropophagic consciousness of the Indians, permitted us to consider the consumption of human flesh, not as an abstract thing, dead and merely remembered, but as present, living desire and longing of the last cannibals of America.

EXTENT AND LIMITS OF ANTHROPOPHAGY

The Guayakí of the Ÿnarö practice systematic endocannibalism. They eat *all* their dead, and have doubtless done so for a very long time since we have ascertained, in gathering genealogies, that anthropophagy was present at the level of the most remote generations. The bodies of only a few individuals were not consumed, not for any ritual reason internal to anthropophagy itself, but always for external, accidental causes, linked to the particular circumstances of the death of one person or another. For example, the body of a woman was abandoned to the vultures because everyone was sick at the time and no one wanted to eat her. Or again, the body of a hunter, killed at the time of a fight with the Paraguayans, remained for several days at the site of the murder. The band had fled and only returned later and the corpse was already too decomposed to be consumed. It should be empha-sized, however, that so strong is the Guayakí taste for human flesh that they do not hesitate to cut whatever seems edible to them from a half rotten corpse. Thus, the leader of one band, Kyrypyragi, was killed by the "Whites" and his group did not return to the site of the ambush until a considerable time later. The body "*iné puté*, stank a lot," nevertheless, the less decomposed portions were cut off to be eaten. The rotten penis of Kyrypyragi could not be recovered, so we were told. It is useless to multiply the few examples of Aché Gatu [the band's name for them-selves] not eaten by their comrades. Those that we have noted suffice to show that when there is no cannibal repast it is, as it were, by default and in spite of the Guayakí themselves. The normal resting place of the dead is the stomach of the living.

Consequently, when a Guayakí dies, he is cooked and he is eaten. Human flesh is not reserved for any particular group within Guayakí society. All members partici-pate equally in the feast: men, women, children, young and old. In addition, human flesh is not subject to any special dietary taboo with the exception, however, of female sex organs which are never eaten and are buried. Aside from this part of female bodies, all the rest is eaten, whether a male or female body. Fairly frequently, however, the intestines are not eaten, not due to any taboo, but because of the very disagreeable odor that this part of the human body emits. When they are not too deteriorated they are eaten. There is no further distinction among the dead. Whatever may be the age or sex of the defunct, he is always eaten. Some

Indians, however, have told us that one does not eat "children with very black bodies" (*kromi braa puté*) or very old women (*waimi puté*). This statement may refer simply to individual preferences, for many old women were eaten. One can, then, say that as a general rule everyone is eaten. Reciprocally, everyone eats excepting the closest relatives of the dead person: a man and a woman do not eat their children, siblings do not eat each other and do not eat their parents. In reality, this taboo is not rigorously respected. We have some cases of sons eating the flesh of their father, of men eating their sons or of brothers eating their brother. On the other hand, a woman never eats her children, a father does not eat his daughter nor a brother his sister, any more than a son eats his mother or a daughter her father. Thus, it can be seen that the taboo is strictly binding on close relatives of opposite sexes and that, in reality, it overlaps the incest prohibitions. Just as exogamy is limited . . . to the nuclear family, so is this unit excluded, for Ego, from anthropophagy. These are the only dietary prohibitions inherent in the essence of cannibalism. Others may occur from time to time, but linked to the temporary situation of the consumer and not to the status of the human flesh. An adolescent boy who has just undergone initiation, or a girl at the time of her first menstruation, does not participate in the cannibal repast but only because he may not eat any kind of meat, either human or animal. To exogamy on the matrimonial plane corresponds an exocuisine on the anthropophagic plane, and this latter is practically the only limitation to generalized endocannibalism.[1]

THE ANTHROPOPHAGIC MEAL

There are two means of preparing human flesh; it is eaten either roasted (*kaimbré, vechy*) or boiled (*baku*); but again not as a result of ritual regulation. It is simply that very young children, too small for their divided body to furnish each person present an appreciable quantity of roast nutriment, are boiled so as to provide a kind of *pot-au-feu*; thus, there is enough liquid for everyone. In such a case, the small body is carved into several large pieces which are set to boil in pottery vessels. The "broth" is consumed by means of a brush (*koto*). In the case of an adult, however, the body is cut into quarters with a bamboo knife (*kyti*).[2] The head and the limbs are separated from the trunk and the various elements are disjointed. The head and the intestines are not treated according to the same "recipe" as the muscular parts or the internal organs. The head is first carefully shaved (beard and hair). In the case of a child it is the mother who shaves it, in the case of a man it is his wife who is, it seems, shaved by her husband. The head is then boiled, as are the intestines, in ceramic cooking pots. Regarding the meat proper and the internal organs, they are placed on a large wooden grill under which a fire is lit. The grill (*byta*) is exactly like that used by the Tupinambá to cook their prisoners of war [cf. Métraux 1948:125, Fig. 14], consisting of four forked uprights about 50 cm. in height upon which are placed the crosspieces that receive the quarters of the butchered body. The meat is roasted slowly and the fat released by the heat is absorbed gradually with the *koto*. When the meat is considered "done" it is divided among all those present. Whatever is not eaten on the spot is set aside in the women's baskets and used as nutriment the next day. As far as the bones are concerned, they are broken and their marrow, of which the women are particularly fond, is sucked.

One very important aspect of the preparation of human flesh, upon which the Guayaki insist especially, is that it must never be eaten alone. It is always accompanied by the pith or the terminal shoot of the pindo palm (*tangy*) which is boiled with the flesh of young children and with the head and intestines of other individuals, or else roasted on the grill. The overriding need for this combination is due, as the Indians explain, to the fact that human flesh is too "hard," too "powerful" (*myrakwa*). Eaten alone it can be very dangerous. It causes *baivwä*, a kind of non-"natural" illness in which there is a great danger of death: "*Aché kyra rö myrakwa; myrakwa rö baivwanvé; Aché kyra jama myrakwa*. Human fat is powerful; this power is the sickness; human fat produces this power." However, mixed with the pith or the shoot of the pindo, neutral foods free of all dietary prohibition, human flesh looses its *myrakwa* and ceases to be dangerous; it can then be eaten without fear.

The distribution of the different body parts seems to obey a very small number of rules, since it scarcely matters who can eat what piece. There are, as far as we know, only two exceptions, one regarding the penis which is always eaten by women and preferably pregnant women, it being supposed that they will thus give birth to male children,[3] the other regarding the head which is reserved for old people, men and women, to the exclusion of the young hunters. These latter . . . should also not suck the heads of animals, under pain of bad luck in the hunt (*pané*). The part of the body unanimously preferred by the Guayaki is the skin because, they explained to us, of the thick layer of fat that it covers: "*kyra wachu!* lots of fat!" When a hunter brings game back to the camp, they begin by ascertaining whether it is good and fat or not and, depending on the case, the comments are enthusiastic: "*piré kyra wachu,* Nice fat skin!" or else disappointed: "*piru, kyra iä,* It's scrawny, no fat." Comments on human skin are made in exactly the same terms, and it is this passion of the Guayaki cannibals for the fat of their fellows that leads them to name themselves Aché Kyravwa, Guayaki eaters of human fat.

When a Guayaki dies, and there will therefore be an anthropophagic repast, one must immediately run to alert the other bands to invite them to the feast or, if they are too far away, to take them some nice fat skin; otherwise the *cheygi* [other bands] are furious and might even try to shoot arrows at those who have forgotten them. It is the young men, the *kybuchuété* [initiated male under 35–40 years old], who are in charge of building the grill on which the dead will be cooked. When the band leaves the site at the end of the feast the builders of the grill must be submitted to a purification rite; they are carefully washed with a decoction . . . of slivers of *kymata* vine. As far as the grill itself is concerned, if it has been used for an adult, it is not destroyed, it is not burned, it remains in place; the Guayaki have given us two kinds of explanation on this matter. They say that Aché strangers will see the grill and thus know that they are in the territory of the cannibals, so they will flee; or else they say that their comrades, seeing the grill, will know that an *irondy* ["those who are comrades"] is dead and they will weep. The two explanations are not, however, contradictory. When the grill has served for a child, it is destroyed or hidden. The anthropophagic meal is followed immediately by the funeral rite proper. . . .

Anthropophagy is not, for the Aché Gatu, a secret rite of which one must not speak to strangers. On the contrary, from the moment the Guayaki perceived that we did not disapprove of this practice, they spoke to us very freely, happy to see a *Béru* [White] place so much attention on a custom so close to˘ their hearts. Unquestionably, on the other hand, it was also close to their stomachs, as it were: "*Aché rö uré uty piré kyra wachu vwä*. We are in the habit of eating Guayaki because of the nice fat skin." And the Indian Kybwyragi confided to us that if he had, 9 or 10 years earlier, eaten the woman Prembégi, it was to nourish himself: "*cho gaipará reko jwe iä*. I did not want to continue to be skinny." The alimentary component of anthropophagy is, then, very important to the Guayaki; it is not, however, the only one and the Indians have given us their own theory of cannibalism.

ENDOCANNIBALISM IN GUAYAKÍ THOUGHT

Although it was relatively easy for us to discover that the Guayaki were cannibals, and simple to obtain a detailed description of this ritual, we found ourselves in serious difficulties in learning the conscious reason for their cannibalism. Certainly it was not due to any dissembling on the part of the Indians since they manifested no reticence at all in evoking the act itself. For several months, however, to the question, "Why do you eat dead Guayaki?" it was impossible for us to obtain any response other than, "Because we are cannibals, Aché kyravwa." This purely alimentary explanation that they apparently gave for their anthropophagy seemed incredible and led to constant questioning on this subject. One day, on asking an Aché Gatu why the Guayaki of the other group were not cannibals, he exclaimed: "*manomba o!* They are all going to die!" Urged to explain, he proceeded to say that if one buries the dead instead of eating them, one falls gravely ill, one has *baivwä*, and one dies; for the souls of the dead remain in the neighborhood of the living, attacking them by penetrating their bodies to make them sick and finally killing them. The only means of disposing of the danger definitively and of driving off the soul of the dead, is to eat the body: "*u iä bu rö, ové tara ikö Aché jachira vwä béru endape; u iä bu rö baivwä, achy puté.* If they are not eaten, the souls arrive in great number to carry off the Aché, thrown over their shoulders, to the abode of the souls of the ancestors; not to eat is *baivwä*, one is very sick." The theory of the Guayaki is very interesting since, to describe the psycho-physiological state in which one finds himself if one does not eat the cadaver of relatives and friends, they use a word that means exactly "very great anxiety, anguish" (*pakryra iä*). The suffix *iä*, indicating privative negation, clearly shows that, for the Guayaki, anthropophagy is above all negative in its function, to banish souls, that is, to avoid the painful state of internal nontranquility (*pakryra iä*). It is, thus, static in its effects. On eating human flesh one does not acquire anything more, there is no positive influence, one simply seeks to maintain the state and situation prior to the death of such and such a person. For the Aché Gatu, it is death that causes change, death that generates imbalance and dangers by liberating souls and their charge of malevolence. The function of cannibalism is to compensate for the negative effects of death and to annul them in order to permit the reestablishment of the *ante mortem* equilibrium. The death of a Guayaki has the effect of causing the members of the group to pass from the state of *pakryra,* internal calm, to the state of *pakryra iä,* noncalm, i.e., anguish, anxiety. The term *pakryra iä* designates, in Guayaki thought, a psycho-physiological condition that is expressed, they explained to us clearly, by a very sharp anxiety and by very strong palpitations of the heart (*pakombo*). The problem, then, consists in removing the new situation of *pakryra iä* to return to the previous state of careless calm. The means of this return is the total consumption of the flesh of the dead person: "*Aché u iä bu rö pakryra iä; Aché o u bu, pakryra gatu, pakombo iä; pakryra iä rö baivwä ruwy; pakryra rö baivwä iä; pakryra rö kyrymba; pakryra iä rö kyrymba iä.* When the Aché are not eaten one becomes anguished; when the meat of the Aché is eaten one is very calm, there is no palpitation; anguish, it is the *baivwä* which is there; calm is nonsickness; calm is courage; anguish is fear." Thus we have a movement limited to the following sequence: death, appearance of the souls, penetration into the bodies of the living, production of anguish, sickness, death. The anthropophagic meal consists in performing the reverse movement, in traveling, in the opposite direction through the symbolic space created by death and we have: consumption of the body, banishment of the souls, suppression of anguish, disappearance of the cause of *baivwä*, return to tranquility and good health. Abolishing the material existence of the cadaver by eating it is to abolish the invisible presence of the soul. The soul is tied to the body; cutting up the body and eating it is to sever the soul from its base in the world of the living, then to expel it and banish it to its distant abode.

The theory of the Guayaki, although their treatise may appear sometimes vague and contradictory to us, implies a double relationship; one, among the living, between the soul and the body, the second between the soul of the dead and the body of the living. The anthropophagy of the Aché returns us, then, to their anthropology, that is, to their concept of man, more or less explicitly apparent in their concept of the soul. We have no desire whatever to give a complete account here, but only to indicate the principal data that relate to the explanation of endocannibalism furnished by the Indians themselves. One comes to see that the concept of soul rests essentially on the idea that the souls of the dead try to attack the living by penetrating the bodies of the living: "*ové ikë o.* The soul is going to go in;" and the only means to prevent this aggression of the soul is to eat the body to which it was linked. On this last point, however, the Guayaki comments are disclosed as at once categorical and unexpected for, they say, as long as the body is alive there is no soul. Only at the death of the body do souls begin to exist. Thus we have in fact much more a "ghost" than a soul. The answers of the Indians were very clear on this point; one speaks of *ové* or *ianvé* only with regard to the dead, never regarding the living. This concept may seem strange since the Guayaki "soul" exists rather as a ghost and nevertheless bears two different names. Although there may be a permanent confusion between *ové* and *ianvé* in the mind of the Guayakí, nonetheless we are dealing with two quite separate entities with different fates. In this sense Aché theory strongly evokes the Guaraní dualism of the soul: *ayvukue* and *asyigua*. These two souls, one good the other evil, contribute to "form" the living being and the second soul, true source of individuation of the person, has its seat in the nape of the neck [cf. Nimuendajú 1914:301–316]. Now according to the Guayakí the soul is not localized in any part of the body and appears only on the death of the individual. We will not dwell any longer on this point which would require greater expansion. We only know that, in spite of the incontrovertible analogies between Guayakí beliefs and Guaraní religion, there also exist very important differences. As far as Guayakí anthropophagy is concerned, several stages in the fate of the soul can be distinguished and elucidated. The first is defined by the simultaneity of death and the coming into being of the soul, that is, in fact, by the separation of the body and the soul. The second movement consists of the effort of the newly freed soul to penetrate the bodies of relatives of the dead person; here we are dealing with an attempt at unification between the soul of the dead and the body of the living. The mortal danger, *baivwä*, of this union is avoided by the collective consumption of the cadaver; as a result the endocannibalistic repast effects a separation between the soul of the dead and the body of the living. To affect the soul the body is eaten and the exclusion of the soul now assumes a definitive character; *ové* goes off toward the sun (*kyrayri*) while *ianvé* wanders in the forest at ground level (*ywyri*).

Do things, however, really always happen thus, and is the Guayakí solution completely effective? On the basis of the evidence it can be determined that occasionally the anthropophagic ritual does not suffice to separate the soul of the dead from the world of the living. For if the noncannibal Guayakí are, in the eyes of the Aché Gatu, irremediably exposed to the undertakings of the souls, they themselves do not always escape. Several of them have died as a consequence of *baivwä* brought on by the penetration of a soul in their body; the cadaver had, nevertheless, been roasted and eaten. It is true, it should be specified, that in this last case the persons attacked by the soul of the departed are very often those who had not been able to eat his flesh because of their close kin ties to the dead person. In other words, the people most directly menaced by the soul of the dead are precisely those to whom the remedy is forbidden. There also remains some uncertainty in the mind of the Indians, less regarding the efficiency and validity of cannibalism than about the malevolence of the souls and their obstinacy in hurting the living.

As to the symptoms that the presence of a soul manifests in the body that it has invaded, they can be extremely varied. We verified one symptom at the request of some Guayakí who showed us an evident case of penetration of *ianvé* in the body of one of them. It was an Indian from a noncannibal group who, for several days, showed a kind of cyst under his skin level with his stomach; he urged us to touch this hard ball that could be felt to roll under the fingers. This was the soul of his wife who had died some days earlier and had penetrated her husband's body in order to cause him to die and to carry him off with her to the sun, her new abode; but he did not die.

Now what do the Guayaki feel individually regarding their *post-mortem* fate? They all know that each of them, once dead, will very certainly be devoured by his relatives and friends. Not only does this certainty not alarm them in the least, but one cannot even speak of resignation. On the contrary, the Aché Gatu *want to be eaten,* and there is truly a very profound accord between the future dead person and the survivors about the ultimate destination of the body. When a Guayaki feels his end to be near, he expresses his last wish and requests that he be eaten; he knows, in fact, that his death is going to be a source of danger to the people of his group, that his soul is going to try to bring them sickness and to kill them. To the somewhat passive compliance with the traditional anthropophagic ritual, thus comes to be added the fear of not being eaten, through concern to do no harm to the existence of the community. This is the short dialogue between an Indian on the point of dying and the members of his band: *"nde mano bu baivwä eme! goburö manové ina: 'baivwä iä; u pa modo!'* When you will be dead don't send us *baivwä!* Then he who is on the point of dying says: 'No *baivwä*; eat me completely!' " Sometimes, also, it is as a sign of affection that the moribund individual beseeches those he loves to eat him. Thus, 4 or 5 years before the establishment of the Aché Gatu at Arroyo Moroti, the woman Prembégi died. She had two husbands, but she felt a particular fondness for the second, the *japétyva* [secondary husband]. Shortly before dying she called him and beseeched him to eat her: *"go nonga baivwä iä, ianvé ikë iä.* That way no *baivwä*, the soul will not get in." And she was eaten.

ACCOUNT OF A CANNIBAL MEAL

Toward the end of July, 1963, the Guayaki held their last anthropophagic meal. A boy, slightly less than two years old, had just died. One of his fathers, Pikygi, former husband of the child's mother, then uttered the *jeproro*, ritual cry intended to drive off the soul. Then he stated: *"cho u vwä; myko eme, kyra wachu.* I'm going to eat him; don't bury him, he's good and fat." He explained: *"cho rö achy puté, mano ruwy, bai o u jwete kwera vwä.* I'm very sick, almost dead, I have a great longing to eat human flesh to get well." The mother, Baipugi, replied: *"pete ro mi!* Cover him with earth!" But she was not annoyed that Pikygi wanted to eat her son. The Indian Kandégi, Baipugi's husband and also father of the child, then said to Pikygi: *"nde pete kaiä bu rö, u modo.* If you don't really bury him, eat him." The mother then shaved the child's head so that the skin of the head might be eaten. Pikygi cut up the body and put it to boil with palm pith. During the cooking, the Aché who were present dipped their palm brushes into the broth and sucked them: *"tapia gatu!* Good fat!" they said after each swallow. When the child was completely cooked he was divided among the guests. Pikygi ate the head, Kandégi ate an arm, Jakugi, the child's *chikwagi*[4], also ate some meat. The internal organs were distributed to the children that were there. The little boy's own brother, some 8 or 9 years old, thus ate his *pavé* [sibling] but *"tara iä*, not very much" he said by way of excuse. The mother attended the meal without eating anything since *"ja memby u iä.* One does not eat one's child." The man Jakugi was the husband of Baipurangi, older sister of the child who was being eaten; he wanted to give her the penis for by consuming it, she would later give birth to a son. She refused, however, *"ja pavé u iä, pa iä; kyrymba íä.* One does not eat one's brother, one is sad; no courage."

The meal finished, the bones were beaten and burned. Then to "avenge" the child, Jakugi beat his wife a little bit with a leather lash. Pikygi said to the mother, Baipugi: *"nde memby mano kaivété.* Your dead child has been completely roasted."[5] She responded: *"pacho bu ja chikwagi javé jepy vwa!* Then beat me at the same time as his *chikwagi* to avenge him!" He did not want to strike, however.

CONCLUSION

The preceding data permit us to establish easily that Guayakí endocannibalism is completely different from that generally practiced by other South American tribes among whom, as we have noted, anthropophagy is reduced in fact to osteophagy. It could be said that Guayakí anthropophagy is a kind of synthesis of endo- and exocannibalism as they have been described in South America. In its intent, that is at the level of the belief system that authorizes, for these Indians, the ritual of eating their dead relatives and friends, Guayakí cannibalism is similar to that of tribes of the Upper Orinoco and Northwestern Amazonia: the act of eating one's relatives is a kind of defense mechanism of the group menaced by the souls of the dead and the ritual terminates in a separation between the world of the dead and that of the living. Consequently, on the plane of the theory that explains it, endocannibalism seems to be at least partially homogeneous in South America.

In its concrete operation, however, on the plane of the ritual proper, the contrast between Guayakí endocannibalism and the endocannibalism of other Indian tribes is shown to be complete. The Guayakí eat the entire dead body, specifically excluding the bones which are abandoned once they are beaten and burned. This amounts to saying that the Aché, while legitimating their anthropophagy by a theory similar to that of the Shiriana, the Tukano, the Amahuaca, etc., celebrate their ritual exactly like the exocannibal tribes (Tupí-Guaraní, Carib, etc.) who consume the flesh of war prisoners but not the bony parts of the body. On the level of "myth" Guayakí anthropophagy reflects endocannibalism, on the ritual level it reflects exocannibalism. The principal contrasts between these two forms of South American anthropophagy pointed out earlier are maintained among the Guayakí, but reversed: the dead relative is treated among his own people as the enemy is among the exocannibals. Should we see in this very strange rule of Guayakí endocannibalism the sign and the survival of a very old model of South American anthropophagy; or are we rather dealing with an institution peculiar to this tribe and indicative of particular historical circumstances? To resolve this problem it would be necessary for the history of the Guayakí to be other than the immense lacuna in which our knowledge of their past is nearly dissipated.

NOTES

1. There is also a prohibition on human flesh when a murder is involved. The "killer" does not eat his victim (any more than the hunter eats his own game).

2. It seems that the task of cutting up the corpse falls by preference to the *jwaré* of the dead person. [The term *jwaré* is applied by a person to the man who, when the individual was born, cut the umbilical cord, bathed the newborn child and deformed its head by modeling.]

3. Similar customs are found elsewhere in South America.

4. [The term *chikwagi* is applied by an individual to the hunter who, shortly before that individual's birth, provided his mother with the animal that provided the name and "nature" of the child after the pregnant woman ate it. The *chikwagi* thereafter stands in a special relationship to the child.]

5. This is doubtless a lapse on the part of the informant; *kai* means to roast, whereas the child was boiled (*baku*).

V REACTIONS TO ENCROACHMENT FROM OUTSIDE

The conquest of South America caused extreme and often fatal changes in the indigenous cultures. That the effects of the conquest are still being felt should be obvious from the preceding material as well as what follows.

In their contact with outsiders the Indians had a choice of two possibilities, adapt or die. Many died. Some died fighting, some of disease, but there were other ways. The following citations from one of the most reliable early chroniclers are self explanatory.

> When we entered this Valley of Aburra [Colombia], such was the loathing its inhabitants felt for us that they and their women hung themselves by their hair or their belts from the trees; wailing with pitiful groans, they left their bodies there, and their souls plunged into hell. (Cieza de León 1922: Chap. XVII, pp. 56–57)

> The Indians [in the area of the first site of Cali] were so determined in not wanting to be friends with the Spaniards, considering their rule oppressive, that they did not want to plant or cultivate their fields, and therefore much privation occurred, and so many died that it is said that the greater part of them are gone. (Cieza de León 1922: Chap. XXVI, pp. 82–83)

> All these plains and the valley [of Popayán] were originally densely populated. . . . Now there are few Indians, because with the war that they had with the Spaniards, they came to eat each other on account of the hunger they suffered, caused by not wanting to plant so that the Spaniards, finding themselves without sustenance, would go away from their provinces. (Cieza de León 1922: Chap. XXX, pp. 99–100)

There are many ways to adapt. Fighting can be successful, as was that of the Araucanians, if one is willing to make the necessary changes in one's old ways. Alliance with the invaders is another way, but generally simply delays the day of reckoning. Withdrawal before the advancing forces is another possibility, but in some cases either impractical or unthinkable. Sometimes it is possible to establish a partial relationship with the invaders without being totally dominated, as did some of the groups mentioned by Roth, the Araucanians as described by Hilger and the southern Quechua. Cieza de León was a most perceptive man and realized some of the factors involved in Indian reaction to the invaders. He attempts to explain why the Indians of the province of Popayán were so difficult to overcome, while those of Perú were submissive.

> All the Indians subject to the jurisdiction of Popayán have always been, and are, without lords. There were no rulers among them who made themselves feared. They are lazy, slothful, and above all loathe serving and being subject, which is sufficient cause for them to distrust being under foreigners and in their service. But this would not be enough for them to attain their purpose; because, forced by necessity, they would do what others do. But there is another much greater cause, which is that all these provinces and regions are very fertile, and on both sides there are dense mountain forests, canebrake and other brush. As the Spaniards close in on them, they burn the houses in which they live, which are of wood and straw, and remove themselves a league or two from there or go as far as they want, and in three or four days they make a house, and in as many more they sow the amount of maize they want, and they harvest it in four months. And if there also they are hunted, they leave that place and go on or go back, and wherever they go or are they find food and fertile land ready and available to give them fruit. For this reason they serve when they want, and war or peace is in their hands, and they never lack food. Those of Perú serve well and are submissive, because they are more intelligent than these others, and because all were made subject by the Inca kings, to whom they gave tribute, serving them always. They were born in that condition; and if they did not want to serve, necessity forced them to it, because the land of Perú is all waste, full of mountains and sierras and snow fields. If they left their towns and valleys to go to these deserts they could not live. The land gives no fruit, nor is there any other place that does so other than their own valleys and provinces; so that in order not to die to the last man, they have to serve and not abandon their lands, . . . (Cieza de León 1922: Chap. XIII, pp. 44–45).

For obvious reasons we have more data about those groups who chose to establish some sort of relationship with the invaders. Such adaptations form a continuum ranging from groups who made relatively few changes in their culture to others who lost everything but a sense of group identity. There appear to be, in each culture, certain elements that are indispensable to its continued existence as a viable system and some cultures seem to be less flexible than others in this respect. The Guajiro, after a period of pearl fishing in the Caribbean, took up cattle raising (and smuggling) and flourished. On the other hand, in 1948 Darcy Ribeiro encountered two Ofaié-Chavante families clinging grimly to all that was left of their previous culture in a situation in which such a reaction was obviously not viable (D. Ribeiro 1951). A similar contrast is offered by the Fulniô and the Guayquerí as compared by Hohenthal and McCorkle (1955). The Fulniô appear to have hung onto their culture just as staunchly as the Ofaié-Chavante but with considerably more success, emphasizing the maintenance of language, religion, and in-group marriage. The Guayquerí, on the other hand, have lost virtually all elements we might consider to differentiate their culture from that of non-Indian Venezuelans, but have managed to maintain their sense of group identity.

The conquest is not yet at an end. Many groups who have retreated time and time again before the invaders are being forced once again to make the decision—adapt or die, and the options open for adaptation are being reduced. With the advent of air transport and the opening of new roads, regions that were previously inaccessible are now subject to encroachment from the outside. With the continual advance of the frontier, the retreating native groups occupy smaller and smaller territories and are forced to compete with one another for resources.

The conquest is no longer being carried forward by the soldier, however. The missionary is the first line of attack against hostile or other refugee groups. Missionaries seek out such groups and, at the cost of much time and sometimes lives, win them over and convince them that they should enter into contact with the outsiders. A second element in the continuing conquest is the trader, who is the purveyor of tempting new items and necessary old ones, such as steel tools. The trader is often connected with a third element, the exploiter of natural resources. Since the newly contacted people have no money to buy coveted items, he will exchange them for whatever it is that is salable at the moment. Traders do not, however, generally organize native labor. Such work is left for the active exploiter, to whom the Indian is a prime resource. In the past the Indian has been hunted and enslaved to provide labor for the exploitation of rubber and other natural resources. Nowadays, although all-out raids and enslavement are not as widespread, even rare, the Indian still provides the best and cheapest means of acquiring rubber, Brazil nuts, lumber, animal skins, or any other item that is found scattered through the area and must be sought rather than produced. The mechanism by which the Indian is brought into this system is clearly indicated by Frikel and by Carneiro (1964b). The exploitation of oil is a relatively new factor in most of the area under consideration, although the Motilones of Colombia and Venezuela have been carrying on guerilla warfare against oil men for decades. The oil man does not need the Indian; he can import labor, but he needs to be able to work in the Indians' territory and build roads and towns and scare the game away. Even more important perhaps, is the fact that up until now the upper tributaries of the Amazon have remained relatively free of pollution since there were no major population centers located upon them. The introduction of oil exploitation all along the eastern edge of the Andes raises the menacing specter of oil spillage into these tributaries. Such occurrences would affect not only the groups near to the site of the work, but possibly thousands of miles of waterways and the immense riverine resources still remaining.

The South American Indian has been subject to waves of exploiters from the time of the first European conquest. These exploiters have come and gone, leaving the areas they occupied open again to use by their original owners, or others that have survived. Livestock raisers and settlers are another problem. The Mataco complain that, "in an area where 500 Mataco still subsist, two Criollo families find it difficult to do so, . . . they populate the Chaco with cattle, not with people" (Fock 1967:94). Livestock raisers occupy areas that were previously hunting grounds for the Indians, sometimes exterminating the original inhabitants, as in the case of the Ona and Yahgan (cf. Bridges 1948). They enlarge grasslands at the expense of the forest, thereby making the areas unsuitable for native farming, and allow their animals to range free and eat or trample Indian crops, as noted by Nimuendajú. Settlers, too, have come and gone, but increasingly, as population pressure grows, they come to stay. To all these people the Indian is at the bottom of the social scale, at best a resource to be exploited, at worst an obstacle to be removed.

The case of the Araucanians must represent one of the most profound and successful adaptations to outside domination to be found in South America, in spite of the fact that the Araucanians lost after 350 years of resistance. It must be noted, however, that in order to fight the Spanish successfully, they found it necessary to effect changes in virtually every aspect of their culture and to go onto a permanent wartime footing. A less spectacular case of stubborn resistance which is still continuing is that of the Campa (Varese 1968).

30   ROBERT CHARLES PADDEN

Cultural Change and Military Resistance in Araucanian Chile, 1550–1730

The term "Araucanian Culture" suggests a definition and unity which is more applicable to present-day aborigines of Chile than to the culture which the Spaniards encountered in the sixteenth century. While the great majority of Chilean Indians were closely related in race, language, and culture, there were minor variations among them.[1] Those differences, however, were infrequently heeded by the Spanish invaders. Thinking in geographical rather than ethnological terms, and measuring culture with reference to military proficiency, the Spanish chroniclers postulated three spatial bands of culture, the first extending from the Aconcagua to the Nuble River; the second from the Nuble to the Imperial River; the third from there to the Gulf of Reloncaví (Olaverría 1852:19–20).[2] Within these regions the Indians were of a single Mapuche culture, as they so identified themselves. Peoples living to the north of any given Mapuche group, although still within it, were identified as Picunche, those to the south as Huilliche (Encina 1940–1952:v. 1, pp. 72–74; Latcham 1928:152–154). The Spaniards applied these denominations to their conception of cultural distribution, thus making them appear to be racio-cultural entities, which, of course, they were not.[3]

The one outstanding difference among these three groups, as the Spaniards saw them, was the ability of the central band to resist effective Spanish settlement, not only through the sixteenth century, but, as it developed, into the late decades of the nineteenth century. The Araucanian culture in which the present paper is interested is limited to the widest Spanish designation, that is, those Indians between the Nuble and Imperial Rivers, and, more precisely, the area which today

Reprinted by permission of the author and publisher from *Southwestern Journal of Anthropology*, vol. 13 (Spring 1957), pp. 103–121.
All material appearing within square brackets [ ] has been added by the editor of this book.

comprises the province of Arauco. This tiny province, some sixty miles long and twenty wide, was the focal point of Araucanian resistance.

The Spanish conquest of Araucanian Chile began in 1550 when Pedro de Valdivia and his followers built a fort and founded the town of Concepción on the northern bank of the Biobío River. From this point they moved south, inflicting military defeats on the Araucanians and dividing them in encomienda. Within three years the Spaniards had ranged below the Calle-Calle River, founding towns and reducing most of the Indians to servitude. The Indians were restive under this imposition of Spanish dominion, but offered no openly unified resistance. On the heels of this initial pacification Valdivia brought in experienced prospectors and miners from Santiago to search out the gold deposits that were believed to exist. The gold-seekers enjoyed incredible success: several strikes were made which yielded nuggets the size of almonds. *"Desde agora,"* quoth Valdivia, *"comienzo a ser señor"* (Marmolejo 1862:33–34).[4]

But the Araucanians were not of like mind. Rapid development of the mines and discoveries of new ones portended undisguised slavery. Under such apprehension the Indians of Tucapel contrived a cunning trap for Valdivia into which he fell, and he was then killed and eaten (Marmolejo 1862:37–39).[5] This signal event inspired a general uprising which lasted for four years, ending with the death of the Indian leader Lautaro in the battle of Peteroa in 1557.[6] Although the general rebellion was ended at this time, the War of Arauco was begun. The Indians of Arauco, Tucapel, Catiray, and Purén (the present province of Arauco and its peripheries) stubbornly resisted effective Spanish settlement. This phase of the struggle lasted until 1598, when the Indians captured and ate Governor Martín García de Loyola (Encina 1940–1952:v. 2, chap. xxiii; also see Serrano 1923). There followed a spontaneous rebellion of subjugated Indians from the Maule River to Osorno in the south: every Spanish town worthy of the designation was wiped out below the Biobío, with the exception of Castro on the Isle of Chiloé (González de Nájera 1889:10–14, 63–65, *passim*).[7] Thus by 1600 the Spaniards, in spite of heavy expenditures of blood and treasure, faced a triumphant foe across the Biobío.

This impasse which marked the turn of the century suggests the central problem in understanding Araucanian culture. What faculty or genius did the Araucanians possess which enabled them to succeed so brilliantly where other indigenous American cultures had failed? How was it possible for the Araucanian warriors to boast rightfully, after some fifty years of warfare, that the Spaniards knew almost as much about the military art as they did? (González de Nájera 1889:93–94). Historians have been prone to avail themselves of superficially reasonable explanations: most cite the numerical superiority of the Indians; some blame the forest because it hampered the functions of the Spanish cavalry; others stress the overly long lines of supply from Peru, coupled with a chronic lack of viceregal interest. These factors are joined to a common belief that the Araucanians simply adopted the Spanish forms and techniques of war, making up in numbers what they lacked in skill. Chilean historians, especially since the nineteenth century when their homeland fought for independence from Spain, have quite happily viewed the historical record as a proof of Araucanian hence mestizo thence Chilean bravery and love of freedom. The point is that it is not merely a question of military science, topography, relative numerical strength, or racial declension. These may be significant particulars, but a war of survival between two ethnic groups implies a conflict of total cultures.

At once we are at a serious disadvantage because we have no such conception of early Araucanian culture, however well we may feel that we know the Spanish. By means of archaeological evidence and brief narratives of exploration we are able to piece together a rather crude notion of what Araucanian culture was like before the Spaniards came, but nothing more. Largely because the area under discussion became almost at once a zone of perpetual conflict, the work of the religious Orders did not develop as it did elsewhere in the Indies, and we keenly feel the lack of Mendicant chronicles. Consequently, most of our information concerning Araucanian life during the first century of conquest is derived from chronicles and histories of the war in which brief glimpses of Indian life all too infrequently appear. There are added limitations. Wherein the Indians were concerned, the chroniclers were seldom efficient observers. In matters of simple fact they tend to be trustworthy, but when the fact becomes interpretive they almost invariably fail to grasp the human thought and action that lie behind it. Rather than as men, they thought of the Indians as wild savages who blindly resisted the sweet yoke of Christianity and Spanish dominion. For this reason they seldom inquired into the possibility of Indian method; rather, Indian resistance was madness. Another weakness inherent in the chronicles is the factor of cultural change. At any given moment the chroniclers made their notations in the belief that what they saw was and had been thus from the beginning of time. Only when contemporaries gave information which contradicted their own observations did they give evidence of change, but without attempting to explain it.

It is seldom wise to take an interpretive fact, as disclosed by one of the chroniclers, at its face value. When we are told, for instance, that the Spaniards lost a given battle because the Indians outnumbered them it is entirely unlikely that the chronicler is telling us the whole truth. We have every reason to doubt him because we already know that the Spaniards, with or without Indian allies, had an enormous talent for winning military victories with inferior numbers. At no time was it normal for Spanish forces to outnumber the enemy anywhere in the Indies. Why, then, did the Indians win not only the battle in question, but a majority of their engagements? The suggestions are several: perhaps the Indians, in their own right, had become superior strategists; perhaps they had improved their own weapons to a point which offset the Spanish advantages of gunpowder and horse; perhaps they had developed a creed for life which made resistance both possible and meaningful. Our questioning of an apparently reliable fact leads us to recognition of a neglected factor, the potentiality of early Araucanian culture. By following these suggestions through and corroborating them with associated evidence, we may well come to an understanding of that particular battle which is far superior to that entertained by the chronicler. More importantly, when the battle is multiplied by 1000 and the conditions of Spanish defeat remain relatively constant, significant conclusions concerning Araucanian culture are inescapable.

By the passing of the first generation of Conquistadores the war had become institutionalized, and observers began to think and write about it historically. In the seventeenth and eighteenth centuries several histories of Chile and its Araucanian War were written which contained a relative abundance of passages describing Indian life. These writers, like their predecessors in the sixteenth century, did not take into account the factor of cultural change, and their judgments were almost entirely based upon the present in which they observed and wrote. Nor did they, with few exceptions, have the opportunity of consulting the major chronicles of the sixteenth century. Most of those manuscripts were sent to Spain for publication, but a good many of them were intentionally or innocently shuttled off to a dark repository to await the dawn of modern historiography on Chilean historians.

There are thus three categories of documentary materials from which to draw an image of Araucanian culture: the chronicles of first contact; the chronicles and documents of the first century of conquest; and the histories of the later colonial period. In past reconstructions scholars have tended to assign cultural forms found in later and better documented periods to earlier periods wherein documentation is not generously provided. With disregard for the depth of time, elements have been taken from documentary sources of the entire colonial period and placed side by side in a synchronic mosaic. At best this type of reconstruction is an abstraction of culture, and, like any abstraction, it is essentially unreal. Nowhere does it give a hint of the potentiality of Araucanian culture: on the contrary, such description lends itself to demonstration of a culture which, by the lessons of historical anthropology, should never have survived the first Spanish onslaught. Such reconstruction follows from a basic assumption of cultural constancy. In some phases of material culture this technique is doubtless warranted and valid, especially in the presence of sufficient archaeological documentation. However this may be, the idea of constancy stands in opposition to the idea of change, and from what can be made of the documents, the strength with which the Araucanians resisted Spanish domination was derived not from a constancy of their cultural forms, but from the ability to change them. It seems valid, therefore, to view the sources of the later colonial period as indication of what Araucanian culture *became* under the stress of the long Spanish war rather than as evidence of what it was before the conquest.

The chronicles of the first century of conflict, when viewed from this position and subjected to critical analysis, provide considerable insight into the design of cultural transformation and suggest a functional hypothesis underlying cultural change. The term culture in the present case does not refer to fine art and letters and the numerous connotations usually associated with the term. Such development was not a concomitant of war, nor, it seems clear, did the Araucanians tend in the direction of refined sensibility. Araucanian cultural development occurred only in those arts which had a survival value, and was canalized by the hostile forces which threatened the total culture. Spanish pressure was exerted in three areas— military, political, and religious. The Araucanians, under the stimulus of this external pressure, turned inward upon themselves and developed their own corresponding forms to a point of equal resistive strength. The Spanish challenge in terms of relative force of impact was first military, secondly political, and lastly religious. Araucanian reaction and response to the challenge followed the same gradient.

The founding of Concepción by Valdivia in 1550 marked the real beginning of Araucanian resistance. Located just across the Biobío, out of Araucanian territory proper, it served as a strategic base of operations and a key position of Spanish strength. Before its foundation the Spaniards posed a transient threat, but after it began to serve as a springboard for trans-Biobío conquest and settlement the Indians better understood the consequences involved. With alarming speed the Spanish moved southward, through the provinces of Arauco, Catiray, Tucapel, Purén, and Marigueño, coming to a temporary halt at the Calle-Calle River. This entire area, bordered on the west by the sea and on the east by the camino real (the easiest passage through the central valley), was divided in encomienda, Arauco, Tucapel, and Purén being retained by Valdivia as the basis of a princely estate (Olaverría 1852:20). These provinces, especially Arauco, were highly prized by the Spaniards as the most heavily populated of the whole kingdom, and as possessing an abundance of food stuffs, fine lands, and a most provident climate (Marmolejo 1862:25; P. Valdivia 1846b:139–146).

Within this area the Indians lived in small, decentralized kinship groups, with no apparent inter-group relationship of an institutional nature. The sources of the sixteenth century are so meagre as to preclude the possibility of clear understanding of the socio-political divisions within the individual group. The local clusters of dwellings, in early chronicles called *levos,* in later ones *reguas,* composed a larger unit known as the *allaregua* (or *aillarewe*). Each allaregua was composed of nine or less levos. Olaverría, writing in 1594, describes this area as consisting of only five allareguas, but the context in which he mentions them suggests that this semi-centralization was of relatively recent origin (Olaverría 1852:20). There is no factual basis for postulating anything but a crude kinship relationship, markedly particularized by geographical isolation, at the time of the Spanish arrival.

These people, albeit ready warriors, were soundly defeated by Spanish arms and remained so for almost four years. Subsequent events, the revolt against Governor Valdivia in December, 1553, and the continuing War of Arauco, indicate quite clearly that this short peace was a period of Araucanian maturation. Through military action, service in encomienda, and free intercourse in the Spanish towns (Concepción, Imperial, Valdivia, and Villa Rica) they observed and learned much about Spanish military organization and strategy, government, social custom, mores, and religious concepts. The lessons they learned were adequately demonstrated in subsequent resistance against the invaders.

This initial period of communication with Spanish culture was constantly amplified throughout the following century. Military action was usually confined to the summer months. During harvest time and winter both Indians and Spaniards tended to refrain from active combat, holding what had been gained and preparing for summer campaigns. Through peaceful Indians, those serving the Spanish, the rebels kept themselves fully informed of all Spanish activity. Never lacking information, the Indians always had a precise idea of Spanish strength or weakness. There was seldom a rigid military perimeter; in those areas where the invader could maintain a fort and military supremacy the Indians were reduced to servitude. With a weakening of Spanish strength, rebellion inevitably occurred, so that the distinction as a peaceful or warlike Indian depended largely upon the state of affairs of the moment. Because the Indians so frequently changed roles, they were never out of personal contact with the Spanish.

The Indians received some aid and encouragement from Spanish deserters. There is no telling how many deserted to enemy ranks in the course of the sixteenth century, but in the year 1600 alone it is known that there were over sixty desertions (Encina 1940–1952:v. 2, p. 306). A good many of these renegades were still living among the Indians in 1607 (González de Nájera 1889:117). In fear of peace and subsequent retribution, the traitors taught the Indians many things that would have been difficult for them to learn themselves, such as the proper use of firearms, building of forges and ironmongering, and even the techniques of political administration. The Spaniards were greatly perturbed when a mestizo powder-maker went over to the other side. With volcanic sulphur, saltpetre, and charcoal in abundance, the Indians could make deadly use of the large stores of field pieces and firearms which they had captured. As luck would have it, the deserter repented and returned to the Spanish fold, whereupon he was forgiven and permitted to return to Peru. There were also clerical renegades who apostatized and urged the Indians on in their own religious beliefs and practices (González de Nájera 1889:117–122, 143–148, 69, 73–75).[8]

It is most important to understand that the motive for Araucanian observation of Spanish cultural forms was not to emulate them and thereby raise the level of their own, but to discover Spanish weaknesses and to mobilize Araucanian strength for forceful opposition. A fundamental weakness of Spanish occupation was its dire need of peace. Exploitation of this weakness became a cornerstone of Araucanian strategy throughout the sixteenth century and beyond. Spanish forces, both civilian and military, were too few and too widely dispersed, and the line of supply from Peru was much too long. Effective occupation and permanent settlement depended upon a guaranteed supply of Indian labor. This, of course, was in turn dependent upon total pacification, which would allow the colonists to concentrate on development of mining and agriculture rather than military defense. As experience in Mexico and Peru had shown, a mere handful of soldiers, colonists, and friars could work great wonders if the Indians would but submit. When they first settled Santiago the Spaniards proved that they could provide their living with their own hands, but full barns and producing mines were impossible of realization without Indian labor.[9] Because of this, the Spaniards always hungered for peace, and, through past experience in the Indies, expected it to follow each victory over the Indians.[10] This was the great error of the Spaniards in the sixteenth century. Whenever the Indians found it advantageous to themselves to live in peace—whether because of famine or disease or military weakness—they willingly surrendered themselves to service in the encomienda, there to repair their fortunes and to watch. The Spaniards, hopeful that this was indeed the dawn of a new day, almost invariably sought immediate expansion of their mining and agricultural activities. With a quickening of economic activity, military vigilance declined to a point which invited rebellion. The Araucanians honored such invitations without fail.[11]

Spanish military strategy was also based upon the gnawing hunger for peace. From past experience the invaders knew that peace would follow the defeat and usurpation of a central authority. In the absence of a central Araucanian authority the only alternative was to instill fear by demonstration of military supremacy, and so the Spaniards constantly sought a definitive battle which, when won, would convince the Araucanians of the futility of resistance. Some civilians differed, advising an Indian policy founded upon kind treatment and remission of personal service, but their voices were seldom heard. Recognizing the Spaniards' willingness to do battle, the Araucanians always chose their own battle sites where the terrain could be used to advantage, where the horse, as a military instrument, could be rendered less effective, and where their own strategies could be best effected. With monotonous regularity the Spaniards, always seeking the big victory, sent an army to defeat a rumored gathering of Indians, which rumor was usually broadcast by the Indians themselves. Upon arrival the Spaniards found themselves outmanned and outmaneuvered, and so were frequently forced to flee for their lives, leaving baggage trains in the hands of the enemy.[12]

It was military planning of this kind that led to the capture and death of Valdivia. Historians generally recognize the death trap into which he fell as the handiwork of Lautaro, the most famous ex-groom in all history. Lautaro has since become one of Chile's great national heroes, symbolizing all that was best in Araucanian culture. Be that as it may, there is considerable reason to believe that Lautaro hailed from the vicinity of Santiago, and was therefore an Araucanian by nothing more than association.[13] His relations with the Araucanians are not clear historically beyond the fact that he led their resistance, aided by other chiefs, until his death in 1557. He was extremely well versed in military strategy, and his deployment of squadrons in place of mass attack and the use of encirclement were valued contributions to Araucanian knowledge, but the fact that many other military techniques were developed after he had passed from the scene would indicate that there were countless Araucanians of equal ability.

Generally speaking, the Araucanians retained their own weapons in the war against the Spanish. Bows and arrows, long lances, spears, long clubs with weighted heads, and slings were the weapons most often used (Olaverría 1852:33–34; González de Nájera 1889:95–98).[14] Strategy was much more important than weapons. As noted above, the Indians never fought in a place that was not of their own choosing if they could avoid it. The horse was their greatest problem and one around which their strategy revolved. They chose battle sites wherein the horse would be difficult to manage; they made use of snares on long poles with which to pull the rider from his horse; they dug pitfalls and trenches, placing sharp stakes upon which rider and mount would be impaled; in all of this their chief aim was to get the Spaniard off his mount (Marmolejo 1862:44–49, 85, 62–63).[15]

Through the spoils of war and peacetime thievery the Indians acquired a vast supply of horses. By 1594 it was not uncommon for them to put several hundred horsemen in the field. It is to be noted, however, that they used the horse as an auxiliary rather than as an instrument of war. Riding as far as thirty miles a night they raided settlements and ranches under the cover of darkness, leaving death and destruction in their wake (Olaverría 1852:34). But acquisition of this new mobility did not alter their basic strategy for fighting Spanish forces. Throughout the sixteenth century they continued to lure Spanish troops into carefully prepared ambuscades, themselves remaining on foot. To have done otherwise would have undone their whole strategy. As the Spanish horsemen approached the main Indian force, their lines of retreat were closed by concentric rings of warriors. If the Spanish were fortunate enough to defeat the enemy they found no difficulty in retracing their steps. If, on the other hand, the Indians proved too strong for them, they could retreat only with great difficulty. Once having forced the Spaniards into retreat, the Indians followed them on foot. When the horses tired sufficiently, their riders could be struck down. A Spanish horseman afoot, because of the weight and bulk of his equipment and his inability to dodge through the forest undergrowth, did not have a chance for his life (Marmolejo 1862:40–43, 47–49).[16]

The idea of Indians running down horses is not as incredible as it at first seems. In the heat of summer, when most of the fighting took place, the Spanish mounts tired quickly, especially after the long trip to the Indian ambuscade. Besides this, the Araucanians were accustomed to hunting wild game by literally chasing it to death. This required a tireless trot, at which they were proficient. Profiting by the lessons of their own strategy, the Araucanians devised an extremely light saddle in order to increase the endurance of their mounts on long rides. When they used captured Spanish saddles they first cut them down so as to make them considerably lighter (González de Nájera 1889:42, 110–116).[17]

Shortly after the turn of the century, by 1611 to be exact, the Indians developed a cavalry that in terms of mobility was superior to the Spanish. They likewise possessed the best horses in the whole of Chile. These advantages were demonstrated in more daring raids on Spanish towns and a willingness to meet the Spanish cavalry on its own ground (González de Nájera 1889:107–110; Xaraquemada 1852b:239, 1852a:247, 1852c:255–257; García Ramón 1852:267). From this time forward the war passed into a new phase in which Araucanian offensive power became an increasingly significant factor. The source of that power, of course, lay in mastery of the horse. In little more than a generation the animal from which the Indians had once fled in terror had been incorporated into their culture, transforming it into a factor of defiant military power, dedicated to the eradication of Spanish culture. The Spaniards were not only dismayed to recognize this development of Araucanian military strength, but were piqued as well at the sight of barbarous savages riding horses with an air of equality. In answer to Spanish resentment the Indians pledged never to quit their war for freedom and their horses to enter serfdom on foot (González de Nájera 1889:116).[18]

The existence of a skilled and effective military force bespeaks the presence of a comparable political organization under whose genius it is formed and directed. In the development of Araucanian political organization the chronicles indicate two major forces at work: the geographical particularism in which the Araucanians traditionally lived and a counter-force provoked by the presence of the enemy and inclining towards Araucanian unity. Throughout the first century of conquest ancient localism clashed with incipient nationalism. This conflict produced a political ambivalence which in itself contributed heavily to the cause of Araucanian independence. Centralization of politico-military authority was achieved to a point where successful resistance was possible, but did not develop to a stage where the Spaniards could defeat and usurp it.

The center of anti-Spanish unity was founded in what the Spanish termed *"el estado."* This was a geographical expression signifying the area that Valdivia held in personal encomienda (Olaverría 1852:20).[19] It was these Indians, particularly those of Arauco, Tucapel, and Purén, who planned and carried out the revolt of 1553, and who assumed leadership of the resistance movement. After the first few years of bitter warfare the Spaniards began to imbue the term estado with political connotations, hence Don Alonso de Ercilla's image of *"el estado indómito"* was much more than a flight of poetic fancy (Ercilla y Zúñiga 1910–1918).[20]

It is virtually certain that the Indians, in pre-Hispanic days, were in the habit of seeking transient familial and friendship alliances in the conduct of war between localities. Upon their first major defeat by Valdivia, following which he recrossed the Biobío and founded Concepción, the more intelligent Indian leaders voiced a wide call to arms (Marmolejo 1862:22 23).[21] The resulting alliance was effective in that it led to the downfall of Valdivia, but it had no permanent character. With each new Spanish thrust the caciques of the estado had to reform alliances and seek wider support for their efforts. In 1556, for example, Lautaro and the chiefs established relations with the Indians of Santiago, attempting to incite them to rebellion (Marmolejo 1862:61–62). Temporary alliances were both frequent and effective. In search of allies the chiefs used glass beads, dogs, and various types of Spanish plunder to effect negotiations (Marmolejo 1862:105, 133). There also developed a type of Indian mercenary who supplied his own weapons and served for a specified length of time at a prearranged scale of pay (Herrera 1862:251).

It seems quite clear that there was no pan-Araucanian sentiment to which the estado could appeal. When local chiefs were asked for troops they not uncommonly rejected the request. If they acceded to the demand, they chose the bravest man for a leader and dispatched the force under his command. Service was performed in the estado's forces for no more consideration than lodging and hospitable treatment. In the event of mortality the close relatives of the fallen warrior were compensated by the residents of the province in whose defense he died (Olaverría 1852:23).

Some of the localities simply did not want to fight the Spaniards, preferring to make the best of conditions under Spanish rule. The Indians around Angol, for instance, joined the Spaniards in war against the estado for a number of years. While the estado leaders accused them of subverting the general Indian cause, the Angol tribes retaliated with accusations of plunder and theft (Marmolejo 1862: 126–127). The estado, with its own crops destroyed by warfare, never hesitated to raid the stores of those who were not immediately allied to the cause. Araucanians who refused to fight were subjected to violent reprisal (Marmolejo 1862:83).[22] Even in the province of Arauco all was not unanimity. An old chief was forced to flee with his family and take refuge in the Spanish fort in Arauco because he would not support the war, thereby giving evidence of pro-Spanish sympathies (Marmolejo 1862:110–113). It is difficult to guess how many others there might have been.

By 1594, according to Olaverría, the estado claimed suzerainty over all of the allareguas from the Biobío to the Imperial River, and was held in dread by all of the Indians as far south as Osorno. The estado was so feared and respected, he said, that Indians in the extreme south would break the peace when the chiefs of the estado so desired (Olaverría 1852:22). Nevertheless, the chiefs never succeeded in gaining effective suzerainty, even for purposes of war. Authority continued to be local, rather than central, and cooperation was most often found in the realm of diplomacy.

With the turn of the century a more precise political and military division was created by the Araucanians. The region between the Biobío and Toltén Rivers was divided into three longitudinal strips called *butanmapos;* they were the sub-Andean range, the central valley, and the coastal strip (including the estado). Each butan-mapo had clearly defined limits and jurisdictions; each had, at least in time of war, a principal chief, or *toque.* It was customary for the chiefs to debate plans for war in a parliamentary junta in which the three territories were represented. Strategy was agreed upon by common consent (Bascuñan 1863:39–41).[23] The relationship between the local chiefs and territorial toques is not clear, but it seems likely that military power was held to both qualify status and to assure authority. When disagreement occurred between toques, war between territories could and did sometimes develop (Latcham 1928:94–99, 144–148; L. Valdivia 1852:281–282).

Gerónimo Pietas, writing around 1729, describes a further development of this general schema. At this time the territorial strips had been increased to four in number. These provinces were still called butanmapos, but they extended farther north and south than did the older territories. This extension of Araucania is mute testimony to the growth of Araucanian strength and confidence. In Pietas' description each butanmapo had a hierarchy of three superior chiefs: a *toqui-guilmen* (commander), a *guinca-guilmen* (field commander), and a *pelqui-guilmen* (diplomatic courier). While these officers assumed absolute authority in their positions within the province, they were inferior to a *toque-general* who apparently wielded a measure of authority over the whole of Araucania. He further describes a conventionalization of diplomacy involving three forms for the calling of war. A general war could be called for only by the toque-general, and at his own discretion. When he desired to begin hostilities word was passed to all chiefs through a group of sub-chiefs called *cones.* Only the toque-general could dispatch the cones, and in the event of hostilities between the provinces, the fact of being called to council by a con was a guarantee of safe conduct. All chiefs attended the councils, wherein strategy was planned and forces drawn up.

War could also be called for by a regional toque. As messenger he sent his pelqui-guilmen to the other butanmapos, asking their aid and support, which they might or might not give. In the third instance war could be initiated by simply attacking the Spaniards. In this event the warring chieftain used force of arms to enlist the support of the local Indians for his designs (Pietas 1846:489–493). As incomplete as this description is, it does give evidence of a relatively sophisticated politico-military organization which stands in sharp contrast against that of the first generation of estado caciques.

Development of religious beliefs among the Araucanians is a most difficult postulation because we know so very little about their pre-Hispanic religious ideas. The chroniclers generally agree that the spirits of Araucanian ancestors formed an important cult, each kinship group having an ultimate progenitor whose spirit was called *Pillán*. This spirit was believed to be immanent, and so could be propitiated. Before going into battle the Indians sometimes sought divination from oracles, and once having gained a victory in a given locality through the intercession of supernatural forces, they believed that they could not lose a subsequent battle in that particular place (Marmolejo 1862:172; González de Nájera 1889:48; see also Latcham 1928:193–194).[24] Given the immediate religious background of the chroniclers of the sixteenth century, one in which religious and nationalistic sentiment were perfectly united, and the omnipresent tradition of the *Reconquista,* one must always wonder if the early chroniclers reported what the Indians actually believed, or if they instead reflected the paths of their own cognition.

As the Spaniards made war in the name of an omnipotent God, the Araucanians appear to have rationalized a deity for their own defense. There were innumerable Pilláns hovering over every locality, and in the absence of concerted missionary effort they doubtless remained. In describing an Araucanian ceremonial that he witnessed in 1629 Bascuñan depicts an interesting bit of symbolism which suggests the evolution of a super-Pillán. The occasion of ceremony was the execution of a Spanish captive. Involved in the execution was a lance with three knives fixed to its end, representing the three butanmapos. After the captive's brains had been dashed out, his captor took from the lance that knife which represented his personal region of Araucania and used it to cut out the victim's heart. He sucked its blood, took tobacco smoke and blew it to the heavens, then passed the heart around to the other chiefs for similar usage, after which it was divided and eaten (Bascuñan 1863:39–43).[25] The three knives symbolized Araucania, and the sucking of blood was a form of thanksgiving to the Pillán for victory. This ceremony closely approaches the abstraction of Home, Country, and God.

Later in his captivity Bascuñan had occasion to spend several days in the company of one of the small sons of a chief. One afternoon he asked the child if he would like to learn how to pray. The boy answered affirmatively; he had already learned something of prayers from a Spanish captive. With little instruction the child recited the Pater Noster in Spanish, but without understanding what it was he was reciting. Bascuñan, speaking Araucanian fluently, decided to teach him in the Araucanian tongue. The child was delighted to understand the recitation. The trenchant Bascuñan then asked him if he understood the idea behind the prayer. Yes indeed, was the reply. God could be none other than a great Pillán, superior to other Pilláns (Bascuñan 1863:155–156; see also Córdoba y Figueroa 1862:26). Bascuñan registered satisfied delight. The question is, should he have been so delighted?

In order to maintain a spirit of unqualified resistance the leaders of the estado, who manipulated majority opinion, instituted indoctrinational forms for boys and youths. Beginning at six years of age boys were taught the use of military weapons. By observing him the boy's tutors would decide which weapon he was most proficient with, and then he would be trained as a specialist in the use of that weapon. At the same time he was arduously trained in running and swimming (Olaverría 1852:23). Another type of training begun at this early age was the torture of Spanish captives. The boys were given knives and living Spaniards, then instructed in the arts of slow dissection, roasting, and eating (González de Nájera 1889:60). They were further required to memorize certain verses which recounted Spanish offenses since the beginning of the war, and were made to recite them at the command of their elders. In this way a boy became a man with a clearly fixed purpose in life. As a youth the Araucanian would speak thus of his lance:

> This is my master: it does not order me to dig for gold, or carry food or firewood, nor to herd cattle, or to follow it about. And since this master sustains my liberty, it is with him that I wish to pass (González de Nájera 1889:61, 105).

There was seldom talk of peace in the estado. Even a chief, if he dared speak of peace in war council, could be cut down on the spot by the nearest soldier. Apparently it was quite common for the warriors to kill any Indian who spoke of peace, or who was suspected of having the word in his mouth. Nájera describes a rigorous "inquisition" by the warriors to suppress the minority who wanted to farm rather than fight. Christianity was also forbidden. In the course of time many Indians were introduced to its tenets through close contact with the Spanish, especially the Indians who lived around the Spanish settlements. After the disaster of 1598, of course, the towns were no more. Many of the Indians had become reconciled to Spanish occupation and were genuinely converted to Christianity. Now they were exposed to the mercy of the estado's inquisitors. From what we know, it did not go well with them (González de Nájera 1889:100, 119, 60, 163, 70; Calderón 1898:13). Standing in opposition to Christianity was an apparently well-defined Araucanian concept, to wit: the Indian way of life is the only one; those who die in war against the Spanish go to another land where they enjoy more women and luxuries than they ever had in this life; there is nothing to fear in death (Olaverría 1852:40).

Araucanian opposition to Spanish intrusion was not confined to the field of battle. At all times they waged psychological warfare with consummate skill. While they always celebrated a victory over the Spaniards, and let the settlers know of their celebration, they never disclosed the identity of the fort or community that had fallen (González de Nájera 1889:75–76, 98, 100). With great finesse they obstructed Spanish intelligence, keeping the enemy in a state of worried ignorance. It is relatively certain that human flesh was not eaten by the Araucanians in pre-Hispanic times except in times of dire necessity (See Cooper 1946a:732; Medina 1952:220–221).[26] With the advent of the Spanish invasion, however, the eating of Spaniards became institutionalized. Time and time again the chroniclers tell of Spaniards being eaten, in whole and in part, and sometimes, their horses with them. Since there does not appear to have been a tradition to support this practice, nor any magical or superstitious belief connected with the act, it seems reasonable to assume that it was developed for its propaganda value. This would represent an intended clash of values. Discovering the abhorrence with which the Christians viewed cannibalism, the Araucanians appear to have developed it as a cultural opposite, a symbol of resistance. The great chief of Arauco, Caupolican, in hurling a challenge at Governor García Hurtado de Mendoza, boasted that he had eaten the previous governor (Valdivia) and would do the same with him (Hurtado de Mendoza 1846:183–184). In some cases, even the well-picked bones of Spaniards were consumed in wine after being burned and powdered, the idea being that no memory of the Spaniards should remain (González de Nájera 1889:54).

Another Araucanian device was the making of flutes from Spanish shinbones, most often extracted while the victim was still alive. On occasion the victim was forced to play his threnody on his own shin bones (González de Nájera 1889:53–54, 54–57). After the Indians developed their own cavalry they used the shinbones in lieu of trumpets. Nájera describes the sound they made as one which was doleful and morose, producing depression in those who heard it (González de Nájera 1889:115). One can but imagine the effect on the settlers produced by a night-riding horde, sweeping over the country side, accompanied by its unearthly music.

The Araucanians had still other ways to indicate their scorn for Spanish culture. On occasions they cut limbs and made crosses upon which to crucify their captives before roasting and eating them (González de Nájera 1889:58). In their treatment of captive Spanish women the Indians made calculated mockery of the enemy's institutions. The conquerors' ladies were highly prized by the chiefs, who used them as concubinary slaves. In 1605 a new Spanish governor, Don Alonso García Ramón, came down from Lima with 1000 troops. With this show of force he opened negotiations with the caciques of the estado for return of female captives, offering Indian hostages in exchange. The chiefs of Arauco decided to part with some of their prizes, and at the appointed time produced the prisoners. Before waiting husbands and fathers the women appeared, calloused, lousy, naked below the waist, and, more often than not, visibly pregnant (González de Nájera 1889: 118, 67–71).[27] Now we know that the Araucanians had the same ideas of physical propriety as did the Spaniards. Both made the same distinction as to public and private parts of the anatomy (González de Nájera 1889:46–47). It was by intention alone that the chiefs of Arauco forced their unfortunate victims to appear thus before their menfolk. The chiefs of Purén, although they liked the Spanish no better, provided coverings with which their captives could hide their shame (González de Nájera 1889:69).

The foregoing brief review of Araucanian culture in its history has embraced the outward manifestations of change rather than its internal mutations. Two principal aims have directed the study: one intended to restore the chronology which is so basic to cultural history; the other to divert study of the problem of Araucanian resistance from narrow analysis of Spanish strength and weakness. It is apparent that understanding is to be found in the sphere of Araucanian cultural experience. In plowing the furrow it is inevitable that questions tentatively answered should suggest a multitude of new ones lying deeper beneath the surface.[28] With more intensified study, surface appearances which now seem to be certainties will doubtless be proved to be more apparent than real. Even so, we can better understand why an observation made by an historian in the middle of the eighteenth century could, with small exception, have been made in the sixteenth:

> In a short time the Spanish conquered the three powerful empires of the American hemisphere, those of Peru, Mexico, and Bogotá, but the hundred and ninety years that have elapsed since the beginning of this conquest have not sufficed to end it with the subjugation of the Araucanians. Nor has the vast expenditure of fifty million pesos and more than 25,000 recruits, nor the effusion of blood that has been spilled done so, even though in the past century the King declared this war to be equal to those of Spain, Flanders, and Italy. Today the Araucanians possess the fairest portions of Chile, from the Biobío River to the Straits of Chiloé, a hundred and fifty leagues stretching between the Cordillera and the sea. In the whole of this area the Spanish hold nothing but the fortified towns of Arauco and Valdivia: the Indians live in independence and enjoyment of their coveted liberty (Córdoba y Figueroa 1862:29).[29]

NOTES

1. For discussion of Chilean pre-history see Encina (1940–1952:v. 1, chaps. ii, iii) and Latcham (1928:147–154, *passim*).

2. Olaverría was an old soldier in Chile when he wrote his chronicle in 1594. His work is both dependable and readable. Also see J. Perez García (1846:224–225).

3. The term Picunche did not come into vogue until the seventeenth century. Writers of the eighteenth and nineteenth centuries accepted and compounded these delineations. In addition to these three areas the Spaniards further differentiated between the Picunche, who extended somewhat south of the Maule River, and the *Promaucaes,* who lived between the Nuble River and the Biobío, including the site of Concepción. The Promaucaes were extremely warlike, but since they lived north of the Biobío they were not Araucanians in the proper sense, nor did they make up any part of the *estado* (see note 19).

4. Marmolejo came to Chile with Valdivia in 1549, hence he wrote with considerable experience and authority. His work is fundamental to the study of Araucanian culture.

5. Marmolejo's account of Valdivia's death is based on an eyewitness account, hence it is more acceptable than are the many others that are based on rumors and hearsay.

6. For a survey of the first general uprising see Encina (1940–1952:v. 1, chaps viii, ix).

7. The author was in Chile from 1601 to 1607. Experienced in military sciences, he made a brave attempt to analyze Araucanian resistance. His work is invaluable for Araucanian study.

8. In spite of Spanish fears, firearms did not play a significant role in Indian strategy until late in the seventeenth century.

9. It should be kept in mind that conquest and settlement were private financial ventures, and very expensive ones. See Governor García Hurtado de Mendoza's complaint in Marmolejo (1862:90).

10. This was Valdivia's experience in Santiago; the Indians tired of "running like beasts" and submitted to reduction (P. Valdivia 1846a:61).

11. This technique of dissembling was practiced widely, both in Spanish towns and on the frontiers. The Indians were so skilled that the Spanish were never able to tell whether they really meant to keep the peace or not. Either way, there was nothing the Spanish could do but accept, driven as they were by the economic imperative of their way of life. The Indians seem to have understood this perfectly. The granting of terminal peace in critical areas as a part of wider strategy became common. Revolts were well planned: the chiefs had the White women divided among themselves in advance; the gold that had been dug for the Whites during peace was thrown into the nearest river, or used to ransom Indian hostages; bloody revenge was visited upon the erstwhile masters. See Marmolejo (1862:58–59, 125) and González de Nájera (1889:46–47, 65).

12. For typical accounts see Marmolejo (1862:35ff, 85, 101, 171–176, 186–187). In the matter of Indian strategy and resistance the Spaniards could not see the forest for the trees. They laid responsibility for their failures on everything but the Indians. A widely prevalent idea, as expressed by Martín Ruiz de Gamboa (1852:123–124), held that more polished peninsular gentlemen were needed to fight the Indians, ignorant creoles being unfit for the task. Discrimination against creoles was a constant source of dissension in Spanish ranks. In 1557, García Hurtado de Mendoza arrived in Chile as Governor with many peninsulars in his train. The abandon with which he handed out encomiendas to his peninsular friends enraged the luckless creoles. In his reply to their complaints he suggested that no more than a handful of the Chileans knew the identity of their fathers, and then insultingly inquired, *"En qué se andan aquí estos hijos de putas?"* (Marmolejo 1862:80). [González de] Nájera (1889:36–37) took a more realistic view. He stated that creoles were born in war and carried the brunt of the fighting, and did it well. Because the chroniclers ignored their deeds, he added, they were unappreciated in Spain. He considered the disparity between creole and peninsular to be utterly inane.

13. Marmolejo simply states that among those who plotted Valdivia's downfall was a *yanacona* named Alonso, who had been Valdivia's servant (1862:36). This brief notice is the only valid evidence of Lautaro's origin. Among the chroniclers in Chile the term yanacona invariably meant a friendly and allied Indian from the north. Chilean historians are prone to begin with the premise that he was an Araucanian, but have difficulty in explaining how he could have become so *españolado* in the brief period between Valdivia's first contact with the Araucanians and his death. It seems much more likely that Lautaro was taken by Valdivia in Santiago when he was a boy. See Vicuña Mackenna (1876) for the standard nationalistic version.

14. For a plausible account of Araucanian reaction to the Spanish danger after 1550 see Latcham (1915). While this study is valuable for purely military affairs, it does not attempt to explore or interpret the force behind Araucanian military organization beyond the factor of Indian bravery. Another weakness is the author's uncritical use of Pedro Mariño de Lovera's *Crónica del reino de Chile* (1865). Lovera was another soldier who came to Chile in 1551, served there for a number of years, and then retired to Lima to write a history of Chile. Ostensibly because it was not well written, the manuscript was turned over to a Jesuit, Bartolomé de Escobar, for rewriting. As a true courtier, he shifted emphasis to flatter his patron, García Hurtado de Mendoza, and otherwise took liberties which rendered the history worthless. After his revision it was probably revised by Hurtado himself. A copy was subsequently disseminated in Spain by Hurtado in suit for royal reward for services rendered. In like vein, Hurtado was ired at publication of Ercilla's *La Araucana,* which he felt slighted his person. In retaliation he commissioned Pedro de Oña to write his dull *Arauco Domado,* an epic in which Hurtado emerged as the conqueror of Arauco. As Nájera remarked, Oña merely made himself a fool in describing Arauco as subdued when in fact Arauco was more victorious and impregnable than ever before (González de Nájera 1889:36–37). See Barros Arana (1884–1902:v. 2, pp. 282–288).

15. John M. Cooper (1946a:697) is in error when he concludes that the Indians mastered European military tactics and strategy, making them their own.

16. These are but representative of many such descriptions.

17. Cooper (1946a:704) gives the impression that Indian saddles and riding gear were nothing more than crude imitations of Spanish models.

18. Whenever the Indians found it necessary or advisable to grant a temporary peace, the Spaniards first insisted that they turn in their horses and move about on foot, as subject persons were expected to do. The Indians invariably turned in their *rocinantes,* keeping their good stock hidden for use after the next rebellion (González de Nájera 1889:128).

19. The area included the Indian localities of Talcamavida, Laucamilla, Catiray, Marigueño, Angol, Arauco, Andalicán, Tucapel, and Purén. After the estado had been recognized as a political entity the term was applied to all or part of it. In essence, the term estado came to mean the center of Indian resistance, whether it embraced all of the above named provinces or merely one of them.

20. Historians and anthropologists seem to be under a strange compulsion to use this poem as a prime documentary source. This is not to say that in select instances the practice is not warranted, but the wide use to which it has been put must certainly be held in question. Everyone knows that there is much truth in it, although seldom is it possible to determine precisely where it resides.

21. It took nearly three years to organize the first rebellion. It is sometimes implied that the Araucanians were introduced to coöperative military effort on a large scale through attempted invasions by the Incas. This seems most unlikely because the Incas were held at the Maule River, and the Indians occupying this area, as nearly as can be ascertained, were the warlike Promaucaes, who were not Araucanians. Nor could the Inca invasions have had anything to do with the formation of the estado, since, as we have seen, it was created by the imposition of Spanish dominion, without which it could have had no meaning.

22. The Indians around the settlements who were friendly towards the Spanish were sorely vexed by the depredations of the estado's warriors. Crops were burned or stolen, and women and children were carried off to be used as drudges. See García Ramón (1852:250, 279), Xaraquemada (1852b:241–242) and González de Nájera (1889:60). Through acts of terror the estado sometimes forced friendly Indians to rebel against the Spanish. Through maladministration the Spanish sometimes achieved the same end. Plundering of Indian stores and raping of their women brought alienation and revolt. See Nuñez de Pineda y Bascuñan (1863:51–52).

23. Latcham (1928:153–154) considers this to be an ancient Mapuche military organization, even though it is first reported almost a century after the Spaniards arrived. From what we know of the ancient Mapuche, this would appear to be an unduly sophisticated organization.

24. Cooper (1946a:742–752) makes a noble attempt to unravel the confused threads of early Araucanian religious belief.

25. The author was a captain of Spanish infantry and the son of Alvaro Núñez de Pineda, *maestro de campo general,* one of Chile's distinguished soldiers. In 1629 the Araucanians crossed the Biobío and fell on Chillán. They captured Bascuñan and took him back to their stronghold. His captivity was one of those story book affairs, almost too romantic and dramatic to be real. He was befriended by Maulican, a powerful chieftain of the estado, and likewise the son of a famous warrior. When the other chiefs learned of Bascuñan's identity they demanded his head to use as a trophy to incite peaceful Indians to war. By chicanery and ruse Maulican saved him, and after some months of comfortable captivity returned him to his own people. His account of the adventure is invaluable, although it is somewhat tiresome to read. He was a creole and educated in Chile. He apparently felt compelled to show that a creole scholar could hold his own with a peninsular, hence his excessive quotation from and reference to classical authors.

26. Marmolejo (1862:57) states that in the spring of 1556 the Indians were visited by a terrible plague (called *chavalongo*). In the aftermath of famine the Indians turned to cannibalism as a means of survival.

27. The author also stated that over 500 Spanish women had been taken captive and at the time of writing some 200 remained in captivity (1889:37–38).

28. One such problem is suggested by the sources. In pre-Hispanic days the Araucanians were sedentary farmers of predominantly vegetarian habits. Frequent mention is made in the documents of a growing cattle economy, especially in Spanish sheep and goats. Inasmuch as warfare disrupted agricultural planting in the valleys, the Araucanians moved their fields to impenetrable sierras. It may be that lower yields in the mountains created a greater need for animal foodstuffs to supplement lowered agricultural production. See, for example, Bastida (1902:498), Olaverría (1852:36–38), Marmolejo (1862:76–77) and González de Nájera (1889: 23). The implications suggested in a shift of basic economy are highly significant and require further investigation.

29. His statistics seem to be far from the mark. In 1664 the casualty figures, as Latcham reports them were 29,000 Spaniards and 60,000 Indian allies (1915:58).

In the preceding article, we saw how contact and conflict with the Spaniards caused dramatic changes in Araucanian culture. It is such dramatic effects of culture ʻcontact that are generally emphasized. In this selection by Hilger and Mondloch, we can see the extent to which outside pressure can penetrate into such seldom recorded aspects of culture as measurements of time and distance. The necessity for Indians to adopt surnames is universal as they come into contact with Europeans, and the different ways in which such surnames are chosen is but another area in which there are few recorded data. One practice is to adopt a Christian first name, using the native name as a surname. Frequently, however, plantation owners, or local traders, will simply give a name to an Indian, much as Negro slaves were given names by their masters in the United States. Such imposed names are frequently accepted by the native because it is easier to do so than to argue, or simply from indifference.

The work of Sister M. Inez Hilger and Margaret Mondloch among the Araucanian has provided us with a wealth of detailed and well documented ethnographic data (cf. Hilger 1957, 1966). Sister Hilger has a talent for collecting data on many topics that are frequently ignored by other investigators (e.g., Hilger and Mondloch 1967), although her primary interest is in child-rearing practices.

31 M. INEZ HILGER AND MARGARET MONDLOCH

Surnames and Time and Distance Measurements Among the Chilean Araucanians

[SURNAMES]

... The man [was reminded] of the importance of identifying heirs by means of surnames. "Until recently no official record anywhere carried a surname for any child or anyone else," he began. "Only the given names of a child's parents were recorded along with the child's name. We have recently learned that surnames are important when clearing titles to land that is being inherited. Parents, therefore,

Reprinted by permission of the senior author and the publisher from *Journal de la Société des Américanistes*, vol. 55 –1 (1966), pp. 207–308.

All material appearing within square brackets [ ] has been added by the editor of this book.

request that surnames be added to their children's names in baptismal records, and all other records." Sister Gerena added, "Every week one or another father asks me to assist him in having surnames added to old records for himself, for his wife, and for his children. In most cases the father's given name becomes the surname of his children."

MEASURING TIME

The man stepped outside to read the time of day by the position of the sun; he had some distance to go before he would be home. He wanted to see too if there were indications of a storm. "Weather has become almost unpredictable," he noted. "Our seasons, too, seem to be changing somewhat. The winter rains should stop and our year should begin when days begin to be longer than nights. From then on until planting time, things of nature show new life, but this no longer holds true. Sometimes buds burst open earlier, and sometimes later. The time for planting wheat is when the leaf buds of the Chilean oak are as large as the kernels on that cob of corn (pointing at a cob riding the raft over the fireplace). When the vine called *paulum (Hydrangea integerrima)* has buds, we plant corn. Then comes sprouting time, and after that comes the period of growing. Then comes the time when there is an abundance to eat, because all things that grow have ripened. Next comes harvest time. And after that a period of time that we know is the forerunner of winter, the rainy season, a time when it rains continuously. The rain stops when days begin to be longer than the nights."

He continued, "We have no weeks, nor months, like the Chileans have; we keep no count of days. We do not understand the Chilean calendar, and have no need for doing so. We like their calendars, however, because of their scenic pictures. Our time of day is measured by the position of the sun. Therefore, on a cloudy day we can only guess at the time: sometimes we guess it correctly; sometimes not. Sometimes I am late in meeting persons with whom I am to catch fish, because I am unable to reckon time; the day is cloudy. We tell time quite accurately, when the sun shines, by taking notice where sunbeams fall, like at the edge of the fireplace or through a certain crack in the wall." Sister Gerena added, "School children call attention to their lunch hour by saying, 'It is past noon. See the sun is already there,' pointing at the sun. Or, if walls obstruct the view of the sun, they point at some object in the room, and say, 'Sunbeams are already shining there.' "

MEASURING DISTANCES

"Formerly it was not important that we measure distances. We would merely say we were going to the Pacific, or to a neighbor over the hill. It was not important to know how *far* we were going, but only *where* we were going. Today, we sometimes use Chilean expressions such as, 'I live about 20 minutes ride on horseback from here,' or 'It takes me one hour on foot to go there,' or 'I live about three kilometers from here.' Every Mapuche who deals with Chileans must have a way of knowing the length of a meter; the meter is a standard measure used by Chileans. One

Mapuche may mark off a meter on his oxcart, or on a pole, or he may measure the length of it on himself, while standing erect. For me a meter is four times this (he indicated distance between tip of thumb and tip of little finger, at greatest stretch). This may not hold for other persons because of differences in the size of hands. This handstretch we call *fücha duke.*

"We have a shorter measure which we call *pichi duke.* Supposing that girl (pointing at [an] eighteen-year-old girl) wants to know how much weaving she has done in one day on that *pontro* (blanket on a frame). She will say that she has woven so many pichi duke. A pichi duke is this distance (between tip of thumb and tip of first finger at greatest stretch)." At this point his sister fetched a stick on which she had measured off a pichi duke; when weaving a saddle cover, for instance, she measured its width with it. The girl added, "The complete measurements for a bed blanket, for me, are those of another blanket; it is only when I want to know how much I have woven in one day that I use the pichi duke to measure it."

This ethnohistoric study of trade in the Ecuadorian Oriente forms an interesting contrast to the article by Roth. Although Roth includes data acquired at different points in time, they tend to cluster within the period from the mid-nineteenth to the early twentieth century and are treated as though they were all contemporaneous. Oberem, using all available material, attempts to emphasize the changes wrought in trade patterns from the period of the conquest to the present.

For those interested in a more recent picture of Jívaro trade than that presented by Oberem, there are considerable data available in Harner's book (1972). Oberem did not pick up the important trade in magical power described by Harner but, as the author notes, it is most difficult to find historical information on trade among and within the various Indian groups, since the "Whites" who were writing the records upon which his study is based were not in the least interested in such matters. Oberem does, however, mention the trade in magical knowledge and curing between the highlands and the Quijo. Belief in the superior "magic" of the tropical forest Indians occurs also in Peru where I observed a highlander who came to the Montaña in order to purchase a magical spell from the lowland Indians. Travel for training in shamanism is also recorded for the Chocó of Colombia, although it is not clear to what extent this travel involved other forms of trade (Reichel-Dolmatoff 1961:151).

Oberem's discussion of the abandonment of coca cultivation and trade in Ecuador is of interest in view of the extent to which coca is vital to Highland religious practices in Perú and Bolivia and has been since before

*the conquest. There is always, however, the possibility of the retention of
some small scale production, or trade in sufficient coca to meet ceremonial
needs.*

32 UDO OBEREM

Trade and Trade Goods in
the Ecuadorian Montaña[1]

Trade is undoubtedly one of the aspects of culture that is easily changed
by outside influence. Since the 16th century the impulse for change in Indian
culture has come primarily from Europeans. In this study we will attempt to
determine how the historic fortunes of the Indian groups of the Ecuadorian
Montaña, that is their contact with and domination by Europeans, is reflected in
trade.

To illustrate the influence of historical events on Indian trade the Montaña, in
this case the Ecuadorian Montaña, serves particularly well since there is documentary evidence about this area spanning a period of nearly 450 years.[2] Unfortunately
the nature of these historical sources is such that they are by no means sufficiently
comprehensive to provide a complete picture of Indian trade through time. Apart
from relatively recent ethnographic reports one is dealing mostly with administrative documents written by Europeans for Europeans, in which the Indians were
only secondary subject matter. This fact explains, for example, why very little is
said about trade among culturally similar groups. The information given is, however, sufficient to provide some examples. The situation in the Montaña is also
more useful for our purposes than that in either the Highlands or the Amazon
lowlands since in the former, although there is undoubtedly more information
available about the Indians, European influence was so far-reaching that Indian
trade can hardly be separated from general trade, while for the latter area not
enough sources exist.

In the following discussion "trade" will be understood as any movement of
goods in which consumer and producer do not coincide as they do in a closed
economy. Excluded are transactions falling under the heading of "exchange" which
is understood as noneconomic or ceremonial gift exchange.[3]

The Indian groups of the Ecuadorian Montaña treated here are, from north to
south: the Yumbo between the southern boundary of Colombia and the Rio Coca;

Reprinted by permission of the author and publisher from *Folk*, vol. 8-9 (1967), pp. 243–258.
Translated by Alegonda M. Schokkenbroek and edited by Patricia J. Lyon with the approval of
the author.
All material within square brackets [ ] has been added by the editor of this book.

the Quijo between the Rio Coca and the Rio Napo; the Jíbaro south of the Rio Pastaza and the Canelo in the area of the Rio Bobonaza. All of these groups are quite similar as far as economic type and social organization are concerned.[4] The Yumbo are mentioned only in the 16th century and may represent either a group related to the Kofán or a division of that tribe. The Canelo are exceptional in being a group formed during the Colonial period consisting both biologically and culturally of a mixture of the original inhabitants of the northern Bobonaza area: Highland Indians; Quijo; Záparo and Jíbaro. Today the Canelo are distinct from their neighbors even linguistically, since they speak Quechua, and are well aware of their homogeneity.

We will now describe trade goods, trade routes and other aspects of culture directly connected with trade insofar as these elements can be determined from the sources. We will then ascertain if, how and why changes have taken place in the sphere of trade since the 16th century.

Hardly any direct information is available regarding pre-conquest Indian trade in the Ecuadorian Montaña. Within certain limits trade goods and routes mentioned in 16th century reports may also apply to the time before the European conquest. To what extent these accounts are also valid for the situation existing before the Inca conquest of the Highlands cannot be stated with certainty. Such an extension is plausible, however, since there existed alliances and other connections between the inhabitants of the Highlands and those of the Montaña. For example, the sister of the Cacique Mayor of Latacunga was married to a chief of the Quijo.[5] Contact between these two areas can also be seen from archaeological remains (See for example Collier and Murra 1943:58–59; Jijón y Caamaño 1952:377; Estrada Icaza 1961:165–172).

A statement in Montesinos refers to trade connections in Inca times. He mentioned six Inca officers sent as spies to the Oriente, that area of Ecuador east of the Andes (Montesinos 1930:108–109). Since they were accompanied by 200 bearers it can reasonably be assumed that they passed themselves off as traders.[6] This interpretation would, however, make sense only if the inhabitants of the Oriente were accustomed to visits by traders. A direct reference to trade goods comes from the report of Toribio de Ortiguera on an expedition made by the Inca Huayna Capac into the Ecuadorian Montaña. He writes that the Inca were particularly interested in finding out about the gold mines there, and exchanged axes and salt for gold (Ortiguera 1909:419–420). The first of the Inca expeditions mentioned above was into the southern Quijo area, the second into the area of the Yumbo or, more likely, the then neighboring Coronado.

In the 16th century the trade of the Yumbo with the Highlanders consisted in supplying planks and wooden agricultural implements. The Yumbo also sold cloth, salt and dogs to the Coronado, their neighbors in the Lowlands, in exchange for medicinal and dye plants, tamed animals, e.g., parrots and monkeys, as well as for young girls and boys. About 1592, when the report on this trade was written, the slave trade had almost stopped since the Coronado would accept only machetes and swords in exchange for slaves, and no one would give them these items (Relación de Pimampiro 1965:248–249, 251).

At that time Hatunquijos, the region around the later town of Baeza, was a center for trade between the Highlands and the Oriente. Markets, called by the Quechua word "gato," were held every eight days [week?] in specially appointed places. Trading was carried on there in "clothing as well as gold jewelry, foodstuffs and other products of the land" (Oberem 1958:235 and 242). The markets also had a social function since there the chiefs were paid tribute in the form of "fruit and food" (Oberem 1958:235 and 242).

In Hatunquijos we also find a currency unit fixed by agreement, a rare occurrence in the Andean and Montaña region. There was a kind of money called "carato" consisting of strings of twenty-four small bone beads. Regarding the value of such a string, it was said to be worth a day's work and that, in exchange for one, a guest had the right to spend the night with the wife of his host (Oberem 1958:235 and 242–243). In commerce between Spaniards and Indians one of these strings was worth one *tomín*.[7]

Suggestions in contemporary sources lead us to the conclusion that there were professional traders among the northern Quijo who traveled to the Sierra selling, for example, coca leaves and receiving, among other things, cotton. There was no cotton in the Baeza region which was known for its textiles in the early Colonial period. The cotton was brought from the Highlands or from the Archidona area known as "Los Algodonales" in southern Quijo territory. Slaves and strings of dried blossoms of the cinnamon tree (*Canela alba*) are mentioned as further trade goods. Cinnamon grew primarily in the area of the "Calientes," a sub-group of the Quijo living on the Rio Payamino (Oberem 1958:234–238, 242–246). The Spanish received their first reports of the Quijo area very early because of the cinnamon trade which extended as far as Peru. For example, in Cajamarca the imprisoned Inca Atahualpa turned over some shipments of cinnamon to Francisco Pizarro (Fernández de Oviedo y Valdés 1851–1855: v. IV, p. 215). In 1535, three years before the first expeditions of the Spanish into the Quijo area, it was known in Quito that cinnamon reached the Highlands by way of Hatunquijos (Quito 1934:107), and La Gasca wrote to the Consejo de Indias in 1549 that Indians were bringing cinnamon to Quito to sell it there (Gasca 1964:335).

All information regarding trade in cinnamon and cotton refers to Hatunquijos. Trade was certainly more extensively organized there than in the rest of the Quijo area. For example, the chiefs of Hatunquijos had asked the Gobernador Gil Ramírez Dávalos, in 1558, to establish a Spanish settlement in their territory in the expectation of a resultant expansion of trade (Rumazo González 1946:86–87). It should not be assumed that the other Quijo did not engage in trade as well; we just do not know anything about it.

Equally little is known about the trade of the Jíbaro in the 16th century. Around 1570 it is reported that those from the Rio Zamora had few trade connections with each other, there were no markets, and when they wanted to buy or sell something they sought each other out (Salinas Loyola 1965:134). In 1582 it is stated that they did not trade with each other, but only with Highland Indians who exchanged animals and other foodstuffs. These Highlanders were Cañari and Palta from the areas of the cities of Cuenca and Loja (Núñez 1965:142; Bello

Gayoso 1965:269). In the same year we are told that the Jíbaro sold salt from the vicinity of the city of Santiago de las Montañas to the Indians living further downriver (Aldrete 1965:148).

Sources for the 17th and 18th centuries are also incomplete. Particulars about the trade connections of the Yumbo are totally lacking. We are better informed about the Quijo and there are also some data about the Canelo and Jíbaro. From the 17th century there are reports about trade of the Quijo only with tribes south of the Río Napo. The town of Puerto Napo served as one of the centers where the Quijo met with their neighbors (Rodríguez 1684:242, 313). The Oa, who had settled in Santa Rosa towards the end of the century, maintained trade relations for a considerable period of time with the Omagua-Yeté who had fled from the Río Sunu to the Tiputini. European tools were traded for food.[8] Sources referring to trade of the Quijo with each other in the 17th and 18th centuries are scanty since this trade passed practically unnoticed by the Spanish. We learn only that in 1754 the inhabitants of San José, the last of the Quijo to weave, sold cloth to other Indians to obtain ready cash for the payment of tribute. A piece of cloth 2.5 varas long and 3/4 vara wide was worth two pesos [A vara is a little less than a yard.] In commerce with the Spanish, chickens were sold in Archidona and gold in Puerto Napo, in exchange for cash or goods (Basabe y Urquieta 1902:62–64).

In 1799 Hernández Bello reports on Indian traders from the Highlands, in particular from the towns of Ytulcachi, Tablón, Pintag and Alangasí. These traders brought cloth, bread, cheese and salt to the Quijo and returned home laden with, for example, calabashes. Hernández Bello points out that the Quijo were slow to settle their debts, since two years often passed before they paid for cloth and tools with *pita* (fiber extracted from the *Agave americana*), wax or gold dust (Hernández Bello 1919:259–261). The Quijo also took to Quito vessels called "pilches" made from calabashes, the fruit of *Crescentia cujete,* as well as tropical fruit and tamed animals. This trade can be seen in a picture, painted in 1783 by Vicente Albán, which is in the Museo de América in Madrid. Stevenson also reports such trade in 1808 (1825–1829:v. 2, p. 353).

Since the Jesuits mostly used the route via Archidona when going to their mission province of Maynas, the Quijo often encountered their boat crews, or themselves made long journeys as paddlers. For instance, it is reported in 1763 that the Omagua of the upper Amazon exchanged salt and dart poison with the Quijo for gold dust (Uriarte 1952: v. I, p. 279). The salt came from the Río Huallaga, the poison from the Peba or the Ticuna (Veigl 1785:90), whose product was known as the very best (Chantre y Herrera 1901:87). Basabe y Urquieta in 1754 and Bermeo about 1780 report that the Canelo collected and sold cinnamon as well as resins, rubber and medicinal plants (Basabe y Urquieta 1902:68–69; Bermeo 1886). It is not indicated whether they were visited by traders from the Highlands or whether they themselves went to the Highlands. It is, however, certain that the Canelo traveled to the Río Huallaga to obtain salt, as reported by Echeverría and Aguilar in 1784. The same authors also mention nets made of palm fibers among the Canelo trade goods (Echeverría and Aguilar y Saldaña 1895:348).

Since the Jíbaro hardly came in contact with the Spanish in the 17th and 18th centuries—they were not conquered—no mention is made of their trade which undoubtedly existed. We know only that, from 1790 on, Jíbaro went to the town of Paute to sell, and in 1792 white traders visited them with tools and other European products (Villavicencio 1860:47).

Naturally, much more information is available from the 19th and 20th centuries due to the more intensive penetration of the Montaña by Europeans. Unfortunately these reports also are confined to the Quijo, Canelo and Jíbaro. The Yumbo, or their neighbors the Kofán, are even now little known ethnographically. With regard to their trade we are therefore limited to relatively vague information. For example, Friede reports that the Kofán traded very little with the whites for fear of being cheated. The main trade item of the Kofán was gold dust, while the white traders that visited them brought tools, among other things (Friede 1955:214–215).

The Quijo maintained their important position as middlemen, procuring goods from the Highlands for other groups of the upper Amazon region, and goods from that area in turn, for the Sierra. In their travels along the Marañón and to the salt mines of the Huallaga, they exchanged beads, balls of colored thread, needles, crosses, religious medals, etc. which they had obtained in the Highlands from white or Indian traders, for foodstuffs. Machetes, knives, glass beads and cloth were used for the acquisition of dart poison or even salt from the Amazon tribes. Although the salt mines of the Huallaga were open to the exploitation of everyone, it was always possible that the way up the Huallaga might be blocked (Villavicencio 1858:388, 1860:47).

In the 19th century the Quijo supplied the Highlanders chiefly with gold, wax, pita, pilches, copal, ornaments and also bird skins;[9] receiving in exchange young pigs, dogs, cloth, needles and other European products.[10] Journeys were undertaken mainly to Quito and towns in the near vicinity of that city. Flemming reports, however, that the Quijo liked to take their gold to Popayán in Colombia to have it melted down because they had more confidence in coins from there (Flemming 1878:374). Many European products also reached the Quijo via travelers passing through their territory whom they supplied with provisions,[11] as well as by way of forced trade called "repartos." The Quijo passed on some of the objects thus acquired to other Indians. The trade connected with journeys for salt and dart poison has already been discussed. Mentioned as further partners in these transactions are the Záparo, Jíbaro, Canelo and some unspecified tribes of the upper Amazon. From the latter tribes the Quijo obtained dried and salted meat of the *vaca marina* [manatee] (*Manatus americanus* Desm.) (Jameson 1858:342) and supplied, among other things, maize and drums in return (Almagro 1866:125). The Záparo went to the towns of Suno, Santa Rosa, Napotoa and Aguano to obtain iron implements in exchange for smoked meat, feather ornaments, baskets, hammocks and slaves, mostly children who they had captured in raids (Villavicencio 1860:37; Osculati 1929: v. II, pp. 11–12). The price for a hammock was one knife. After the Záparo had used a knife for a considerable length of time they sold it to some group living further in, obtaining four to five hammocks for the used knife (Villavicencio 1858:366). The Canelo and Jíbaro traded mainly in blowguns. In 1864 Jiménez de la Espada encountered eleven Canelo in Puerto Napo who had come to exchange blowguns for gold (Jiménez de la Espada 1927–1928: v. LXVIII, pp. 358–359). The Quijo traded some of the blowguns further along to their northeastern neighbors, the Ciona [Siona] on the Putumayo whence they were traded to the Quechua-speaking Indians of Mocoa in Colombia who called themselves "Ingas," and still further north to the "Ingas" of Santiago, a small town on the way from Pasto to Putumayo (Hardenburg 1912:59, 81). Little is mentioned in the sources about the trade of the Quijo with one another although, for example, those returning from journeys certainly resold part of their acquisitions. Direct mention is made, as an oddity, of the lard trade carried on by the inhabitants of San José. The rendered fat was supplied in bamboo tubes called "pima" which cost four *reales,* and was traded in particular to the neighboring villages of Concepción, Avila and Loreto (Jiménez de la Espada 1927–1928: v. LXVIII, p. 464; Villavicencio 1858:402).

The Indians of Loreto in Quijo territory probably carried on a lively trade with those Loretanos who had earlier fled to the Rio Huiririma, a southern tributary of the Rio Napo. Villavicencio was unable to obtain direct information on this matter, but he believed that he could draw this conclusion on the basis of the purchase by the Loretanos of tools and cloth far in excess of their needs (Villavicencio 1858:400–401).

Present day trade relations of the Quijo still resemble, in general outline, those of the last century, as the author was able to observe. Gold and craft products are sold in the Highlands and, for example, young pigs or dogs are brought back from there. Blowguns, dart poison, quivers and some blowgun darts are obtained from the Canelo, often in exchange for European type fiddles made by the Quijo. European goods and a small amount of dart poison from the Amazon are also obtained from resident and transient white traders against payments in labor.

The professional activity of the *sagra,* the Quijo "sorcerer," may also be viewed as the acquisition of goods in exchange for labor. The sorcerers exercise their profession not only among the Quijo themselves, but are also called into the Highlands to heal the sick, and are well paid for this service since it is generally believed that the sorcerers of the Oriente are more powerful than those of the Sierra. This belief is why, for example, Highland Indians take their training among the Quijo or obtain ingredients from them. Such behavior is reported from the last century as well as from this one.[12] Karsten reports the sale by the Quijo to a Canelo, at a high price, of a stone found in the stomach of a big fish. This stone served as a goodluck charm in fishing (Karsten 1920:57). According to Tessmann the Quijo also acquired pottery drinking bowls from the Canelo, and according to Porras Garcés there is a trade in "poison, lances and other things" from the Quijo to the Colorado on the western slopes of the Andes (Tessmann 1930:243; Porras Garcés 1961:142). The author was, however, unable to obtain details anywhere about these trade connections or objects.

Aside from the above mentioned trade relations with the Quijo, the Canelo also maintained a separate trade with the Jíbaro. The exchange of blowguns for drums is important. The two groups depend on one another for these goods. Apart from drums, the Jíbaro obtain dart poison and blowgun darts from the Canelo, although they also manufacture both themselves, giving dogs and salt in return.[13] Within Canelo territory, for example, gold dust and tobacco from the Rio Villano are sold to the inhabitants of the Rio Bobonaza (Canelo, Sarayacu, Pacayacu) in exchange for tools and clothing.[14] The Canelo who travel as paddlers for whites use every occasion to take trade goods with them. For example, on the lower Bobonaza they trade alcohol, gunpowder and small metal objects for blowguns, poison, unfinished blowgun darts, tamed animals and smoked fish.[15] Some of the goods obtained are passed on to the Quijo, Jíbaro and white traders. The Canelo also travel to the Highlands taking rubber, wax, gold dust, medicinal plants, etc., and bringing back, especially, tools and clothing. Journeys to the Huallaga to collect salt were still undertaken until the end of the 1930's.[16] Today salt is provided only through purchase from white or Indian traders from the Highlands, or from the Jíbaro northeast of Macas. The same is true of dart poison. The Canelo know how to make poison themselves, but value that made by other groups more highly.

On the whole, the Jíbaro trade much less than do the Quijo and Canelo. Exceptions to this generalization are the groups in the Macas region and a very few from Méndez and Gualaquiza. They supply pork, salt, chickens, etc., to the whites in exchange for guns, clothing, ammunition and iron tools. A portion of these goods is traded to other Jíbaro (Villavicencio 1858:365–366; Valladares 1912:25; and others). The sale of lances with which a person has been killed is also a part of Jíbaro trade. The lances are disposed of because it is believed that otherwise the game would smell of human flesh (Karsten 1935:159). The Jíbaro themselves seldom visit Highland towns to offer their products for sale. They generally obtain European goods from transient or resident traders. Peculiar to the Jíbaro is the trade in shrunken human heads. Although this trade has long been forbidden, tsansas are still exchanged for rifles (Bastian 1878–1889: v. II, p. 88; Karsten 1935:81).

One can readily see from the preceding review of Indian trade in the Ecuadorian Montaña that change has taken place since the 16th century, in spite of the somewhat unsatisfactory nature of the evidence from sources and the fact that the list of trade goods is incomplete. We will now demonstrate by some typical examples what were the bases of this change and what the eventual effects of the changes were on other cultural domains.

The most striking among the new trade goods were the objects made of iron or steel. Axes, knives and particularly the machete which had become an all-purpose tool, were so widely dispersed at an early time that here, as in no other cultural sector, an almost total dependence on "imports" resulted. The manufacture of stone tools was soon abandoned and is today forgotten. Since the use of metal tools makes many tasks much easier, the relatively high price which the Záparo, who were not in direct contact with the whites, were still paying in the last century is understandable, as is the 16th century boycott of the Coronado who would supply slaves to the Yumbo only in exchange for machetes.[17]

With regard to the supply of textiles, the Quijo and Canelo today find themselves totally dependent on trade. This fact is the more surprising as the Quijo area enjoyed a certain fame for textile production in early Colonial times. A large portion of tribute had to be delivered in woven goods. Later, *encomenderos* found it more profitable to import cheap cloth from the Highlands and receive tribute in gold dust. The Quijo became so accustomed to the purchased cloth, or, today, ready-to-wear European styles, partly through lack of time due to increased gold washing and partly due to fashion, that the manufacture of cloth was completely abandoned and they no longer master this skill at all. As noted earlier, the last Quijo who were still weaving, around 1754, were the inhabitants of San José. Along with weaving, the cultivation of cotton and the cotton trade reported in the 16th century were also abandoned. The Canelo were still weaving in the last century but today they also wear only imported clothing. The reason for their abandonment of textile manufacture must be sought simply in their close contact with the whites. Direct pressure cannot be shown. In their entire history they have never been completely dependent as have the Quijo, nor were they under the coercion of the repartos [forced trading], nor were they dependent upon *patrones* except in the case of a few families during the rubber boom around the turn of the century.[18]

The Jíbaro still make the greater part of their own textiles themselves, though they also buy some clothing.

The manufacture of barkcloth, which until rather recently was used for blankets, was widely abandoned by all three groups in favor of imported woven goods. Lately the Canelo are again making barkcloth with bright painted patterns which they sell in the Highland cities where a demand, albeit not great, exists for it in tourist shops.

Today the Quijo and Canelo are finally dependent on the import of salt which they get from the Highlands or from the Jíbaro of the Macas area. The Jíbaro, except for those that have been Christians for a long time, use salt largely for medicinal purposes and very little as seasoning.

In the 16th century the Quijo laboriously made bitter tasting salt from plants. This supply could hardly have been sufficient, however, since it is reported, in the description of the journey of the Inca Huayna Capac to the Ecuadorian Oriente, that gold was obtained there in exchange for salt and, in 1542, the companions of Gonzalo Pizarro complained that the greatest "nuisance" in the Quijo territory was lack of salt. The Quijo probably gave up salt production in the 17th century after the Jesuits had taken over the Archidona pastorate. The missionaries brought salt from the mines on the Rio Huallaga to supply the Indians under their tutelage. The Quijo, too, learned in the course of time to make trips to the upper Amazon and Huallaga for salt.

When the Jesuit expeditions to and from the upper Amazon ceased with the expulsion of this order from Spanish possessions, the Quijo began to travel to this area on their own account as well as on commission for white traders. These trips are mentioned in many 19th century sources. When traveling on commission, at the beginning of the trip each Indian received in payment about twenty-five to thirty meters of plain cloth. From this cloth were made a poncho, a pair of pants and a mosquito net, and any remainder was left for wives and children to use. The trip to the Huallaga was begun at the end of June or the beginning of July. The route followed was down the Napo to the Amazon, up the Amazon to the mouth of the Huallaga, and up the Huallaga to where rock salt occurs, especially beyond Chasuta about halfway up the river. Arriving about the end of August, the men worked there until about the end of September when the waters of the Huallaga began to rise. With the aid of the current, the return trip was easy as far as the mouth of the Napo. Then, heavily laden with salt blocks, the boats had to be slowly poled up the Napo. The travelers usually returned toward the end of November. As previously mentioned, during the trip items of European manufacture were exchanged for provisions.

The Canelo also made journeys for salt. They had the advantage of a shorter route than the Quijo, traveling down the Bobonaza and the Pastaza to the Amazon, and from there on down to the Huallaga. Difficulties for the Quijo and Canelo in their travels arose from disputes between the republics of Ecuador and Peru regarding the boundary line in the Amazon region. In 1851 the authorities of both countries agreed that even Indians must possess a valid passport to travel in the area of the other country. About 1908 the salt-collecting trips had to be stopped completely for a while because the Peruvian government had granted exploitation rights in the Huallaga salt mines to a private company.

During that period the Quijo and Canelo were dependent on the Highlands for their salt supply, and members of both groups undertook trading trips to that region. The Quijo could also obtain salt from their patrons.

Since the Canelo were not subject to patrons, the Dominican missionaries made great efforts to channel to their Canelos mission part of the salt produced, by means of salt water evaporation, by the Jíbaro northeast of Macas. The missionaries were so successful in their efforts that, to the present day, not only the town of Macas, but also the Canelo territory is supplied from this source. This trade between the Canelo and Jíbaro could not, however, meet the demand. Therefore, around 1914, both the Canelo and the Quijo again began to make successful salt trading journeys. Increasingly, however, they became the victims of political difficulties. The number of trips decreased and they have stopped completely since the Peruvian-Ecuadorian War of 1941.

All Indians of the Montaña are enthusiastic hunters. Guns are presently in use for hunting throughout the region. Generally these guns are muzzle loaders which are still being manufactured especially for the Indian trade. The Indians prefer this type of gun as a hunting weapon because it requires only relatively cheap gunpowder, and not the more expensive ammunition of more modern models. Only the Jíbaro are also interested in rifles which they use on their raids. These weapons are obtained in exchange for tsansas [shrunken heads], the only Jíbaro product of great value due to the lively demand for them on the part of tourists. It can hardly be established that this demand has led to an increase in headhunting, but such a result could be very possible.

The gun has almost completely replaced the lance for hunting large animals. For hunting monkeys, birds and other such smaller animals, however, the Indians still prefer the noiseless blowgun. Trade in blowguns and dart poison has, therefore, not decreased at all. The previously described salt trading journeys served simultaneously for the purchase of dart poison since that of the Ticuna, Peba and also of the Indians of the salt mine area of the Huallaga, was considered better than that of the Canelo and Jíbaro. At times dart poison served as the preferred medium of exchange.

Further new trade goods owing their introduction to white influence are chickens and pigs, adopted as domestic animals and integrated into the Indian cultures, although more as trade goods than for personal consumption.

In the same way that some Jíbaro groups exploit salt only for sale, they have also started to hunt deer. They themselves do not eat deer for religious reasons, but the deer serve as trade items in dealings with the whites.

The cultivation of tobacco was also taken up by some Quijo groups about the end of the 18th century and by the Canelo since the beginning of the present century only because of white demand. The small amount needed by the Indians themselves is supplied by wild tobacco. The same is true of pita, the fibers of the *Agave americana*. In the 18th and 19th centuries many parts of Quijo territory specialized in the production of pita. Trade in this product, as in tobacco, has decreased today because it is easier and cheaper to supply the Highlands from other areas.

Because the alcoholic drinks of the Indians are not as strong as distilled spirits, the latter form a popular trade item. The distilling of alcohol by the Quijo, since the first half of the last century, may be viewed as an effort to free themselves from dependence on the whites as a source of supply. The Quijo use a very simple pottery still with a brass condensing cover.

Examples of trade goods mentioned in 16th century documents but no longer in existence are gold ornaments, coca and slaves. The manufacture of gold ornaments and the trade in them is mentioned only for the Quijo, who ceased both activities soon after the conquest of their territory. The reason for this abandonment may be that the Spanish were so interested in this metal. It is more difficult to explain why the Quijo had coca, at most, until the end of the 16th century. This item was grown and consumed by them as well as being traded. In fact, it cannot be said with certainty why the consumption of coca, and coca trade generally, stopped in Ecuador. A decisive factor may possibly have been that, in contrast to Peru and Bolivia, the Spanish in Ecuador did not engage directly in coca trade and cultivation, but rather left them to the Indians. Only for this reason was it possible to implement the royal decrees directed against coca, which failed in Peru and Bolivia due to Spanish resistance. The abandonment of coca growing and coca trade by the Quijo may perhaps also be explained as a result of upheavals in their economic and social organization due to the wars and uprisings of the 16th century. The slave trade of the Montaña tribes, reported in the 16th century for the Yumbo and the Quijo, officially stopped soon after the conquest since the Spanish Crown allowed the enslavement of Indians only under specific conditions, which, however, did not prevail in Ecuador. More or less unnoticed by the Spanish or Ecuadorian authorities, a kind of trade in people continued. Children were given by one family to another, by one Indian group to another, and even by Indians to whites. This activity can be considered as trade insofar as it involved payment.

The old forms of trade reported to us, especially from Hatunquijos, are not found after the 17th century. This statement applies to the markets held at eight day intervals, currency in the form of strings of bone beads, and professional traders. It cannot be demonstrated in detail why these institutions were, or had to be, given up. In general it can be said only that the disruption of Quijo social structure caused by the Spanish conquest led to their disappearance.

New forms of trade developed, such as the trading journeys for salt and poison that have already been mentioned, and also the introduction of money as a medium of exchange. This latter was by no means accomplished everywhere, and where accomplished then only in the form of coins, with paper money still being widely refused by the Indians. The acquisition of goods in exchange for labor should also be seen as a new form of trade. In addition to the voluntary contracts of paddlers and bearers, for instance, there were and still are the special forms of *reparto* and *patronazgo*. Both forms are typical for the Quijo while the other groups were hardly touched by them. Repartos refer to the forced transfer of items from the authorities or priests to the Indians who, in turn, had to deliver, within a fixed period of time, a certain quantity of their products, among the Quijo mainly gold dust or pita. Under this system, the prices paid by the Indians were three to four times the market value. The system of repartos lasted throughout the 19th century. The circulation of goods increased by leaps and bounds, in part so much so, however, that the requirements of the Indians were far exceeded. Large groups of Quijo fled to other areas at that time to escape being provided with unwanted goods.

As more and more whites settled in Quijo territory, the system of repartos was modified to that of patronazgo. Since about 1910 almost all Indians are dependent upon a *patrón,* a white settler or trader. The patrón gives "his" Indians goods on credit in payment for which they put their labor at his disposal either directly, or indirectly in the form of manufactured products. Even today it is almost impossible to obtain bearers or boat crews in Quijo territory without dealing through a patrón. He is paid by the traveler and deducts the money received from the account of indebtedness of the Indians. The dependence of the Quijo on their patrons is so great that whole families can be forced to give up their old homesteads and live as laborers on haciendas on the middle Napo or the Putumayo. Such treatment entails, of course, a severe disruption of the social structure, especially when only a few nuclear families are displaced from an extended family.

The Indians of the Ecuadorian Montaña have here provided an example of how, since the 16th century, white contact has resulted in change in one sector of culture, trade. In the process described, the culture type as such has been maintained, namely that of farmers with extended family organization subsisting mainly on slash and burn cultivation but with the importance of hunting and fishing not to be underestimated. However, due to the functional interrelation of all aspects of culture, the changes in trade goods and forms of trade also led to changes in other aspects of culture.

NOTES

1. The author is greatly indebted to the Deutschen Forschungsgemeinschaft which made possible his two trips to Ecuador for ethnographic research and the survey of historical materials.

2. Montaña is here used following Steward (1948). [The region in question is commonly called "Oriente" in Ecuador, Montaña being the Peruvian term.]

3. The author follows the definitions of Hartmann (1968) where the question of the terminology of economic anthropology is discussed in detail.

4. Those wishing further detail on the culture of the groups mentioned in this article should refer to the corresponding sources: for the Jíbaro and Canelo, for example, Karsten (1935), and for the Quijo, Oberem (1971).

5. Informaciones de D. Sancho Hacho (ms.: f. 26 v.). Details on these Indian nobles and their families in Oberem (1967).

6. Cieza de León (1880:230) also reports on the sending, by the Inca Tupac Yupanqui, of spies disguised as traders to the area lying east of the Andes. [It should be noted that the passage from Cieza here cited refers to the area of the Montaña immediately to the east of Cuzco, and that the purpose of the spying was to obtain military intelligence prior to an invasion of the region.]

7. Lobato de Sosa ms.: f. 1 v. The tomín is an old silver coin (= 1 real = 1/8 peso).

8. Maroni 1889–1892: v. XXVI, p. 244. On these Omagua see Oberem (1961).

9. Uhle 1889–1890: v. II, pp. 2, 7; Orton 1870:193; Simson 1883:25; Gerstäcker 1906: 133.

10. Bollaert 1860:295, Villavicencio 1858:387; Simson 1886:154; and others.

11. Wiener 1884:38–39; Jameson 1858:342; Jiménez de la Espada 1927–1928: v. LXVIII, p. 194; and others.

12. Jiménez de la Espada 1927–1928: v. LXVIII, p. 364; Disselhoff 1940:304–305. The author also carried out research among the Canelo in 1955.

13. E.g., Karsten 1935:46, 145, 156–157, 1920:57; Mission report of 1887/88 in "El Oriente Dominicano," 36/37, Quito 1935, p. 90.

14. Mission report in "El Oriente Dominicano," 58/59, Quito 1938, p. 241.

15. In contrast to the Rio Napo where the author could observe only trade in small quantities, it is not uncommon to see three or four canoes laden with trade goods on the Rio Bobonaza.

16. E.g., Mission report in "El Oriente Dominicano," 42, Quito 1936, p. 247, 43/44, Quito 1936, p. 317, etc.; Valladares 1912:21–24.

17. Bibliographical references will not be repeated in the following sections. The sources already cited are those referred to.

18. [The forced sale called *reparto* and the system of *patronazgo* will be discussed later.]

Although the problems of Brazil's Indian populations have become world knowledge in recent years, Brazilian anthropologists have been aware of them for much longer and have been attempting both to call attention to the problem and to do something about it. A major effort in this direction has been the "Study of areas of inter-ethnic friction in Brazil" initiated and directed by Roberto Cardoso de Oliveira. This project has resulted in publications such as Laraia's studies of the "marginal man" (1967) and inter-ethnic friction on the middle Tocantins (1965), Laraia and Matta's book on Indians and Brazil nut gatherers (1967), and Oliveira's book on the Tukúna (1964).

Frikel's presentation of the material in historical perspective is necessary if one is to understand the many factors that enter into contact situations. His comments on changes in settlement plan, the loss of the men's house, and the resultant problems are significant in the light of the following excerpt from Nimuendajú regarding the eastern Timbira:

> One of the most characteristic features of Timbira culture—in the natives' own opinion—is the circular village plan. So long as their aboriginal life retains a spark of vitality they cling to this mode of settlement, which is most intimately bound up with their sociocere-monial organization. Notwithstanding their ignorance of Indian usage, the Baptist missionaries in Brazil correctly recognized the social signifi-cance of this feature and did their utmost to effect its abandonment; for as long as it survives the ancient social order, too, lives on, and within that there is no place for missionaries. (1946:37)

Lévi-Strauss made similar observations regarding the Bororo (1962:189).

Although Frikel has been unable to return to the Xikrín since the visits reported on in this article, he was kind enough to provide a postscript to the article including more recent information. What the present situation of this group may be awaits further investigation as suggested by the author.

In addition to the postscript, Frikel also made some minor additions and corrections to the original text. He has also written a monograph on Xikrín manufactures and subsistence activities (1968) as well as numerous works on other Brazilian groups.

33 PROTÁSIO FRIKEL

Notes on the Present Situation of the Xikrín Indians of the Rio Caeteté

The Xikrín or Djóre belong to the Gê linguistic family and are, at present, the northernmost group of the Kayapó Indians. They inhabit the lands of the Rio Caeteté, a left affluent of the Rio Itacaiunas which is, in turn, a tributary of the

Reprinted by permission of the author and publisher from *Revista do Museu Paulista*, n.s., vol. 14 (1963), pp. 145–158. Translated and edited by Patricia J. Lyon with the approval of the author.

All material appearing within square brackets [ ] has been added by the editor of this book.

Tocantins. The county seat is Marabá, situated at the confluence of the last named rivers. We visited these Indians twice, observing the changes that are occurring among them. We think it appropriate to present here some notes on their present situation.

It should be noted that the present account is based on a more condensed report on the same topic sent by the Division of Anthropology of the Museu Paraense "Emilio Goeldi" to the Office of the Director of the Indian Protection Service [Serviço de Proteção aos Índios].

HISTORICAL REMARKS

Little is known about the origin of the Xikrín, or even of the Kayapó groups in general. It is certain, however, that they are not autochthones of the region of the Caeteté and Itacaiunas rivers to which they migrated. We can base our interpretations of the circumstances on tribal tradition and on the depositions of old people of the region of Marabá and the Itacaiunas who went up these rivers as far as the headwaters by the beginning of the century, as well as on the records of the SPI [Indian Protection Service] since 1952.

Tribal tradition reports the following: In ancient times the Xikrín or Djóre were also Gorotire, together forming a single large block. Details of the location of the groups at that time are not mentioned. Because of disagreements over a corn field, however, part of the group split off. The Gorotire then called the dissidents "Djóre," that is, *aramã*, which is a small black bee. The Djóre adopted that name, continuing to call the old group "Goroti" or "Gorotire," that is, "sleepyheads" (*ngoro* = to sleep; *ti* = great, much). Another version says that the meaning of the term "Gorotire" is "great group, principal band or faction" (derived from *goro* = group; *ti* = great, much), which makes more sense. It may be added here that the Xikrín's name for themselves is *mebênokre* (real, brave people), à name common to all the Kayapó, or even Djóre-aramã, but never Xikrín, since they say that this term does not exist in their language and that it was applied to them by the neo-Brazilians.[1]

The Djóre, due to disagreements with the main group, emigrated from the territory then shared with the Gorotire and went to live, initially, in the Campos do Triunfo (Victory Plains). During their stay in the plains, fights with the original Gorotire are mentioned. Since the Djóre were the weaker group, they were partially decimated. They resolved, therefore, to abandon the Campos do Triunfo and emigrate again. We know neither how long a time nor how many generations the Djóre remained in the region of the plains, but the end of that phase should coincide, more or less, with the end of the last century, a period in which the Djóre also made their first contacts with the rubber gatherers of the Xingú. These events are confirmed by the fact that Bepkarotí, the *benadjure-rai* or principal chief, one of the oldest people of the present Xikrín group, being approximately 80 years old, was born in the Campos do Triunfo where, also, his father died by the bullet of a rubber gatherer.

It appears that the Rio Fresco was always considered to be the northern limit of the Kayapó, since to the north of this river began territory inhabited principally by Tupí groups (*Assurini*) who extended in semicircles to the Tocantins, including the Caeteté and Itacaiunas. In their migration, the Djóre entered this new realm and broke the barriers formed by the Kuben Kamrektí and other Tupí groups residing there. The Djóre went up the Trairão River and from there reached the affluents of the upper Caeteté to which they then descended. Establishing themselves there, they first endeavored to drive out all the other inhabitants of the middle and lower Caeteté and upper Itacaiunas. These groups retired to the regions of the headwaters of the northern affluents of the Itacaiunas: the Rio Cinzento; the Tapirapé; the Prêto and others. Groups called Akokakóre are designated as the original inhabitants of the region, the last remnants of which are identified by the Xikrín as Paracanã.

In 1903 we find the Xikrín—already known by this name—as fixed residents on the Caeteté. We have, on this point, a deposition from Sr. Manuel Pernambuco da Gama, now more than 80 years old and residing in Marabá. We cannot, here, present his entire account. He states that he worked on the Rio Caeteté from 1903 to 1913 in a place called "Cachoeira Feia," always maintaining peaceful contacts with the Indians. He recounts, however, that by 1903 the hostilities between the Xikrín and the invading rubber gatherers had already begun, with deaths on both sides. These fights continued, with some interruptions, until 1954.

It appears that there were three critical phases of more acute hostilities. The first was in 1913. In the opinion of Manuel Pernambuco, although without specifying numbers or the circumstances of the killings, this was the year in the decade prior to World War I in which there were the most deaths in the Xikrín region. And it was because of Indian hostilities in general that he resolved to abandon his work on the upper river.

During World War I there was a period of greater calm. Because of the difficulties of exportation, the products of the river were not sought. Rubber production also fell because of inferior quality. It never recovered from the sudden fall, and rubber is no longer being exploited in that region. After the war, however, the search for Brazil nuts increased, causing new assaults against Xikrín territories, rich in the nuts. New conflicts arose between the Xikrín and the nut gatherers, reaching a climax shortly before 1930 on the occasion of a great increase in the price of Brazil nuts. This period, which we may consider the second critical phase, was perhaps the most difficult year for the Xikrín. To avenge two labor contractors, killed by the Xikrín, a certain Antonio Borges Pires Leal mobilized 60 men, went up river with them, and assaulted the Xikrín in their own village, reducing their population by half. It is believed that the total of Indians massacred at that time was about 180. No one was spared, not even infants.

As a consequence of the enormous losses suffered, the Xikrín resolved to abandon the Caeteté. It is probable that it was this occasion that resulted in a schism within the group based on a lack of agreement regarding which direction to take. One group, the smaller, continued north and established itself later on the Pacajá River, an affluent of the Xingú. The larger group, however, went to settle in the region of the headwaters of the right affluents of the Itacaiunas: the upper

Branco (Paraopeba); the Arraias; the Vermelho and the Sororozinho. But since these were also Brazil nut areas, the encounters between nut gatherers and Indians were not slow in repeating themselves, bringing on the third phase of hostilities about 1952. We do not know what motives induced the Indians to aggression, but in that year the Xikrín killed 10 neo-Brazilians in a single day, although in different places. The records of the SPI mention this killing, calling it the "first hostilities of the Indians of that region of the Rio Vermelho." Again a retaliatory expedition was formed which killed a number of Indians.

It was after this episode that the attempts of the SPI to pacify the Xikrín began. Also in 1952, the SPI first penetrated to the Rio Vermelho under the direction of Inspector Dorival Pamplona who, although not unaware of the fights and reciprocal killings between Indians and nut gatherers, still made the following deposition with respect to the Xikrín in one of the written statements now in I.R. 2 in Belém: "Of the existing bands, the most tamable is the 'Xikrí' who, for many years have lived, . . . surrounded by civilized folk, explorers for natural products. . . . Settled in the area of the Igarapé Sororozinho, affluent of the Sororó, in the municipality of Marabá, they never menaced the white element in spite of the fact that, though they are peaceful by nature, they have suffered barbarous armed incursions. They frequently appeared in the nut gatherers' camps carrying off machetes and small household utensils, certainly because they needed them, and from this comes the saying that the Chikrí are thieves . . . " (Dorival Pamplona, Relatório de 1952). It is possible that these small, repeated thefts may have been one of the causes of the disagreements and hostilities.

Somewhat later, in 1953, Hilmar Harry Kluck of the SPI visited several Xikrín villages in the course of a four month trip. In 1954 we find a group of Xikrín at the SPI Post of Las Casas. Evidently they did not adapt to the regime of the Post, abandoning it shortly. Only a few families remained. Still, this contact, however brief, produced its fruits, because, since 1954, after a full 50 years of conflict, (1903–1954), open hostilities between neo-Brazilians and Indians ceased in that region. Some Xikrín returned after that, and others in several stages, to the Rio Caeteté, absorbing the survivors from the Sororó, Vermelho and Branco rivers, forming a new common village on the same site as that of 1903 where we found them still in 1962 on the occasion of the first visit that we made to them.

CHANGES IN THE SITUATION OF THE XIKRÍN
FROM 1962 TO 1963

In February of 1962 when we met the Xikrín of the Caeteté, the Indians were carrying on a regular and normal tribal life. According to a count made on that occasion the group comprised 164 persons: 65 men, 50 women, 21 boys who did not yet frequent the men's house, and 28 girls. This group of people lived in 11 houses disposed in a circular fashion, forming a village of the traditional type (Banner 1961:3–4). The social institutions were still functioning. The major division into work cycles for both sexes, one of the bases for the internal development of the material culture and social life of the group, was observed intact. Economic life likewise functioned. Men and women worked equally to obtain sustenance for their families. The Xikrín are not lazy, and they clear and plant large fields. To guarantee the subsistence of the group they had several fields within a radius of one day's travel. The most distant of these fields was on the banks of the Rio Sêco which they called Kam-Krokró, an affluent of the upper Caeteté. We mention it since it must be one of the most advanced points of the Xikrín, a place that served them as a point of departure for the lands of the Kuben Kamrektí, a Tupí group against whom they warred from time to time. Moreover, both sexes contributed directly to subsistence. Men and boys daily went out hunting and to search for land turtles, and women to collect *babassú* palm hearts, fruits, or other edible items. In other words, the system of economic activities functioned in such a way that no one need be hungry, although not all always had a "full belly." Equilibrium in the distribution of food was based on kinship. The importance of the maternal family is revealed primarily by matrilocality in marriage. The married couple normally continues to live in the house of the mother of the woman. Diniz (1962:22, 35), and, indirectly from context, also Banner, are inclined to consider the Kayapó as matrilineal, an opinion to which we are not inclined to subscribe without reservation, at least regarding the Xikrín. Kayapó-Xikrín kinship terminology is not absolute proof of the existence of a type of matrilineality, but can be fitted into a system of double, or even multiple, descent, since Kayapó, and also Xikrín, "compadrio" is nothing other than a system that functions in terms of patrilineal kinship always and exclusively inherited in the male line. Moreover, the offices of chieftainship are normally transmitted through the paternal line (father-son-grandson) without considering maternal descent. And even the conditions of kinship from which a child is named indicate, according to the sources (Métraux and Dreyfus-Roche 1959:377; Diniz 1962:19), a basis that is probably double descent rather than purely matrilineal. We have here a vast field for new investigation.

Another aspect of tribal life, intimately related to the economic and social life of the group, is revealed in the functioning of the men's house or, as the Xikrín themselves call it, the "unmarried men's house." It can be said, without fear of exaggeration, that the social functioning of the group depends on the proper functioning of the men's house. It is there that all the men meet, although only single men live there permanently, from boys who have reached puberty to aged widowers. For the boys the men's house is the place of instruction and learning where they learn not only affairs of practical life, e.g., how to make the objects and utensils of daily life, but also proper attitudes respecting social relations with the various groups within their own society, with foreign groups, the customs of war, behavior in festivals, etc. A great part of the preparations for festivals are carried out in the men's house: the making of masks, dance and song rehearsals, etc. Through living in the men's house, we know that festivals were planned within the group of the young men. We were able to attend the celebration of the harvesting of the first maize. Other festivals such as the fish poison festival, the festival of the groups identified by the addition of such prefixes as Bep-,Tokok-,Nyok-,etc., the festival of the Bo (a kind of *Araunã* [a festival of the Karajá Indians]) were already being planned with considerable anticipation in order to have time to make the feather adornments and other festival outfits. At night the oldest men or the chief of the group pronounce discourses of instruction, admonition and orientation with the young men seated before them forming a semicircle or an open square, the fourth side being occupied by the instructor.[2]

The system of lectures, especially at night, belongs to Xikrín life. The most frequent speaker is the chief, giving orders for the following day, distributing duties, protesting irregularities that have occurred. But it is not only the chiefs who speak. Any and all men, as well as women, have the right to speak. The listeners, on the one hand frequently make suggestions respecting the matter being expounded, encourage and spur on, and on the other hand they reply. Thus, there sometimes even occur disputes in public. For the warriors, the discourses serve, along with trips they have made and deaths they have caused, as a means to increase their prestige within the group. We observed Indians with real talent for oratory, with gestures and mimicry as expressive as any we have seen in our own civilized medium.

The brief notes presented here are necessarily incomplete, a fact of which we are perfectly aware. What we are attempting to point out, in summary, is the following: In 1962, on the occasion of our first visit to the Xikrín, their tribal life was functioning normally. There was an equilibrium between the activities of men and women on behalf of the group, and the various social factors and their manifestations (such as the division in work cycles, the tribal economy together with the subsistence bases, kinship and matrilocality, festivals and ceremonies and the function of the men's house) were so interwoven that there existed a truly ordered whole.

In the space of a single year, however, there occurred notable changes, not simply demographic but also in the realm of organization. In the first place there was a schism within the group based on attitudes toward the neo-Brazilians or, in more general terms, toward the products of civilization. One part of the Xikrín went to live at the mouth of the Rio Caететé, this group representing the younger generation or, at least, those more disposed to adapt themselves to the national society and desirous of being integrated, on the basis of work, into the local economic system of the Itacaiunas, the only way for them to obtain means to satisfy the new cultural needs acquired with contact.

We know, on the basis of what has happened to other Kayapó groups, that schisms are almost always due to intergroup disagreements (Diniz 1962:33, note 2). Here this was not the case. The schism was not due to internal rivalry within the group, but to differential economic motivation between the sector most disposed to accept new ways of life and the other, more conservative, sector. This attitude is revealed in manifest form by the behavior of the factions. The village was burned leaving a single house standing to shelter those with occasion to travel through or pass by the site. And while the group of young people moved closer to the neo-Brazilians, the conservative group retired further into the forest toward the region of the already mentioned Kam-Krokró or Rio Sêco. Although the younger group had previously planted a field at the mouth of the Caетété, they still lacked sufficient fields to guarantee them sustenance. Moreover, on the banks of the major river they could more easily acquire tools and other necessary items that the interior group lacked. As a consequence of these facts, a certain social division of labor came to be established between the two factions. The "traditionalist" segment provided the other with foodstuffs and, through it, sold articles such as animal skins, receiving in return utensils and iron objects such as knives, machetes, axes, etc., from the "progressive" group.

It is worth noting, however, that the schism mentioned did not imply, at least directly, any break in the internal cohesion of the group, but only a formal alteration in the social organization, since the principal basic structures of the group were maintained relatively unchanged, thus leaving the way open for an eventual reunification of the Xikrín.

Although there is not yet any break in group cohesiveness, a series of changes is noticeable in the situation of the group and in the functioning of tribal life. The new village, located below the confluence of the Caetete and the Itacaiunas, no longer follows the spatial and residential pattern defined by tradition. The word "village" no longer has its original meaning to the group, but instead refers to a large "camp" with the houses disposed in a line along the river bank, an arrangement that surely contributes to the disruption of the functioning of the traditional social system. Whereas previously the families were spread out and slept in 11 dwelling houses, they now live together in only 5 huts. Under these circumstances the more closely related families are congregated and, by joining together, originate nuclei that, in social life, act as small "political groups," contending among themselves for power and influence. The weakest, those of the "minority," have to submit, against their will, to the stronger groups. Thus, discontent ferments in the atmosphere, resulting in the continual emergence of new group leaders. We observed that, already within this dissident group there are again two factions: one, inclined to total commitment to civilization or, worse yet, to the so-called "civilized people," representatives of the vanguard of Brazil nut gatherers in the region; and the other desiring to restrict contact, taking advantage of the goods of civilization insofar as these are necessary for their work, without, however, sacrificing their autonomy. These attitudes are already quite well marked and will probably result in a new schism if not in the complete disintegration of the group. It is natural that, along with these internal biases and conflicts, the economic aspects of native society also suffer. The Xikrín necessarily go hunting, collecting and to their fields as long as there is something to be obtained from these activities. But the men no longer want to absent themselves from the village for very long. They want to remain nearby, especially in the Brazil nut season when motor launches and nut gatherers go up and down the river, the occasion for business dealings. The Indians no longer want to miss these occasions when they can even obtain *farinha* [manioc flour]. In summary, they are neglecting hunting and gathering, sometimes spending entire days hungry, hoping for the arrival of the launches, thus aggravating their situation of dependency on the neo-Brazilians and increasing the tensions that we have already mentioned.

The festivals and ceremonies are no longer held. Questioned about this, they respond that they can no longer perform them since there is no appropriate site in the new village.

What most disrupts the life of the group, however, is the lack of a men's house. In addition to interrupting all the social functions linked to it, as we have already seen, the unmarried men themselves feel superfluous in the village. The married men are with their wives and children. But the young men and unmarried men have no right to occupy the family mats; they have nowhere to stay. This fact explains why, since we were also single, the young men grouped themselves around us and, after a few weeks, our house began to function as a men's house. A large number of the young men who felt ashamed to sleep among the women in the family houses slept on the porch of our house, or along side of it in the open.[3] The absence of a men's house, causing lack of cohesion among the young men, warriors and hunters, also explains the constantly increasing tendency for young men to want to go off to the stands of Brazil nut trees or other places, abandoning the village.[4]

Comparing the situation of the Xikrín in 1962 and 1963, it can be seen that, through contact with civilization, the possibilities of disintegration of the group were greatly increased.[5]

PRESENT CONTACTS WITH THE VANGUARD OF BRAZIL NUT GATHERERS

We spoke, at the beginning of this article, of the first contacts between the Xikrín and the neo-Brazilians and the hostilities resulting therefrom. We have said little, however, about the relationships that the Xikrín presently have and maintain with these people. In comparison with past decades, here too there have been changes in attitude, these being, perhaps, the most profound. It is from these changes in attitude, in the final analysis, that the entire situation of the Xikrín in these last two years emerged. Before 1962 there was no lack of contacts with the neo-Brazilians, but these were not very frequent and could be considered sporadic. One or another nut gatherer, once a year, would send his outboard motor to the village to pick up Brazil nuts cut by the Indians or to buy some skins. Moreover, because of the lack of women in the stands of Brazil nut trees, they took advantage of the occasion to "know the village broads," to use regional jargon. From this activity arose the introduction of prostitution, in the civilized pattern, because these favors were paid for in knives, machetes, etc., or even in farinha. Avid for metal implements, the Xikrín endeavored to link themselves to the economy of the neo-Brazilians: the men searching for Brazil nuts or working, occasionally, in the stands of Brazil nut trees; the women giving themselves in exchange for remuneration.

Whereas in the old village, until 1962, this state had an "occasional, sporadic" character, after the movement of the group to the mouth of the Caeteté the picture changed completely. The function of the Xikrín "camp," with relation to the caboclo population, took on a new aspect. As a consequence of its location, and because of the intensity of traffic of nut gatherers working the upper Itacaiunas, that settlement was transformed into a kind of rest stop and trading post. It was not, however, simply a rest stop. In reality, the village became, simultaneously, a "hotel and bordello" for the population of Brazil nut gatherers who adjusted their trips so as to pass the night in the village.[6] The power of the firearms, from which the Brazil nut gatherer is practically never parted, a feeling of their own inferiority to the "civilized people," and their cultural dependence with relation to the national society, led the Xikrín to surrender their women without greater resistance. At present, however, as the discrepancies between the two societies in contact become more acute, the Xikrín are beginning to present resistance to this practice, as well as because they now see that, through sexual contact of their women with the gatherers, the group has contracted venereal diseases, common within the caboclo population.[7]

The damaging effects, as far as disease is concerned, are not limited to venereal complaints alone. The constantly increasing contact also unleashed epidemics of influenza, skin diseases, etc. In January of this year (1963), a wave of influenza was at its peak, and the only reason it did not cause greater harm was that we carried a substantial reserve of medicine in our luggage. There were days in which we administered more than 50 injections of antibiotics. The last epidemic, of a still unidentified disease, caused 12 deaths between January and the middle of March, and 5 cases of paralysis of the left side of the body. With 6 more deaths among the interior group, the contacts of less than one year reduced the Xikrín population by 10 percent.

We stated that the Xikrín are beginning to present resistance to certain demands of the neo-Brazilians. This resistance is extending, also, to the economic and commercial sector. They are beginning to feel the frustration of their aspirations in the face of the negative results of interaction with caboclo society. Contact was desired, initially, and the Xikrín believed that with it would come transformations advantageous to the group. Some few, however, are recognizing the negative effects of this contact. For example, those who were engaged in collecting Brazil nuts are beginning to see how they are exploited. The same is happening with those who "sell" skins of jaguar, peccary or other animals to the Brazilians. Thus, for example, in exchange for a jaguar skin worth more than Cr$ 20,000.00, they receive a handful of bullets or a machete with a maximum value of Cr$ 500.00. The Xikrín are beginning to recognize the exchange value of their articles, however. Commercial relations, initially a source of social well-being, are coming to constitute, given their highly exploitative character, foci of social tension between Indians and neo-Brazilians.

Some renters [arrendatários] of stands of Brazil nut trees have gotten Indians to cut trails for the purpose of exploring for new stands. Even considering the low level of payment for labor in the area, payment to the native worker, to the "animal" as he is called, is always less than that paid to a "Christian." On the other hand, merchandise sold to the Indian regularly suffers a surtax by means of which the patron manages to retain an additional part of the product of native work. The result of these factors is, obviously, a state of permanent indebtedness. On still other occasions the Indian is openly and scandalously robbed.[8] On the part of the Indian there is a progressive realization of the situation, which may result, in the near future, in armed conflict. Meanwhile, they are compelled to accept the situation due to the need to obtain commercial products, especially arms. We have examples of Indians who are trying to store up ammunition to confront what they call the Kuben punú (wicked people, worthless civilized people).

In addition to this situation, there are other indications that the tension between Indians and neo-Brazilians is progressively increasing. Nevertheless, the local authorities refuse to admit, formally, the possibility of the emergence of a situation of conflict. They always state that the problem does not exist, which may be a means of avoiding "officializing" such a danger and, by implication, the exploitative mechanisms described, making the adoption of radical measures easier. One of the authorities of Marabá stated that, in case the problem did arise, "he would know how to resolve it." The methods that would be employed can be easily predicted: massacre of the indigenous population.

The intensification of antagonism on the one hand, and, on the other, the Xikrín's awareness of their inferiority in both equipment and numbers to the neo-Brazilians in the event of a new armed conflict, led to the adoption of a tension relieving mechanism, that is, an "escape valve." This mechanism consists in developing a climate of animosity directed against the neighboring Indian groups, the Kre-ankóre (Arara) and Kuben-Kamrektí (Assurini), a climate that could, with the accumulation of tensions, lead to the actual opening of intertribal hostilities.

In summary, it may be said that the approach of the Xikrín to the national pioneer frontier had two kinds of repercussion on them, both negative.

a. With relation to their own tribal and social life: from the disruption of tribal institutions, causing them to fail to function, resulted incipient tribal disorganization.

b. With relation to contact with the neo-Brazilians: from the exploitative system employed by the nut gatherers and the frustration, felt and now understood, of their aspirations to acculturation (including, as well, an important psychological factor, namely racial discrimination, maintained by the neo-Brazilians on the basis of the terms "animals" for Indians and "Christians" for themselves), resulted a tension that does not explode only because of the manifest inferiority of the material equipment, chiefly armaments, of the Xikrín.

It is not incumbent upon us to predict the future of these Indians. We can, however, suggest the following: if native life and institutions were so shaken in a single year of more frequent contact, in view of the circumstances described, the Xikrín will probably not have enough strength to defend themselves effectively against the influences of the Brazil nut collecting frontier. Therefore, the period of existence of the Xikrín as a group or society will be very limited.[9]

POSTSCRIPT—DECEMBER, 1972

Since this paper was written ten years ago, many changes have occurred in Xikrín life and society. The Indians saw that the situation in 1963 was untenable. They left the mouth of the Caeteté River to return to the old site on the middle Caeteté, and the two factions, the "progressives" and the "traditionalists," reunited. In addition, the aforementioned Catholic priest, Father Caron, O.P., established a small mission among these Indians to control the social and commercial relations between the Xikrín and the Brazilians. The FUNAI (Fundação Nacional do Indio = Indian Office) also became interested in the Xikrín, so that the situation of these Indians is no longer the same as that reported for 1963. This fact suggests that new observations are needed.

NOTES

1. Darcy Ribeiro (1957:72, 98) refers separately to the Diore (Djóre) and the Xikrín, the former on the Rio Paraopeba (Branco), right affluent of the Itacaiunas, the latter also on the right bank of that river, apparently considering the two groups as separate, when in reality, as explained above, they constitute a single tribal group calling itself Djóre.

2. We disagree with Banner (1961:20) when he refers to the men's house as a locale where "the young women, men-kurerére, are grabbed by the warriors and violated, time after time, in everyone's view. It is not only the single women who suffer, but also the wives of the younger and less valiant men." This statement is probably due to poor interpretation or a misunderstanding. Diniz (1962:92) also allows exaggeration to confuse the issue in his exploration of the matter. If a case of this kind occurs, it is doubtless an exception that should not be generalized, since this is not the significance of the men's house.

3. There was mutual advantage in this situation. The young men went to hunt and collect turtles for us, and we paid for the service in farinha and rice, preparing the meal in common and eating together.

4. Perhaps this fact may also explain the frequency with which young Timbira men (Canela, Xerente, etc.) organize trips sometimes reaching as far as the capitals of the South and of the Northeast.

5. We are convinced that the Xikrín will not resist the pressure of the Brazil nut gathering frontier and its disintegrative influence unless a program of assistance is immediately put into effect. We have as yet no knowledge of preparations that might indicate the presence of either the SPI, to whom we sent a very detailed report, or of either Catholic or Protestant missions. Thus, the Xikrín, from this moment, are condemned to perish within a few years just as is happening to other Kayapó groups such as those cited in the report of Moreira Neto (1959).

6. On one occasion we ourselves resisted one of these owners of stands of Brazil nut trees who wanted to take two Xikrín women up river to serve as prostitutes to his laborers.

7. An article by Darcy Ribeiro on "Convívio e contaminação" is worth mentioning here. His examples and conclusions regarding contact and diseases such as influenza, measles, etc., fit in here, showing, among other things, the repetition of events. As one of the most striking examples, and one that coincides with the Xikrín situation, we will cite what he writes about the introduction of gonorrhea among the Xokleng: "It was introduced by an Indian woman. . . . Through the system of sexual relations, within the tribe, she passed the disease to her husband, and he to other women, finally contaminating a great number of persons. When the epidemic was discovered many were in a grave state, several cases of death, sterility and blindness resulting" (D. Ribeiro 1956:14).

8. We would like to add here a typical example. In April of this year of 1963, after our return from the Xikrín, P. Caron, O.P., visited the Xikrín for some days. An Indian brought him a statement of accounts that had been provided by his patron. P. Caron was present, personally, at the delivery of 29 hectoliters of Brazil nuts. In the statement only 16 appeared at Cr$ 400 each, or a total of Cr$ 6,400.00, when the local price was over Cr$ 2,000.00 per hectoliter. In the same statement there appeared purchases made by the Indian totaling Cr$ 7,700.00, including 1/2 *quarta* [15 kg.] of farinha for Cr$ 1,000.00, two pairs of shorts that were neither ordered nor delivered for Cr$ 800.00 and other things. Thus, the Indian ended up owing his "patron" Cr$ 1,300.00, while the patron still obtained a profit of nearly Cr$ 25,000.00 on the 13 hectoliters of stolen Brazil nuts.

9. We want to put on record, as have other ethnologists working with Kayapó groups, especially Carlos Moreira Neto (1959), our opinion that, in order to resolve the problems of

conflict and tension existing between Indians and neo-Brazilians, the following would be necessary: immediate and permanent health care, rigorous control of individual and commercial contacts and the guarantee, given to the Indians, of the possession of the lands of the Caeteté River and of the stands of Brazil nut trees that are their source of subsistence and income. The guiding role in this problem, therefore, belongs to the authorities that were constituted for this purpose. Our intention was, simply, to describe and render comprehensible a series of problems that the changes, originated by contact with the neo-Brazilians, brought about in the short space of one year. It remains to express here our sorrow and our sympathy for the Xikrín, one of the last groups of independent Kayapó, now on the way to total disintegration.

The following three articles deal with depopulation from different points of view. Drastic loss of population has been recorded for native groups from the first days of contact, the effects of disease far surpassing those caused by armed conflict, and disease is a continuing factor in depopulation.

One of the unexplored facets of South American Indian demography that, to my knowledge, has never been investigated, is the frequency with which a shortage of women appears to occur. Factors that may contribute to this sexual disequilibrium are a reduction in warfare, which would cut down on the death of men of marriageable age, the attachment of women of marriageable age willingly or unwillingly to the households of outsiders, as well as the practice of female infanticide as noted by Ribeiro for the Kadiwéu. In some cases such an imbalance may be corrected by robbing women from neighboring groups but another possible adjustment is that with which this article deals, namely some form of polyandry. The Guayaki have also opted for polyandry as a solution but with quite different social arrangements from those of the Suruí (cf. P. Clastres 1970:19–25).

Further publications by the author resulting from two field seasons with this group are to be found in Laraia (1965, 1967, 1972) and Laraia and Matta (1967).

"Polyandrous Adjustments" in Surui Society

The purpose of this study is to describe the effect of depopulation on the marriage regulations of the Suruí Indians. The Suruí are a tribal group of the Tupí linguistic stock, known until recently as Mujetire, located on the headwaters of the Sororó in the southeast of the state of Pará.[1]

The process of depopulation is not a new phenomenon in Suruí society. Tribal tradition retains a record of various intertribal fights, primarily with Kayapó groups, with disastrous results for the Suruí. Internal strife, such as a bitter dispute over women between two of their five clans, also contributed to the depopulation which reached its height when, in 1960, having established permanent contact with the national society, the Indians were practically decimated by a flu epidemic.

Depopulation affected the female element most strongly. The genealogies obtained show that it was frequent for one woman to have been the wife, successively, of two or three men without having herself been widowed. At present there are fourteen adult men for seven women, two of whom are already in the menopause. There are ten male children and nine female children, one of the former suffering from tuberculosis of the bone and unlikely to reach adulthood. Thus, the number of children of each sex will be equal. Since five of the girls are already engaged to adult men, however, the demographic imbalance tends to persist.

For this reason, the native society sought to create a mechanism capable of satisfying single and widowed men while avoiding the repetition of the serious conflicts of the past. It is this mechanism that we are calling "polyandrous adjustments."

We should explain that we are using this term in order not to speak of polyandry, since to do so we would have to satisfy the conditions set forth by Murdock that, "the term 'polyandry' be reserved exclusively for a form of marriage which is socially sanctioned and culturally patterned and which involves economic cooperation and residential cohabitation as well as sexual rights" (Murdock 1949: 25–26). Since this pattern does not occur in Suruí society, we will not use the term to avoid falling into the error, pointed out by Murdock, of various ethnologists who applied it, "to sporadic instances of the association of several men with one woman in contravention of cultural norms . . ." (1949:25). For example, among both the Shoshoni (North America) and the Kota (India) the fact that a man occasionally permitted his wife to have sexual relations with his brother was considered as polyandry (Steward 1936b; Mandelbaum 1938). To accept such cases would lead to polyandry being considered quite common when, in fact, it is very rare, being

Reprinted by permission of the author and publisher from *Revista do Museu Paulista*, n.s., vol. 14 (1963), pp. 71–75. Translated and edited by Patricia J. Lyon with the approval of the author.

All material appearing within square brackets [ ] has been added by the editor of this book.

known only among the Toda in India and the natives of the Marquesas Islands in Polynesia.

Therefore, the present use of the term "polyandrous adjustments" refers only to the occasional association of two men with one woman, based on the tacit acceptance of the group. It is such association that occurs in Suruí society as we will now describe.

Every married woman at present possesses an *amutehéa* with whom she maintains sexual relations during the absence of her husband, or even during his presence in the village. All members of the tribe know of these relationships which are considered normal. The husband, nevertheless, pretends to be ignorant of them in an attempt to reconcile the strongly patrilineal traditions of the group with the present situation. Every married man of the village can name the participants in all the other arrangements but always refuses to say who is the amutehéa of his own wife, alleging that she does not have one.

The only two widows in the group also have amutehéa, but neither of these men wants to transform his relationship into that of marriage because to do so would involve an intense economic cooperation determined by the marriage, a cooperation from which the parties are excused by the "adjustment." Kuarijuara, *mourobixawa* [chief] of the group, however, collaborated in the agricultural work of the husband of Ariheira, his amutehéa. He also permitted that Koimoá and the woman Múrua, both widowed and joined by this type of arrangement, engage in agricultural tasks performed only by persons properly married. The justification for this concession was that the tribe needed large fields.

The fact that a single man participates in these "adjustments" does not prevent his contracting new marriages. Four participants in this type of union are "engaged" to young girls in the tribe.

One problem arising from this type of union is that of paternity. This question raised doubts among our informants. Some think that the child belongs to both the sexual partners of the woman, a solution in accord with neither the descent rule nor the Suruí concept of paternity. Others think that the child belongs only to the husband, but all agree with the mourobixawa when he states that the child belongs to the clan of its mother's husband.

These "polyandrous adjustments" are apparently recent in Suruí society. In no case were they reported in the genealogies. By their very nature, however, and especially by their inability to determine descent, they seem to be a mechanism which would not be detected by the genealogical method. The Suruí consider them to be a type of complementary union much less desirable than matrimony. Thus in one case an Indian proposed to the husband of his amutehéa that this man give up the woman in exchange for one of his daughters. The proposal was accepted and the exchange will be carried out when the daughter reaches puberty.

We believe that the factor making matrimony preferable to an "adjustment" is linked to the recruitment of new members for the clan. Whereas matrimony is the agency that provides the clan with new members through sexual reproduction, the "adjustment" causes a man to beget new elements for the clan of the husband of his amutehéa, which is not always his own clan. In a society that worships its ancestors, begetting children that will belong to a clan different from oneself is not really ideal behavior. Much less desirable, then, is the bestowal of one's children on another man, when the rites to the ancestors, which appear to be very important for the prolongation of a man's afterlife, depend on his descendants.

Another problem is related to the fact that a man can only have as amutehéa a woman whom he could marry. Rules of clan exogamy apply as well as kinship prohibitions. A brother's spouse is a potential wife since the levirate occurs within the group. But the marriage makes a woman prohibited as amutehéa of her husband's brother. Formally there is no reason for this to occur, and our limited control of the language, in what is a practically monolingual group, prevented our understanding the explanations of our informants. However, on the basis of the vehement reactions to the possibility of a union with a brother's wife, and the fact that a husband pretends to be unaware of the extramarital relations of his wife, we can formulate the hypothesis that a man would consider himself to "betray" his brother if he were to have relations with his brother's wife.

We can conclude, finally, that this type of union is an adjustment, as we have called it, which exists to ameliorate the problems arising from the scarcity of women in the tribe. We are not dealing with a completely sanctioned form, simply one that is tolerated, perhaps only as long as the demographic imbalance lasts.

There does not exist between the participants in the "adjustment" any obligation to cooperate economically. In only two cases was any kind of cooperation noted. In one of these, as we saw, the participants in the supplementary union could, although they were widowed, participate in an agricultural activity performed only by married persons. The situation of poverty which the group was then facing, however, must have caused the chief to permit this infraction.

The "polyandrous adjustments" have prevented fights over the possession of women thus serving to maintain group solidarity intact.

The solution is not, however, ideal since it is in conflict with various elements of Suruí society. It is in conflict, as we have said, in the first place with descent rules, in the second place with the concept of paternity and in the third place with the rights a man desires to the exclusive possession of his wife, an attitude common to the various known Tupí groups.

NOTES

1. We were among the Indians in the second half of 1961 in company with Marcos Magalhães Ribinger, then a student at the Museu Nacional, to whom we here express our gratitude for his efficient collaboration.

The present article presents a striking picture of the extent to which depopulation can effect a culture. It deals, as do the following two articles, with the Tapirapé, among whom Wagley spent a considerable amount of time. There is probably no other group in South America for whom we have a similar longitudinal record during a period of intensive culture change. Over a period of almost thirty years, Wagley and Baldus, visited the group alternately at sufficiently short intervals so that the intervening events could be easily remembered. The bibliography of most of the major works on the Tapirapé is to be found in the references cited in the next two articles.

35   CHARLES WAGLEY

The Effects of Depopulation upon Social Organization as Illustrated by the Tapirape Indians

In recent years, there has been an increasing interest in the general processes of culture change resulting from contacts between European and native peoples. Such studies are part of the study of "acculturation," a term recently defined by Professors Linton, Redfield, and Herskovits: "The crux of the definition lies in the phrase, 'Those phenomena which result when groups of individuals having different cultures come into continuous first-hand contact' " (Linton, ed. 1940:464). This period of continuous first-hand contact historically follows upon a period of sporadic contact between the native peoples and some few Europeans (fur traders, explorers, missionaries, and even occasional single settlers), which in a sense has prepared the ground for a more intense influence of European culture when relations between the two peoples have become continuous. Few ethnologists have witnessed this period of sporadic contact and histories have little to tell us of it. But during this period, borrowing of European material culture generally occurs. Often the value system of the native culture is shifted, as objects having minor value take on major value for purposes of trade. Of great importance is the introduction of foreign disease, which frequently wipes out large numbers, or even the major part of the native population.

The Tapirape Indians, among whom the author lived for more than a year,[1] are a

Reprinted by permission of the author and publisher from *Transactions of The New York Academy of Sciences*, vol. 3, series 2 (1940), pp. 12–16. © 1940 by The New York Academy of Sciences.

Tupi speaking people living between the Araguaya and Xingu Rivers of Central Brazil near an affluent of the Araguaya which bears their name. They are a forest people and their village lies some fifty miles back from the Tapirape River. They have had only sporadic contact with Europeans. About 1909, the first Brazilians visited them in their village, and, each July or August since 1914, the Dominican priests meet them at a port on the Tapirape River and bring them presents—axes, hoes, salt, etc. Between 1930 and 1935, a Scotch Protestant missionary made three trips to the village, staying there two to three months at a stretch. During the dry season, the Tapirape regularly go down to the river for fishing and collecting turtle eggs and to wait in hope that the Dominican priests will come with a new supply of presents. There they sometimes meet trappers and hunters, and occasionally a Brazilian hunter will make the long trip to their village as an adventure, or—rarely— a Tapirape will go back with a missionary or hunter to the Araguaya—some 200 miles away—and return to the village loaded with presents and tall stories. These few contacts, the only ones which these people have had with Europeans, have nevertheless affected the Tapirape culture profoundly and in many ways. For lack of time, however, I shall describe only the effects resulting from the introduction of foreign diseases, which even antedated European contact, and the consequent wiping out of the great part of the Tapirape population.

In the memory of one Tapirape informant, there were five villages (about 1890), each of which must have contained well over two hundred people. The introduction of smallpox about 1895[2] caused one village to disband, since most of the inhabitants had died. About 1900, another European disease, probably influenza, caused a second village to break up through loss of people. Yellow fever must have taken its toll among the Tapirape at various times, as it did among the neighboring Caraja Indians, and, in 1920, the world-wide influenza epidemic came belatedly to the Araguaya and on to the Tapirape. In 1932, the survivors of a third village, depopulated by disease, joined the most southern village, Tampitawa, and, during my residence there in 1939, the survivors of a fourth village joined us. As a result of this wholesale depopulation from disease, there remained only one village and only 147 inhabitants. This is an extraordinary example of the ravages of European diseases among a native American people.

Tampitawa (Village of the Tapir) is composed, therefore, of a residue from all of the five original villages. All of the customs and ceremony attached to inter-village relations have of course disappeared. People remember their former village affiliation, or that of their parents. They still speak of a person as being "the son of Fish Village," but village loyalty, once strong, has disappeared. Formerly, villages were basically endogamous, but some marriage outside of the village did take place. Today, only three people can say that they are descendants of people from Tapir Village. Ancient inter-village antagonism existed, especially between Tapir and the village which joined with it in 1900. Today, this conflict is only remembered under the stress of some quarrel and is referred to only as a taunt.

Depopulation has had little effect on the economic life of the Tapirape. They are basically a forest agricultural people with large plantations. Manioc is their staple. Plantations are large enough, and the economic organization fluid enough, to allow for the support of large numbers of refugees for a year or so until they can make gardens for themselves. Refugees have joined one of the large households, at present eight, each with some twenty-five to thirty people. Formerly these households were matrilineal groups headed by a man of high prestige. His wife's relatives formed the matrilineal group and he demanded labor from his numerous sons-in-law (husbands of daughters of wife, including extended "daughters"). The coming of refugees disrupted these matrilocal households. If a refugee woman lacked a close female kin, her husband often arranged for habitation with a friend or a relative of his. Men of high status offered the hospitality of their houses to incoming men of rank. Today, therefore, many reassortments of relatives live under one roof, and two and even three separate groups of female relatives live under as many older men, whereas formerly they would have formed one household under the leadership of one household head. In no one case, does a man control a complete household as he would have done under the old system.

The men's moieties form the basis for Tapirape ceremonial and for cooperative gardening and hunting. Each moiety is divided into three age grades. Thus, in the village, there are two groups of "boys" and "youths" (up to sixteen years of age), two of mature men or "warriors" (up to approximately 45), and two groups of "older men." Really old and inactive men give up moiety activity and have no affiliation. A boy belongs automatically to the moiety of his father and formerly he progressed through the three age grades of that moiety. All ceremonies involve the moiety age grades, which dance against each other, race against each other, and give reciprocal feast exchanges. Cooperative hunts and clearing of the forest likewise involve reciprocal activities. However, with the great loss of population, and especially a loss of men of the oldest age group, this organization was thrown out of balance. In order to continue ceremonial life, several youths, who were spoken of as "lazy" and who were not capable hunters or workers, passed into the "older men's" age groups, in which there is little active cooperative hunting and gardening, in order to give those groups sufficient numbers for ceremonial activity. This rapid passing from boys' age grade to that of older men has influenced native thought in two ways:—First, young men are losing the idea of automatic progression through the three age grades, and there is a tendency now to think that the better young men become "warriors," while less capable ones pass rapidly to the older men's group. Second, the older men's age grades, formerly the groups of highest prestige, tend to be looked on with little favor, and only those individuals are thought of with respect who have status for other reasons.

Depopulation has also affected the second Tapirape social grouping—the feast groups. These are made up of all men and women. They are matrilocal for women and patrilocal for men. These feast groups meet periodically during the dry season for ceremonial meals. At present, three of the original ten feast groups have disappeared because of lack of members.

Chieftainship has changed under the influence of both depopulation and the sporadic contacts with Brazilians. All men of status are, today, called "capitaoes" (The Tapirape use the Portuguese word. There is no equivalent in their language.) These "capitaoes" are village elders (who were village "favorite children" in their youth, and therefore people of prestige), leaders of the warriors, age grades, and able shamans. Formerly, there were only two village elders, two warrior leaders, and ideally, two favorite children in a village. Today, with congregation of people from all villages in one, several "noble" families are present and there is an oversupply of "capitaoes."

Marriage arrangements, too, have been affected by depopulation. At present, there are some ten men of marriageable age, for whom there are no possible wives, and immediate families are so broken up that there are no possible groups of women to care for these unattached men. A man must have a wife to cook for him and perform women's tasks. To do any woman's work would play complete havoc with a man's personal prestige, which is a matter of greatest importance. Most of these Tapirape men have solved their problem by contracting convenient "social" marriages with extremely young girls. They attach themselves to a household, in which they perform a man's customary economic duties, and, in turn, their mothers-in-law do women's work for them.

Lack of time prevents mention of many other aspects of native life pertaining to marriage, kinship, and leadership, which have been profoundly affected by depopulation. Possibly, in other cultures, the effects of introduced disease have not been quite so disastrous, nor the loss of people so important to the social life, as in the case of the Tapirape. Without a doubt, however, wherever there have been sporadic contacts with Europeans, these or other alien factors have been introduced and have caused important changes in the structure of native life.

NOTES

1. This research extended from January 1939 to June 1940, and was made possible by a grant from the Social Science Research Council, Columbia University.
2. Probably through the Caraja.

This article overlaps somewhat the preceding one, but uses the data in an entirely different way. In this comparison of two Tupí groups, Wagley suggests some reasons why depopulation may affect some groups more violently than it does others, or why some groups seem to recover from depopulation while others do not. Once stated, it seems obvious that cultural attitudes toward population would play a major role in the ultimate recovery of a group. Reasons for maintaining small populations may differ greatly from one group to another, as demonstrated by the Tapirapé and the Kadiwéu, but the Kadiwéu population is not increasing any more than is the Tapirapé.

36 CHARLES WAGLEY

Cultural Influences on Population: A Comparison of Two Tupí Tribes

Contact with European civilization has had a varied effect upon the population trends of native societies. Frequently conquest warfare, slavery, bad labor conditions, disruption of aboriginal subsistence methods, and above all foreign disease have brought a rapid population decline which has led in many cases to the total disappearance of aboriginal groups as distinct ethnic units. In other instances, native groups have made an adjustment to the new circumstances. After an initial epoch of sharp decline in population, a few native groups have not only regained their former population level but actually increased in number several times fold. The depopulation of many Melanesian Islands, the decimation of the coastal Tupí speaking peoples of Brazil, and the rapid disintegration of the aboriginal groups of the Antilles are well known examples of sharp population decline following European contact from which the groups never recovered. The multiplication of the Navajo during the last century and the population growth of the Polynesian Island of Tikopia after European contact are examples of recovery and expansion (cf. Firth 1939:39–49).

In many cases, these differences in population trend following European contact may be explained in terms of the nature of contact with Europeans to which the different native groups have been subjected. Epidemics have varied in frequency and in intensity among native groups and the systematic exploitation of native peoples through slavery and other forms of enforced labor has taken heavier toll upon native population in some areas than in others. On the other hand, introduced crops, domesticated animals, new instruments, and new techniques have sometimes raised the aboriginal subsistence level and made possible an expansion of population.

Yet, the causes of such different trends in population among native groups after European contact cannot always be sought in the contact situation alone. The variables which allowed one group to absorb the shock of new disease and other disrupting accompaniments of European contact and to revive, or which led to quasi—or total extinction of a people may also be found in the culture and the society of peoples concerned. Each culture has a population policy—an implicit or explicit set of cultural values relating to population size. The social structure of each society is closely inter-related with a specific population level. A modification of the external environment, such as that brought about by contact with Europeans, generally calls for change both in cultural values as well as in social structure. In addition to environment, technology, and other material factors, cultural values

Reprinted by permission of the author and publisher from *Revista do Museu Paulista*, n.s., vol. 5 (1951), pp. 95–104.

and social structure act also to determine population size and demographic trends in the face of modified external circumstances. A rapid decrease in population due to new disease or an increase in population resulting from an increased food supply calls for adjustments in population policy (implicit or explicit) and in social structure. It is the purpose of the present paper to examine the relationship between these social and cultural factors and the population trends following European contact of two Tupí speaking tribes of Brazil.

The two Tupí speaking tribes in question are the Tenetehara of northeastern Brazil and the Tapirapé of central Brazil.[1] After more than 300 years of contact with Luso-Brazilians the Tenetehara in 1945 still numbered some 2000 people—not much less, if at all, than the aboriginal population. On the other hand, by 1947 the Tapirapé with less than forty years of sporadic and peaceful contact with Luso-Brazilians had been reduced to less than one hundred people, the remnant of an aboriginal population which must have numbered more than one thousand. While the Tenetehara still maintained a functioning social system and continued as a distinct ethnic group, Tapirapé society was in 1947 almost totally disorganized and the Tapirapé as a distinct people were clearly on the road to extinction.[2]

A partial answer to this very different reaction to Luso-Brazilian contact may be found in the nature of the acculturation process which each has experienced. Although the first decades of Tenetehara relations with Europeans were marked by slave raids, massacres, and epidemics, the protection of the Jesuits during more than one century (1653–1759) seems to have given the Tenetehara time to make adjustments in their culture and society to changing external circumstances. The missionaries were able to prevent the movement of colonists into Tenetehara territory; and after the expulsion of the Jesuits in 1759, the increased importation of African slaves into Maranhão eased the pressure for Indian slaves. Close relations with the missionaries, and later with the civil authorities and the rural Luso-Brazilian population, presented the Tenetehara with new culture patterns, new attitudes which either replaced aboriginal elements or were incorporated in their culture as alternative patterns. The missionaries urged larger families in order to have numerous innocents to baptize. Warfare was prohibited in the area.[3] The Tenetehara learned that children might be useful in collecting babassu nuts for sale to Luso-Brazilians. Steel instruments and new plants (such as rice, bananas, lemons, etc.) made agriculture more productive. The sale of babassu nuts, copaiba oil, and other forest products brought the Tenetehara imported products. Although Tenetehara culture and society were modified, the aboriginal and the borrowed elements slowly combined to form a new culture and a new social system which at least met the minimum requirements for survival.

The Tapirapé, on the other hand, have had only intermittent contact with Luso-Brazilians. Since about 1911, the Tapirapé have had occasional contact with Luso-Brazilians. A few Tapirapé have visited Luso-Brazilian settlements and missionary stations on the Araguaya River and a few Luso-Brazilians have visited Tapirapé villages. Tapirapé contact with Luso-Brazilians has been limited to relatively short periods and to small groups of people. They have acquired a few axes, hoes, some salt, cloth, beads, and other material objects from their occasional visitors but, on the whole, their culture was little modified by borrowed patterns and elements from Luso-Brazilians. Yet the presence of Luso-Brazilians brought about a crucial modification in their environment. With the arrival of Luso-Brazilians in the area, the Tapirapé were subjected to a series of foreign diseases. If the memory of older Tapirapé informants may be trusted, foreign disease (common colds, measles, and smallpox) came at first via the neighboring Karajá sometime before their first meeting with Luso-Brazilians. Since about 1911 to 1914, however, foreign disease acquired directly from Luso-Brazilians has steadily decimated the Tapirapé. Unlike the Tenetehara, before the Tapirapé were presented with a broad segment of Luso-Brazilian culture, which might have provided them with alternative patterns and values with which they might have made adjustments to their new circumstances, they have been practically wiped out.

Still, the difference in population trends after Luso-Brazilian contact of these two tribes cannot be explained entirely in terms of the differences in the contact continuum. The first fifty years of contact between the Tenetehara and Europeans was more violent than anything the Tapirapé have experienced. In the early 17th century organized slave raiding parties penetrated into Tenetehara territory and armed forces such as the one led by Bento Maciel Parente in 1616 made war upon the Tenetehara. Epidemics, which raged in the early 17th century among the Indian populations of northeast Brazil, certainly reached the Tenetehara. From time to time smallpox, measles, and other diseases have taken a heavy toll among these Indians. The impact of the dominant culture upon the Tenetehara was more intense than it has been upon the Tapirapé. In addition to differences in the nature of the contact continuum, factors inherent in the society and the culture of the two tribes were responsible for the reaction of these societies to Luso-Brazilian contact and for the population trends which followed. Since the Tenetehara and the Tapirapé have historically related cultures sharing many patterns and institutions common to most Tupí speaking tribes, a comparison of the two societies and cultures should allow us to determine the variables responsible for their contrasting reactions.

The subsistence methods of the tribes were in aboriginal times basically similar. Both were tropical forest horticulturalists depending upon hunting, fishing, and forest fruits to supplement their diet. For fishing, the Tenetehara had an advantage since their villages were normally situated near rivers and streams while the Tapirapé villages were located inland many kilometers from the river. In hunting, the Tapirapé had the advantage of nearby open plains country where hunting was more productive than in the tropical forest. Neither tribe had a land problem: the nearest village of the Karajá, who were Tapirapé neighbors, was at least two hundred kilometers away and the Timbira neighbors of the Tenetehara were savanna people offering no competition for forest land. Both tribes during aboriginal times had sufficient territory to move their villages every five or six years when suitable garden sites near their villages had been used up by the slash-and-burn system of horticulture. The two tribes inhabited similar physical environments and they had approximately the same technological equipment to cope with it. Their technology and their subsistence methods must have limited the maximum population of any one village and there are indications that approximately two hundred people was the average village size for both groups. On the other hand, a lack of territory evidently did not enforce a limitation on the number of villages for the tribe. Yet while the Tapirapé tell of only five villages in aboriginal times many times that number are reported by early observers for the Tenetehara. Although specific data is not available, it seems that in aboriginal times Tapirapé population was relatively small and stable while the Tenetehara population was at least twice as large and probably expanding.

This difference in population level between the two tribes in aboriginal times was related to the population policies held by the two groups as well as to differences in social structure of the groups concerned. These cultural values relating to population level are explicit in attitudes toward family size and in positive actions to limit families. Among the Tenetehara infanticide is indicated only in the case of the birth of twins since they are believed to be the result of sexual relations between the mother and a dangerous supernatural and in the case of infants with certain supernaturally caused abnormalities. Since there is a low incidence of twins and since in several known cases "abnormal" children have been allowed to live, infanticide has had little or no effect upon Tenetehara population trends. The Tenetehara tell of one or two formulas thought to produce abortion. The long taboos imposed on both parents during the pregnancy of the mother and during the early infancy of the child are a source of irritation and discomfort which would seem to tend to discourage large families. But, in general, there is little planned effort among the Tenetehara to limit family size. Men seem proud of several children; women are eager to bear children and they will leave a husband whom they believe to be sterile.

In contrast, the Tapirapé value small families. They take specific steps to limit their families and have explicit ideas as to maximum family size. Not only do the Tapirapé bury twins at birth as do the Tenetehara (and for similar reasons) but they believe that a woman should not have more than three live children.[4] In addition, the three children of a woman should not be of the same sex. In other words, if a woman has two living daughters and her third child is also a girl, it is usually buried at birth. Similarly, if she has two male children and her third is a male, infanticide is in order. Furthermore, all men who have sexual relations with a woman during her pregnancy are considered fathers to her child. More than two co-fathers leads to complications. All co-fathers are expected to observe taboos on sexual relations and on the eating of certain meats during the pregnancy of the woman and the early infancy of the child. If there are three, four or more co-fathers one of them is certain to break these taboos thus endangering the health of the infant; consequently the woman is urged to bury the child.[5]

On an overt level, the Tapirapé justify these checks on population by saying, "We do not want thin children" or "They would be hungry." They enlarge upon such statements by adding that it is difficult for a father to supply a large family with meat from hunting. In aboriginal times, manioc was plentiful and no one lacked the tubers with which to manufacture flour but meat was especially scarce during the rainy season when the forest is partially flooded and the paths to the savanna country are impassable. In addition, a complex set of food taboos make the job of supplying meat for a family more difficult. Children before adolescence are allowed to eat only specific meats and women are prohibited others. When a Tapirapé says "I am hungry" he generally means by implication: "hungry for meat." Although empirical data are not available, it is my impression that meat is (and was in the past) just as scarce in Tenetehara villages, and during the rainy season fish are extremely difficult to catch. The Tenetehara, with roughly the same food supply as the Tapirapé, do not feel called upon to impose drastic limitations upon the family size. Population control among the Tapirapé seems not to result from a direct limitation imposed by food supply but from culturally derived values. In other words, although family limitation among the Tapirapé has a basis in subsistence, it does not derive from a minimum starvation situation. Family limitation seems to be related to a desire for a specific food, which the organism needs but which is also selected by Tapirapé culture as particularly desirable.

This population policy of the Tapirapé with its explicit concept of maximum family size and the use of infanticide to limit the number of children must have maintained Tapirapé population in aboriginal times on a stable level. Even then, the balance between a stable and a declining population must have been a delicate one. With an increase in the death-rate from new disease for which they did not have an acquired immunity, this delicate equilibrium was thrown off balance. After Luso-Brazilian contact, the population declined rapidly. Tapirapé concepts of population limitation remained unchanged in the face of modified circumstances and families were not large enough to replace the adult population. The less rigid population policy of the Tenetehara was conducive to a large population during aboriginal times and it made the Tenetehara less vulnerable than the Tapirapé to modifications in the external environment. Without doubt numerous Tenetehara died from new diseases, from war, and from slavery after contact with Luso-Brazilians, but their desire for large families must have allowed them to replace their population in at least sufficient numbers to survive until they were able to adjust to the new circumstances.

Secondly, differences in social structure between the two tribes were also important in determining aboriginal population size as well as population trends after Luso-Brazilian contact. An extended family based upon at least temporary matrilocal residence and a widely extended bilateral kin group were basic social groupings of both the Tapirapé and the Tenetehara in aboriginal times. Tenetehara social structure was in fact limited to the extended family and the bilateral kin group. The Tapirapé, on the other hand, also had two other sets of social groups which were lacking in Tenetehara society. First, there were patrilineal ceremonial moieties limited to men. Each moiety was divided into three age grades—boys, young men or warriors, and older men. Second, both men and women among the Tapirapé belonged to one of eight "Feast Groups" which were non-exogamous. Membership in these "Feast Groups" was patrilineal for men and matrilineal for women, although these rules were often modified by the personal desires of a parent. Both Tapirapé men's moieties and age grades and the "Feast Groups" were basic to all ceremonials and important in economic production and distribution. The masked dances with impersonation of forest spirits performed by the men during the dry season were a function of the men's moieties. The "Feast Groups" met at intervals during the dry seasons at their traditional stations in the central plaza for ceremonial meals. At such times, as Herbert Baldus has shown, these "Feast Groups" functioned as a mechanism for food distribution in a season when more food was available than a family would normally consume (Baldus 1937: 88ff.). The "Feast Groups" sometimes formed to collect honey and to hunt. The age grades of the men's moieties also frequently acted together economically; they organized work parties for clearing of large garden sites and they went out on large cooperative hunts after herds of wild pigs.

In aboriginal Tapirapé society ceremonial life and many important cooperative subsistence activities were based upon this balanced set of associations. A Tapirapé village in order to assure adequate representation in the various age grades of the men's moieties as well as in the "Feast Groups" by necessity had to consist of about 200 people or more. A small village of fifty to a hundred people, for example, would not have provided a sufficient number of males of the proper ages to allow the age graded moieties to carry out their ceremonials nor to organize their cooperative subsistence activities. Tapirapé village organization was therefore not conducive to a process of "splitting off" of groups from one village to form another. The size of Tapirapé villages was limited by their technological equipment within their tropical forest environment yet the social structure made the formation of numerous small villages difficult. In contrast, the less formalized social structure of the Tenetehara allowed for villages of varying size within the limits of their ecological adjustment. Extended family groups easily might break off from a larger village to form a new settlement fully able to carry out the cooperative economic activities and even ceremonials of the society. This process is constantly occurring in contemporary Tenetehara society. When tensions arise between extended families, one group simply splits off from the parent village to join another or to form a separate village without serious effects on the ceremonial or economic system. Tenetehara social structure offered a favorable condition for an expanding population after Luso-Brazilian contact among the Tapirapé seriously affected population.

Tapirapé social structure seems also to have been more vulnerable to disorganization in the face of a rapid change in population size. Rapid depopulation after Luso-Brazilian contact among the Tapirapé seriously affected the normal functioning of their highly segmented and balanced social structure. By 1940, the lack of men had thrown the system of reciprocal and competitive activities of the men's age graded moieties out of balance. There were not enough men of the "older" age grade of either moiety nor of the young men "warrior" age grade of one moiety to form functioning units to reciprocate in cooperative garden clearing and to participate in group hunts. Several of the "Feast Groups" had been disbanded for lack of numbers. Ceremonials in 1940 had not been abandoned but they were performed in an attenuated and disheartened manner. There was little motivation to accumulate the meat, the forest fruits, and the garden products which important ceremonials require among the Tapirapé.

Ceremonials and cooperative economic activities in Tenetehara society are organized by extended family and kin groups. Lack of numbers, of course, creates difficulties in carrying out ceremonials and in organizing economic activities but it does not have the effect of disorganizing the society. Cooperation of large extended families in gardening and in collecting babassu nuts and copaiba oil is still the general pattern among the Tenetehara. Tenetehara social structure was malleable to change. Adjustment to new circumstances after Luso-Brazilian contact must have been easier for the Tenetehara than for the Tapirapé.

This brief comparison of the cultural values and of those aspects of social structure of the Tenetehara and of the Tapirapé in terms of their effect upon population size and on population trends after Luso-Brazilian contact suggest several general hypotheses. First, the available information concerning the population size of these two tribes in aboriginal times indicates that the Tenetehara were much more numerous than the Tapirapé. Yet both tribes were tropical forest peoples with roughly similar technological equipment. It seems to the writer that this difference in population size between the two tribes was functionally related to ideological values and to social structure and not to differences in technology and environment. In other words, such differences in population can hardly be interpreted strictly in Malthusian terms. While population potentials are certainly limited by food supply, the level of technology, the application of medical knowledge, and other material factors, social institutions and culturally derived values are influential in determining trends in population size within the limits set by such "natural" factors.

Second, the social structure and the cultural values of any society are functionally related to a given population level. With change in population size, both the cultural values regarding population size and social structure must be adjusted. The Tapirapé concept of family size remained unchanged in the face of modified conditions (i.e., higher death-rate caused by foreign disease) with the result that the adult population was no longer replaced by births. A rapidly declining population disrupted Tapirapé socio-ceremonial organization and affected the internal system of production and distribution. The Tenetehara with a more malleable social structure than that of the Tapirapé were able to survive the initial impact of Luso-Brazilian contact until the protection of the Jesuits allowed them to make necessary adjustments to the new circumstances.

Finally, this comparison between the Tapirapé and the Tenetehara calls to mind other primitive societies whose social structure must have been functionally related to population level and to demographic trends in the face of European civilization. In Brazil, the Ramkokamekra (Eastern Timbira) with their complex moiety system and the Apinayé with their kiye marriage classes, to mention only two examples, had social systems comparable to that of the Tapirapé. Such social structures depended upon a balanced representation of population in each of the numerous social units. A sudden decline of population might easily throw such highly segmented societies out of balance, so to speak. Without sufficient representation in one or more of these social units reciprocal socio-ceremonial affairs become impossible or may be carried out in a highly attenuated manner. Again, the social structure of the Karajá of the Araguaya River is based essentially upon extended family and kinship ties and lacks the highly segmented social units which crosscut villages and even family groups. Like that of the Tenetehara, Karajá social structure would seem to be less vulnerable to change in population size and more conducive to population growth. In addition to technological equipment and subsistence methods, social structure and cultural values also influence strongly the final adjustment of each society to its environment. Differences in social structure and of value systems between societies must be taken into account in studies of population size and of population trends in any natural area, such as the Tropical forest of South America.

NOTES

1. Basic descriptions of the Tapirapé and the Tenetehara have been published elsewhere: Cf. Wagley and Galvão (1948a, 1948b, 1949), Baldus (1937, 1944–1949, 1948, 1949, 1952). Only directly pertinent descriptive data is present in this paper.

2. Cf. Wagley (1940) and Baldus (1944–1949:v. CIII, 1948, 1949) for discussion of Tapirapé depopulation and disorganization. Baldus (1948:137–138), who found the village called Tampiitáua inhabited by 130 individuals in 1935, and only 62 in 1947, mentions that during this lapse of time several inhabitants had emigrated to another Tapirapé village very far from Tampiitáua, but that their number seems to be lower than the number of those who came from there to Tampiitáua. According to information received by this author, the other village is smaller than Tampiitáua, so that in 1947 the whole tribe probably counted less than a hundred members. In the same year, shortly after Baldus' visit, the Tapirapé were attacked by Kayapó Indians and lost several individuals.

3. There are no indications that the Tenetehara shared the warfare-cannibalism complex of the Tupinambá, but the lower reaches of the Mearim-Grajaú-Pindaré River system and the Island of Maranhão at its mouth were inhabited by Tupinambá groups (Métraux 1948:95 ff.; see also Fernandes 1949).

4. Baldus (1944–1949:v. CXXIII, p. 55) was told the same thing regarding the limitation of number of children of the Tapirapé family, but the contrary in relation to twins. According to information given to him by these Indians, the Tapirapé appreciate twins and, therefore, husband and wife eat twin or double bananas, i.e., with two fruits in the same peel.

5. Genealogies indicated that these rules are adhered to almost without exception. In 1939, during my residence in a Tapirapé village, one woman hesitated in allowing her third male child to be buried. Less than a month after its birth, she appeared one day without the infant and announced that he had died of a cold. Another woman whose child had four fathers allowed the child to live only to have it die of an intestinal disorder. The villagers took a definite "I-told-you-so" attitude.

This article by the late Herbert Baldus is only one of many that he wrote on the Tapirapé. Shortly before his death, he published a monograph on this group (Baldus 1970).

In the present article the author presents the shaman in a different light from the previous articles on shamans. The presentation is anecdotal in nature but conveys a feeling for the personality and function of the shaman that one might not get from a more formal presentation.

In the original, Baldus' references to Wagley's article on Tapirapé shamanism (1943) were to the Portuguese version. I have changed these references to the corresponding portions of the English version.

37   HERBERT BALDUS

Shamanism in the Acculturation of a Tupí Tribe of Central Brazil

Thirty years ago, that is, in 1935, there existed between the Araguaia and the Xingú, great rivers of Central Brazil, a village of Indians belonging to the numerous Tupí linguistic family. It was Tampii-táua, "Tapir village." The stream running by it emptied into a left affluent of the Araguaia known as the Rio Tapirapé, "Tapir trail," among the whites, who also called the forest dwellers by that name.

Access to Tampii-táua required several days travel by canoe on unknown waters and lengthy marches through savannas and flooded forests. This isolation, however, had not prevented sporadic contact between the Tapirapé and hunters and missionaries, either along the homonymous river or in the village itself. Thus, they had already received from our civilization, as well as from their neighbors the Karajá, objects to adorn their throats or, on occasion, cut them, e.g., glass beads, knives and machetes. They had also received European diseases.

The necklaces of imported beads did not acquire great importance in economic and social life, but the tools, because of the need for continual replacement, placed the Indians in a situation of dependence on the manufacturers. The modifications produced by these tools in the preparation of cultivated fields must undoubtedly be viewed as phenomena of acculturation without, however, being the result of continuous, or even always direct, contact.

Even more disturbing to the order of things were the epidemics that exterminated a great part of the population. This disaster resulted in the survivors of other Tapirapé villages joining those of Tampii-táua. As a consequence, not only did all the cultural features connected with interaction among these local groups disappear, but also the traditional conditions for family composition and ceremonial associations. Disturbance of the social organization was not directly reflected in material culture. On the other hand, if mythical themes were better known previously than in 1935, the year in which the Tapirapé told me of the loss of such

Reprinted by permission of the publisher from *Revista do Museu Paulista*, n.s., vol. 15 (1964), pp. 319–327. Translated by Patricia J. Lyon.
All material appearing within square brackets [ ] has been added by the editor of this book.

knowledge that was beginning to occur, it was perhaps not simply a consequence of the mass deaths but of inter-ethnic pressure arising from the proximity of the whites, whose constantly increasing power caused the Indians to lose interest in some traditions that did not seem to be of immediate value in the struggle for survival. It is certain, however, that anguish, whether a consequence of the deaths or of fear of their neighbors, did not make them forget the importance of an institution that integrated the Tapirapé world, that is, shamanism, but rather placed it more in evidence. In explaining the abandonment of three villages the inhabitants of which moved to Tampii-táua, informants from these places did not refer to the exterminating catastrophe in demographic terms, but emphasized only one of its aspects, the fact that there were no more shamans in these local groups. There is nothing more indicative of the state of Tapirapé culture at that time than this explanation. In spite of all the threats of social disintegration, shamanism continued to be considered the foundation of life, since life could only be conceived as forming a whole with the supernatural. Thus, the decisive patterns of tribal behavior were preserved.

How did the bearers of this Tapirapé world confront our world when I visited them for the first time in 1935? Some with curiosity, others with apparent indifference, but many, doubtless, with terror and repugnance. This fact did not, however, prevent women, children and even men from surrounding me with attentions. Rarely I noted a certain constraint; I was received everywhere with hospitality. From some whites who had visited Tampii-táua and some residents of the village who had traveled to the Araguaia, the Tapirapé knew of the power and the "riches" of our world; that it also brought them sickness and death they also knew. What was to me a true revelation, transporting me into a world completely different from our own, was the fact that, in 1935, they questioned me about whether we, the whites, would have to die, too. When a human condition like death is not known to be universal, I think it justifiable to speak of different worlds, thus characterizing the profound difference in views of the totality of natural and supernatural things. Contacts with us had not been, at that time, sufficiently frequent and prolonged to give the Tapirapé a better biological knowledge of us. The atmosphere of our influence, advancing toward them like a suffocating wind, could have caused them to consider us to be invulnerable to the dangers that threatened the life of the Indians. Such dangers were magical even when they came in the form of sickness brought by the whites. Even in cases where they were aware of such alien origin, the Tapirapé looked for, and found the magical originator of the sickness, always among themselves. Not that the inhabitants of Tampii-táua considered us to be devoid of magic. On the contrary, they never doubted my shamanistic qualities since, by analogy, they believed that a society as powerful as that of the whites could not exist without shamans. They believed in my ability to travel great distances in dreams and were even convinced that I had brought, by supernatural means, a baby boy born several months after my departure from the village.

What I managed to ascertain about the Tapirapé shaman in 1935 showed him, primarily, as defender of the community against evil spirits. It is worthy of note that the shaman, representative of a tribe so opposed to warlike actions on earth, became so combative in the journeys to the heavens. No doubt the change was an outlet for the tribe's repressed aggression, as were the practices of killing shamans alleged to be evil, dreaming the supernatural journeys, ill-treating orphans and parodying their dreaded neighbors, the Kayapó. Filling his empty stomach with tobacco smoke, the Tapirapé shaman achieved a kind of ecstasy that enabled him to find, and to extract by suction from the body of a sick person, the substance of the illness that had been shot at him, like an arrow, by an evil spirit. These cures, which I attended almost every night since my hammock was hung next to those of two shamans, always had the appearance of a fierce battle with moans and groans issuing from the mouth of the savior. There were also innumerable spirits of various kinds that surrounded the Tapirapé, so that there was never any lack of work for the shamans in protecting their fellow tribesmen. In addition to all this, the shaman had to know how to dream in order to undertake, in dreams, the great journeys to terrestrial and celestial regions for the purpose of localizing groupings of game, learning other facts of interest for the community life and bringing back the spirits of children. The most spectacular of these journeys was that which took place annually to the house of Thunder, in the season when violent thunderstorms with rain threatened the new plantings. This journey took place during a four day ceremony observed in January, 1940, by the North American ethnologist, Charles Wagley, who, in his masterful description, considers it "the culmination of sha-manistic activity among the Tapirapé" (Wagley 1943:78). On this occasion the shaman is the warrior disposed to give his life for his companions in defense of the crops against the attacks of Thunder and his followers, invisible to the eye of the layman. Alternately inhaling tobacco smoke and vomiting, he challenges that powerful supernatural being with his song until, shot with an arrow by this being, he "dies" in battle, that is, he falls intoxicated, his body remaining rigid after some contortions. Thus, it is in the active form of the ecstasy, that is, in the form physically provoked by the shaman himself, that the process of excorporation is achieved, the soul abandoning the body to go to the sky in search of the house of Thunder. Thunder and his sons wear the same attire as does the shaman, their terrestrial adversary, a headdress of red macaw feathers on the head and a small lip plug in the lower lip.

During my stay in Tampii-táua in 1935, I saw four men act as shamans in the treatment of illness. They differed considerably among themselves. The two who were my hammock neighbors, Kamairahó, head of the house, and Urukumy, had quite different personalities. The former, with delicate features, was expansive, voluble, disinclined to physical effort, preferring to appear timid and acquiring by diplomacy the position of the most powerful man in the village. Urukumy was calm and discreet, always even tempered and a good executor of his duties as a Tapirapé man and a shaman. Almost equal to Kamairahó, politically, was Vuatanamy, head of the house that was second in numerical importance, that is, it sheltered slightly fewer people than did ours. He was robust, withdrawn, averse to outsiders, hard-working, a good hunter with a great knowledge of animals, rather a warrior type than a diplomat. The fourth and youngest of the shamans was Maninohó, a tragic figure, sad, treated like an enemy in his own house, polite to me. All four were affectionate husbands but only Urukumy had children.

The Tapirapé did not restrict the exercise of the office of shaman to a determined human type as do certain other peoples. The fact that extroverts as well as introverts, pyknics as well as leptosomes occupied the office gave a broad base to shamanism, providing it a better chance for survival. Further evidence of the integrative function of this institution was the fact of the continuing existence of persons who, serving the collectivity in that office in obedience to the tribal pattern of behavior, did not take into consideration their individual destiny, in spite of the knowledge of the fatal end that normally awaited the shaman, that is, his execution as an evil sorcerer. They would become ambivalent through the supernatural power that they bore within themselves, a power capable, on the one hand, of defending the community against malign forces and, on the other, of attacking it as if it were one of those forces; power at the same time good and evil and, as a consequence, capable of arousing suspicion and fear. It is true that even then there was perhaps a slight tendency to emancipation when the astute Kamairohó told me suavely that he knew only how to "dream small," that is, to be a weak shaman and, therefore, inoffensive. Acculturation in this respect may be noted in the declaration made five years later to Wagley by a young Tapirapé well acquainted with the life of the whites on the Araguaia, who categorically refused to assume the dangerous office, saying that his people had killed many shamans (Wagley 1943:94). Indeed, Wagley recounts the execution of Urukumy (1943:71, note 15) which I confirmed in 1947 on the occasion of my second visit to Tampii-táua.

In that year I ascertained that 62 inhabitants existed in the village. Twelve years before there had been 130. The surplus of vegetable foods had disappeared and, with it, the unlimited hospitality. The women, previously completely nude, tied pieces of cloth around their waists when whites visited, and some of them even wore dresses. But the influence of our civilization seemed to be limited to these externals, although contact with the frontiersmen [sertanejos] was becoming more frequent. What most impressed me at that time was precisely to see and feel in the actuality what we all know so well theoretically—the superindividual nature of culture in the sense that it survives individuals, continuing to function beyond their existence. For example, I attended the same dances performed twelve years previously but now with other dancers. Those who had been, at that time, between eighteen and thirty years old were almost all dead. With a few exceptions, the Tapirapé do not normally reach a more advanced age. Not even this fact had caused the loss of their 1935 culture in any of the aspects that I could observe in 1947.

Since my second visit coincided with the dry season, I was unable to attend the Thunder ceremony, that important component of shamanism that belongs, however, to another season of the year. With depopulation the number of shamans had also diminished. I noted the existence of just one, but he was very powerful. Wagley mentions him as a very active participant in the Thunder ceremony when it took place in 1940, adding that he had already been treating the sick "for several years" (1943:93). The name Pančeí indicated by Wagley corresponds to the "Pantxai" noted by me in 1935. I also noted his Christian name, Antonio Pereira, bestowed by a missionary and maintained until the death of the bearer, whereas the Tapirapé name was replaced in 1947 by that of "Vuatanamy" by which the influential leader and shaman, now dead, was called in 1935.

The first time I saw Pantxai I calculated that he must be about 20 years old. He danced in a row of adult men. He shared his hammock with a girl about thirteen, not yet menstruating. He lived in the same house as Maninohó but did not seem to like that shaman very much. When I saw Pantxai again twelve years later his appearance as well as his name had changed. The insignificant adolescent was transformed into a strong and vigorous Vuatanamy, warrior against enemies on earth and in the heavens. But what distinguished him from the previous bearer of this name was his viciousness. The previous Vuatanamy had attracted many people to live in a large house under his protection; he would go hunting in the morning as happily as a little boy and was a tender husband as were almost all the Tapirapé. The present bearer of the name lived in a small hut with only his wife and a small daughter. Just before arriving at the village in 1947, in Porto Velho on the Tapirapé River, I had encountered Maretiã, a Tapirapé woman about 38 years old, who, as a refugee from Tampii-táua, lived disconsolate and alone under a wretched shelter. While, with a hand so light it seemed more like a caress, she delicately killed the mosquitoes that lit on me, she told her sad story. She was separated from her people because Antonio Pereira had beaten her on the head with a large knife, threatening to kill her because she did not want to work. The brutality of this man was further proved later when I visited his house. I found him beating his young wife, Maeteraó, on the back with a bundle of bamboo rods while she sat, bent over and sobbing loudly. Seeing her back begin to bleed, I could not contain myself and threatened the tormentor, shouting that I would beat him, too, if he did not stop that thrashing immediately. He stopped, laughing, but from then on when he was in my presence he carried a long dagger, accompanying me thus armed even on my return trip. I knew at that time that he was the killer of the great and generous shaman, Urukumy, having murdered him when, maddened by the death of his wife and son, he accused the shaman of the deed. To execute an evil sorcerer consecrates a young Tapirapé shaman. The adoption of the name Vuatanamy increased his prestige and, in 1947, the power of this intrepid man was further indicated by the fact that he had two wives, Maeteraó and Eiróa, the latter a girl about 20 years old who lived in the next house but accompanied him when he traveled and was considered to be "his other wife." Bigamy, not being the norm among these Indians, was in his case proof of strength.

But this violent man seemed destined to suffer misfortune. At least that is what we can deduce from a letter sent to me by Frei M.-H. Lelong who describes how, after my departure, the Kayapó Indians attacked Tampii-táua in the absence of the male inhabitants, sacking it, burning two houses, killing and stealing women. Among the dead the French Dominican mentions "Perera's wife," and among the stolen "Perera's daughter" (cf. Baldus 1948:142). I was later told that the unhappy shaman began a solitary persecution of the enemy, making long treks until he was shot in the leg. Tampii-táua was definitively abandoned by its inhabitants who, having lost their tools and food stores, looked for protection to the whites established on the banks of the Tapirapé River.

Thus, in 1953 when Wagley returned to these Indians, he found them reduced to

51 individuals who had built a new village near the mouth of that affluent of the Araguaia (Wagley 1955:99–106). The North American ethnologist observed that, from 1947 to 1950, these Indians were so dispersed that they had ceased to exist as a society, but since their culture persisted in their minds they could rebuild the social life, although with modification, a fact presenting "a striking example of the difference between a society and its culture" (1955:101–102). The cultural losses noted by Wagley in 1953 were manifested in the increasing abandonment of the art of basketry (1955:105), the failure to observe food taboos (1955:105) and the disappearance of shamanism (1955:104). Thus, no one was willing to admit to being a shaman although two men, one of them Antonio Pereira, were said to be able to "cure" a little without, however, having the formidable powers of the old shamans (Wagley 1955:104).

Nuns of the order of "Little Sisters of Jesus" installed themselves next to the new Tapirapé village. According to information given to me by Brother Francisco, assistant to this mission, in 1955 Antonio Pereira was still not living in Tapirapé fashion in a maloca along with several other families but continued, as he had in 1947, to live with only his wife and offspring in a house located outside the circle of the other houses of the village and hidden behind some bushes. In 1957 he was also found living in this way by the photographer Erwin von Dessauer (1960:27) who calls him, significantly, "the old chief"; and as Dessauer informed me personally, he continued to live in this way until 1960, the year in which he was killed by a rifle, shot by another Tapirapé. The death of the last shaman and the manner in which it occurred indicate the point acculturation had reached by the time of this event: the traditional culture functioned in the execution itself, being modified, however, by the instrument of execution, now a firearm.

The last data on the Tapirapé were given to me in 1963 by the aforementioned Brother Francisco. Their number had increased to 62. They practiced neither shamanistic acts nor intoxication by smoke to induce trance. They called what Wagley had written about the Thunder ceremony "nonsense" (in spite of the excellent photographic documentation of that description).

Thus, the old inhabitants of Tampii-táua and their descendants, having preserved their language and important features of their material culture, having reorganized their society and begun to increase, cut the heroic relationships of the Tapirapé world with the supernatural in order increasingly to tighten the bonds that join them to a world they still do not understand and one which does not understand them. They now know that whites also have to die but are no longer aware of the greatest spiritual factor in the old tribal culture. Obtaining that biological knowledge on passing from their culture to ours, they lost the manner of believing that they had received from their ancestors, and with it the means of channeling ambivalence. The shamanistic combination of tendencies for good and for evil cannot function in a Christian environment; there you do not travel to the sky to do battle nor do you, at least at the present time, execute evil sorcerers. Acculturation finished shamanism, but it will simply give "escapism" a new form, since, for us mortals, good and evil appear to be eternal forces.

As Miller notes, it is rare for an anthropologist to write about missionary activities aside from mentions of missionization or discussion of the possible effect on the native religious system. Since missionaries have been and still are an important factor in the culture of many South American Indian groups, we should pay as much attention to their effect on all aspects of native culture as we do to that of other outsiders. Surely it would not occur to most of us to consider the missionary as an agent of secularization as has Miller. Further information on the Toba and their religion may be found in Miller (1966, 1971, ms.), and he is actively continuing fieldwork with the group.

38 ELMER S. MILLER

The Christian Missionary, Agent of Secularization

Anthropologists tend to view Christian missionaries as conveyers of a supernaturalistic world view. This paper argues, in contrast, that missionaries are primarily agents of secularization. Socialized in a largely secular society, Western missionaries look to science for the explanation of most day-to-day experiences of human existence. Naturalistic, rather than supernaturalistic, beliefs form the organizing basis for viewing the vast majority of human events and experiences. For example, missionary attitudes and teachings concerning disease, accidents, catastrophies, the learning experience, even cosmology, reflect largely naturalistic rather than supernaturalistic beliefs. Consequently, events and experiences which were traditionally a part of the supernaturalistic universe are given naturalistic explanations and credence. This observation has relevance for the anthropologist studying culture change, particularly when religious movements are involved. It is important to note that the missionary's world view tends to support secularistic pressures on the folk society rather than to reinforce traditional supernaturalism, even while legitimating this view with a restricted supernaturalism. . . .

In spite of frequent off-the-record comments about the activities of missionaries, anthropologists have done little to document the role of missionaries as agents of culture change. What little they have written focuses on the religious aspects of missionary work but rarely on the missionary as agent of Westernization generally. Here, I shall attend to the missionary as purveyor of a naturalistic world view as

Reprinted by permission of the author and publisher from *Anthropological Quarterly*, vol. 43, no. 1 (1970), pp. 14–22.

opposed to a supernaturalistic one. By naturalistic, I refer to cause and effect explanations based on natural laws rather than explanations which rely on supernatural powers of intervention in human affairs. I shall draw on my own field work among the Toba Indians of the Argentine Chaco.

Naturalistic beliefs form the organizing basis for the missionary's comprehension of the vast majority of day-to-day events and experiences. Rather than reinforce or expand traditional supernaturalistic beliefs, the missionary, in fact, supports the many naturalistic orientations Westerners tend to impose on non-Western cultures.[1] Socialized in a largely secular society (i.e., one which depends upon naturalistic rather than supernaturalistic beliefs and activities for its raison d'être), missionaries actually assign supernaturalistic beliefs and actions a minor role in describing and explaining the everyday experiences of human existence. For them, the arena of direct supernatural involvement is generally restricted to past events (such as the "Creation" and the Old and New Testament periods of "revelation") or to individual experiences which they cannot readily trace to naturalistic causes. In contrast, traditional supernaturalistic world views tend to encompass all of life's experiences with no comparable cognitive distinction between the natural and supernatural or between temporal epochs of differential supernatural activity.

The extent to which the missionary is successful in communicating his secularized world view depends to a great extent, of course, upon the conditions existing in the target culture at the time of mission contact. The Toba Indians referred to here are presently located in approximately fifty semi-sedentary communities scattered throughout the Chaco and Formosa provinces of northern Argentina. The latest census data indicate a population of eight to nine thousand (Ministerio del Interior 1968:116). Prior to the Argentine military conquest of the Chaco region in 1884–85, the Toba had traditionally roamed the area in bilateral bands subsisting on hunting, gathering, and fishing. After the conquest and subsequent colonization of the Chaco, however, huge landholdings were fenced off and game became less readily available. The Toba were obliged to depend upon wage-earning tasks in the cotton fields, on sugar farms, and at lumbering projects for their subsistence needs. Several attempts were made during the early decades of this century by traditional Toba leaders to recoup lost ground and to frustrate the foreign incursions into Toba territory. In 1924 a major attempt of this sort resulted in the slaughter of several hundred Toba men, women and children by government forces. It was this incident which set the stage for Protestant mission penetration.

The first foreign Protestant Mission to the Argentine Toba of the Chaco province was the British Emmanuel Mission at El Espinillo from 1934 to 1949. The only other foreign Protestant group to establish mission headquarters in the province was the Mennonite Mission at El Aguará from 1943 to 1955.[2] Following established missionary procedures, both groups conducted what they considered an essentially four-pronged approach. At the mission centers, four major buildings were constructed—a store, a school, a clinic, and a chapel—and missionary personnel were assigned to some extent on this basis. The missionary considered the first three approaches essentially "service" activities. That is, their involvement in economic, education, and medical programs was viewed as supplementary to the primary task of communicating the "spiritual" message associated with chapel activities. I will show, however, that all four areas were traditionally of supernaturalistic concern to the Toba.

The Emmanuel store was established in order to supply the Toba with provisions at reasonable prices since local traders reputedly exploited the Indians (Sockett 1966:58). In addition to supplying the Toba with trade items, the Mennonite store was also designed to teach the Toba the "economic facts of life." At one time, bank accounts were kept for individual families in order to instruct them in the value of saving but this practice had to be abandoned as the Toba persistently complained that they were being cheated—an unwarranted accusation, in the eyes of the missionary. In connection with both stores, there was instruction in crop cultivation, especially corn, vegetables, and cotton, as well as in the keeping of chickens. The missionary idea was that the store program would instill the Protestant ethic that "he who does not work shall not eat."[3] This philosophy stood in direct contrast to the traditional Toba belief that human welfare depended not so much upon human technological responsibility as upon maintaining a proper relationship of balance with the animistic world.

Traditionally, Toba men hunted and fished while the women collected wild fruits and vegetables. The local chief-shaman had the responsibility of leading his bilateral band to areas where game and fruit were most plentiful. He decided where the band should go primarily by means of communication with his spirit companion (ltaxayaxaua). When the food supply became scarce and the game unavailable, it was assumed that the harmony between humans and spirits had been jeopardized. This may have resulted from witchcraft by a competing shaman or from some specific individual error, such as contamination by a menstruating woman. On these occasions, Toba leaders lost prestige and authority, and some band members occasionally joined relatives in other locations.[4]

The contrast between traditional Toba and missionary attitudes toward economic subsistence is obvious. The Toba had depended upon a proper relationship with spirit beings for access to food resources. When food became scarce, greater physical exertion was not necessarily required, but rather a restoration of balance and harmony with the spirit world. The missionary insisted, on the other hand, that improved productive techniques and expanded agricultural efforts were the keys to solving the problems of food scarcity. It was man's responsibility to improve his food supply by increased physical activity and only on occasions of extreme drought or excessive flooding were appeals made for supernatural intervention. For the missionary, the sun and rain were considered phenomena of nature which conformed to the laws of cause and effect whereas for the Toba they were spirit-like beings with the ability to directly influence human existence. The missionary contributed to the breakdown of the Toba's traditional dependence upon the spirit world for subsistence needs by placing food in the category of items produced solely by human energy to be bought and sold like any other trade goods.

A new philosophical base for viewing subsistence was required by the Toba with the introduction of a wage-earning economy and the breakdown of reliance upon the chief-shaman. It was at this juncture that the missionary appeared with his secular view of economics. That he was successful is attested to by the fact that the contemporary Toba, while actively participating in a Pentecostal-type religious movement, do not include economic concerns as part of their religious activities.

In the mission schools, classes for all ages were conducted (in Spanish) in the basic subjects. Naturalistic interpretations were involved both in method and content. In method, the missionaries insisted that the learning process required studious concentration and cogitation. In contrast, the traditional Toba attitude toward learning was that of power infused or revealed through one's Itaxayaxaua (spirit companion). The Toba frequently expressed their frustration at the missionary for not sharing the deepest knowledge and insights into his religious faith. For example, they repeatedly asked for Bible study—for that special knowledge of the Bible which the foreign pastor reserved for himself—as though this knowledge was an object to be exchanged rather than concepts to be learned. This attitude led one missionary to exclaim in exasperation, "They seem to expect us to unlock their skulls and deposit the information."[5]

Traditionally, the Toba acquired the ability to perceive the unusual or extraordinary by means of dreams and visions, or by direct communication with an Itaxayaxaua. Even when an elder shaman wished to instruct an apprentice, he did so by infusing "power" (*napinshic*) into the novice. Not until the missionary, and later provincial, schools were established in Toba communities did the notion of studying to acquire knowledge become comprehensible. In treating learning as a natural process, dependent primarily upon one's willingness to concentrate and cogitate rather than insights revealed through dreams, visions, or contacts with spirit beings, the missionary served to "disenchant" or "intellectualize" the Toba, in the sense that Weber used the terms.[6]

In addition to the methods of learning, the subjects taught also involved disenchantment. For example, the Toba traditionally conceptualized the cosmos as a three-layered universe, with one layer situated on top of the other. These layers included the sky, land surface, and earth interior. Waters were located off to the side and some mythological accounts implied that the waters enabled one to move from one level to another. Along with spirits of the dead and animals, the sun, moon, and lightning all possessed an animistic quality and were part of Toba ontology. These beings, classified into sky, land, earth, and water beings, were both potentially dangerous and potentially helpful to humans. Since they significantly influenced human existence, it was important to maintain a proper relationship with them.[7]

Although the missionary also taught that a supernatural being created and controlled the universe, it was a Copernican universe which he conceptualized, one based upon physical laws and natural cause and effect relationships. Thus, when the jeep failed to function properly, or a mishap of some sort occurred, the missionary tended to explain the incidents as accidents or natural failures, whereas the Toba were much more inclined to suspect omens and seek other-than-natural explanations. By introducing globes and maps, the missionary managed to discredit the three-layered Toba view of the universe. At the very least he caused the Toba to raise serious questions about their own mythology. The sun, rain, and lightning were said to be objects of nature and not personally responsible for the effects they produced on humans. Thus, the missionary's view of the cosmos represented again a naturalistic interpretation of what the Toba had previously considered supernaturalistic phenomena. The influence of missionary teaching is demonstrated by the fact that traditional Toba myths are no longer repeated and the young are now told myths with a Christian interpretation.

Perhaps the most intense mission efforts toward modifying the Toba dependence upon supernaturalism occurred in the clinics where nurses worked with a highly naturalistic view of disease and medicine. In the traditional Toba view, illness resulted from witchcraft and sorcery involving object intrusions and soul loss. An individual became ill because someone aimed to harm him, not because of chance encounters with germs. Only shamans (pi'oxonaq) or sorcerers ('enaxanaxai) could cure and cause illness or other kinds of physical ailment. They accomplished this by power objects, by contagious magic, or by communication with their spirit helpers (Itaxayaxaua). Although the precise methods for causing injury were not generally known to all, the techniques for curing were. To cure, the shaman consulted his Itaxayaxaua who, in turn, provided a healing song and determined whether the patient would recover or die. In former times, when the shaman declared that there was no hope of recovery, the extremely ill or aged were sometimes abandoned or buried while still alive. In sum, the cause and cure for illness among the Toba traditionally involved supernatural power and power objects. A more or equally powerful shaman could generally protect and undo the damage caused by another shaman. Occasionally, several shamans combined forces to perform a feat requiring an extraordinary amount of power. There was no remedy, however, for the accomplished work of a sorcerer; the result was sure death.

In contrast, the missionary understanding of illness involved making the proper diagnosis (which in turn depended upon proper training) and obtaining the required remedies. Germs caused sickness by moving, more or less predictably, in humans. They could, with a few exceptions, be controlled and destroyed by natural means. Although appeals were made to divine powers in particularly difficult cases, the healing process itself was basically considered a naturalistic one. Given time, the proper treatment would have its beneficial effect. The missionaries themselves relied on aspirin and penicillin in times of illness and readily shared of their supply with the Toba.

The similarities of the Christian and Toba techniques, that of diagnosing and counteracting the harm in one's body, should not obscure the basic conceptual difference of disease as a naturalistic versus a supernaturalistic process. This conceptual distinction was not lost on the Toba. In recent years government clinics have come to play an increasingly important role in treating Toba illness. The role of the missionary in breaking down resistance to medical aid, by transporting the sick to clinics and by insisting upon the use of prescribed remedies, significantly modified Toba attitudes toward disease and its treatment.[8]

The three mission approaches, then,—store, school, clinic—all served to impose naturalistic orientations on the Toba. Furthermore, even the one mission approach that directly and immediately concerned the supernatural—the chapel—involved a secularizing influence. Neither the Emmanuel nor the Mennonite missionaries experienced, or claimed to experience, direct contact with the supernatural by means of ecstasy, or what the Toba term *gozo* (literally, "joy"). Missionary prayers lacked the emotional content and the supernatural interaction appreciated by the Toba. Their attitude toward the Bible had also been influenced by textual criticism and by a secular world view. In contrast, the Bible made more sense to the Toba in terms of a fetish. They tied it to their side while dancing and placed it over the bodies of sick people for healing. Furthermore, in his desire to translate the Bible into the Toba language, the missionary served to remove the mystic halo associated with a Spanish text which was only poorly understood, thus undercutting the fetish quality. In practice, if not in theory the removed and "cool" God of the missionary was confined to a small arena of operation in contrast to the traditional Toba view of the involvement of spirit-like beings in everyday affairs.

The contrast of world views, particularly in regard to disease and direct communication with the supernatural, was not as immediately apparent among the Pentecostal ministers who also had contacts with the Toba. In most other areas, however, such as general cosmology, attitudes toward the learning process, and toward food acquisition, Pentecostal notions were much more closely aligned with the missionary than with the Toba world view. Thus, Pentecostal preachers, who actually had a greater ideological impact upon the Toba than did the Emmanuel and Mennonite missionaries, also contributed to the breakdown of traditional reliance upon supernaturalism.

While individual missionary programs vary from country to country and among denominations, Christian missionary ideology constitutes a radically different kind of belief system than that of the folk societies it contacts. This ideology represents a highly institutionalized operation in which supernaturalism's sphere of influence has been increasingly narrowed and circumscribed in the sending community (Western World). It was Weber's opinion, of course, that the process of disenchantment has continued to exist in Occidental culture for millennia. Generating few values uniquely its own, mission ideology reflects and even legitimates many of the values being forced at the same time upon the folk society by a colonial administration or a national government.

Although governmental administrators and educators openly pursue secular objectives, they may actually be less effective in achieving them than the missionary, who claims supernatural backing for his beliefs and actions even while communicating a highly secular point of view. Consequently, Christian missionaries serve to accelerate the breakdown of traditional animistic world views perhaps to a greater extent than any other agent of change.

NOTES

1. Throughout this paper I refer only to Christian missionaries, and to Protestant missionaries in particular.
2. There were other Protestant groups (Pentecostal Baptist, and others) which established significant contacts with the Toba but their work was essentially *criollo* in orientation.

Approximately eight individuals were associated with the Emmanuel Mission; six married couples and two single girls (nurses) served in the Mennonite Mission, although only about half that number at any one period of time.

3. A slight paraphrase of II Thessalonians 3:10.

4. This is not to imply that the Toba had no notion of seasonal abundance. It refers rather to times of extended bad luck or unexpected scarcity.

5. This reaction parallels reports from Melanesia where cargo cult believers frequently accused Christian missions of withholding prime information.

6. By disenchantment, Weber referred to the tendency to "master all things by calculation" rather than to rely on "mysterious incalculable forces," to resort to technical rather than "magical means," in order to accomplish human ends (Gerth and Mills 1958: 139).

7. The early satellites caused a great deal of excitement among the Toba. They appeared to accept my attempts at explanation uncritically, although with little enthusiasm. In this instance the two world views came into clear focus. I claimed the light moving across the sky was an object placed there by human ingenuity while the Toba were inclined to believe it was a spirit on the move with some omen or message which only a knowledgeable old shaman would be able to interpret. Perhaps the shaman himself had caused the "sky being" (*piguem l'ec*) to move.

8. When I first went to the Chaco in 1958, the Toba rarely attended the public health clinics. They certainly did not attend of their own initiative. Upon my return in 1966, however, the Toba were conspicuous by their presence in waiting lines and the nurses were seeking ways to discourage their daily visits for minor ailments, due to overcrowding.

The only change in this article from the original, excepting translation, is the omission of a photograph with the caption, "Interesting group of Toyeris, on the day following their arrival at the Mission of Lago Valencia. P. Arnaldo is seen among them. Fr. Francisco has a baby in his arms." At least 22 adult Indians are shown in the photograph as well as a number of infants and small children.

39 JOSÉ ALVAREZ, O.P.

A New Tribe of Toyeri Savages

It is inexpressibly gratifying, a splendid summation and complete fulfillment of all our aspirations, to see a new tribe of savages arrive at the Mission. And if, as in the present case, one sees them come happily with the desire to settle at our side to enjoy the advantages that Christian civilization always provides to her

Reprinted by permission of the publisher from *Misiones Dominicanas del Peru*, vol. 17, no. 93 (1936), pp. 64–67. Translated by Patricia J. Lyon with the permission of the publisher.

beloved children, our satisfaction passes all bounds and our soul must bless God who is always splendid and magnificent in His manifestations.

How many prayers and hidden sacrifices must have been needed for the hour of their conversion finally to sound on the great clock face of the Eternal Will? We do not know; but P. Arnaldo, during his long and dangerous expedition, tangibly felt the powerful effect of those constant prayers and pleas that so many spiritual souls, true apostles, make for our cause so that the cross of Christ, in the hands of the missionary, may advance and triumph, conquering for His kingdom these sons of the jungle, sad victims of barbarism and misfortune.

This step forward, this promising triumph, this enthusiastic and joyful reception that a totally barbarous tribe of savages gives to the missionary, should stimulate us beyond measure to others, greater and more difficult, should convince us once more of the ease of their conversion.

With reason the Cardinal Prefect of the Propaganda Fide, in his message to all missionaries, tells us, "Let all those who suffer to follow the orders of Christ and build the kingdom of God always maintain the certainty of victory!" And let them not forget either that question, full of wonderment, with which a savage, surprised at my delay in going to convert him, chided me lovingly: "Why didn't you come sooner?" And the other, no less tender and affectionate: "Now are you going to be my father?"

DAYS OF JOY, OF MOURNING, OF DESOLATION

Upon the arrival of the new tribe at the Mission, missionaries, semicivilized Indians and savages rivaled each other in heaping upon them all kinds of affection and attention in order to convince them that the offers of good treatment, abundance of food and all kinds of gifts that had been so extolled to them when they were invited to come live at the Mission, had not been false promises.

As for them, although timid and frightened (they trembled on seeing any cow, dog or pig), they made themselves loved for their frank, sweet and affable character, completely free of those instincts for criminality and thievery of other tribes.[1] They were extremely satisfied, pleasantly surprised by the affection and dignity with which they were treated: clothing, blankets and mosquito netting[2] instead of crude barkcloth; machetes, knives and axes of steel[3] forced them to look with ridicule on their primitive stone axes; porcelain plates and bowls instead of the clay pots they had so reluctantly left on abandoning their huts. Their food, consisting until then of natural products of the forest, was now made up of enormous quantities of bananas, plantains and manioc and, especially, sugar cane which they had never before seen.

But how brief are the days of happiness on earth!

Whether they already carried the germ or whether it was the change in diet, the bites of flies and mosquitoes that so tormented them (where they had been living, as in a truly paradaisical place, there had apparently been not a single one to molest them), at the end of about a week at our sides they were overcome, especially the adults, by fevers so pertinacious and malignant that, in spite of all the efforts we made to combat them, we could not avoid the frightful havoc that was on the point of making an end of all of them.

It is so difficult properly to administer medicine, purgatives, sudorifics, quinine, to totally barbarous savages who have more faith in cold baths, that in spite of the most careful vigilance day and night their habitual customs prevailed, and finally our exhaustion from attending them was so great that only the power of God could sustain us and prevent our being swept away by the terrible contagion.

Above all, from the time they began to die in so fast, sometimes startling, so sadly irremediable a manner, those days were a truly painful period for us. This anguish that afflicted our hearts so rudely was intensified unbearably at each step by the cries of pain and demonstrations of affection and confidence that they showed us constantly when they asked our help in their need and suffering, when we gave them holy Baptism, when we saw them die in our arms.

And now, as evening falls, these sixteen little orphans, seeing that their parents do not arrive from the forest loaded with game and fruit as usual, burst into tears and the smallest ones stretch out their trembling hands to us, calling, between sobs, for their beloved mothers who no longer live.

What sad scenes, full of tender emotion and bitterness!

Poor Toyeris, who at one moment appeared before us so satisfied and so good, like a smiling hope, and suddenly disappeared again forever, struck down by the mysterious hand of the destiny in which the eternal purposes of the justice and mercy of God make us tremble.

I wonder what is the fate of the soul of those so beloved children at this moment!

This is the sorrow that afflicts and tortures us, and the only reason for these lines is to ask for them a fervent prayer to merciful God that he grant eternal rest to their poor souls.

NOTES

1. They had never been visited by anyone, nor had they ever made any kind of raid on other tribes.

2. What had frightened them most (they stated later) was to see people wearing clothing.

3. Such was the esteem in which they held these very valuable instruments of defense and of work, that for days they did not let them out of their hands.

A GUIDE TO THE BIBLIOGRAPHY
OF SOUTH AMERICAN ETHNOLOGY

This guide is a descriptive list of the major sources of published information on the anthropology of South America.

The "Bibliography of Anthropological Bibliographies: The Americas" by Gibson (1960) is arranged by geographical area and has an author and subject index. Each entry is annotated with the topics covered, number of entries and a library where the item can be found. Jaquith's "Bibliography of Anthropological Bibliographies of the Americas" (1970) contains 344 additional items. It is arranged alphabetically by author, with a topic-area index; most entries are annotated. A guide to ethnographic bibliographies (O'Leary 1970) is arranged by geographical area with an additional section on subject bibliographies.

The *Handbook of South American Indians* (Steward, ed. 1946–1959) contains a number of references at the end of each article; these references are to entries in a bibliography arranged alphabetically at the end of each volume. It should never be assumed, however, that the references for any given article represent the entire literature on that subject.

The *Ethnographic Bibliography of South America* (O'Leary 1963) contains more than 24,000 references arranged according to Murdock's *Outline* (1951a). There is an introductory section on bibliographic aids as well as a section on works about South America in general. This invaluable resource is rumored to be in the process of revision.

The *Catalogue of the Library of the Peabody Museum of Archaeology and Ethnology, Harvard University* was published in 1963. The catalogue is divided into twenty-six volumes alphabetically arranged by author, and twenty-seven volumes arranged by subject. A twelve-volume supplement was issued in 1970 and a second supplement of five volumes in 1971. Of special value is the analytical cataloguing of journals, each article having a separate entry. Although this catalogue is an exceptionally useful research tool, it must be borne in mind that it contains references only to those items contained in the library and, hence, is not exhaustive.

In addition to single bibliographical treatments such as those listed above, there are several periodical sources of bibliographical material on South America. Of special interest is the *Handbook of Latin American Studies* published annually since 1936. From 1936 to 1963 (nos. 1–25) each volume covered every subject. Since 1964 (no. 26), however, the even-numbered volumes have contained publications in the humanities (art, history, language, literature, music, and philosophy) and the odd-numbered volumes cover the social sciences (anthropology, economy, education, geography, government, and international relations, law, and sociology). The *Handbook of Latin American Studies* provides an annotated bibliography of selected books and articles, together with comments by the contributors on the general trend within each specialty.

The *Boletín Bibliográfico de Antropología Americana* has been published by the Instituto Panamericano de Geografía e Historia in Mexico quarterly or annually from 1937. Its comprehensiveness varies, but it is always worth checking. The *Latin American Research Review,* published three times a year since 1965, contains review articles, reviews and listings of current publications, as well as an inventory of current research in Latin America.

The most comprehensive of the annual bibliographies is the "Bibliographie Américaniste" which appeared in the *Journal de la Société des Américanistes* (Paris) through Tome LIII, 1964. Since that time it has been issued as a separate publication by the Société. Although this bibliography is not annotated, it is arranged by topic and geographical area and has an author index.

Surely the most useful tool in South American anthropological bibliography must be the two volumes of Baldus' monumental *Bibliografia Crítica da Etnologia Brasileira* (1954, 1968). Although the title indicates that the bibliography is limited to Brazilian materials, in fact the author has included many works that are peripheral to Brazil. Not only are all the entries annotated, sometimes extensively, but translations and later editions are indicated as well as reviews. The contents are arranged alphabetically by author with indexes by subject, geographical area, tribe, and author. The second volume contains a supplemental listing of later editions and translations of works originally noted in volume I. The first volume, long out of print, has recently been reprinted as volume IV of the *Völkerkundliche Abhandlungen,* a publication series of the Niedersächsisches Landesmuseum, Hanover.

BIBLIOGRAPHY

Only two abbreviations are used in the bibliography.

HSAI Handbook of South American Indians. Julian H. Steward (ed.). Smithsonian Institution, Bureau of American Ethnology, Bulletin 143. 7 vols. Washington: United States Government Printing Office.

Volume 1. 1946. The marginal tribes.
Volume 2. 1946. The Andean civilizations.
Volume 3. 1948. The tropical forest tribes.
Volume 4. 1948. The circum-Caribbean tribes.
Volume 5. 1949. The comparative ethnology of South American Indians.
Volume 6. 1950. Physical anthropology, linguistics and cultural geography of South American Indians.
Volume 7. 1959. Index.

RMP Revista do Museu Paulista. Nova série. São Paulo.

Since there is no fixed rule for distinguishing surnames in Portuguese, wherever possible references to Portuguese surname authors follow the usage of Herbert Baldus (1954, 1968).

Adam, Lucien
    1890 Arte de la lengua de los indios Antis o Campas; varias preguntas, advertencias, i doctrina cristiana, conforme al manuscrito original hallado en la ciudad de Toled [sic] por Charles Leclerc; con un vocabulario metódico i una introducción comparativa por . . . Bibliothèque Linguistique Américaine, t. XIII. Paris: J. Maisonneuve, Libraire-Editeur.
Aldrete, Juan
    1965 Relación de la gobernación de Yahuarzongo y Pacamurus. [1582] Relaciones Geográficas de Indias—Perú, t. IV, pp. 147–153. Biblioteca de Autores Españoles, t. 185. Madrid: Ediciones Atlas.
Allan, William
    1965 The African husbandman. Edinburgh, London, New York: Oliver & Boyd.

Allen, William L., and Holshouser de Tizón, Judy
1973　Land use patterns among the Campa of the Alto Pachitea, Peru. *In* Variation in anthropology: Essays in honor of John C. McGregor. Donald W. Lathrap and Jody Douglas (eds.), pp. 137–153. Urbana: Illinois Archaeological Survey.

Almagro, Manuel de
1866　Breve descripción de viajes hechos en América por la comisión científica enviada por el gobierno de S.M.C. durante los años de 1862 á 1866. Acompañada de dos mapas y de la enumeración de las colecciones que forman la exposición pública por Don . . . Publicada por órden del Ministerio de Fomento. Madrid: Imprenta y Estereotipia de M. Rivadeneyra.

Andrée, Richard
1887　Die Anthropophagie. Eine ethnographische Studie. Leipzig: Veit & Co.

Anonymous
1874　Die Götter der wilden Indianer in Brasilien. Globus, Bd. XXV, no. 19, pp. 296–298. Braunschweig.
1965　Lethal kokoi venom related to hormones. M.D., Medical News Magazine, v. 9, no. 4, April, p. 112. New York.

Appun, Carl Ferdinand
1871　Unter den Tropen. Wanderungen durch Venezuela, am Orinoco, durch Britisch Guyana und am Amazonenstrome in den Jahren 1849–1868. 2 vols. Jena: Hermann Costenoble.

Azara, Félix de
1809　Voyage dans l'Amérique méridionale, par Don . . . , depuis 1781 jusq'en 1801, contenant la description géographique, politique et civil du Paraguay et de la rivière de La Plata . . . publiés d'après les manuscrits de l'auteur, avec une notice sur sa vie et ses écrits, par C.A. Walckenaer, enrichis de notes par G. Cuvier . . . suivis de l'histoire naturelle des oiseaux du Paraguay et de la Plata, par le même auteur, traduite, d'après l'original espagnol, et augmentée d'un grand nombre de notes, par M. Sonnini; accompagnés d'un atlas de 25 planches. 4 vols. and atlas. Paris: Dentu.

Baldus, Herbert
1937　Ensaios de etnologia Brasileira. Biblioteca Pedagógica Brasileira, série 5ª. Brasiliana, v. 101. São Paulo.
1939　Herrschaftsbildung und Schichtung bei Naturvölkern Südamerikas. Archiv für Anthropologie Völkerforschung und kolonialen Kulturwandel, n.F., Bd. XXV (LIII. Bd.), 2. und 3. Heft, pp. 112–130. Braunschweig.
1943　Sinopse da cultura guayakí. Sociologia, v. V, no. 2, pp. 147–153. São Paulo.
1944–1949　Os Tapirapé, tribo Tupí no Brasil central. Revista do Arquivo Municipal, 1944, v. XCVI, pp. 155–166; v. XCVII, pp. 45–54; v. XCVIII, pp. 105–126; v. XCIX, pp. 63–77; 1945, v. C, pp. 191–198; v. CI, pp. 67–75; v. CII, pp. 123–130; v. CIII, pp. 183–189; v. CIV, pp. 93–100; v. CV, pp. 77–90; 1946, v. CVII, pp. 107–120; v. CVIII, pp. 121–137; v. CIX, pp. 75–88; v. CX, pp. 191–202; v. CXI, pp. 105–119; 1947, v. CXII, pp. 51–62; v. CXIII, pp. 191–199; v. CXIV, pp. 185–199; v. CXV, pp. 255–260; v. CXVI, pp. 55–61; 1948, v. CXVII, pp. 91–98; v. CXVIII, pp. 117–125; v. CXIX, pp. 79–87; v. CXX, pp. 51–57; 1949, v. CXXI, pp. 79–82; v. CXXII, pp. 167–172; v. CXXIII, pp. 53–56; v. CXXIV, pp. 139–143; v. CXXVII, pp. 234–236. São Paulo.
1948　Tribos da bacia do Araguaia e o Serviço de Proteção aos Índios. RMP, v. II, pp. 137–168.
1949　Akkulturation im Araguaya-Gebiet. Anthropos, Bd. XLI–XLIV, Heft 4–6, 1946–1949, pp. 889–891. Freiburg.
1952　Caracterização da cultura Tapirapé. *In* Indian tribes of aboriginal America. Sol Tax (ed.), Selected Papers of the XXIXth International Congress of Americanists (New York, Sept. 5–12, 1949), v. 3, pp. 311–313. Chicago: University of Chicago Press.
1954　Bibliografia crítica da etnologia Brasileira. São Paulo: Comissão do IV centenário da cidade de São Paulo.
1967　Synopsis of the critical bibliography of Brazilian ethnology, 1953–1960. *In* Indians of Brazil in the twentieth century. Janice H. Hopper (ed.), ICR Studies 2, pp. 207–228. Washington: Institute for Cross-Cultural Research.
1968　Bibliografia crítica da etnologia Brasileira, Volume II. Völkerkundliche Abhandlungen, Bd. IV. Hannover.

1970   Tapirapé: Tribo tupi do Brasil central. Brasiliana (Série Grande Formato), v. 17. São Paulo: Companhia Editora Nacional and Editora da Universidade de São Paulo.

Baltasar de Lodares
1922   Los Franciscanos en Venezuela. Caracas: Empresa Ediorcil.

Bamberger, Joan
1971   The adequacy of Kayapó ecological adjustment. Verhandlungen des XXXVIII. Internationalen Amerikanistenkongresses, Stuttgart-München, 12. bis 18. August 1968, Bd. III, pp. 373–379. München: Klaus Renner Verlag.

Bancroft, Edward
1769   An essay on the natural history of Guiana, in South America; containing a description of many curious productions in the animal and vegetable systems of that country; together with an account of the religion, manners and customs of several tribes of its Indian inhabitants. . . . London: T. Becket and P.A. DeHondt.

Banner, Horace
1961   O índio Kayapó em seu acampamento. Boletim do Museu Paraense Emílio Goeldi, n.s., Antropologia, setembro, no. 13. Belém-Pará.

Barcia, Roque
1881–1883   Primer diccionario general etimológico de la lengua española. 5 vols. Madrid: Estab. Tip. de Alvarez Hermanos.

Barrau, Jacques
1958   Subsistence agriculture in Melanesia. Bernice Pauahi Bishop Museum of Polynesian Ethnology and Natural History, Bulletin 219. Honolulu.

Barrère, Pierre
1743   Nouvelle relation de la France équinoxiale, contenant: la description des côtes de la Guiane; de l'Isle de Cayenne; le commerce de cette colonie; les divers changemens arrivés dans ce pays; & les moeurs & coûtumes des différens peuples sauvages qui l'habitent. Paris: Piget, Damonneville, Durand.

Barrett, Otis Warren
1928   The tropical crops. A popular treatment of the practice of agriculture in tropical regions, with discussion of cropping systems and methods of growing the leading products. New York: The Macmillan Company.

Barros Arana, Diego
1884–1902   Historia jeneral de Chile. 16 vols. Santiago: Rafael Jover, Editor [and others].

Basabe y Urquieta, Josseph de
1902   Informe sobre las provincias de Quijos, Avila, Canelos y Macas. In Colección de documentos sobre límites Ecuatoriano Peruanos. 2 vols. Enrique Vacas Galindo (ed.), t. I, documento quinto, pp. 61–70. Quito: Tipografía de la Escuela de Artes y Oficios por R. Jaramillo.

Bascuñan: See Nuñez de Pineda y Bascuñan, Francisco

Basso, Ellen Becker
1970   Xingu Carib kinship terminology and marriage: Another view. Southwestern Journal of Anthropology, v. 26, no. 4, winter, pp. 402–416. Albuquerque.

Bastian, Adolph
1878–1889   Die Culturländer des alten America. 3 vols. Berlin: Weidmannsche Buchhandlung.

Bastida, Julián de
1902   Carta original de Julián de Bastida á Don García de Mendoza. [Nov. 15, 1563] Colección de Historiadores de Chile y Documentos Relativos a la Historia Nacional, t. XXIX, pp. 469–501. Santiago de Chile: Imprenta Elzeviriana.

Bates, Henry Walter
1864   The naturalist on the river Amazons. A record of adventures, habits of animals, sketches of Brazilian and Indian life, and aspects of nature under the equator, during eleven years of travel. London: John Murray. 2nd edition.
1892   The naturalist on the river Amazons. A record of adventures, habits of animals, sketches of Brazilian and Indian life, and aspects of nature under the equator, during eleven years of travel. London: John Murray. [reprinting of 1864 edition]

Becher, Hans
1968   Endocanibalismo Yanonámi. Actas y Memorias, XXXVII Congreso Internacional de Americanistas, República Argentina—1966, v. III, pp. 41–49. Buenos Aires. [Distributed by Librart S.R.L.]

Bello Gayoso, Antonio
   1965   Relación que enbió a mandar Su Magestad se hiziese desta ciudad de Cuenca y de toda
          su provincia. [1582] Relaciones Geográficas de Indias–Perú, t. III, pp. 265–290.
          Biblioteca de Autores Españoles, t. 184. Madrid: Ediciones Atlas.
Benitez, Leopoldo A.
   1942   Supuestos túmulos en Ybytymí. Revista de la Sociedad Científica del Paraguay, t. V,
          no. 6, pp. 77–89. Asunción.
Bennett, Charles F. Jr.
   1962   The Bayano Cuna Indians, Panama: An ecological study of livelihood and diet.
          Association of American Geographers, Annals, v. 52, no. 1, March, pp. 32–50.
          Lawrence, Kansas.
Bermeo, Manuel
   1886   Informe del misionero Fray Manuel Bermeo [1778]. In Varones Ilustres de la Orden
          Seráfica en el Ecuador; desde la Fundación de Quito hasta Nuestros Dias. Francisco
          María Compte (ed.), t. II, pp. 278–282. Quito: Imprenta del Clero. [dated 1885 on
          title page]
Bird, Junius Bouton
   1946   The archeology of Patagonia. HSAI, v. 1, pp. 17–24.
Bloomfield, Leonard
   1946   Algonquian. In Linguistic structures of native America. Viking Fund Publications in
          Anthropology, no. 6, pp. 85–129. New York.
Bödiger, Ute
   1965   Die Religion der Tukano im nordwestlichen Amazonas. Kölner ethnologische Mit-
          teilungen, 3. Köln: Kölner Universitäts-Verlag.
Bodley, John H.
   1969   The last remaining independent Campa. Andean Air Mail and Peruvian Times, v.
          XXIX, no. 1498, Sept. 5, pp. 8–10. Lima.
   ms.   Campa socio-economic adaptation. Dissertation . . . for the degree of Doctor of Philos-
          ophy in Anthropology . . . the University of Oregon, Eugene. 1970.
Boggiani, Guido
   1945   Os Caduveo. Biblioteca Histórica Brasileira, v. XIV. São Paulo: Livraria Martins
          Editôra.
Bohannan, Paul
   1967   The differing realms of the law. In Law and warfare; studies in the anthropology of
          conflict. Paul Bohannan (ed.), American Museum Sourcebooks in Anthropology, pp.
          43–56. Garden City, New York: The Natural History Press.
Bollaert, William
   1860   Antiquarian, ethnological and other researches in New Granada, Equador, Peru and
          Chile, with observations on the pre-incarial, incarial, and other monuments of peru-
          vian nations. London: Trübner & Co.
Bonino Nieves, Marco
   ms.   Unpublished data on the community of Wanqara. [1968]
Borde, [Father] de la
   1886   History of the origin, customs, religion, wars, and travels of the Caribs, savages of the
          Antilles in America. Translated from the French and condensed by G.J.A. Bosch-
          Reitz. Timehri, v. 5, pp. 224–254. Demerara, British Guiana.
Brand, Donald D.
   1941   A brief history of Araucanian studies. New Mexico Anthropologist, v. V, no. 2,
          April-May-June, pp. 19–35. Albuquerque.
Brass, L. J.
   1941   Stone age agriculture in New Guinea. Geographical Review, v. XXXI, no. 4, October,
          pp. 555–569. New York.
Brett, William Henry
   n.d.   Mission work among the Indian tribes in the forests of Guiana. London: Society for
          Promoting Christian Knowledge.
   1868   The Indian tribes of Guiana; their condition and habits. London: Bell and Daldy.
Bridges, E. Lucas
   1948   Uttermost part of the earth. New York: E.P. Dutton and Company, Inc.; London:
          Hodder & Stoughton.

Brinton, Daniel Garrison
   1946   La raza americana; clasificación lingüística y descripción etnográfica de las tribus indígenas de América del Norte y del Sur. Translated by Alejandro G. Perry. Biblioteca Americanista. Buenos Aires: Editorial Nova.
Bristol, Melvin L.
   1968   Sibundoy agricultural vegetation. Actas y Memorias, XXXVII Congreso Internacional de Americanistas, República Argentina—1966, v. II, pp. 575–602. Buenos Aires. [Distributed by Librart S.R.L.]
Broadbent, Sylvia Marguerite
   1969   A prehistoric field system in Chibcha territory, Colombia, Ñawpa Pacha 6, 1968, pp. 135–148. Berkeley.
Brookfield, Harold C.
   1968   New directions in the study of agricultural systems in tropical areas. In Evolution and environment; a symposium presented on the occasion of the one hundredth anniversary of the foundation of Peabody Museum of Natural History at Yale University. Ellen T. Drake (ed.), Yale University, Mrs. Hepsa Ely Silliman Memorial Lectures, v. 40, pp. 413–439. New Haven and London: Yale University Press.
Brown, Charles Barrington
   1877   Canoe and camp life in British Guiana. London: Edward Stanford. 2nd edition.
Brown, Paula, and Brookfield, H.C.
   1959   Chimbu land and society. Oceania, v. XXX, no. 1, September, pp. 1–75. Sydney.
Brüzzi Alves da Silva, Álcionílio
   1962   A civilização indigena do Uaupés. São Paulo: Linográfica Editora Ltda.
Cabrera, Angel, and Yépes, José
   1940   Historia natural Ediar. Mamíferos sudamericanos (vida, costumbres y descripción). Buenos Aires: Compañía Argentina de Editores.
Cadogan, Léon
   1961   Algunos textos guayakí del Yñarö. Boletín de la Sociedad Científica del Paraguay y del Museo Etnográfico, v. IV, 1ª pt., Etnografía, 4. Asunción.
Calderón, Melchor
   1898   Tratado de la importancia y vtilidad que ay en dar por esclauos a los Indios rebelados de Chile. Dispvtase en el, si es licito, o no el darlos por esclauos: y ponense razones por ambas partes, y sus respuestas: dexando la determinación a los señores Visorey, y Audiencia de los Reyes. A qvienes el Licenciado Don Melchor Calderon Tesorero de la Cathedral de Santiago, Comissario del santo Oficio, y de la santa Cruzada, Prouisor, Vicario General deste Obispado. En sedeuacante lo dirige. [1599] In Biblioteca hispano-chilena, 1523–1817. José Toribio Medina (ed.), t. II, pp. 5–21. Santiago de Chile: Impreso y grabado en casa del autor.
Carneiro, Robert L.
   1959   Extra-marital sex freedom among the Kuikuru Indians of Mato Grosso. RMP, v. X, 1956/58, pp. 135–142.
   1960   Slash-and-burn agriculture: A closer look at its implications for settlement patterns. In Men and cultures; selected papers of the Fifth International Congress of Anthropological and Ethnological Sciences, Philadelphia, September 1–9, 1956, pp. 229–234. Philadelphia: University of Pennsylvania Press.
   1962   The Amahuaca Indians of eastern Peru. Explorers Journal, v. 40, no. 4, December, pp. 26–37. New York.
   1964a The Amahuaca and the spirit world. Ethnology, v. III, no. 1, January, pp. 6–11. Pittsburgh.
   1964b Logging and the patrón system among the Amahuaca of eastern Peru. Actas y Memorias, XXXV Congreso Internacional de Americanistas, México 1962, v. 3, pp. 323–327. México: Editorial Libros de México, S.A.
   1964c Shifting cultivation among the Amahuaca of eastern Peru. Beiträge zur Völkerkunde Südamerikas, Völkerkundliche Abhandlungen, Bd. I, pp. 9–18. Hannover.
   1970   The transition from hunting to horticulture in the Amazon Basin. Proceedings, VIIIth International Congress of Anthropological and Ethnological Sciences, Tokyo, 1968, v. III, pp. 244–248. Tokyo: Science Council of Japan.
Carneiro, Robert L., and Dole, Gertrude E.
   1959   La cultura de los índios Kuikurus del Brasil central. Runa, v. VIII, pt. 2ª., 1956–57, pp. 169–202. Buenos Aires.

Carter, William E.
1968   Secular reinforcement in Aymara death ritual. American Anthropologist, v. 70, no. 2, April, pp. 238–263. Menasha.
Carvalho, João Braulino de
1931   Breve noticia sobre os indígenas que habitam a fronteira do Brasil com o Perú elaborado pelo medico da comissão, Dr. . . . , e calcada em observações pessoais. Boletim do Museu Nacional, v. VII, no. 3, setembro, pp. 225–256. Rio de Janeiro.
Casaverde Rojas, Juvenal
1970   El mundo sobrenatural en una comunidad. Allpanchis Phuturinqa; Orakesajj Achukaniwa, v. II, pp. 121–243. Cuzco. [Instituto de Pastoral Andina]
Cassidy, N.G., and Pahalad, S.D.
1953   The maintenance of soil fertility in Fiji. Agricultural Journal, v. 24, nos. 3 & 4, December, pp. 82–86. Suva, Fiji.
Castellví, Marcelino de
1937   Proyecto de organización de encuestas aplicadas al acopio metódico de materiales para la lingüística, la etnografía y el folklore o demosafia del Ecuador. Boletín de la Academia Nacional de Historia, v. 16, nos. 46–49, julio-diciembre, pp. 62–66. Quito.
Castelnau, Francis de
1850–1851   Expédition dans les parties centrales de l'Amérique du Sud; de Rio de Janeiro à Lima, et de Lima au Para; exécutée par ordre du gouvernement français pendant les anées 1843 à 1847, sous la direction de. . . . Première partie; histoire du voyage. 6 vols. Paris: P. Bertrand, Libraire-Éditeur.
Chanca, Diego Alvarez
1907   The letter of Dr. Diego Alvarez Chanca, dated 1494, relating to the second voyage of Columbus to America (being the first written document on the natural history, ethnography, and ethnology of America). Translated and edited by A.M. Fernandez de Ybarra. Smithsonian Miscellaneous Collections, v. 48, v. III, pt. 4, pp. 428–457. Washington.
Chantre y Herrera, José
1901   Historia de las misiones de la Compañía de Jesús en el Marañón español, por el Padre . . . de la misma Compañía, desde 1637 hasta 1767. Madrid: Imprenta de A. Avrial.
Chapple, Eliot Dismore, and Coon, Carleton Stevens
1942   Principles of Anthropology. New York: Henry Holt and Company.
Chiara, Vilma
1962   Folclore Krahó. RMP, v. XIII, pp. 333–375.
Childe, Vere Gordon
1953   Old World prehistory: Neolithic. In Anthropology today, an encyclopedic inventory prepared under the chairmanship of A.L. Kroeber, pp. 193–210. Chicago: The University of Chicago Press.
Chomsky, Noam
1965   Aspects of the theory of syntax. Cambridge: Massachusetts Institute of Technology Press.
Chrostowski, Marshall S.
1973   The eco-geographical characteristics of the Gran Pajonal and their relationships to some Campa Indian cultural patterns. Actas y Memorias del XXXIX Congreso Internacional de Americanistas (Lima, 2–9 de agosto, 1970), v. 4, 1972, pp. 145–160. Lima: Instituto de Estudios Peruanos.
Chrostowski, Marshall S., and Denevan, William Maxfield
1970   The biogeography of a savanna landscape: The Gran Pajonal of eastern Peru. McGill University Savanna Research Project, Savanna Research Series, no. 16. Montreal.
Cieza de León, Pedro de
1880   Segunda parte de la crónica del Perú, que trata del señorío de los Incas Yupanquis y de sus grandes hechos y gobernación. [1553] Biblioteca Hispano-Ultramarina, t. V, pp. 1–279. Madrid.
1922   La crónica del Perú. [1550] Madrid: Calpe.
1959   The Incas of Pedro de Cieza de León. Translated by Harriet de Onis, edited, with an introduction by Victor Wolfgang von Hagen. Norman: University of Oklahoma Press.
Clastres, Hélène
1970   Rites funéraires Guayaki. Journal de la Société des Américanistes, t. LVII, 1968, pp. 63–72. Paris.

Clastres, Pierre
1966   L'arc et le panier. L'Homme, t. VI, num. 2, Avril-Juin, pp. 13–31. Paris.
1968a   Ethnologie des indiens Guayaki; la vie sociale de la tribu. L'Homme, t. VII, num. 4, Octobre-Décembre, 1967, pp. 5–24. Paris.
1968b   Mission au Paraguay et au Brésil. L'Homme, t. VII, num. 4, Octobre-Décembre, 1967, pp. 101–108. Paris.
1970   Ethnographie des indiens Guayaki (Paraguay-Brésil). Journal de la Société des Américanistes, t. LVII, 1968, pp. 8–61. Paris.
1972   Chronique des Indiens Guayaki: Ce que savent les Aché, chasseurs nomades du Paraguay. Collection Terre Humaine. Paris: Librairie Plon.
Clastres, Pierre, and Sebag, Lucien
1963   Cannibalisme et mort chez les Guayakis. (Achén). RMP, v. XIV, pp. 174–181.
Coe, William R.
1957   Environmental limitation on Maya culture: A re-examination. American Anthropologist, v. 59, no. 2, April, pp. 328–335. Menasha.
Collazos, Carlos, and others
1957   La composición de los alimentos peruanos. By: Carlos Collazos Chiriboga, Philip L. White, Hilda S. White, Eduardo Viñas T., Enrique Alvistur J., Renán Urquieta A., Juan Vásquez G., César Días T., Alfonso Quiroz M., Amalia Roca N., D. Mark Hegsted, Robert B. Bradfield. Universidad Nacional Mayor de San Marcos, Anales de la Facultad de Medicina, v. XL, no. 1, julio, pp. 232–266. Lima.
Collier, Donald
1959   El desarrollo de la civilización peruana. Revista Colombiana de Antropología, v. VII, año de 1958, pp. 271–287. Bogotá.
Collier, Donald, and Murra, John Victor
1943   Survey and excavations in southern Ecuador. Field Museum of Natural History, Anthropological Series, v. 35. Chicago.
Collío Huaiquilaf, Martín
1941   A tri-lingual text by. . . . Introduction by Donald D. Brand. New Mexico Anthropologist, v. V, no. 2, April-May-June, pp. 36–52. Albuquerque.
Conklin, Harold C.
1957   Hanunóo agriculture; a report of an integral system of shifting cultivation in the Philippines. F.A.O. Forestry Development Paper, no. 12. Rome: Food and Agriculture Organization of the United Nations.
Cook, Orator Fuller
1916   Staircase farms of the ancients; astounding farming skill of ancient Peruvians, who were among the most industrious and highly organized people in history. The National Geographic Magazine, v. XXIX, no. 5, May, pp. 474–534. Washington.
Cooper John Montgomery
1942a   Areal and temporal aspects of aboriginal South American culture. Primitive Man, v. XV, nos. 1 and 2, January and April, pp. 1–38. Washington.
1942b   The South American marginal cultures. Eighth American Scientific Congress, Washington May 10–18, 1940. Proceedings, v. II, pp. 147–160. Washington.
1946a   The Araucanians. HSAI, v. 2, pp. 687–760.
1946b   The culture of the northeastern Indian hunters: A reconstructive interpretation. In Man in northeastern North America. Frederick Johnson (ed.), Papers of the Robert S. Peabody Foundation for Archaeology, v. 3, pp. 272–305. Andover, Massachusetts.
1949a   Games and gambling. HSAI, v. 5, pp. 503–524.
1949b   Traps. HSAI, v. 5, pp. 265–276.
Córdoba y Figueroa, Pedro de
1862   Historia de Chile. Colección de Historiadores de Chile y Documentos Relativos a la Historia Nacional, t. II, pp. 1–329 [second paging]. Santiago: Imprenta del Ferrocarril.
Coudreau, Henri Anatole
1886–1887   La France équinoxiale. 2 vols. Paris: Librairie Coloniale.
Coudreau, O.
1901   Voyage au Cuminá; 20 Avril 1900–7 Septembre 1900. Paris: A. Lahure, Imprimeur-Éditeur.
Craig, Alan K.
1967   Brief ethnology of the Campa Indians, eastern Peru. América Indígena, v. XXVII, no. 2, abril, pp. 223–235. México.

Crévaux, Jules Nicolas
1883 Voyages dans l'Amérique du Sud. Paris: Hachette et Cie.
Crocker, William H.
1958 Os índios Canelas de hoje; nota prévia. Boletim do Museu Paraense Emílio Goeldi, n.s., Antropologia, julho, no. 2. Belém-Pará.
1961 The Canela since Nimuendajú: A preliminary report on cultural change. Anthropological Quarterly, v. 34, no. 2, April, pp. 69–84. Washington.
1964 Conservatism among the Canela: An analysis of contributing factors. Actas y Memorias, XXXV Congreso Internacional de Americanistas, México 1962, v. 3, pp. 341–346. México: Editorial Libros de México, S.A.
1965 A preliminary analysis of some Canela religious aspects. RMP, v. XIV, pp. 163–173.
1967 The Canela messianic movement: An introduction. Atas do Simpósio sôbre a Biota Amazônica (Belém, Pará, Junho 6–11, 1966). Herman Lent (ed.), v. 2: Antropologia, pp. 69–83. Rio de Janeiro: Conselho Nacional de Pesquisas.
1971a The Canela (Brazil) taboo system: A preliminary exploration of an anxiety-reducing device. Verhandlungen des XXXVIII. Internationalen Amerikanistenkongresses, Stuttgart-München, 12. bis 18. August 1968, Bd. III, pp. 323–331. München: Klaus Renner Verlag.
1971b Observations concerning certain Ramkokamekra-Canela (Brazil) Indian restrictive taboo practices. Verhandlungen des XXXVIII. Internationalen Amerikanistenkongresses, Stuttgart-München, 12. bis 18. August 1968, Bd. III, pp. 337–339. München: Klaus Renner Verlag.
Darwin, Charles Robert
1936 The origin of species by means of natural selection; or, The preservation of favored races in the struggle for life; and, The descent of man and selection in relation to sex. New York: The Modern Library.
Denevan, William Maxfield
1970a The aboriginal population of western Amazonia in relation to habitat and subsistence. Revista Geográfica, no. 72, junho, pp. 61–86. Rio de Janeiro.
1970b Aboriginal drained-field cultivation in the Americas. Science, v. 169, no. 3946, 14 August, pp. 647–654. Washington.
Depons, F. See Pons, F.R.J. de
Der Marderosian, Ara H., and others
1970 The use and hallucinatory principles of a psychoactive beverage of the Cashinahua tribe (Amazon Basin). By: Ara H. Der Marderosian, Kenneth M. Kensinger, Jew-ming Chao, Frederick J. Goldstein. Drug Dependence, issue no. 5, October, pp. 7-14. Chevy Chase, Maryland.
Dessauer, Erwin von
1960 Vaniní. Tage im Urwald. München: Prestel Verlag.
Diniz, Edson Soares
1962 Os Kayapó-Gorotíre; aspectos sócio-culturais do momento atual. Boletim do Museu Paraense Emílio Goeldi, n.s., Antropologia, 13 dezembro, no. 18. Belém-Pará.
Disselhoff, Hans Dietrich
1940 "Brujos" im Hochland von Ekuador. Zeitschrift für Ethnologie, 71. Jahrgang, Heft 4–6, 1939, pp. 300–305. Berlin.
Dobrizhoffer, Martin
1784 Historia de Abiponibus, equestri, bellicosaque Paraquariae natione, locupletata copiosis barbararum gentium, urbium, . . . ferarum, . . . observationibus. 3 vols. Viennae: typis J. nob. de Kurzbek.
Dole, Gertrude E.
1959 Ownership and exchange among the Kuikuru Indians of Mato Grosso. RMP, v. X, 1956/58, pp. 125–133.
1964 Shamanism and political control among the Kuikuru. Beiträge zur Völkerkunde Südamerikas, Völkerkundliche Abhandlungen, Bd. I, pp. 53–62. Hannover.
1966 Anarchy without chaos: Alternatives to political authority among the Kuikuru. In Political anthropology. Marc J. Swartz, Victor W. Turner, and Arthur Tuden (eds.), pp. 73–87. Chicago: Aldine Publishing Company.
1969 Generation kinship nomenclature as an adaptation to endogamy. Southwestern Journal of Anthropology, v. 25, no. 2, summer, pp. 105–123. Albuquerque.

Dole, Gertrude E., and Carneiro, Robert L.
1958   A mechanism for mobilizing labor among the Kuikuru of central Brazil. Transactions
        of the New York Academy of Sciences, ser. 2, v. 21, no. 1, pp. 58–60. New York.
Duke, James A.
1970   Ethnobotanical observations on the Chocó Indians. Economic Botany, v. 24, no. 3,
        July-September, pp. 344–366. New York.
Duviols, Pierre
1971   La lutte contre les religions autochtones dan le Pérou colonial. "L'extirpation de
        l'idolâtrie" entre 1532 et 1660. Travaux de l'Institut Français d'Etudes Andines, t.
        XIII. Lima, Paris: Institut Français d'Etudes Andines. [distributed by Editions
        Ophrys, Paris]
Echeverría, Mariano, and Aguilar y Saldaña, Francisco de
1895   Relación geográfica, etc., de la provincia de Maynas [1784?]. In Antología de
        Prosistas Ecuatorianos. Pablo Herrera (ed.), t. I, pp. 346–364. Quito: Imprenta del
        Gobierno.
Eder, Francis Xavier
1791   Descriptio provinciae moxitarum in regno peruano, quam e scriptis posthumis Franc.
        Xav. Eder e Soc. Jesu annis XV. sacri apud eosdem curionis digessit, expolivit, &
        adnotatiunculis illustravit Abb. & Consil. Reg. Mako. Budae: Typis Universitatis.
Eliade, Mircea
1954   The myth of the eternal return. Translated by Willard R. Trask. New York: Pantheon
        Books.
Encina, Francisco Antonio
1940–1952   Historia de Chile desde la prehistoria hasta 1891. 20 vols. Santiago: Editorial
        Nascimento.
Ercilla y Zúñiga, Alonso de
1910–1918   La Araucana de D. . . . Edición del Centenario; ilustrada con grabados, docu-
        mentos, notas históricas y bibliográficas y una biografía del autor. La publica José
        Toribio Medina. 5 vols. Santiago de Chile: Imprenta Elzeviriana.
Escobar Moscoso, Mario
1958   Reconocimiento geográfico de Q'ero. Revista Universitaria, año XLVII, no. 115, 2º
        semestre, pp. 159–188. Cuzco.
Estrada Icaza, Emilio
1961   Cerámica de diferentes sitios del valle de los Quijos, proveniente de las excavaciones
        realizadas por el Padre Porras. Appendix to: Contribución al estudio de la arqueología
        e historia de los Valles de Quijos y Misagualli (Alto Napo) en la región oriental del
        Ecuador, by Pedro Ignacio Porras Garcés, pp. 165–172. Quito: Editora Fénix.
Evans, Clifford
1955   New archeological interpretations in northeastern South America. In New interpreta-
        tions of aboriginal American culture history. 75th Anniversary Volume of the Anthro-
        pological Society of Washington, pp. 82–94. Washington.
Farabee, William Curtis
1922   Indian tribes of eastern Peru. Papers of the Peabody Museum of American Archae-
        ology and Ethnology, Harvard University, v. X. Cambridge, Massachusetts.
Faron, Louis C.
1961   Mapuche social structure; institutional reintegration in a patrilineal society of central
        Chile. Illinois Studies in Anthropology, no. 1. Urbana: University of Illinois Press.
Fast, Pedro W.
1962   Naciones aborígenes en la Amazonía peruana. La Montaña, v. 5, no. 56, pp. 6–7. La
        Merced, Peru.
Favre, Henri
1968   Tayta Wamani: Le culte des montagnes dans le centre sud des Andes péruviennes.
        Études Latino-Américaines, III, 1967, pp. 121–140. Université d'Aix-Marseille, Fac-
        ulté des Lettres & Sciences Humaines d'Aix-en-Provence.
Félix José de Augusta
1916   Diccionario Araucano-Español y Español-Araucano. 2 vols. Santiago de Chile: Im-
        prenta Universitaria.
Fernandes, Florestan
1949   A análise funcionalista da guerra: Possibilidades de aplicação à sociedade tupinambá.

Ensaio de análise crítica da contribuição etnográfica dos cronistas para o estudo sociológico da guerra entre populações aborígenes do Brasil seiscentista. RMP, v. III, pp. 7–128.

1952   La guerre et le sacrifice humain chez les Tupinamba. Journal de la Société des Américanistes, n.s., t. XLI, fasc. I, pp. 139–220. Paris.

Fernández de Oviedo y Valdés, Gonzalo
1851–1855   Historia general y natural de las Indias, islas y tierra-firme del Mar Océano. [1548] 4 vols. Madrid: Imprenta de la Real Academia de la Historia.

Fiasson, Raymond
1947   Algunos aspectos científicos del Apure. El Agricultor Venezolano, año XII, no. 127, noviembre, pp. 3–12. Caracas.

Figueroa, Francisco de
1904   Relación de las misiones de la Compañía de Jesús en el país de los Maynas. [1661] Colección de Libros y Documentos Referentes á la Historia de América, t. I. Madrid.

Firth, Raymond
1939   Primitive Polynesian economy. London: George Routledge and Sons, Ltd.

Flemming, Bernhard
1878   Die Provincia del Oriente (Ecuador). Aus allen Weltteilen, Jahr 9, Heft 12, pp. 374–375. Leipzig.

Fock, Niels
1963   Waiwai. Religion and society of an Amazonian tribe. Nationalmuseets Skrifter, Etnografisk Roekke, VIII. Copenhagen.
1967   Mataco Indians in their Argentine setting. Folk, v. 8–9, 1966/67, pp. 89–104. København.
1972   Regulation of conflicts in Amerindian societies. In Conflict control and conflict resolution. Bengt Höglund and Jørgen Wilian Ulrich (eds.), Interdisciplinary Studies from the Scandinavian Summer University, v. XVII, pp. 143–155. Copenhagen.

Fried, Morton H.
1966   On the concepts of "tribe" and "tribal society." Transactions of the New York Academy of Sciences, ser. 2, v. 28, no. 4, pp. 527–540. New York.

Friede, Juan
1955   Los Kofán: Una tribu de la alta Amazonia Colombiana. Proceedings of the Thirtieth International Congress of Americanists, held at Cambridge, 18–23 August 1952, pp. 202–219. London: The Royal Anthropological Institute.

Frikel, Protásio
1968   Os Xikrín; equipamento e técnicas de subsistência. Conselho Nacional de Pesquisas, Instituto Nacional de Pesquisas da Amazônia, Museu Paraense Emílio Goeldi, Publicações Avulsas, no. 7. Belém-Pará.

Fulop, Marcos
1955   Notas sobre los términos y el sistema de parentesco de los Tukano. Revista Colombiana de Antropología, v. IV, pp. 121–164. Bogotá.

Furst, Peter T. (ed.)
1972   Flesh of the gods; the ritual use of hallucinogens. New York and Washington: Praeger Publishers.

Galvão, Eduardo
1959   Aculturação indígena no Rio Negro. Boletim do Museu Paraense Emílio Goeldi, n.s., Antropologia, no. 7, setembro. Belém-Pará.
1960   Áreas culturais indígenas do Brasil; 1900–1959. Boletim do Museu Paraense Emílio Goeldi, n.s., Antropologia, no. 8, janeiro. Belém-Pará.
1963   Elementos básicos da horticultura de subsistência indígena. RMP, v. XIV, pp. 120–144.
1967   Indigenous culture areas of Brazil, 1900–1959. In Indians of Brazil in the twentieth century. Janice H. Hopper (ed.), ICR Studies 2, pp. 169–205. Washington: Institute for Cross-Cultural Research.

García, Secundino
1935   Entre los salvajes Machiguengas—gente sin Dios? Misiones Dominicanas del Perú, año XVII, no. 88, mayo-junio, pp. 95–99. Lima.
1935–1937   Mitología Machiguenga. Misiones Dominicanas del Perú, año XVII, 1935, no. 90, setiembre-octubre, pp. 170–179; no. 91, noviembre-diciembre, pp. 220–228; año

XVIII, 1936, no. 92, enero-febrero, pp. 2–13; no. 94, mayo-junio, pp. 86–97; no. 95, julio-agosto, pp. 131–139; no. 96, setbre.-octubre, pp. 166–176; no. 97, novbre.-dicbre., pp. 212–219, año XIX, 1937, no. 98, enero-febrero, pp. 11–17. Lima.

García Ramón, Alonso
1852   Carta de Alonso García Ramón al rey de España, 1613. *In* Gay, 1846-1852, v. II, pp. 265–279.

Gasca, Pedro de la
1964   Relación de La Gasca al Consejo de Indias. De los Reyes, a 2 de mayo de 1549. Documentos relativos a Don Pedro de la Gasca y a Gonzalo Pizarro. Edición por Juan Pérez de Tudela Bueso. Archivo Documental Español, publicado por la Real Academia de la Historia, t. XXI, II, [doc.] no. CLXIV, pp. 326–342. Madrid.

Gay, Claudio
1846–1852   Historia física y política de Chile, según documentos adquiridos en esta república durante doze años de residencia en ella y publicada bajo los auspicios del supremo gobierno por . . .; documentos sobre la historia, la estadística y la geografía. 2 vols. Paris: En casa del autor; Santiago, Chile: Museo de Historia Natural.

Gerstäcker, Friedrich Wilhelm Christian
1906   18 Monate in Süd-Amerika. Neu durchgesehen und hrsg. von Dr. Carl Döring. Berlin: Neufeld & Henius.

Gerth, Hans Heinrich, and Mills, C. Wright
1958   From Max Weber: Essays in sociology. Translated, edited, and with an introduction by. . . . New York and Oxford: Oxford University Press.

Giaccaria, Bartolomeu, and Heide, Adalberto
1972   Xavante (Auwẽ Uptabi: Povo Autêntico); pesquisa histórico-etnográfica. São Paulo: Editorial Dom Bosco.

Giacone, Antônio
1939   Pequena gramática e dicionário da lingua Tucana. Manáos: Papelaria Velho Lino.
1965   Gramática da língua "Dahceié ou Tucana," dicionário "Dahceié ou Tucano-Portu-guês," dicionário "Português-Dahceié ou Tucano," vade-mecum para os missionários e fraseologia usual tucana no rio Uaupés, Tiquié e Papurí. Belém-Pará.

Gibson, Gordon D.
1960   A bibliography of anthropological bibliographies: The Americas. Current Anthropology, v. 1, no. 1, January, pp. 61–73. Chicago.

Gilij, Filippo Salvadore
1780–1784   Saggio di storia Americana, o sia storia naturale, civile, e sacra de regni, e delle provincie Spagnuole di Terra-ferma nell' America meridionale; descritta dall' Abate. . . . 4 vols. Roma: Luigi Perego Erede Salvioni.

Gilmore, Raymond M.
1950   Fauna and ethnozoology of South America. HSAI, v. 6, pp. 345–464.

Goeje, Claudius Henricus de
1908   Verslag der Toemoekhoemak-expeditie. (Tumuc-Humac-expeditie.) Tijdschrift van het Koninklijk Nederlandsch Aardrijkskundig Genootschap, 2ᵉ ser., Deel XXV. Leiden.
1910   Beiträge zur Völkerkunde von Surinam. Internationales Archiv für Ethnographie, Bd. XIX, Heft I & II, 1909, pp. 1–34. Leiden.
1943   Philosophy, initiation and myths of the Indians of Guiana and adjacent countries. Internationales Archiv für Ethnographie, Bd. XLIV, pp. vi-xx, 1–136 [first paging]. Leiden.

Goldman, Irving
1948   Tribes of the Uaupés-Caquetá region. HSAI, v. 3, pp. 763–798.
1963   The Cubeo; Indians of the northwest Amazon. Illinois Studies in Anthropology, no. 2. Urbana: The University of Illinois Press.

Góngora Marmolejo, Alonso de
1862   Historia de Chile desde su descubrimiento hasta el año de 1575. Colección de Historiadores de Chile y Documentos Relativos a la Historia Nacional, t. II, pp. xi–xiii, 1–212 [first paging]. Santiago: Imprenta del Ferrocarril.

González de Nájera, Alonso
1889   Desengaño y reparo de la guerra de Chile. Colección de Historiadores de Chile y Documentos Relativos a la Historia Nacional, t. XVI. Santiago de Chile: Imprenta Ercilla.

Gourou, Pierre
1953   The tropical world: Its social and economic conditions and its future status. Translated by E.D. Laborde. London: Longmans, Green and Co.

Greenberg, Joseph H.
1960   The general classification of Central and South American languages. *In* Men and cultures; selected papers of the Fifth International Congress of Anthropological and Ethnological Sciences, Philadelphia, September 1–9, 1956, pp. 791–794. Philadelphia: University of Pennsylvania Press.

Griffin, James B.
1946   Cultural change and continuity in eastern United States archaeology. *In* Man in northeastern North America. Frederick Johnson (ed.), Papers of the Robert S. Peabody Foundation for Archaeology, v. 3, pp. 37–95. Andover, Massachusetts.

Guevara Silva, Tomás
1911   Folklore araucano; refranes, cuentos, cantos, procedimientos industriales, costumbres prehispanas. Santiago: Imprenta Cervantes.

Gumilla, Joseph
1791   Historia natural, civil y geográfica de las naciones situadas en las riveras del Rio Orinoco. 2 vols. Barcelona: Imprenta de C. Gibert y Tutó. New edition.

Gumperz, John J.
1961   Speech variation and the study of Indian civilization. American Anthropologist, v. 63, no. 5, pt. 1, October, pp. 976–988. Menasha.

Hallowell, A. Irving
1943   Araucanian parallels to the Omaha kinship pattern. American Anthropologist, v. 45, no. 3, pt. 1, July-September, pp. 489–491. Menasha.

Hanke, Lewis
1959   Aristotle and the American Indian; a study in race prejudice in the modern world. Chicago: Henry Regnery Company.

Harcourt, Robert
1906   A relation of a voyage to Guiana. *In* Hakluytus posthumus, or, Purchas his pilgrimes. Samuel Purchas (ed.), v. XVI, pp. 358–402. Glasgow: James MacLehose and Sons.

Hardenburg, Walter Ernest
1912   The Putumayo, the devil's paradise; travels in the Peruvian Amazon region and an account of the atrocities committed upon the Indians therein. London: T. Fisher Unwin.

Harner, Michael James
1962   Jivaro souls. American Anthropologist, v. 64, no. 2, April, pp. 258–272. Menasha.
1968   Technological and social change among the eastern Jívaro. Actas y Memorias, XXXVII Congreso Internacional de Americanistas, República Argentina–1966, v. I, pp. 363–388. Buenos Aires. [Distributed by Librart S.R.L.]
1972   The Jívaro; people of the sacred waterfalls. Garden City, New York: Doubleday/Natural History Press.

Harner, Michael James (ed.)
1973   Hallucinogens and shamanism. New York: Oxford University Press.

Harrington, John Peabody
1943   Hokan discovered in South America. Journal of the Washington Academy of Sciences, v. 33, no. 11, November 15, pp. 334–344. Menasha.

Hartmann, Roswith
1968   Märkte im alten Peru. Inaugural-Dissertation zur Erlangung der Doktorwürde der Philosophischen Fakultät der Rheinischen Friedrich-Wilhelms-Universität zu Bonn. Bonn: Rheinische Friedrich-Wilhelms-Universität.

Hassel, Jorge M. von
1905   Las tribus salvajes de la región amazónica del Perú. Boletín de la Sociedad Geográfica de Lima, año XV, t. XVII, trimestre primero, pp. 27–73. Lima.

Haugen, Einar
1955   Review: Fjoldemålets lydsystem, by Anders Bjerrum. København: Ejnar Munksgaard. 1944. Houlbjergmålet . . ., by Ella Jensen. (Udvalg for Folkemaals Publikationer, serie A, Nr. 6.) København: J.H. Schultz. 1944. Synchronisk beskrivelse af Aabenraa bymaal, by Karen Marie Olsen. Danske folkemål 1–67. 1949. Brøndum-malet . . ., by Inger Ejskjaer. (Udvalg for Folkemaals Publikationer, serie A, Nr. 10.) København:

J.H. Schultz. 1954. Language, v. 31, no. 1, pt. 1, January-March, pp. 141–147. Baltimore.

1966a Dialect, language, nation. American Anthropologist, v. 68, no. 4, August, pp. 922–935. Menasha.

1966b Semicommunication: The language gap in Scandinavia. Sociological Inquiry, v. 36, no. 2, spring, pp. 280–297. Lincoln, Nebraska.

Herderschee, A. Franssen

1905a Verslag van de Gonini-expeditie. Tijdschrift van het Koninklijk Nederlandsch Aardrijkskundig Genootschap, 2ᵉ ser., Deel XXII, no. 1, Januari, pp. 1–159. Leiden.

1905b Verslag van de Tapanahoni expeditie. Tijdschrift van het Koninklijk Nederlandsch Aardrijkskundig Genootschap, 2ᵉ ser., Deel XXII, no. 4, Juli, pp. 847–985. Leiden.

Hernández Bello, Miguel

1919 Descripción del govierno de Quijos; formada en compendio por su actual-Gefe el Capitan de Dragones Voluntarios de la Septima Compañia de Guaranda Dn Miguel Hernandez Bello, acompañada de una brebe noticia o derrotero del camino, dispuesta en Archidona Capital de esta Governacion, y firmada en Quito; 1799. La publica C. de Gangotena y Jijón. Boletín de la Sociedad Ecuatoriana de Estudios Históricos Americanos, no. 9, noviembre-diciembre, pp. 257–263. Quito.

Herndon, William Lewis, and Gibbon, Lardner

1854 Exploration of the Valley of the Amazon, made under the direction of the Navy Department, by . . . . Part I. By Lieut. Herndon. Washington: Robert Armstrong Public Printer. Part II. By Lt. Lardner Gibbon. Washington: A.O.P. Nicholson Public Printer.

Herrera, Juan de

1862 Relación de las cosas de Chile, dada por el licenciado . . . Colección de Historiadores de Chile y Documentos Relativos a la Historia Nacional, t. II, pp. 250–253 [first paging]. Santiago: Imprenta del Ferrocarril.

Hilger, M. Inez

1957 Araucanian child life and its cultural background. Smithsonian Miscellaneous Collections, v. 133. Washington.

1966 Huenun Ñamku: An Araucanian Indian of the Andes remembers the past. By . . . with the assistance of Margaret A. Mondloch. The Civilization of the American Indian Series. Norman: University of Oklahoma Press.

Hilger, M. Inez, and Mondloch, Margaret A.

1967 The Araucanian weaver. Boletín del Museo Nacional de Historia Natural, t. XXX, pp. 291–298. Santiago de Chile.

Hilhouse, William

1832 Notices of the Indians settled in the interior of British Guiana. Journal of the Royal Geographical Society of London, v. II, pp. 227–249. London.

1834 Memoir on the Warow-land of British Guayana. Journal of the Royal Geographical Society of London, v. IV, pp. 321–332. London.

Hissink, Karen, and Hahn, Albert

1961 Die Tacana. Ergebnisse der Frobenius-Expedition nach Bolivien 1952 bis 1954. I. Erzählungsgut. Veröffentlichung des Frobenius-Instituts an der Johann Wolfgang Goethe-Universität, Frankfurt am Main. Stuttgart: W. Kohlhammer Verlag.

Hockett, Charles F.

1948 Implications of Bloomfield's Algonquian studies. Language, v. 24, no. 1, January-March, pp. 117–131. Baltimore.

Hoebel, Edward Adamson

1964 The law of primitive man; a study in comparative legal dynamics. Cambridge, Massachusetts: Harvard University Press.

Hohenthal, William Dalton, Jr.

ms. The concept of cultural marginality and native agriculture in South America. Dissertation submitted in partial satisfaction of the requirements for the degree of Doctor of Philosophy in Anthropology in the Graduate Division of the University of California [Berkeley]. January 1951.

Hohenthal, William Dalton, Jr., and McCorkle, Thomas

1955 The problem of aboriginal persistence. Southwestern Journal of Anthropology, v. 11, no. 3, autumn, pp. 288–300. Albuquerque.

Holmberg, Allan R.
1950   Nomads of the long bow: The Siriono of eastern Bolivia. Smithsonian Institution, Institute of Social Anthropology, Publication no. 10. Washington.
1969   Nomads of the long bow: The Siriono of eastern Bolivia. American Museum Science Books. Garden City, New York: The Natural History Press.
Hopper, Janice H.
1967   Translator's preface. In Indians of Brazil in the twentieth century. Janice H. Hopper (ed.), ICR Studies 2, pp. 69–75. Washington: Institute for Cross-Cultural Research.
Hrdlička, Aleš
1911   Cannibalism. In Handbook of American Indians north of Mexico. Frederick Webb Hodge (ed.), Smithsonian Institution, Bureau of American Ethnology, Bulletin 30, pt. 1, pp. 200–201. Washington. Third impression.
Humboldt, Alexander von
1852–1853   Personal narrative of travels to the equinoctial regions of America during the years 1799–1804. By Alexander von Humboldt and Aimé Bonpland. 3 vols. London: Henry G. Bohn.
Hurault, Jean
1968   Les indiens Wayana de la Guyane Française; structure sociale et coutume familiale. Office de la Recherche Scientifique et Technique Outre-Mer. Memoires O.R.S.T.O.M., 3, pt. 5. Paris.
Hurtado de Mendoza, García
1846   Relación que envia el señor Garcia de Mendoza, gobernador de Chile, en 24 de enero de 1558, desde la ciudad de Cañete de la Frontera, que nuevamente se ha poblado en Arauco. In Gay, 1846–1852, v. I, pp. 180–186.
Hymes, Dell
1964   Directions in (ethno-) linguistic theory. In Transcultural studies in cognition. A. Kimball Romney and Roy Goodwin D'Andrade (eds.), Special Publication, American Anthropologist, v. 66, no. 3, pt. 2, June, pp. 6–56. Menasha.
Im Thurn, Everard F.
1883   Among the Indians of Guiana; being sketches chiefly anthropologic from the interior of British Guiana. London: Kegan Paul, Trench and Co.
Informaciones de D. Sancho Hacho
ms.   Informaciones de méritos y servicios de D. Sancho, Cacique de La Tacunga 1559–79. (Quito 20/2) Archivo General de Indias, Sevilla.
Izaguirre, Bernardino
1922–1929   Historia de las misiones franciscanas y narración de los progresos de la geografía en el Oriente del Perú. Relatos originales y producciones en lenguas indígenas de varios misioneros. 14 vols. Lima: Talleres Tipográficos de la Penitenciaría [and others]. [Some sets of this work are dated 1923–1929]
Izikowitz, Karl Gustav
1935   Musical and other sound instruments of the South American Indians: a comparative ethnographical study. Göteborgs Kungl. Vetenskaps- och Vitterhets-Samhälles Handlingar, femte Följden, ser. A, Bd. 5, N:o 1. Göteborg.
Jameson, William
1858   Excursion made from Quito to the river Napo, January to May, 1857. Journal of the Royal Geographical Society, v. XXVIII, pp. 337–349. London.
Jaquith, James R.
1970   Bibliography of anthropological bibliographies of the Americas. América Indígena, v. XXX, no. 2, abril, pp. 419–469. México.
Jijón y Caamaño, Jacinto
1940–1947   El Ecuador interandino y occidental antes de la conquista castellana. 4 vols. Quito: Editorial Ecuatoriana.
1952   Antropología prehispánica del Ecuador; resumen. Quito: La Prensa Católica.
Jiménez de la Espada, Marcos
1927–1928   Diario de la expedición al Pacífico llevada á cabo por una comisión de naturalistas españoles, durante los años 1862–1865, escrito por D. . . ., miembro que fué de la misma. Publícalo ahora por vez primera, adicionada con notas, el P. Agustín Jesús Barreiro, agustino. Boletín de la Real Sociedad Geográfica, t. LXVII, 4º trimestre, 1927, pp. 341–406; t. LXVIII, 1º trimestre, 1928, pp. 72–103. Madrid.

Jones, Robert B., Jr.
   1961   Karen linguistic studies; description, comparison, and texts. University of California
          Publications in Linguistics, v. 25. Berkeley.
Kaplan, Joanna Overing
   1972   Cognation, endogamy, and teknonymy: The Piaroa example. Southwestern Journal of
          Anthropology, v. 28, no. 3, autumn, pp. 282–297. Albuquerque.
Kappler, August
   1854   Sechs Jahre in Surinam; oder, Bilder aus dem militärischen Leben dieser Colonie, und
          Skizzen zur Kenntniss seiner socialen und naturwissenschaftlichen Verhältnisse. Stutt-
          gart: E. Schweizerbart'sche Verlagshandlung und Druckerei.
Karsten, Rafael
   1920   Contributions to the sociology of the Indian tribes of Ecuador; three essays. Acta
          Academiae Aboensis, Humaniora, v. I, no. 3. Helsingfors. [For Abo Akademi, Turku,
          Finland]
   1935   The head-hunters of western Amazonas; the life and culture of the Jibaro Indians of
          eastern Ecuador and Peru. Societas Scientiarum Fennica. Commentationes Human-
          arum Litterarum, VII, 1. Helsingfors.
Kelsey, Harlan P., and Dayton, William A. (eds.)
   1942   Standardized plant names. A revised and enlarged listing of approved scientific and
          common names of plants and plant products in American commerce or use. Prepared
          for the American Joint Committee on Horticultural Nomenclature by its Editorial
          Committee. . . . Harrisburg, Pennsylvania: J. Horace McFarland Company. 2nd edi-
          tion.
Kensinger, Kenneth M.
   1973   *Banisteriopsis* usage among the Peruvian Cashinahua. *In* Hallucinogens and shamanism.
          Michael J. Harner (ed.), pp. 9–14. New York: Oxford University Press.
Kidder, Alfred II
   1940   South American penetrations in Middle America. *In* The Maya and their neighbors,
          pp. 441–459. New York and London: D. Appleton-Century Company, Inc.
Killip, Ellsworth P., and Smith, Albert C.
   1930   The identity of the South American fish poisons, "cube" and "timbó." Journal of the
          Washington Academy of Sciences, v. 20, no. 5, March 4, pp. 74–81. Baltimore.
   1931   The use of fish poisons in South America. Annual Report . . . of the Smithsonian
          Institution . . . for . . . 1930, pp. 401–408. Washington.
Kirchhoff, Paul
   1948a Food-gathering tribes of the Venezuelan llanos· The Yaruro. HSAI, v. 4, pp. 456–463.
   1948b The Guayupe and Sae. HSAI, v. 4, pp. 385–391.
Kloos, Peter
   1968   Becoming a pïyei: Variability and similarity in Carib shamanism. Antropológica, no.
          24, diciembre, pp. 3–25. Caracas.
   1971   The Maroni River Caribs of Surinam. Studies of Developing Countries, 12. Assen, The
          Netherlands.
Kluckhohn, Clyde
   1941   Patterning as exemplified in Navaho culture. *In* Language, culture, and personality;
          essays in memory of Edward Sapir. Leslie Spier, A. Irving Hallowell, Stanley S.
          Newman (eds.), pp. 109–130. Menasha: Sapir Memorial Publication Fund.
   1949   The philosophy of the Navaho Indians. *In* Ideological differences and world order.
          F.S.C. Northrop (ed.), pp. 356–384. New Haven: Yale University Press.
Koch-Grünberg, Theodor
   1899   Die Anthropophagie der südamerikanischen Indianer. Internationales Archiv für Eth-
          nographie, Bd. XII, pp. 78–110. Leiden. [Author's name given as Theodor Koch]
   1909–1910   Zwei Jahre unter den Indianern; Reisen in Nordwest-Brasilien 1903/1905. 2
          vols. Berlin: Ernst Wasmuth.
   1917–1928   Vom Roroima zum Orinoco; Ergebnisse einer Reise in Nordbrasilien und
          Venezuela in den Jahren 1911–1913. Unternommen und herausgegeben im Auftrage
          und mit mitteln des Baessler-Instituts in Berlin. 5 vols. Berlin: Dietrich Reimer (Ernst
          Vohsen) [vol. I]; Stuttgart: Strecker und Schröder [vols. II–V].
Kok, P.
   1922   Ensayo de gramática Dagseje o Tokano. Anthropos, Bd. XVI–XVII, Heft 4, 5, 6,
          Juli-Dez., 1921–1922, pp. 838–865. St. Gabriel-Mödling bei Wien.

Krickeberg, Walter
1935   Beiträge zur Frage der alten kulturgeschichtlichen Beziehungen zwischen Nord- und Südamerika. Zeitschrift für Ethnologie, 66. Jahrgang, Heft 4/6, 1934, pp. 287–373. Berlin.
Kroeber, Alfred Louis
1952   The nature of culture. Chicago: The University of Chicago Press.
Laraia, Roque de Barros
1965   A fricção interétnica no médio Tocantins. América Latina, v. 8, no. 2, pp. 66–76. Rio de Janeiro.
1967   O "homem marginal" numa sociedade primitiva. Revista do Instituto de Ciências Sociais, v. IV, no. 1, pp. 143–157. Rio de Janeiro.
1968   O sol e a lua na mitologia Xinguana. Actas y Memorias, XXXVII Congreso Internacional de Americanistas, República Argentina—1966, v. III, pp. 75–93. Buenos Aires. [Distributed by Librart S.R.L.]
1972   Akuáwa-Asurini e Suruí: Análise de dois grupos Tupí. Revista do Instituto de Estudos Brasileiros, Universidade de São Paulo, no. 12, pp. 7–30. São Paulo.
Laraia, Roque de Barros, and Matta, Roberto Augusto da
1967   Índios e castanheiros; a emprêsa extrativa e os índios no médio Tocantins. Corpo e Alma do Brasil, XXI. São Paulo: Difusão Européia do Livro.
Latcham, Ricardo Eduardo
1915   La capacidad guerrera de los Araucanos: Sus armas y métodos militares. Revista Chilena de Historia y Geografía, año V, t. XV, 3er trimestre, no. 19, pp. 22–93. Santiago de Chile.
1928   La prehistoria chilena. Santiago de Chile: Soc. Imp. y Lit. Universo.
Lathrap, Donald W.
1968   The "hunting" economies of the tropical forest zone of South America: An attempt at historical perspective. In Man the hunter. Richard B. Lee and Irven DeVore (eds.), pp. 23–29. Chicago: Aldine Publishing Company.
1970   The upper Amazon. Ancient Peoples and Places, v. 70. New York and Washington: Praeger Publishers.
1971   The tropical forest and the cultural context of Chavín. In Dumbarton Oaks conference on Chavín, October 26th and 27th, 1968. Elizabeth P. Benson (ed.), pp. 73–100. Washington: Dumbarton Oaks Research Library and Collection, Trustees for Harvard University.
Lave, Jean
1973   A comment on "A study in structural semantics: The Siriono kinship system." American Anthropologist, v. 75, no. 1, February, pp. 314–317. Washington.
Lawes, John Bennet, and Gilbert, Joseph Henry
1895   The Rothamsted experiments; being an account of some of the results of the agricultural investigations conducted at Rothamsted, over a period of fifty years. From the Transactions of the Highland and Agricultural Society of Scotland.... Printed for private circulation. Edinburgh: William Blackwood and Sons.
Le Besnerais, Henry
1948   Algunos aspectos del Río Capanaparo y sus índios Yaruros. Memoria de la Sociedad de Ciencias Naturales La Salle, año VIII, no. 21, enero-abril, pp. 9–20. Caracas.
1954   Contribution a l'étude des indiens Yaruro (Venezuela); quelques observations sur le territoire, l'habitat et la population. Journal de la Société des Américanistes, n.s., t. XLIII, pp. 109–121. Paris.
Leeds, Anthony
1961   Yaruro incipient tropical forest horticulture; possibilities and limits. In The evolution of horticultural systems in native South America, causes and consequences; a symposium. Johannes Wilbert (ed.), Antropológica, Supplement Publication, no. 2, September, pp. 13–46. Caracas.
Lehnertz, Jay F.
ms.   Cultural struggle on the Peruvian frontier: Campa-Franciscan confrontations, 1595–1752. Master's thesis. University of Wisconsin, Madison. 1969.
Leigh, Charles
1906   Captaine Charles Leigh his voyage to Guiana and plantation there. In Hakluytus posthumus, or, Purchas his pilgrimes. Samuel Purchas (ed.), v. XVI, pp. 309–323. Glasgow: James MacLehose and Sons.

Leung, Woot-Tsuen (Wu)
1961   Food composition table for use in Latin America; with the cooperation of Marina
        Flores. Sponsored jointly by the Institute of Nutrition of Central America and
        Panama . . . and the Interdepartmental Committee on Nutrition for National Defense.
        Bethesda, Maryland.

Lévi-Strauss, Claude
1950   The use of wild plants in tropical South America. HSAI, v. 6, pp. 465–486.
1958   Anthropologie structurale. Paris: Librairie Plon.
1962   Tristes tropiques. Le Monde en 10–18, 12/13. Paris: Union Générale d'Editions.
1964   Mythologiques * Le cru et le cuit. Paris: Librairie Plon.
1966   Mythologiques ** Du miel aux cendres. Paris: Librairie Plon.
1968   Mythologiques *** L'origine des manières de table. Paris: Librairie Plon.
1971   Mythologiques **** L'homme nu. Paris: Librairie Plon.

Lima, Pedro E. de
1950   Os índios Waurá; observações gerais. A cerâmica. Boletim do Museu Nacional, n.s.,
        Antropologia, no. 9, 8 de maio. Rio de Janeiro.

Linné, Sigvald
1929   Darien in the past; the archaeology of eastern Panama and north-western Colombia.
        Göteborgs Kungl. Vetenskaps- och Vitterhets-Samhälles Handlingar, femte Följden,
        ser. A, Bd. 1, N:o 3. Göteborg.

Linton, Ralph
1936   The study of man; an introduction. New York and London: D. Appleton-Century
        Company, Inc.

Linton, Ralph (ed.)
1940   Acculturation in seven American Indian tribes. New York and London: D. Appleton-
        Century Company, Inc.

Lobato de Sosa, Diego
ms.   Memorial de algunas cosas que se han de remediar en la gobernación de los Quijos. [ca.
        1595] (Quito 25) Archivo General de Indias, Sevilla.

Loeb, Edwin M.
1930   Cannibalism. Encyclopaedia of the Social Sciences, v. 3, pp. 172–173. New York: The
        Macmillan Company.

Lothrop, Samuel K.
1942   Sud América vista de América Central. Actas y Trabajos Científicos del XXVII⁰
        Congreso Internacional de Americanistas (Lima, 1939), t. I, pp. 191–204. Lima:
        Librería e Imprenta Gil, S.A.

Loukotka, Čestmír
1935   Clasificación de las lenguas sudamericanas. Lingüística Sudamericana, no. 1. Praha:
        Tipografía Josef Bartl.
1941   Roztřídění jihoamerických jazyků. Druhé opravené a rozmnožené vydaní, doplněné
        mapou. Clasificación de las lenguas sudamericanas. Segunda edición, augmentada [sic]
        y corrigida [sic]. Con un mapa de distribución. Lingüística Sudamericana, no. 3.
        Praha: The author.
1944   Klassifikation der südamerikanischen Sprachen. Zeitschrift für Ethnologie, 74. Jahr-
        gang, Heft 1–6, 1942, pp. 1–69. Berlin.
1950a   Les langues de la famille Tupi-Guarani. Universidade de São Paulo, Facultade de
        Filosofia, Ciências e Letras, Boletim CIV. Etnografia e Lingua Tupi-Guarani, no. 16.
        São Paulo.
1950b   La parenté des langues du bassin de la Madeira. Lingua Posnaniensis, v. 2, pp.
        123–144. Poznan.
1968   Classification of South American Indian languages. Reference Series, v. 7. Latin
        American Center, University of California, Los Angeles. Los Angeles.

Lyon, Patricia Jean
ms. a   Dislocación tribal y clasificaciones lingüísticas en la zona del Río Madre de Dios. Actas
        y Memorias del XXXIX Congreso Internacional de Americanistas (Lima, 2–9 de
        agosto, 1970), v. 5. Lima: Industrialgráfica, S.A. (in press)
ms. b   Singing as social interaction among the Wachipaeri of eastern Peru. Dissertation
        submitted in partial satisfaction of the requirements for the degree of Doctor of
        Philosophy in Anthropology in the Graduate Division of the University of California,
        Berkeley. 1967.

Malinowski, Bronislaw
1954 Magic, science and religion and other essays. Doubleday Anchor Books. Garden City, New York: Doubleday & Company, Inc.
Mandelbaum, David G.
1938 Polyandry in Kota society. American Anthropologist, n.s., v. 40, no. 4, pt. 1, October-December, pp. 574–583. Menasha.
Mariño de Lovera, Pedro
1865 Crónica del reino de Chile. Colección de Historiadores de Chile y Documentos Relativos a la Historia Nacional, t. VI. Santiago, Imprenta del Ferrocarril.
Markham, Clements R.
1910 A list of the tribes of the valley of the Amazons, including those on the banks of the main stream and of all the tributaries. Journal of the Royal Anthropological Institute of Great Britain and Ireland, v. XL, January to June, pp. 73–140. London.
Marmolejo: See Góngora Marmolejo, Alonso de
Maroni, Pablo
1889–1892 Noticias auténticas del famoso río Marañón y mission apostólica de la Compañía de Jesús de la provincia de Quito en los dilatados bosques de dicho río. Escribíalas por los años de 1738 un misionero de la misma Compañía y las publica ahora por primera vez Marcos Jiménez de la Espada. Boletín de la Sociedad Geográfica de Madrid, t. XXVI, primer semestre 1889, pp. 194–270, 397–430; t. XXVII, segundo semestre 1889, pp. 47–101; t. XXVIII, primer semestre 1890, pp. 175–203, 383–454; t. XXIX, segundo semestre 1890, pp. 73–119, 220–266; t. XXX, primer semestre 1891, pp. 111–161, 193–235, 381–405; t. XXXI, segundo semestre 1891, pp. 22–77, 235–282; t. XXXII, primer semestre 1892, pp. 113–143; t. XXXIII, segundo semestre 1892, pp. 24–79. Madrid.
Martius, Carl Friedrich Philipp von
1867 Beiträge zur Ethnographie und Sprachenkunde Amerika's zumal Brasiliens. 2 vols. Leipzig: Friedrich Fleischer.
Mason, John Alden
1950 The languages of South American Indians. HSAI, v. 6, pp. 157–317.
Matta, Roberto Augusto da
1971 Myth and anti-myth among the Timbira. In Structural analysis of oral tradition. Pierre Maranda and Elli Köngäs (eds.), Publications in Folklore and Folklife, 3, pp. 271–291. Philadelphia: University of Pennsylvania Press.
Maybury-Lewis, David
1965 The savage and the innocent. London: Evans Brothers Limited.
1967 Akwẽ-Shavante society. Oxford: Clarendon Press.
Mayntzhusen, Friederich C.
1913 Über Gebräuche bei der Geburt und die Namengebung der Guayaki. International Congress of Americanists. Proceedings of the XVIII. Session, London, 1912. Part 1, pp. 408–412. London: Harrison & Sons.
1926 Guayaki-Forschungen. Zeitschrift für Ethnologie, 57. Jahrgang, Heft 3–6, 1925, pp. 315–318. Berlin.
McQuown, Norman A.
1955 The indigenous languages of Latin America. American Anthropologist, v. 57, no. 3, pt. 1, June, pp. 501–570. Menasha.
Medina, José Toribio
1952 Los aborígines de Chile. Santiago de Chile: Fondo Histórico y Bibliográfico José Toribio Medina. 2nd edition.
Meggers, Betty Jane
1954 Environmental limitation on the development of culture. American Anthropologist, v. 56, no. 5, pt. 1, October, pp. 801–824. Menasha.
1957 Environment and culture in the Amazon Basin: An appraisal of the theory of environmental determinism. In Studies in Human Ecology; a series of lectures given at the Anthropological Society of Washington. Social Science Monographs, III, pp. 71–89. Washington: Panamerican Union.
1971 Amazonia; man and culture in a counterfeit paradise. Chicago and New York: Aldine Atherton, Inc.
1972 Prehistoric America. Chicago and New York: Aldine Atherton, Inc.
Melatti, Julio Cezar
1967 Indios e criadores: A situação dos Krahó na área pastoril do Tocantins. Monografias

do Instituto de Ciências Sociais da Universidade Federal do Rio de Janeiro, v. 3. Rio de Janeiro.

1971   Nominadores e genitores: Um aspecto do dualismo Krahó. Verhandlungen des XXXVIII. Internationalen Amerikanistenkongresses, Stuttgart-München, 12. bis 18. August 1968, Bd. III, pp. 347–353. München: Klaus Renner Verlag.

1972   O messianismo Krahó. São Paulo: Editora Herder and Editora da Universidade de São Paulo.

Menzel, Brigitte
1957   Deformierender Gesichtsschmuck südamerikanischer Naturvölker. Baessler-Archiv, n.F., Bd. V (XXX. Bd.), Heft 1, Juli, pp. 1–120. Berlin.

Menzel, Dorothy
1964   Style and time in the Middle Horizon. Ñawpa Pacha 2, pp. 1–105. Berkeley.

Métraux, Alfred
1946   Ethnography of the Chaco. HSAI, v. 1, pp. 197–370.

1947   Mourning rites and burial forms of the South American Indians. América Indígena, v. VII, no. 1, enero, pp. 7–44. México.

1948   The Tupinamba. HSAI, v. 3, pp. 95–133.

1949a   Religion and shamanism. HSAI, v. 5, pp. 559–599.

1949b   Warfare, cannibalism, and human trophies. HSAI, v. 5, pp. 383–409.

Métraux, Alfred, and Baldus, Herbert
1946   The Guayakí. HSAI, v. 1, pp. 435–444.

Métraux, Alfred, and Dreyfus-Roche, Simone
1959   La naissance et la première enfance chez les indiens Cayapó du Xingú. Miscellanea Paul Rivet Octogenario Dicata, II. XXXI Congreso Internacional de Americanistas [São Paulo, 1954]. Universidad Nacional Autónoma de México, Publicaciones del Instituto de Historia, primera serie, núm. 50, 1958, pp. 363–378. México.

Meyer de Schauensee, Rodolphe
1970   A guide to the birds of South America. Published for the Academy of Natural Sciences of Philadelphia. Wynnewood, Pennsylvania: Livingston Publishing Company.

Migliazza, Ernesto
1965   Fonologia Máku. Boletim do Museu Paraense Emílio Goeldi, n.s., Antropologia, no. 25, março 8. Belém-Pará.

1966   Esbôço sintático de um corpus da língua Máku. Boletim do Museu Paraense Emílio Goeldi, n.s., Antropologia, no. 32, agôsto 29. Belém-Pará.

Miller, Elmer S.
1966   Toba kin terms. Ethnology, v. V, no. 2, April, pp. 194–201. Pittsburgh.

1971   The Argentine Toba Evangelical religious service. Ethnology, v. X, no. 2, April, pp. 149–159. Pittsburgh.

ms.   Los Tobas argentinos y su culto. Buenos Aires: Paidos. (in press)

Miller, M.F., and Hudelson, R.R.
1921   Thirty years of field experiments with crop rotation, manure and fertilizers. University of Missouri, College of Agriculture, Agricultural Experiment Station, Bulletin 182, April. Columbia, Missouri.

Ministerio del Interior
1968   Censo indígena nacional. Tomo II. Buenos Aires: Secretaria de Estado de Gobierno.

Miracle, Marvin P.
1967   Agriculture in the Congo basin; tradition and change in African rural economies. Madison: University of Wisconsin Press.

Mishkin, Bernard
1946   The contemporary Quechua. HSAI, v. 2, pp. 411–470.

Montesinos, Fernando de
1930   Memorias antiguas historiales y politicas del Peru. [after 1628] Colección de Libros y Documentos Referentes a la Historia del Peru, 2ª serie, t. VI. Lima.

Moreira Neto, Carlos de Araújo
1959   Relatório sôbre a situação atual dos índios Kayapó. Revista de Antropologia, v. 7, nos. 1 and 2, junho-dezembro, pp. 49–64. São Paulo.

Morley, Sylvanus Griswold
1947   The ancient Maya. Stanford University, California: Stanford University Press. 2nd edition.

Mors, Walter B., and Rizzini, Carlos T.
1966   Useful plants of Brazil. San Francisco, London, Amsterdam: Holden-Day, Inc.

Moser, Brian, and Tayler, Donald
1963   Tribes of the Piraparaná. The Geographical Journal, v. 129, pt. 4, December, pp. 437–449. London.
Münzel, Mark
1971   Medizinmannwesen und Geistervorstellungen bei den Kamayurá (Alto Xingú-brasilien). Arbeiten aus dem Seminar für Völkerkunde der Johann Wolfgang Goethe-Universität, Frankfurt am Main, Bd. 2. Wiesbaden.
Murdock, George Peter
1949   Social structure. New York: The Macmillan Company.
1951a   Outline of South American cultures. Behavior Science Outlines, v. II. New Haven: Human Relations Area Files, Inc.
1951b   South American culture areas. Southwestern Journal of Anthropology, v. 7, no. 4, winter, pp. 415–436. Albuquerque.
1958   Outline of world cultures. New Haven: Human Relations Area Files Press. 2nd edition, revised.
1967   Ethnographic atlas. Pittsburgh: University of Pittsburgh Press.
Murphy, Robert F.
1957   Intergroup hostility and social cohesion. American Anthropologist, v. 59, no. 6, December, pp. 1018–1035. Menasha.
1959   Social structure and sex antagonism. Southwestern Journal of Anthropology, v. 15, no. 1, spring, pp. 89–98. Albuquerque.
1960   Headhunter's heritage: Social and economic change among the Mundurucú Indians. Berkeley: University of California Press.
Murphy, Robert F., and Steward, Julian H.
1956   Tappers and trappers: Parallel process in acculturation. Economic Development and Culture Change, v. IV, 1955–1956, pp. 335–355. Chicago.
Nájera: See Gonzáles de Nájera, Alonso
Naroll, Raoul
1964   On ethnic unit classification. Current Anthropology, v. 5, no. 4, October, pp. 283–291. Glasgow.
Nietschmann, Bernard Quinn
1971   The substance of subsistence. In Geographic research on Latin America: Benchmark 1970. Barry Lentnek, R.L. Carmin and T.L. Martinson (eds.), Proceedings of the Conference of Latin Americanist Geographers, v. 1, pp. 167–181. Muncie, Indiana: Ball State University Press.
ms.   Between land and water: The subsistence ecology of the Miskito Indians, eastern Nicaragua. Ph. D. dissertation, Geography, University of Wisconsin, Madison. 1970.
Nimuendajú [Unkel], Curt
1914   Die Sagen von der Erschaffung und Vernichtung der Welt als Grundlagen der Religion der Apapocúva-Guaraní. Zeitschrift für Ethnologie, 46. Jahrgang, Heft 2 und 3, pp. 284–403. Berlin.
1939   The Apinayé. Translated by Robert H. Lowie. Edited by Robert H. Lowie and John M. Cooper. The Catholic University of America, Anthropological Series no. 8. Washington.
1946   The eastern Timbira. Translated and edited by Robert H. Lowie. University of California Publications in American Archaeology and Ethnology, v. 41. Berkeley and Los Angeles.
1956   Os Apinayé. Boletim do Museu Paraense Emílio Goeldi, t. XII. Belém-Pará.
Nimuendajú, Curt, and Guérios, Rosário Farani Mansur
1948   Cartas etno-lingüísticas. RMP, v. II, pp. 207–241.
Noble, G[ladwyn] Kingsley
1965   Proto-Arawakan and its descendants. Indiana University Research Center in Anthropology, Folklore, and Linguistics, Publication 38. Also Part II of the International Journal of American Linguistics, v. 31, no. 3, July. Bloomington.
Nordenskiöld, Erland
1931   The origin of the Indian civilizations in South America. Comparative Ethnographical Studies, 9, pp. 1–153. Göteborg.
Núñez, Alvaro
1965   Relación de la dotrina e beneficio de Nambija y Yaguarsongo. [probably ca. 1582]

Relaciones Geográficas de Indias—Perú, t. IV, pp. 139–142. Biblioteca de Autores Españoles, t. 185. Madrid: Ediciones Atlas.

Núñez de Pineda y Bascuñan, Francisco
1863   Cautiverio felíz, del maestro de campo jeneral Don . . . , y rázon individual de las guerras dilatadas del reino de Chille, compuesto por el mismo, y dedicado al rei N.S. Don Cárlos II, que dios guarde muchos años para gloria nuestra. Colección de Historiadores de Chile y Documentos Relativos a la Historia Nacional, t. III. Santiago: Imprenta del Ferrocarril.

Núñez del Prado B., Juan Víctor
ms.   El hombre y su mundo sobrenatural en la comunidad de Qotobamba. 1968.

Núñez del Prado C., Oscar
1957   El hombre y la familia: Su matrimonio y organización político-social en Q'ero. Cuzco: Editorial Garcilaso.
ms.   Unpublished data on Q'ero. 1955.

Oberem, Udo
1958   Diego de Ortegóns Beschreibung der "Gobernación de los Quijos, Zumaco y la Canela." Ein ethnographischer Bericht aus dem Jahre 1577. Zeitschrift für Ethnologie, Bd. 83, Heft 2, pp. 230–251. Braunschweig.
1961   Über die Omagua des Río Napo. In Kulturhistorische Studien; Hermann Trimborn zum 60. Geburtstag von seinen Schülern gewidmet, pp. 94–114. Braunschweig: Albert Limbach Verlag.
1967   Don Sancho Hacho, ein cacique mayor des 16. Jahrhunderts. Jahrbuch für Geschichte von Staat, Wirtschaft und Gesellschaft Lateinamerikas, Bd. 4, pp. 199–225. Köln Graz: Böhlau Verlag.
1971   Los Quijos: Historia de la transculturación de un grupo indígena en el Oriente ecuatoriano, (1538–1956). Memorias del Departamento de Antropología y Etnología de América, 1 and 2. Facultad de Filosofía y Letras, Universidad de Madrid. Madrid.

Oberg, Kalervo
1949   The Terena and the Caduveo of southern Mato Grosso, Brazil. Smithsonian Institution, Institute of Social Anthropology, Publication no. 9. Washington.
1965   The marginal peasant in rural Brazil. American Anthropologist, v. 67, no. 6, pt. 1, December, pp. 1417–1427. Menasha.
ms.   The social economy of the Tlingit Indians. Ph.D. dissertation, Anthropology, University of Chicago, Chicago, Illinois. 1937.

O'Brien, Patricia J.
1972   The sweet potato: Its origin and dispersal. American Anthropologist, v. 74, no. 3, June, pp. 342–365. Washington.

Oficina de Evaluación
1968   Inventario, evaluación e integración de los recursos naturales de la zona del río Tambo-Gran Pajonal. Lima: Oficina Nacional de Evaluación de Recursos Naturales.

Olaverría, Miguel de
1852   Informe de Don Miguel de Olaverria sobre el Reyno de Chile, sus indios y sus guerras. [1594] In Gay, 1846–1852, v. II, pp. 13–54.

O'Leary, Timothy J.
1970   Ethnographic bibliographies. In A handbook of method in cultural anthropology. Raoul Naroll and Ronald Cohen (eds.), pp. 128–146. Garden City, New York: Natural History Press.

Olien, Michael D.
1973   Latin Americans: Contemporary peoples and their cultural traditions. New York and so forth: Holt, Rinehart and Winston, Inc.

Oliveira, Roberto Cardoso de
1964   O índio e o mundo dos brancos; a situação dos Tukúna do Alto Solimões. Corpo e Alma do Brasil, XII. São Paulo: Difusão Européia do Livro.

Opler, Morris Edward
1945   Themes as dynamic forces in cultures. American Journal of Sociology, v. LI, no. 3, November, pp. 198–206. Chicago.

Oppenheim, Victor
1936   Notas ethnographicas sobre os indígenas do Alto Juruá (Acre) e valle do Ucayali (Perú). Annaes da Academia Brasileira de Sciencias, t. VIII, nº 2, 30 de junho, pp. 145–155. Rio de Janeiro.

Ortiguera, Toribio de
1909 Jornada del Río Marañón; con todo lo acaecido en ella, y otras cosas notables dignas de ser sabidas, acaecidas en las Indias Occidentales. [after 1585] Historiadores de Indias, t. II, pp. 305–422. Nueva Biblioteca de Autores Españoles, v. 15. Madrid.
Ortíz, Alejandro
n.d. En torno a los mitos andinos. Tesis doctoral, Universidad Nacional Mayor de San Marcos, Lima. Mimeograph. [ca. 1971]
Orton, James
1870 The Andes and the Amazon; or, across the continent of South America. New York: Harper & Brothers, Publishers.
Osculati, Gaetano
1850 Esplorazione delle regioni equatoriali lungo il Napo ed il fiume delle Amazzoni; frammento di un viaggio fatto nelle due Americhe negli anni 1846–1847–1848. Milano: Tipografia Bernardoni.
1929 Esplorazioni nell'America equatoriale. 2 vols. Milano: Ediz. Alpes. 2nd edition.
Ossio A., Juan M. (ed.)
1973 Ideología mesiánica del mundo andino. Antología de . . . Colección Biblioteca de Antropología, dirigida por Ignacio Prado Pastor. Lima: Edición de Ignacio Prado Pastor.
Owen, Roger C.
1965 The patrilocal band: A linguistically and culturally hybrid social unit. American Anthropologist, v. 67, no. 3, June, pp. 675–690. Menasha.
Parsons, James Jerome
1969 Ridged fields in the Rio Guayas Valley, Ecuador. American Antiquity, v. 34, no. 1, January, pp. 76–80. Salt Lake City.
Parsons, James Jerome, and Bowen, William A.
1966 Ancient ridged fields of the San Jorge floodplain, Colombia. The Geographical Review, v. LVI, no. 3, July, pp. 317–343. Burlington, Vermont.
Parsons, James Jerome, and Denevan, William Maxfield
1967 Pre-Columbian ridged fields. Scientific American, v. 217, no. 1, July, pp. 92–100. New York.
Paz Soldán, Carlos Enrique, and Kuczynski-Godard, Maxime
1939 La selva peruana: Sus pobladores y su colonización en seguridad sanitaria. Lima: Instituto de Medicina Social de la Universidad de San Marcos.
Perez García, J.
1846 Viaje de García Hurtado de Mendoza al sur de Valdivia, y fundación de Osorno. In Gay, 1846–1852, v. I, pp. 221–225.
Petrullo, Vincenzo
1939 The Yaruros of the Capanaparo River, Venezuela. Smithsonian Institution, Bureau of American Ethnology, Bulletin 123, Anthropological Papers no. 11, pp. 161–290. Washington.
Pietas, Gerónimo
1846 Noticia sobre las costumbres de los Araucanos. [June 11, 1729] In Gay, 1846–1852, v. I, pp. 486–512.
Pinckard, George
1816 Notes on the West Indies, including observations relative to the creoles and slaves of the western colonies, and the Indians of South America; interspersed with remarks upon the seasoning or yellow fever of hot climates. 2 vols. London: Baldwin, Cradock, and Jay. 2nd edition.
Ploetz, Hermann, and Métraux, Alfred
1930 La civilisation matérielle et la vie sociale et religieuse des indiens Žè du Brésil méridional et orientale. Revista del Instituto de Etnología de la Universidad Nacional de Tucumán, t. I, entrega 2ª, pp. 107–238. Tucumán.
Pompeu Sobrinho, Thomas
1934 Os Tapuias do Nordeste e a monografia de Elias Herckman. [ms. 1639] Revista do Instituto do Ceará, v. 48, pp. 7–28. Forteleza.
Pons, F.R.J. de
1806 Travels in parts of South America, during the years 1801, 1802, 1803, and 1804; containing a description of the Captain-Generalship of Carracas, with an account of

the laws, commerce, and natural productions of that country; as also a view of the customs and manners of the Spaniards and native Indians. London: Printed for Richard Phillips by J.G. Barnard.

Porras Garcés, Pedro Ignacio
1961 Contribución al estudio de la arqueología e historia de los Valles de Quijos y Misagualli (Alto Napo) en la región oriental del Ecuador. Quito: Editora Fénix.

Prado, Francisco Rodrigues do
1839 História dos Indios Cavalleiros ou da Nação Guaycurú. Em que descreve os seus usos e costumes, leis, allianças, ritos e governo domestico, e as hostilidades feitas a differentes nações barbaras, aos Portuguezes e Hespanhoes, males que ainda são presentes na memoria de todos. [1795] Revista do Instituto Histórico e Geográfico do Brazil, primeira serie, t. I, no. 1, 1º trimestre de 1839; 2ª edição, 1856, pp. 25–57. Rio de Janeiro.

Quito
1934 Libro primero de cabildos de Quito; tomo primero [1529–1538]. Descifrado por José Rumazo González. Publicaciones del Archivo Municipal. Quito.

Radcliffe-Brown, Alfred Reginald
1930–1931 The social organization of Australian tribes. Oceania, v. I, no. 1, April 1930, pp. 34–63; no. 2, July 1930, pp. 206–246; no. 3, October-December 1930, pp. 322–341; no. 4, January-March 1931, pp. 426–456. Melbourne.
1965 Structure and function in primitive society. London. 5th edition.

Ramírez, Balthasar
1906 Descripción del reyno del Pirú, del sitio, temple, prouincias, obispados y ciudades; de los naturales, de sus lenguas y traje. Año de 1597. Juicio de Límites entre el Perú y Bolivia. Prueba peruana presentada al Gobierno de la República Argentina por Víctor M. Maurtua, t. 1º, Virreinato peruano, pp. 281–363. Barcelona: Imprenta de Henrich y Comp.
1936 Description del Reyno del Piru del sitio temple. Prouincias, obispado. y ciudades. de los Naturales de sus lenguas y trage . . . Año de 1597. Bearbeitet von Wilhelm Petersen. Quellen zur Kulturgeschichte des präkolumbischen Amerika, Studien zur Kulturkunde, 3. Bd., pp. 1–122 [text pp. 10–68]. Stuttgart: Strecker und Schroeder, Verlag.

Reichel-Dolmatoff, Gerardo
1950 Los Kogi; una tribu de la Sierra Nevada de Santa Marta—Colombia. [Tomo I] Revista del Instituto Etnológico Nacional, v. IV, entregas 1ª and 2ª, 1949–1950. Bogotá.
1951a Datos histórico-culturales sobre las tribus de la antigua Gobernación de Santa Marta. Bogotá: Imprenta del Banco de la República, Instituto Etnológico del Magdalena, Santa Marta.
1951b Los Kogi; una tribu de la Sierra Nevada de Santa Marta—Colombia. Tomo II. Bogotá: Editorial Iqueima.
1953 Contactos y cambios culturales en la Sierra Nevada de Santa Marta. Revista Colombiana de Antropología, segunda época, v. I, no. 1, junio, pp. 15–122. Bogotá.
1961 Notas etnográficas sobre los índios del Chocó. Revista Colombiana de Antropología, v. IX, 1960, pp. 73–158. Bogotá.
1963 Review: The Cubeo: Indians of the northwest Amazon. Irving Goldman. (Illinois studies in anthropology no. 2.) Urbana: The University of Illinois Press, 1963. . . . American Anthropologist, v. 65, no. 6, December, pp. 1377–1379. Menasha.
1968 Desana; simbolismo de los indios Tukano del Vaupés. Bogotá: Universidad de los Andes.
1971 Amazonian cosmos. The sexual and religious symbolism of the Tukano Indians. Chicago: University of Chicago Press.

Relación de Pimampiro
1965 Relación en suma de la doctrina e beneficio de Pimampiro y de las cosas notables que en ella hay, de la cual es beneficiado el P. Antonio Borja. [ca. 1592] Relaciones Geográficas de Indias—Perú, t. II, pp. 248–253. Biblioteca de Autores Españoles, t. 184. Madrid: Ediciones Atlas.

Ribeiro, Darcy
1950 Religião e mitologia Kadiuéu. Ministério da Agricultura, Conselho Nacional de Proteção aos Índios, Serviço de Proteção aos Índios, Publicação no. 106. Rio de Janeiro.

1951 Notícia dos Ofaié-Chavante. RMP, v. V, pp. 105–135.
1955 Os Indios Urubús; ciclo anual das atividades de subsistência de uma tribo da floresta tropical. Anais do XXXI Congresso Internacional de Americanistas, São Paulo, 23–28 de agôsto de 1954, v. 1, pp. 127–155. São Paulo: Editora Anhembi.
1956 Convívio e contaminação; efeitos dissociativos da depopulação provocada por epidemias em grupos indígenas. Sociologia, v. XVIII, no. 1, março, pp. 3–50. São Paulo.
1957 Culturas e línguas indigenas do Brasil. Educação e Ciências Sociais, v. 2, no. 6, novembro, pp. 1–102. Rio de Janeiro.

Ribeiro, Francisco de Paula
1841 Memoria sobre as nações gentias; que presentemente habitam o continente do Maranhão: analyse de algumas tribus mais conhecidas: processo de suas hostilidades sobre os habitantes: causes que lhes tem difficultado a reducção, e unico methodo que seriamente poderá reduzil-as. Escripta no anno de 1819 pelo Major Graduado. . . . Revista Trimensal de Historia e Geographia; ou Jornal do Instituto Historico Geographico Brasileiro, t. III, reimpreso 1860, no. 10, julho, pp. 184–197; no. 11, outubro, pp. 297–322; no. 12, dezembro, pp. 442–456. Rio de Janeiro.

Rivera, José Eustasio
1948 La vorágine. Santiago: Zigzag Press.

Rivet, Paul
1943 La influencia karib en Colombia. Revista del Instituto Etnológico Nacional, v. 1, entrega 1, pp. 55–93. Bogotá.

Rivière, Peter
1969 Marriage among the Trio: A principle of social organisation among a South American forest people. Oxford: Clarendon Press.

Roark, R.C.
1931 Excerpts from consular correspondence relating to insecticidal and fish-poison plants. Washington: United States Department of Agriculture, Bureau of Chemistry and Soils.
1933 Rotenone. Industrial and Engineering Chemistry, v. 25, no. 6, June, pp. 639–642. Easton, Pennsylvania.

Robles Rodríguez, Eulojio
1912 Costumbres i creencias araucanas. República de Chile, Anales de la Universidad, t. CXXX, año 70º, enero-febrero, pp. 343–369. Santiago de Chile.

Rodrigues, Aryon Dall'Igna
1958a Classification of Tupi-Guarani. International Journal of American Linguistics, v. XXIV, no. 3, July, pp. 231–234. Baltimore. [Author's name given as Arion D. Rodrigues]
1958b Die Klassifikation des Tupí-Sprachstammes. Proceedings of the Thirty-second International Congress of Americanists, Copenhagen 8–14 August 1956, pp. 679–684. Copenhagen: Munksgaard.
1960 Über die Sprache der Surára und Pakidái. Mitteilungen aus dem Museum für Völkerkunde in Hamburg, v. XXVI, pp. 134–138. Hamburg.
1963 Os estudos de lingüística indígena no Brasil. Revista de Antropologia, v. 11, pp. 9–21. São Paulo.
1964 A classificação do tronco lingüístico tupí. Revista de Antropologia, v. 12, pp. 99–104. São Paulo.

Rodríquez, Manuel
1684 El Marañón y Amazonas; historia de los descubrimientos, entradas y reducción de naciones; trabajos malogrados de algunos conquistadores y dichosos de otros, assi temporales, como espirituales, en las dilatadas montañas, y mayores rios de la América. Madrid: Imprenta de A. Gonçalez de Reyes.

Roquette-Pinto, Edgard
1950 Rondônia. Brasiliana, v. 39, série 5ª da Biblioteca Pedagógica Brasileira. São Paulo: Companhia Editora Nacional. 5th edition.

Roth, Walter Edmund
1915 An inquiry into the animism and folk-lore of the Guiana Indians. Thirtieth Annual Report of the Bureau of American Ethnology, . . . 1908–1909, pp. 103–386. Washington.
1924 An introductory study of the arts, crafts, and customs of the Guiana Indians. Thirty-eighth Annual Report of the Bureau of American Ethnology, . . . 1916–1917, pp. 25–745. Washington.

1929   Additional studies of the arts, crafts, and customs of the Guiana Indians; with special reference to those of southern British Guiana. Smithsonian Institution, Bureau of American Ethnology, Bulletin 91. Washington.

Rowe, John Howland
1946   Inca culture at the time of the Spanish Conquest. HSAI, v. 2, pp. 183–330.
1969   The sunken gardens of the Peruvian coast. American Antiquity, v. 34, no. 3, July, pp. 320–325. Salt Lake City.

Ruddle, Kenneth
1970   The hunting technology of the Maracá Indians. Antropológica, no. 25, pp. 21–63. Caracas.

Ruiz de Gamboa, Martín
1852   Carta de Martin Ruiz de Gamboa al rey de España. [1580] In Gay, 1846–1852, v. II, pp. 119–124.

Rumazo González, José
1946   La región amazónica del Ecuador en el siglo XVI. Anuario de Estudios Americanos, t. III, pp. 1–268. Sevilla.

Rydén, Stig
1950   A study of South American Indian hunting traps. RMP, v. IV, pp. 247–352.

Salinas Loyola, Juan de
1965   Relación de la ciudad de Zamora de los Alcaides. [before 1582] Relaciones Geográficas de Indias Perú, t. IV, pp. 125 135. Biblioteca de Autores Españoles, t. 185. Madrid: Ediciones Atlas.

Salzano, Francisco Mauro (ed.)
1971   The ongoing evolution of Latin American populations. Springfield, Illinois: Charles C. Thomas.

Salzano, Francisco Mauro, and Freire-Maia, Newton
1970   Problems in human biology; a study of Brazilian populations. Detroit: Wayne State University Press.

Salzmann, Zdaněk
1951   Review: Klassifikation der südamerikanischen Sprachen. By Čestmír Loukotka. Zeitschrift für Ethnologie 74.1–69 (1942). International Journal of American Linguistics, v. 17, no. 4, October, pp. 259–266. Baltimore.

Sánchez Labrador, José
1910   El Paraguay católico. 2 vols. Buenos Aires: Imprenta de Coni Hermanos.
1917   El Paraguay católico. Tomo 3. Buenos Aires: Comp. Sud-Americana de Billetes de Banco.

Sapper, Karl
1936   Geographie und Geschichte der indianischen Landwirtschaft. Ibero-americanische Studien. I. Hamburg.

Sauer, Carl Ortwin
1950a   Cultivated plants of South and Central America. HSAI, v. 6, pp. 487–543.
1950b   Geography of South America. HSAI, v. 6, pp. 319–344.

Schaaffhausen, H.
1870   Die Menschenfresserei und das Menschenopfer. Archiv für Anthropologie, 4. Bd., pp. 245–286. Braunschweig.

Schaden, Egon
1965   Aculturação indígena. Ensaio sôbre fatôres e tendências da mudança cultural de tribus índias em contacto como mundo dos brancos. Revista de Antropologia, v. 13. São Paulo.

Scheffler, Harold W., and Lounsbury, Floyd G.
1971   A study in structural semantics: The Siriono kinship system. Englewood Cliffs, New Jersey: Prentice-Hall, Inc.

Schmidt, Max
1905   Indianerstudien in Zentralbrasilien; Erlebnisse und ethnologische Ergebnisse einer Reise in den Jahren 1900 bis 1901. Berlin: Dietrich Reimer.
1914a   Die Guato und ihr Gebiet. Ethnologische und archäologische Ergebnisse der Expedition zum Caracara-Fluss in Matto-Grosso. Baessler-Archiv, Bd. IV, Heft 6, pp. 251–283. Leipzig and Berlin.
1914b   Die Paressi-Kabichi. Ethnologische Ergebnisse der Expedition zu den Quellen des Jaurú und Juruena im Jahre 1910. Baessler-Archiv, Bd. IV, Heft 4/5. Leipzig.

1929 Kunst und Kultur von Peru. Berlin: Propyläen-Verlag zu Berlin.
1940 Hallazgos prehistóricos en Matto-Grosso. Revista de la Sociedad Científica del Paraguay, t. V, n. 1, pp. 37–62. Asunción.
1941 Los Barbados o Umotinas en Matto Grosso (Brasil). Revista de la Sociedad Científica del Paraguay, t. V, n. 4. Asunción.
1942a Estudos de etnologia brasileira; peripécias de uma viagem entre 1900 e 1901; seus resultados etnológicos. Tradução directa do alemão de Catharina Baratz Cannabrava. São Paulo: Companhia Editora Nacional.
1942b Resultados de mi tercera expedición a los Guatós efectuada en el año 1928. Revista de la Sociedad Científica del Paraguay, t. V, n. 6, pp. 41–75. Asunción.

Schmidt, Wilhelm
1913 Kulturkreise und Kulturschichten in Südamerika. Zeitschrift für Ethnologie, 45. Jahrgang, Heft 6, 1913, pp. 1014–1124. Berlin.

Schomburgk, [Moritz] Richard
1847–1848 Reisen in Britisch-Guiana in den Jahren 1840–1844. 3 vols. Leipzig: Verlagsbuchhandlung von J. J. Weber.

Schomburgk, Robert Hermann
1841 Robert Hermann Schomburgk's Reisen in Guiana und am Orinoko während der Jahre 1835–1839; nach seinen Berichten und Mittheilungen an die geographische Gesellschaft in London, herausgegeben von O. A. Schomburgk. Leipzig: Verlag von Georg Wigand.

Schultz, Harald
1950 Lendas dos índios Krahó. RMP, v. IV, pp. 48–163.

Sebag, Lucien
1964 Analyse des rêves d'une indienne Guayaki. Les Temps Modernes, 19e année, no. 217, Juin, pp. 2181–2237. Paris.

Serra, Ricardo Franco de Almeida
1845–1850 Parecer sobre o aldêamento dos Indios uaicurús e guanás, com a descripção dos seus usos, religião, estabilidade e costumes. Resposta do general Caetano Pinto de Miranda Montenegro a este parecer. [Apr. 5, 1803] Revista de Historia e Geographia, ou Jornal do Instituto Historico e Geographico Brasileiro, no. 25, abril de 1845, t. 7°, 2^a ed., 1866, pp. 204–218; v. 13, 2^a ed., 1872, pp. 348–395. Rio de Janeiro.

Serrano, Gregorio
1923 Relación de lo subcedido en Chile desde veinte de diciembre de noventa y ocho hasta primero de mayo de noventa y nueve . . . Colección de Historiadores de Chile y Documentos Relativos a la Historia Nacional, t. XLIV, pp. 227–233. Santiago de Chile: Imprenta Universitaria.

Siemens, Alfred H., and Puleston, Dennis E.
1972 Ridged fields and associated features in southern Campeche: New perspectives on the Lowland Maya. American Antiquity, v. 37, no. 2, April, pp. 228–239. Washington.

Simmel, Georg
1955 Conflict. Translated by Kurt H. Wolff. The web of group-affiliations. Translated by Reinhard Bendix. Glencoe, Illinois: The Free Press.

Simposio
1968 Etnobotánica de América. Actas y Memorias, XXXVII Congreso Internacional de Americanistas, República Argentina–1966, v. II, pp. 505–656. Buenos Aires. [Distributed by Librart S.R.L.]

Simson, Alfred
1883 Notes on the Napo Indians. Journal of the Anthropological Institute of Great Britain and Ireland, v. XII, pp. 21–37. London.
1886 Travels in the wild of Ecuador and the exploration of the Putumayo River. London: S. Low, Marston, Searle, and Rivington.

Snethlage, Emil Heinrich
1931 Unter nordostbrasilianischen Indianern. Zeitschrift für Ethnologie, 62. Jahrgang, 1930, pp. 111–205. Berlin.

Sockett, B.
1966 A stone is cast. Birkenhead, Cheshire: Wrights Ltd.

Spencer, Joseph Earle
1966 Shifting cultivation in southeastern Asia. University of California Publications in Geography, v. 19. Berkeley and Los Angeles.

Steinen, Karl von den
1894   Unter den Naturvölkern Zentral-Brasiliens. Reiseschilderung und Ergebnisse der Zweiten Schingú-Expedition 1887–1888. Berlin: Geographische Verlagsbuchhandlung von Dietrich Reimer.
Steinmetz, Rudolf S.
1896   Endokannibalismus. Mittheilungen der Anthropologischen Gesellschaft in Wien, XXVI. Bd. (n.F. XVI. Bd.), pp. 1–60. Wien.
Stevenson, William Bennet
1825–1829   A historical and descriptive narrative of twenty years' residence in South America . . . containing travels in Arauco, Chile, Peru, and Colombia; with an account of the revolution, its rise, progress, and results. 3 vols. London [and so forth]: Hurst, Robinson, and Co. [and others].
Steward, Julian H.
1936a   The economic and social basis of primitive bands. In Essays in anthropology presented to A.L. Kroeber in celebration of his sixtieth birthday, June 11, 1936, pp. 331–350. Berkeley: University of California Press.
1936b   Shoshoni polyandry. American Anthropologist, n.s., v. 38, no. 4, October-December, pp. 561–564. Menasha.
1937   Petroglyphs of the United States. Annual Report . . ., Smithsonian Institution . . . for . . . 1936, pp. 405–425. Washington.
1948   Tribes of the Montaña: An introduction. IISAI, v. 3, pp. 507–533.
1949   South American cultures: An interpretative summary. HSAI, v. 5, pp. 669–772.
Steward, Julian H. (ed.)
1946–1959   Handbook of South American Indians. Smithsonian Institution, Bureau of American Ethnology, Bulletin 143. 7 vols. Washington.
Steward, Julian H., and Faron, Louis C.
1959   Native peoples of South America. New York: McGraw-Hill.
Strong, William Duncan
1943   Cross-sections of New World prehistory. A brief report on the work of the Institute of Andean Research, 1941–1942. Smithsonian Miscellaneous Collections, v. 104, no. 2. Washington.
1947   Finding the tomb of a warrior-god. The National Geographic Magazine, v. XCI, no. 4, April, pp. 453–482. Washington.
Sumner, William Graham
1906   Folkways; a study of the sociological importance of usages, manners, customs, mores, and morals. Boston: Ginn and Co.
Sumner, William Graham, and Keller, Albert Galloway
1927   The science of society. 4 vols. New Haven: Yale University Press.
Swadesh, Morris
1959   Mapas de clasificación lingüística de México y las Américas. Cuadernos del Instituto de Historia, Serie Antropológica no. 8. Universidad Nacional Autónoma de México. México. [Author's name given as Mauricio Swadesh]
Swanton, John R.
1946   The Indians of the southeastern United States. Smithsonian Institution, Bureau of American Ethnology, Bulletin no. 137. Washington.
Symposium
1971   Recent research in central Brazil. Verhandlungen des XXXVIII. Internationalen Amerikanistenkongresses, Stuttgart-München, 12. bis 18. August 1968, Bd. III, pp. 333–391. München: Klaus Renner Verlag.
Tastevin, Constant
1925   Le fleuve Murú. Ses habitants—Croyances et moeurs kachinaua. La Géographie, t. XLIII, nos. 4–5, Avril-Mai, pp. 403–422; t. XLIV, no. 1, Juin, pp. 14–35. Paris.
Tax, Sol
1958   Indian, Latin American. Encyclopaedia Britannica. [Also appears in later editions.]
1960   Aboriginal languages of Latin America. Current Anthropology, v. 1, nos. 5–6, September-November, pp. 430–436. Chicago.
Tessmann, Günter
1930   Die Indianer Nordost-Perus: Grundlegende Forschungen für eine systematische Kulturkunde. Veröffentlichung der Harvey-Bassler-Stiftung. Hamburg: Friedrichsen, de Gruyter & Co. M.B.H.

Thomas, Northcote Whitbridge
  1910   Cannibalism. The Encyclopaedia Britannica, v. 5, pp. 184–185. Cambridge, England: University Press. 11th edition.
Thompson, J. Eric S.
  1943   A trial survey of the southern Maya area. American Antiquity, v. IX, no. 1, July, pp. 106–134. Menasha.
  1945   A survey of the northern Maya area. American Antiquity, v. XI, no. 1, July, pp. 2–24. Menasha.
Tippett, A.R.
  1958   The nature and social function of Fijian war (Focus—1839–1846). Transactions and Proceedings of the Fiji Society, v. 5, no. 4, 1954, pp. 137–155. Suva, Fiji.
Titiev, Mischa
  1943   The influence of common residence on the unilateral classification of kindred. American Anthropologist, v. 45, no. 4, pt. 1, October-December, pp. 511–530. Menasha.
Tovar, Antonio
  1961   Catálogo de las lenguas de América del Sur; enumeración, con indicaciones tipológicas, bibliografía y mapas. Buenos Aires: Editorial Sudamericana.
Towle, Margaret A.
  1961   The ethnobotany of pre-Columbian Peru. Viking Fund Publications in Anthropology, no. 30. Chicago: Aldine Publishing Company.
Uhle, Max
  1889–1890   Kultur und Industrie südamerikanischer Völker; nach den im Besitze des Museums für Völkerkunde zu Leipzig befindlichen Sammlungen von A. Stübel, W. Reiss und B. Koppel. 2 vols. Berlin: Verlag von A. Asher & Co.
  1942   Procedencia y origen de las antiguas civilizaciones americanas. Actas y Trabajos Científicos del XXVIIº Congreso Internacional de Americanistas (Lima, 1939), t. I, pp. 355–368. Lima: Librería e Imprenta Gil, S.A.
Ule, Ernst Heinrich Georg
  1913   Unter den Indianern am Rio Branco in Nordbrasilien. Zeitschrift für Ethnologie, 45. Jahrgang, Heft 2, pp. 278–298. Berlin.
Uriarte, Manuel Joaquín
  1952   Diario de un misionero de Mainas. Transcripción, introducción y notas del P. Constantino Bayle, S.J. 2 vols. Madrid: Instituto Santo Toribio de Mogrovejo, Ediciones Jura.
Vaillant, George C.
  1944   The Aztecs of Mexico; origin, rise and fall of the Aztec nation. The American Museum of Natural History, Science Series. Garden City, New York: Doubleday, Doran & Company, Inc.
Valdivia, Luis de
  1852   Relación de lo que sucedio en la jornada que hicimos el Sr. preste Alonso de Ribera gobernador deste reyno y yo desde Arauco á Paycavi á conducir las paces de Ilicura última regua de Tucapel y las de Puren y la Imperial, escrita por mi el padre . . . al salir de Paycavi de vuelta á Lebo. [Oct. 25, 1613] In Gay, 1846–1852, v. II, pp. 281–296.
Valdivia, Pedro de
  1846a   Carta de D. . . . á S.M. Cárlos V, dándole noticia de la conquista de Chile, de sus trabajos y del estado en que se hallaba la colonia. [Sept. 4, 1545] In Gay, 1846–1852, v. I, pp. 49–73.
  1846b   Carta de . . ., escrita á S.M. desde la ciudad de la Concepción del Nuevo Estremo, á 25 de setiembre de 1551. In Gay, 1846–1852, v. I, pp. 139–146.
Valladares, Alvaro
  1912   Carta de Fray . . . al Dr. Jacinto Angel Scappardini. In Cartas sobre Misiones Dominicanas en la Región Oriental del Ecuador, 2ª ser., carta 2ª. Quito.
Varese, Stefano
  1968   La sal de los cerros: Notas etnográficas e históricas sobre los Campa de la selva del Perú. Lima: Universidad Peruana de Ciencias y Tecnología.
Veigl, Franz Xavier
  1785   Gründliche Nachrichten über die Verfassung der Landschaft von Maynas, in Süd-Amerika, bis zum Jahre 1768. In Reisen einiger Missionarien der Gessellschaft Jesu in Amerika, pp. 1–324. Christoph Gottlieb von Murr (ed.). Nürnberg: Johann Eberhard Zeh.
Viagem
  1848   Viagem de Thomaz de Souza Villa Real pelos rios Tocantins, Araguaya e Vermelho;

acompanhada de importantes documentos officiaes relativos á mesma navegação. [1797] Revista Trimensal de Historia e Geographia, ou Jornal do Instituto Historico e Geographico Brazileiro, t, XI, volume supplementar, 1872, pp. 401–444. Rio de Janeiro.

Vicuña Mackenna, Benjamín
1876   Lautaro y sus tres campañas contra Santiago, 1553–1557. Santiago: Imprenta de la Libreria del Mercurio.

Villanueva, Manuel Pablo
1902   Fronteras de Loreto. Lima: Imprenta y Librería San Pedro. [Also published in:] Boletín de la Sociedad Geográfica de Lima, t. XII, año XII, trimestre 4°, 31 diciembre 1902, pp. 361–479; t. XIII, año XIII, trimestre 1°, 31 marzo 1903, pp. 30–54. Lima.

Villavicencio, Manuel
1858   Geografía de la república del Ecuador. New York: Imprenta de Robert Craighead.
1860   Apéndice a la jeografía del Ecuador y de los terrenos baldíos. Valparaiso: Imprenta y Librería del Mercurio de S. Tornero.

Vine, H.
1953   Experiments on the maintenance of soil fertility at Ibadan, Nigeria, 1922–51. The Empire Journal of Experimental Agriculture, v. XXI, no. 82, April, pp. 65–85. Oxford.

Voegelin, Charles F., and Harris, Zellig S.
1951   Methods for determining intelligiblity among dialects of natural languages. Proceedings of the American Philosophical Society, v. 95, no. 3, June, pp. 322–329. Philadelphia.

Voegelin, Charles F., and Florence M.
1965   Languages of the world: Native America fascicle two. Anthropological Linguistics, v. 7, no. 7, pt. I, October. Bloomington.

Wagley, Charles
1940   The effects of depopulation upon social organization as illustrated by the Tapirapé Indians. Transactions of the New York Academy of Sciences, ser. 2, v. 3, no. 1, pp. 12–16. New York.
1943   Xamanismo tapirapé. Tapirapé shamanism. Boletim do Museu Nacional, n.s., Antropologia, no. 3, 15 de setembro. Rio de Janeiro.
1953   Amazon town: A study of man in the tropics. New York: The Macmillan Company.
1955   Tapirapé social and culture change, 1940–1953. Anais do XXXI Congresso Internacional de Americanistas, São Paulo, 23–28 de agôsto de 1954, v. 1, pp. 99–106. São Paulo: Editora Anhembi.
1964   The peasant. In Continuity and change in Latin America. John J. Johnson (ed.), pp. 21–48. Stanford, California: Stanford University Press.

Wagley, Charles, and Galvão, Eduardo
1946   O parentesco Tupi-Guarani. Boletim do Museu Nacional, n.s., Antropologia, no. 6, 31 de janeiro. Rio de Janeiro.
1948a   The Tapirapé. HSAI, v. 3, pp. 167–178.
1948b   The Tenetehara. HSAI, v. 3, pp. 137–148.
1949   The Tenetehara Indians of Brazil: A culture in transition. Columbia University Contributions to Anthropology, no. 35. New York.

Wagner, Erika
1973   The Mucuchíes phase: An extension of the Andean cultural pattern into western Venezuela. American Anthropologist, v. 75, no. 1, February, pp. 195–213. Washington.

Waitz, Theodor
1859   Anthropologie der Naturvölker. 3. Theil. Leipzig: Friedrich Fleischer.

Wallace, Alfred Russel
1889   A narrative of travels on the Amazon and Rio Negro. London: Ward, Lock & Co. 2nd edition.

Wassén, [Sven] Henry
1935   Notes on southern groups of Chocó Indians in Colombia. Etnologiska Studier, v. 1, pp. 35–182. Göteborg.
1955   Algunos datos del comercio precolombino en Colombia. Revista Colombiana de Antropología, v. IV, pp. 87–109. Bogotá.
1957   On dendrobates-frog-poison material among Emperá (Chocó)-speaking Indians in western Caldas, Colombia. Etnografiska Museet, Göteborg Årstryck för 1955 och 1956, pp. 73–94. Göteborg.

Watt, George
1908 The commercial products of India; being an abridgement of "The dictionary of the economic products of India." London: John Murray.
Weinreich, Uriel
1953 Languages in contact; findings and problems. Publications of the Linguistic Circle of New York, no. 1. New York.
1968 Unilinguisme et multilinguisme. In Le Langage. André Martinet (ed.), Encyclopédie de la Pléiade, v. 25me, pp. 647–684. Paris: Éditions Gallimard.
Weiss, Gerald
1973 Shamanism and priesthood in light of the Campa *ayahuasca* ceremony. In Hallucinogens and shamanism. Michael J. Harner (ed.), pp. 40–47. New York: Oxford University Press.
ms. The cosmology of the Campa Indians of eastern Peru. Ph.D. dissertation, Anthropology, University of Michigan, Ann Arbor. 1969.
White, Leslie A.
1959 The evolution of culture: The development of civilization to the fall of Rome. New York, Toronto, London: McGraw-Hill Book Company, Inc.
Wiener, Charles
1884 Viaje al río de las Amazonas y á las Cordilleras; 1879–1882. In América Pintoresca; descripción de viajes al nuevo continente, por los más modernos exploradores, pp. 1–112. Barcelona: Montaner y Simon.
Wilbert, Johannes
1972 Survivors of Eldorado: Four Indian cultures of South America. New York, London, Washington: Praeger Publishers.
Wilbert, Johannes (ed.)
1961 The evolution of horticultural systems in native South America, causes and consequences; a symposium. Antropológica, Supplement Publication, no. 2, September. Caracas.
Willey, Gordon R.
1946 The Chiclín conference for Peruvian archaeology, 1946. American Antiquity, v. XII, no. 2, October, pp. 132–134. Menasha. [Author's name given as G.R.W.]
1966–1971 An introduction to American archaeology. 2 vols. Englewood Cliffs, New Jersey: Prentice-Hall, Inc.
Wilson, John
1906 The relation of Master John Wilson of Wanstead in Essex, one of the last ten that returned into England from Wiapoco in Guiana 1606. In Hakluytus posthumus, or, Purchas his pilgrimes. Samuel Purchas (ed.), v. XVI, pp. 338–351. Glasgow: James MacLehose and Sons.
Wissler, Clark
1917 The American Indian; an introduction to the anthropology of the New World. New York: Douglas C. McMurtrie.
Wistrand, Lila M.
1969 Music and song texts of Amazonian Indians. Ethnomusicology, v. XIII, no. 3, September, pp. 469–488. Middletown, Connecticut.
Xaraquemada, Juan de
1852a Carta de Xaraquemada al rey de España. [Jan. 29, 1611] In Gay, 1846–1852, v. II, pp. 245–253.
1852b Informe de Xaraquemada sobre las cosas de Chile. [May 1, 1611] In Gay, 1846–1852, v. II, pp. 234–244.
1852c Otra carta del mismo presidente. [Jan. 28, 1612] In Gay, 1846–1852, v. II, pp. 253–264.
Yde, Jens
1965 Material culture of the Waiwái. Nationalmuseets Skrifter, Etnografisk Roekke, X. Copenhagen.
Zerries, Otto
1954 Wild- und Buschgeister in Südamerika. Eine Untersuchung jägerzeitlicher Phänomene im Kulturbild südamerikanischer Indianer. Studien zur Kulturkunde, 11. Bd. Wiesbaden.
1960 El endocanibalismo en la América del Sur. RMP, v. XII, pp. 125–175.

A NOTE ON THE TRIBAL DISTRIBUTION MAP

The map of *Indian Tribes of South America* by John Howland Rowe that is included at the end of this book has been revised for this publication. Tribal locations are based on first-hand research in primary sources for Venezuela, Colombia, Ecuador, Peru, highland Bolivia, and Patagonia. For Brazil and the Guianas, Koch-Grünberg and Nimuendajú have been followed as far as possible, supplemented by data from the *Handbook*. Locations in the Chaco and eastern Bolivia are based on the work of Métraux, and those in Chile on Cooper. The criteria for tribal definition are linguistic where possible, so that the map may be used to show linguistic classification. Boundaries between languages known to be related are shown by broken lines, other tribal boundaries by solid lines.

Boxes are provided for a linguistic color key, so that each reader may color the map according to the linguistic classification of his or her own choice. The linguistic groupings represented by the boxes are those that are most widespread and those with a discontinuous distribution according to Rowe's classification.

Users of the map are urged to read the General Information note in the lower right-hand corner of the map.